Rethinking Evidence
Exploratory Essays

WILLIAM TWINING

Basil Blackwell

Copyright © William Twining, 1990

First published 1990

Basil Blackwell Ltd
108 Cowley Road, Oxford OX4 1JF, UK

Basil Blackwell Inc.
3 Cambridge Center,
Cambridge, Massachusetts 02142, USA

British Library Cataloguing in Publication Data

A CIP catalogue record for this book is available
from the British Library.

Library of Congress Cataloging in Publication Data

Twining, William L.
  Rethinking evidence: exploratory essays/William Twining.
    p.   cm.
  Bibliography: p.
  Includes index.
  ISBN 0–631–17001–4 (U.S.)
  1. Evidence (Law)   I. Title.
K2261.T847   1990
347′.06—dc20   89–15014
[342.76]   CIP

Typeset in 10 on 11pt Ehrhardt
by Footnote Graphics, Warminster, Wiltshire
Printed in Great Britain by
T. J. Press Ltd, Padstow, Cornwall

Contents

Acknowledgements

One of the blessings of academic life is the collegiality that transcends institutions, countries and disciplines. These essays were written over a period of sixteen years during which I have benefited from the comments, advice, criticisms and friendship of more students, colleagues, editors, librarians and others than it is possible to list. A few of these debts have been acknowledged in the endnotes of individual essays either here or, in some cases, where they were first published. Thanks are also due to The Law Book Company, Australia, Basil Blackwell Ltd, Butterworth and Co., Toronto and London, and John Wiley and sons for permission to reproduce copyright material (for details see the endnotes). A more general debt is due to Terry Anderson, Ian Dennis, Neil MacCormick, David Schum, Alex Stein, Peter Tillers and Adrian Zuckerman. As usual I owe most to my wife for more support, advice and practical help than I deserve.

W.L.T.
Iffley

List of Abbreviations

Analysis	T. Anderson and W. Twining, *Analysis of Evidence* (tentative edition, University of Miami, 1987)
Bentham *Works*	*The Works of Jeremy Bentham*, published under the superintendence of John Bowring (Edinburgh, 1838–43)
Bentham *CW*	*The Collected Works of Jeremy Bentham*, prepared under the supervision of the Bentham Committee, University College, London (London, 1968–82; Oxford, 1983–)
Cross on Evidence	R. (later Sir Rupert) Cross, *Evidence* (London, 1st edn, 1958; 6th edn by C. Tapper, 1985)
FL	W. Twining (ed.), *Facts in Law*, ARSP Beiheft No. 16 (Wiesbaden, 1983)
JSPTL	Journal of the Society of Public Teachers of Law
LTCL	W. Twining (ed.), *Legal Theory and Common Law* (Oxford, 1986)
TEBW	W. Twining, *Theories of Evidence: Bentham and Wigmore* (London and Stanford, 1985)
Thayer *Treatise*	J. B. Thayer, *A Preliminary Treatise on Evidence at the Common Law* (Boston, 1898; reprinted, 1969)
Wigmore *Science*	J. H. Wigmore, *The Principles of Judicial Proof* (Boston, 1st edn, 1913; 2nd edn, 1931; 3rd edn, sub nom. *The Science of Judicial Proof*, 1937)
Wigmore *Treatise*	*A Treatise on the System of Evidence in Trials at Common Law*, Boston (1st edn, 1904–5), cited as 1 Wigmore *Treatise*, s.—; later editions cited as 1 Wigmore *Treatise* (Tillers rev., 1983), s.—.

For Peter

1
Introduction: The Story of a Project

Once upon a time a jurist in mid-career decided that the time had come to test and explore the implications and applications of some of his more general ideas at less abstract levels. The starting-point was an interest in 'broadening the study of law from within' as part of a conception of the discipline of law as an intellectual activity primarily concerned with the creation and dissemination of knowledge and critical understanding within 'legal culture'.[1]

The first step was to select a traditional field that seemed ripe for rethinking. There were several candidates. Torts, which he had taught for several years and which was in process of being deconstructed and redistributed; Contract, which was coming to be perceived almost as the paradigm or test case of legal scholarship; Land Law, on which several colleagues had done some promising ground-clearing work without having yet established a clear path out of the thickets of feudal arrangements and medieval doctrine; and Evidence, which had some intriguing ancestors in Bentham, Wigmore, Thayer and Frank, but which seemed to have been going through a somewhat stagnant phase in recent years.

The choice of Evidence was sealed by an epiphanic moment. In 1972, during a heated debate about proposed reforms of Criminal Evidence, Sir Rupert Cross, the leading English Evidence scholar of the post-war era said: 'I am working for the day when my subject is abolished.'[2] This was provocative at several levels. In the immediate context it was ideologically offensive to one who saw at least some of the surviving rules of evidence as symbolizing important civil libertarian values and providing some, admittedly fragile, safeguards for persons suspected or accused of crime. At a personal level, it was intriguing to speculate about the seeming ambivalence or masochism underlying the remark. Successful expositors have a vested interest in the survival of their chosen field(s). Even more intriguing was the suggestion that if the rules of evidence were abolished there would be nothing left to study. The conception of the subject implied in this remark was that the Law of Evidence was co-extensive with the subject of Evidence – a school-rules view of the field.[3] This naturally raised further questions: How much of evidence doctrine consists of rules? What would we study if there were no rules? What should we be studying about evidence or 'evidence plus' in addition to the rules? What would be the place of the Law of Evidence within a broadened conception of the subject? And by what criteria might one judge what parts of our existing heritage of evidence doctrine might be worth preserving or extending?

This casual remark provided an almost ideal starting-point for my project. For was not the enterprise of 'broadening the study of law from within' directed specifically to constructing alternatives to this kind of narrow, rule-bound 'formalism'? And was not Evidence – narrowly conceived, riddled with technicality, relatively neglected as a subject of academic study in England, and prone to cyclical, repetitious, deeply unsatisfying political debates – ripe for rethinking in this way?

About six years later, but still at a relatively early stage of my explorations, I reported on my project thus:[4]

One central problem may be restated as follows: most Evidence scholarship in the Anglo-American tradition (and here I would include courses on Evidence and public debate on evidentiary issues) has concentrated on and been organized around the *rules* of evidence, especially the exclusionary rules, and their rather limited framework of concepts. Within that tradition work on other aspects of evidence, proof and fact-finding has at best been fragmented and spasmodic. Work in such fields as forensic science, witness psychology, the logic of proof, probability theory, and the systematic study of fact-finding institutions and processes has proceeded largely independently, not only of the study of evidence doctrine, but also of each other. All these lines of enquiry – and many others – seem to be related, but the exact nature of the relationships is often puzzling and obscure. From the point of view of a broadened conception of legal scholarship it is worth asking: Is it possible to develop a *coherent* framework for the study of evidence, proof and related matters within academic law?

As a first step towards confronting this question, I sought to analyse and diagnose the main reasons for my dissatisfaction with the prevailing tradition of Evidence scholarship and debate. After all if one is able to articulate one's own grounds for dissatisfaction with a corpus of literature, this can at least suggest some implicit criteria for a more satisfying approach. These criteria may then be articulated, refined and systematized. After some reflection I concluded that, at a general level, at least four main charges could be made against the orthodox literature as it was a few years ago: First, it was too narrow. Because it had focused almost exclusively on the rules of admissibility, it had almost systematically neglected a whole range of other questions, such as questions about the logic and psychology of proof. Secondly, it was atheoretical: the leading theorists of Evidence, such as Bentham or Gulson or Jerome Michael, have in recent years either been ignored entirely or have been used or abused extraordinarily selectively; most discussions of evidentiary issues have proceeded without any articulated and coherent theoretical framework for describing, explaining or evaluating existing rules, practices and institutions. By and large orthodox Evidence scholarship had assumed a rather naïve, commonsense empiricism, which failed to confront a variety of sceptical challenges to orthodox assumptions, ranging from Jerome Frank's fact-scepticism, through politico-ideological critiques, to various forms of epistemological relativism. It had proceeded in almost complete isolation from developments in relevant branches of philosophy. Thirdly, in so far as orthodox academic discourse has moved beyond simple exposition, it has tended to be incoherent: for the conceptual framework of legal doctrine often does not provide an adequate basis for establishing links with other kinds of discourse; by and large this is true of the Law of Evidence. For instance, the orthodox expository framework cannot easily accommodate even something as central as the nature of reasoning about probabilities in forensic contexts, a topic which has recently been given prominence in this country by Jonathan Cohen, Glanville Williams and Sir Richard Eggleston.[5]

Fourthly, the expository orthodoxy can lead to distortions and misperceptions of key evidentiary issues and phenomena. A weak version of this charge is that by concentrating on some issues to the neglect of others, a misleading impression is given of the subject as a whole. A stronger version is that such imbalances actually lead to misperceptions and error. Here one illustration must suffice: because of the concentration on the exclusionary rules, nearly all of the existing literature on confessions treats retracted confessions as the norm; yet retracted confessions surely represent only a small minority of all confessions. Typically, neither the scholarly literature nor public debate gives a balanced and realistic total view of the role of confessions in the criminal process; for example, the significance of confessing as an important stage en route to a guilty plea. Evidence scholarship has failed to give a systematic account of confessions in criminal process as *phenomena*. As a result, it provides no clear answers to such questions as who confesses to whom about what under what conditions, in what form and with what results? Yet it is difficult to see how one can hope to make sensible and informed judgments about the issues of policy relating to confessions and interrogation without at least tentative working answers to such questions.

This kind of criticism suggests some criteria which a broader approach to the study of evidence would need to satisfy in order to meet these objections, in so far as they are well-founded. To meet the charge of narrowness, it would be necessary to identify at least the most important questions which ought to be tackled in a systematic and comprehensive approach to the study of evidence. This requires an adequate theoretical and conceptual framework.

To meet the charge of incoherence, the relationships between the different lines of enquiry would need to be charted carefully and explicitly – there are, for example, some puzzling questions about the connections between the logic and the psychology of proof, or again, between the study of evidence and proof on the one hand and of criminal and civil procedure on the other.

To meet the charges of theoretical naivety, important theoretical puzzles and disagreements would need to be identified and considered. It is not good enough to dismiss the sceptics, however exaggerated their views may be, by pretending that they do not exist or that what they say is irrelevant.

And to meet charges of distortion and misperception, it is important to paint as realistic a total picture as possible of the phenomena under consideration, so that particular issues can be set in the perspective of some reasonably balanced and realistic overview of the whole. That is part of what is meant by studying law in context. For example, one of the main objections to the CLRC Eleventh Report is that it tended to treat trials on indictment as representative of all trials and professional criminals as representative of all suspects, and was silent about the scale of many of the phenomena and types of behaviour which it was purporting to discuss.[6] To a lesser extent similar criticisms might also be made of the Devlin Report on Identification.[7] If recent public debate about the exclusionary rules and about particular problems of fact-finding, such as problems related to identification, had been set in the context of a broad and balanced total picture, it would have been much easier to make confident judgements about the problems and some of the recommended solutions. Within that perspective it would have been difficult for the CLRC to ignore almost entirely evidentiary problems in

Magistrates' Courts and for the Devlin Committee to overlook the fact that the problem of misidentification of juveniles, which rarely reaches the stage of trial on indictment, may be one of the most serious aspects of the total problem of misidentification. Such considerations suggest that in order to develop a broader approach to the study of evidentiary questions it would be helpful, perhaps necessary, to develop a working theory of evidence, proof and fact-finding in adjudicative processes.[8]

Having reached this stage, an obvious next question to ask was: Has anyone tried to develop such a theory before? It did not take long to discover that this was by no means a novel enterprise, even within the Anglo-American tradition of Evidence scholarship. In particular, Bentham's *Rationale of Judicial Evidence*, and his other very extensive writings on evidence and procedure, and Wigmore's *Principles of Judicial Proof* could both be viewed as attempts to develop a working theory for a broad approach to the study of the problems of evidence and proof respectively.[9] Whatever their short-comings, each of these works ranks among the major achievements of our scholarly heritage. Each of them can provide a rich and convenient starting-point for attempting to develop a contemporary theory which seeks to satisfy the kind of criteria suggested above. Yet they have been largely ignored.

It was not surprising, indeed it was rather encouraging to find that there had been previous attempts to tackle the problem that I had posed to myself. But there were some aspects of the history of the study of evidence which were surprising and ultimately very daunting.

The intellectual history of Evidence scholarship is full of fascinating twists and turns. It could, I suspect, be treated as a representative case study of the intellectual history of Anglo-American academic law. It includes many ironies and paradoxes: orthodox study of the law of evidence has been one of the least empirically oriented branches of academic law. The work of specialists in Evidence, such as Wigmore and Cross, ranks among the highest achievements of legal scholarship. Yet does not much of the secondary writing on Evidence, to borrow a phrase from Holmes, rank 'high among the unrealities'?[10]

One aspect of this history is particularly relevant to my present theme: there has been a natural tendency within the Anglo-American tradition to treat Evidence scholarship as starting in the eighteenth century, first with the early expository treatises of Gilbert and Peake, and then with Bentham's writings on evidence.[11] According to this account the judges developed the common law rules piecemeal; the early expositors tried to reduce the case law to at least partial order and in so doing gave Bentham a clear target to attack: the technical system of procedure and the whole corpus of evidentiary rules. Although he was conscious of the logical and psychological aspects, even Bentham's work is to a large extent rule-centred, for the core is an obsessive and repetitious attack on the very idea of having formal rules of adjective law.

I suggest that this view of the intellectual history of Evidence scholarship is a good example of the kind of distortion that a narrowly rule-centred conception of academic law can produce. For the study of problems of evidence and proof in forensic contexts does not start with Gilbert and Peake and Bentham. It has a very much longer history than that. For example, the study of the logical and psychological aspects of the subject can be traced back all the way to classical rhetoric. Rhetoric, viewed as the study of persuasive discourse, was a central part of the humanistic tradition of Western learning from Corax of Syracuse in the 5th century BC right through until the early nineteenth century. It was part of the trivium of logic, grammar and rhetoric; the intellectual histories of, for example, inductive logic, literary criticism and the study of communication are inextricably bound up with the long and complex story of rhetoric as an academic subject.[12] Now, one of the most important stimuli for the development of classical rhetoric, perhaps the single most important one, was a practical concern with the art of pleading in court: many of the classical texts, *The Murder of Herodes*, some of the speeches of Demosthenes and Cicero, are examples of forensic oratory. Similarly persuasive discourse and concern with probability are as important as ever for contemporary legal practice. The irony is that although legal processes provided one of the most important stimuli for the early development of rhetoric as a subject, contemporary legal scholarship and legal education have, with some notable exceptions, recognized neither its historical nor its contemporary significance. Although this may be a simplification, I would suggest that there is a single main reason for this: it is that legal scholarship has taken legal dotrine as its *starting-point* – thus even the two subjects which are most closely concerned with the issues which lie at the centre of the rhetorical tradition, the study of evidence and probability and the study of reasoning in forensic contexts, do not treat these questions. The modern study of evidence is largely equated with the study of the rules of evidence, just as the study of legal reasoning (and the traditional moot) are confined almost entirely to reasoning about disputed questions of law. The study of rhetoric on the other hand was concerned with reasoning and persuasion in regard to disputes about facts, arguments about policy and arguments about law making and, only rather peripherally, with questions about legal doctrine. This is just one instance of an over-concentration on rules of law contributing to the dual divorce of legal scholarship from a central part of the tradition of humanistic learning on the one hand, and from the concerns and realities of some important aspects of legal practice on the other. This in turn suggests that a redefinition of the boundaries of academic law, including both legal scholarship and legal education, would not involve embarking on uncharted waters; rather it would involve a return to a place in the mainstream of the humanistic tradition of learning.

Now there is a danger that all of this may sound rather grandiose. So let me make a confession. If [someone] had asked: 'How far have you got?' the answer would have been: 'The project has at least ten years to go.' If she had asked: 'Are you not opening a Pandora's box?' it would have been dishonest to deny it. The prospect of developing a framework for the study of evidence and proof which is broad and coherent and has some prospect of satisfying reasonable standards of scholarship is extremely daunting. It is calculated to bring on recurrent attacks of that familiar disease 'the sabbatical blues'.

That was written in 1978.

Ten years on, I can up-date this report as follows. The enterprise has made progress on three main fronts: first, a fairly extensive, but selective, review of one part of our heritage of evidentiary texts – specialized secondary Anglo-American writings about evidence – has been completed. The most detailed part of this, case-studies of two of the leading figures in the tradition, has been published as a book: *Theories of Evidence: Bentham and Wigmore*.[13] This was a quite limited enterprise in that it was restricted to an introductory account, 'more expository than critical', of two specific works, Bentham's *Rationale of Judicial Evidence* and Wigmore's *Principles of Judicial Proof*, set in the context of an argument that our received heritage of specialized secondary texts about evidence has been dominated by a remarkably homogeneous set of ideas and assumptions that have their roots in eighteenth-century Enlightenment rationalism. The restricted nature of that book deserves emphasis. Apart from limitations of time, space and expertise, I did not attempt a full-scale contextual intellectual history because this was meant to be a preliminary stock-taking of the central tradition of our received ideas as part of a contemporary exploration of the subject. Bentham's writings on evidence in particular deserve a much more detailed and genuinely historical treatment, as does the development of the underlying ideas, legal doctrine and legal practice in this area. Three early essays in this volume (chapters 2, 3 and 6) – an extended version of the essay on the Rationalist Tradition, an exploration of some seemingly sceptical challenges to this ideal type, and a critical re-interpretation of the Thayerite conception of the Law of Evidence – are also quasi-history. They too represent a critical stock-taking of selected parts of a rich heritage rather than intellectual history *stricto sensu*.[14]

The second sub-project that has been brought to completion is a set of teaching materials on *Analysis of Evidence* prepared in collaboration with an American law teacher and litigator, Terence Anderson, and an English Professor of Statistics, Philip Dawid.[15] This work is based on Wigmore's account of the logic of proof (including his Chart Method of analysing mixed masses of evidence) and seeks to interpret, develop and to some extent subvert it. The materials are intended as a vehicle for developing some intellectual awareness and analytical skills in intending American practitioners. It is not necessary to describe the work here, but it is relevant to give a brief account of some lessons I have learned from this experience of preparing and using the materials and working with an American attorney, a statistician and the ghost of Wigmore.

One of the central themes of the essays that follow relates to the uses and limits of 'reason' in fact-determination. The experience of extensive and intimate collaboration over several years has not resolved all of my doubts, uncertainties and confusions. Indeed, it has opened up some others. What it has done, however, has been to exorcize certain spectres. For example, at first sight the secondary discourse of advocates often suggests a fundamental scepticism about the relevance of 'rational' analysis and intellectual skills to the task of selecting, seducing, impressing, and persuading jurors in the adversary system. 'The hard-nosed practitioner' claims to be concerned with 'winning, not justice', 'proof, not truth', 'persuasion, not reason', 'experience, not logic', 'Art not Science', 'feel, not analysis', 'theatre, not ...' and so on.[16] Manuals of advocacy emphasize body language, eye-to-eye contact, rhetorical devices, manipulative and diversionary tactics, making a good personal impression, gaining and keeping attention, brevity and simplicity. The more explicit American treatments of jury selection exhibit an uninhibited concern for the exploitation of all kinds of bias, prejudice and stereotyping – race, gender, class, religion, nationality.[17] On the surface, most say almost nothing about rational argument. The discourse of advocacy is a rich source of ammunition against sharp distinctions between fact and value, fact and law, reason and intuition, and other similar discriminations. My experiences suggest that the hard-nosed practitioner's 'and nots' just do not work – either way. Even the crudest cook-books on advocacy presuppose, build on, and even pay homage to a basic, indeed somewhat formalized rationality. My collaborator, Terry Anderson, was independently attracted to Wigmorean analysis because it offered a means of injecting some intellectual rigour into modes of training that he considered were too dominated by the 'touchy-feelies'. Some of those who know him might wish to dismiss his faith in reason as utopian or eccentric, but he can hardly be accused of indifference to the theatrical and rhetorical aspects of advocacy. The reactions of students, especially those who have had extensive practical experience of litigation, are perhaps better evidence. Almost without exception, even the most laborious form of Wigmorean analysis converts them – 'I wish I had had that before I tried my first case.' For me the first lesson of this experience is that neither simple faith in reason nor brute scepticism will do.

Another fallacy that has been exposed by this project has been the idea that Wigmore's Chart Method and one or other versions of the calculus of probability are rigid, 'mechanical' devices based on doctrinaire versions of pseudo-science – at best of little practical use for legal practitioners, at worst dangerous instruments of delusion of self and others.[18] Wigmore's 'logic of proof' was indeed rooted in a particular intellectual tradition and presented in a rather formal manner. But experience of using and teaching them – for the purpose of reconstructing, constructing and criticizing arguments – suggests that Wigmore's method, Bayes's Theorem and other axioms of probability, are extraordinarily flexible and powerful intellectual tools which, if used with sensitive awareness of their nature, make clear the operation of 'subjective' values, biases and choices at almost every stage of complex intellectual procedures.

Again, it could be pointed out that my other collaborator, Philip Dawid, is a distinguished subjectivist and so not typical of proponents of 'misplaced mathematicization'[19] whose influence on evidentiary theory is often sharply attacked as politically dangerous as well as philosophically wrong. But, in my experience, the main messages of statisticians to the non-expert consist of warnings about the misuse of statistical analysis. The dangers are real, but they lie with the half-educated, the innumerate and those unable to spot elementary statistical fallacies. I remain unpersuaded by claims that either in principle or in practice lawyers' reasonings can be subordinated to Bayes's Empire, but that is for different reasons than the idea that they are 'mechanistic'.[20]

Theories of Evidence represented an attempt to take stock of this part of our intellectual heritage through a detailed study of two of its leading figures. *Analysis of Evidence* is intended as a set of learning materials for developing a group of flexible intellectual skills of potential value to practitioners. This third product of the continuing enterprise is more varied. The essays in this volume were written over nearly fifteen years. While the general project has remained fairly stable, over time my ideas have developed and changed; each essay was written in a particular context for a specific audience. In selecting and revising them for inclusion, I have tried to reduce repetition and to make the book more coherent than a mere anthology. Although they are presented in an orderly sequence, each essay is intended to be self-standing and it is not necessary to read them in order. It may help to say something about each of them.

The first essay, 'Taking Facts Seriously', was written for a Canadian audience in 1980. It was intended to arouse interest in the general area and to make the case for giving it more attention within academic law. Although the paper is ostensibly about legal education, the central thesis, that questions of fact deserve as much attention as questions of law, applies to legal scholarship and legal discourse generally. This was in essence a consciousness-raising exercise. At the time, Evidence as an academic subject was in the doldrums. In North America nearly all courses on Evidence focused almost exclusively on the Law of Evidence and were strongly influenced by traditional bar examinations which tested doctrinal knowledge rather than fact-handling skills. In the United Kingdom, Evidence was eccentrically considered to be 'a barrister's subject'; it was studied only by a small minority of undergraduates and was given little emphasis in solicitors' training. The situation has greatly improved in the last ten years, but the case for taking facts more seriously is still worth making.

'The Rationalist Tradition of Evidence Scholarship' (chapter 3) was originally written for a *Festschrift* in honour of Sir Richard Eggleston, an Australian judge and scholar, who has contributed as much as anyone to the recent revival of interest in the subject. The essay is in two parts: an historical survey of specialized Anglo-American secondary writings on evidence from 1750 to about 1970, and a reconstruction of common basic assumptions about the aims and nature of adjudication and about what is involved in reasoning about disputed questions of fact in this context. The essay thus has an historical and an analytical aspect. The historical thesis is that by and large leading specialized writings on evidence have approximated sufficiently to this ideal type to justify talking about a single, remarkably homogeneous tradition of Evidence scholarship. The analytical thesis is that this ideal type is a useful starting-point for interpreting and evaluating any discourse about evidence and is not restricted to secondary writings or the common law world. The test of success of this analytical construct is its clarity, coherence and utility as a tool of analysis of evidence discourse and doctrine. A much abbreviated version of the original essay formed the first chapter of *Theories of Evidence* in order to set detailed studies of the ideas of Bentham and Wigmore in the context of the intellectual tradition of which they were the leading figures. In revising the essay for this volume, I have expanded it to include some additional material (especially on Stephen, Chamberlayne and Moore), and to respond to criticisms and questions from commentators on the earlier versions.

The next chapter, 'Some Scepticism about Some Scepticisms', was written as a sequel to 'The Rationalist Tradition'. It explores whether and in what respects a direct challenge to central ideas in that tradition is offered by a sample of seemingly sceptical or relativist writings that bear directly or indirectly on fact-finding and adjudication. This study highlights some contrasts between specialized writings on evidence – homogeneous, intellectually isolated and rooted in a particular brand of eighteenth-century optimistic rationalism – and the more varied, iconoclastic and modernist approach of many writers about legal processes. The general conclusion is that few, if any, of the writers surveyed present a direct challenge to the core *concepts* (notably Truth, Reason and Justice) embodied in the Rationalist Model, but that the particular *conceptions* associated with this tradition are not the only possible ones and appear somewhat simplistic and old-fashioned today. In short, there is much worth preserving in our heritage of Evidence scholarship and there are no coherent alternative models in sight, but the subject is ripe for rethinking and up-dating.

'Identification and Misidentification in Legal Processes: Redefining the Problem' (chapter 5) develops and illustrates the application of a contextual total process model of litigation to a familiar topic. It was originally intended to point out to researchers into witness psychology that concentration on the reliability of eyewitness identification in contested jury trials was unduly constricted and that there are richer, more suggestive and more realistic models of legal processes available as a starting-point for their enquiries. The essay can also be read as a case study of the narrowing and distorting effects of the expository orthodoxy referred to above.

Chapter 6, 'What is the Law of Evidence?' was originally conceived as an attempt to present an overview of the subject to foreign lawyers, emphasizing the point that our Law of Evidence is neither as extensive nor as important nor as peculiar as its popular image abroad might suggest. Having presented this paper successively to audiences in Italy, China and Poland, I now offer it with only minor modifications to students of the common law as a way of seeing the subject whole. The interpretation could be described as a modified and up-dated version of Thayer's vision of the common law of evidence as a series of rather limited exceptions to a principle of free proof, meaning in this context free enquiry and 'natural reason'. Thayer's key perception was that the rules, standards, guidelines, instructions and other evidentiary norms serve mainly to structure arguments about disputed facts and to modify and to constrain general canons of practical reasoning in a particular kind of context. The idea that the Law of Evidence is primarily concerned with reasoning links this essay with a central theme of this book – the nature, uses and limitations of reasoning about questions of fact. It is hoped that this chapter will also serve to dispel some misconceptions: I have sometimes argued that the Law of Evidence is only one part of the subject of Evidence.[21] This has been variously interpreted to mean that, like Bentham, I believe that all rules of evidence should disappear, or like radical indeterminists, I think that they have already disappeared or that they are uninteresting or unimportant. This essay should put such canards to rest.

'Lawyers' Stories' (chapter 7) is a preliminary exploration of some possible functions of story-telling by judges and advocates with particular reference to the relations between narrative and argument and between rational and irrational means of persuasion. The relationship between narrative, analysis and reasoning is further explored in 'Anatomy of a *Cause Célèbre*' (chapter 8), a detailed study of *R. v. Bywaters and Thompson*. This is the most complex case used in *Analysis of Evidence* as a vehicle for learning a particular method of analysis pioneered by Wigmore and for critically exploring its validity, uses and limitations. After the essay was completed, two very different works appeared which bore directly on its central themes; they provided an opportunity to develop these a bit further in a postscript (chapter 9) comparing modified Wigmorean analysis with two other approaches.

In a lighter vein 'The Way of the Baffled Medic' (chapter 10) satirizes the modes of argumentation about reform of the law of evidence used by the Criminal Law Revision Committee and its critics in 1972. The particular controversy about the right to silence has resurfaced yet again in 1988. While the political motive behind the essay was to criticize the misuse of Bentham by the law-and-order lobby, especially in relation to the right to silence, its significance is not confined to one sector of the political spectrum nor to that particular debate.

'Rethinking Evidence' (chapter 11) draws some themes together and outlines one possible way of looking at and redefining the field. It can even be interpreted as delivering on a rash promise to construct a mapping theory that at least indicates the main points of connection between the many different lines of enquiry that have emerged from this particular version of Pandora's Box. However, it ends not with answers, but with questions. And if I am required to justify this let me borrow the final paragraph from a piece not included in this volume, my inaugural lecture at University College, London in 1983:

It is tempting to move from a critique of past theories to a bold clarion call proclaiming the need for a new theory. My remarks on evidence could be interpreted as a call for a Brand New Theory of Evidence for the Modern Age. But this is also too neat and too simple. In sketching one possible way of developing a different perspective on evidence and information in litigation, I have been suggesting that legal theorists have a constructive role to play in building bridges, sculpting syntheses or hatching theories. The study of evidence also reminds us that all such structures are built on shifting sands. We may have to wait many years for a new theory of evidence to emerge, probably as the work of many minds. If it does, however useful or illuminating it may be, it will not be difficult to show up the flimsiness of its foundations, whatever its particular form and content. Meanwhile, there is one further job for the jurist to undertake in his daily work – to examine critically the underlying assumptions of all legal discourse and to question established ways of thought, especially those that are becoming entrenched. One task of the theorist is to pick away at all assumptions, including his own. Whether he adopts the role of court jester or the Innocent in *Boris Godunov* or the child in the story of the Emperor's clothes or any other form of hired subversive – his first job is to ask questions and, with the greatest respect to the greatest of our gurus, to let the consequences take care of themselves.[22]

NOTES

1   See generally my essays entitled 'Some Jobs for Jurisprudence' (1974), 'Goodbye to Lewis Eliot' (1980) and 'Evidence and Legal Theory' (1984); for full citations see the Bibliography.
2   I cannot be certain of the precise words used. For Cross's position in that debate see Cross (1973); for an alternative view see below, ch. 10.
3   Simpson (1986).
4   From 'Goodbye to Lewis Eliot', op. cit., n. 1, at 9–14.
5   L.J. Cohen (1977); Williams (1979a and b); Eggleston (1978, 1979).
6   Criminal Law Revision Committee, 11th Report (Evidence) (1972).
7   Devlin Report (1976).
8   This formulation of the organizing concept for such a theory is tentative. Bentham advanced a theory of evidence; Wigmore a theory of proof in trials at Common Law. What is being suggested here is much broader than that: it would extend at least to all types of litigation, to all stages in such processes, and would not necessarily be confined to common law systems. See below, ch. 11.
9   See esp. Bentham VI and VII *Works*; Wigmore *Science* (1913, 1931, 1937). The Bentham papers contain an extensive collection of unpublished manuscripts on Evidence. See *TEBW, passim*.

10 Holmes (1897), 475.
11 E.g. Wigmore (1908), 695–7; cf. Montrose (1968), 286ff. See below, ch. 3.
12 On the history of rhetoric, see Kennedy (1963, 1972); J.J. Murphy (1974). A useful overview is included in Corbett (1965).
13 See List of Abbreviations for full citation.
14 On the distinction see Twining (1985a), 336, n. 13.
15 See List of Abbreviations for full citation.
16 See below, 97–9. For an extreme version of the view of trials as political theatre see Graham (1987).
17 A classic example is Darrow, 'Selecting A Jury' (1936), reprinted in Jeans (1975), 167–72. The following quotation gives some of the flavour of the whole piece: 'Beware of Lutherans, especially the Scandinavians; they are almost always sure to convict ... As to Unitarians, Universalists, Congregationalists, Jews and other agnostics, don't ask them too many questions; keep them anyhow; especially Jews and agnostics. It is best to inspect a Unitarian, or a Universalist, or a Congregationalist, with some care for they may be prohibitionists; but never the Jews and the real agnostics!' (id., 170).
18 E.g. Graham, op. cit., n. 16, at 1222–5.
19 The phrase is L.J. Cohen's (1980), 91. For Prof. Dawid's views see *Analysis*, Appendix.
20 See 68 Boston U.L. Rev. (1986), 391–9.
21 E.g. ch. 2 below.
22 Twining (1984), 282–3.

2

Taking Facts Seriously[1]

Once upon a time, on the eastern seaboard of Xanadu, a brand new law school was established. An innovative, forward-looking, dynamic young dean was appointed, and he quickly recruited a team of innovative, forward-looking dynamic young colleagues in his own image. At the first faculty meeting – there were as yet no students to complicate matters – the only item on the agenda was, naturally, curriculum. The dean opened the proceedings: 'Persons,' he said, 'there is only one question facing us today: What can we do that is new, creative, innovative, path-breaking ...?' His colleagues nodded assent; being young and forward-looking they had not yet learned that even in legal education there is nothing new under the sun. Suggestions followed quickly: law and the social sciences, a clinical programme, psycho-legal studies, eco-law, computer-based instruction, law and development, and many of the fads, fashions, follies, and frolics of the 1970s and 1960s, and even some from the 1950s (for how far back does the history of legal education stretch?) were all quickly rejected as old hat. They were, in Brainerd Currie's phrase, 'trite symbols of frustration'.[2] For our subject is governed by a paradox: In general education there is no reported example of an experiment that has ended in failure; in academic law no movement or programme has ever achieved success.

Eventually the Oldest Member spoke up. He had actually looked backward into past numbers of the Journal of Legal Education and other forgotten sources:

'It was once suggested that 90 per cent of lawyers spend 90 per cent of their time handling facts and that this ought to be reflected in their training.[3] If 81 per cent of lawyer time is spent on one thing, it follows that 81 per cent of legal education ought to be devoted to it. There have been some isolated courses on fact-finding and the like, but no institution has had a whole programme in which the main emphasis was on facts. I propose that we base our curriculum on this principle and that we call our degree a Bachelor of Facts.'

Opposition to this proposal was immediate and predictable.

'We do it already.'
'Illiberal!'
'It's only common sense. Therefore it is unteachable.'
'Fact-finding can only be learned by experience.'
'None of us is competent to teach it.'
'There are no books.'
'You cannot study facts in isolation from law.'
'Law schools should only teach law.'
'The students would not find it interesting or easy.'
'The concept of a fact is a crude positivist fiction.'
'Who would want to go through life labelled a BF?'

The Oldest Member was an experienced academic politician; he had studied not only the *Journal of Legal Education* but also Cornford's *Microcosmographia Academica* which, as you know, is our special supplement to Machiavelli's *The Prince*. Adapting the tactic of the Irrelevant Rebuttal, he seized on the objection to the title of the degree and made a crucial concession: 'It need not be a bachelor's degree,' he said; 'there are good American precedents for calling the undergraduate law degree a doctorate. To call our graduates Doctors of Facts will not only attract students and attention, it will also signal that we are well aware that reality is a social construction and not something out there waiting to be found.'

The opposition having been routed, a curriculum committee was set up to work out the details. To their surprise they learned that the range of potential courses was virtually limitless and, what is more, that there already existed an enormous, if scattered, literature. They submitted a detailed plan for the curriculum, including a full range of options, and added a recommendation that the length of the degree should be increased to five years.

This fantasy was concocted for a seminar on legal education, with two objectives in mind. Professional educators should have no difficulty in satisfying the first objective, that is spotting the dozen (or more) standard educational fallacies illustrated by this hypothetical example. The second objective was to underline the point that the study of evidence, broadly conceived, is potentially a rather large subject. My purpose is to explore some aspects of this latter suggestion and to examine why it has been relatively neglected in most programmes of legal education.

The problem might be stated as follows: At least since the time of Jerome Frank it has been widely acknowledged that an imbalance exists between the amount of attention devoted to disputed questions of law in upper courts and the amount devoted to disputed questions of fact in trials at first instance, in other tribunals, and in legal processes generally. Frank might be interpreted as suggesting that the amount of intellectual energy devoted to a subject varies inversely with its practical importance. His thesis was not restricted to legal education, but covered legal discourse generally: legal research, legal literature, debates about law reform and lawyers' perceptions of the law, and their underlying assumptions about it. He was inclined to overstatement and used some vulnerable arguments to bolster his case; but it is now very widely accepted that his central thesis was sound.[4]

Frank's crusade is by no means unique; it is the most sustained polemic in what has been an almost continuous tradition: this includes the German scholar Hugo Muensterberg's campaign for scientific experimental psychology;[5] Albert Osborn's proposal for a Chair of Facts;[6] and numerous pleas from leading judges, practitioners, and committees. The Ormrod Committee on Legal Education in England explicitly included as one major objective of the first or academic stage 'the intellectual training necessary to enable [the student] to handle facts and apply abstract concepts to them'.[7] In addition to such general prescriptions, there have been numerous calls for more attention to be paid to specific aspects of fact-handling: recently, for example, Eggleston, Finkelstein, Barnes, and others[8] have echoed Holmes's argument that 'the man of the future is the man of statistics'[9] and that the calculus of chances, Bayes's Theorem, and a general ability to spot fallacies and abuses in statistical argument should be part of the basic training of every lawyer. Similarly, numerous specific suggestions are to be found in the literature on clinical legal education[10] and the recent debates in the United States on lawyer competence.[11] Thus, even before Frank, attempts had been made to right the imbalance that he pinpointed; such attempts have continued, but they do not seem to have caught on in the sense that Evidence, Proof and Fact-finding (hereafter EPF) does not seem to be generally accepted as an integral and central part of the core curriculum nor of legal discourse generally.[12]

Before considering some specific attempts to deal with the problem, we might at least provisionally indicate the potential scope of the subject. Jerome Michael, who is one of the heroes of our story, summarized his view of the theoretical bases of the arts of controversy as follows:

... since legal controversy is conducted by means of words, you need some knowledge about the use of words as symbols, that is, some grammatical knowledge. Since issues of fact are constituted of contradictory propositions, are formed by the assertion and denial of propositions, and are tried by the proof and disproof of propositions, you need some knowledge of the nature of propositions and of the relationships which can obtain among them, and of the character of issues of fact and of proof and disproof, that is, some logical knowledge. Since the propositions which are material to legal controversy can never be proved to be true or false but only to be probable to some degree and since issues of fact are resolved by the calculation of the relative probabilities of the contradictory propositions of which they are composed, you need some knowledge of the distinction between truth or falsity and probability and of the logic of probability. Since propositions are actual or potential knowledge, since proof or disproof is an affair of knowledge, since, if they are truthful, the parties to legal controversy assert, and witnesses report, their knowledge, and since knowledge is of various sorts, you need some knowledge about knowledge, such, for instance, as knowledge of the distinction between direct or perceptual and indirect or inferential knowledge. Since there are intrinsic and essential differences between law and fact, between propositions about matters of fact and statements about matters of law, and between issues of fact and issues of law and the ways in which they are respectively tried and resolved, you need some knowledge about these matters. Since litigants and all those who participate in the conduct and resolution of their controversies are men and since many of the procedural rules are based upon presuppositions about human nature and behavior, you need some psychological knowledge. Finally, of course, you need such knowledge as is necessary to enable you to understand the tangential ends which are served by procedural law and to criticize the rules which are designed to serve them.[13]

Michael's list is impressive: it includes the classic trivium of logic, grammar and rhetoric; epistemology; forensic psychology; the detailed exploration of probabilities; the interconnections between law and fact; and the basic concepts, doctrines and policies of the law of evidence. Other pioneers in the field have outlined similar schemes which differ in detail and emphasis. Indeed, there is a continuous intellectual tradition from Bentham, through Wills, Best, Stephen, Thayer, Gulson, Wigmore, Michael and Adler to Leo Levin, Irvin Rutter, and contemporary teachers of law who have treated EPF as an important focus of attention.[14]

When one contemplates the history of this particular tradition, however, one sometimes wonders whether it has been the subject of some peculiar curse. For it reads like the story of Sisyphus who was condemned for ever to roll a heavy boulder up a hill, only to see it roll down just before he reached the top.[15] The study of rhetoric, which had its origins in forensic situations, has been the inspiration of important developments in several disciplines – inductive logic, literary criticism, semantics, even parts of psychology, for example – but it has been forgotten by the discipline of law.[16] James Mill edited Bentham's *Introductory View of Judicial Evidence*, and one third of the work was in proof when the printer took fright because of Bentham's views on jury packing (and possibly his potentially blasphemous critique of oaths), with the result that publication was delayed by some thirty years.[17] Immediately after the young John Stuart Mill had completed the herculean feat of editing Bentham's *magnum opus*, the *Rationale of Judicial Evidence*, he suffered his famous breakdown and substituted Wordsworth's poetry for Bentham's relentlessly intellectual pushpin.[18] Most of Bentham's concepts and basic theoretical analysis have been thoroughly absorbed into the Anglo-American tradition of Evidence scholarship, but his main argument – that all exclusionary rules should be abolished and that fact-finding should be treated as a quintessentially rational process – has gained only limited acceptance.

In 1908, Hugo Muensterberg trumpeted a new era for forensic psychology,[19] only for John Henry Wigmore, the rising star of evidence, to write a satire, laced with most un-Wigmorean wit, which was so effective that it helped to dampen the budding enthusiasm of psychologists – and forensic psychology went to sleep for several decades.[20] Ironically Wigmore himself then moved into the field,[21] but more in the mode of a dilettante anthologist, drawing almost as heavily on writings by lawyers and the work of a member of the Indian Civil service, G. F. Arnold, who was neither a lawyer nor a psychologist, as he did on serious empirical research.[22] During the heyday of the realist movement, the young Robert Maynard Hutchins collaborated with a psychologist, Donald Slesinger, for a number of years; but after he had been translated precociously to the presidency of the University of Chicago, Hutchins recanted, suggesting in a remarkable paper entitled 'The Autobiography of an Ex-Law Student' that he had been wasting his time.[23] In the 1930s Jerome Michael and Mortimer

Adler prepared the most elaborate account of the logical and analytical aspects of EPF, entitled *The Nature of Judicial Proof.*[24] This actually reached the stage of being privately printed for limited circulation, but the full version never received full publication, perhaps because commentators, including Wigmore, dismissed it as being of no practical value.[25] Wigmore's own *Principles* [later *Science*] *of Judicial Proof* suffered a rather more bizarre fate. For many years he taught a course on proof at Northwestern University which remains the most systematic and intellectually sophisticated attempt of its kind to deal with the analytical and psychological dimensions of proof in forensic contexts. While Wigmore was dean, his course on proof was a regular part of the curriculum, first as a required course and latterly as an option; after he ceased to be dean, it was relegated to the summer programme. The book of the course was first published in 1913.[26] It was well received critically, but so far as I have been able to discover it was never adopted more than once in any other law school during Wigmore's lifetime. The reason why it went into three editions appears to have been that his publishers, Little, Brown, valued their relationship with Wigmore (for good reason) and Little, Brown salesmen found a modest market among practitioners who treated it as good bedside reading.[27]

Since the 1930s the pattern has continued. For example, in the late 1950s Leo Levin of the University of Pennsylvania Law School prepared an excellent set of materials, *Evidence and the Behavioral Sciences*, but this too was never published as a book.[28] In the 1970s an ambitious project to produce a definitive edition of Bentham's very extensive writings on evidence – in the eyes of some, one of the most important and least known aspects of his work – was frozen *sine die* for lack of funds.[29]

So far as legal education is concerned, a similar, less dramatic, pattern is to be discerned. Before 1960, there were some attempts to establish courses on fact-finding and the like in law schools, particularly in America. Almost without exception, like all educational experiments, these have been reported as successes; Jerome Michael at Columbia, Jerome Frank at Yale, Wigmore at Northwestern, Judge Marx and Irvin Rutter at Cincinnati, Marshall Houts at UCLA, and Leo Levin at Pennsylvania are among those who have attempted to develop courses on fact-finding.[30] These are fascinating in their diversity, but the more striking fact is that they did not become established; almost without exception they stand as monuments to the ephemeral contributions of individual teachers. They did not become institutionalized, nor did the lessons of experience cumulate. The pattern was perhaps symbolized by staged witness 'experiments'. The literature abounds with reports along the following lines: A student dressed in a top hat and tails, with a monocle in his left eye, a bottle of champagne on a silverplated salver in the right hand and a gun in the left hand, rushes into the classroom, shouting, 'You bounder, I have got you at last'; he shoots the teacher and rushes out again, still carrying the champagne. The teacher then rises from the dead and asks the class to write down an account of what they have just witnessed. Almost invariably they put the monocle in the wrong eye, forget about the champagne, and substitute some other word for 'bounder'. No doubt these so-called eyewitness experiments taught a simple lesson vividly, but even in respect of the method of staging them, knowledge did not *accumulate* on the basis of experience. They remained idiosyncratic, spasmodic, and essentially amateur.[31]

Some years ago I suggested that legal education had been strongly influenced by two sharply contrasting images of the lawyer: on the one hand, the lofty image of Pericles, the lawgiver, the enlightened policy maker, the wise judge; on the other hand, the image of the lawyer as plumber, a no-nonsense, down-to-earth technician.[32] My argument, which has sometimes been misunderstood, was that neither image was suitable as a model for the end products of a sane system of legal education and training, and that the influence of these two images, typically in the form of unstated assumptions, has contributed to unnecessary controversy and tensions within legal education. In a nutshell: the academics have often been too lofty, but practitioners have tended to be too mundane. Understanding and practising law are more difficult, more varied, and more interesting than the plumbing image implies; but legal education has no special claim to be suited to the mass production of statesmen.

In respect of EPF there may be something in the view that the plumbing image has been too influential on attempts to respond to calls to take facts more seriously. At least some of the courses described in the literature seem to have concentrated more on specific techniques than on basic, transferable skills, and to have tried to instil skills without an adequate theoretical base. Some have also tried to cover too much ground in a very limited time. In so far as this has been the case, it is hardly surprising. Much of the pressure for teaching courses on fact-handling and the like has come from the practitioners and judges who typically, but by no means universally, express the need in terms of securing minimum competence in respect of immediately usable techniques. The standard academic response to such requests is that formal legal education should concentrate on matters that represent a long-term investment, on understanding as well as skill, on transferable *skills* rather than narrowly focused techniques.[33]

Let us consider briefly one of the more carefully worked out courses from this perspective – Wigmore's course on proof. His starting point is a sharp distinction between the rules of admissibility and proof – what he termed 'the ratiocinative process of contentious persuasion'.[34] He adopts the standpoint of the trial advocate at the point when the questions of admissibility have been dealt with and the evidence is all in and 'the counsel sets himself to the ultimate and crucial task, i.e., that of persuading the jury that they should or should not believe the fact alleged in the issue.'[35] Stated like this, it sounds as if Wigmore is reviving the ancient art of forensic oratory; in fact his primary educational aim was quite different: it was to develop *'skill in thinking about evidence'*[36] and, in particular, of mastering a limited number of types of mental process which bear on systematically analysing a mixed mass of evidence in order to come to a judgement about its probative force for the case as a whole. To this end Wigmore developed a particular method which is designed, in his words, 'to enable us to lift into consciousness and to state in words the reasons why a total mass of evidence does or should persuade us to a given conclusion and why our conclusion would or should have been different or identical if some part of the total mass had been different'.[37]

The basis of this method is inductive logic, as expounded by John Stuart Mill, Alfred Sidgwick and Stanley Jevons. The core of the course was a series of exercises in applied inductive logic. The initial exercises deal with analysing examples of different kinds of evidence according to this method, in the course of which Wigmore introduces a considerable amount of psychological and scientific material. All these particular sections are only preliminaries to the finale – an elaborate exercise of analysing a mixed mass of evidence, using records of famous trials as examples. Put simply, a two-stage process is involved: First, all the evidence which the student considers to be potentially relevant, directly or indirectly, to a fact in issue has to be expressed in the form of simple propositions of fact. Each proposition is given a number and becomes part of a 'key list of evidence' for the case. The second stage is to map, using a limited number of symbols, all the significant relationships between all the propositions, and to indicate the author's *belief* about the probative force (or otherwise) of each proposition in relation to its immediate *probandum*. The final result should represent a rational reconstruction of the chart-maker's belief about the significance of each item of evidence and its bearing on the case as a whole.

For several years past I have set undergraduates exercises based on a modified and somewhat diluted version of Wigmorean analysis. Typically, selected *causes célèbres* have provided the raw material – Sacco and Vanzetti, Alger Hiss, Tichborne, Hanratty, and, above all, Bywaters and Thompson, have turned out to be reasonably suitable for this kind of exercise.[38] To keep matters under control I have had to lay down a set of artificial ground rules, for example, that no key list should contain fewer than 250 or more than 500 propositions and (after receiving a chart that extended for thirty-seven feet) that no chart should be more than ten feet long.

This is not the place to give a full account of my impressions of the value and the limitations of such exercises. Suffice it to say that although they are extremely time-consuming and are clearly both artificial and academic (in a non-pejorative sense), I am convinced that they are an excellent pedagogical device for a number of purposes: doing such exercises should drive home the lesson that analysis of evidence involves careful exploration of *relations between propositions*; it should help to make the student aware of the complexity of such relations and of the many possibilities of logical jumps and of fallacious reasoning when a mass of evidence is involved. Wigmore's method lays a foundation for a systematic approach to analysing disputed questions of fact; it sets forth a disciplined approach to charting the overall structure of a case, to digging out unstated, often dubious, propositions, and to mapping all the relations between all the relevant evidence. It is not merely a vehicle for giving a grounding in some elementary techniques of analysis, for it also provides a perspective – a way of looking at evidence and at complex cases which does not come naturally to most students. My impression of student reactions to Wigmore exercises is that many either groaned while they were sweating it out or became obsessed with their particular cases, but that nearly all have been glad to have been through the process and have learned a great deal from it.[39]

In the present context, Wigmore's *Science* is significant for a number of reasons. First, it represents the most concrete and developed version of an analytical, non-mathematical, approach to problems of forensic proof. Second, it purports to integrate logic, forensic psychology, and forensic science into a single coherent scheme. Some of the psychological and scientific material looks rather dated and, to a lesser extent, the same may be said of the logic. But that does not undermine the validity of the general approach. Third, Wigmore's educational objectives are unashamedly vocational, but the main lessons that can be learned from such a study would satisfy the criteria of most liberal educators. There is no conflict.[40] However, Wigmore's approach is narrowly focused – it concentrates on one standpoint, the trial advocate, at one moment of time. It concentrates on one point in the totality of legal process. Wigmore filters out many questions and factors that the process school and sceptical students of legal processes would consider to be very important. This, I think, signals a limitation, but does not undermine the validity or the value of the enterprise. Fourth, it provides a coherent, if not fully argued, theory within a central intellectual tradition – English empiricism – which can be compared and contrasted with perspectives and ideas that fit more easily with other philo-sophical traditions, such as neo-Kantian, Hegelian, or Marxian approaches.[41] This last point deserves emphasis: for Wigmore's *Science* provides as good a starting-point as any for exploring a wide range of theoretical issues which he did not himself explore, such as the nature of probabilistic reasoning in forensic contexts, how judgments about the weight of different items of evidence are to be combined, 'holistic' versus 'atomistic' approaches, how 'reality' is con-structed in the courtroom, and the nature and purposes of different kinds of legal processes.[42]

Wigmore's 'science' is only one – but indubitably the most important – example of an attempt to deal with factual questions seriously and systematically within legal education. Other precedents, of course, are worthy of attention – though none, in my view, are sufficiently comprehensive to go beyond showing what can be done by a systematic approach to one or two particular aspects of this broad field. We do not yet have a blueprint for a comprehensive approach to EPF within legal education, but in the courses and writings of Wigmore, Michael, Levin, Rutter,[43] Eggleston, Anderson, Schum, and others we have a valuable heritage of relatively sophisticated and diverse precedents. One lesson to be learned from this past experience is that it is unwise to expect to be able to tackle even the basics of all that is encompassed by EPF satisfactorily within the confines of one or two courses.[44]

Given the quality of much of the thinking and the avowed success of a number of individual courses, why has EPF not been more firmly entrenched in the law schools? I shall address this question, without attempting to give a comprehensive answer, by looking first at some arguments which are sometimes advanced against extending the study of EPF and then at some other factors in the intellectual climate of law schools that may have contributed to the neglect of an important dimension of academic law.

In the hypothetical example of the Xanadu Law School I implied that the objections that were raised against the proposal for a BF degree were all either fallacious or seriously defective. If we put forward a more modest proposal – that the systematic study of facts in law should have a central, but not dominating, place in undergraduate legal education, for example, there are some rational objections that at least deserve a response. The main arguments can be divided into three categories: (a) the subject is dealt with adequately already; (b) the subject is important but is not dealt with extensively in most law schools because it is unnecessary to devote valuable class time to it; (c) in theory one should devote more time to it, but there are severe difficulties in doing so. Let us call these respectively: the 'we do it already', the 'too soft', and 'too hard' arguments.

The first argument, that enough is done already to teach students the fundamentals of handling facts, was cogently put by Jack B. Weinstein in commenting on issues raised by Jerome Frank and Judge Marx.[45] Speaking of Columbia in the 1950s, but by implication more generally, he argued that three fundamental 'fact skills' were already being taught and that was all that could be expected in a three-year degree. First, students are taught 'to differentiate between facts which are and which are not materially significant'.[46] The main vehicle for this was the case method which, claimed Weinstein, 'is uniquely conceived and designed to build a foundation for an understanding of the relationship of facts to law and for skilful handling of facts'.[47] This was supplemented at Columbia by Jerome Michael's more theoretical approach which, alas, has since been largely forgotten.[48] The second skill, 'knowledge of how courses of conduct may be planned to shape the material facts', is dealt with in courses on contracts, tax, trusts and estates, and the like. The third skill, 'an awareness of how evidence of the facts may be gathered and used in litigation', is adequately dealt with in courses on procedure and evidence and reinforced by such electives as legal aid work, trial moot courts, and specialized seminars. Beyond that, instruction in fact-handling is unnecessary or else is best left to be learned in practice.[49]

Even in this simplified version (he makes a number of other points), Weinstein's argument deserves respect. At the very least it suggests that Jerome Frank had exaggerated the extent of the imbalance and that, in its turn, Columbia in the 1950s had implemented at least some of Frank's suggestions.

A modern successor to Weinstein could with some justification claim that in many law schools his argument could be put with even greater force today: in particular, clinical programmes and trial practice courses have since become more sophisticated and more widespread, and the post-realist 'process school' has stimulated a much greater academic awareness and attention to pre-trial aspects of civil and criminal litigation and to such matters as sentencing, parole and arbitration.

I can make only a peremptory reply here to this line of argument. One can readily concede both that Jerome Frank overstated his case and that the situation has improved significantly since his day. But it is just not true that the pleas of Frank and others have been met in a systematic and satisfactory manner. First, Weinstein's conception of the field is narrowly vocational. It is confined to the fundamental 'fact skills' of private practitioners and omits nearly all of the broad or theoretical dimensions outlined by his colleague Jerome

Michael. He concentrates on techniques and says almost nothing of more general understanding and criticism.

Second, even in respect of the unashamedly vocational teaching of elementary skills, his account of what is involved is too simple. If one takes as baseline for the claim 'we do it already' a more systematic job analysis of what is involved in 'fact-handling' by private practitioners, such as that by Irvin Rutter, few programmes of legal education and training can claim systematically to deal even at an elementary level with the whole range of basic skills of private practitioners – let alone at a more advanced level or with other skills or with the concerns of other participants. It is difficult to generalize, of course, for both programmes and the experience of individual students within a programme even now vary considerably, and there have been significant advances in recent years. What I wish to suggest in general terms is that fact-handling skills, in so far as they are taught directly, are taught less systematically and at a more elementary level than rule-handling skills, and that there is anyway more to legal education than the inculcation of basic skills.

Third, Weinstein was writing about Columbia in 1954, which may in some respects have been exceptionally well off. In particular, Jerome Michael's courses on procedure and analytical aspects of proof represent one of the clear cases of a model that did not catch on. At best his ideas were accepted in a watered-down form, without the rigorous analytical approach on which he insisted; on the whole they have been largely ignored or forgotten.

Weinstein also raises one important issue: How far is it sensible to isolate the study of fact-finding from other substantive and procedural issues? His answer is clear: 'It ought to be distributed throughout the curriculum so that students begin to think of a case in the many different ways that a lawyer might.' This raises a familiar issue over which first-year teachers regularly disagree: the 'direct' versus the 'pick-it-up' approaches to the study of legal method. Suffice it to say here that I am as committed to the direct approach in respect of EPF as I am in respect of orthodox legal analysis and interpretation.[50] The 'pick-it-up' approach to basic skills typically confuses laying a foundation for mastery of a skill and reinforcing it through practice. Moreover, picking things up tends to proceed in a theoretical vacuum.

The second argument against direct and extensive teaching of EPF is that it is neither necessary nor appropriate for law schools to undertake to teach it. There are several versions of this argument. One is that fact-handling is largely a matter of clear thinking and general knowledge, which should have been adequately developed before law school by general education. Law schools, so the argument goes, should not take on the mantle of general education, but should confine themselves to law. Accordingly they should deal only with matters which are peculiar to law or which involve special problems of application.

A variant of this argument is more fundamental: we are told that the logic appropriate to reasoning about evidentiary issues is the ordinary inductive reasoning used in everyday practical affairs; that judgements about relevance and about probabilities are based on common sense and the common course of experience;[51] after all, we entrust some of our most important fact-finding decisions to jurors, ordinary citizens who are without any training – indeed, perhaps because they are untrained. You cannot teach common sense and you should not try to do so.

Some support for this view is to be found in Bentham, who apologized for the obviousness of much of his *Rationale of Judicial Evidence* in the following terms:

So obvious are most of the considerations above presented, so much in the way of everybody's observation, that, under the name of instruction, they have scarce any pretension to be of any use. But, what a man has had in his mind, he has not always at hand at the very moment at which it is wanted: what conveys no instruction, may serve for reminiscence.[52]

Another variant is that some aspects of EPF may be considered to be soft options, less intellectually demanding or stimulating than traditional law courses. This is a criticism, often implicit rather than explicit, that has sometimes been made about courses on forensic science and forensic psychology in American law schools and about largely descriptive courses on institutions generally. The argument might be stated as follows: Much of the material central to fact finding is undoubtedly important, but one does not need a course in it to learn the main lessons. It is of course important to be aware, for example, that memory is unreliable, perception is unreliable and is subject to distortion through bias, inattention, and lapse of time, that interrogation can be intrinsically coercive, and that decision makers are likely to have unconscious biases. Do we need to spend scarce and expensive time and resources in a law school to create such awareness? Even when it is not just a matter of common sense, can it not be done just as efficiently through self-education? Provide the student or lawyer with a list of recommended reading – Frank's *Courts on Trial*, Wellman's *The Art of Cross-Examination*, some manuals of advocacy, and standard works on forensic science and forensic psychology – and let them get on with it.[53]

Perhaps the most important objection to direct teaching of basic skills of fact-handling is an ethical one. Many techniques of the effective advocate are inimical to the traditional values of a university, for they involve the undermining of rational argument rather than its promotion: they include techniques for keeping relevant information out, for trapping or confusing witnesses, for 'laundering' the facts, for diverting attention or interrupting the flow of argument, and for exploiting means of non-rational persuasion. The teacher of advocacy within the academy has an ethical dilemma: it may be appropriate to discuss the ethics of such techniques in class, but is it compatible with our calling to train students in the skills of non-rational or anti-rational means of persuasion which are a part of *effective* advocacy? Or, for the university teacher, is this a form of *trahison des clercs*?

The argument may be restated as follows:

1   In so far as certain skills and knowledge of a general kind need to be taught at all, they should be made a prerequisite for entry to law school.
2   In so far as much of what is involved in fact-finding is based on common sense, it is unnecessary to teach it.
3   In so far as some relevant knowledge and awareness is easily acquired through general reading or experience, valuable law school time should not be devoted to it.

4 In so far as effective fact-handling involves unethical, non-rational, or anti-intellectual skills and techniques and perspectives, it is inappropriate for these to be taught in the academy.

These arguments are powerful and need to be taken into account in planning a sensible programme of education and training and in assessing priorities. But they are by no means dispositive. First, some aspects of clear thinking and general knowledge need to be developed to an especially high standard. To put the same point differently: one of the main claims of case method teaching and of analytical jurisprudence is that they develop *general* powers of reasoning and analysis – distinguishing the relevant from the irrelevant, handling abstract concepts, constructing and sustaining an argument, drawing precise distinctions. Much of the Langdellian tradition depends on the dual claim that lawyers need to be trained to think clearly and that legal materials are a particularly good vehicle for this purpose. Similar claims can be made for the analytical aspects of EPF, but the skills and techniques are not identical. Elucidating the concepts of 'fact' or 'proof' or 'relevance' poses somewhat different problems from elucidating basic legal concepts, such as 'right' or 'cause' or 'intention' or 'justice' or 'law'; and different lessons may be learned in analysing a mixed mass of evidence from analysing a series of reported cases.

Similarly, while some aspects of EPF are indeed quite easily understood and could provide the basis for 'soft options', many of its analytical and theoretical dimensions are at least as demanding as anything to be found in the expository and Langdellian traditions of legal education. Furthermore, the problems of understanding the special applications to legal contexts of general principles of clear thinking or general concepts affect questions of fact as well as questions of law.

Nor is it realistic to throw the burden back on general education and law school entrance requirements. To take but one example: most law students and lawyers readily confess to being innumerate; some even boast of it. Yet the mathematicists claim that in arguing about disputed issues of fact one is reasoning about probabilities, and that this kind of reasoning is always in principle mathematical and requires at least an elementary command of basic statistical and related techniques.[54] I am not concerned here about the validity of the mathematicist thesis; but I would suggest that the serious study of reasoning in regard to disputed matters of fact is at least as important and can be at least as intellectually demanding as the study of reasoning in respect of disputed questions of law. In short, the answer to the 'too soft' argument is that the claims of EPF, far from diluting the rigorous core of traditional legal education, would involve a broadening of the scope of analytical studies and, if done well, would make legal education more rather than less demanding.

This also provides at least a partial response to the ethical objection. No doubt, in dealing with advocacy and other aspects of lawyering, teachers as well as practitioners are regularly faced with moral dilemmas, as is illustrated by some of the classic debates in the history of rhetoric. But if one believes that an intellectually sound argument is often the most persuasive argument or even that good advocacy involves a subtle combination of rational and non-rational means of persuasion, then one has at least a partial answer to the objection. A rigorously intellectual approach to the skills of fact-handling may help to further the cause of promoting rationality in legal processes. A direct approach to the analysis of evidence (and related matters) may also help to illuminate the relations between rational and non-rational factors and different conceptions of rationality. Such an approach belongs to the mainstream of Western university education, for fact-handling is as much a basic human skill as rule-handling. That some such skills may be amoral, immoral, or open to abuse is not a sufficient reason for not dealing with them in the academy. All skills give rise to ethical problems; how to cope with such problems is an issue facing every educator.

The next and converse objection – is that the systematic study of fact finding is not too soft, but that it is too hard. This argument is more commonly expressed in terms of feasibility rather than of intellectual toughness.[55] Let us put on one side perennial questions of priorities and of teacher competence, which are best discussed in the context of specific programmes. Two robust maxims will suffice here: 'Questions of priorities should be debated on the merits' and 'If competent teachers cannot be found, they must be made.' Let us rather consider two different versions of the argument about feasibility – the 'no literature' argument and the 'Pandora's Box' argument.

In a rational and orderly world one might expect the natural sequence of development in education to be, first, some initial theorizing; then, research into and a new understanding of narrow areas leading to the publication of specialized studies; next, the publication of general books based on these particular studies; then, the establishment of courses based on the general books. In legal education the process is sometimes reversed: courses precede research and theorizing; general educational books grow out of the courses; detailed particular research follows the general studies. This need not be the case today in respect of EPF, for there is an extraordinarily rich literature – from Aristotle's *Rhetoric* to Perelman's *The New Rhetoric*; from Bentham's great *Rationale* to Wigmore's marvellously entertaining and instructive *Science*; from Mill's *Logic* to Jonathan Cohen's *The Probable and the Provable*. Forensic science is reasonably well served and there is a burgeoning literature on forensic psychology, on legal process, and on particular topics such as probabilities, identification evidence, and the ethics of advocacy. It may be that manuals on cross-examination and some other aspects of trial practice have not evolved much beyond the cook-book stage,[56] but there is an enormous and varied secondary legal literature. Orthodox evidence scholarship, although it has tended to be rather narrowly focused, has often been of outstandingly high quality, and there is, of course, the vast heritage of relevant literature from the humanities and social sciences – on epistemology, on logic, on historiography, on the sociology of knowledge, for example.

In addition to the secondary literature, a body of primary material remains to an extraordinary degree underexploited from the point of view of legal research and education – trial records and accounts of *causes célèbres*. It is a striking fact of our intellectual life that these are seen more as a source of entertainment (note, for example, the fate of Wigmore's *Science*) than as raw material for systematic study and analysis. The law teacher's relatively well-developed ex-pertise in using appellate cases as rich, stimulating, and demanding educational material has not been extended to records of trials. The potential uses of this kind of course, the criteria for selection, and the kinds of skills and awareness it can help to develop are, in some respects, significantly different from the law reports.[57] The human element is more clearly displayed in trial records, for example; the law reports are more compact and have special status as authorities. But, from a pedagogical point of view, they are quite closely related species of the same genus – case-studies; they are concrete, often dramatic, dialectical examples, which can be analysed in numerous ways. They can be used to illustrate general ideas, but they are anecdotal and as such they can be almost systematically misleading. The most interesting cases are typically atypical and, as has often been pointed out, the case-trained lawyer is in danger of having a distorted picture of the world in which the pathological and the exotic obscure the healthy and the routine.

Thus it is just not true that there is not an adequate literature on which to base a significantly expanded study of EPF within a broadened conception of academic law. It is nearer the mark to say that a potentially rich body of literature has been almost systematically neglected. It is symptomatic of this neglect that some of the most significant works in the field have either gone out of print or were never even published.[58] It is also symptomatic of neglect that, by and large, law teachers have so far failed to develop anything like the same level of pedagogical sophistication in selecting, presenting, and using trial records as they have done in respect of the law reports. The literature is there, but it has yet to be exploited.

But, it will be objected, you are opening Pandora's Box. Pursue this line and all knowledge becomes your province: epistemology, logic, statistics, historiog-raphy, psychology, all the behavioural sciences, and heaven knows what else will escape and swamp us. Let us stick to what we can do well; let us keep the clamp down on the lid or we shall be assaulted by reality. Maybe I dismissed too summarily the notion that the gods are angry. Could it be that the sad story of the publishing history of theorizing about evidence by lawyers, of all those aborted projects and *culs-de-sac*, were small thunderbolts from heaven, shots across the bows warning academic lawyers to keep off? There is after all the precedent of Prometheus who stole fire from Olympus and opened the eyes of humankind by asking a lot of awkward questions. Is not taking a serious interest in facts rather like that? What is truth? What is proof? What part can reason play in adjudication? Is judicial process really concerned with truth? All the endless concerns of the humanities with knowledge, reality and reason are threatening to break in. Start opening up these questions and you are lost.

Back to earth. There are no gods to anger, but the fears are not groundless: it is the case that the potential ramifications of EPF are endless and taking facts seriously is a daunting prospect. Jerome Frank's position on this is quite clear: the elusiveness and complexity of the world of facts is a central part of the lawyer's world. One can either duck or confront reality. Frank is a confronter *par excellence*, his recipe the American equivalent of the stiff upper lip, a Freudian notion of maturity.[59] The completely adult jurist acknowledges the difficulties and gets on with the job. In this view the main objection to the orthodox tradition of Evidence scholarship is that it evades the difficult problems. It is a tradition of relatively complacent commonsense empiricism that concentrates on the most formal and most public part of judicial processes and has devoted far more attention to the rules of admissibility than to questions about the collection, processing, presentation and weighing of information that reaches the decision makers. The rationality of the process is by and large assumed; the elusiveness of reality is barely acknowledged. There is again a good precedent in jesting Pilate. What is truth? asked the evidence scholars, and would not stay for an answer.

Let me restate my response to the four main arguments against a modest version of the Frank thesis. To the claim 'we do it already', my reply is that this is only partly true and that rarely is fact-finding as such directly studied in a systematic, comprehensive and rigorous manner. To the 'too soft' or 'unnecessary' argument, my reply is that this is also partly true, but that there are important aspects of EPF for which almost identical claims can be made as for those aspects of traditional legal education, which are considered to be both practically important and intellectually demanding. To the 'unethical' argument, my reply is much the same: the problem is not peculiar to fact studies. To the 'too hard' argument, my response is that in so far as these are arguments about feasibility they are unconvincing; in so far as they are objections on grounds of intellectual difficulty they are despicable; and in so far as they are objections on grounds of absence of a suitable literature they are incorrect. The strongest response to 'it can't be done' is to point out that it has been done – often rather well. In so far as the argument is one about priorities – for example, that there is no time to fit this extra material in – I merely wish to suggest that the claims of EPF should be considered on the merits. It is not self-evident that the study of the rules of evidence deserves a higher priority than the principles of proof or that appellate cases are *ipso facto* better pedagogical material than trial records.

While there is some force in the objections so far considered, I do not accept them as satisfactory justifications for the *status quo*. Nor on their own do they provide a plausible explanation for the relative failure of responses to the repeated pleas for a righting of the imbalance. Nor do I think that academic conservatism and inertia, no doubt potent factors, provide the missing link. Without claiming to be exhaustive, I wish to consider briefly two further related contributory factors: the gravitational pull of the rule-centred tradition of academic law and the failure of its critics to construct a *coherent* theoretical alternative in respect of EPF.

One interpretation of the American realist movement, of which Frank is generally regarded as a leading member, is that it represented a rather diverse and loosely coordinated series of reactions against rule-dominated notions of academic law, exemplified by Langdellism in the United States and the expository orthodoxy in the United Kingdom. According to this view the realists were reacting against an orthodoxy, but their grounds for criticizing or rejecting that orthodoxy were diverse. On the positive side they shared one single idea, which can be expressed as a truism: there is more to the study of law than the study of rules. It is a caricature of almost all realists to attribute to them the view that rules are a myth or are merely predictions or are unimportant, just as it is a caricature of many expositors to suggest that they seriously deny the central truism that united realists. The reasons for the dissatisfaction of the realists with the orthodoxy were diverse in crucial respects – one basic concern was practitioner-oriented: how to narrow the gap between academic law and the day-to-day realities of legal practice? Another was scientistic: how to develop an empirical, research-oriented science of law quite far removed from the day-to-day concerns of practitioners? Some realists were concerned to criticize existing legal institutions, rules, and practices with a view to reform. Failure to perceive this diversity of concerns obscured the crucial point that a corresponding diversity of alternative solutions or programmes was indicated. Constructing a more enlightened system of vocational training is a very different enterprise from developing an empirical science of law or a basis for a reformist or radical critique of the legal order.[60]

Part of the toughness of the expository orthodoxy was that it had (or was thought to have) a strong internal coherence; law is a system of rules, and the study of law involves the exposition, the analysis, and occasionally the evaluation of those rules. The raw material for this study is primary sources of law; the central questions were disputed questions of law. Concessions could be, and were, made to demands to raise wider issues, to include non-legal materials and so on, but it was clear that these belonged to the periphery rather than the centre. In respect of the core curriculum the starting-point and the main subject of study were rules. It was accordingly natural that the study of evidence was equated with reasoning about questions of law. The toughness of the tradition was due in large part to its coherence.

When such realists as Holmes, Frank and Llewellyn opened Pandora's Box they seemed to be letting loose an almost limitless number of possible avenues of enquiry. If the study of rules alone is not enough, what is enough? The danger was that nothing was to be excluded, everything was relevant. In order to cope, this problem had to be confronted and new *coherences* had to be developed. Unfortunately some of the leaders, such as Holmes and Frank, were stronger on diagnosis than they were on prescription – neither of them ever worked out the full implications of their position in terms of coherent programmes for legal education, legal research or law reform.[61] Karl Llewellyn, it has been suggested with some justification, retreated in his later years to the relatively safe ground of the Uniform Commercial Code and the study of appellate courts. Scientists such as Cook and Moore underestimated the magnitude and difficulty of the tasks they had set themselves. There were some notable particular achievements, but they were fragmented and diverse. No new core or cores were established.

One reason for this failure was a failure of theory. For one major function of theorizing is to provide coherence – to map connections and to develop a systematic, internally consistent overview. But, by and large, the realists failed to do this. They pursued some of the particular hares (and other creatures) that they had let loose when they lifted the lid, but they failed to marshal these diverse creatures into any sort of order.

In respect of this kind of organizing theory, evidence has been better served than most. Bentham's theory of evidence purports to integrate the logic, psychology and philosophy of evidence, and makes the case for having no binding exclusionary rules. Moreover, Bentham's theory of evidence is subsumed under a theory of adjudication which in turn has its place within the Constitutional Code as part of his general theory of law.[62] Wigmore's theory of proof, although more narrowly focused, integrates the study of the logic and psychology of proof and forensic science with evidence doctrine. Both belong to a tradition of rather optimistic rationalism about legal process, are unduly court-minded and, as one would expect, are outdated in a number of ways. Nevertheless the legacy of Bentham and Wigmore (and of other theorists) provides an impressive foundation from which to start to develop a systematic mapping theory of EPF as part of a broadened conception of academic law. Such a theory may help to provide the coherence that is needed if alternatives to the rule-dominated tradition are to have much staying power. Such a theory needs to be conceived, in first instance, independently of its educational implications[63] – for over-concern with the day-to-day realities and constraints of academic life can have a distorting effect on theory construction. But some of the basic foundations exist for the development of a coherent theory of EPF within the framework of a broad approach to academic law.[64] When such a theory is developed, then it may be that Jerome Frank's vision – in its saner aspects – will be realized in practice.

NOTES

1   This essay, a revised version of an address delivered at the ceremonies celebrating the opening of the Begbie Building, Faculty of Law, University of Victoria, BC, in November 1980, was published in N. Gold (1982) and in 34 Jo. Leg. Ed. 22 (1984). It is reprinted here by kind permission of Butterworth & Co., Toronto. The informal style of an address has been retained.
2   Currie (1955), 4.
3   Recent research suggests that the Oldest Member may have been exaggerating. A particularly suggestive study which has a bearing on several issues in this paper is Zemans (1980). The findings of Zemans, and of other studies cited in her paper, provide a useful starting-point for informed discussion of educational priorities in a coherent scheme of vocational training. On their own, they cannot, of course, resolve complex issues of priorities and programming in a multifunctional system of legal education. See further Zemans and Rosenblum (1981).
4   See generally Frank (1930, 1933, 1949). See further below, ch. 4.
5   Muensterberg (1908).
6   Osborn (1922).
7   Report of the Committee on Legal Education, HMSO Cmnd. 4595 (1971), 94; for other examples see Marx (1953). See now the Marre Report (1988). This lists twenty-four legal skills, including '(6) An ability to isolate elementary logical and statistical fallacies', '(9) An ability to ascertain and verify the relevant facts of any legal problem' and '(10) An ability to analyse facts and to be able to construct and criticise an argument on a disputed question of fact'. Strangely, it concludes that (6) and (9) should be taught at the academic stage, but that (10) should be among those taught at the vocational stage (paras. 12, 21–3).
8   Eggleston (1983); Finkelstein (1978); Cullison (1969); Barnes (1983). For a critique

of 'mathematicist' approaches, see L. J. Cohen (1977). See further below, 70, 119–22 and Twining (1980a).
9 Holmes (1897).
10 See the useful bibliography by Snyman (1979). See now Watt (1988).
11 See, for example, American Bar Association (1979).
12 It is argued below (ch. 11) that for some purposes a broader category, covering the processing and uses of information in important decisions in litigation (IL), is preferable to EPF.
13 Michael (1948).
14 On Bentham see n. 18 below; on Wigmore see n. 21 below; on Michael see n. 24 below; on Levin see n. 28 below; on Rutter see n. 30 below. Classic works in the Anglo-American tradition include: Wills (1838); Best (1849); J. F. Stephen (1872); Gulson (1905). For a useful historical survey see 1 Wigmore *Treatise*, s. 8. Almost without exception these concentrate on disputed questions of fact in litigation ('legal controversy') on the basis of a number of largely shared assumptions about the nature of adjudication and of what is involved in 'rational' fact determination. This shared perspective can be characterized as 'optimistic rationalism', see below, ch. 3.
15 A similar pattern in law and the social sciences is discussed by Kalven (1958).
16 Below, ch. 3, at 70.
17 Bentham vi *Works*. The proof of the unpublished printing of 1812 of approximately the first third of *An Introductory View* survives in the Bentham MSS at University College, London. A sheet dated 1822 states that the printing was stopped 'owing to the disappearance of some papers which have since been recovered'. James Mill's biographer suggests that booksellers feared prosecution because of Bentham's critique of jury packing (Bain, 1882, 120); Bentham's famous discussion of oaths, *Swear Not at All*, was originally written as part of the *Introductory View*. It was separately printed in 1813, but publication was postponed until 1817. For Bentham's account, see v *Works* 189. I am indebted to Ian Morrison for much of the information in this note. Recent research by Andrew Lewis casts doubt on the claim that James Mill edited *An Introductory View*.
18 Bentham, *Rationale* (1827); J. S. Mill, *Autobiography* (1873).
19 Above, n. 5.
20 Wigmore (1909). See also C. C. Moore (1907); Moore, a practitioner, was himself author of a remarkable work, *A Treatise on Facts* (1908). Wigmore, while praising the work in general terms, criticized Moore for suggesting that rules of law can determine the weight or credibility of testimony (1909). See below, 65–7.
21 Wigmore *Science*.
22 Arnold (1906) (2nd edn, 1913).
23 Hutchins and Slesinger (1928, 1928a, 1929, 1929b); Hutchins (1933). These articles are discussed in Schlegel (1979).
24 Michael and Adler (1931). The foreword states: 'This is not a book. It is merely galley proof, which after considerable revision and elaboration will become a book, and it is being put forth in this form so that the authors can use it in classes which they are now conducting. It is not intended for wider circulation.' Some of the material was later used in articles and other writings by the two authors; see especially Michael and Adler (1934, 1952) and Michael (1948).
25 Wigmore, above, n. 21; 3rd edn, 6, n. 1.
26 Wigmore, above, n. 21.
27 The information about the fate of Wigmore's *Science* is taken from the Wigmore Papers at Northwestern University Law School and Roalfe (1977).
28 A. Leo Levin (1956), discussed in Levin (1958).
29 On the Bentham Project see reports in the *Bentham Newsletter*, 1978–88. Editorial work has been restarted on *An Introductory View*.
30 Marx, above, n. 7; Houts (1955, 1956); Michael, n. 24; Rutter (1961); Levin, above, n. 28. The coverage of Frank's course at Yale approximated to the topics dealt with in *Courts on Trial* (1949).

31   For published accounts of demonstrations and 'experiments' in the classroom, see e.g. Wigmore, above, n. 20 (2nd edn), 532ff.; Roalfe (1977), 56; Houts (1956), ch. 1; Merrills (1971). On research in this area see especially Trankell (1972); Damaska (1975); Clifford and Bull (1978); Loftus (1979); Lloyd-Bostock (1988). See further below, ch. 5.

32   Twining (1967).

33   On the distinction between 'skills' and 'techniques', see Rutter (1961), Gold et al. (1989).

34   Wigmore *Science* (1937), 5.

35   Id., 6.

36   Id., 7.

37   Id., 8.

38   Wigmore provides a list of trials useful for study in the appendices of the 2nd and 3rd editions of the *Principles of Proof*, together with a list of historical problems susceptible to the same kind of analysis. Professor Terence Anderson of the University of Miami Law School has used National Trial Competition problems and other such materials as the basis for exercises in Wigmorean analysis from the standpoint of a lawyer preparing for trial. Although Wigmore *claimed* to be adopting the standpoint of the trial attorney during trials, by using inert records he often switched to the standpoint of a historian. See also *TEBW* and *Analysis* and below, chs. 8 and 9.

39   Lord Wright (1938) in an enthusiastic review of Wigmore's *Science*, wrote: 'I have asked myself whether I should have done my work any better if I had studied the book in earlier days, not merely for information, but for living mastery of the principles so as to apply and use them. I think the answer should be in the affirmative. Rule of thumb is all very well, especially in a subject like legal proof ... But all the same, the logic is there. A workman is all the better if he knows and understands his tools as scientifically as he can.'

40   This theme is developed in Twining (1988b).

41   For an evaluation of the educational and other uses and limitations of Wigmore's method see *TEBW*, *Analysis*, and chs. 8 and 9 below.

42   These themes are developed in later essays in this book.

43   The 1982 version of this paper, op. cit. n. 1, contains a discussion of Rutter's approach.

44   In addition to those already mentioned, contemporary precedents include Sir Richard Eggleston's courses at Monash University, Terence Anderson's Evidence Workshop at the University of Miami, David Schum's work at Rice University (see Schum and Martin (1983)), and my own courses at Warwick and London. These are just a sample of university-based courses. Anderson, Schum and Twining all build on Wigmore *Science*. Some relatively new types of vocational training courses that developed during the 1970s in many common law jurisdictions devote a substantial amount of time to aspects of 'fact management', typically without resort to such terms. An exception is the new Vocational Course for the Bar, run by the Council of Legal Education in London, which emphasizes the attainment of minimum competence in the practical skills expected of junior barristers. See generally, Gold, Mackie and Twining (eds) (1989).

45   Weinstein (1955), discussing Marx, above, n. 7, and Frank's thesis, above, n. 4.

46   Weinstein, id. 464.

47   Id., 465.

48   Ibid.

49   Id., 464.

50   See Twining and Miers (1982), Preface. In respect of skills, a direct approach postulates the need to allocate time (a substantial part of a course on legal method would, in some contexts, be adequate) and to isolate relevant aspects of EPF for study. This is not inconsistent with advocating 'a pervasive approach' in other courses for purposes of reinforcing and extending such basic skills. A strong case can be made for direct study of several aspects of EPF, in addition to what is already done in curricula of the kind postulated by Weinstein.

51 See below, ch. 3 and 4.
52 Bentham (1827), 182; cf. Bentham (1825), 269: 'There would be no absurdity in inserting in a course of law, and, above all, in a treatise on the judicial art, a summary of the laws of nature, as applicable to different questions which may arise before judges; but it ought to be presumed, that the men who are elevated to high judicial functions, have passed through the schools of philosophy.'
53 See *Works*, cited above, n. 17.
54 On the debate between 'mathematicists' and Baconians, see below, 117–22.
55 In conversation with teachers of evidence in the United Kingdom, the United States and Canada I have found that the two most commonly articulated objections to extending the study of evidence and proof beyond the rules of evidence are that (1) professional examinations concentrate on the rules and (2) law teachers are not competent to teach the logical, psychological and other aspects of a broadened conception of EPF. In respect of (1), one object of this paper is to make the case for change in the long term; meanwhile professional requirements need not so directly limit the extension of the study of EPF within law schools. In respect of (2) my impression is that lack of confidence is more of an obstacle than lack of competence. Several reviewers of Wigmore *Science* attributed its neglect to 'the real or imagined incompetence' of law teachers to deal with the subject; see, for example 30 Mich. L. Rev. 1354 (1932).
56 See Rutter (1961), 312–16. Since this essay was first published there have been very significant developments in the literature, as is illustrated by references in the footnotes above.
57 This thesis is developed in Twining (1986c) and *The Reading Law Cook-Book* (forthcoming).
58 However, Bentham's *Rationale of Judicial Evidence* has been reprinted in a facsimile edition as part of *Classics of English Legal History in the Modern Era* (New York, 1978); Wigmore *Science* (3rd edn) is available in photocopy or microfilm from University Microfilms International. Michael and Adler's work is not so accessible, except in their excellent series of articles cited above, n. 24. Levin's mimeographed materials are to be found in a number of law libraries in the US.
59 See especially Frank (1930).
60 See generally, Twining (1973).
61 On Holmes, see Twining (1973a). See Frank (1949), ch. 16 and at 422–3, and (1947) for his prescriptions.
62 See especially Halévy (1928), 1955 edn, 373 ff. and Postema (1977).
63 *TEBW*, ch. 2.
64 Cf. Kalven, op. cit., n. 15, on the odd and mistaken view 'that the only test of relevance of research in the law school world is whether you can teach it'.

3

The Rationalist Tradition of Evidence Scholarship

What was formerly 'tried' by the method of force or the mechanical following of form is now tried by the method of reason.

Thayer[1]

At the start of Shakespeare's *Richard II* Bolingbroke and Mowbray, Duke of Norfolk, are called before the King 'to appeal each other of high treason'. Each of the disputants is anxious to defend his honour and to prove the other a traitor in the lists. Before they come before him, Richard asks Gaunt if this dispute is based on ancient malice or 'worthily, as a good subject should, on some known ground of treachery in him'. Gaunt replies that, 'as near as I could sift him on the argument', there is no inveterate malice, but apparent danger to the King. Richard responds:

> Then call them to our presence; face to face
> And frowning brow to brow, ourselves will hear
> The accuser and the accused, freely speak.

Only after they have had their say and Richard and others have failed to persuade them to make up, does he reluctantly agree to let

> ... your swords and lances arbitrate
> The swelling difference of your settled hate.[2]

They reassemble at Coventry ready for battle, but the King intervenes at the last moment to stop the fight and to banish both disputants, a classic example of a disastrous attempt at peaceful dispute-settlement.

We need not here concern ourselves with the detailed accuracy of Shakespeare's account of the proceedings, nor with whether this mode of dispute-settlement can appropriately be said to have involved a 'trial', political or otherwise.[3] But it is worth noting some of the ingredients of this example of a manner of proceeding which is conventionally termed 'irrational': insistence on a specific charge; confrontation of accused and accuser before authority; the opportunity for each side to be heard; arguments 'sifted' (twice);[4] attempts to persuade the parties to settle the dispute peacefully; ultimate control over each stage of the proceedings by lawful authority in the person of the King, but the original initiative and some of the decisions on how to proceed in the control of the parties. It is a formal adversary process, supervised by authority, involving argument and decision at most stages. The main 'irrational' element, the proof by force of arms, is seen as a last resort and is framed in terms of appeals to God to defend the righteous contender.

In given circumstances there may be reasons for choosing to settle a dispute or disagreement or competition or game by means other than reasoning and argument, for example by tossing a coin or by fighting or by granting victory to the side which scores the most goals or by considering the result of plunging a person's arm in boiling oil. One may seek to justify the choice of means with reasons, but the means are not themselves considered 'rational' in Thayer's sense. The 'rational' system is one which uses reason, so far as is feasible, in determination of disputed questions of fact and law. This particular view of rationality is succinctly summarized by Thayer as follows: 'Any determination by a court which weighs (the) testimony or other evidence in the scale of reason, and decides a litigated question as it is decided now'.[5]

The purpose of this chapter is to examine some of the background to contemporary studies of evidence and proof, by considering both historically and analytically some highlights of the development of the specialized study of evidence in England and the United States. The next section presents an historical overview in the form of brief surveys of the work of selected writers within this tradition. The third section contains a restatement of some of the basic assumptions about fact-finding in adjudication that appear by and large to have been shared by almost all of the leading specialist writers on evidence. They can be said to have a shared underlying theory that may be characterized as optimistic rationalism. There is a sharp contrast both in tone and emphasis between orthodox literature on evidence and much recent writing on judicial process, but it will be argued in chapter 4 that the differences may not be so great as they appear on the surface.

Anglo-American Evidence Scholarship: An Historical Overview

It is not necessary for present purposes to attempt to trace all aspects of the intellectual history of the study of Evidence. Such an account would have to include the contributions of classical and medieval rhetoric, the debates on the numerical system of proof in Europe, the history of probability theory, the emergence of forensic science and forensic psychology in the late nineteenth century and much else besides.[6] But it is instructive to consider in outline the history of the *specialized* study of evidence in the Anglo-American tradition between the publication in 1754 of Gilbert's *The Law of Evidence* and the death of Wigmore in 1943. For convenience of exposition, the story can be roughly divided into four periods: (a) the period before 1800; (b) the period 1800–50, marked by the writings of Bentham, the establishment of the first generation of English treatises, and the first round of public debates on reform of the law of evidence; (c) the period 1850–1900, during which further debates on reform took place in England, India and the United States, and the first generation of American Evidence scholars emerged and began to dominate the field; and (d) the period 1900–60 which is dominated by Wigmore.[7] The survey which follows deals with selected writers from Gilbert to Wigmore with a few deviations from strict chronological order for convenience of exposition.

Before 1800

Problems of proof are as old and as pervasive as the law itself: one would accordingly expect them to be reflected even in the earliest legal literature. So far as England is concerned this is true only in a very restricted sense. For the development of a substantial body of literature devoted to evidence and proof as such is a relatively late phenomenon. There are several reasons for this: for a remarkably long time the main methods by which disputed questions of fact were dealt with did not require a system of *evidence*; the early methods of ordeal, battle and compurgation and the emerging jury did not require decisions by tribunals that had no first-hand knowledge of the alleged facts. The early history of the rules of evidence is the story of the emergence of different doctrines in different periods; the conclusiveness of documents under seal was an early development; the rules concerning competency of witnesses – an important battleground in the nineteenth century – were largely established in the sixteenth century; the privilege against self-incrimination took root in the common law in the seventeenth century; there is much debate about the origins of the hearsay rule, but it is reasonably clear that it did not become firmly established until after 1600. Each rule of evidence has its own, sometimes obscure, often convoluted, history. Sometimes isolated precedents anticipate the recognition of a practice, and practice precedes the articulation of doctrine. In the case of the law of evidence what is sometimes referred to as 'the modern system' was to a large extent a late eighteenth-century and early nineteenth-century creation, fashioned by secondary writers from materials spanning several centuries.

In 1794 at the trial of Warren Hastings, Burke is reported as saying: 'It was true, something had been written on the law of Evidence, but very general, very abstract, and comprised in so small a compass that a parrot he had known might get them by rote in one half-hour and repeat them in five minutes.'[8]

Making due allowance for the rhetorical exaggeration of a non-lawyer advocate, this is not far removed from contemporary professional perceptions of the law of evidence. The first important treatise, by Gilbert, attempted to subsume the whole of the law under a single principle, the 'best evidence rule'. Buller's *Nisi Prius*, a very influential work, summarized the rules of evidence first in nine and later in twelve propositions; if one looks in Comyn's *Digest* under 'Evidence', even as late as the edition of 1822, one is referred to 'Testmoigne', which takes up less than forty pages of what was by then an eight-volume encyclopaedia. Blackstone devoted little more than ten pages to the subject.

There are several reasons for this perception of evidence as a rudimentary branch of law. First, precedents later seen to be relevant were scattered throughout the reports and digests. In the seventeenth century, practice books such as those of Style and Duncombe collected together some cases under the heading of 'Evidence'; early treatises on criminal law by Hale (1682) and Hawkins (1716) had separate chapters devoted to the topic. But before 1800 lengthy treatments of evidence as a distinct subject were almost unknown. A digest of the *Law of Evidence*, published in 1717 and attributed to William Nelson, may have been the earliest example. An anonymous work on *The Theory of Evidence* was published in 1761 and was later blamed, along with Gilbert, for the popularization of the 'best evidence rule', a source of continuous difficulty for nineteenth-century writers. The author is thought to be Henry Bathurst, who later became Lord Chancellor (1771–8); much of his work was subsequently incorporated in an introduction of the *Law of Evidence Relative to Trials at Nisi Prius*, first published, also anonymously, by Bathurst's nephew, Francis Buller, in 1772. A few works, long since forgotten, such as Morgan's *Essays of the Law of Evidence* (1789), in three volumes, appeared, but seem to have made little impact. By far the most important separate work on evidence before 1800 was Gilbert's treatise, *The Law of Evidence*, which will be discussed below.

Neither the separate treatises nor the works which devoted attention specifically to evidence as part of some broader topic, presented the subject in a systematic fashion. Even Gilbert, by far the most systematic, is not much more than a digest of cases collected together under a few pithy, loosely connected, general propositions. At the time Burke spoke there was some justification for believing that Evidence, as reflected in the secondary literature, deserved to be treated as a 'non-subject'.

There is one further factor which helps to explain professional perceptions of the matter at the end of the eighteenth century. This was the expansion of law reporting, especially at Nisi Prius. Wigmore puts the matter as follows:

A.D. 1790–1830. The full spring-tide of the system had now arrived. In the ensuing generation the established principles began to be developed into rules and precedents of minutiae relatively innumerable to what had gone before. In the Nisi Prius reports of Peake, Espinasse, and Campbell, centering around the quarter-century from 1790 to 1815, there are probably more rulings upon evidence than in all the prior reports of two centuries. In this development the dominant influence is plain: it was the increase of printed reports of Nisi Prius rulings.[9]

Gilbert

Gilbert was Lord Chief Baron of the Court of Exchequer from 1722 until his death in 1726. He was a prolific writer, but nearly all of his works were published posthumously. *The Law of Evidence* was published in several editions, the first in Dublin in 1754, the last in London in 1801, edited by J. Sedgwick. It is a tribute to the quality and originality of the work that it survived a thirty-year delay in publication to become what was perhaps the single most important work on evidence before Bentham. Gilbert's style is simple and cogent, but the key to his success lay in the fact that he set out to establish a tightly integrated theory of evidence based on the notion of probability. *The Law of Evidence* begins with Locke:

In the first Place, it has been observed by a very learned Man, that there are several Degrees from perfect Certainty and Demonstration, quite down to Improbability and Unlikeliness, even to the Confines of Impossibility; and there are several Acts of the Mind proportion'd to these Degrees of Evidence, which may be called the Degrees of Assent, from full Assurance and Confidence, quite down to Conjecture, Doubt, Distrust and Disbelief.[10]

Demonstration is based on the clear and direct perception of permanent things by 'a Man's own proper senses'. The affairs of life allow only exceptionally of demonstration because they are generally concerned with transient actions which often are not clearly perceived or are reported by others. Accordingly the rights of men in civil life have to be determined on the basis of something less than demonstration, that is judgments of probability. Gilbert set out to erect a theory of evidence in trials on the foundation of this explicitly Lockean theory of knowledge:

The first therefore, and most signal Rule, in Relation to Evidence, is this, That a Man must have the utmost Evidence the Nature of the Fact is capable of; for the Design of the Law is to come to rigid Demonstration in Matters of Right, and there can be no Demonstration of a Fact without the best Evidence that the Nature of the Thing is capable of.[11]

Taking this very general and rather rigid formulation of the 'best evidence rule', which he purported to derive from Holt, Gilbert proceeded to establish various categories of evidence and to grade them in terms of probabilities in something approaching a formal hierarchy, with Public Records at the top, as the very best evidence.

The Law of Evidence was recognized as the leading work on the subject for about fifty years after its first publication in 1754 and was re-issued on at least four occasions between 1791 and 1801. This was not merely a commercial success. Bathurst used it as a model; Peake, the author of the first important nineteenth-century treatise, made handsome acknowledgement of Gilbert's influence, as did several other later writers. Blackstone, who delicately side-stepped 'the numerous niceties and distinctions' of the law of evidence, referred his readers to Gilbert's treatise as 'a work which it is impossible to abstract or abridge without losing some beauty and destroying the chain as a whole'.[12] Gilbert was seen by his admirers as having presented the law of evidence within a coherent theoretical framework and in a clear, succinct and useful form. It was partly for this reason that Bentham was provoked into a venomous attack.

'False Theory of Evidence (Gilbert's)' is the subject of chapter 31 and Appendix C of Bentham's *An Introductory View*, written between 1802 and 1809, but not published until some thirty years later.[13] According to Bentham the efficient cause of Gilbert's error was a defective scheme of arrangement; the final cause was the sinister interest of the legal fraternity to throw and keep the subject in confusion; the result a false theory which, *inter alia*, erroneously gives precedence to written over oral evidence. By making the distinction between written and oral evidence the foundation of their system, Gilbert and his successors were led into several errors: they overlook real evidence, give insufficient attention to circumstantial evidence and ignore several crucial distinctions. For example, Gilbert failed to discriminate between various kinds of makeshift and pre-appointed evidence. The error of ranking written evidence above unwritten is based on confusing verity and authenticity of documents. It may be the case that few records are not authentic, but many of them are clearly unreliable. Gilbert had placed first in his hierarchy of probability the legal memorials of the legislature and of the king's courts of justice deposited at the Treasury of Westminster. Mocking the Chief Baron's love of mathematics, Bentham suggests that Gilbert treats records as 'a diagram for the demonstration of right' produced by a 'supersacred and super-human class of persons'.[14] But officials are but men, whose trustworthiness needs to be determined by the same tests as any other men; and legal records are notoriously unreliable, 'compounds or reservoirs of truths and lies undistinguishably shaken together, penned by nobody knows who, and kept under the orders, how seldom soever, if ever, actually subjected to the eyes of the judges of Westminster Hall'.[15] They are, moreover, the repositories of legal fictions and so, in Bentham's eyes, particularly suspect.[16] After criticizing other aspects of Gilbert's hierarchy, he concludes: 'In the same strain of anility, garrulity, narrow-mindedness, absurdity, perpetual misrepresentation, and indefatigable self-contradiction, runs the whole of this work, from which men are to understand the true theory of evidence.'[17]

Bentham's attack on Gilbert's theory is as sharp as any to be found in his often polemical writings on evidence. *En passant* he takes sideswipes at some familiar targets – legal fictions, judge-made law, the double-fountain of Law and Equity, and the sinister interest in mystification of 'Judge and Co.'. The main target is ostensibly Gilbert's scheme of classification, but the real object of attack is the attempt to regulate judgments of probability by formal rules.

In an important sense one of Gilbert's principal achievements was to provide Bentham with an identifiable target to attack. Before Gilbert there was hardly a 'law of evidence' to criticize. As the most coherent and the most influential expositor of this branch of law Gilbert provided an important focus of attention. Furthermore his theory was clearly false in Bentham's eyes. The immediate source of error was a defective scheme of classification, but the core of the matter was the suggestion that the weighing of evidence could be governed by rigid rules. By talking in terms of 'rules of probability' Gilbert had conflated questions of admissibility and questions of weight, and had suggested that both kinds of question could be governed by formal rules, whereas Bentham believed that the former should not be and the latter could not be. What a modern commentator has termed 'misplaced mathematicization'[18] was just one more symptom of a generally flawed attempt to formalize a subject that was literally ungovernable. The attractive simplicity and seeming elegance of Gilbert's theory no doubt made it seem all the more dangerous.

To a large extent Bentham's critique has been confirmed by the judgement of history, even though his own arguments were not published until after his death, and have since attracted little attention. Most of Gilbert's successors, both judges and treatise writers, including Peake, Phillipps, Starkie, Greenleaf, Taylor, Best, treated the 'best evidence rule' as a fundamental principle. Some struggled to free themselves from the straitjacket, first by restricting its scope and then by reducing its status from a rigid rule to a prudential maxim. But during the nineteenth century, as Thayer was eventually to point out, it became even more rigid by being transformed from a positive admonition to adduce the most reliable kind of evidence, especially in respect of documents, to a rigid rule of exclusion, sometimes leading to the loss of valuable evidence, sometimes to complicated distinctions and exceptions.[19] Thayer concludes that 'Gilbert in his premature, ambitious and inadequate attempt to adjust to the philosophy of John Locke the rude beginnings and tentative, unconscious efforts of the courts in the direction of a body of rules of evidence, hurt rather than helped matters'.[20]

This is an unduly harsh judgment on the first serious attempt to provide a coherent and principled theory of evidence, which was not published in the author's lifetime and which was then interpreted more rigidly than he probably intended. Nevertheless, the view that Gilbert's theory was false and had exercised a baneful influence prevailed; similarly during the nineteenth century it was Bentham's conceptual scheme rather than Gilbert's which prevailed, not because of his attack on Gilbert (which was hidden in the little-known *Introductory View*), but because this was one part of Bentham's theory of evidence that was picked up by most later writers.

Bentham[21]

Bentham's main work on evidence was done in the period 1802–12, but his interest in the subject spanned the whole of his working life. His writings on evidence and procedure are vast: in addition to the main published works, *Traité des preuves judiciaires* (ed. Dumont), *An Introductory View of the Rationale of Evidence* (ed. James Mill), *Rationale of Judicial Evidence* (ed. J. S. Mill), and *Principles of Judicial Procedure* (ed. Richard Doane), there are several important other works in which the subject is discussed; the surviving unpublished manuscripts are almost as extensive as the corpus of published works, although many of them represent earlier versions of the latter.[22]

Elie Halévy wrote: 'Of all Bentham's works *The Rationale of Judicial Evidence* ... is the most voluminous and also without doubt the most important.'[23] In the John Stuart Mill edition it runs to nearly three thousand pages. It is not possible here to do justice to the richness, diversity and crankiness of its arguments, but the central thesis can be succinctly stated: the direct end of adjective law is rectitude of decision, that is the correct application of valid laws (presumed to be consonant with utility) to true facts. The collateral end is to minimize the pains of vexation, expense and delay. Conflicts between the direct and collateral ends are to be determined on the basis of utility, but Bentham leaves no doubt that in this calculation he placed a high value on the pursuit of truth in adjudication. Judgments about the truth of allegations of fact are to be made by considering the relevant evidence – 'Evidence is the basis of justice.'[24] Such judgments are based on estimates of probabilities, which estimates in turn are based on experience. The system of adjudication most conducive to promoting the ends of judicature is the Natural System as opposed to the Technical System. The Natural System takes as its prototype the wise father adjudicating in the bosom of the family, the disputants face to face, giving *viva voce* testimony and subject to cross-examination. No witness, including the parties themselves, and no relevant evidence is excluded, subject to preponderant vexation, expense or delay: 'Be the dispute what it may, – see everything that is to be seen: hear everybody who is likely to know anything about the matter: hear everybody, but most attentively of all, and first of all, those who are likely to know most about it – the parties.'[25]

Much of Bentham's central thesis is negative in import. It consists of a sustained polemic on the unnecessary complication, absurdity and obscurity of the Technical System and on the sinister interests of the judiciary and the legal profession ('Judge and Co.') which sustain the system in England. Bentham also attacks all exclusionary rules of evidence ('the non-exclusion principle') and the very idea that the weighing of evidence is susceptible to regulation by formal rules, what I shall refer to hereafter as the anti-nomian thesis. There is, however, a positive side to the *Rationale,* for Bentham deals at length with such matters as the means of securing the forthcomingness of witnesses and of evidence, with securities for correctness and completeness of evidence, and with guidance by way of instructions to the judge about the weighing of evidence.

Bentham's *Rationale* and assorted writings still represent the most ambitious and fully developed theory of evidence and proof in the history of legal thought. The nearest rival is Wigmore's 'science of judicial proof', which underlies his great *Treatise* and is more fully, but still only partially, expounded in his neglected work *The Principles* [later *Science*] *of Judicial Proof* (hereafter referred to as Wigmore's *Science*). Wigmore deals more comprehensively (and in a more up-to-date fashion) with some of the logical and psychological dimensions of proof, as well as dealing in far more detail with the history, content and underlying rationales of particular evidence doctrines. But Bentham's theory is more extensive in several key respects: first, his theory of evidence and proof is more explicitly and fully integrated with a theory of adjudication, which in turn is part of a general constitutional theory and ultimately of a general theory of law. Wigmore did not develop a rounded theory of procedure or of adjudication comparable to Bentham's. Secondly, Bentham's prescriptions on evidence represent a direct and relatively straightforward application of the principle of utility. As such they are based on an explicit theory of value, albeit a highly controversial one. Most other theorists of evidence, including Wigmore, are less explicit and less coherent about the basis of their evaluations and recommendations. Thirdly, Bentham's writings on evidence contain some of his most extensive discussions of epistemology and psychology and, to a lesser extent, of logic. In the *Rationale* he expounds what might be characterized as a cognitivist, empirical epistemology, based on a correspondence theory of truth, which owes a great deal to Locke. Rather less clearly he advances a theory of induction, including a rather obscure account of reasoning about probabilities, which has been interpreted – probably correctly – as being non-mathematicist.[26] Except on the vexed issue of the nature of probabilistic reasoning, nearly all leading Anglo-American writers on evidence have adopted, more often than not *sub silentio*, epistemological and logical views which are similar to Bentham's. I shall return to this later.

It is also pertinent here to say something about Bentham's anti-nomian thesis. At first sight it seems surprising that the jurist who more than any other believed in the desirability and feasibility of a complete code of substantive laws, leaving no discretion to judges to make law, should also have been an extreme opponent of the view that judicial discretion in respect of deciding questions of fact should be limited by rules. Whether there is a fundamental inconsistency in Bentham's views on substantive and adjective law in this respect is a matter of controversy among specialists.[27] But there is no doubt about his opposition to rules of evidence:

> To find infallible rules for evidence, rules which insure a just decision is, from the nature of things, absolutely impossible; but the human mind is too apt to establish rules which only increase the probabilities of a bad decision. All the service that an impartial investigator of the truth can perform in this respect is, to put the legislators and judges on their guard against such hasty rules.[28]

Although in the *Rationale* he placed particular emphasis on the non-exclusion principle, Bentham was opposed to all rules of evidence: rules governing credibility, weight and quantum of evidence are all mischievous. The apparent extremism of the anti-nomian thesis is subject to two major caveats. First, Bentham concedes that in theory a time may come when judging the closeness of the connection between a principal fact and an alleged evidentiary fact might profitably be subjected to rules: 'To take the business out of the hands of instinct, to subject it to rules, is a task which, if it lies within the reach of human faculties, must at any rate be reserved, I think, for the improved powers of some maturer age.'[29] But he consistently maintains that such a task, even if it is conceivable, is not yet feasible.

A second concession is more significant: what Bentham is opposed to is 'unbending rules' addressed to the will of the judge; it is, however, the role of the legislator to provide 'instructions' addressed to the understanding – general guides which he even sometimes refers to as 'rules'.[30] This is significant, for several subsequent writers on evidence have questioned the desirability of having binding rules of evidence, as opposed to guiding principles. Some have even gone so far as to doubt whether rulings on points of evidence should ever have the force of precedent and whether such rulings should be subject to appeal. Even Wigmore, in debating the Model Code of Evidence, went so far as to suggest that its rules should be 'directory, not mandatory'[31] to the judge, whose rulings should be subject to review only in extreme instances. Viewed in this light Bentham's anti-nomian thesis has some distinguished allies.

Subsequent Anglo-American writers on evidence have been selective in their reception of the anti-nomian thesis. With relatively minor exceptions, they have rejected the idea that weight of evidence is susceptible to formal regulation. Perhaps the classic formulation is that of Wigmore: 'The principles of Proof, then, represent the natural processes of the mind in dealing with the evidential facts after they are admitted to the jury: while the rules of Admissibility represent the artificial legal rules peculiar to our Anglo-American jury system.'[32]

In respect of rules of weight, Bentham's views have largely prevailed. There are two main exceptions. First, the law of evidence still lays down some formal minimum requirements concerning sufficiency of evidence: for example, the requirement of corroboration in cases of perjury, in relation to the evidence of accomplices, and to certain sexual offences. (In the case of child witnesses, reference should be made to the Criminal Justice Act, 1988, s. 34.) Moreover the civil and criminal standards of proof could be interpreted as rules of quantum. Secondly, there has been a controversy as to whether questions of relevancy are ever questions of law. Thayer advanced the view that 'the law furnishes no test of relevancy'.[33] Stephen, Best and Wigmore have variously argued that 'natural evidence' is restrained or modified by rules of positive law, with the result that the courts sometimes treat as irrelevant matters which are logically relevant (for example, because it is of insufficient probative force or in order to avoid a multiplicity of issues) and that some judicial decisions on relevance have value as precedents. The dispute is largely one of terminology, with few important practical consequences, for no clear formal lines are drawn and judges tend to exercise their discretion in this area along lines that are quite compatible with Bentham's thesis. There are few formal rules governing questions of weight or credibility of evidence and, in this respect, Bentham's victory is substantial, if not complete.

The position with regard to exclusionary rules is less simple. Many of Bentham's particular arguments have been accepted and some of his main targets, notably the exclusion of parties and others as competent witnesses, have virtually disappeared.

Nearly all the changes made since his day have been in the direction of abolishing or diminishing the importance of the exclusionary rules. This trend has generally gone further in England than the United States, especially in respect of civil evidence. However, Bentham's general principle of non-exclusion has not been accepted. Certain doctrines, such as legal professional privilege, parts of hearsay, the rule about previous convictions, and some other safeguards for the accused are still firmly entrenched, while others remain the subject of continuing controversy. The exclusionary rules have been eroded, but there is no immediate prospect of their complete abolition.

Nevertheless, Bentham's anti-nomian thesis has immense historical significance. Since his day protagonists of the common law rules of evidence have generally been on the defensive; the actual scope of the law of evidence, in the sense of those matters which are governed by mandatory rules, has steadily diminished and is today a good deal narrower than is sometimes supposed; and, haunting every expositor of the rules and challenging those who favour a broader approach to law is the question: 'What would we study in respect of evidence and proof if there were no rules?'[34] But this is to run ahead of my theme. We must first look briefly at the main English treatise writers in the period 1800–50.

The early nineteenth-century treatises

The start of the nineteenth century saw the first of a succession of practical reference works on evidence for practitioners, which has continued until the present day. The first of these was *A Compendium of the Law of Evidence* by Thomas Peake (1771–1838), a barrister of Lincoln's Inn who later became a Serjeant at Law. Peake edited a series of reports of Nisi Prius cases starting in 1790, a period in which decisions on evidence became very prominent. Peake's *Reports* had an excellent reputation for clarity and accuracy. So did his *Compendium*, which was first published in 1801. It immediately became a standard work. It was intended as a book of practical reference, excluding 'every thing which was not practically useful', but emphasizing principle. The early chapters, including his statement of 'the general rules', followed Gilbert and Buller very closely, but he also included a great deal of new material on proof of private instruments, on parole testimony and on witnesses, thereby reflecting recent developments in the law, not least the establishment of a clear distinction between competence and credibility of witnesses. There is little that is original in Peake's ideas or approach, but the conciseness and accuracy of his exposition were praised, even by Bentham.[35] There were five English editions of Peake's *Compendium*, the last in 1822, by which time further changes in the law had rendered it obsolete.

The first edition of Peake's *Compendium* was quickly followed by an Irish work for practitioners, Leonard MacNally's *The Rules of Evidence on Pleas of the Crown*, published in Dublin in 1802. This was rather longer than Peake, although confined to criminal cases, but it does not seem to have been so successful. These two books can be seen as forerunners of a long line of compact works published in the nineteenth century, ranging from those of Harrison (1825), Saunders (1828) and Garde (1830), all of which appear to have made less impact than standard works that ran to many editions. The most successful of these were by Roscoe and Archbold. All of these books had limited, severely practical aims mainly as handy works of reference and they had little or no pretensions to influence the development of the law – although in the case of Archbold it probably did exert considerable influence, partly by its power of survival and by its convenience for and familiarity to practitioners and judges.[36]

Sir W. D. Evans

In 1806 an English translation of R. Pothier's treatise[37] on the law of obligations was published in London, accompanied by a lengthy introduction and a commentary in the form of 'Notes, illustrative of the English Law on the subject'. The commentary was substantially longer than the translated text. The translator and commentator was William David Evans, who was at the time a special pleader and conveyancer practising on the Northern Circuit.[38] Evans was an energetic, ambitious man who seems never quite to have fulfilled his potential as either lawyer or author. He served successively as a stipendiary magistrate in Manchester, as Vice-Chancellor of the County Palatine of

Lancaster and finally as Recorder of Bombay, where he died at the age of fifty-four. He was a prolific editor and writer mainly, but not exclusively, on legal topics. He published several legal works, besides his edition of Pothier, and left several unfinished manuscripts at his death. A man of broad intellectual and legal interests, he was an enthusiastic proponent of the value of general jurisprudence and comparative law. In 1803 he had published a two-volume study of Lord Mansfield's decisions in civil cases,[39] which he complained, in his introduction to Pothier, had 'remained three years almost entirely unnoticed'. This work reveals him as an ardent, if not entirely uncritical, disciple of Mansfield. He shared his hero's view of 'jurisprudence as a rational science, founded upon the universal principles of moral rectitude, but modified by habit and authority'.[40] This notion provided both the inspiration and the basis for his treatment of Pothier.

Evans's Pothier has been widely recognized as a seminal influence on the development of English contract doctrine during the nineteenth century. His appendix on evidence, which ranges far beyond its application to contracts, was described by Wigmore as 'epoch-making'[41] on the ground that it was the first reasoned analysis of the rules and provided the theoretical foundation for the next phase of English writing about evidence. This probably exaggerates the importance of Evans's 'Notes'. Nevertheless it was a significant contribution, not least because it marked a much less rigid approach than Gilbert's.

Evans's study of Mansfield consisted largely of a descriptive survey of his more important decisions, with occasional comments. There was a strong emphasis on general principles. The section on evidence is one of the longest in the book. Similarly the appendix in Pothier's *Obligations* takes up nearly 200 pages, almost twice the length of the relevant sections by Pothier. There is also a substantial appendix on the distinction between law and fact. Not surprisingly there is considerable affinity and some overlap between the earlier and later treatments of evidence. It is fair to say that Evans's general approach and his ideas on evidence are Mansfieldian.

Evans was an early exponent of general jurisprudence, which he seems to have equated with the *ius gentium*. He justifies his introduction of Pothier to the English lawyer on the ground that the study of foreign systems helps him to discern 'those great and fundamental principles which being deduced from natural reason are equally diffused over all mankind and are not subject to alteration by any change of time or place ...'[42] Pothier's approach was based on similar ideas and it has been remarked that he drew 'an idealised picture of contract in eighteenth century France'.[43] Evans's commentary stresses the similarities of English and French principles, sometimes to a point which stretches credulity: it is surely misleading to suggest that the differences between the common law and civilian approaches to evidence and proof amounted to little more than some modifications of particular jurisprudence, even though the theory of evidence in England was in a sufficiently undeveloped state to allow some latitude in its interpretation.

Evans's commentary follows Pothier's arrangement fairly closely. After a brief consideration of general matters, including the 'best evidence rule', he deals first with written evidence, in which the French rules regarding notarized documents are observed to be more systematic and more formal than their English equivalents. In treating verbal evidence Evans notes that the law of France goes much further than English law in not allowing oral testimony to be admitted either to vary or explain written contracts. Furthermore no verbal evidence could be given in respect of the making of a contract, the delivery of goods or the payment of debts where the matter involved exceeded 100 livres.[44] The French rules requiring two witnesses were much more extensive, as were their provisions for excluding witnesses on such grounds as infamy, partiality, enmity or relation to a party to a dispute. Finally, the French rules governing confessions, presumptions and oaths are shown to be generally more formal than their English counterparts.

It is strange that Evans should conclude that a very great proportion of the rules of evidence 'answers the description of Sir William Jones of being equally good law at Westminster as at Orleans'.[45] For not only does he document a number of very striking differences of substance, but he interprets the English rules in a much more liberal spirit than Gilbert and Peake, thereby sharpening the contrast between the rigidities of the French and the relative flexibility of the English approach. This is particularly clearly illustrated by his treatment of the best evidence rule and of rules governing competence and number of witnesses. Gilbert, as we have seen, made the 'best evidence rule' the unifying principle of his whole system. Evans quotes with approval an unnamed North Carolina case which both restricted its scope and emphasized its flexibility:

There is but one decided rule in relation to evidence, and that is, that the law requires the best evidence. But this rule is always relaxed upon two grounds, either from absolute necessity, or a necessity presumed from the common occurrences amongst mankind. The rule is not so stubborn but that it will bend to the necessities of mankind, and to circumstances not under their control. The rule is adopted only to obviate the fraud of mankind.[46]

Evans accepts the 'best evidence rule' as a general starting-point, but unlike Gilbert he draws a sharp distinction between rules of admissibility, which are 'absolute and imperative', and questions of weight, on which he is not far from being an anti-nomian.[47] He is emphatic that in weighing contradictory testimony 'the mere consideration of number is held subordinate to that of the indications of individual veracity',[48] but he adds: '... although nothing can be more remote from the subject in discussion than the application of the strict rules of mathematical equality or proportion, a fair attention to the principles of those rules is often of considerable importance.'[49] Evans openly criticizes some of the exclusionary rules of competency, arguing cogently that factors such as infamy or interest should go to credit rather than competency; exclusion of a witness for mere suspicion, he suggests, 'is a very disproportionate sacrifice of a certain advantage to the avoidance of a contingent evil'.[50]

It is difficult to estimate the significance of Evans's contribution. In respect of contract, his main achievement was to make Pothier's text available in English. But even Pothier could not conceal the extreme rigidity of the French rules of evidence. There is a tension between Evans's concern to emphasize the similarities of English and French principles and his plea for limiting rules of exclusion and for a flexible approach to weighing evidence. It is true that he sought to establish some notion of universal principles as a basis for evaluating English doctrine and that he urged that law in general and the rules of evidence in particular should be expounded in a systematic manner. But his treatment of evidence in his commentaries on Mansfield and Pothier is more discursive than analytical; it does not compare in intellectual rigour with the attempts of Gilbert or Bathurst or even Peake to expound a reasonably coherent statement of principles. While some of his language echoes the natural law tradition of Grotius and Puffendorf, there are passages that could be interpreted as being distinctly utilitarian.[51]

In so far as one can extract a coherent general theory from Evans's work it is that a rational science of law should be based on universal moral principles reflected in the *ius gentium*, but modified in particular systems by tradition, authority and considerations of utility and convenience. Evans, unlike Gilbert and Peake, was prepared to criticize rather than merely rationalize existing doctrine, but his evaluation of the English rules of evidence was strikingly cautious; he advanced mild criticisms of some of the rules governing competency, confessions and comparison of hands, but he also tried to show that the great bulk of English rules, if interpreted as fairly flexible principles, were based on principles of natural reason. As he made clear in presenting his work on Mansfield to Lord Ellenborough, he was a moderate reformist, respectful of authority: 'It has been my aim ... to do justice to that spirit of liberal improvement, which is equally remote from timid servility and wanton innovation.'[52]

Wigmore suggests that Evans provided the first reasoned analysis of the rules of evidence and that his work was 'epoch-making'. For, when Phillipps and Starkie combined 'Evans' philosophy with Peake's strict reflections of the details of practice ... [t]here was now indeed a system of Evidence, consciously and fully realized.'[53] This seems to exaggerate both Evans's originality and his influence. Much of his inspiration came from Mansfield. Several of his predecessors were familiar with Roman Law, if not with contemporary French doctrine. Gilbert and Bathurst in particular were concerned to develop a systematic and principled account of the law of evidence; indeed their attempts at systematization were later seen as premature and over-rigid. Evans's concern to promote a more flexible, less formal approach represents a cautious attempt to reverse this trend. But he was not conspicuously successful. Bentham seems to have ignored him and in any event would have considered his philosophy muddled and his suggestions for reform absurdly cautious. Subsequent writers such as Phillipps, Starkie and Archbold drew from a wide range of sources. It is not clear how much, if at all, they were influenced by Evans's ideas (he complained that he was 'more often quoted than acknowledged'),[54] but their interpretation of the 'best evidence rule' and other rules was a good deal more rigid than his.

Phillipps

A Treatise on the Law of Evidence by Samuel March Phillipps of the Inner Temple, appears to have achieved instant success with practitioners. First published in 1814, new editions, each time 'with considerable additions', were published in 1815, 1817, 1820, 1822, 1824, 1829, 1838 and 1843. The stated purpose of the book was 'not so much to enquire minutely into particulars, as to take a general view of the system of the Law of Evidence; entering occasionally into details, for the purposes of illustration'.[55] But it was clearly used as a practitioners' handbook and it steadily increased in girth over the years, as new cases were fed into it, but old ones were generally not eliminated. In the first three editions Phillipps concentrated on attendance and competency of witnesses and on written evidence; with the fourth edition an entirely new second volume was added dealing with the nature of proofs required for various kinds of actions. Even as late as 1843 the principal general rules of evidence were dealt with in a single chapter occupying less than one twelfth of the whole work. As the author admitted, much of the second volume dealt with the rules of substantive law.[56] Until the publication of *Greenleaf on Evidence* in 1855, several editions of Phillipps's *Treatise* with American annotations, occupied a dominant place among practitioners' works in the United States.

Wigmore saw the works of Phillipps and Starkie as marking a transition from handbooks of practice to systematic treatises. Phillipps was not entirely insular, in that he cited Evans, Burnet's *Treatise of the Criminal Law of Scotland* and a few civilian writers. More important, he set out to expound the principles of his subject in a clear and systematic way. Rather than trying to provide a compendium of all authorities, he mainly used cases as examples to illustrate problems and points of practice as well as legal rules. For this purpose he drew on accounts of trials which did not necessarily have precedent value, in addition to reported authorities. However, there is little to suggest that he shared Evans's conceptions of universal jurisprudence and natural law. He consciously set out to expound and not to criticize the existing rules, and in giving explanations it is in terms of reasons stated in cases and older authors, the official view of the rationale for the rules rather than his own justifications for them. It is an attempt at systematic exposition which sticks closely to English law and practice, with utility to the practitioner as its primary aim. Its success may be attributable to this deliberate restraint as well as to the fact that he was accepted as accurate, perspicuous and well-organized.

Starkie

Thomas Starkie's *A Practical Treatise on the Law of Evidence* fits Wigmore's dictum more closely. Starkie was born in 1782. He was a Senior Wrangler at Cambridge and he practised as a Special Pleader on the Northern Circuit for a number of years.[57] In addition to his treatise on evidence he published two other substantial treatises and a three-volume series of *Reports at Nisi Prius*. In 1823 he was elected to the Downing Chair at Cambridge, but teaching was not his forte: it is reported that he was not successful as a lecturer in Common Law and Equity at the Inner Temple and, according to one of his successors, Professor Kenny, he did not deliver any lectures at Cambridge during his last twenty years as Downing Professor.[58] However, he was more successful in the world of affairs as a barrister, law reformer and eventually as a County Court Judge.

The Preface to Starkie's *Treatise on Evidence* (1824) is much closer to Evans than was Phillipps's. Law is regarded as a science, governed by universal principles, which are modified by the positive law of particular systems. Every rational system of judicial investigation shares with pure science 'the common aim ... of discovery of truth'. Positive rules of evidence and procedure act as constraints on the operations of natural reason, often in a manner that is arbitrary and unjust. Starkie was not afraid to expound a general theory of evidence and to criticize current English law and practice in terms of universal principles. But, mindful of his audience, he was careful to state that he considered the English law of evidence by and large to be 'founded on just and liberal principles'[59] and to emphasize that his work was intended to be of practical utility rather than to provide a critique of the remaining imperfections.

Starkie differs from Phillipps in several other respects. There is a long theoretical introduction, much more emphasis on the exclusionary rules of evidence and rather less on competency of witnesses. He exhibits a greater breadth of learning (although Phillipps was broadly read) and his style is more elegant, if more diffuse. Like Phillipps, his second volume contains a digest of proofs centred on the forms of action. Both deal with civil and criminal proceedings. Both became the standard works in the United States until superseded by local authors. Perhaps because of fiercer competition, perhaps because it was more obviously a work of scholarship as well as a practical treatise, Starkie did not achieve quite the same commercial success as Phillipps. He published four English editions at approximately ten-year intervals between 1824 and 1853, compared with Phillipps's nine editions in thirty years (1814–43).

Wills

In 1838 a Birmingham solicitor, William Wills, published *An Essay on the Principles of Circumstantial Evidence*, the product of his practical experience and of wide reading in his leisure hours. It is quite appropriately called an essay, for it does not fit into any of the standard categories of law books. It was not designed either as a reference work for practitioners nor as a student's textbook, nor as a polemic. Nor is it a work of high theory in the manner of Gulson or Michael and Adler. The author did set out to give a coherent account of 'the leading principles of circumstantial evidence'. He was not afraid to venture into philosophy, drawing extensively on Locke, Hampden, Butler and various writers on logic and probability. But much of his text is occupied with illustrations taken from famous trials and his own experience as well as from the law reports. Indeed, like two later writers, Ram and Moore,[60] he appears to have believed that the study of records of cases of controverted fact could provide the basis 'for consistent and immutable principles of reason and natural justice'.[61] He presents what he considers the principles governing circumstantial evidence as 'rules of induction', but it is not entirely clear whether he considered them to have the status of rules of law. He hardly mentions exclusionary rules of evidence and makes an eloquent argument against 'imperative formulae descriptive of the kind and amount of evidence requisite to constitute legal proof'.[62]

A charitable interpretation of Wills's book is to treat it not as a work on the law of evidence, but rather as a reflective essay on the logical and practical aspects of handling circumstantial evidence – in Wigmore's terminology, a contribution to a science of proof. As such, if not particularly profound or original, it is eminently readable, and this may account for its subsequent popularity in the United States and India as well as in England. Later editions contained extensive treatments of scientific evidence and in time it became established as a popular practitioners' handbook, although it dealt hardly at all with legal doctrine.

Best

In 1844 William Mawdesley Best (1809–69), a barrister of Gray's Inn, published *A Treatise on Presumptions of Law and Fact*, a work primarily concerned with circumstantial proof in criminal cases. Five years later this was followed by a more general treatise on *The Principles of Evidence* (hereafter *Best on Evidence*), which soon became a classic. Best was a scholar as well as a practising lawyer, and his research goes beyond the English authorities to draw on philosophical writings, continental jurists, Romanists and others. It is a rounded and elegant work of scholarship which deservedly established itself as a standard advanced textbook and, in time, as an authority. Best's avowed aim was to examine the principles underlying the rules of evidence rather than to provide another practical treatise, but the work gained sufficient favour with the Bar that by the twelfth and last edition, published in 1922, it had expanded to include references to over three thousand cases.

Best managed to integrate theoretical and historical analysis with principled exposition in a way which has since been bettered only by Wigmore and which has not been repeated in England in this century. He drew freely on Butler, Heineccius, Hume, Locke, Paley and other theoretical writers, and the final chapter sets out elementary rules for conducting examination and cross-examination modelled closely on Quintilian. Best had made a careful study of Bentham's *Rationale*, and much of the organization and terminology of the theoretical parts followed Bentham quite closely. But he is also one of his most judicious critics. According to him Bentham was mistaken in his distrust of judge-made law and of the legal profession, and in his faith in codification and in publicity as a security against misdecision.[63] Bentham's principal error was to fail to take account of the peculiar nature of judicial evidence, several characteristics of which give rise to the need for special rules; exclusionary rules and investitive rules, i.e. those 'investing natural evidence with artificial weight'. Unlike the *paterfamilias*, the judge is concerned solely with *expletive* justice, that is, the enforcement of strict legal rights and duties, and to this end the discretion of tribunals in determining facts must be limited. The need for prompt and final decision requires rules regulating the burden of proof and presumptions. The evil consequences of possible conviction of the innocent also require special safeguards. The differences between historical and judicial inquiries lead to the need for special legal securities against misdecision, in addition to publicity, such as oaths, prescribed forms for pre-appointed evidence and the rejection of testimony of suspected persons, all of which were undervalued by Bentham. Best also defended the lawyer–client privilege and took a *via media* between the existing law and Bentham on rules governing competency.

Best's most scathing criticism was reserved for Bentham's moral thermometer, 'a plan so extraordinary that it is but justice to give his own words'.[64] He adopts the criticisms made by Dumont and Bonnier; one of his later editors, J. M. Lely, omitted the passage devoted to this 'fantastic suggestion' on the grounds that the thermometer was 'one of the few follies of a very wise man'.[65]

Despite his attacks on some of Bentham's central doctrines, Best did as much as anyone to keep his influence on thinking about evidence alive. He became the main conduit for a moderate version of Benthamism. The terminology and much of the organization of *Best on Evidence* are inspired by Bentham, as are some of his statements of principle and his criticisms of the exclusionary rules. Where Bentham's conclusions are rejected, it is usually in his own terminology and on utilitarian grounds; some of his arguments were adopted by Best but in a more moderate tone. Thus it could be said that some of Bentham's ideas lived on in a moderate form in a work which prospered for over seventy years and which, more than nearly all other treatises on evidence, seems to have satisfied simultaneously the needs of students, practitioners and scholars.

The later history of *Best on Evidence* is a good example of the influence of the market on the form of treatises and textbooks. The author's original claim that this was not intended as a practical treatise was submerged in its success. The first edition was 540 pages long and cited under 600 cases. In 1876 Stephen pointed out that it had swollen to 908 pages and cited about 1400 cases, providing some justification for the launching of a new students' work.[66] By 1923 the reviewer in the *Harvard Law Review* could justly complain that it was being kept alive for a purpose for which it was not originally intended and that an English barrister might be better occupied in preparing an English edition to Wigmore's *Treatise*, just as American reviewers had suggested that Taylor's editors would have been better occupied in doing something similar.[67] In fact *Best on Evidence* remained in print for many years beyond this. Two of his editors, Sydney Phipson and Charles Chamberlayne, eventually produced leading treatises of their own.

Greenleaf

Simon Greenleaf (1783–1853) was one of the first of the great series of treatise writers associated with Harvard. He was a disciple of Joseph Story.[68] The first edition of *A Treatise on the Law of Evidence* was published in 1842. It was originally planned as a student text, but from the start the author 'was naturally led to endeavour to render the work acceptable to the profession as well as useful to the student'.[69] Up to that time the field had been dominated by the English works of Phillipps and Starkie, supplemented by notes on American cases. These had become increasingly inconvenient to use and less and less satisfactory as the rules of evidence in England and the various American jurisdictions diverged through both legislation and judicial activity. Up to that time the only indigenous American treatise had been a short work by Chief Justice Swift of Connecticut, published in 1810.[70]

Greenleaf's aim was 'to state those doctrines and rules of the Law of Evidence which are common to all the United States'[71] without trying to note all local variations. In later editions, recent decisions in England and Ireland, as well as in the United States and Canada, were included. The first volume dealt with theoretical matters and general principles, but the second (and latterly subsequent volumes) dealt with details of the evidence requisite in certain particular actions and issues at common law, matters of great value to the practitioner, but belonging more to substantive law and procedure than to the law of evidence. Thus *Greenleaf on Evidence* was a hybrid: it dealt not with the law of any one jurisdiction, but rather with the principles of the Anglo-American law of evidence; it was designed to meet the needs of both students and practitioners, two rather different audiences, especially after the rise of teaching by the case method. It soon became established as the leading American practitioners' treatise on the subject. The fact that it went through sixteen editions in less than sixty years is a measure both of its success and of the pace of change in this branch of the law during this period.

After Greenleaf's death in 1853, his editors made little attempt to do more than keep it up to date through annotations, so that like many works it suffered a steady decline in quality and utility, until the young John Henry Wigmore took over as editor of the sixteenth edition. As we shall see, this led on directly to Wigmore's own *Treatise*; but before that *Greenleaf on Evidence* made an impact in England in rather unusual circumstances.

Taylor

John Pitt Taylor's *A Treatise on the Law of Evidence as Administered in England and Ireland* (first edition 1848), is an interesting case-study in publishing history. The author's original intention was merely to edit Greenleaf's American treatise for use in England and Ireland, but he found that English case and statute law had diverged too far to make mere annotations satisfactory. Accordingly he published the work in his own name, despite the fact that substantial portions of the original text were Greenleaf's *ipsissima verba*.[72] This led Thayer to remark some years later: 'If Mr. Taylor ... had indicated the real nature of his book, not merely in the ample acknowledgments found in his preface and elsewhere, but in the title of the book; if, for instance, he had called it "Taylor's Greenleaf", – less dissatisfaction with his course would have been felt on this side of the water.'[73] This doubt about Taylor's originality may have led to an underestimation of the real worth of his work.

Taylor, a barrister who in due course became a County Court judge, was a dedicated scholar with a deep interest in his subject. His work soon acquired the reputation for combining comprehensive coverage of the English authorities with Greenleaf's 'terse and luminous' writing. If anything, he was more of an intellectual than Greenleaf, and he was less impatient of philosophical and other non-legal literature than his American precursor. But *Taylor on Evidence* was conceived and executed as a work for practitioners. It lasted for over eighty years, for forty of them with Taylor himself as editor. For nearly fifty years it was regarded as the leading practitioners' treatise, replacing Starkie and Phillipps and in due course being overtaken by Phipson.

The editor of the ninth edition (1895), G. Pitt-Lewis QC, was quite bold in cutting and up-dating the work, but by the eleventh edition (1920), the editors rather pointedly claimed 'to have as far as possible, reverted to the very words used by the author in his final edition'.[74] Whether this was done because it was felt that to preserve the actual words of a dead author would maintain its status as an authority, or for some other reason, the later editions drew fire from academics. Zachariah Chafee suggested in the *Harvard Law Review* that English barristers might spend their time better than in 'warming over for the eleventh time the words of an American ... long superseded in his own country'.[75] Eventually, an unusually long and acerbic review by Stallybrass in the *Law Quarterly Review* administered the *coup de grâce*. He contrasted 'the perfunctory editing of great books by busy practitioners who perhaps have not made any profound study of the subject' with Taylor's own deep interest in the history and the rationales behind the rules as well as in their practical application.[76] The demise of *Taylor on Evidence* marks the end of a period in England in which concern with the history and underlying theory of the subject was not regarded as incompatible with the production of works of practical utility to the practitioner.

Burrill and Appleton

Greenleaf's treatise was first published in 1842. During the next fifty years it dominated the field, its nearest rivals being American versions of standard English works. Best appeared with relatively sparse American annotations; Wills was plagiarized by one William Will; Phillipps and Starkie survived for a time; even Taylor, itself based on Greenleaf, eventually reached an international edition. Stephen's *Digest* also seems to have been popular in some parts of the United States in the latter years of this period.

The two most interesting American works published on evidence in this period are by Alexander Burrill and John Appleton, both of whom were influenced by Bentham. Burrill, a New York practitioner, first published *A Treatise on the Nature, Principles and Rules of Circumstantial Evidence* in 1856. In some respects it is an American counterpart of Wills and Best, a learned, somewhat discursive essay on the theory and practical applications of circumstantial evidence. Burrill was more concerned with principle than with detail and treated cases more as illustrations than as authorities. The book was intended for the general public, as well as for professional use. It is an admirable work, elegantly written and drawing extensively on civilian writers and philosophers as well as on the standard English legal authorities. Burrill seems to have been as familiar with Beccaria and Hume as with Bentham. Wigmore, in his *Science of Judicial Proof*, referred to 'Burrill's masterly work',[77] but did not cite him in his *Treatise*. Although it reached a second edition in 1868, Burrill's work does not seem to have made much impact. Strangely, it is ignored by Thayer in his classic essay on presumptions, for Burrill's views were close to his own.

Burrill took Bentham as his starting-point, but did not accept him uncritically. By contrast, John Appleton, who in time became Chief Justice of Maine, was an ardent and effective disciple. Over a period of years Appleton published a series of articles forcefully criticizing particular exclusionary rules. He collected and revised some of these in a book, *The Rules of Evidence Stated and Discussed*, which was published in 1860. His stated aim was to examine 'the more important rules of law, as to admission and exclusion of evidence, and the differing modes adopted in its extraction', in the light of Bentham's reasoning and principles.[78] More than half of the book was devoted to competency of witnesses and of parties, the remaining chapters dealing with privileged communications, confessions, hearsay, examination and cross-examination of witnesses and judicial oaths.

Appleton stuck closely, but judiciously, to the substance of Bentham's arguments, without falling into the trap of imitating either his style or his lack of diplomacy. His efforts at reform were remarkably successful. Between 1857 and 1860 a series of enactments in Maine swept away most of the rules of incompetency affecting parties, spouses, slaves and coloured persons, and greatly reduced the scope of exclusionary rules based on interest and religious belief. In 1864, largely due to the efforts of Appleton, Maine took the lead in enabling the accused to give evidence in criminal cases; most States soon followed suit and it became part of federal law in 1878.[79] Some of the reform legislation in Maine had been anticipated in other States and by Denman's reforms in England, but it was not until 1898 that England reached the same point as most American jurisdictions in allowing the accused to testify. Appleton was not alone in promoting legislation on evidence between 1850 and 1880, but he was one of the most effective reformers and he provides one of the clearest examples of the influence of Bentham's ideas.

Stephen

From the mid-nineteenth century onwards American scholars began more and more to dominate the study of evidence. The trend was started by Greenleaf, consolidated by Thayer and Wigmore, and carried on by Chamberlayne, Moore, Morgan, Maguire, McCormick and others. There was, however, one significant English writer who deserves mention: Sir James Fitzjames Stephen (1829–94).

During his life-time Fitzjames Stephen was known as a prolific writer upon many subjects, as a friend of Sir Henry Maine, as Carlyle's executor, as a champion of codification, and as a forceful, if somewhat simple-minded, judge. He is remembered today mainly for his works on criminal law, especially for his three-volume *History of the Criminal Law of England* (published in 1883), for his harsh views on punishment and as the man who narrowly failed to secure the codification of our criminal law.[80]

Stephen was an ambivalent utilitarian, as befits one who was a student of Bentham and John Austin, a disciple of Mill on logic but not on liberty, and a friend of Maine and Carlyle. Of Bentham he wrote:

He was too keen and bitter a critic to recognise the substantial merits of the system which he attacked; and it is obvious to me that he had not that mastery of the law itself which is unattainable by mere theoretical study, even if the student is, as Bentham certainly was, a man of talent, approaching closely to genius.

During the last generation or more Bentham's influence has to some extent declined, partly because some of his books are like exploded shells, buried under the ruins which they have made, and partly because, under the influence of some of the most distinguished of living authors, great attention has been directed to legal history and in particular to the study of Roman Law.[81]

This cautious attitude is reflected in Stephen's approach to the law of evidence. He was impatient of technicality, he welcomed the changes that had been brought about in respect of competency, and he agreed that the English law was unsystematic and confusing. But he did not share Bentham's dislike of judge-made law nor his opposition to all exclusionary rules and he was particularly critical of what he regarded as Bentham's failure to recognize the dangers of prejudicial evidence.[82] In Stephen's view the rules of evidence had an important role to play in excluding everything that is irrelevant and in requiring the production of the best evidence available. Bentham had praised courts martial as embodiments of the natural system of procedure; Stephen observed that absence of rules of evidence led them into pursuing many irrelevant and vexatious questions. The English law of evidence needed some amendment and considerable simplification, but on the whole 'it is full of sagacity and practical experience, and is capable of being thrown into a form at once plain, short and systematic.'[83]

Stephen had written briefly, but perceptively, about the merits and demerits of the English law of evidence in his *General View of The Criminal Law*, first published in 1863.[84] His main work in this field began when he succeeded Sir Henry Maine as Legal Member of Council in India in 1869. This was the great period of the drafting and enactment of the Indian codes. The Code of Civil Procedure had been passed in 1859, the Penal Code in 1860, and a Code of Criminal Procedure in 1861. Drafts for general laws on contract and evidence had been prepared by the time that Stephen arrived. In three years of intensive activity he was responsible for twelve Acts (including redrafting the Indian Contracts Act and revising the Criminal Procedure Code). He played a major part in the preparation of eight more.[85] He drafted the Indian Evidence Act almost entirely on his own and he prepared a lengthy introduction and commentary which was published shortly after its enactment in 1872.[86] This contains the fullest and clearest statement of his general theory of and approach to evidence, although he later modified his views on some important points in response to criticism.[87]

An Evidence Bill had been prepared in 1868, but it was dropped after the first reading.[88] Stephen criticized it as being incomplete and not sufficiently elementary for those who had to administer it, for much of it presupposed a prior knowledge of the English law of evidence. He also agreed with those members of Council who felt that it went too far in relaxing the exclusionary rules of evidence. So he set about drafting an entirely new Bill, condensing material to be found in 1508 pages of *Taylor* into 167 crisp sections. There were a few modifications and omissions, but it was designed as a virtually complete Code applicable to Indian conditions.[89]

The Indian Evidence Act, 1872 has generally been regarded as a masterpiece of compression, although it is doubtful whether it quite satisfied Stephen's own standards of intelligibility and completeness. It is still in force in India and has served as a model for many other jurisdictions. A century after its enactment the authors of the leading commentary on the Act may have had some justification in complaining that it had stagnated with virtually no amendment,[90] but by and large it is thought to have stood the test of time and translation to different environments remarkably well. The succinctness and clarity of the Act have not prevented elephantiasis: the 1971 edition of *Sarkar* fills 1477 pages of small print and is, if anything, larger than the edition of *Taylor* that Stephen took as his starting-point.

Stephen's aim was to adapt and to codify the English Law of Evidence without making sweeping reforms. It was, he said, 'little more than an attempt to reduce the English law of evidence to the form of express propositions arranged in their natural order, with some modifications rendered necessary by the peculiar circumstances of India'.[91] The debate on the codification of evidence was the occasion for the often quoted remark, made to Stephen: 'My Evidence Bill would be a very short one; it would consist of one rule, to this effect: All rules of evidence are hereby abolished.'[92] Stephen argued strenuously against this, insisting that the Rules of Evidence had an important negative role to play in excluding everything that is irrelevant and in requiring the production of the best available evidence.

Stephen's Indian experience converted him to codification, confirmed his belief in strong government and led him to be highly critical of the casual and unsystematic approach to law reform in England. Shortly after his return he was invited by the Attorney-General, then Sir John Coleridge, to prepare an Evidence Bill for enactment at Westminster. The Bill, based on the Indian Act, was ready early in 1873, but Coleridge was unable to introduce the subject until the last day of the Parliamentary Session. Shortly afterwards he was elevated to the House of Lords, and the Bill was never even officially published. Stephen was later to remark: 'It would be as impossible to get in Parliament a really satisfactory discussion of a Bill codifying the Law of Evidence as to get a committee of the whole House to paint a picture.'[93] He was disappointed by the failure of his Evidence Bill, but in the words of Radzinowicz, 'not discouraged, and in a truly Benthamite spirit embarked upon the business of codification as a private enterprise'.[94] Parliament was not interested in the law of evidence, and traditional common lawyers were strongly opposed to codification. The Courts were in no position to simplify and systematize the Law, so the task must fall on 'private writers'.

Shortly after being appointed Professor of Common Law in the Inns of Court in 1875, Stephen set out to produce a book that would meet this need. The outcome was *A Digest of the Law of Evidence*, published in June 1876. In the introduction he stated his aims as follows:

My object ... has been to separate the subject of evidence from other branches of the law with which it has commonly been mixed up; to reduce it into a compact systematic form, distributed according to the natural division of the subject matter; and to compress into precise definite rules, illustrated by examples, such cases and statutes as properly relate to the subject-matter so limited and arranged. I have attempted, in short, to make a digest of the law, which, if it were thought desirable, might be used in the preparation of a code, and which will, I hope, be useful, not only to professional students, but to every one who takes an intelligent interest in a part of the law of his country bearing directly on every kind of investigation into question of fact, as well as on every branch of litigation.[95]

Stephen's first objective was to make as clear a separation as possible of the Law of Evidence from other parts of Procedure and Practice and from substantive law.[96] His classification follows Bentham's division between substantive and adjective law and sharpens the distinction between evidence and other parts of adjective law, such as rules of procedure and rules of practice. Thus, Stephen sought to exclude a great deal of material that had been dealt with by other writers on evidence. First, he treated the question: 'What may be proved under particular issues?' (for example, what must or may be put in issue in respect of a charge of murder) as belonging to the subject of pleading rather than of evidence. A very considerable portion of the treatises of Starkie, Roscoe, Taylor, Greenleaf and others was taken up with such matters.

Secondly, he treated most 'presumptions' as belonging to different branches of the Substantive Law 'and to be unintelligible, except in connection with them'.[97] This excluded from consideration such maxims as *Ignorantia iuris haud excusat* and various presumptions as to rights of property. He did include, after some hesitation, a number of presumptions and estoppels in his *Digest*, notably the presumption of innocence, of legitimacy, of death from seven years' absence, of lost grant and of regularity. Subsequently, Thayer, in a famous essay, was to challenge whether most of these were properly termed 'presumptions' and whether any of them belonged to the Law of Evidence.[98] Debate has continued over the perplexing questions about the classification and place of presumptions in the law, but almost all leading writers on evidence have followed Stephen in treating at least some of them as belonging to the Law of Evidence.

Thirdly, Stephen argued that rules concerning the attendance of witnesses, the taking of depositions, interrogatories and statutory provisions making particular documents evidence of certain facts all belonged to the subject of Procedure rather than that of Evidence. However, some later editions included an Appendix, borrowed from Wills, containing a Table of Statutes governing the mode of proof of public documents, because of its utility to practitioners. This indicates that what had started out as a students' work was being widely used as a handy practical manual.

Stephen acknowledged the difficulty of drawing a sharp boundary between the Law of Evidence and other branches of law. But he was largely successful in substantially reducing the scope of the subject and most academic writers subsequently followed his lead. This not only enabled him to make a succinct statement of the law of evidence, but also to give it a coherent theoretical base.

Stephen's second objective was to ground his exposition on a single unifying principle, the doctrine of relevancy. Here he was less successful and, ironically, was later accused of unjustifiably extending the scope of the Law of Evidence.[99] The attempt is of great historical significance. It marked a break with the legacy of Gilbert and the starting-point of most modern treatments of the subject.

Stephen boldly tried to restore order to the study of evidence, substituting a new unifying principle. Earlier writers, he suggested, had failed adequately to distinguish between 'evidence' in the sense of testimony and 'evidence' as facts relevant to the facts in issue:

The great bulk of the Law of Evidence consists of negative rules declaring what, as the expression runs, is not evidence.

The doctrine that all the facts in issue and relevant to the issue, and no others, may be proved, is the unexpressed principle which forms the centre of and gives unity to all these express negative rules. To me these rules always appeared to form a hopeless mass of confusion, which might be remembered by a great effort, but could not be understood as a whole, or reduced to a system, until it occurred to me to ask the question, What is this evidence which you tell me hearsay is not? The expression 'hearsay is not evidence' seemed to assume that I knew by the light of nature what evidence was, but I perceived at last that was just what I did not know. I found that I was in the position of a person who, having never seen a cat, is instructed about them in this fashion: 'Lions are not cats, nor are tigers nor leopards, though you might be inclined to think they were'. Show me a cat to begin with, and I at once understand both what is meant by saying that a lion is not a cat, and why it is possible to call him one. Tell me what evidence is, and I shall be able to understand why you say that this and that class of facts are not evidence. The question 'What is evidence?' gradually disclosed the ambiguity of the word. To describe a matter of fact as 'evidence' in the sense of testimony is obviously nonsense. No one wants to be told that hearsay, whatever else it is, is not testimony. What then does the phrase mean? The only possible answer is: It means that the one fact either is or else is not considered by the person using the expression to furnish a premiss or part of a premiss from which the existence of the other is a necessary or probable inference − in words, that the one fact is or is not relevant to the other. When the inquiry is pushed further, and the nature of relevancy has to be considered in itself, and apart from legal rules about it, we are led to inductive logic, which shows that the judicial evidence is only one case of the general problem of Science − namely, inferring the unknown from the known. As far as the logical theory of the matter is concerned, this is an ultimate answer.[100]

Stephen's *Digest* was immensely popular. The first edition was reprinted three times in 1876 and 1877, and new editions followed fairly regularly during the next decade. It increased in weight and girth conspicuously less than most books on evidence as it passed through a total of twelve English editions, the last in 1948. It was also well known in the United States and in other parts of the Commonwealth and Empire, where its closeness to the Indian Evidence Act enhanced its popularity and its influence. Clearly it filled a felt need for a compact and systematic treatment of the subject.

The *Digest* was more than just a successful effort by a respected author to fill a gap in the literature. Rather it was a bold attempt to base a systematic treatment of the law of evidence on a single principle. For over a hundred years the ghost of Gilbert's formulation of the 'best evidence rule' had haunted the exposition of the law. Peake, Phillipps, Starkie, Greenleaf, Taylor and Best had all stated it as the main underlying principle of the law of evidence, but had then hedged it round with so many qualifications and exceptions that it served almost no useful purpose. Indeed, it had created much confusion. As Thayer argued in his brilliant essay on the rule, Burke interpreted it as leaving no rules of evidence at all; some nineteenth-century writers converted it from a rule of permission, allowing inferior evidence when other evidence was not available, to a rule of exclusion forbidding substitutionary evidence; they thereby conflated several different specific rules with different origins and different rationales.[101] Thus Gilbert's original unifying principle of the law of evidence had become at best unhelpful, at worst misleading. Stephen offered a fresh start, substituting Mill for Locke as the philosophical starting point, and the doctrine of relevancy for the 'best evidence rule' as the unifying principle.[102] Stephen's unifying principle was also rejected; but whereas Gilbert's attempt may have caused some harm,[103] Stephen stimulated some of his critics to make some important clarifications of the basic concepts of the law of evidence[104] and some of his immediate successors, notably Thayer, Wigmore and Chamberlayne, to take up the challenge of reducing the law of evidence to order on sound principles. It was a fruitful failure.

Thayer[105]

In 1874 James Bradley Thayer (1831–1902) was appointed to the Royall Professorship of Law at Harvard and a new era of Evidence scholarship began.[106] Before entering academic life Thayer had divided his energies between legal practice, literary reviewing and some legal editing. During his twenty-eight years at Harvard, Thayer made contributions of profound importance to both Evidence and Constitutional Law, but in one sense he never really fulfilled his potential. Soon after he joined Harvard Thayer resolved to write a major practical treatise on evidence, but the more he delved into the subject the more he was impressed by the general confusion surrounding both the case law and the literature in the field:

> The chief defects in this body of law, as it now stands, are [the] motley and undiscriminated character of its contents ...; the ambiguity of its terminology; the multiplicity and rigor of its rules and exceptions to rules; the difficulty of grasping these and perceiving their true place and relation in the system, and of determining, in the decision of new questions, whether to give scope and extension to the rational principles that lie at the bottom of all modern theories of evidence, or to those checks and qualifications of these principles which have grown out of the machinery through which our system is applied, namely, the jury.[107]

Thayer admired Fitzjames Stephen for his brave attempt to cut through the jungle of detail and confusion to establish a systematic foundation for the subject on the basis of principle. But Stephen's chosen principle, his doctrine of relevancy, failed to perform the task. It was, as Pollock called it, 'a splendid mistake'.[108] Thayer told his pupils that 'a more excellent way' was still needed.[109] As a preliminary to writing a practical treatise he embarked on detailed historical research which took him further and further away from his original project. The result was one of the classic works of legal history, but no systematic treatise.

Some of Thayer's main theses are familiar: he linked the origin and continuance of the exclusionary rules of evidence to the survival of the jury, a view adopted by Wigmore, but challenged by Edmund Morgan.[110] More firmly and clearly than his predecessors he emphasized the narrowness of the scope of the common law of evidence:[111] it was a mistake to treat presumptions and the burden of proof as rules of evidence; the most common grounds for exclusion of evidence were materiality – a matter of substantive law – and relevance, which was a matter of logic, not law. Stephen's basic error was to treat the logical presuppositions of a rational system of evidence as formal rules of evidence. Bentham's *Rationale* was not a law book.[112]

Thayer's main approach was not anti-nomian but he did favour an extension of judicial discretion and a radical simplification of the law of evidence. Rather he was concerned to clarify, both historically and analytically, the differences between rules of evidence, on the one hand, and rules of substantive law and precepts of logic on the other. In this view the core of the law of evidence was an essentially negative 'set of regulative and excluding precepts' based on policy,[113] which set certain artificial constraints on what witnesses and what classes of probative facts may be presented to a jury and how certain types of fact may or must be proved. For Thayer the modern system of proof is essentially rational, but 'the law has no mandamus to the logical faculty.'[114] Some legitimate constraints are placed on the operation of natural reason by substantive law, by the exigencies of litigation, by extrinsic policy and, above all, by the institution of the jury. But the scope and functions of the law of evidence are quite limited and could be reduced to a simple system, based on two principles: '(1) that nothing is to be received which is not logically probative of some matter requiring to be proved; and (2) that everything which is thus probative should come in, unless a clear ground of policy of law excludes it.'[115]

Thayer is mainly remembered today for his *Preliminary Treatise,* but his influence may have been at least as great, if not greater, through his teaching. His academic career coincided with the era of the blossoming of the Harvard Law School as the home both of the Langdellian system of legal education and of the inspired and varied scholarship of Holmes, Langdell, Ames, Gray, Williston and Thayer himself. Three of the leading Evidence scholars of the next generation – Charles Chamberlayne, John McKelvey and John Henry Wigmore – were his pupils. Several more, including Edmund Morgan, John Maguire and Zechariah Chafee, narrowly missed being taught by him, but lived in the shadow of his influence, modified perhaps by the more down-to-earth approach of the great John Chipman Gray, who reluctantly took over teaching Evidence after Thayer's death. Perhaps the main medium of Thayer's continuing influence was his *Select Cases on Evidence at the Common Law.* This was first published in 1892. It was revised by Thayer in 1900, shortly before his death, and in this form it became the leading casebook on Evidence in American law schools for a quarter of a century. In 1925 John Maguire produced a revised edition, by arrangement with the Thayer family.[116] Then in 1934 it was transformed, under the direction of Edmund Morgan, into what was in most respects a new book, but with an acknowledged and legitimated parentage. Morgan and Maguire's *Cases on Evidence* lasted through successive editions until 1965, when it was succeeded by the Foundation Press casebook, *Cases and Materials on Evidence*, the latest edition of which appeared in the names of Maguire, Weinstein, Chadbourn and Mansfield in 1973.[117] This explicitly claims to trace its lineage directly back to Thayer's *Cases*. It is still one of the leading casebooks used in American law schools. Thus almost since the beginning of the American casebook as a major form of student literature, Thayer's *Select Cases on Evidence at Common Law*, and its direct descendants, have continuously occupied an important, sometimes a commanding, position in American legal education. Although the scope of the book and the range of materials used have both expanded, perhaps even in ways that Thayer might not have approved, the main focus is still consciously on the rules of evidence, rather than on all aspects of proof – the bulk of the materials consists of appellate cases and the leading contemporary American 'codes' – the Federal Rules of Evidence, the California Evidence Code, and the Uniform Rules of Evidence.

Thayer never got round to expounding the simple system of evidence doctrine that he advocated. Whether he was too fastidious or otherwise temperamentally unsuited to the task, or whether it was a contingent fact that he died before completing it, is uncertain.[118] It was left to three of his pupils, Wigmore, Chamberlayne and McKelvey, to continue the search for 'a more excellent way'. He inspired each of them to do this in strikingly different fashions.

McKelvey produced a successful and provocative black letter text which was widely used as a companion to Thayer's casebook, but which made no visible impact on the development of the law of evidence nor on legal scholarship.[119] Wigmore and Chamberlayne deserve more detailed treatment.

Wigmore

Few, if any, legal scholars have been praised so often or in such extravagant terms as John Henry Wigmore (1863–1943), for many years Dean of North-western Law School and author of *A Treatise on the Anglo-American System of Evidence in Trials at Common Law*.[120] Of the first edition John Henry Beale wrote: 'It is hardly too much to say that this is the most complete and exhaustive treatise on a single branch of our law that has ever been written.'[121] Wigmore's most persistent critic, Edmund Morgan, wrote of the third edition: 'Not only is this the best, by far the best, treatise on the Law of Evidence, it is also the best work ever produced on any comparable division of Anglo-American law.'[122] Other commentators have been even more lavish in their praise.

It is not possible to do justice here to Wigmore's many achievements. He was an essentially simple-minded man who combined exceptional industry with a clear mind, broad interests and a methodical approach.[123] His unrivalled mastery of his field was attributable in large part to his simplicity of vision: the world is full of a marvellous diversity of things, but with application and a systematic approach they can be reduced to order; supremely self-confident and untroubled by doubt, he reduced more material to order than any other legal scholar.

Wigmore began his career as an Evidence scholar as the editor of the first volume of the sixteenth, and last, edition of *Greenleaf on Evidence*. This was so well received that he was immediately commissioned to produce an entirely new treatise to replace Greenleaf. This, in turn, was so successful that not only is it still the leading Anglo-American treatise on evidence, but no one has yet dared to try to produce a serious rival.

In the preface to the first edition, Wigmore stated the aims of the work:

First, to expound the Anglo-American Law of Evidence as a system of reasoned principles and rules; secondly, to deal with the apparently warring mass of judicial precedents as the consistent product of these principles and rules; and, thirdly, to furnish all the materials for ascertaining the present state of the law in the half a hundred independent American jurisdictions.[124]

From the outset Wigmore was concerned to go beyond the bare exposition of evidence doctrine: he explored in detail and depth the history and rationales of all the main rules and he included a considerable amount of material on forensic psychology and forensic science. At the same time, following Thayer, he generally excluded matter that he felt belonged to substantive law or the law of procedure.[125]

Wigmore's *Treatise* succeeded in being both a monumental work of scholarship and a highly successful practitioners' treatise. However, the constraints of the treatise form inhibited him from dealing as systematically or as fully as he would have liked with what he termed 'the science of proof'. Accordingly, he set out to remedy this in a separate work, *The Principles* [later *Science*] *of Judicial Proof as Founded on Logic, Psychology and General Experience*.[126] At the start of *The Science* Wigmore stated with typical forthrightness:

The study of the principles of Evidence, for a lawyer, falls into two distinct parts. One is Proof in the general sense, – the part concerned with the ratiocinative process of contentious persuasion, – mind to mind, counsel to Judge or juror, each partisan seeking to move the mind of the tribunal. The other part is Admissibility, – the procedural rules devised by the law, and based on litigious experience and tradition, to guard the tribunal (particularly the jury) against erroneous persuasion. Hitherto, the latter has loomed largest in our formal studies, – has, in fact, monopolized them; while the former, virtually ignored, has been left to the chances of later acquisition, casual and empiric, in the course of practice.[127]

Wigmore proceeded to argue that 'the science of proof' is both anterior to and more important than the trial rules of evidence. Moreover, it had been neglected in legal education and legal scholarship and, since the rules of evidence were destined to decline in importance, it was vital to try to develop a science of proof: 'All the artificial rules of Admissibility might be abolished; yet the principles of Proof would remain, so long as trials remain as a rational attempt to seek the truth in legal controversies.'[128]

Both commercially and in terms of intellectual influence Wigmore's *Science* was almost as much a failure as his *Treatise* was a success. It never caught on, and systematic Evidence scholarship continued to concentrate largely on the rules; indeed, for most of the twentieth century there has been proportionately less interest in the historical and philosophical aspects of evidence than there was in the nineteenth. This is illustrated by the fact that Thayer remains our leading historian of Evidence, and Bentham and Wigmore its most important theorists.

What is significant, in the present context, is that the leading Evidence scholar of the twentieth century based his whole approach to his subject on a rounded and relatively well-articulated theory of evidence and proof, which went beyond concentration on the rules of evidence to encompass, in an integrated fashion, both legal doctrine and the logical, psychological and scientific aspects of proof. It is misleading to present the *Treatise* as dealing with rules and the *Science* as dealing with the 'non-legal' aspects: both are based on a shared conceptual framework and the same underlying theory, which received its fullest exposition in a largely forgotten work. Wigmore claimed that his was the first attempt in English since Bentham to deal with the principles of proof 'as a whole and as a system'.[129] This was true when he wrote it and it is still true today. There has been valuable theoretical work by Gulson, Michael and Adler, Jonathan Cohen and others, but none of these has set out to produce comprehensive theories. Thus Bentham and Wigmore are still our two leading theorists of evidence.[130] In the next section I shall suggest that, despite important differences between them, they and nearly all Anglo-American writers on evidence, belong to a single intellectual tradition. However, before doing so, it is illuminating to consider briefly two of Wigmore's forgotten contemporaries, Charles F. Chamberlayne and Charles C. Moore.

Chamberlayne

Charles Frederick Chamberlayne was born in Cambridge, Massachusetts in 1855 and died in 1913.[131] He went to Harvard College and Harvard Law School from which he graduated *cum laude* in 1881. As a student he fell under the spell of James Bradley Thayer, and for the rest of his life Evidence was his main interest. From 1884 to 1890 he was a trial judge, but for most of his career he divided his time between practice in New York and Boston and writing about Evidence. Soon after he graduated he was recommended by Thayer to be the American editor of Best's *Principles of the Law of Evidence* and between 1883 and 1908 he was responsible for American notes for three editions of that work, which was commended by Thayer 'as the most authoritative and reliable treatise on the subject of evidence in the English language'.[132] In 1897 he produced the American notes to the three-volume edition of *Taylor on Evidence*, which was at the time still the leading practitioners' treatise in England. Chamberlayne's notes were succinct, precise and to the point and he soon established an excellent reputation among both practitioners and academics. His last years were devoted to writing his *magnum opus, A Treatise on the Modern Law of Evidence* in five volumes, three of which were published posthumously.[133]

It is interesting to consider Chamberlayne's work in the context of his own interpretation of the immediate past history of the development of evidence in the United States.[134] He accepted, with only minor modifications, Thayer's interpretation of the historical development of the law of evidence and of the defects to which it had given rise.[135] In Chamberlayne's view the feud, trial by combat, ordeals and the duel were not just primitive methods awaiting the development of a superior, more rational technology for ascertaining the truth. They also represented the expression of a primitive, individualistic ethos. 'The natural man understands fighting. He loves its self-assertiveness, its excitement, its triumphs ... Naturally, all that this individualistic conception of the proper purposes of litigation has ever demanded of society is that it should stake out and maintain the lists, enforce the rules, and make the victory effective to the victor.'[136] The adversary process and the technical rules of evidence represented a non-violent extension of the sporting view of litigation based on the same ethos. 'The American elevation of the jury at the expense of the court' was a legacy inherited from England, where it was 'a direct result of the conscious rebellion of the Democracy of England against the power of the Crown as represented by the royal judges'.[137]

The law of evidence and the administration of justice had not kept pace with social change. 'Happily, the battles of Democracy have been won; – completely and forever.' The domination of Individualism is being replaced, if not by Socialism, at least by 'an insistence that individualistic action shall be directed to socially beneficial ends'.[138] It is generally recognized that the administration of justice in modern democratic society requires the ascertainment of truth as an essential means of implementing the law. But the surviving structure of the adversary process, the jury system and rules of evidence led to a pernicious formalism for which society pays a heavy price in terms of injustice in individual cases, loss of popular respect for law, an impairment of the instinct for justice, and unnecessary expense and delay. There is furthermore a loss of intelligibility: 'A complex civilisation can scarcely avoid an intricate system of substantive law. But it need have no complicated system of procedure.'[139]

Thayer had eloquently summarized the failings of the law of evidence. In Chamberlayne's view the situation had deteriorated in the previous twenty-five years:

The multiplicity of connotations for a single term has increased; the admixture of substantive law has grown more pronounced; the attenuated lines of hair-splitting decisions have become yearly more numerous; the percentage of reversal to trial has crept steadily higher; the length of time required for final adjudication against an alert opponent with adequate financial resources has extended; the average expense of litigation has increased. In fact, the administration of justice, especially of criminal justice, is, in many parts of the country, obviously breaking down; the courts have necessarily lost much in popular respect. Indeed, they are the object of open, grave and continued political attack. And the end is not yet reached.[140]

Given this diagnosis of the situation, Chamberlayne considered that there was a crying need for a more rational and more flexible system of administration of justice.

Stephen's *Digest* represented the first modern attempt to produce a radical simplification suited to modern conditions. Its instant popularity with the legal profession on both sides of the Atlantic showed that lawyers appreciated the need for change, but his doctrine of relevancy had been shown to be inadequate for the purpose.[141] Thayer had urged his pupils to seek 'a more excellent way' and had himself set out to confront the challenge.[142] But he had not completed his work. His *Preliminary Treatise* was an historical masterpiece, but it was only preliminary to the constructive task of placing the modern law of evidence on a scientific and flexible basis. If he had lived, Thayer might perhaps have done the job. But, Chamberlayne suggests, he was too much in love with history. The historical method is '*in*structive rather than *con*structive'.[143] So it was left to his pupils to complete the task.

Unfortunately, Thayer's most talented pupil, Wigmore, had followed his teacher too closely. He, too, had adopted the historical method: 'indeed it is obvious but well-merited praise to say of Dean Wigmore's work that he has written very much such a treatise as Professor Thayer has led us reasonably to believe he might have written had he lived to finish his work in this respect.'[144] But the historical method is not suited to producing fundamental change; knowledge alone does not constitute reform; and an emphasis on the past and on precedents as authorities almost inevitably has a conservative tendency. Accordingly the search for 'a more excellent way' must continue.

Chamberlayne recommended the adoption of a quite different approach, based on what he termed 'the principle of administration'. He succinctly summarized the main ideas underlying his general approach as follows:

That the rules of Evidence are canons of judicial administration and not properly within the real scope of the doctrine of *stare decisis*; that the social objects of litigation outweigh in importance the personal; that Society has a transcendent interest in the ascertainment of truth and should remove all barriers across the path of its tribunals in reaching it; that the interests of justice should be intrusted to the Court rather than to the jury; – these are the fundamental propositions which I venture to commend to the favorable attention of the profession.[145]

Chamberlayne explicitly, though discreetly, attributes 'the principle of adminis-tration' to Bentham.[146] Like Bentham he draws a sharp distinction between substantive and adjective law; the former must inevitably be governed by complex and detailed rules, the latter should be confined by very few formal regulations. The end of adjective law is to implement rights and duties under substantive law. The main test is whether it promotes the discovery of truth and by this test there should be no strict rules of admissibility. Generally speaking, unreliable evidence is better than no evidence. Chamberlayne's notion of 'administration', the granting of a wide discretion and ultimate responsibility to the judge to control the trial by reason rather than regulation, is strongly reminiscent of Bentham's 'doctrine of the single Judge'.[147] His attack on the abuse of technicalities and on the sporting conception of the trial is little more than a restatement of Bentham's own attack on the 'fox hunter's argument'.[148] Chamberlayne's primary concerns were similarly to minimize expense and delay, and to secure the conviction of the guilty as well as the acquittal of the innocent.[149] Above all his general strategy was anti-nomian: 'In connection with the law of evidence, the nerve of the octopus can readily be cut. It is the theory that judicial administration must be regulated by rigid rules.'[150]

Chamberlayne summarized his constructive thesis as follows:

1　The social objects of litigation are vastly more important than the personal.
2　The transcendently important end which the community seeks to accomplish by litigation is not that the dispute between A and B should be settled by the use of reason and without violence; but that truth should be discovered and justice done as accurately and speedily as possible.
3　While old terminology is best retained, the connotation of terms should so far as practicable, be restricted to a single meaning.
4　Substantive law, including the determinate probative force of any given inference of fact, should be eliminated from the field of evidence.
5　The parol evidence rule and presumptions of law should not be treated as part of the law of evidence.
6　Any rule which excludes probative or constituent facts actually necessary to proof of the proponent's case is scientifically wrong.
7　Any privilege accorded a witness which prevents the ascertainment of truth is scientifically wrong.
8　The presiding judge should be strengthened in the exercise of the administrative function, and not subordinated to the prestige of the jury.[151]

Chamberlayne's *A Treatise on the Modern Law of Evidence*, published in five volumes between 1911 and 1916, was the main vehicle for the development of his ideas. This was a work on the grand scale, comparable in size and heroic conception to Wigmore's *Treatise*. Unfortunately several factors conspired to diminish its impact. First, Wigmore's *Treatise* had been published several years earlier and had already begun to dominate the field. It required both courage and commitment to set out to produce a rival to that great work. Chamberlayne was an able, dedicated and learned man, but it hardly belittles him to say that he was not in the same class as Wigmore.

Secondly, the author died before the completion of the last three volumes. They seem to have been edited rather hastily with only the short-term needs of practitioners in mind. Remarkably, the publishers did not even mention the author's demise.[152] Possibly because of this shoddy treatment of the work after his death, there were relatively few reviews, and some of them were sharply critical of the publisher's and editors' behaviour.[153]

Apart from his controversial political views, there is another reason why Chamberlayne made no lasting impact. His basic concern was to advance an argument for far-reaching changes in the law of evidence and the prevailing approach to it. But the literary form which was chosen as the vehicle for this was an encyclopaedic treatise. In the Preface he was at pains to stress that he had two aims in mind: first, to provide a severely practical work of reference for the busy practitioner, 'without any considerable indulgence in the delightful work of tracing historical developments or establishing true perspectives'[154] (a dig at Thayer and Wigmore). Secondly, 'that the building should present so much of precision in design and symmetry of arrangement as might supplement, and in a sense, increase its utilitarian advantages'.[155] Like Stephen, his aim was to simplify the law, by placing it on a rational basis, but without the confusions in Stephen's doctrine of relevance. Unlike other writers on evidence, he would approach the subject from the standpoint of administration rather than that of procedure, treating the rules merely as illustrations of 'the few simple and primary canons of judicial administration'.[156] These somewhat opaque phrases concealed the fact that this work claimed at once to be a practical work of reference and a sustained argument for change in the substance and the spirit of the American approach to evidence. Chamberlayne was justified in emphasizing the differences between his and Wigmore's treatises, but he failed to resolve the tension between his concern to provide practical detailed information about existing doctrine and his desire to develop a coherent theory and polemic *de lege ferenda*. His argument for change led him to step beyond the latitude for interpretation available to the expositor into statements that could only fairly be interpreted as straightforward recommendations for change or as merely wishful thinking about what the law might be. This is particularly the case in respect of his treatment of the role of precedent in dealing with evidence. Thayer had argued that it was still open to treatise writers and the courts to impose order and system on the tangled jungle of case law without recourse to the legislature.[157] He had suggested that one cause of the trouble had been that some specific rulings at Nisi Prius had been wrongly treated as binding although they had 'no general element or principle which should make it a precedent'; other cases which should have been regarded merely as illustrations of a general principle had been treated as binding authorities on narrow technical points. Chamberlayne went much further in that he argued forcefully that it was 'unscientific' to treat rules of evidence as being subject to *stare decisis*. Thayer had suggested that the case law could be reinterpreted and expanded to yield a coherent body of principles; he was attracted by Stephen's model of restating the law, but rejected crucial aspects of his formulation. Chamberlayne was much closer to Bentham in advocating almost complete judicial discretion unregulated by formal rules of evidence. Unfortunately this reflected neither American practice nor professional opinion and severely undermined the value of a book that was presented and packaged as a practical work of reference in five substantial volumes. Chamberlayne's model was closer to Bentham's *Rationale* than to Wigmore's *Treatise* and it deserves attention as a work of theory.

Chamberlayne's *Treatise* was mainly discredited by being ignored. Ezra Ripley Thayer (his teacher's son), while welcoming Chamberlayne's attack on formalism, suggested that the book was 'marred by a faulty terminology and a tantalising diffuseness'.[158] More significantly there is not a single reference to it listed in the later editions of Wigmore, and it was almost completely ignored by other writers. This is unfortunate, for even today Chamberlayne's *magnum opus* is a rich source of arguments and ideas as well as of information and references. It may not be quite the 'masterpiece' that Harry Shulman of Yale, an early realist, proclaimed it to be,[159] but it deserved a better fate. Chamberlayne's fault was not so much that he followed the advice, 'When preaching radical ideas, wear a suit', but rather that he forgot the corollary, 'and don't shout'.

Moore on Facts

One of the most remarkable publications of the first decade of this century was *A Treatise on Facts or Weight and Value of Evidence*, by Charles C. Moore, published in two volumes in 1908.[160] The author was a New York practitioner, who had joined Wigmore in attacking Muensterberg's claims for forensic psychology.[161] His treatise was a labour of love, the fruit of years of combing the law reports and other literature for material which no orthodox index or system of classification would reveal. His aim was to make available reported discussions by judges and others of the weight and value of evidence and the credibility of witnesses. The first volume contained chapters on such topics as 'Sound and hearing', 'Light and sight', 'Speed', 'The weather', 'Course and bearing of vehicles', as well as on more conventional topics such as 'Degree of proof', and 'Presumptions, inferences and circumstantial evidence'. The second volume could be seen as a compendium of lawyers' psychology as it collects together in one place a mass of judicial statements on observation, memory, bias, confessions, and other topics of witness psychology. The bulk of the work is taken up with material from the law reports. But there are also extensive quotations from the Bible, literature, philosophy, poetry and any other source that the author could lay his hands on. At first sight the book looks like an elephantine version of Wills on *Circumstantial Evidence* or Ram's *Treatise on Facts*.[162] But it is less analytical than Wills and more scholarly and discriminating than Ram; it is the product of considerably more effort than either.

Moore's *Treatise* represented a lifetime's work based on a category mistake. Whereas Chamberlayne had attacked the idea that *stare decisis* applied to any aspects of evidence, Moore gave the impression that the law reports could provide authoritative guidance on the weight and value of particular kinds of evidence as well as on questions of admissibility. His conception of the enterprise was rather confused and invited different interpretations. In the opening paragraph of the Preface Moore states that arguments on questions of fact can be as fully supported by reference to judicial authorities as arguments on questions of law and that his aim is to exhibit what American, Canadian and English judges have said 'concerning the causes of trustworthiness and untrustworthiness of evidence, and the rules for determining probative weight'.[163] A few pages later he modifies this by suggesting that only some such statements have become established as propositions of law,[164] but the preface and the book as a whole readily create the impression that it could provide authoritative material for arguments by counsel and rulings by judges on the proper weight to be attached to particular kinds of evidence. At first sight this might seem to be an example of the passion for indiscriminately collecting facts of which some of the scientific realists, such as Cook and Underhill Moore, were later accused.[165] This would be a caricature of Charles Moore, for his mistake was to collect non-existent rules rather than samples of facts.

The reviews of Moore's *Treatise* were interesting. An English reviewer saw it as 'an elaborate, exhaustive and successful assault' on Best's notion – which was, of course, really Bentham's – that questions of weight and credibility cannot be governed by rules.[166] Significantly several American reviewers doubted whether most of Moore's quotations from the law reports were 'really declarations of law and within the doctrine of *stare decisis*'.[167] Most pointed this out gently, while commending the book as a rich storehouse of information which would be useful to practitioners by way of general instruction and in preparing cases, even if most of the material could not be explicitly cited in argument – ammunition for pocket pistol law. Wigmore, who was fond of Moore, felt bound to attack his work quite sharply, for he saw it as dangerous: 'This treatise,' he began, 'is in performance exhaustive, in scope novel, in utility large, in avowed purpose it is partly good; partly it is what we should consider as bad as possible.'[168] For, he suggested, it is based on a fallacy, which is beginning to regain some ground, the idea that there are rules of weight:

If there is one thing for which the common law system of judge and jury stands, it is that the rules of evidence, as determined and applied by the judge, are rules of admissibility alone, and for the judge alone; the weight or credibility is for the jurors untrammelled by any rules of law ... The counsel who uses this book to induce the judge to a ruling of law upon credibility is committing moral treason to our system.[169]

Wigmore's view has generally prevailed. Moore seems to have made little impact and was soon forgotten. This is unfortunate for, as Wigmore acknowledged, it is a rich and fascinating compendium, in essence a judicial dictionary of quotations, full of delights and insights, certainly enjoyable, possibly useful, and dangerous only if misused.[170] As one reviewer suggested, it is a lawyers' book, if not a law book.[171] Thus Chamberlayne and Moore both failed for converse reasons: Chamberlayne went too far in trying to free the administration of evidence from all rules; Moore erred in the opposite direction, trying to subordinate all aspects of evidence to the governance of rules. Anglo-American practice, and its commentators, took a middle way, accepting most of Bentham's thesis with regard to competency, weight and credibility, but rejecting it with regard to admissibility – at least in part.[172]

After Thayer[173]

Thayer's failure to produce his promised treatise and the absence of serious competitors provided Wigmore with his opportunity. He took it with such conspicuous success that he earned more praise than his mentor and overshadowed all other writers on evidence for the next fifty years. It is, of course, quite misleading to depict Wigmore merely as a disciple of Thayer. Wigmore explicitly adopted Thayer's general theory of the law of evidence and drew heavily on his historical researches; both belong to the central tradition of Evidence scholarship and share most of its basic assumptions, but the resemblance ends here. Thayer was a subtle intensive thinker; his forte lay in the penetrating analysis of sharply focused questions; he was a lawyer who became obsessed by a rather narrow kind of history. Wigmore's talents were more extensive and systematic: he had broad legal interests and he was insatiably curious about other disciplines and other countries; he was an efficient and well-organized scholar with a great capacity for synthesis and simplification.

Their contributions to the theory of evidence are correspondingly different: Thayer provided the prevailing rationale for the *law* of evidence; Wigmore adopted Thayer's theory as one part of a much broader inter-disciplinary 'Science' of Evidence and Proof.[174] The nature and quality of Wigmore's achievements have been explored elsewhere. Here it is worth noting one negative impact of his success. The next generation of specialists in evidence in the United States contained some men of outstanding ability: Morgan, Chafee, McCormick and several others. They worked in the shadow of the master. Only one of them, McCormick, attempted to write a systematic treatise. This was quite modest in its stated aims and hid its light under a bushel, for McCormick was respected as a subtle and original thinker.[175] Whether Wigmore's dominance was the sole or even the primary cause, the first fifty years of the twentieth century represent a relatively fallow period, marked by much excellent and sophisticated work on particular topics, but more remarkable for the absence of attempts to develop general theories or to write systematic treatises as alternatives to Wigmore's.

There are, of course, some exceptions to these broad generalizations. Two deserve mention here. First, in this period a great deal of the energy of leading American evidence scholars, of whom Morgan was the most prominent, was channelled into drafting and debating proposed codes of evidence. The products of this long and complicated process were a series of consolidations and codes, notably the Model Code of Evidence (1942), the Uniform Rules of Evidence (1953), the California Evidence Code (first implemented 1965–7), the Federal Rules of Evidence (enacted 1975) and legislation based on one or other of these.[176] Although this movement towards codification represents the general trend in the direction of simplification and further narrowing of the scope of the formal rules of evidence, these codes represent achievements of pragmatic, incremental change based on compromise rather than a clear victory for Thayerism, let alone Benthamism.

One theorist who wrote in this period was Jerome Michael of Columbia, who for many years explored the theoretical foundations of evidence and civil procedure, including the logical and psychological dimensions of proof.[177] Much of the work was never completed, but a tentative edition of an ambitious theoretical book, written in collaboration with a philosopher, Mortimer Adler, was privately printed in 1931, as *The Nature of Judicial Proof: an Inquiry into the Logical, Legal, and Empirical Aspects of the Law of Evidence*.[178] Of this Wigmore wrote somewhat harshly: '[it] is a metaphysical analysis of the elements of probative reasoning; but its remarkable subtleties seem to have no more service for the practitioner than do the mathematical and physical formulas on which the physicist constructs his practicable microscope.'[179]

The period 1900–60 was also a fallow period for English Evidence scholarship and theorizing.[180] The most notable contribution was the first edition of *Cross on Evidence*, which soon became recognized by practitioners and academics alike as the leading English work in the field.[181] Its success was in part indicative of a need: it helped to fill a vacuum. Its limitations are equally revealing of the state of the subject at the time. Cross was pragmatic in respect of both form and substance: he set out to cater for two rather different markets, students and practitioners, simultaneously.[182] He sought to go beyond simple exposition to provide 'an up-to-date account of the theory of the subject'. But his notion of theory stopped at giving purported explanations for particular doctrines. Cross was a good expositor, clear and concise and with an excellent command of the case law. He also had a good sense of what issues practitioners thought important. But he set himself rather modest aims, he concentrated almost exclusively on the rules of evidence, and he exhibited little interest in the broader dimensions of the underlying theory of the subject or in its logical, psychological and empirical aspects.[183] The first edition of *Cross* contains no references either to Bentham or to Wigmore's *Science*.[184] His robust no-nonsense approach was typified by his remark, made in my presence: 'I am working for the day that my subject is abolished.'

Since 1960 there has been a slow, but steady, revival of interest in the study of evidence. In England a series of reports by the Law Reform Committee culminated in the Civil Evidence Acts of 1968 and 1972 which significantly reduced the scope and practical importance of the Law of Evidence in civil cases. On the criminal side, the Eleventh Report of the Criminal Law Revision Committee (1972) and the Report of the Royal Commission on Criminal Procedure (Philips Commission, 1981) both invoked Benthamite utilitarianism in rather dubious ways and stimulated public debates with strong echoes of the 1830s.[185] The main outcome was the Police and Criminal Evidence Act, 1984, which represents a compromise that satisfies few people. During this period some notable contributions have been made by Commonwealth scholars and law reformers, but without producing any radical breaks with the predominant tradition.

In selecting only a few highlights from a vast mass of material I have no wish to slight either the learning or sophistication of much of the case law and secondary writings, especially in the periodicals, that appeared in the years between the establishment of Wigmore's supremacy and the late 1960s. Evidence has tended to attract some of the finest minds among legal scholars and, in the United States in particular, there has been great strength in depth. But most of the learning has been particularistic and much of it has proved to be relatively ephemeral. The enactment of the Federal Rules and other quasi-codes of evidence has also created some hitherto unresolved problems for teachers of the subject. By simplifying the old law they have made some of the old learning obsolete, yet the new codes may not provide such a satisfactory basis for teaching skills of statutory interpretation as the Uniform Commercial Code or the Inernal Revenue Code. Writing in 1977, shortly after the enactment of the Federal Rules, two leading commentators remarked: '... the field of evidence can use a bit of shaking up; it has become stagnant since the defeat of the last generation of reformers. It would be only a slight exaggeration to say that there has not been one significant contribution to the field in the last twenty-five years.'[186]

From the perspective of 1984, this seemed to be a bit of an exaggeration. Today it no longer holds true. One of the reasons for this relative stagnation is that in England, the United States and other parts of the common law world, teaching, writing and thinking about evidence centred on the *law* of evidence. The scholars tended to follow the rules. These have diminished in scope and declined in importance over the years; they have also tended to become simpler. A number of recent developments have taken the subject out of the doldrums. Significantly each of these is concerned with aspects of evidence and proof that are largely independent of the technical rules.

First in time was the development of 'the new rhetoric' by Chaim Perelman and his associates.[187] This was a useful reminder of the close historical connection of questions of proof with classical and medieval rhetoric, which itself originally developed in large part in the forensic arena. It also showed that questions of fact pose as interesting and important problems of 'lawyers' reasonings' as questions of law.

A second, connected development was a series of debates about the nature of probabilistic reasoning in forensic contexts. It is a commonplace of evidence discourse that triers of fact are concerned with 'probabilities, not certainties'. For many years almost no attention was given by lawyers to the nature of the probabilities that were involved, despite enormous interest in probability theory in several adjacent disciplines. Then, stimulated in part by some elementary statistical errors in the California case of *People* v. *Collins*, a lively debate developed in the United States about the potential uses and abuses of mathematics in litigation.[188] To begin with the main participants took it for granted that all reasoning about probabilities is in principle mathematical; they disagreed about the correct way of applying the calculus of probability to particular situations and about the feasibility and desirability, as a matter of policy, of explicit resort to mathematical arguments in the courtroom. In the late 1970s whole books began to appear devoted to the application of statistics and mathematical probability to law.[189] In 1977 a British philosopher, Jonathan Cohen, advanced the thesis that not all reasoning about probabilities is in principle mathematical (Pascalian) and that some judgements of probability can be appropriately justified and criticized on the basis of objective, non-mathematical (Baconian) criteria. He further argued that most, but not all, arguments about probabilities in forensic contexts fitted his Baconian theory of induction better than any of the standard versions of mathematical probability, and that most leading theorists of evidence, including Bentham and possibly Wigmore, were probably Baconians. Cohen's thesis stimulated lively debates in several disciplines, including law. These debates have not yet run their course.

A third, largely independent development has been a revival of interest in law and psychology including, but not confined to, witness psychology. Between about 1890 and 1920 there was considerable interest in this field, especially in Germany and the United States. Then, for rather obscure reasons, interest almost completely died out for nearly fifty years. It began to revive in the 1960s, partly through the work of Lionel Haward, James Marshall, Arne Trankell and others. To begin with, much of the research was narrowly empirical and highly particularistic; but over time more critical and analytical approaches began to develop. By 1980 'Law and Psychology' had developed into an established field, especially in the United States.[190] As we shall see, in the past fifteen years the interests of specialists in fields as diverse as forensic science and conversation analysis, phenomenology and statistics, literary theory and expert systems have converged on the processing and uses of information in litigation, and questions were being asked about the relations between these lines of enquiry and about their general significance. Theory was becoming respectable again.

The Rationalist Tradition

This survey of some of the highlights of the intellectual history of the specialized study of Evidence in England and the United States should at least be enough to suggest that the story is by no means a straightforward case-study of the development of a specialized branch of expository scholarship. From an early stage there was a continuing uneasiness about whether there were or should be any formal rules of evidence, what precisely might be the status of such rules (and, in particular, of judicial rulings on points of evidence) and about the scope of Evidence as a subject. There were recurrent tensions between authors' concerns and the demands of the market, so that there was often an uneasy fit between substantive content and literary form. Most writers could hardly fail to be aware of the artificiality of isolating the study of evidence from the study of procedure, of substantive law and of 'non-legal' dimensions, especially the logical, epistemological and psychological aspects. Yet the desire to systematize, to simplify and, in some instances, to codify generated equally strong pressures to draw the boundaries of evidence doctrine precisely and narrowly. The systematic exposition of the law of evidence on the basis of principle was a primary concern of Gilbert and most of his successors. For some, like Bentham and Chamberlayne, the fundamental principle was some version of free proof. Gilbert, Peake and several leading nineteenth-century writers each tried to subsume the rules of evidence under different versions of the 'best evidence rule'. Stephen purported to find a single unifying principle in the notion of 'relevance'. All of these efforts failed and, since Thayer, the modern tendency has been to see the law of evidence largely as a collection of disparate constraints on freedom of proof and free evaluation of evidence.[191]

Evidence scholarship has also been a forum for a series of protracted controversies. Some of these belong fairly specifically to the study of evidence – conceptual disagreements, the debates about presumptions, hearsay and the best evidence rule, for example. Others represent particular applications of standard legal or juristic controversies, such as debates about the pros and cons of the jury or the adversary system or judge-made law or codification. Some, such as disagreements between utilitarians and deontologists, between civil libertarians and proponents of 'law and order', between Pascalians and Baconians, and more recently between atomists and holists, reflect wider differences. There is a remarkable degree of continuity about some of these controversies: for example, a reader of the *Edinburgh Review* in the eighteen-twenties and thirties would have found a great deal that was familiar in recent debates in England about the reform of criminal evidence and procedure.[192]

Despite these strains and disagreements there is a truly remarkable homogeneity about the basic assumptions of almost all specialist writings on evidence from Gilbert through Bentham, Thayer and Wigmore to Cross and McCormick. Almost without exception Anglo-American writers about evidence share very similar assumptions, either explicitly or implicitly, about the nature and ends of adjudication, about knowledge or belief about past events and about what is involved in reasoning about disputed questions of fact in forensic contexts. They differed about such matters as the scope of and the need for rules of evidence, about the role and rationale of the law of evidence in general, about the details of particular rules and about many other things. But these disagreements have by and large taken place within a shared framework of basic assumptions and concepts.[193]

These assumptions can be conveniently summarized in the form of two models or ideal types which are set out in table 1. The first Model reconstructs a Rationalist Model of Adjudication; the second attempts to articulate the main epistemological and logical assumptions of standard evidence discourse to be found in specialized secondary writings about evidence in the Anglo-American tradition.

If the propositions of the second Model represent standard elements in rationalist theories of evidence, it should be clear that it is artificial to make a sharp distinction between theories of evidence and theories of adjudication: generally speaking the former presuppose or form part of the latter. However, it is necessary to proceed with caution, partly because by no means all evidence scholars articulated clear and developed statements of their views about adjudication, and partly because there appears to be less of a consensus in the relevant literature about the ends and the achievements of the Anglo-American system of adjudication than about the logic and epistemology of proof. It is, however, possible to postulate a rationalist model of adjudication as an ideal type which both fits a rationalist theory of evidence and is recognizable as a reasonably sophisticated version of a widely held, if controversial, view. The first Model is a modified version of a Benthamite model of adjudication, presented in a way which suggests a number of possible points of departure or disagreement. Although by no means all leading Evidence scholars have been legal positivists and utilitarians, a rationalist theory of evidence necessarily presupposes a theory of adjudication that postulates something like Bentham's 'rectitude of decision' as the main objective. There is scope for divergence on a number of points of detail, but not from what might be called 'the rational core'.[194]

It is reasonable, and sufficient for present purposes, to assert that by and large the leading Anglo-American scholars and theorists of evidence from Gilbert to Wigmore (and, for the most part, until the present) have either implicitly or explicitly accepted such notions as these, although not in this particular formulation. Central to this model are two ideas: first that the Anglo-American system has adopted a 'rational' mode of determining issues of fact in contrast with older 'irrational' modes of proof.[195] Secondly, a particular view of 'rationality' was adopted or taken for granted. This found its classic expression in English empirical philosophy in the writings of Bacon, Locke and John Stuart Mill. But for the ungainliness of the term, it would be appropriate to refer to this 'intellectual mainstream' as the Classical Rationalist Tradition of Evidence Scholarship, in order to emphasize 'rational proof' as its central idea and a particular view of rationality as one of its basic assumptions.[196]

The characteristic assumptions of discourse about evidence within the Rationalist Tradition can be succinctly restated as follows: epistemology is cognitivist rather than sceptical; a correspondence theory of truth is generally preferred to a coherence theory of truth; the mode of decision making is seen as

Table 1 The Rationalist Tradition: basic assumptions

Model I A Rationalist model of adjudication	Model II Rationalist theories of evidence and proof: some common assumptions
A *Prescriptive* 1 The direct end 2 of adjective law 3 is rectitude of decision through correct application 4 of valid substantive laws 5 deemed to be consonant with utility (or otherwise good) 6 and through accurate determination 7 of the true past facts 8 material to 9 precisely specified allegations expressed in categories defined in advance by law i.e. facts in issue 10 proved to specified standards of probability or likelihood 11 on the basis of the careful 12 and rational 13 weighing of 14 evidence 15 which is both relevant 16 and reliable 17 presented (in a form designed to bring out truth and discover untruth) 18 to supposedly competent 19 and impartial 20 decision-makers 21 with adequate safeguards against corruption 22 and mistake 23 and adequate provision for review and appeal. **B** *Descriptive* 24 Generally speaking this objective is largely achieved 25 in a consistent 26 fair 27 and predictable manner.	1 Knowledge about particular past events is possible. 2 Establishing the truth about particular past events in issue in a case (the facts in issue) is a necessary condition for achieving justice in adjudication; incorrect results are one form of injustice. 3 The notions of evidence and proof in adjudication are concerned with rational methods of determining questions of fact; in this context operative distinctions have to be maintained between questions of fact and questions of law, questions of fact and questions of value and questions of fact and questions of opinion. 4 The establishment of the truth of alleged facts in adjudication is typically a matter of probabilities, falling short of absolute certainty. 5 (a) Judgments about the probabilities of allegations about particular past events can and should be reached by reasoning from relevant evidence presented to the decision-maker; (b) The characteristic mode of reasoning appropriate to reasoning about probabilities is induction. 6 Judgments about probabilities have, generally speaking, to be based on the available stock of knowledge about the common course of events; this is largely a matter of common sense supplemented by specialized scientific or expert knowledge when it is available. 7 The pursuit of truth (i.e. seeking to maximize accuracy in fact-determination) is to be given a high, but not necessarily an overriding, priority in relation to other values, such as the security of the state, the protection of family relationships or the curbing of coercive methods of interrogation. 8 One crucial basis for evaluating "fact-finding" institutions, rules, procedures and techniques is how far they are estimated to maximize accuracy in fact-determination—but other criteria such as speed, cheapness, procedural fairness, humaneness, public confidence and the avoidance of vexation for participants are also to be taken into account. 9 The primary role of applied forensic psychology and forensic science is to provide guidance about the reliability of different kinds of evidence and to develop methods and devices for increasing such reliability.

Note: Prescriptive rationalism: acceptance of A as both desirable and reasonably feasible. No commitment to B.
Complacent rationalism: acceptance of A & B *in re* a particular system.

'rational', as contrasted with 'irrational' modes such as battle, compurgation, or odeal; the characteristic mode of reasoning is induction; the pursuit of truth as a *means* to justice under the law commands a high, but not necessarily an overriding, priority as a social value.

This account of the Rationalist Tradition has both an analytical and an historical aspect.[197] Analytically it is an attempt to reconstruct in the form of an 'ideal type' an account of a set of basic assumptions about the aims and nature of adjudication and what is involved in reasoning about disputed questions of fact in that context. The test of success of this ideal type is its clarity, coherence, and usefulness as a tool of analysis of evidence discourse and doctrine.

The historical thesis is more cautious. It advances the hypothesis that, by and large, the works of most of a list of named writers on evidence either articulated or assumed ideas that were close to the ideal type. The historical claim should be treated with caution for two main reasons. First, it is a tentative hypothesis based on selective sampling of works of a few writers. Even in respect of those named individuals the hypothesis needs to be tested and refined by much more detailed research. For example, no systematic attempt has been made to test the hypothesis in respect of judicial discourse in appellate cases or in writings by continental European writers on evidence.[198] It would be surprising if there were not some significant deviants,[199] but I would also be surprised if sufficient evidence were adduced to refute the claim that the predominant Anglo-American tradition of *specialized* discourse about evidence is remarkably homogeneous in respect of its basic underlying assumptions which are rooted in eighteenth-century Enlightenment Rationalism.

The emphasis on *specialized* discourse is crucial. For it is part of my wider thesis that there is a sharp contrast between writings about evidence and the much more varied, often sceptical, literature(s) about litigation, legal processes, and procedure. Part of the argument is that our heritage of specialized evidence discourse became artificially isolated from these other bodies of literature and from broader movements in ideas and that the time is ripe for a rethinking.

The second caveat about the historical thesis relates to the first part of the ideal type. This is based explicitly on Bentham's ideas, deliberately set out in a way that signals clearly and provocatively a whole range of possible points of departure from this model. One reason for constructing it in this way was to try to facilitate the pinpointing of differences between Bentham's powerful, but simplistic, theory of procedure, and existing and possible alternatives.[200] A second reason is that, as we have seen, it is much harder to make confident assertions about evidence specialists' underlying theories of adjudication and procedure, because these are relatively rarely articulated in a coherent fashion.[201] There are clearly some tensions between the first Model and the 'ideal type' of adversarial procedures. One could expect detailed research to reveal such tensions and more divergences by writers on evidence from Model I than from Model II.[202]

The claim that the modern system of adjudication is 'rational' is a statement of what is considered to be a feasible *aspiration* of the system; it does not necessarily involve commitment to the view that this aspiration is always, generally, or even sometimes, realized in practice. It is commonplace within the

Rationalist Tradition to criticize existing practices, procedures, rules and institutions in terms of their failure to satisfy the standards of this aspirational model.

Part A of Model I is prescriptive: it states an aspiration and a standard by which to judge actual rules, institutions, procedures and practices. Acceptance of such standards involves no necessary commitment to the view that a particular system, or some aspect of it, at a particular time satisfies these standards either in its design or in its actual operation. Part B of the model is intended to represent typical claims or judgments of the kind 'on the whole the system works well.' None of the leading theorists in the Rationalist tradition were perfectionists who expected one hundred per cent conformity with the ideal. Some were highly critical of existing arrangements and practices. Indeed Bentham, whose *Rationale of Judicial Evidence* is the main source of the model, made his theory of adjudication the basis for a radical and far-ranging critique of English (and, to a lesser extent, Scottish and continental) procedure, practice and rules of evidence in his day. It is, of course, possible to explore how far any individual writers have been complacent, either generally or in particular respects, about the design or practical operation of their own system; but this kind of judgement involves an additional step – moving from prescribing general standards to applying them to particular examples.

Thus it is important to distinguish clearly between *aspirational* and *complacent rationalism* in respect of adjudication. It is also useful to differentiate a third category, which might be referred to as *optimistic rationalism*. For in invoking prescriptive standards one often makes some judgement about the prospects for attaining or approximating to such standards in practice in a given context: in the case of many writers on evidence and judicial process who accepted some variant of Part A of the rationalist model of adjudication, it is reasonable to attribute to them the view that its standards represent a feasible aspiration rather than a remote or unattainable Utopian ideal. Even virulently critical writers such as Bentham and Frank can be shown to have believed that their own favoured recommendations would in practice lead to significant increases in the level of rationality in adjudication. They were optimistic rationalists. Nearly all of the literature on evidence that has been discussed in this essay is generally optimistic in this sense. In brief: almost all the leading writers in the mainstream of Anglo-American Evidence scholarship were aspirational rationalists, most were optimistic rationalists most of the time, and many, but by no means all, were fairly complacent about the general operation of the adversary system in their own jurisdiction in their day.

The general tendency of Anglo-American Evidence scholarship is not only optimistic, it is also remarkably unsceptical in respect of its basic assumptions. Hardly a whisper of doubt about the possibility of knowledge, about the validity of induction, or about human capacity to reason darkens the pages of Gilbert or Bentham or Best or Thayer or Wigmore or Cross or other, leading writers. Confident assertion, pragmatic question-begging or straightforward ignoring are the characteristic responses to perennial questions raised by philosophical sceptics. At first sight this may seem rather surprising, given the sceptical tone of a great deal of writing about judicial processes since the time of Holmes.

There is thus a sharp contrast in tone between the optimistic, often bland, rationalism of specialized writings on evidence and the sceptical tendencies in much recent writing about judicial process. The contrast, however, may be more of style than of substance, for the main thrust of critical writings is directed at the design and the actual operation of a particular system and the claims that are made for it, rather than at the underlying philosophical assumptions and aspirations of the Rationalist Tradition. The principal target is complacent rather than aspirational rationalism. In the next chapter I shall argue that many seemingly sceptical writers about judicial processes invoke standards which are identical or similar to those outlined in the rationalist model of adjudication and that, in law as elsewhere, genuine philosophical sceptics are rare birds. In brief they are not so far removed from aspirational, even optimistic, rationalism as the sceptical tone of some of their writings suggests. If this is correct, it suggests that the obstacles to a reintegration of the literature on evidence and on the processes which constitute the context of disputed questions of fact about particular past events may not be as great as appears on the surface. There are genuine difficulties and disagreements, but they are shared by several specialized fields of enquiry that have grown apart.

Reintegration is surely needed. For the Rationalist Tradition of Evidence scholarship, by dint of its artificial isolation, has paradoxically produced a corpus of literature which is notable both for scholarly excellence and conceptual sophistication and for a series of recurrent controversies which even some of the leading protagonists acknowledge are 'high among the unrealities'. Evidence scholarship has a lot to offer and a lot to learn.

The Rationalist Tradition: A Postscript

Since the original version of this essay was published in 1982 it has been the subject of a good deal of comment and discussion in print and in seminars and conferences.[203] The historical thesis has so far been accepted as generally correct although, as I have suggested, detailed investigation and analysis is likely to yield a more complex story.[204] The two models have also been accepted as a coherent and analytically useful ideal typical reconstruction of an orthodoxy and have been subject to only a few verbal amendments. However, commentators have raised three general questions that deserve a response: First, have there been any significant deviants from the orthodoxy? Secondly, what is the political or ideological significance of the Rationalist Tradition? What is its relationship, both historical and logical, to a particular 'ideology' or creed, such as Benthamism or 'Liberal Legalism'?[205] To what extent can this ideal type accommodate substantial internal political disagreements on important issues? Finally, several civilian proceduralists have posed in a sharp form a question that had already troubled me.[206] The point may be restated as follows: although this ideal type has been reconstructed from Anglo-American writings it seems to fit an 'inquisitorial' model of procedure better than an 'adversarial' one. For it is generally recognized that inquisitorial systems are more directly and consistently concerned with the pursuit of truth and the implementation of law than adversarial proceedings, the primary purpose of which is legitimated conflict-resolution. Is there not, therefore, a tension between adversarial proceedings and the formulation of the ends of procedure in Model I?

These are all worthwhile and complex questions which deserve attention. Without trying to do justice to them here, it may be helpful to give some preliminary indications by way of response.

Deviants

The Rationalist Tradition is presented in the form of an 'ideal type' to which the ideas of the authors discussed in the text, and many other Anglo-American writers about evidence, appear to conform more or less closely. The historical thesis is cautious, partly because of the danger of generalizing about the ideas (many of them implicit) of authors writing at different times in different contexts and partly because more detailed research and analysis than I have undertaken could be expected to uncover some significant refinements and deviations. Even Bentham's epistemology, as embodied in his theory of fictions, is a good deal more complex and subtle than is suggested by the bald formulations in Model II, 1–6.[207] Of *specialist writers* on evidence who published before 1980, the two leading candidates for treatment as deviants seem to be James Glassford and Kenneth Graham Jr.

James Glassford (obit 1845) was a Scottish Advocate and Sheriff-Depute.[208] His work *An Essay on the Principles of Evidence and Their Application to Subjects of Judicial Enquiry* (1820) was originally intended as a contribution to the *Supplement of the Encyclopaedia Britannica*, but was published separately because of its length. This interesting work has been well described and analysed by Dr M. A. Abu Hareira.[209] He convincingly shows that Glassford was a pioneering exponent of a 'holistic' approach to the evaluation of judicial evidence and that he challenges the 'atomistic' approaches of writers in the Rationalist Tradition (including *both* Baconians and Pascalians in recent debates about probabilities and proof). I shall argue later that, while a sound theory of reasoning about disputed questions of fact needs to take account of narrative coherence and other 'holistic' ideas, it is a mistake to treat atomism and holism as rival or incompatible approaches.[210] However, 'holism' does raise questions about the acceptability of the particular conceptions of rationality adopted or assumed by writers in the Rationalist Tradition. The significant point is that at least one Scottish writer on evidence belonged to a different philosophical tradition (the common sense school) from that of early English writers on evidence, such as Gilbert, Bentham and Evans; a similar challenge is mounted by contemporary theorists who draw some of their inspiration from Continental European philosophy (e.g. Hegel or Habermas)[211] or, in the case of Abu Hareira, Islamic ideas.

Professor Kenneth Graham Jr. has launched a series of attacks on what he calls 'Progressive Proceduralism', which invites interpretation as the twentieth-century American branch of the Rationalist Tradition.[212] Graham characterizes Progressive Proceduralism as being based on 'Benthamite ideology'. The motives and methods of his attack are overtly political. However, he acknowledges that its opponents have so far not developed an 'alternative model'[213] and his own version of an 'Irrealist Theory of Evidence', while revealing, can most charitably be interpreted as parody.[214] Graham's most substantial contribution to date has been the four volumes and supplements on evidence in the encyclopaedic *Federal Practice and Procedure*.[215] The constraints of compiling a reference work for practitioners have not entirely curbed Graham's ebullience nor concealed his values, but it is not yet possible to reconstruct a coherent alternative theory from his published work, which could be located on the fringes of critical legal studies. Graham offers a sharp political challenge to orthodox evidence theory, but whether acceptance of his political views would necessarily involve rejecting any central ideas of the Rationalist Tradition is an open question.

Ideology

Graham's attitude to 'Progressive Proceduralism' and his interpretation of 'Benthamite ideology' at least have the virtue of raising some important issues about the ideological significance of the basic assumptions of the Rationalist Tradition. His account of 'the Progressive Paradigm' in the United States emphasizes several ideas: 'the purpose of Litigation is to vindicate the substantive law so as to make relationships predictable and certain'; fact-finding is best done by scientific experts rather than lay jurors; it favours increase of judicial discretion in admitting evidence; and, as part of a more general concern to establish 'the neutrality' of law and procedure, it disguises the infusion of repressive values into procedural arrangements by treating the latter as neutral instruments of positive law. In short, the Rationalist Tradition is an obfuscating ideology which has been used to legitimate institutions and doctrines that uphold an ethos of social control, which is technocratic, hierarchical, centralized and statist.[216]

The details of Graham's challenge have been considered and criticized at length elsewhere.[217] Stripped of its excesses it can be interpreted as raising some important questions about the political significance of the Rationalist model viewed as a reconstruction of the basic assumptions of a rather stable intellectual tradition. First, if the historical thesis is correct, does it follow that all of our leading writers on evidence were, consciously or unconsciously, committed to an ideology of centralized statist social control? Secondly, to what extent does adherence to the central tenets of the Rationalist Tradition preclude significant political disagreements? These are important and complex questions and I cannot hope to do justice to them in brief compass. However, it is worth responding to the challenge by outlining my position on them.

The central tenet of the Rationalist Tradition is that the direct end of adjective law is the achievement of rectitude of decision in adjudication. In respect of questions of fact, that involves the pursuit of truth about particular past events through rational means. Rectitude of decision is given a high, but not an overriding, priority as a means to securing justice under the law (expletive justice). The model is instrumentalist in that the pursuit of truth through reason is a means to expletive justice, i.e. the implementation of substantive law.[218]

Does acceptance of such basic ideas necessarily involve commitment to centralized statist social control? Some clues to this complex question are to be found in Mirjan Damaska's masterly analysis of procedural systems.[219] Any procedural system, he suggests, can be interpreted in terms of the interaction between ingredients of three ideal types relating to *systems of government* ('the managerial state' and 'the reactive state'); hierarchical and coordinate *systems of authority*; and inquisitorial (inquest) and adversarial (contest) *systems of procedure*. Damaska suggests that nearly all historical examples of actual systems of each kind are hybrids, combining elements of each ideal type in complex ways, and that there is no stable correlation between the different ideal types: for example, while one might expect a managerial state to have a hierarchical system of authority and a primarily inquisitorial system of procedure, this is not a matter of logical or historical or institutional necessity. Most actual systems reflect complex compromises, some of which are more 'comfortable' than others. Thus, in the present context, the Rationalist model is compatible with coordinate as well as hierarchical authority and even with adversarial systems of procedure, although there are some admitted tensions in the latter case.[220] Thus, at this very abstract level, there is no necessary incompatibility between the central tenets of the Rationalist Tradition and democratic systems of government, de-centralized coordinate authority and adversary proceedings.

Before moving to a more concrete level, it is worth making two theoretical points: first, like Damaska's three models, the Rationalist Tradition is an 'ideal type'; that is an interpretative tool, to be evaluated in the first instance by its clarity, coherence and explanatory power. The historical claim that by and large most Anglo-American specialized writings on evidence have approximated to that type is an application of that tool to particular data. This claim could be refuted or modified or re-interpreted by more detailed research and analysis without invalidating the model.

Secondly, the distinctions between aspirational, optimistic and complacent rationalism are important in interpreting our heritage of evidence scholarship.[221] My ideal type is in first instance normative and aspirational: it reconstructs a prescriptive design theory. Writers within this tradition diverge as to the feasibility of the aspiration and even more on the extent to which they believe that the aspiration is realized in practice at a particular time and place. Bentham, for example, used his theory of adjective law as the basis for a radical critique of early nineteenth-century English institutions, doctrines and practices. Frank, while emphasizing the obstacles in the way of ever achieving the ideal, invoked much the same values in advocating somewhat less sweeping reforms of the American system of his day.[222] Other writers have varied both in the degree of their complacency about existing arrangements in their own systems and in respect of optimism or pessimism about the feasibility of change. The essays in this book explore critically and selectively how far some ingredients of the aspirational model, or the model as a whole, require more fundamental rethinking in the light of recent intellectual developments.

Against this background, it is worth asking how far genuine political or ideological differences can be (and have been) accommodated within the tenets of the Rationalist Tradition. I shall defer until later consideration of examples of radical ideological scepticism, such as that all our inherited evidence discourse is little more than a form of bourgeois mystification which serves to legitimate a system that is rotten to the core, or the slightly more subtle thesis that this inheritance is just another example of 'liberal legalism' that is irreparably flawed by inescapable contradictions.[223] Here some more specific examples will suffice to illustrate two related points: first, that the model of the Rationalist Tradition has been constructed in such a way as to accommodate some genuine political differences; secondly, that not all the disagreements and differences between writers within the tradition are sensibly characterized as 'political', except in some trivial sense.

The most familiar disagreements about evidence relate to the position of persons suspected of or charged with criminal offences. In England such debates have been a recurrent feature of public life for over two hundred years, with the polemical battle lines being drawn with monotonous regularity and very similar arguments being adduced by each side when the issues periodically resurface.[224] In the United States, and more recently in Canada, an additional constitutional dimension has featured in a similar recurrent cycle.[225] While the details and the rhetoric may change, the central issues remain relatively stable and can generally be formulated in terms compatible with the Rationalist model: What priority should be given to rectitude of decision on the one hand and process values and the avoidance of vexation on the other? What priority should be given to the principle of avoiding conviction of the innocent over the objective of crime prevention? When, if ever, should rules of evidence be used as means of preventing or deterring illegal or improper police behaviour, even at the expense of rectitude of decision? And so on. Most of these debates can be interpreted as debates *within* the Rationalist Tradition although, as I shall argue later, my particular formulation is sufficiently Benthamic to put non-utilitarians at a disadvantage.[226] This general claim applies *pari passu* to debates about particular topics such as the privilege against self-incrimination, the right to silence, 'fruits of the poisoned tree', the presumption of innocence and many other familiar, regularly contested matters.

A rather different set of debates relates to what constitute valid and cogent modes of reasoning about disputed questions of 'fact'. There is, first, the recent debate about probabilities and proof.[227] This seems to me to be in the first instance an apolitical debate about fundamental issues in the theory of probabilities. Interestingly, it has an important political dimension. Jonathan Cohen (the leading modern Baconian) has conducted a sustained campaign against the cult of the expert in psychology and diagnostic medicine, as well as in law.[228] Ordinary adults, such as jurors, patients, and subjects of psychological experiments have a 'general cognitive competence' to make rational judgments about questions of fact, because the appropriate form of reasoning in this context is ordinary practical reasoning which conforms to Cohen's model of inductive probability better than the less accessible mathematical models. But the grounds for his logical theory are independent of his (political) argument about the dangers of misuse of statistical theory by experts. Similarly, Laurence

Tribe has argued against the overt use of mathematical argument in courts as politically dangerous even though, unlike Cohen, he assumes that the correct model for such reasoning is in principle mathematical.[229] In short Pascalians and Baconians can become political allies in defending juries and other participatory institutions against the potential misuse of specialist knowledge by decision theorists and other 'experts'. These disagreements also fit within the framework of the Rationalist Tradition.

The debate between 'atomists' and 'holists' similarly has political as well as analytical dimensions. Whether 'holistic' elements can be accommodated within our conception of rationality is in the first instance a philosophical question which can and should be separated from one's political preferences. However, in the context of litigation, I shall argue that there is a tendency for holistic thinking to subvert sharp distinctions between fact and law, fact and value, and law and value.[230] For me this presents a political dilemma: on the one hand I am sympathetic to the introduction of community values in the administration of justice; on the other hand, such values may include social, sexual or other 'prejudices' that offend my liberal beliefs, and giving free play to holism may subvert important principles, such as the principle 'judge the act, not the actors.'

The Rationalist model and adversary proceedings

Finally, it has been suggested that the two models of the Rationalist Tradition taken together, fit inquisitorial systems better than adversarial ones.[231] This raises important questions both about the internal coherence of the Rationalist Tradition and about the implications of my story for interpretation of civilian systems. The issues are complex and deserve to be explored further on another occasion. Here I shall merely sketch the outline of a possible answer. First, it is widely acknowledged that both Anglo-American and Continental European systems contain hybrid mixtures of adversarial and inquisitorial features.[232] In so far as the Anglo-American system fits the model of inquest rather than contest, the specific question under discussion does not arise.

Secondly, 'inquest' and 'contest' as ideal types are total process models of procedural systems. Models I and II, on the other hand, focus on the adjudicative stage of litigation, a stage which is generally not reached in practice in the Anglo-American system because of such devices as settlement out of court and guilty pleas. If we were to widen the subject of 'judicial evidence' to encompass all aspects of the processing and uses of information in litigation, a much more complex set of assumptions would be indicated.[233]

Thirdly, within a general theory of dispute-settlement, third-party adjudication is one recognized means among many for achieving the goal of resolution of conflict. Legal process scholarship recognizes this with varying degrees of clarity: for example, non-prosecution, freely negotiated compromise, pressured settlement, abandonment and surrender.[234] It need not occasion surprise if the standards of correct decision by adjudicators in contests are not fundamentally different from the standards for adjudication in inquests. Adjudicative decisions that serve different procedural ends may share many key features.

Finally, some of the leading evidence writers in the Rationalist Tradition, including Bentham and Wigmore, were either highly critical of or deeply ambivalent about many adversarial aspects of common law proceedings. Conversely, some apologists for the adversary system claim, *inter alia*, that it has the more efficient methods of ascertaining the truth, even if it is less committed to this end.[235] It is not possible to do justice to these complex issues here. Perhaps enough has been said to indicate the problematic nature of the relationship between discourse about evidence and proof on the one hand and different procedural contexts on the other.

NOTES

This essay, which appears in a revised and extended form in this book, was first published as a festschrift for Sir Richard Eggleston in Campbell and Waller (1982). An abbreviated version appeared in Twining (1985). The author wishes to thank the Law Book Co., Australia, for kind permission to reproduce the essay.

1 Thayer *Treatise*, 198–9.
2 The quotations are from Shakespeare, *Richard II*, I. i.
3 Standard accounts of 'irrational' modes of dispute-settlement include Thayer *Treatise*, ch. 1; Lea (1878); Goitein (1923); Caenegem (1973), ch. 3; Diamond (1971), esp. ch. 21; Roberts (1979); Hyams (1981). In an amusing article Ireland (1980) develops the theme, found elsewhere in the literature, of the marginality and unpopularity of ordeal and battle in many contexts. Cf. Harman J in *Serville* v. *Constance* [1954] 1 WLR 487, at 491, regretting that conflicting claims to the title of Welterweight Champion of Trinidad could not be settled by battle. On Judge Bridlegoose, see below, 117–22.
4 There was, however, no attempt to call or examine witnesses or adduce other evidence in support of the facts alleged.
5 Thayer, op. cit., 10, n. 1.
6 On rhetoric see, e.g. Kennedy (1963, 1972, 1980); Perelman and Olbrechts-Tytecha (1971); Goodrich (1986). On the numerical system of proof see Kunert (1966/7). On the history of probability theory see Hacking (1975) and Shapiro (1969, 1983). On the history of forensic science see Smyth (1980) and Lambourne (1984). On forensic psychology see Lloyd-Bostock (1980, 1988) and Trankell (1982). On the comparative study of procedure see Damaska (1973, 1986). On the history of Criminal Procedure see Langbein (1974, 1978, 1983).
7 General surveys of the history of the law of evidence, including writers on evidence, are to be found in 1 Wigmore *Treatise* (Tillers rev., 1983), s.8, which also contains a useful bibliography; Holdsworth (1903–38), esp. 1, 299–312; 9, 127–222; 12, 365–7; 13, 466–8, 504–10; 15, 138–42, 307–10; Holdsworth (1925), 116ff.; Nokes (1967), ch. 2. Thayer *Treatise* remains the classic study of many aspects of the history of evidence. See also Wright and Graham (1977), ch. 1. 'Some of the most fundamental attributes of modern Anglo-American criminal procedure for cases of serious crime emerged in England during the eighteenth century: the law of evidence, the adversary system, the privilege against self-incrimination, and the main ground rules for the relationship of judge and jury,' Langbein (1983), 2. Much of the evidence for this claim is gathered in Langbein (1978). Short biographies of several of the writers discussed in this chapter can be found in Simpson (ed.) (1984).
8 Lords' Journal, 25 February 1794. On Burke's interpretation of the 'best evidence rule' and Christian's challenge to it, see Thayer *Treatise* 492–5. Cf. 1 Wigmore *Treatise*, 237.
9 Wigmore, id., 238.
10 Gilbert (1754), 1. On the relationship of Gilbert's treatise to Hale and to broader

intellectual developments in the seventeenth century see Shapiro (1983), ch. 5. See also Abu Hareira (1984, 1986).

11 Id., 4.
12 3 *Commentaries*, ch. 23.
13 vi *Works*, 142–5, 183–7.
14 Id., 144.
15 Id., 186.
16 Id., 144.
17 Id., 186–7.
18 L. J. Cohen (1980).
19 Thayer *Treatise*, ch. 11.
20 Id., 506.
21 For a detailed account of Bentham on Evidence see *TEBW*.
22 The most important of these are *Scotch Reform* and *Court of Lords Delegates*. An attenuated version of the former appears in v *Works*, 1–53; recent research by Ms Claire Gobbi suggests that there is much of interest in these works which survives unpublished in the Bentham papers. For details see Twining (1986) and *TEBW*.
23 Halévy (1928), 1955 edn, 383.
24 vii *Works*, 384.
25 vii *Works*, 599. On the anti-nomian thesis see below, 216 n. 71.
26 L. J. Cohen (1977), 54ff. Bentham's epistemology, as embodied in his theory of fictions, is generally regarded as ahead of its time. Most evidence writers have adopted a less sophisticated version of Lockean empiricism, e.g. Postema (1983), 37ff. *TEBW*, 52–68.
27 Postema (1977); see further Postema's excellent work, *Bentham and the Common Law Tradition* (1986), cf. *TEBW*, 74–5.
28 Bentham (1825), 180 (hereafter *Treatise*).
29 vi *Works*, 216.
30 See generally Bentham (1838–53), App. A; vi *Works*, 151–2; (1827), B. 6; *Treatise*, 180–3. See further below, ch. 6.
31 Wigmore (1942), 26 *ABAJ*, 476, 477.
32 Wigmore *Science*, 5 qualified on hearsay, id., 944.
33 Thayer *Treatise*, 265. See further below, ch. 6.
34 Twining (1980), 8–9. The argument of exaggerated importance in respect of the modern Law of Evidence is examined in ch. 6 below.
35 See e.g. vi *Works*, 6n.
36 Archbold (1822). On treatises of this period see Shapiro (1986), 175ff.
37 Pothier (1761, 1806).
38 Article on W. D. Evans in the *Dictionary of National Biography*.
39 W. D. Evans (1803).
40 Id., Preface, iv.
41 1 Wigmore *Treatise*, 238.
42 W. D. Evans in Pothier (1806), 40.
43 Cheshire and Fifoot (1969), 20–1.
44 W. D. Evans in Pothier (1806), 95.
45 Id., 96.
46 Id., 148.
47 Id., esp. 148–9.
48 Id., 262.
49 Ibid.
50 Id., 301.
51 See e.g. 40–1, 225, 300–1. Evans and Bentham were contemporaries and corresponded briefly. See *The Correspondence of Jeremy Bentham*, vol. 8 (ed. S. Conway, *CW*, 1988), 442, 525. How far either author influenced the other in respect of evidence is uncertain – there is almost no direct evidence on the point.

52   W. D. Evans (1803), iv.
53   1 Wigmore *Treatise*, 238.
54   Op. cit., n. 40.
55   Preface.
56   Ibid.
57   See the article on Starkie in the *Dictionary of National Biography*.
58   Kenny (1928), 319.
59   Preface.
60   Ram (1861); C. C. Moore (1908). On Moore, see below; of the former one reviewer wrote: 'Mr Ram has achieved the triumph of making romance and poetry the staple materials of a legal treatise. Extracts from the novelists, varied with hexameters, epigrams, odes and blank verse, are scattered broadcast upon its pages ... A couplet or an epigram *à propos* of the subject frequently imparts grace and piquancy to the style of a writer; but when paltry truisms are solemnly enunciated to foist upon the reader long passages from *Noctes Ambrosianae* or the *Satires* of Juvenal, it is not simply bad taste, but pedantry' (12 Law Mag. and Law Rev., 1861–2, 163).
61   Preface to 1st edn.
62   Ch. 8.
63   See Best (1849), *passim*, esp. 32–3, 49–50, 60, 72–5, 98, 114, 165. See also Best (1856–8), 209, which contains a general critique of Bentham's attitude to codes and to the legal profession, including 'Judge and Co.'. See further *TEBW*.
64   Best (1849), 72.
65   8th ed. (1893), Preface.
66   J. F. Stephen (1876), Introduction.
67   Chafee (1922–3). Cf. Chafee (1920–1).
68   See generally Greenleaf (1842). The Preface to the sixteenth edition, by Wigmore, contains a brief account of Greenleaf and of the history of his work. See also the *Centennial History of the Harvard Law School, 1817–1917* (1918), 215–19; Sutherland (1967), 122–3, 137.
69   Preface.
70   Swift (1810).
71   Preface.
72   Preface.
73   J. B. Thayer (1927), 210.
74   11th edn (1920) (ed. J. B. Matthews and G. F. Spear).
75   Chafee (1920–1), 901.
76   Stallybrass (1933), 127.
77   Wigmore *Science*, 5n.
78   Preface. See also J. B. Thayer (1927), 323–4; 2 Wigmore *Treatise*, 687, n.1; 12 Law Mag. and Law Rev. (1861–2), 44; 7 The Green Bag (1895), 510–16; D. M. Gold (1979). I am grateful to Chief Justice Vincent L. McKusick of Maine for information and references concerning his predecessor.
79   20 US Stat. at Large, 30.
80   For an excellent general account, see Radzinowicz (1957). See also L. Stephen (1895). See now K. J. M. Smith (1988).
81   J. F. Stephen (1876), Introduction, xxii. Cf. Fifoot (1959), 115–17.
82   L. Stephen, op. cit., 209–11; J. F. Stephen (1890), 206–7.
83   (1876), xxiii. See also L. Stephen, op. cit., 207–10.
84   J. F. Stephen (1863).
85   Radzinowicz (1957), 54–5; Fifoot (1959), 115.
86   J. F. Stephen (1872). The Introduction ran to 134 pages and, although somewhat discursive, remains one of the classic contributions to the theory of evidence. On the Indian Evidence Act, see Gledhill (1964), 241–5.
87   Sarkar (1971), 15.

88 L. Stephen, op. cit., 275.
89 Id., 271–5.
90 See Elias (1962), 253n; Sarkar (1971), Preface.
91 Sarkar, op. cit., ch. 1, quoting Bayley CJ in *Smith* v. *Ludhia* 17.B, 129, 141.
92 Cited 1 Wigmore *Treatise* (3rd edn), Preface, xx.
93 (1876), xx.
94 Radzinowicz (1957), 9.
95 (1876), x.
96 (1876), Introduction.
97 Id., xvii–xviii.
98 Thayer *Treatise*, ch. 8.
99 Stephen's original account of relevancy was criticized by George Clifford Whitworth of the Bombay Civil Service in a pamphlet which I have not been able to trace. Whitworth's argument was discussed and developed by Pollock (1876). Pollock argued that it would not be appropriate to treat logical relevancy as part of the law of evidence for two reasons: first, it mixes up legal propositions with propositions which are common to all knowledge; second, that there was no consensus on the principles of logic: 'If the law of evidence is to embody the canons of inductive logic to the extent of Mr Whitworth's rules or Mr Stephen's ninth article, I do not see why it should stop short of giving a complete exposition of them, and landing us, perhaps in the thick of a purely metaphysical controversy on the true meaning of cause' (id., 388). Thayer followed Pollock in treating relevance as a matter of logic which was presupposed by, but not part of, the law of evidence. Chamberlayne discusses the debate at length and concludes that 'No Particular Theory of Relevancy [is] Imposed on the Law of Evidence' (1 *Treatise*, s. 59). Stephen explicitly states that '[t]he logical theory was cleared up by Mill' (1876, xii). Pollock and Chamberlayne recognized that there is more than one theory of logic. Unfortunately, at least until recently, most writers in the Rationalist Tradition have *assumed* Mill's account of induction uncritically. A major theme of the present work is that there are competing conceptions of rationality abroad in evidence discourse and that to *understand* the subject one cannot beg the metaphysical questions. Whether one classifies this as part of 'the law of evidence' for purposes of codification or exposition is another, secondary, issue (see below, ch. 6).
100 (1876), xi–xii. He continues: 'The logical theory was cleared up by Mr Mill. Bentham and some other writers had more or less discussed the connection of logic with the rules of evidence. But I am not aware that it occurred to any one before I published my "Introduction to the Indian Evidence Act" to point out in detail the very close resemblance which exists between Mr Mill's theory and the existing state of the law.'
101 Thayer *Treatise*, ch. 11.
102 (1876), x *et seq.*
103 Thayer, *Treatise* ch. 11.
104 See esp. (1876), x *et seq.*
105 For a detailed account of Thayer's view of the Law of Evidence, see below, ch. 6.
106 On Thayer's life, see especially the *Centennial History of the Harvard Law School, 1817–1917* (1918). A fascinating interpretation is to be found in Chamberlayne (1908), 758–63.
107 Thayer *Treatise*, 527.
108 Pollock (1899). Both Pollock and Thayer criticized Stephen for lacking a clear conception of admissibility, distinct from relevance on the one hand and materiality on the other.
109 Chamberlayne, op. cit., 760.
110 See esp. Morgan (1956).
111 See Thayer *Treatise*, *passim*; (1927), 305–9.
112 *Treatise*, 279n.
113 Id., 535.

114   Id., 314n.
115   Id., 530.
116   A brief account is given in Maguire et al. (1973), Preface.
117   There is a 1980 supplement.
118   See Chamberlayne, loc. cit. After the original version of the essay was published, I had
       access to a valuable unpublished paper by J. Hook, then a student at Harvard Law
       School, entitled 'A Preliminary Treatise on Thayer' (1986). This contains a good deal
       of interesting new material about Thayer's intellectual background, associations and his
       political and religious beliefs. Hook emphasizes Thayer's admiration of Maine,
       Emerson and the early pragmatists, some of whom he knew well. He also had a close
       association with the young Oliver Wendell Holmes Jr. Hook presents Thayer as a
       forerunner of legal realism; he was also committed to a particular form of intuitionist
       morality. This paper suggests that there is still scope for a full-scale intellectual
       biography of Thayer. I found the following passage particularly revealing:

> Thayer's favourite maxim was: 'The law of evidence is the creature of experience
> rather than logic.' The most important reason, however, is based in Thayer's
> fundamental sympathy with Jacksonian democracy and Emersonian intuitive indi-
> vidualism. The official determination of matters which are essentially logical was a
> form of elitism. It suggests that local judges and jurors are not very intelligent.
> Thayer, who once appended a two page footnote on the origin of the fact that
> Americans are called citizens, and English subjects, to an innocent sentence in an
> article about Indians, was probably embarrassed by any appearance of elitism. Also,
> the idealist tendency, some of which Thayer received from Emerson, has always
> been to tie morality and logic together. Morality is not beaten into the child, but
> discovered by the child as his logic matures. Since Thayer was anxious to show that
> the law is a positive creation, not an expression of higher morality, it made sense for
> him to divorce logic from the law as well. (Hook, 43)

       The interpretation of Thayer's views of the Law of Evidence advanced in ch. 6 below is
       similar to Hook's, although the emphasis is different.
119   McKelvey (1897). The 1924 edition was criticized by Morgan for doing little more than
       putting 'the new wine of current decisions ... in the old bottle of his original text and
       thereby ruining the wine', 34 Yale LJ (1924–5), 223. A similar fate befell *Jones on
       Evidence* (1896), which was destined for most of its lifespan to be dwarfed by Wigmore.
       It is an example of an unpretentious but competent book which expanded from a
       compact textbook to a single-volume reference work for practitioners, to a four-volume
       reference work. Although its scope was extended to cover criminal evidence, the
       organization and content remained remarkably static, the main contribution of
       successive editors being to make minor verbal amendments to the text and to cram
       more and more cases into the footnotes.
120   See List of Abbreviations. On Wigmore generally see Roalfe (1977); *TEBW*, ch. 3; and
       the entry in Simpson (ed.) (1984).
121   Beale (1905).
122   Morgan (1940).
123   See above, n. 120. For an interesting interpretation of Wigmore's political significance
       see Graham (1987), discussed below, 77–9.
124   Preface to the 1st edn.
125   Wigmore was more pragmatic about this than Thayer, and in the *Treatise* dealt with a
       number of topics which he acknowledged belonged to substantive law or procedure
       rather than the law of evidence.
126   See List of Abbreviations.
127   Wigmore *Science*, 1.
128   Id., 5.

129 Ibid. On the relationship between the Science and the Trial Rules see id. Appendix I and *TEBW*, 151–64.
130 See generally *TEBW*.
131 Note in Chamberlayne (1908).
132 Ibid. Chamberlayne is described in his *Treatise* as the 'American Editor of Best's *Principles of the Law of Evidence*, and American Editor of the International Edition of *Best on Evidence*, and the American Editor of *Taylor on Evidence*'.
133 Chamberlayne (1911–16) (hereafter, Chamberlayne *Treatise*), vol. 1, *Administration*, 1911; vol. 2, *Procedure*, 1911; vol. 3, *Reasoning and Witnesses*; vol. 4, *Relevancy*, 1913; vol. 5 *Media of Proof*, 1916 (edited by Howard C. Joyce). The work was published by Matthew Bender, Albany, New York, and Sweet and Maxwell, London. On the unhappy publishing history of the last volumes, see below.
134 Chamberlayne's general views and approach are conveniently summarized in his paper (1908). See also the Preface and Introduction to the first volume of his *Treatise*, 18 Green Bag (1906), 677, and *Trial Evidence* (1936).
135 Thayer *Treatise*, 527, quoted above.
136 Op. cit., n. 134, at 766–7.
137 Id. 771–2. There seems to be less of a tension between the adversarial model and the aims of adjective law in Chamberlayne's thought than in Bentham's.
138 Chamberlayne 1 *Treatise*, Preface, xi.
139 Id., s. 772. This section draws heavily on Salmond (1907).
140 Chamberlayne (1908), 773.
141 Id., 759–60.
142 Id., 773.
143 Id., 761.
144 Id., 762.
145 Id., 772. Chamberlayne's explicit ground for differing from Thayer and Wigmore relates to the role of precedent in the law of evidence – a theme, the importance of which is regularly underestimated in the literature; however, a more important implicit difference is ideological. Chamberlayne's approach to precedent is usefully summarized as follows:

> Perhaps the most fundamental difference is that I cannot concede the scientific propriety of applying the doctrine of *stare decisis* to the rules regulating the admissibility of evidence. I at once agree that there is a large element of substantive or positive law which is covertly or openly within the scope of the rules of evidence; and, as to this, I make no question as the right of an aggrieved party to carry an adverse ruling up to a higher court. But I feel convinced that the control of precedent should extend only to matters of the substantive rights or duties of the parties; and that the admissibility of evidence is not a question of substantive right, but an incident in the administration by the court of its judicial function for the doing of justice. In my view, the presiding judge has the administrative duty of protecting and enforcing the substantive rights of the parties; but that in connection with the trial of a disputed proposition of fact the substantive right of the party is practically limited to insisting upon the opportunity of trying to establish, by the most probative evidence at his command, the truth of his contention, and that the evidence in the case shall be received and weighed according to the rules prescribed by reason. So long as reason is followed, it is not, according to my view, part of the substantive right of a litigant to insist that it should be exercised in a particular way, merely because in the most closely analogous case such a ruling was made. In other words, the admissibility of evidence, so long as reason is applied, is a matter of administration. (Id., 763; cf. 1 *Treatise*, s.68)

146 Id., 770–1; 1 *Treatise*, *passim*. Like Best and Appleton, Chamberlayne no doubt realized that it was impolitic to present himself as an unqualified Benthamite.

147 *TEBW*, 48, 82–66; Bentham, e.g. vi *Works*, 557–9.
148 Chamberlayne (1908), 769; cf. 1 *Treatise*, Preface and chs. 6 and 7.
149 One of Chamberlayne's list of defects of judicial administration is: 'the ability of the well-paid criminal lawyer to outwit the efforts of society to punish its law-breakers, of high or low degree or position, by laying traps for overworked judges on points of evidence, almost too fine for statement, and springing them in an appellate court, until outraged society sees its only hope for safety in the convenient branch of a tree …' (id., 759). There is no mention in this context of the risks of conviction of innocent suspects, but Chamberlayne called the presumption of innocence an 'overstated rule' and a 'pseudo-presumption' (2 *Treatise* ss. 1172–5). Chamberlayne's treatment of the burden of proof in criminal cases, silence, the privilege against self-incrimination, and other matters of concern to civil libertarians are generally unsympathetic to the accused. For an examination of Bentham's views on the evils of wrongful conviction see *TEBW*, 95–100, where it is suggested that he can be criticized on both utilitarian and non-utilitarian grounds.
150 1 *Treatise* s.172, at 222.
151 Chamberlayne (1908), 764–5.
152 Chamberlayne had earlier been involved with litigation with the publishers of the *Cyclopedia of Law and Procedure* (1905) 'as to their right to publish his unfinished manuscript [an article on Evidence] without consent, and with addition of matter written by others; to the accuracy of which he was unable to agree' (note, 42 Am. L. Rev., 755, 756). He gained widespread support in his campaign during his lifetime, but lost out after his death.
153 The work had a mixed reception. For reviews of Chamberlayne see esp. (1911–12) 25 Harv. L. Rev., 483; (1913–14) 27 Harv. L. Rev., 601 (E. R. Thayer); (1913–14) 23 Yale LJ, 384 (Shulman); (1915–16) 1 Cornell LQ, 14 (Wyckoff).
154 1 *Treatise*, ix.
155 Ibid.
156 Id., xiii.
157 Thayer *Treatise*, 511–12.
158 E. R. Thayer (1913–14).
159 Shulman (1913–14).
160 C. C. Moore (1908), clxviii, 1612 (hereafter Moore *Treatise*).
161 C. C. Moore (1907).
162 Above, n. 60.
163 Moore *Treatise*, Preface.
164 Id., vi.
165 Discussed Twining (1973), 60–7.
166 14 *Law Notes* 35 (1910). Ironically the key-note quotation on the title page is from Bentham (1827), bk. i, ch. 9.
167 8 Michigan L. Rev. 80 (1909–10) (V. H. L.); see also 9 Col. L. Rev. 570 (1909); 20 Green Bag, 627 (Chamberlayne).
168 Wigmore (1909). This is one of the clearest passages in which Wigmore, while denying that there are rules of weight, acknowledges the value of the law reports as sources of general (or lawyers') experience. See *TEBW*, 154–5 and 236n.
169 Id.
170 Wigmore *Science* (1937), 5, n. 1.
171 V. H. L. in 8 Michigan L. Rev. 80; cf. Thayer on Bentham, cited above.
172 See below, ch. 6.
173 This section is a slightly modified version of pages 8–12 of *TEBW*. Its purpose is to bring the story up to date without attempting a comprehensive overview.
174 Op. cit., n. 120.
175 On McCormick see 40 Texas L. Rev. 176 (1961). Graham (1987) took me to task for calling McCormick's hornbook 'pedestrian' in *TEBW* and for overlooking the point that

'it was butchered by its revisors' (1208). The text indicates that I have revised my opinion on McCormick's intellect, but not on the point about the constraints imposed by commercial publishing pressures.

176 On the history of these codes, see Wright and Graham (1977), ss. 5001–7; Lempert and Saltzburg (1977), 1191–2000.

177 On Michael and Adler, see 1 Wigmore *Treatise* (Tillers rev., 1983), s. 371. Tillers suggests that Michael and Adler were indirectly influential through the writings on relevancy of Professors James, Trautman and Ball.

178 Michael and Adler also wrote a series of articles that were more influential: see especially (1934), (1952); also Michael (1948).

179 Wigmore *Science*, 6.

180 Apart from periodical literature, perhaps the most significant contributions were Nokes (1967), in my view an underrated work; Cowen and Carter (1956) and Williams (1963). The paucity of scholarly writing on Evidence in England is directly attributable to its relative neglect in the law curriculum in university degrees and The Law Society's examinations, which in turn is partly due to the absurd idea that Evidence is essentially a 'barrister's subject'.

181 A. R. N. (later Sir Rupert) Cross, *Evidence* (1st edn, 1958; 5th edn, 1979; the latest edition is by Colin Tapper, 1985).

182 Preface to the first edition (1958). Stephen's *Digest* was 'extremely condensed'; Cross refers to *Phipson on Evidence*, the leading practitioners' treatise which his work partly displaced as 'the repository of evidentiary law' (ibid.).

183 On Cross, see Hart (1984), 405–37; Tapper (ed.) (1981), esp. the Memorial Address by A. M. Honoré.

184 Cross was familiar with at least some of Bentham's writings on evidence; he cited Gulson (1923) in two places in the first edition. The fifth edition contains a few references to recent debates on probabilities and proof. On the misuse of Bentham by the Criminal Law Revision Committee, see ch. 10.

185 *TEBW*, 100–8. See now The Criminal Justice Act, 1988.

186 Wright and Graham, op. cit., 13.

187 See especially Perelman (1963); Perelman and Olbrechts-Tyteca (1971).

188 *People* v. *Collins* 68 Cal. 2d. 319. 438 P. 2d. 33, (1968). A select bibliography on probabilities and proof is included in Twining (1983), 156–7.

189 Eggleston (1983); Barnes (1983); M. D. Finkelstein (1978).

190 Useful surveys are to be found in Tapp (1976, 1980, 1982); 17 Law and Society Review, No. 1 (1982); Lloyd-Bostock and Clifford (1983); Saks and Hastie (1978); Lloyd-Bostock (1988, 1988a).

191 See below, ch. 6.

192 See *TEBW* 100–8.

193 On the relationship between disagreements within and disagreements about these frameworks of assumptions see Postscript below, 79–81.

194 See Fuller (1978), 358.

195 Thayer *Treatise*, 199 (cited above); cf. J. B. Thayer (1927), 307. Most claims to 'rationality' imply something more positive than a rejection of traditional 'irrational' modes of dispute-resolution.

196 I am grateful to Kenneth Casebeer for this suggestion.

197 This passage is adapted from 86 Michigan L. Rev., 1531–2, where the point is developed further.

198 On the possible extension of the models to discourse about evidence and proof in civilian and socialist legal systems see below, 81–2.

199 On deviants see Postscript below, 77–8 and Tillers (1983) at 1018.

200 Model I allows for non-utilitarian views and for disagreements about the priorities between rectitude of decision and other values. It is, however, clearly instrumentalist and has the effect of anchoring debates on Benthamite territory.

201   Cf. Wright and Graham, op. cit., 147:

> The Progressive proceduralists considered themselves pragmatists, rather than theoreticians, so they seldom troubled to develop their model in any systematic fashion. While the fundamental principles of the Progressive school are easily deduced from the works of its leading writers, modern critics attribute much of the weaknesses of the paradigm to this inattention to theory. They say the reason there has been so little successful empirical work on questions of procedure is due to a failure to develop any model of the procedural system other than a simple chronology of the steps in a lawsuit. In terms of evidence the failure to consider basic theory means that use is still made of a set of concepts evolved a hundred years ago as a method of categorizing the existing caselaw although they have little relevance to the issues that arise in modern litigation.

202   Several civilian proceduralists have suggested to me that the Rationalist Model fits civilian discourse even better than Anglo-American. This raises some interesting questions about the compatibility of Model I with adversarial proceedings. A good starting point for such an enquiry is the theoretical framework presented in Damaska (1986). See further Postscript below, 81–2.

203   In addition to helpful discussions in seminars in several universities, I have found the following particularly stimulating: Weinberg (1984); Galligan (1988); J. Jackson (1988, 1988a); Stein (1987, 1988). And, in a different vein, the exchange between Graham, Tillers and myself in 85 Michigan Law Rev. 1204 (1987); 86 id., 768 (1988a); and 86 id., 2901.

204   See Weinberg (1984), 136–8, doubting, *inter alia*, whether Morgan accepted Bentham's epistemology. Weinberg cites Frank *Courts on Trial* (1963 edn) in support of this. However, even some of Frank's discussions of Morgan as a possible 'fact-sceptic' suggest that he was implicitly invoking the standards of aspirational rationalism in giving a 'realist' account of how trials are in fact conducted – see e.g. 'Morgan commented *sadly*' (id., 102). Another possible candidate is some of the work of Weinstein (e.g. 1966). In playing the game of 'spot-the-deviants' from my historical hypothesis it is probably wiser to focus on particular texts rather than authors.

205   'Liberal legalism', as used by critical legal writers, seems to be so broad as to encompass almost all Anglo-American legal thought in the past two centuries. 'Benthamism', while narrower, is also open to a variety of interpretations, on which see Twining (1988), 1536–41. The question about the ideological and political significance of the Rationalist Tradition is nevertheless important.

206   I am particularly grateful to Professors J. Wroblewski and M. Taruffo for raising this issue.

207   On the theory of fictions, see R. Harrison (1983), *TEBW*, 52–64, and Postema (1983).

208   Glassford (1820).

209   Abu Hareira (1984, 1986).

210   Below, chs. 4 and 7–9.

211   E.g. Peter Tillers and Bernard Jackson below, 241, 258 n. 113–4.

212   Wright and Graham (1977), 143–54; Graham (1983, 1987). Graham and I have many differences, but we are both agreed that his model of 'Progressive Proceduralism' fits a Benthamite version of the Rationalist Tradition almost exactly, the main differences being that my formulation also allows space for differing interpretations of Bentham and for non-utilitarian process values.

213   Wright and Graham (1977), 149.

214   Graham (1987), 1231–4.

215   Wright and Graham (1977).

216   Reconstructed from Graham's writings cited in n. 212.

217   Tillers (1988a); Twining (1988). Graham misinterpreted my reconstruction of the Rationalist Tradition and my account of the theories of Bentham and Wigmore as

evangelical promotion rather than as a relatively detached attempt to expound and clarify the nature of our received heritage of thought about evidence as a preliminary to considering critically to what extent and in what respects it requires rethinking.

218 Graham is correct in pointing to the sharp distinction made by Bentham between substantive and adjective law and some possible political implications of this (e.g. that adjective law should not be used to nullify or mitigate bad laws); see further *TEBW*, 80, 82–3, 94–5.

219 Damaska (1986); see further below ch. 6 and Stein (review) (1988).

220 See below, 81.

221 Above, 73.

222 See below, 109–12.

223 Below, ch. 4. On the self-refuting nature of 'irrealism' see Twining (1988), 1544–46.

224 On the parallels between debates on Criminal Evidence in England in the 1820s and 1970s, see *TEBW*, 100ff.

225 On the implications of the Charter on Canadian procedure see Schiff (1988) and N. Finkelstein and Rogers (1988).

226 Below, 129–32.

227 See below, 117–22.

228 See e.g. L.J. Cohen (1983). See also (1980a) on medical diagnosis. See further 86 Michigan L. Rev. (1988), 1528, n. 16.

229 Tribe (1971).

230 Below, ch. 7.

231 See above, n. 206. This passage was prompted by discussions at a conference on semiotics and law at Messina, Sicily in 1987. See symposium in 2 Int. Jo. Semiotics and Law (1988–9).

232 Damaska (1986), *passim.*

233 See below, chs. 5 and 11.

234 Cover and Fiss (1979).

235 E.g. Thibaut and Walker (1975); cf. Landsman (1984).

4

Some Scepticism about Some Scepticisms

Introduction

As dependent variable, the law is potentially a particularly vulnerable target for what Berger has termed the 'debunking motif inherent in sociological consciousness'. This is perhaps especially true of the criminal law and criminal justice systems, which offer the promise of a particularly rich harvest to the sociologist anxious to indulge his perennial preoccupation with irony, latent function and the overlap and interpenetration of vice and virtue. For here are to be found society's most solemn proscriptions of unrighteousness on the one hand, and on the other its most formal procedural prescriptions as to how to deal with it.

Colin Low[1]

There is a sense in which we are all relativists of one kind or another. In order to distinguish between different kinds we need a map. The sceptical, debunking tendency which is said to make sociology 'particularly at home in the temper of the modern era',[2] also runs through much recent literature about legal processes. It is appropriate that the jurist who urged us most forcefully to study fact-finding in law, called his theory 'fact-scepticism' and devoted a whole book to the study of historical relativism.[3] Jerome Frank is, of course, by no means unique. Rabelais's Bridlegoose throws dice to decide cases;[4] some logicians point to the limited role of closed system logic in reasoning towards particular conclusions of fact;[5] some doubt whether induction and paraduction deserve to be classified as 'reasoning' at all;[6] the recent debate about probabilities is set within a framework in which there is general agreement that mathematical probabilities have at best a very limited practical application in law;[7] Eggleston, for example, points to the fallacies, logical jumps and pitfalls for the unwary that can be found in actual examples of practical reasoning in legal contexts.[8] The main lessons of psychology also appear to be cautionary: memory is unreliable, perception is unreliable, honest witnesses are suggestible, bias is unavoidable, non-rational techniques of persuasion are potent, and so on.[9] From the Left comes the steady chant that the whole system is repressive and that notions such as the rule of law, justice under the law, and rights of the accused are a facade, part of a mystifying ideology which masks a very different reality.[10] From the Right comes the equally steady chant that many traditional safeguards of individuals, such as the right to silence and the jury, are irrational sacred cows.[11] As is suggested in the quotation from Colin Low, much recent research on criminal justice – not only by sociologists – has been dominated by a debunking motif. Many of the exposés are familiar: for example, legal process as a degradation ceremony,[12] defence lawyers as double agents,[13] the arcane role of the judiciary in plea-bargaining,[14] the myth of the so-called 'helping' professions,[15] and the essentially routine, bureaucratic and cooperative nature of allegedly 'adversary' proceedings.[16]

Some of these ideas are not new; epistemological scepticism and relativism (the latter has had a strong recent resurgence in, for example, phenomenology) are as old as philosophy itself. The notions of a forensic lottery, of gaps between aspiration and reality, between law in books and law in action, and between theory and practice, are perennial themes within legal discourse. Recently there has been more talk of obfuscation, demystification and grim realities hidden behind 'official views'. Current legal scholarship and public debate have been going through a fairly robust phase in which not only are alleged versions of 'common sense' and 'the official view' under regular attack, but strongly held beliefs of civil libertarians and of the Left have also been challenged intellectually as well as politically.

These trends in literature about legal processes, especially on the criminal side, seem very different from the optimistic and complacent rationalism of the mainstream of Anglo-American evidence scholarship.[17] I argued in the last chapter that nearly all specialized Anglo-American literature about evidence – both theoretical and expository – has been remarkably homogeneous and narrowly focused.[18] To put the matter simply: nearly all Anglo-American scholars and theorists of evidence, from Gilbert's *The Law of Evidence* (1754), through Bentham, Stephen, Thayer and Wigmore, to the writings of Sir Rupert Cross, have broadly shared a common set of assumptions or postulates about the nature and purpose of adjudication and what is involved in proving allegations of fact in forensic contexts.[19] We are, therefore, justified in talking of a single Rationalist Tradition of Evidence scholarship that by and large shares a common perspective that can be characterized as *optimistic rationalism*.[20]

This contrast between the unsceptical assumptions of the central tradition of Evidence scholarship and the sceptical tone of much modern writing about legal processes is puzzling. Of course, it is hardly surprising that the ideas of Hegel and Darwin, of Freud and Marx, of Nietzsche and Schutz, should find some echoes in legal thought after a predictable intellectual lag.[21] Nor is it surprising that such echoes should vary in volume and content, if rather less in tone. And why should it seem strange to find what might be interpreted as an enclave of bourgeois legal liberalism, or an untouched relic of Enlightenment optimism, co-existing with the confused uncertainties of a later era? Is this too not just a reflection of our general culture in which *Waiting for Godot* can be sandwiched between a chat show and a book at bedtime? A continuous bombardment of seemingly contradictory messages is what one expects of our modern Babel.

For the scholar trying to make sense of his intellectual environment just to accept, even relish, such diversity is not enough. One must still strive for coherence. Also, some of the contrasts seem too neat: Marxist demystification versus liberal obfuscation or 'contradiction';[22] modern sophistication versus Lockean common sense; pessimistic scepticism versus optimistic rationalism; students of judicial process versus evidence scholars. Some of these dichotomies just do not fit the facts; none does justice to complex cross-currents. The student of evidence who is concerned to feel his way towards a new alignment for the subject must come to terms with this confusing scene. The apparent contrast between mainstream evidence scholarship and the more diverse literature on judicial processes at least raises some questions: Is a direct challenge being presented to any of the key assumptions of the Rationalist Tradition? If so, at what points and with what implications? Are modern versions of scepticism and relativism merely a matter of mood and tone and rhetoric, masking some residues of common sense rationalism? Or are Reason, Truth and Justice seen as outdated illusions of a past age that have no place in a sophisticated and enlightened perspective on legal processes? Does contemporary thought mandate relativist or irrationalist theories of evidence? What would such theories look like?[23]

This essay grew out of such concerns. It is the product of a first attempt to impose some order on a vast and confusing landscape. As such it claims to be little more than a report on a preliminary exploration of a few selected scenes of modern intellectual life. The result will be a preliminary sketch rather than a comprehensive map. Clarification of standpoint is important for such a venture.[24] In this essay I shall adopt the posture of a Thursday Sceptic, that is to say one who most of the time believes that the chair he is sitting on exists in a real world, that reason and persuasion are to be valued, and that a scholar should at least strive for relative detachment – but who is beset by doubts at a number of levels, most often, but not entirely regularly, between 2 a.m. and 4 a.m. on some Thursdays.

This is not just an ironic ploy. The Thursday Sceptic acknowledges that it is notoriously difficult consistently to sustain a genuinely sceptical position. Like lying and truth-telling, scepticism is hard work.[25] Belief is at least as insidious as doubt. The Thursday Sceptic tends to look quizzically at all claims to scepticism, including his own. He recognizes that doubt can operate at many levels; that in so complex and fallible an area as litigation the conditions of doubt are many and potent;[26] and that a single kind or condition of doubt may have wide ramifications. As Berger acknowledges, the law is particularly vulnerable as a target for debunking. For present purposes Thursday scepticism may be more than enough.

So far I have used the terms 'scepticism' and 'relativism' generically to encompass a wide range of positions in which confident or widely accepted views are made the subject of doubt.[27] From now on we need to be rather more discriminating, but it is important to cast the net widely for the reasons stated in the last paragraph. There are many varieties of scepticism. For example, philosophical scepticism typically refers to fundamental doubts about the *possibility* of knowledge or of reason or of objective values; religious scepticism involves doubt or disbelief about the tenets of some or all religions or about the existence of God; 'scepticism' may also refer either to a generally sceptical attitude or to doubt about the possibility of any kind of knowledge or about some specific branch of knowledge or about some particular assertion or supposed fact or about something else. Accordingly, it is always important to ask: sceptical *about what?* Sceptics can be tough-minded or tender-minded, sincere or insincere, genuine or spurious. There are also degrees of doubt ranging from clear disbelief (e.g. the atheist), to agnosticism, to doubt (which may include the doubts of a true believer on the way to achieving faith), to mere questioning, however open-minded, of some belief or assumption which is commonly taken for granted. Accordingly it is important to ask: *how* sceptical? 'Scepticism' may apply, *inter alia*, to dispositions, to attitudes, to style or tone or demeanour, to methods or to a proposition or belief. For the most part we are here concerned with sceptical positions or beliefs which can be expressed as propositions. The Thursday Sceptic, dubious of all claims to scepticism, always asks: who is being how sceptical, about what, in what context(s), and for how long?

For the most part I shall concentrate on fairly familiar general forms of scepticism, such as philosophical scepticism and historical relativism, and typically in their stronger versions. I shall be particularly concerned to differentiate between very broad sceptical claims (as exemplified by epistemological scepticism or doubts about the reachability of fact in any legal system) and claims which turn out on examination to be about something much more specific (such as a doubt about the actual operation of a particular institution in a particular system).

This chapter, then, is a preliminary attempt to explore in general terms what bearing, if any, some apparently sceptical approaches have on the study of evidence and proof in adjudication. The central question addressed is how far the central underlying assumptions of the predominant Anglo-American tradition of theorizing, writing and debating about evidentiary issues are challenged by one or more varieties of scepticism or relativism so as to undermine the very notion that studying such matters as the reliability of testimony, the logic of proof or the efficiency of fact-finding institutions is both feasible and worth while.[28]

The proposed itinerary is as follows: after a preliminary inspection of four kinds of trivial or spurious scepticism, we shall look briefly and in general terms at five related 'strategies of scepticism' and their possible bearings on a theory of evidence. First, philosophical scepticism with particular reference to the theory of knowledge as discussed by A.J. Ayer. Next historical relativism, as exemplified by the Americans Carl Becker and Charles Beard, who in turn influenced the leading protagonist of 'fact-scepticism' in law, Jerome Frank. Our fourth stop will be phenomenology, as exemplified by Berger and Luckmann's *The Social Construction of Reality* and some recent applications of 'constructionist perspectives' to law. Next, we shall observe the implications of the position of some mathematicists in the current debate on the nature of

reasoning about probabilities in forensic contexts. This leads on to a consideration of how far emphasis on differentiation of standpoint in legal discourse
involves commitment to some kind of 'relativism'. In Part III I shall consider
what general lessons might be drawn from this survey and what implications
they may have for developing a 'modern' theory of evidence and proof in
adjudication that belongs to a broadened conception of the discipline of law,
which in turn still draws its theoretical inspiration largely from late ninteenth-
century thought and its heirs.

Exposition

Spurious scepticism and artificial polemics

False polemics feature prominently in the Great Juristic Bazaar.[29] Indeterminate attribution, ismatizing, Aunt Sallyism, non-joinder of issue and the
repetitious exaggeration of minute differences are all familiar features of juristic
debate.[30] In searching for serious challenges to the Rationalist Tradition we
need to be particularly wary of becoming involved in artificial polemics
prompted by spurious or trivial scepticism – that is to say versions of purported
'scepticism' or 'relativism' that are not worth taking seriously. These are
sufficiently common that it is worth identifying and disposing of four characters
who present little threat to the Rationalist Tradition. Let us call them the
Sophomore, the Disappointed Perfectionist, the Caricaturist and the Hard-
nosed Practitioner.

The 'sceptical' Sophomore is familiar to teachers of philosophy. This is the
student who poses or misposes an important philosophical question and then
either refuses to play the philosophical game or is merely playing some trivial
game of his or her own or gets caught in an infinite regress or commits some
elementary fallacy, such as begging the question or assuming what has to be
proved. Trivial, self-contradictory or otherwise fallacious sceptical noises are
common in legal discourse, but they present no serious intellectual threat to the
Rationalist Tradition.

Another kind of spurious scepticism that is particularly prevalent in jurisprudential debate is the alleged scepticism of the Disappointed Perfectionist (or
Absolutist). H. L. A. Hart in *The Concept of Law* identifies this as one of the
factors behind 'rule-scepticism', which he defines as 'the claim that talk of rules
is a myth':

> The rule-sceptic is sometimes a disappointed absolutist; he has found that rules are not
> all that they would be in a formalist's heaven, or in a world where men were like gods and
> could anticipate all possible combinations of fact, so that open-texture was not a
> necessary feature of rules. The sceptic's conception of what it is for a rule to exist may
> thus be an unattainable ideal, and when he discovers that it is not attained by what are called
> rules, he expresses his disappointment by the denial that there are, or can be, any rules.[31]

This passage has a double significance: it usefully identifies a tendency to
exaggeration which is endemic in juristic debate, in this case scepticism about

an unattainable ideal to which few, if any, subscribe. It also illustrates the related tendency of caricaturing what one is criticizing by attributing absolutist views to one's opponents, for it is difficult to find a serious jurist who held the views attributed to rule-scepticism by Hart.[32]

The Disappointed Perfectionist and the Caricaturist are often united in one person in polemical jurisprudence.[33] Attributing extreme views to one's opponents and then rushing to the other extreme is a familiar pattern of juristic discourse: because complete certainty is unattainable in law, it follows that law is totally unpredictable; because no human being can be completely neutral or impartial, it follows that all judges are biased. Such *non-sequiturs* are easily spotted when stated explicitly. Typically they are merely assumed or suggested by innuendo. A useful, but often misunderstood, corrective is Karl Llewellyn's robust maxim: ' "And-not" is bad Jurisprudence'.[34]

Here it is pertinent to look for such tendencies in the context of seemingly sceptical attacks on alleged 'official' or 'common-sense' or 'orthodox' views in respect of fact-finding in adjudicative processes. A good example is Jerome Frank's attack on the 'myth of certainty'.[35] Of course, the rhetoric of aspiration and unthinking assumptions in the ordinary discourse of laymen and of lawyers can provide numerous examples of loose talk of 'certainty' both in respect of rules and, less commonly perhaps, in respect of fact-finding. But, one may ask, if 'certainty' is interpreted strictly to mean a probability of 1 (as in the doctrine of chances), who believes in certainty in fact-finding? Is 'the myth of certainty' a worthwhile target to attack? In respect of fact-finding it is surely a caricature to equate 'the myth of certainty' with 'the official view'. It is widely and openly acknowledged that evidentiary issues are to be conceived in terms of relative probabilities rather than certainties. The standards of proof 'beyond reasonable doubt' and 'on the balance of probabilities' explicitly set standards below 'certainty' in this literal sense. The elaborate paraphernalia of doctrines concerning the burden of proof and presumptions can plausibly be interpreted as fairly sophisticated guides to decision in situations of *uncertainty*. The provision of safeguards and appeals is an acknowledgement of the general possibility of mistakes, even though officialdom often finds it difficult openly to admit to mistakes in particular cases. It is disingenuous to interpret terms like 'certainty' literally when they are used as part of the rhetoric of aspiration.[36]

The 'ideal type' of a 'rational' approach to evidence does not postulate a set of impossible ideals. Rather it should be seen as an attempt to articulate some of the standard working assumptions of an intellectual tradition that was strongly oriented to the needs, attitudes and views of practising lawyers and judges. As such one might expect their views to be just as liable to attack for being simple-minded, insincere and unduly pragmatic as for being hopelessly idealistic or naive. We shall return to this in connection with the Hard-nosed Practitioner.

It is important to emphasize the qualified nature of the central assumptions of this ideal type; it is equally important to identify the unsceptical core: rectitude of decision is seen as the primary end of adjudication, as a necessary means to enforcement of law and vindication of rights (expletive justice); expletive justice is an important, if not necessarily an overriding, social value;

the concept of 'rectitude of decision' leads directly to such notions as truth, facts, relevance, evidence, and inference and to a number of assumptions about the possibility of knowledge (or at least of warranted conclusions of fact) and about valid reasoning. Thus there are plenty of points of potential disagreement and difference between adherents of this model and others without our having to waste time on caricatures or unattainable ideals.

The Hard-nosed Practitioner is less easily dismissed. This is the professional who makes such statements as 'I am not concerned with justice or truth, my aim is to win cases' or 'The adversary trial *is* a game' or 'My task is to persuade, not to reason.' After one has made due allowance for rhetorical exaggeration and false contrasts (e.g. the assumption that justice and winning are mutually incompatible), there may still be some substantial points that survive: there is often a conflict between winning and truth-seeking from the standpoint of the advocate in adversary proceedings; those features of some trials that make them like some games may be subversive of rationalist aspirations; non-rational means of persuasion may sometimes or often be more effective than reasoned argument.[37]

It is difficult to know how to interpret such simplistic assertions. Is an emphasis on winning to be taken as merely indicating a tension within the adversary process, or does it indicate a rejection of the stated values of the system or a cynicism about any claims to such values or what? Is pointing to the operation of non-rational factors in adjudicative fact-finding, such as the attractiveness of one's client or the appeal of one's body language, to be taken as a denial of the value or feasibility of rationality? The difficulty about such statements is not that they are necessarily untrue or insincere, it is rather that their precise meaning and status are unclear. Before their validity and significance can be assessed for present purposes they need to be restated in a form that is less vague and less ambiguous. In short, the folk-wisdom of the Hard-nosed Practitioner needs to be academicized. This has been done to some of the standard examples. The notion of the trial as a game, the ethical dilemmas of advocacy, the tensions between winning and truth have been canvassed in the academic literature. Some of them will reappear in a different form later in this essay.

There is, however, an alternative interpretation of standard pragmatic disclaimers – commonplace in treatises and the law reports – that the law is not concerned with ultimate questions about philosophical concepts of truth and proof. In this view, the law proceeds *as if* there is a real world, accessible to the human mind, and that the truth of statements can be tested by evidence. Just as for some purposes we treat 'the facts' of a case or 'stipulated facts' in litigation as if they are true, even if we are not sure or do not know or even believe them to be false, so, it might be argued, the assumptions of the Rationalist Tradition are pragmatic working hypotheses which all participants, including treatise writers, accept as if they were so, irrespective of their personal beliefs. Thus a scholar in the Rationalist Tradition, as well as a practitioner or judge, might be a genuine philosophical sceptic (about knowledge or rationality or ethics or all three) and yet, in order to participate in legal processes, adopts unsceptical premises as pragmatic working hypotheses.[38]

To dismiss some sceptics as disappointed absolutists or as caricaturists should not be taken as a sign of complacency about our legal institutions or about the human condition. Nor is it a plea for consensus. The object is to clear the ground of rhetoric and artificial polemics in order to clarify what may be in issue in serious non-rhetorical debates. The Disappointed Perfectionist typically ends up in a position as absurd and untenable as the one from which he reacted. The Caricaturist typically fails to join issue at all. There is enough room for disagreement and doubt among reasonable and informed people in the areas under discussion for there to be no need for the artificial polemics of traditional jurisprudence nor untenable forms of extremism.

Philosophical scepticism

The contrast between the unsceptical assumptions of the Rationalist Tradition and the sceptical tone of much recent writing about judicial processes needs to be clarified at a number of levels. In this section I shall try to suggest some points of contact between the central assumptions of the Rationalist Tradition and the persistent phenomenon of scepticism in philosophy by reference to A. J. Ayer's treatment of scepticism in *The Problem of Knowledge*.[39] Later I shall consider whether any of the writers being surveyed might count as philosophical sceptics of one kind or another in a strong sense. Once again the object is to map possible points of contact rather than to explore complex issues in depth.

For present purposes it is useful to distinguish three broadly different kinds of philosophical scepticism. First, epistemological scepticism which denies the possibility of any kind of knowledge; secondly, ethical scepticism, or subjectivism, which holds that judgements of value are merely a matter of individual preference or are entirely relative to time or place or circumstance, and, thirdly, irrationalism, in the sense of scepticism about all claims to the possibility of objectively valid reasoning or, as Peter Unger puts it, 'the thesis that no one is ever *justified* or at all *reasonable* in anything'.[40]

There are, of course, many varieties within these broad categories and complex relations between them. In order to keep the presentations simple, I shall focus on strong or extreme forms of each variety – the denial that *any* knowledge is *possible*; the claim that all judgements of value are *solely* a matter of individual preference, not susceptible to rational appraisal or justification; and the denial of the *possibility* of valid reasoning. I shall concentrate on epistemological scepticism and scepticism about one kind of reasoning, induction, as these have the most direct and obvious connections with the assumptions of the Rationalist Tradition.

A theory of Evidence, Proof and Fact-finding (hereafter EPF) is a middle order theory. The philosopher of knowledge is concerned with ultimate questions about the possibility and the nature of knowledge in general. The historiographer is concerned with the specific nature of historical knowledge and the standards and methods of proof or the canons of evidence on which such 'knowledge' is allegedly based. The theorist of evidence is, in a sense, concerned with 'legal knowledge of past facts'.[41] The philosophical sceptic who questions the possibility of any kind of knowledge, thereby questions the

100 Some Scepticism about Some Scepticisms

possibility of both historical and legal knowledge. A theory of history or a theory of EPF which takes the possibility of historical knowledge or legal knowledge as a given presupposes some theory of knowledge. Thus epistemological scepticism offers a direct challenge to such a theory.

'It is now often said that philosophical scepticism is not serious, and there is a sense in which this is true', writes Ayer at the start of an essay on the subject.[42] This statement is not as dismissive as at first sight may appear. For Ayer's approach to the problem of knowledge is based on taking the arguments of scepticism seriously. He suggests that the pattern of a sceptic's argument is essentially the same when he casts doubt on the validity of our belief in the existence of physical objects or of scientific entities or of the minds of others or of the past or on the validity of inductive reasoning.[43] The sceptic uses an argument which seeks to show that the belief in each case depends upon an illegitimate inference.[44] The applications to each particular kind of belief are different, showing that the justifications for each may stand on different levels, but the pattern is the same: 'The first step is to insist that we depend entirely on the premises for our knowledge of the conclusion; ... the second step ... is to show that the relation of premises and conclusion is not deductive...' The third step is to show that these inferences are not inductive either, even if inductive inference is legitimate at all; '[t]he last step is to argue that since these inferences cannot be justified either deductively or inductively they cannot be justified at all.'[45] Ayer continues:

The problem which is presented in all these cases is that of establishing our right to make what appears to be a special sort of advance beyond our data ... For those who wish to vindicate our claim to knowledge, the difficulty is to find a way of bridging or abolishing this gap.

Concern with the theory of knowledge is very much a matter of taking this difficulty seriously. The different ways of trying to meet it mark out different schools of philosophy or different methods of attacking philosophical questions. Apart from the purely sceptical position, which sets the problem, there are four main lines of approach. It is interesting that each of them consists in denying a different step in the sceptic's argument.[46]

Thus, according to Ayer, the Naive Realist denies the first step; the Reductionist denies the second; the Scientific Approach denies the third; and the method of Descriptive Analysis, favoured by Ayer, denies the fourth. 'Here one does not contest the premises of the sceptic's argument, but only its conclusion ... we can give an account of the procedures that we actually follow. But no justification of these procedures is necessary or possible.'[47] The sceptic's conclusion is not acceptable because 'it is by insisting on an impossible standard of perfection, that the sceptic makes himself secure.'[48] Ayer's argument, then, is that the philosophical sceptic's *arguments* should be taken seriously, for refuting them is central to a theory of knowledge, but his conclusion should not.[49]

Ayer's approach to the problem of knowledge is useful for present purposes for a number of reasons. First, it suggests that we should question whether particular allegedly sceptical or relativist positions need to be taken seriously at the level of philosophy. Or, to put the matter differently, not all sceptics are *philosophical sceptics* in Ayer's sense. Later I shall try to show that few, if any, of the 'strategies of scepticism' considered in this essay necessarily involve rejection of a cognitivist position.

Secondly, Ayer's account provides a useful way of mapping the relationship of a wide variety of different theories and approaches to the problem of knowledge on the one hand and to a theory of EPF on the other. We can identify two immediate points of contact between a theory of EPF and philosophical scepticism. According to the orthodox view fact-determination in adjudicative processes is typically, but not exclusively, concerned with ascertaining the truth about *particular* past events.[50] In this respect it is closely analogous to historical enquiry. Thus a possible direct connection is established with both historical relativism and with scepticism about the possibility of historical knowledge. Furthermore, there seems to be a general consensus among theorists of evidence that the mode of argumentation appropriate to proof in legal contexts is induction, as it is found in everyday practical reasoning.[51] Thus scepticism about the possibility of induction and theories of induction is also directly relevant to a theory of EPF. Conversely questions about the existence of physical objects or of other minds or scientific laws, although they may have particular applications in legal contexts, seem at first sight to be less generally relevant to a theory of EPF.

Thirdly, Ayer's account suggests another important link between the philosophy of knowledge and theories of evidence. Concepts such as 'fact', 'truth', 'objectivity', 'proof', 'inference', 'probability', 'canons of evidence', and 'induction' are important, in some cases central, concepts in epistemology as they are in the legal literature on evidence. At the very least this suggests a possibility of cross-fertilization between two bodies of literature that have developed largely independently of each other in modern times. Indeed, it is fair to say that epistemology has been very largely neglected by Anglo-American legal philosophers.

Finally, there is a direct historical connection beween Ayer's approach and the central intellectual tradition of theorizing about evidence in the Anglo-American context. For they are both out of the same philosophical stable – English empiricism. Bentham's epistemology, which was only partially developed, is directly traceable to the tradition of Bacon, Locke and Hume, but without Hume's fundamental scepticism.[52] Mill built on Bentham and nearly all subsequent English-speaking writers on Evidence, such as Stephen, Wigmore, Michael and Adler,[53] and Cross built on Bentham and Mill. Ayer, as a theorist of knowledge, is perhaps the leading contemporary critic of Humean scepticism among English analytical philosophers. Not all Anglo-American evidence scholars have shared identical epistemological assumptions, but it is fair to say that none was a philosophical sceptic and that most, like Ayer, can be located within the general tradition of English empiricism.

It is not true to say that philosophical scepticism is dead. Indeed, Anglo-American philosophers pay tribute to its persistence both explicitly and, more important, implicitly by treating it as their main target of attack. There are, however, surprisingly few leading philosophers who accept the label of 'sceptic' in any strong sense of the term – the Norwegian philosopher Arne Naess is perhaps the most important exception.[54] Instead there is a widespread, but not universal, consensus among contemporary Anglo-American philosophers that philosophical scepticism – as exemplified by Sextus Empiricus and Hume – is unacceptable, but that there are some important elements of truth in scepticism that account for its tenacity. In this view, 'the sceptic has won many battles ... [but] has lost the war.'[55] Nicholas Rescher, a prominent exponent of this view, summarizes the alleged core of truth in scepticism as follows:

> To begin with, the sceptic is quite right on the issue of the demanding absolutism of knowledge. When something is claimed as known it is indeed thereby claimed to be certain, exact, incorrigible, etc. And this absolutism – however 'realistically' construed – makes the substantiation of knowledge claims a relatively demanding enterprise. (To be sure, the sceptic is wrong to inflate these difficulties into impossibilities, construing the absolutes at issue in an unrealistic and hyperbolic sense which quite improperly loads the argument decisively in his favour from the very outset.) Again, the sceptic is right in his assault against foundationalism and the idea of absolutely certain irrefrangible premises on which the whole structure of objective factual knowledge can be erected. He is right in contending that insofar as such absolutely secure data are available to us through the phenomenal certainties of immediate experience, they cannot yield *objective* knowledge. Moreover, the sceptic is right in his insistence on the 'evidential gap' as a fact of life that assures the theoretical fallibility of all objective factual claims. These must – in view of their very objectivity – inevitably be such that their assertive content transcends the supportive data we can ever secure on their behalf. The sceptic is also right in holding that what we vaunt as our 'scientific knowledge' must always be conceived of as containing a substantial admixture of error. (To be sure, scepticism goes too far in construing such a concession of fallibility as to destroy any and all prospects of the realization of knowledge.) Finally, the sceptic is right that we cannot claim the completeness or the correctness and indeed not even the consistency of our knowledge of the world ...
>
> The concession that 'the body of our knowledge' contains various errors and deficiencies does not make it in order to withdraw each and every one of the particular claims to knowledge that lie within its precincts.
>
> Yet the sceptic has certainly not struggled in vain. Much essential clarification of the nature of knowledge can only be attained by analysing how the key arguments deployed by the sceptic fail in the final analysis to establish his governing conclusion of the illegitimacy of claims to knowledge. What the sceptic's argumentation has managed to achieve is not to establish the unattainability of knowledge but to exhibit the inherent limitations of such knowledge as we can properly lay claim to. In this way, the sceptic has – no doubt to his own discomfiture – rendered a highly useful and constructive service to the cognitivist position.[56]

The cognitivist is unsceptical only about the *possibility* of knowledge; it is entirely consistent with this position to be highly sceptical about particular claims to knowledge, about complacent claims for the efficiency of particular institutions, procedures and techniques as instruments for discovering the truth or about any of 'the subsidiary issues regarding the inadequacy of our knowledge'.[57] Indeed, the thoughtful cognitivist should be particularly aware of the difficulties in practice of satisfying his own standards of 'knowledge'. The philosophical cognitivist is both entitled and well-qualified to adopt sceptical stances on many specific issues.

It should be reasonably clear that the premisses of the Rationalist Tradition are generally incompatible with each of these kinds of philosophical scepticism, at least in their more extreme forms. To put the matter very simply: the mainstream of Evidence scholarship has been cognitivist, in that it has assumed the possibility of warranted knowledge about the external world, its leading exponents have either been utilitarians or non-utilitarian deontologists who have accepted, and argued for, such values as expletive justice, the pursuit of truth, the preservation of the family, due process and the avoidance of vexation. The core assumption of the tradition is that adjudicative decisions on questions of fact should be based on evidence and argument, typically induction. In short, we try to arrive at warranted judgments about the truth of allegations of fact on the basis of rational evaluation and analysis of evidence in order to further the ends of justice and/or utility.

It is not my purpose in this paper to attack or defend a cognitivist position. Rather, I wish to suggest three points. First, that the leading Anglo-American theorists of Evidence are all cognitivists in the tradition of British empiricism. Secondly, that cognitivists have made a number of important concessions to sceptical arguments and some of these have potential implications for any theory of EPF. Finally, that genuine *philosophical* sceptics are rather rare birds today and, in the context of law, we should examine carefully the credentials of those who make such a claim. In the following sections I shall question *en passant* whether any of the sceptics or relativists under consideration deserve to be treated seriously as sceptics in respect of their basic epistemological or other philosophical assumptions.

Historical relativism

Modern historical relativism is generally associated with a reaction by historians and philosophers against some of the claims of the nineteenth-century objectivist school of historiography.[58] The latter is often exemplified or caricatured by the dictum of Leopold von Ranke that the aim of the historian is to describe things '*Wie es eigentlich gewesen*' ('exactly as they happened').[59] Leading proponents of this version of historical relativism – there are, of course, many varieties – included Croce, Mannheim, Collingwood and E. H. Carr. Each of these had different concerns and developed distinct positions, but all of them sought to disassociate themselves from 'extreme relativism'.

In the United States the leaders of historical relativism in the early twentieth century were James Harvey Robinson, Carl Becker and Charles Beard. It is useful for present purposes to look specifically at Becker and Beard, for it is they who have the most direct historical connection with scepticism in law. Becker and Beard were important figures in the general intellectual revolt against formalism in the United States, associated with Holmes, Dewey, William James, Peirce and Thorstein Veblen.[60] Charles Beard's *An Economic Interpretation of the Constitution* (1913) stimulated interest and controversy among lawyers as well as historians. More directly Carl Becker, who was primarily an historian of ideas, was one of the sources of inspiration of Jerome Frank.[61]

Becker and Beard were unusual among American historians of the time in

trying to develop theories of historiography.[62] Each stuck his neck out in his Presidential Address to the American Historical Association (Becker, 1926; Beard, 1933). I shall follow the example of other commentators in treating these as convenient summaries of their respective views.[63] Becker's is the more carefully considered statement; Beard's, being more vulnerable, has attracted more critical attention. Although both men were influenced by and contributed to the climate of opinion (one of Becker's favourite phrases) of the revolt against formalism, their theoretical ideas were more in tune with European writers, such as Nietzsche, Croce and Pirenne from whom – Morton White acidly suggests – they derived most of their confusions.[64]

Becker's explicit target was all forms of 'objectivist' history – including Ranke, Foustel de Coulanges, and Acton's claims for the *Cambridge Modern History*.[65] But his historical scepticism was rooted in more general concerns. In his presidential address he asked three questions: '(1) What is the historical fact? (2) Where is the historical fact? (3) When is the historical fact?'[66]

Becker acknowledges that 'simple facts', such as the statement 'In the year 49 BC Caesar crossed the Rubicon' or 'Indulgences were sold in Germany in 1517', 'can be proved down to the ground'.[67] He does not doubt that such facts are 'hard', 'objective', not susceptible to reasonable doubt. He is not, in short, a philosophical sceptic in Ayer's sense. But, he asks, are such facts as simple as they seem? And are they, on their own, historical facts? The answer to each of these questions is negative:

> ... a thousand and one lesser 'facts' went to make up the one simple fact that Caesar crossed the Rubicon; and if we had someone, say James Joyce, to know and relate all these facts, it would no doubt require a book of 794 pages to present this one fact that Caesar crossed the Rubicon. Thus the simple fact turns out to be not a simple fact at all. It is the statement that is simple – a simple generalisation from a thousand and one facts.[68]

Becker's argument can perhaps be restated as follows: history is necessarily incomplete; even the statement of a 'simple fact' involves *selection*;[69] and the task of the historian is to give meaning and significance to past facts. The picture of his task as merely piling up 'hard facts' for someone else to use is accordingly trebly misleading: *selection* is involved both in formulating statements of past facts and in deciding what statements to include; the idea of 'history' also involves *interpretation* and *arrangement*. Accordingly, 'the historian cannot eliminate the personal equation.'[70]

Becker's emphasis on selection, interpretation and arrangement is typical of most relativist writings. His answers to the idiosyncratically expressed questions: 'Where is the historical fact?' and 'When is the historical fact?' have been more controversial. By drawing a sharp distinction, which has been much criticized, between past events and statements about past events, he is able to say that 'the historical fact is in someone's mind or is nowhere... We say that it *was* an actual event, but is *now* an historical fact.'[71] It follows that historical facts are part of the present. These statements have been criticized as being a misleading way of stating and explaining the truism that history is rewritten in every generation. As a description this is obscure; as an explanation it is inadequate; it is obscure about the exact nature of the relations between historical statements and actual past events; and it begs the question whether there are acceptable criteria for evaluating and criticizing particular historical statements.[72]

Charles Beard's account of the writing of history is similar in spirit and tone to Becker's, but the arguments he uses are rather different. Like Becker he emphasizes the necessity for selection, interpretation and ordering and he emphasizes 'that any written history inevitably reflects the thought of the author in his time and cultural setting.'[73] He distinguishes between history as past actuality, as record, and as thought. He defines 'history' as 'thought about actuality, instructed and delimited by history as record and knowledge – record and knowledge authenticated by criticism and ordered with the help of the scientific method.'[74] More than Becker, Beard emphasized the contemporary significance of history and the need for the historian to clarify his personal values and his frame of reference.

One of Beard's central concerns was to reconcile his rejection of 'the pretensions of the scientific method in history and his awareness that some standards of truth and objectivity are necessary in order to be a responsible historian'. He was also concerned to argue that history should throw light on contemporary issues and to justify his own, albeit ambivalent, espousal of a particular ideology. Beard's response to these problems was unsatisfactory, involving on the one hand a naïve exaggeration of the objectivity of physical science in contrast with history and an equally dubious espousal of a belief in progress: 'History as actuality is moving ... on an upward gradient towards a more ideal order.'[75] Beard's final profession of faith was hardly sceptical in spirit.

Some of the standard criticisms of Becker and Beard and their European precursors have been usefully summarized by Fischer: first, they confuse the way knowledge is acquired and the validity of that knowledge; second, they mistakenly argue that because an account is incomplete, it follows that it must be false; third, 'relativism makes false distinctions between history and the natural sciences' as, for example, when Beard attacked the use of hypotheses in history; fourth, relativists such as Beard and Mannheim either inconsistently or implausibly sought to exempt themselves from relativism in some degree. Finally:

the idea of subjectivity which the relativists used was literal nonsense. 'Subjective' is a correlative term which cannot be meaningful unless its opposite is also meaningful. To say that all knowledge is subjective is like saying that all things are short. Nothing can be short, unless something is tall. So, also, no knowledge can be subjective unless some knowledge is objective...[76]

It is not necessary here to consider which, if any, of these criticisms are valid, or whether they can fairly be applied to Becker or Beard. The common ground between the relativists and their critics is as interesting as their differences. Most critics of relativism are prepared to concede that nineteenth-century historicism, at least in its extreme form, was naïve and untenable; they acknowledge that a 'complete' account of past events is impossible and that history involves selection, interpretation and arrangement (some would add explanation), thus opening the way for the personal element. They acknowledge that historians are influenced by circumstances of time and place and interest and that there are many obstacles in practice to attaining objectivity in history.

For their part Becker and Beard and their modern counterparts would probably not have condoned some of the practices which may have been encouraged or even justified in the name of relativism: a cavalier attitude to factual detail, the politically motivated doctoring of history or the squeezing of the facts to fit simplistic and rigid prejudices masquerading as frames of reference. As we have seen, neither Becker nor Beard was a philosophical sceptic, in that both acknowledged the possibility of objectively true facts; Beard expressly argued that 'extreme relativism is self-refuting' and neither, so far as I know, has he been accused of 'disrespect for facts'.[77]

The central points at issue between the historical relativists and their detractors seem to be 'whether there is any possibility of formulating criteria for deciding about the scientific adequacy of different histories'[78] (White) and whether there is any possibility of 'warranted explanation' in history (Nagel).[79] One of the harshest critics of relativism, Fischer summed up his position as follows:

There is, of course, something that is profoundly right in relativism. It is true that history is something which happens to historians. And it is correct to argue that no historian can hope to know the totality of history as it actually happened. But it is wrong to conclude that objective historical knowledge is therefore impossible. The conventional wisdom of contemporary historiography still consists in the common idea that 'a historian cannot know what *really* happened, but he has a duty to try.'[80]

What are the similarities and the differences between historical and adjudicative enquiries into issues of fact? In the legal literature this question has tended to receive a fairly standard answer,[81] which might be restated as follows: the historiographer and the legal scholar have a shared interest in such questions as: Is knowledge of (particular) past events possible? What is involved in proving that a particular conclusion about the past is true? What kinds of reasoning are involved in reasoning towards conclusions of fact? Is it possible to formulate canons of evidence and standards of proof in such contexts? But there are also important differences between historical and legal approaches to the pursuit of truth about the past. The aims of each process are different; typically the judge has a duty to decide every case before him, however incomplete the evidence; no such duty is imposed on the historian;[82] the methods, the resources, the timing and the procedures of each type of enquiry are characteristically different. Particularly important in the present context is the point that in legal contexts the selection and interpretation of past facts is characteristically governed, at least in theory, by relatively precise pre-existing rules which provide both standards of materiality and a set of categories for classifying particular events. The historian is typically concerned with describing, explaining and attributing significance to unique past events; in judicial process similar objects of enquiry (unique past events)[83] have to be described in terms of concepts and at a level of generality which makes it possible to determine whether or not they fall within or outside the scope of general rules. Thus the historian's task of selection and interpretation and the lawyer's task of categorization of past facts are rather different. There is an important sense in which fact-determination in adjudication is concerned very largely with trivial or platitudinous truths (Plattheit), that is to say with statements of the kind: 'X died on 20 December 1930' or 'It was Y who killed Z.'[84] These are not trivial in the sense that they are necessarily unimportant or insignificant to the individuals affected. But establishing such facts does not involve explanation nor interpretation nor the establishment of general truths – all major sources of concern to relativists. Nor, typically, is the person charged with determining the truth of alleged facts responsible for selection – what are the material facts in a particular case is typically determined by the rules of law and by the pleadings, which often remove another source of indeterminacy familiar to lawyers, the choice of an appropriate level of generality. Thus, in this view, at the point of decision about disputed issues of fact in adjudication (in the narrow sense it is used here), most of the difficulties which lie at the root of the central concerns of historical relativism have been filtered out – selection, interpretation, explanation and arrangement are not normally involved in determining the truth or otherwise of facts in issue.

This account is both attractive and plausible given the assumptions on which it rests. But is not rather a lot being taken for granted?

First, it is assumed that there is a typical or standard case for each type of enquiry. The standard case of adjudication is assumed to be an untrained trier of fact deciding on the truth of one or more allegations about *particular* past events. 'The historian' is also concerned with 'describing, explaining and attributing significance to *unique* past events'. These are, indeed, recognizable examples of each type of enquiry, but in what sense are they 'typical' or 'standard'? Surely not all triers of fact are non-expert, not all facts in issue are particular or unique.[85] Nor are triers of fact only concerned with facts in issue: as we have seen, the structure of reasoning in adjudication typically involves appeal to intermediate propositions, many of which will be generalizations of one kind or another. Similarly there is not one type of historical enquiry: do Herodotus and Namier and Toynbee and E. P. Thompson and Sir Mortimer Wheeler all conform to the same model of the typical historian? And, does each of these pursue only one type of enquiry? The orthodox comparison of standard cases of historical and legal enquiries can be illuminating, but it needs to be recognized that it rests on a very simple view of both historiography and adjudication.

Secondly, the notion of 'fact' in adjudication is more problematic than the orthodox view suggests. While it is true that for certain purposes, for example making probabilistic calculations, we have to proceed as if questions of fact can be and have been sharply differentiated from questions of value – an is/ought distinction has to be postulated – even within the Rationalist Tradition it is widely acknowledged that triers of fact are regularly and unavoidably involved in making evaluations.[86] Thus it is misleading to suggest that legal enquiries into questions of fact are value-free in the way that historical enquiries are not. Evaluation is regularly involved in both types of enquiry, though not necessarily in identical ways. In so far as some historiographers are concerned about the possibility of objectivity or detachment in the writing of history their concerns are at least analogous to questions about the possibility of impartiality or objectivity in adjudication.

Thirdly, it may be objected, a false comparison is being made between historical and legal enquiries in that the total process of historical investigation is being compared with one point only in legal processes, the adjudicative decision. Thus, in so far as it is the case that triers of fact are typically not involved in selection, interpretation, explanation and arrangement (and this is at best an overstatement), this is partly because some such difficulties or choices have been resolved at earlier stages in the process, often by other participants. The adjudicator's 'givens', the rules of law, the particular allegations, the levels of generality, the conceptual framework have been 'given' by other participants in the process. In making the rules the legislator was neither constrained nor helped by any notion of materiality; the prosecutor or plaintiff may have had a range of choices as to the precise content of the charges or allegations; the litigants framed the issues, with or without the intervention of third parties and so on. Thus while it may be the case that some of the central concerns of historical relativism to some extent do not apply directly to adjudicators, it does not follow that they are irrelevant to fact-handling in legal processes seen as a whole. It is strange to equate 'legal enquiries' with adjudicative decisions.

This is a powerful argument which leads, interestingly, to the conclusion that historical enquiries may have more similarities to factual enquiries in law than the orthodox view allows; it follows from this that the concerns of historical relativists cannot be so easily dismissed.[87] The argument can, of course, be overstated. It does not totally invalidate the comparison of historical enquiries and adjudicative decisions and, at the very least, the orthodox account highlights an interesting and highly suggestive point: historians lack the lawyers' concept of 'materiality'.

To sum up: what I have called the standard way of comparing legal and historical enquiries needs to be treated with caution, for it over-simplifies the complexity and the variety of both kinds of process and it too readily dismisses some of the central concerns of historical relativism. In so far as the orthodox view is acceptable, it suggests that the main point of contact between historical and legal concerns about proof of past facts falls largely, if not entirely, in the area where there appears to be no significant disagreement between historical relativists, such as Beard and Becker, and their critics. Where disagreement is sharpest – over the implications for historiography of the need for selection, interpretation, explanation and arrangement – the tasks and problems of adjudicators and historians are rather different. The historians' debates are suggestive in their exploration of the obstacles to obtaining accurate accounts of past events, on the dangers latent in such notions as 'hard facts' and 'simple facts', and no doubt on many points of detail about historical method and the weight to be accorded different kinds of evidence. But historical and legal enquiries into past facts take place in different contexts and for different purposes. Historical relativism is concerned not so much with the possibility of knowledge about past events as with the practical difficulties of attaining such knowledge – a theme also central to Jerome Frank's fact-scepticism. There is little in the debates we have considered which casts serious doubt on such notions as 'established facts', 'reasoning towards particular conclusions of fact' or 'standards of proof'. On the other hand, both critics of relativism and those robust practising historians who are dismissive of these debates are concerned to rescue notions such as 'respect for facts', 'deciding on the basis of the evidence', and 'canons of evidence' from what most of them consider to be the excesses of extreme relativists.

Jerome Frank and legal fact-scepticism

It may seem paradoxical to suggest that the greatest dilettante in American Jurisprudence was essentially a man of one idea – a hedgehog rather than a fox. Jerome Frank may have read more widely and written about more topics, legal and non-legal, than most jurists; but a single thread runs consistently and repetitively through his work: an obsessive concern with the uncertainty of fact-finding in law.[88]

Frank is one of the main sources of inspiration for the enterprise of taking facts seriously. It was he, more than anyone else, who directed attention to a striking imbalance in academic law and, more generally, in our legal consciousness. While over 90 per cent of contested cases are decided on disputed issues of fact in courts of first instance, a similar proportion of academic attention is paid in traditional legal education and literature to disputed questions of law.[89] Frank's successors, notably the process school, have convincingly shown that in some ways Frank understated this aspect of his case. For only a small percentage of disputes ever reaches trial, most of the 'action' in legal process taking place outside the courtroom in transactions which culminate in settlements, guilty pleas or decisions not to proceed and in subsequent stages of the process, such as sentencing, post-conviction decisions and enforcement of judgments.[90] The impetus to develop a theory of evidence, proof and fact-finding is rooted not only in the recognition of a need for a new framework for the study of this general area, but also in the notion that a balanced conception of academic law would place much greater emphasis on it. If Frank is right, the study of fact-finding deserves much more of our attention.[91]

Frank's main argument hardly needs to be restated. The central notion is the unreachability of fact, that is to say the obstacles, some inevitable, some avoidable, to reaching objectively true judgements about past events and to predicting what the courts will find the facts to be:

The axiom or assumption that, in all or most trials, the truth will out, ignores, then, the several elements of subjectivity and chance. It ignores perjury and bias; ignores the false impression made on the judge or jury by the honest witness who seems untruthful because he is frightened in the court-room or because he is irascible or over-scrupulous or given to exaggeration. It ignores the mistaken witness who honestly and convincingly testifies that he remembers acts or conversations that happened quite differently than as he narrates them in court. It neglects also, the dead or missing witness without whose testimony a crucial fact cannot be brought out, or an important opposing witness who cannot be successfully contradicted. Finally, it neglects the missing or destroyed letter, or receipt, or cancelled check.[92]

A great deal of *Law and the Modern Mind* is devoted to exploring why lawyers and the general public continue to believe in the utterly implausible myth of certainty. In *Courts on Trial*, a more mature, richer, but less coherent work, Frank was more concerned with artificial or removable obstacles to arriving at the truth in judicial processes – the jury, the adversary process, the exclusionary rules of evidence, the obfuscating rituals and so on. Frank's polemical writings and his controversial activities during the New Deal made him 'the *enfant terrible* of American law'.[93] His elevation to the bench shocked many lawyers, but pleased his admirers one of whom compared it 'to the choice of a heretic to be a bishop of the Church of Rome'.[94] But, one may ask, was Frank the profound sceptic and the radical extremist that he is sometimes depicted to be?

In what sense was Frank a sceptic? First of all there is a generally iconoclastic and doubting spirit about his approach: he hated dogma and all forms of absolutism; he emphasized the part played by chance and choice in history; he revelled in the diversity, the complexity and the unpredictability of human affairs and he suggested that acceptance of the situation – whether with stoicism or positive interest – is the hallmark of personal maturity. In respect of law his main emphasis was on the practical obstacles to attainment of accuracy, consistency and predictability in fact-finding.

Such ideas and attitudes indicate a lively, critical, doubting mind, but they do not by themselves establish Frank as a philosophical sceptic in any strong sense of that term. Yet most commentators, including the most sympathetic, treat him as an out-and-out sceptic and relativist at the most fundamental level.[95]

Frank's biographer, Volkomer, argues that he was a sceptic because he was hostile to dogmatism; because, following Erich Fromm, he believed that there are few uniformities in human nature, and above all, because he believed in the relativity of knowledge.[96] The first two points are easily disposed of. It is a caricature of the cognitivist position to equate it with dogmatism: to accept the possibility of knowledge, to accept that 'we are indeed in a position to stake rationally warranted claims to objective knowledge about the world'[97] involves no commitment to dogmatic or absolutist beliefs, including the doctrinaire versions of Marxism and Fascism that Frank was concerned to attack.[98] Similarly cognitivism does not entail a simplistic belief in a uniform human nature. Volkomer's first two points correctly identify Frank's position, but do not *ipso facto* put him in the ranks of the philosophical sceptics, as the term is used in this paper.

Frank's belief in the relativity of all knowledge requires closer examination. The nearest Frank got to a sustained development of an epistemological position was in his book *Fate and Freedom*, revealingly subtitled *A Philosophy for Free Americans*.[99] The main concern of this work is to attack dialectical materialism and, in particular, deterministic theories of history. Frank emphasizes the operation of individual choice and of chance in history; he makes great play of the point that in numerous instances historical narratives once accepted as beyond question have later proved false or misleading;[100] and, in developing his own version of a free will theory, he goes quite far in rejecting the principle of causality (here he purports to follow Hume).[101] *Fate and Freedom* and some of Frank's other writings certainly contain some bold remarks – 'all human interpretations of experience are "just-so" stories';[102] 'facts are guesses',[103] 'the "facts" ... are not objective. They are what the judge thinks they are',[104] 'facts are human achievements, human feats';[105] and most history is 'twistory'.[106]

Taken on their own such remarks give the impression both of a fairly extreme relativism and of some form of epistemological scepticism. Frank was neither a precise nor an analytically consistent thinker and he was prone to exaggerated statement. But a careful study of the context of many such remarks would suggest that, interpreted liberally, they are not a necessary part of his argument nor consistent with others of his statements and assumptions. As such it may be sensible to dismiss them as rhetorical exaggerations and lapses, not central to his main concerns. For Frank's main targets – in history, dogmatic versions of historical materialism; in law, complacency about the predictability, the uniformity and the efficiency of judicial 'fact-finding' – did not require him to adopt strong sceptical or relativist positions at a fundamental level. Many of his targets were specific – the jury, the exclusionary rules, 'fight' elements in the adversary process, the Langdellian system of legal education.[107]

Sceptical about what? On this interpretation Frank was not a philosophical sceptic in Ayer's sense.[108] He clearly accepted the possibility of objective knowledge about particular past events;[109] he delighted in William James's notion of 'wild facts', but this implied an acceptance of 'tame' or 'hard' facts with which 'wild facts' are contrasted.[110] He talks of 'avoidable mistakes',[111] of 'real objective past facts';[112] his scepticism about logic relates to the role of *deductive* logic in the law;[113] he explicitly claims to be concerned with making judicial processes 'more rational'.[114] There is little in his writings which seriously questions the use of the language of 'evidence', 'inference', 'standards of proof' or 'rectitude of decision' in discussing evidentiary issues, except some provocative dicta such as that 'facts are guesses'[115] and his more plausible suggestion that 'it is misleading to talk .. of a trial court "finding" the facts ... More accurately, they are processed by the trial court – are, so to speak, made by it on the basis of its subjective reactions to the witnesses' stories.'[116]

The main objects of Frank's scepticism are (a) optimistic aspirations (and claims) to unattainable ideals of objectivity and uniformity and (b) belief in a number of widely held axioms which, in his view, misdescribe the realities of legal processes.[117] Frank in part shared similar concerns to the historical relativists about the difficulties of attaining accurate accounts of the past, but a great deal of his fire is directed to specific, contingent features of the American legal system which were in his view capable of being improved.

How sceptical was he? While there is undoubtedly a strain in Frank which relishes the uniqueness of individual events and the elusiveness of reality, I would suggest that he was far from being the cynic or extremist that some critics have depicted. In *Courts on Trial*, responding to his critics, Frank went out of his way to reject 'absolute relativism', 'nominalism', 'anti-rationalism' and various other forms of extreme 'isms' of which he had been accused.[118] Even in *Law and the Modern Mind* his model is the mature adult 'questioning – not hastily, angrily, rebelliously, but calmly and dispassionately – our bequests from the past, our social heritage ...'[119] 'The stage of complete maturity is reached when the relativity of all truths is accepted but seen to be compatible with their provisional validity.[120] He would have strongly denied that he was a disappointed absolutist. Today Frank hardly seems to fit the image of a radical – his prescriptions to modern eyes might seem to be a rather optimistic blend of measures designed to make decision making fit more closely to a rational model of truth-seeking (abolish exclusionary rules, substitute truth-theory for fight-theory) linked to a characteristically American faith in education as a cure-all. He looks more like a reformist than a radical by the standards of today.[121] There is little in Frank that seriously and consistently challenges any of the central assumptions of the Rationalist Tradition.

Thus contrary to his image, Frank is not far from the mainstream of the Anglo-American tradition, without sharing the complacency of some of its leading exponents. By drawing attention to the distorting influence of 'appellate court-itis' and to the importance of disputed issues of fact, he raised some key questions that need to be confronted by a theory of EPF. He can claim some credit for building bridges between law and psychology, especially Freudian psychology. But he failed to develop systematically or in detail what would be involved in a sustained study of 'fact-finding'. His course on fact-finding at Yale was too abstract and jurisprudential really to come to grips with the detailed implications of the questions he had raised; having pointed to an imbalance in our legal culture, he allowed himself to be side-tracked first into psychological speculations about why lawyers cling to untenable myths and later into a not very carefully thought out programme of reforms. Holmes never worked out in detail the full implications of his 'bad man' insight for the practice of legal education;[122] similarly Frank failed to follow through the full implications of his one great idea for a broader and richer perspective on law. He sowed the seed for the present enterprise, but he failed either to sell the idea or to give it a solid theoretical base.

The Sociology of Knowledge and the social construction of reality

Pressures of space and my own ignorance make it impossible to do justice here to the complex history of the Sociology of Knowledge and the possible bearing on law and on a theory of EPF of some of its offshoots such as phenomenology and ethnomethodology.[123] But it is appropriate to make at least a brief reference to some of this work, for it is making a significant impact on the study of judicial processes.

One of the main jumping off points for a Sociology of Knowledge is the fact that what passes for 'knowledge' varies from society to society. Perhaps the *locus classicus* is Aristotle: 'Fire burns both in Hellas and Persia; but men's ideas of right and wrong vary from place to place.'[124] So do their ideas of fact and fiction. The very notion that 'knowledge' is itself a social product at least raises questions about claims to objectivity of particular examples of knowledge. It is not surprising to find most sociologists of knowledge and phenomenologists explicitly claiming to be relativists of some sort. It is also natural that questions about the possibility of objective knowledge are central to the concerns of leaders in the field, such as Mannheim. If all knowledge is in some sense a product of social processes can there be objective knowledge of reality independent of particular social contexts? If not, can the sociologist of knowledge claim any special status for his relativist thesis?

The centrality of the concern about basic epistemological issues does not seem to have led the pioneers in the field into positions of philosophical scepticism in a strong sense: few seem to deny the possibility of objective knowledge. Thus Marx, if I understand his thesis about ideology correctly, while maintaining that what has passed for 'knowledge' in pre-industrial and capitalist societies has been systematically distorted and conditioned, both consciously and unconsciously, by class interests, nevertheless envisages the possibility of attaining objective, impartial knowledge of the external world in a classless society. [125] Nor, at a more specific level, does he deny the possibility of objective knowledge of particular 'hard facts' even in capitalist society. He is not, in short, a philosophical sceptic *au fond*. Similarly, Karl Mannheim introduced the term 'relationism' to distinguish his position from that of extreme relativists and devoted a good deal of effort to developing the thesis that intellectuals, by virtue of their detachment and alienation from society, are less prone to the distortions of ideology and are charged with the task of moving towards 'a correct understanding of human events'[126] through the accumulation of different perspectives. [127] Although the problems of epistemology were central to Mannheim's concerns, he was hardly in either his attitudes or his conclusions a philosophical sceptic in Ayer's sense of the term.

The same appears to be true of Berger and Luckmann's *Social Construction of Reality*, which has stimulated a lot of interest within the sociology of law. They start their work with an express disclaimer of 'any pretention to the effect that sociology has an answer' to the philosophical preoccupations of the epistemologist. [128] The philosopher asks: What is real? How is one to know? The sociologist asks: How did what passes for 'knowledge' in any given society come to be socially established as 'reality'?[129] 'The sociology of knowledge must concern itself with whatever passes for "knowledge" in a given society, regardless of the ultimate validity or invalidity (by whatever criteria) of such "knowledge".'[130] Thus Berger and Luckmann expressly beg 'ultimate' philosophical questions about the possibility of knowledge and there is ample evidence from their writings that they themselves need notions of accuracy, distortion, and falsification, as well as more general notions of 'objectivity' in their own analysis. [131] They are concerned to explore certain questions about what is involved in the social processes of knowledge formation and construction of different 'realities'.

One of the main objectives of Berger and Luckmann was to help to shift the focus of attention of the sociology of knowledge from the study of theoretical ideas (the main concern of most of the early pioneers) to the study of everyday 'realities': '*The Sociology of Knowledge must concern itself with everything that passes for "knowledge" in society* [authors' italics] ... Common sense "knowledge" rather than "ideas" must be the central focus for the sociology of knowledge.'[132] This shift of attention has helped to bring the concerns of sociologists of knowledge much closer to legal concerns. For not only are all forms of 'legal knowledge' and specifically 'legal realities', whatever those may be, brought within the scope of the sociology of knowledge, but more importantly, both a theory of EPF and the kind of approach advocated by Berger and Luckmann have a special interest in what passes for 'common sense' or 'everyday knowledge'.

Let us take an example that is not immediately obvious – the lawyer's concept of 'relevance' in fact-finding. The first rule of admissibility of evidence is that all evidence which is irrelevant is to be excluded; only relevant evidence is admissible.[133] What is the test of relevance in this context? This is one of the more problematic questions in the subject of Evidence, even within the expository tradition. On one view, that I am inclined to favour, an evidentiary fact is relevant or potentially relevant to a *probandum* (i.e. a fact to be proved), whether intermediate or ultimate, if it has some connection with it – the test is: does it tend to support (or negate) the *probandum* at all?[134] On what basis do we establish this connection? The answer is largely on the basis of what Berger and Luckmann call 'the available social stock of knowledge' in a given society.[135] Jonathan Cohen in discussing inductive probabilities puts the matter as follows:

> The inductivist analysis, however, has no difficulty at all here. It presupposes only that when a juryman takes up his office his mind is already adult and stocked with a vast number of commonplace generalizations about human acts, attitudes, intentions, etc., about the more familiar features of the human environment, and about the interactions between these two kinds of factors, together with an awareness of many of the kinds of circumstances that are favourable or unfavourable to the application of each such generalization. Without this stock of information in everyday life he could understand very little about his neighbours, his colleagues, his business competitors, or his wife. He would be greatly handicapped in explaining their past actions or predicting their future ones. But with this information he has the only kind of background data he needs in practice for the assessment of inductive probabilities in the jury-room ... The main commonplace generalizations themselves are for the most part too essential a part of our culture for there to be any serious disagreements about them. They are learned from shared experiences, or taught by proverb, myth, legend, history, literature, drama, parental advice, and the mass media. When people ceased to believe that those who had insensitive areas of skin were in commerce with the Devil, it was symptomatic of a major cultural change.[136]

In this view the main source of criteria of relevance in legal contexts at any given time is the social stock of knowledge.

Let me illustrate this by an absurd example. In the jurisdiction of Sodom there is an offence of fomenting earthquakes. X and Y, two homosexuals, are accused of this offence, in connection with an earthquake that occurred on 31 March. The only evidence against them is that on 30 March they committed a homosexual act in private. In our culture it is 'known' that there is no connection between homosexuality and earthquakes. But in Sodom it is known that homosexuality causes earthquakes – indeed, this is the basis for the offence. Thus in Sodom the evidence is relevant to the charge, in our culture it is not. We 'know' that there is no connection between the two events.

There is no denying the strong relativistic currents within the field nor the generally sceptical spirit noted by Berger of much of the writings. Berger and Luckmann, for instance, take the relativity of knowledge as their starting-point: 'Sociological questions about "reality" and "knowledge" are thus initially justified by the fact of social relativity. What is "real" to a Tibetan monk may not be "real" to an American businessman.'[137]

There is then a sceptical tendency – but how sceptical about what? We have seen that there is little evidence of philosophical scepticism in the strong sense. But it is claimed that belief is a function of time, place and circumstance and there is plenty of questioning of *particular* claims to objectivity, especially in respect of 'official views'.[138] At a general level Peter Berger reminds us of possible gaps between legal and sociological perspectives:

The lawyer is concerned with what may be called the official conception of the situation. The sociologist often deals with very unofficial conceptions indeed. For the lawyer the essential thing is to understand how the law looks upon a certain type of criminal. For the sociologist it is equally important to see how the criminal looks at the law.[139]

A broadened conception of legal scholarship involves, *inter alia*, a broadening of lawyers' perspectives to include much more than merely official points of view.[140] It should include the standpoints and perspectives of all participants in legal processes and transactions – and here the work of writers like Schutz and Collingwood clearly has direct relevance. In respect of EPF there are many specific points of contact: how official records are created, how some deaths are classified as suicides, and how information is processed *en route* to presentation to decision makers, are examples of points of shared concerns between lawyers and sociologists of knowledge. One of the main contributions that sociologists can make in this area is to make us question the claims to objectivity and reliability of *particular kinds* of evidence. In this context a sceptical, questioning approach is likely to be immensely useful.[141]

There are, however, some dangers. The general sceptical spirit or style of some writings in this vein may at least give the impression that the writer is a philosophical sceptic or a suicidal relativist. Such an impression may be quite misleading or the writer may have been carried away by debunking enthusiasm to make statements which imply a fundamental scepticism which is neither logically necessary nor internally consistent with the basic points he is making.[142]

To take one example: In an interesting paper entitled 'The Social Construction of Truth: Some Thoughts on Jury Trials and Current Research into Juries', Michael Freeman argues that much recent jury research is based on naïve assumptions both about the role of the jury and about the processes by which jurors reach decisions.[143] Much of the research, he points out, assumes that the only role of the jury is to act as a fact-finder according to some rational model of adjudication. This, he argues, overlooks the symbolic functions of the jury and in particular its role in allowing community sentiment to exercise some check on the rational bureaucratic 'output of justice'.[144] Furthermore, Freeman argues, it is naïve to assume that the decision-making process of juries is to seek 'a right answer, an objective truth almost ... [by] a uniquely correct method of ascertaining of this truth.'[145] Rather, using Garfinkel's model of the trial as a degradation ceremony, Freeman suggests that in contested trials the jury 'constructs its own reality' from the conflicting versions of reality which are presented to it.[146]

I have a good deal of sympathy with Freeman's criticism of some of the simplistic assumptions of much jury research; I also find his analysis of notions such as 'perverse' and 'lawless' verdicts illuminating. But in the process of debunking some simplistic views, Freeman appears to commit himself to some converse simplicities.

First, he sets up some artificially soft targets in his account of 'the official view' and 'the rational legal model of legal authority'.[147] Who seriously maintains that in practice jurors are concerned *only* with determining facts on the basis of reasoning from the evidence presented to them or that there is a uniquely correct method of ascertaining the truth? Neither jury researchers nor EPF theorists in the Rationalist Tradition need to be saddled with such simple-minded views. What they do claim is that attempting to determine the truth of particular past events by rational means on the basis of evidence is one central aspiration of any system of adjudication and that it is a ground for criticism if the system in practice falls far short of or does not accept this as an aspiration. To acknowledge a role for the jury in frustrating unpopular laws or restraining official zeal in other ways does not involve a denial that its central task is to try to make accurate determinations of fact.

Secondly, Freeman scornfully dismisses the idea 'that there is a right answer, an objective truth almost'.[148] What precisely is Freeman denying here? Taken at its face value this kind of statement has some extraordinary implications – it suggests for example that no court has ever made a mistake, that no one has ever been wrongly convicted, that there never has been a miscarriage of justice. For this kind of descent into irrationalism allows no room for concepts like 'mistake' or 'error' or 'falsehood' or 'wrongful conviction'. We are left with no basis for criticizing decisions on questions of fact. This looks very like suicidal relativism.

Thirdly, Freeman substitutes for a caricature of a rationalist view an account of jury decision-making which is equally simplistic:

> But always in contested trials two or more competing pictures of reality confront the jury. From this material the jury must construct its own reality. It is confronted with a plethora of conflicting claims. Its job is to make sense of the situation, to make it meaningful. It by no means follows that the jury will pick one side's story. It is quite possible for it to take segments of competing versions of the truth and to weld the whole into a composite picture. It selects using criteria of its own commonsense, everyday understandings of situations. What it repeatedly asks itself is whether the defendant conforms to its conception of the stereotype of whatever criminal he is alleged to be. Alan Blum, in an essay on the sociology of mental illness, put it like this: 'jurors use the act as an occasion for reviewing the defendant's biography to determine whether the character of the action is discrepant with some conception of the defendant based on a reading of his biography ... an insane defendant should have a biography that supports such conception'. If the jury, then, decides that the defendant does so conform, then the label of deviant is successfully fixed.[149]

To substitute for the picture of twelve rational men objectively reasoning towards objective conclusions a picture of twelve entirely subjective creatures intuitively picking one side's story and arbitrarily constructing stories of their own is surely to trade one caricature for another. Now, it is clear that there is an enormously rich, complex and fascinating field of enquiry into what is involved in constructing, presenting, receiving, testing and taking with a pinch of salt 'plausible stories'. The connections between the advocate's concept of 'the theory of a case', ideas about 'coherence', historians' concerns about narration, sociological interest in constructing reality and many other notions that float around in our confusing intellectual world are crying out to be mapped and explored. In respect of adjudication of disputed issues of fact such notions *prima facie* seem to be both important and neglected. But it is just not good enough to throw out by implication all the accumulated lessons of the logic and psychology of proof and what professional lawyers claim to have learned by experience, by substituting a simple picture of choosing between plausible stories purporting to present competing versions of reality – perhaps between two *gestalts?* This does justice neither to the complexity of the subject matter nor to the sophistication of the intellectual heritage of the Rationalist Tradition.[150]

This criticism may be based on an unfairly literal reading of Freeman's paper; nor is it reasonable to treat one paper as representative of the rich variety of approaches to the study of legal processes that have been stimulated by different ideas derived from the sociology of knowledge.[151] Furthermore, I readily concede that within this enormously diverse branch of social theory there are strands which have strong claims to be regarded as genuinely sceptical at the level of philosophy or which present direct challenges to the epistemological premises of English empiricism. However, the main points in this section still stand: first, that some of the sociologists of knowledge who have been influential on legal thought, such as Mannheim and Berger and Luckmann, have dissociated themselves from philosophical scepticism and extreme relativism. Secondly, that such notions as constructing reality (or conviction or stories) or processing information or manufacturing evidence are not *necessarily* inconsistent with standard forms of empiricism and so do not *ipso facto* present a direct challenge to the fundamental assumptions of the Rationalist Tradition. Thirdly, there is a strong tendency to rhetorical exaggeration in writings of this kind: this often leads to artificial polemics or self-contradiction. The potential of various forms of constructionist and related approaches is more likely to be reached sooner, if their exponents confronted the most sophisticated versions of aspirational rationalism rather than being satisfied with debunking caricatures of common sense and official views.[152]

The Bridlegoose challenge and the forensic lottery

When Pantagruel came to Mirelingues he was invited to attend at the Trial of Judge Bridlegoose, who was being called on to explain why he had pronounced a sentence on the Subsidy-Assessor, Toucheronde 'which did not seem very equitable to that Centumviral Court'.[153] Bridlegoose's principal defence was that his sight was failing by virtue of old age with the result that he may have misread the dots on his small dice which, having read the papers several times, he threw in order to decide causes and controversies at law: small dice for complex cases and large dice for simpler ones. As 'the Imperfections of Nature should never be imputed unto any for Crimes and Transgressions', he had a complete defence, if he had indeed misread the dice.[154] Since you decide by the chance of the Dice, he was asked, why do you spend so long studying the writings and 'Papers and Other Procedures contained in the Bags and Poaks of the Law-Suitors'?[155] In response, Bridlegoose gives three reasons: for the sake of Formality, which alone can validate the proceedings; in lieu of corporeal exercise; and because 'Time ripeneth and bringeth all things to maturity ... Time is the Father of Truth and Vertue.' After adequate delay the losing parties will with much greater patience and more mildly bear their misfortunes at the hands of chance.[156]

Rabelais was specifically concerned to satirize the minutiae of the Pandects[157] as well as the more familiar targets of the chicaneries of lawyers and the defects of legal procedures.[158] But Judge Bridlegoose is sometimes interpreted as throwing down a broader challenge to the law – to do better than the dice, that is to get correct results in more cases than could be obtained by chance.[159]

Interest in Bridlegoose has recently revived in connection with discussions about the potential uses and abuses of mathematical reasoning in legal processes.[160] If decisions on questions of fact have to be based on assessments of probabilities, then surely the correct criteria for such judgments must be one or other versions of the calculus of probabilities? But the conditions for making such calculations are strict: for example, in the classical doctrine of chances, when applied to estimating the chances of throwing ten sixes in succession with a dice, the multiplication rule applies if and only if a number of conditions are satisfied: for example, that the dice is unweighted; that the throwing is fair; that the outcomes are mutually exclusive at each throw; that each throw is independent of the previous one; that the report of each outcome is correct and is accurately recorded; that the person making the calculation is able to apply the calculus correctly, and so on.[161]

It is significant that at his trial Judge Bridlegoose felt no need, and was not asked, to justify his method of decision. However, it is not difficult to reconstruct a possible justification from Rabelais's account of the trial. The conditions for the application of the doctrine of chances are satisfied, if one completely divorces the throwing of the dice from the merits of the evidence and the arguments of the parties and postulates that the prior probabilities are even. From the standpoint of the judge, there was an equal chance in every case that either party might be right.[162] Throwing dice ensured that in every case each side had an exactly equal chance of winning. Over the long run it was statistically highly probable that he would get the right result in about half the cases;[163] whereas given the arbitrary confusion of the Pandects, the obfuscations and chicaneries of lawyers and the possibility of his own fallibility or corruption, there was no such guarantee that he would achieve this level of justice by purporting to decide on the merits. The method of deciding could be adjusted to reflect the different standards of proof; for example, 50 per cent in civil cases, longer odds against conviction in criminal cases.[164] Interpreted thus, Judge Bridlegoose challenges any system of adjudication and, in the present context, adherents of Rationalist theories of adjudication to demonstrate that both in design and actual operation the system gets the correct result in more cases than would be achieved by a game of chance.[165]

We can now consider the Bridlegoose Challenge in the context of recent debates about probabilities in the law. The debate falls roughly into two stages. Initially a number of writers, notably Kaplan, Finkelstein and Fairley, Tribe, Eggleston and Cullison, discussed at length the scope, limitations and dangers of mathematical reasoning about probabilities in respect of disputed issues of fact in litigation.[166] While there have been disagreements on specific issues – for example, whether mathematical reasoning, in particular Bayesian analysis, should be allowed in legal argument as a matter of policy – all seem to have been agreed on three main points: first, that reasoning about probabilities is in principle a form of mathematical reasoning; secondly, that the conditions for the use of such reasoning are rarely satisfied in practice in legal contexts; thirdly, that it would be undesirable as a matter of policy to permit widespread use of this kind of argument, even where theoretically appropriate, at least until lawyers and decision makers have had an adequate basic training in the appropriate mathematical techniques.[167]

Since 1977 the debate has shifted ground to a more fundamental issue. Jonathan Cohen has suggested that there is a non-mathematical mode of probabilistic reasoning (what he calls Baconian probability) in addition to the mathematical (Pascalian) mode and that Baconian probability is characteristically used by lawyers in reasoning about disputed questions of fact in forensic contexts, at least in the common law system.[168] The view that all reasoning about probabilities is Pascalian is mistaken. Cohen concedes that there is some scope for Pascalian probability in legal contexts, but it is much more limited in theory as well as in practice than the Pascalians admit. In particular they are mistaken in thinking that the appropriate mode of reasoning is mathematical in respect of standards of proof, convergence and corroboration and in assessing the weight or cogency of evidence in respect of ultimate *probanda* and the case as a whole.

Cohen's thesis provoked sharp retorts from Eggleston and Glanville Williams in the *Criminal Law Review*[169] and similar, sometimes hostile, reactions have come from mathematicians, lawyers and others in the United States.[170] Two main lines of attack on Cohen's thesis need to be distinguished. First, one approach is to deny the proposition that there is or can be more than one kind of probabilistic reasoning; a second approach is to argue that, whether or not there is a coherent and valid method of non-Pascalian probability, Cohen's reasons do not support his conclusions. In particular, it has been suggested that his arguments about standards of proof and convergence and corroboration are mistaken and that several of his particular examples are explicable in terms of Pascalian probabilities. A third, moderate position is that Cohen's Baconian principles can be accommodated within a sophisticated version of the Pascalian calculus.

For present purposes the validity or otherwise of the various arguments is not in issue. My own tentative position is that Cohen is correct both in maintaining that there is a valid form of non-mathematical probability and that this mode of reasoning is appropriate to many arguments about evidentiary issues in forensic contexts. I suspect, however, that he may have overstated the case against the application of Pascalian probabilities in these contexts and that some of his specific arguments are not as dispositive as he suggests. What is of immediate interest is the implications of the view, such as that of Glanville Williams, that any reasoning about probabilities which is not notionally translatable into mathematical form is not reasoning at all. For, if this is correct, it suggests an extreme form of scepticism about the prospects for rationality in fact-finding in adjudication. Put simply the argument goes as follows:

1   the characteristic argument in legal contexts about disputed questions of fact is an argument about probabilities;
2   all valid arguments about probabilities are Pascalian arguments;
3   Pascalian arguments are usable only if certain stringent conditions are satisfied;
4   these conditions are only exceptionally capable of being satisfied in legal contexts;
5   it follows that the conditions for valid reasoning about disputed questions of fact in legal contexts are only exceptionally capable of being satisfied − or, to put it differently, most of what passes for argument about evidentiary issues is not reasoning at all.

If this is correct it puts at least some defenders of the mathematical thesis in the position of sceptics in the debate about the problem of induction. It also seems that they may be more sceptical about the prospects for rationality in adjudication than any of the theorists we have considered to date. For they are committed to the proposition that it is only very exceptionally that the conditions for the only valid kind of reasoning are satisfied in practice. If this is correct, it plays straight into Bridlegoose's hands: 'On your own admission, most of what passes for argument in litigation is not rational. It is merely a facade or a delusion. My method ensures 50 per cent correctness and eliminates judicial bias; given the possibilities for chicanery, bias and inequality of resources between the parties, we cannot be nearly so confident about the outcomes secured by so-called "rational" methods. So my method is superior to yours.'

The matter is not quite as simple as that, for there are at least two different lines of escape for Pascalians. The first is to resort to estimates of frequency; the second is to treat judgments about particular past events as subjective probabilities, but then to argue that these can be translated into a form which is susceptible to the mathematical calculus by resorting to the notion of laying odds in a fair system of betting.

To concretize the discussion let us take as our starting-point a quotation from a work on the philosophy of history which states a view similar to that of Jonathan Cohen. Atkinson postulates two premises in dealing with judgments of probability about particular past events (simple facts):

The first is that the probability which may be enjoyed, or suffered, by historical statements is not the probability of the mathematical theory of chances: there is no possibility of putting a numerical value on the probability that Napoleon's illness contributed to his defeat at Waterloo in anything like the way in which one can put a value of one-half on the probability of obtaining a head with any toss of a fair coin. The second, and for present purposes more important, premise is that non-mathematical probability assessments are not merely expressions of subjective confidence but rather to be founded on evidence. (To couple a subjective view of probability with the notion that history is exclusively a matter of probability is, of course, fatal to history.)[171]

How might a Pascalian react to this? One response is that any event which is normally viewed as unique 'can be conceived as recurrent'.[172] Thus in Atkinson's example we can make some more or less informed estimates about such matters as the correlation between illness of commanders and defeat in battles of a certain kind and the correlation between points of time when Napoleon was similarly ill and his efficiency in performing tasks of the kind that he was called on to perform at Waterloo and so on. In short, arguing by analogy from previous similar instances one constructs generalizations of the kind: 'The outcome of battles is very rarely affected by the health of generals' or of a more particular kind, such as, 'Napoleon's efficiency was frequently impaired by bouts of illness.' Such more or less speculative generalizations can then be translated into numerical terms as estimates of frequency. The fact that, in this kind of example, such estimates are very largely guesswork based on almost no evidence does not undermine the mathematicist theory; rather it brings to light the largely speculative and unreliable nature of such judgments. What the mathematicist suggests is that a rational reconstruction of probability judgments about unique past events necessarily involves reliance on such estimates, however speculative and unreliable they may be. Typically such estimates are implicit; the process of making them explicit may serve to indicate both how well or ill-founded a particular judgment may be and what kind of information would be helpful in making the estimates, and hence the judgments, more reliable.[173] 'Rationality' from this point of view requires the strengthening of the empirical basis for such estimates of probability.

Most people would concede that estimates of frequency are often relevant to the formation of judgments about the probability of unique past events. The relationship between the health of commanders and the outcomes of battles of a certain kind *is* relevant. But is it the case that estimates of frequency are the *only* kind of premise on which such judgments may be based? An alternative approach for the mathematicist is to resort to subjective probabilities. A statement about the 'probability' of a unique past event is a statement about the strength of belief about the likelihood that such an event in fact occurred. In short it is a judgment in terms of subjective probability. It may be based on intuition, informed estimates about frequencies, pure guesswork or different kinds of reasons. But such subjective probabilities can be operationalized for the purpose of making mathematical calculations by expressing them in terms of the odds that a rational man would lay on the proposition in a fair system of betting.[174]

It is not my intention here to plunge into the theoretical morass of decision theory and the foundations of mathematics. My concern is to map a series of different positions. It seems to me that the first line of escape sketched above represents the route taken by Glanville Williams, the second that taken by Finkelstein. An inductivist response might proceed along the following lines: estimates of frequency represent one, but not the only, kind of reason which may support a judgment of probability about unique past events. Such estimates are themselves capable of rational appraisal and justification and such estimates may be arrived at in whole or in part on the basis of reasoning which may be in principle mathematical or non-mathematical or a combination of the two. Accordingly not all probability judgments of this kind are based on Pascalian premises.

Similarly while it may be conceded that judgments of subjective probability may be translated into mathematical form by the device of postulating a system of wagers, this involves an extra step in the process of rational reconstruction of probability judgments and this step may be either problematic or unnecessary or both. For the allegedly 'subjective' belief of the rational betting man is conceded to be capable of being based on reason (how else is he a rational man?) and such reasons, argues the inductivist, are not necessarily mathematical. Such judgments are capable of being non-Pascalian inductive probability judgments and it is misleading to suggest that it is either necessary or unproblematic to take the additional step of converting them into mathematical form. The judgments *are* judgments of probability, they can be supported by reasons some of which are governed by non-Pascalian principles of reasoning. Since they are based on reasons governed by principles of valid reasoning they are not in principle subjective.

A third version of the Pascalian position is that the Pascalian calculus, and particular aspects of it, such as Bayes's Theorem, provide a model for argument even when the conditions for application of the calculus are not strictly satisfied.[175] The rationalist aspiration merely requires us to use 'the best reason we can muster'. Arguments which approximate to the Pascalian model still deserve to be called 'rational', because we often have to be satisfied with something short of perfection. On one view, the Baconian thesis represents an acceptable second-best when some of the conditions for a more rigorous kind of reasoning are absent. Whether or not this is a tenable position, this and other moderate types of Pascalians, along with Baconians, accept some version of 'soft rationality' and, in so doing, have a basis for a response to the Bridlegoose challenge.

To sum up: some, but by no means all Pascalians, by setting very strict standards for rationality which are rarely attainable in practice make serious concessions to the Bridlegoose challenge. They are analogous to disappointed absolutists. Bridlegoose has the last laugh. For he has revealed that of all the varied types of potential sceptics and relativists that we have considered, it is the most enthusiastic rationalists who are the nearest, among writers on law, to a genuinely sceptical position.

Standpoint and relativism

For our next step we return to territory familiar to lawyers. It is sometimes claimed that law is inevitably to a large extent a participant-oriented discipline and that many differences within legal discourse can be usefully explicated, perhaps even explained away, by careful clarification of standpoint.[176] In this view, most legal discourse is oriented more or less explicitly and more or less directly to the standpoint of one or more participants in legal processes of one kind or another. Holmes's Bad Man, Bentham's legislator, appellate court judges, the juror, the advocate and the office lawyer (or 'counsellor') are standard examples of types of participant each of whom has different, but overlapping, vantage-points, roles and purposes. In this view, most legal discourse is *relative* to one or more standpoints with different criteria of relevance, significance and appropriateness and different ways of perceiving facts. This looks like some kind of 'relativism'; but does this kind of approach tend to lead to relativism or scepticism in the sense in which we have already encountered these terms? And what are the implications of analysis of standpoint for our perceptions of the Rationalist Tradition?

In legal theory differentiation of standpoint is recognized as having enormous explanatory potential. Hart's 'internal point of view' is the best-known modern example.[177] A core of truth in the generally vulnerable 'prediction theory of law' can be rescued by restricting it to the particular concerns of some actors;[178] Rawls has shown how the controversy between retributivist and utilitarian views of punishment can be narrowed, but not completely dissolved, by pointing out that the former focus on the judge's question (Why punish this man?), while the latter are concerned with the legislator's question (Why prescribe punishment for offences?);[179] some of the puzzlements underlying debates about the *ratio decidendi* of a case can be clarified by switching from the standpoint of the judge to that of the advocate, because the latter's role in interpreting cases is less problematic;[180] the narrow focus of expository textbooks is in part attributable to their tendency to adopt almost identical criteria of relevance to those of appellate court judges.[181] Failure to differentiate standpoint has perhaps been the single most fertile source of artificial polemics in jurisprudence.

Such differentiations are crucial in studying evidence. A fundamental difference between Bentham's theory of evidence and Wigmore's science of proof is that the former consistently takes the form of advice to the legislator, while the latter is addressed, mainly but not entirely, to the advocate and the adjudicator at a particular stage during trial. Most expository works on evidence tend to adopt, more or less consistently, the same criteria of relevance and of significance as appellate court judges. Traditional discussions of the notion of 'relevance' itself concentrate on relevance to already formulated facts in issue and say little about ways in which particular items of information may be relevant, according to *different criteria*, in investigation, in drafting statements of claim or formulating criminal charges, in plea-bargaining and other negotiations, and in a host of other operations in litigation, including sentencing.[182] To put the matter in general terms: a coherent account of evidence and information in legal processes within a broadened conception of the study of law would, at the very least, need to deal systematically with the perception and handling of facts by all the main participants in those processes.

A distinction is sometimes drawn between observer and participant perspectives on law.[183] The participant views legal phenomena from the inside, typically with a view to action; the observer views them from the outside, typically with a view to description, explanation, understanding and, sometimes, criticism. Even in this extremely crude version, this distinction is potentially illuminating.[184] *Inter alia*, it helps to explain some of the different tendencies of evidence scholarship and many modern studies of judicial processes. As a very broad generalization one might suggest that by and large the Rationalist Tradition has been participant-oriented, while many, but by no means all, writers on judicial processes have adopted observer or outsider perspectives. Thus Bentham's theory of evidence and Wigmore's science of proof are first and foremost working theories for different participants. The primary audience for almost all expository work on evidence is actual and intending participants in legal processes notably judges, practising lawyers, the police and law students. Naturally their standpoints and concerns predominate.[185] Much of the legal literature on evidence, especially in periodicals and official reports, is concerned with the reform or codification of the law of evidence. It is addressed to, or adopts the standpoint of, the law-maker (whether legislator or judge) within a particular system (and hence on a particular set of assumptions). Thus the great bulk of specialized writing on evidence, despite its variety, shares two characteristics: it is normative or prescriptive and it is addressed to a range of participants within a given legal system.[186]

While some writing about judicial processes shares these characteristics, there is a discernible strand that does not. Sociological and other empirical writings about judicial processes often claim to try to describe or explain such phenomena from the outside.[187] Similarly much recent 'critical' legal scholarship expressly disclaims any concern to give practical advice to participants or to make recommendations for reform within the existing order (hence the use of 'reformist' as a derogatory term). 'Criticism' in this context is typically more concerned to challenge fundamental assumptions or claims of the system as a whole than to evaluate particular phenomena within a framework that takes such assumptions for granted.[188] Looked at in this way, it is hardly surprising that those who adopt observer perspectives should tend to be more concerned with the realities of the law in action and more inclined to question what is normally taken as given. Systematic description and sustained scepticism – at any level – are luxuries from the point of view of regular participants. It is not a coincidence that many of the examples cited at the start of this essay come from outsider perspectives.[189]

In so far as much legal discourse is participant-oriented, does this mean that it is also relativistic? Is it a necessary or merely a contingent fact that most specialized evidence scholarship has been participant-oriented in this sense? The answers to these questions are quite closely related. Because most legal discourse is directly relevant to the standpoint of one or more types of participants in legal processes, there is a sense in which it is relativistic and partial. It is directly affected by the vantage-points, roles and purposes of particular participants in a particular kind of enterprise. Each standpoint generates its own standards of relevance, of significance and of appropriateness. For example, a given 'bit' of information might be crucial in the process of eliminating a suspect or in leading to further information, yet it might turn out at a later stage to be irrelevant to the facts in issue, or inadmissible, though relevant, or superfluous or not very important for the particular theory of the case that the advocate is trying to develop. Its relevance, its importance and the appropriateness of making use of it vary according to the standpoints of the detective, the advocate, the judge and other participants. It may get filtered out or translated into a different terminology or distorted or 'processed' in other ways as it moves through the process.[190]

It may be objected that this kind of differentiation of standpoint is too particularistic – that particular statements of 'fact' (e.g. X saw Y leave the house at 6 p.m.) or statements of 'the facts' of a case transcend particular standpoints – that they can be true or valid or important independently of the standpoint of any particular participant. Several different considerations may lie behind such objections. First, it is clear that the standard standpoints of participants in legal processes overlap to a considerable extent. What is relevant for the purposes of the advocate is to a large extent, but not entirely, also relevant for the judge or other trier of fact. A single textbook statement of the hearsay rule can be equally *valid* for the detective, the solicitor, the advocate and the judge; but it will be *relevant* to their purposes and be of more or less *importance* to them in different ways. Of course, there is considerable overlap between different standpoints, but this is not an objection to emphasizing the general value of clarification of standpoint.[191]

Another concern behind this kind of objection is that some legal standpoints are more important or central than others. A common example is the claim that the judge is *the* fulcrum of legal processes. Differentiation of standpoint is neutral about the relative importance of one standpoint against another – importance is itself relative to one's purposes or other standards. Judicial decisions cast a long shadow.[192] For many purposes, the judge does occupy an especially important point in legal processes; for example, a central preoccupation of practising lawyers is to anticipate and influence particular judicial decisions; or again, a great deal of negotiating takes place 'in the shadow of the law'. But unqualified, the claim that the judge is the fulcrum of all legal processes is a great over-simplification. There are many contexts in which the likely or actual decisions of judges are of little or no importance; the bad man about to embark on a course of action may be much more concerned about the likelihood of detection than about any possible judicial decision; many decisions in legal processes are taken in contexts where the chances of the matter ever coming before a court are less than one in a thousand; a tax consultant may be far more concerned about the reaction of his local inspector than about what might happen if the case reached the Commissioners or the courts. In many such instances the possibility of a judicial decision exists in the background; even if it is remote, an official or other participant *may* use a hypothetical judicial decision as a standard, but it is often the case that this is not treated as a relevant factor or is only one of a number of factors taken into account.[193]

If the point being made is that some standpoints are more important than others, this is not an objection to differentiation of standpoints. If the objection is that this kind of analysis overlooks the centrality of the judge in legal processes, this objection is invalid because it is based on a false assumption about what is involved in clarification of standpoint and an over-simplified view of legal processes.

A third possible concern is that differentiation of standpoint leads to extreme relativism. The argument might be stated as follows: emphasis on different standpoints with different criteria of relevance and significance leads on to talk of 'multiple realities' and 'different worlds'. This is a short step from extreme statements of the kind 'members of different cultures live in different worlds', 'all that we have is multiple realities', or 'Ethnomethodology treats social science as one more reality among the many.'[194] It has been suggested that if such statements are correct, one wonders 'why anyone should pay attention to ethnomethodology', or how or whether crosscultural studies are possible.[195]

Whether or not such examples of 'extreme relativism' are defensible need not detain us. For such propositions do not follow inexorably from insistence on differentiation of standpoints in legal discourse. Such analysis is neutral on the issue of objectivity. To say that the bad man, the advocate and the judge have different vantage points, purposes, roles and concerns and hence have different criteria of relevance, significance and appropriateness involves neither acceptance nor denial of objective standards of truth or trans-subjective notions of reality.[196] Because even a quite simple event can be differently perceived, interpreted and reported by those who witness it, it does not follow that there are no criteria for assessing or criticizing what they report. Differentiation of standpoint may indeed have a tendency to make us cautious about particular claims to objectivity or to a monopoly of the truth, but that is a far cry from philosophical scepticism or extreme relativism.

Some Strategies of Scepticism

What general lessons are suggested by this tour of selected scenes from modern intellectual life? Some of them present no discernible threat to the view that notions of reason, truth and justice under the law form 'the rational core' of all adjudication; some indeed can be shown to share the same or very similar values. Thus the Sophomore and the Caricaturist can be dismissed as irrelevant; the standards of optimistic rationalism fall sufficiently short of any absolutes as hardly to offer a target to the Disappointed Perfectionist. Genuine philosophical sceptics present a direct challenge to the core notions of rationalism, but philosophical scepticism is a difficult posture to maintain consistently, except perhaps in silence; very few, if any, of those considered here seem to be serious sceptics at this level. The folk-wisdom of the Hard-nosed Practitioner is typically either too simplistic or too vague to be interpreted as attacking aspirational rationalism, but lurking behind talk of 'fight theories', 'the trial as a game', 'laundering the facts', or 'effective advocacy' may be ideas that represent a genuinely different way of looking at things; for issue to be joined such ideas need to be articulated much more precisely.[197]

Many of those who point to gaps between the law in books and the law in action or between aspiration and reality, go beyond pointing out such lacunae to invoking, more or less explicitly and clearly, the very standards they are discussing. When they do so their complaint is in essence that a particular system or some feature(s) of it regularly fail to achieve truth or to deliver justice under the law or to attain an acceptable degree of rationality in practice. Such criticisms present a challenge to complacent claims for a particular system, but not to aspirational rationalism. Those who dismiss talk of the Rule of Law and due process *merely* as the mystifying ideology of bourgeois or liberal legalism are often in danger of becoming victims of their own rhetoric: in relation to adjudication, notions of reason, truth and expletive justice – especially the latter – are intimately related to the classical ideal of the Rule of Law. Without care, an attack on one may take on the character of an attack on the others. Undiscriminating critiques of the Rule of Law risk throwing some important babies out with the bath-water for, if taken at face value, the critics seem to be straying into some wilderness of irrationalism, arbitrariness or self-defeating scepticism. Such deviations are often implied or suggested by critical attacks on orthodox theories or official views, although it is not always easy to separate the substance from the rhetoric.

However, irrationalism is not a necessary option for inheritors of late nineteenth-century social thought. Writing in the 1950s about the generation of European thinkers of the 1890s and after – who included such different figures as Freud, Croce, Sorel, Collingwood and Mannheim – Stuart Hughes observed:

The question of rationality is the crucial one – the final test of what was viable and what was transitory in the intellectual labors of this generation. In defining their attitude toward reason, the social thinkers of the early twentieth century were obliged to walk the edge of a razor. On the one side lay the past errors of the eighteenth century and of the positivist tradition. On the other side lay the future errors of unreason and emotional thinking. In between there remained only the narrow path of faith in reason despite and even because of the drastic limitations with which psychological and historical discovery had hedged it: however much 'intuition', free association, and the other unorthodox techniques of investigation might have broadened the criteria of evidence in social thought, reason alone remained the final control and arbiter.[198]

It was for such reasons that Mannheim talked of 'relationism' and that historiographers, sceptical jurists and many sociologists were so anxious to dissociate themselves from 'extreme relativism'.[199] For Max Weber the tensions between rational method and subjective meaning, between 'the sphere of logic and the sphere of value,'[200] were central. As Hughes suggests: '[H]e alone invariably held to the central understanding of his whole generation. He alone never wavered in his insistence that *both* reason and illogic were essential to the comprehension of the human world. While reality, he implied, was dominated by unreason it was only through rational treatment that it would be made comprehensible.'[201] Perhaps the main conclusion suggested by my own explorations is that the vast majority of 'critical' studies of judicial process and of other sceptical or debunking motifs listed at the start should be interpreted as posing far more of a threat to complacent rationalism than to the aspirational core of the Rationalist Tradition. Reason, Truth and Justice, as central notions of adjudication and proof, may not be under such direct attack as first impressions suggest; but they are, of course, subject to reinterpretation in each generation.

To put the matter differently: few, if any, of the sample of texts studied for this essay need to be interpreted as involving an outright rejection of the *concepts* of Truth, Reason or Justice as central aspirations of adjudication, representing its 'rational core'; however, the particular *conceptions* associated with the Rationalist Tradition are by no means the only ones to be found in our current stock of theories and, in the light of more general intellectual developments, they seem rather old-fashioned and simplistic by virtue of their roots in eighteenth-century Enlightenment thought.[202]

Another general lesson of this enquiry concerns concepts. 'The field of evidence is no other than the field of knowledge', wrote Bentham.[203] It is hardly surprising that some of the basic concepts of the law of evidence and theories of judicial evidence should be shared with other disciplines: proof, truth, facts, evidence, relevance, probability, credibility, reliability, common sense, rationality, practical reason, belief and decision are all obvious, if not straightforward, candidates for the status of fundamental concepts of any theory of evidence. Some are, perhaps, less obvious: stock of knowledge, cognitive competence, cognitive consensus, criteria of relevance, criteria of significance, materiality, efficiency, narrative coherence for example. Philosophers of knowledge, historians, scientists, phenomenologists, probability theorists, and information scientists are among those who, in this respect, use what looks like a common language.[204] How far such terms have shared meanings across disciplines and how far they are necessary or central in each context are debatable questions.

So far, I have suggested, the central underlying assumptions of the Rationalist Tradition have stood up rather well in the face of a series of potentially destructive or subversive intellectual trends. There are, however, some other general themes in this essay that point in a different direction. Two of the more important ones are cautionary.

First, at several points we have encountered powerful reminders of the difficulty of the enterprise of seeking after truth. Rescher, a cognitivist, readily concedes that the sceptic has managed 'to exhibit the inherent limitations of such knowledge as we can properly lay claim to'.[205] Fischer, one of the sharpest critics of historical relativism, acknowledges that completeness ('the whole truth') is an unattainable ideal and that the obstacles in the way of accurate history are formidable.[206] Similarly, the need for selection, interpretation and arrangements of 'facts' is almost universally accepted as an inevitable part of the writing of history. The trier of fact in adjudication may have his task simplified for him by prior definitions of what is material, by pleadings and by all the other kinds of filtering that have taken place before trial. But the tasks of selection, interpretation, arrangement and many other aspects of information-processing face legal enquiries seen as total processes; even judges and other triers of fact are by no means totally exempted from such operations. Jerome Frank may have overstated his case from time to time; his criticisms of particular institutions and devices are still controversial; but it is difficult to contest the core of truth in his identification of practical obstacles to arriving at correct decisions and the inevitability of 'the personal element' at every stage of judicial processes. Nor is there much room for disagreement about the central thesis of phenomenology that all that passes for knowledge is affected by its social environment and that, in some sense, all judgements or statements of fact are 'constructed': disagreement centres mainly on the meaning and implications of such notions. Finally, the leading exponents of mathematical analysis of probabilities are careful to acknowledge how rarely the conditions for the kinds of calculations they favour are satisfied in practice in forensic contexts. Thus in various ways these representatives of different kinds of scepticism and relativism all emphasize the complexities and the practical difficulties of fact-determination. That the pursuit of truth is a difficult enterprise deserves the status of a truism; it is fair to say that within Evidence scholarship this has sometimes been part of 'the neglected obvious'.

A second warning note is, perhaps, less obvious. This relates to the dangers of over-simplification. To put the matter simply: there *is* something simplistic about the Rationalist Tradition. This is illustrated in extreme form by its greatest scholar, Wigmore, whose view of the world looks quaintly simple-minded to modern eyes. Even Bentham, in many respects a complex and incisive thinker, espoused a form of common sense empiricism in his approach to evidence. One example of over-simplification will suffice. The standard contrast (by lawyers) between historical and legal enquiries discussed above is based on an extraordinarily simple and monolithic view of both historiography and adjudication as enterprises. 'The historian' is a single character. All types of judicial process are treated as similar, jury trials tend to be seen as the paradigm, the focus is on the adjudicative decision rather than on the complex flows of decisions that characterize most kinds of legal processes. What has happened, one wonders, to such elementary discriminations – familiar to lawyers in other contexts – as the distinctions between criminal and civil procedure; between contested and uncontested cases; between jury trials, other trials, and proceedings in other tribunals; between legislative and adjudicative facts; between multi-million dollar anti-trust suits, political trials and simple consumer claims, or between private and public law litigation – to say nothing of more recondite differences? Can an adequate theory of evidence conflate all types of proceeding, all types of tribunal, all types of case and all the stages in each type of proceeding within a single model of adjudication (including its basic assumptions about evidence)? In any given jurisdiction can there be only *one* law of evidence which applies across the board, subject to a few exceptions and modifications? In the Anglo-American system can there be just one 'typical' or 'paradigm' case and if that is conceded, is the contested jury trial an appropriate choice?

Most writers on evidence give some place to some of these distinctions and modifications – especially the distinction between criminal and civil proceedings. There *may* be some justification for treating contested jury trials as paradigmatic in some contexts, even if they are atypical. The search for principle and for coherent frameworks is a worthy one. The 'ideal type' of the assumptions of the Rationalist Tradition is my own construction and I have, perhaps rashly, treated some quite different individuals as belonging to a single intellectual mainstream. I have also indulged in other simplifications. Nevertheless, it is worth asking whether the great bulk of writing about evidence is not seriously over-generalized and whether a theory of evidence suited to the modern temper does not need to be much more differentiated than its predecessors. These questions are pursued in later chapters. What I want to suggest here is that one important source of scepticism about some of the assumptions and claims of the Rationalist Tradition is that it has tended to adopt a picture of adjudication that is both over-simple and over-generalized. We may still wish to move towards a general theory of adjudication (or litigation) and a general theory of evidence as part of that theory, but the implications of even the most elementary distinctions (and many others) need to be explored in a questioning spirit. There are many types of judicial processes; each type of legal process is itself an extremely subtle and complex kind of social process involving numbers of participants. The heritage of orthodox evidence scholarship does not make sufficient allowance for such complexities.

When an orthodoxy is under challenge from a number of different directions at a number of different levels it is foolish to expect or to wish for a single new orthodoxy to emerge to replace the old one. Our intellectual environment is more complex than that. The orthodoxy that I have identified as the Rationalist Tradition has an internal coherence yet it is sufficiently flexible to accommodate some important disagreements[207] – for example, the running debate about safeguards in criminal procedure or the wide spectrum of views about the scope and justifications for deviations from a principle of free proof. By making some important concessions to the fallibility of human deciders and the practical exigencies of litigation, the Rationalist Tradition has been well protected from simplistic attack by disappointed perfectionists or absolutists. By concentrating very largely on the aspirational and the normative, it has made few empirical claims that can be directly refuted. Orthodox evidence scholarship tells us almost nothing about how the rules of evidence operate in practice, about the actual mental processes of witnesses, triers of fact or other participants, nor about any other aspects of the actual dynamics of information-processing in litigation. Although it has been less narrow and less rule-obsessed than other fields of law that have been dominated by the Expository Orthodoxy (Bentham and Wigmore have ensured that), it is *par excellence* an unempirical tradition. As such it is open to attack on grounds of narrowness, triviality and, above all, neglect of important questions, but it is less obviously vulnerable to charges of distortion, misperception and error.[208]

If some notions of Truth, Reason and Justice are worth preserving, are those versions espoused by the Rationalists the only, or the most acceptable, ones? Can this narrow focus or some of its key assumptions be shown to lead to significant error in treatment of particular topics? For example, has not 'the problem of misidentification' been misposed and does the orthodox literature not give a systematically misleading picture of the nature and role of confessions in the administration of criminal justice?

I have emphasized that the statement of the underlying assumptions about evidence and the Rationalist model of adjudication are both ideal types, to which the views of nearly all leading Anglo-American writers have more or less approximated. The historical thesis is thus a restricted one – the claim is that by and large these writers have subscribed to most of the elements in the scheme, though not in this specific formulation. It is an approximate reconstruction of common ideas in an intellectual tradition that is remarkably homogeneous without being doctrinaire or monolithic. That will suffice for present purposes.

In chapter 3 the main underlying assumptions of the Rationalist Tradition were articulated in the form of two ideal types, a Rationalist Model of Adjudication (Model I) and a series of common assumptions underlying orthodox theories of evidence and proof (Model II) (p. 73).[209] Even if it were possible to be exhaustive, it would be tedious to try to identify all possible deviations from each element in the two models. But some of the main possible strategies of different kinds of scepticism about aspirational rationalism can be quite simply depicted by restating Model II in simplified form and indicating some important variants (table 2). It is difficult to evaluate the potential significance of many of the variants in isolation from some more general theory or line of argument. Some can fairly be interpreted as particular moves or ploys or tactics that belong to a more general strategy. To return to the mapping analogy: these charts are like town plans that indicate a number of stations and other points of departure without providing much information about what destinations might be reached by precisely what routes.

From the variety of perspectives and bodies of literature that we have glanced at in these preliminary explorations, perhaps five main strategic approaches can be singled out as either presenting direct challenges to the central notions of the Rationalist Tradition or as offering starting-points for alternative theories of evidence:

1 *Philosophical Scepticism*, that is strong scepticism about the possibility of knowledge or rational argument or objective values. Genuine scepticism at this level presents a direct challenge to *any* theory of evidence; but there are good grounds for doubting the genuineness of most claims to philosophical scepticism.

2 *Ideological scepticism*, that is a stance that treats the assumptions and central ideas of the Rationalist Tradition as mere ideology (usually as part of the ideology of 'liberal legalism') which wholly or largely masks a very different reality – for example, that what is presented as the rational pursuit of justice under the law is in practice part of the repressive machinery of an unjust social order. In its more moderate or more refined forms, for example in E. P. Thompson's much debated claims for the Rule of Law, some place is accorded to law as being more than mere ideology, even in a declining capitalist society. In so far as this is acknowledged, the core notions of the Rationalist Tradition may survive, albeit in circumscribed, modified or attenuated forms, in both descriptive accounts of existing arrangements and in prescriptive theories of evidence within some new social order.[210]

3 *Nature-of-the-enterprise scepticism*, that is scepticism about claims that adjudication is about implementation of law and vindication of rights as opposed, for example, to the termination of disputes by peaceful means or the routine bureaucratic processing of people who have been unfortunate enough to fall into the clutches of the agencies of repression or social control. In its extreme forms this kind of scepticism about adjudication can barely accommodate such notions as 'miscarriage of justice', 'reliability', or even 'evidence' or 'proof' in any recognized sense. One can only remain sceptical of accounts of any legal order that allow no place for the notion of 'rectitude of decision' and its associated concepts. In more moderate forms – including accounts that emphasize the essentially bureaucratic and cooperative aspects of many

Table 2   Rationalist theories of evidence and proof, with selected variants

Aspirational rationalism (ideal type)	Selected variants
1 Cognitivist epistemology.	Epistemological scepticism.
2 Correspondence theory of truth.	Coherence theory of truth.
3 Rational decision making as aspiration.	(a) Scepticism about the possibility of rationality in (a) any context, (b) adjudication (this cannot be the aspiration); (b) claims to aspire to rationality in adjudication are a pretence or a delusion (this is not in fact the end which is pursued); (c) some other end should be pursued (this should not be the aspiration).
4 Decisions based on relevant evidence.	(a) Relevance a meaningless concept; (b) lawyers' conceptions of relevance are unduly narrow or otherwise strange.
5 Common sense appeals to a shared social stock of knowledge about the common course of events.	(a) Scepticism about common sense; (b) scepticism about general cognitive consensus; (c) scepticism about general cognitive competence.
6 Inductive reasoning the norm.	(a) Scepticism about the possibility of rationality in (a) any context, (b) adjudication; (b) scepticism about induction; (c) mathematical (Pascalian) reasoning the only valid kind of reasoning; (d) alternative conceptions of 'rationality' (e.g. holistic rather than atomistic; Hegelian rather than Baconian).
7 The pursuit of factual truth (as part of rectitude of decision) commands a high priority (as a means to Justice under the law).	(a) Scepticism about all claims to 'truth' (cognitivist epistemology); (b) fact and value cannot be separated in normative enquiries (anti-positivism); (c) truth is (largely) irrelevant in conflict-resolution; (d) the adversary system does not give a high priority to the attainment of truth.
8 Justice under the law.	(a) Ethical relativism or subjectivism; (b) other ends should be or are in fact pursued.

so-called 'adversary' proceedings – such scepticism serves as a useful corrective against simplistic or complacent views. It is one thing to argue for the retention of notions of reason, truth and justice in adjudication, it is quite another to postulate a single direct end as an aspiration, let alone as the achievement, of so complex an enterprise as litigation.[211]

4 *Legal fact-scepticism*, that is doubt about the feasibility in practice of designing institutions, procedures and rules which will in practice regularly

maximize rectitude of decision, in so far as that is an important goal of a given system; that will, for example, meet the Bridlegoose Challenge to a satisfactory standard. It is common ground that the pursuit of truth in adjudication, as elsewhere, is a difficult enterprise. There is a spectrum of views as to *how* difficult it is in various contexts. Even Jerome Frank, when one pares away the rhetoric, proves on examination to be an optimistic rationalist – in so far as he maintains a consistent posture. It is remarkable how little has been done to develop and refine Frank's central insight in a sustained and systematic fashion. Judge Bridlegoose remains the archetype of the fact-sceptic. He offers a constant and inescapable challenge to both optimistic and pessimistic rationalists. One ironic finding of this tour has been that mathematical purists are, perhaps unwittingly, the leading proponents of the view that the Bridlegoose Challenge is not, and most probably cannot be, met in practice.

5   *Contextualism*, that is the broad, and avowedly open-ended, thesis that for most purposes law, and particular aspects of it, cannot sensibly be studied in isolation, but need to be set in some broader context. In respect of adjudication, a standard precept is that adjudicative decisions need to be seen in the context of total legal processes, which in turn need to be set in the context of other social processes and of some broad vision of a particular social order (and, indeed, of an increasingly interdependent world). In the present context this kind of perspective mandates scepticism of the isolationist tendencies of specialized evidence scholarship. This is not only a matter of keeping a close watch on the interactions between rules of evidence, procedure and substantive law, but also of setting the study of adjudicative decisions firmly in the context of some model of total processes of litigation and other modes of dispute-settlement. The approach also draws attention to the fact that intellectual movements in law have a close, but complex, relationship to broader intellectual trends – as should be clear from this essay.

Such elementary precepts do not, on their own, involve any necessary commitment to even quite moderate forms of scepticism or relativism at a fundamental level. Nor do they lead inexorably to rejection of specialized studies nor of such projects as drafting codes of evidence. They do, however, suggest that a theory of evidence as part of a broadened conception of law as a discipline must inevitably be integrated with some general view of dispute-settlement, adjudication, procedure and much else besides. Moreover, like most of the other strategies already discussed, contextualism almost inevitably raises doubts about monolithic or simplistic views of the subject: *the* end of adjudication? *one* law of evidence? *the* judicial process? ... Since this travelogue has been written by a committed contextualist some of the tendencies and biases of this kind of approach should be apparent in all that has gone before.

These five strategies of scepticism are clearly not exhaustive of all possible strategies. Nor are they mutually exclusive; indeed some of them can be combined in a variety of ways. They do, however, provide a rough sketch of some of the more persistent patterns that can be discerned in the bewildering panorama presented by our intellectual heritage.

In any worthwhile expedition the tourists are exhausted before they have exhausted the sights. It is time to conclude. What is the Thursday Sceptic to make of all this? Given his lack of stamina, two final observations based on this survey will suffice: first, the individual scholar – whether he likes it or not – when confronted with so vast a heritage must accept inevitability of pluralism as a fact. Second, for rethinking evidence, Thursday scepticism is quite enough as a start.[212]

NOTES

This essay was first written during 1979–82 as a sequel to the essay on the Rationalist Tradition and published in the *British Journal of Law and Society* (Basil Blackwell, 1984). Since it is in part a report on wide exploratory reading in several disciplines, I have made only a few minor changes to the text. To have attempted to up-date the essay would have involved reporting on a further sample of diverse writings by Dworkin, Foucault, Geertz, Putnam, Ricouer, Rorty and above all, Mensonge, as well as various contributions to and comments on critical legal studies, feminist legal theory and writings about the relations between law, semiotics and narratology. Had I written the essay in 1988 there would have been some differences in tone, emphasis and position. I would possibly have devoted more attention to the Hard-nosed Practitioner, nature-of-the-enterprise scepticism, the role of narrative in constructing and reconstructing reality and the interplay of fact, law and value. Under the tutelage of Philip Dawid I have also developed a more sympathetic appreciation of the flexibility of certain kinds of statistical analysis than is suggested by the text. Some of these developments are explored in later chapters. However, I am still prepared to stand by the central thesis, viz. that the literature sampled here (a) poses few threats to the centrality of the concepts of Truth, Reason and Justice in any theory of Evidence and Proof and Fact-finding (EPF) (or even of the broader field of Information in Litigation (IL) that is developed in later chapters), but (b) suggests that the particular conceptions and focus built into the assumptions of the Rationalist Tradition are ripe for rethinking.

1   Low (1978), 7. The reference to Peter Berger comes from his *Invitation to Sociology* (1963), 51. The whole passage is germane to the present paper:

> We would contend, then, that there is a *debunking motif* inherent in sociological consciousness. The sociologist will be driven time and again, by the very logic of his discipline, to debunk the social systems he is studying. This unmasking tendency need not necessarily be due to the sociologist's temperament or inclinations. Indeed, it may happen that the sociologist, who as an individual may be of a conciliatory disposition and quite disinclined to disturb the comfortable assumptions on which he rests his own social existence, is nevertheless compelled by what he is doing to fly in the face of what those around him take for granted. In other words, we would contend that the roots of the debunking motif in sociology are not psychological but methodological. The sociological frame of reference, with its built-in procedure of looking for levels of reality other than those given in the official interpretations of society, carries with it a logical imperative to unmask the pretentions and the propaganda by which men cloak their actions with each other. This unmasking imperative is one of the characteristics of sociology particularly at home in the temper of the modern era.

2   Berger, ibid.
3   Frank (1945; revised edn, 1953).
4   Rabelais, *Gargantua and Pantagruel*, chs. 37–43 (trans. Sir Thomas Urquhart, 1913).
5   The *locus classicus* is J. S. Mill, *System of Logic*, Bk. II, ch. 3.
6   Hume (1748), s. IV; Rescher, (1980), chs. XI and XII. See further, below, 99.
7   See Twining (1980), 51. For references to contributions to the debate see n. 166 below.
8   Eggleston (1983).
9   See e.g. Wigmore *Science* (3rd ed.); Marshall (1980); Lloyd-Bostock (1980).

10　Above, n. I and works cited there. Scholarly works that explore contrasts between the ideology or rhetoric of the legal system include Blumberg (1967); Carlen (1976); and McBarnett (1981). Mere rhetorical statements that balance the 'official rhetoric' are commonplace in contemporary political discourse. A more sophisticated debate within Marxism about the Rule of Law as ideology has been provided by Edward Thompson's defence of the Rule of Law in *Whigs and Hunters* (1975).

11　See e.g. Cross (1970), 66; and response by Field, id., 76.

12　Garfinkel (1956), 420.

13　E.g. Blumberg, op. cit., 65–9; cf. Baldwin and McConville (1977), 111.

14　A selection of writings on plea-bargaining in England is included in Baldwin and Bottomley (eds) (1978), 71ff. See also Baldwin and McConville, op. cit., 13.

15　E.g., Blumberg, (1967), 65–9.

16　E.g., Blumberg (1967), *passim*.

17　See ch. 3, above.

18　Ibid. On the argument about narrowness see below, n. 361–5.

19　The historical claim is stronger in respect of the epistemological and logical assumptions than in respect of the underlying view of the nature of the enterprise of adjudication, for two reasons. First, writers on evidence tend to be much more explicit about the former than the latter. Secondly, there has probably been less agreement in fact about the nature of the enterprise than about what is involved in proving facts in that context. See further above, 72–6.

20　Debunking, ironic contrasts, doubt and despair are alien to the Rationalist Tradition from Sir Jeffrey Gilbert through Jeremy Bentham to most other contemporary writers on evidence. Even Bentham at his most savagely polemical treated the Technical System of Procedure as absurd, arbitrary and outrageously unjust *because* it offended common sense, reason and utility. Bentham was not a sceptic about knowledge, values or reason and he was a rule-sceptic only in a restricted sense. His ideas on adjudication belong to the Enlightenment in substance and spirit. As a theorist of evidence he is an optimistic rationalist, clearly within the mainstream of evidence scholarship (see further *TEBW*, ch. 2). Despite differences and disagreements, Thayer and Wigmore, Cross and Cohen, even secular natural lawyers such as Michael and Fuller belong to the same mainstream. Truth, reason and justice under the law (expletive justice) are the core concepts of the Rationalist Tradition.

21　One of the best studies of the intellectual history of post-Enlightenment social thought, from which many of the trends discussed in this essay emerged, is Hughes (1958).

22　On the affinities between Marxian and Benthamite 'demystification' see Hart (1973), 2; also *TEBW*, 75–88.

23　See now Kenneth Graham Jr.'s 'Manifesto of Legal Irrealist Disbelief' (1987), 1231–4.

24　On standpoint see Twining (1973a), 275 and below, 122 ff.

25　Cf. Bentham VI *Works*, 249.

26　On the notion of conditions of doubt, see Twining and Miers (1982), ch. 6.

27　See generally Hollis and Lukes (1982).

28　A brief comment on the doubts which lie behind such questions. A philosophical sceptic who doubts whether it is possible to have knowledge about the past, is likely also to be sceptical of a theory which purports to answer questions about logical aspects of proof of past facts; someone who doubts whether judicial processes are in any important sense concerned with fact-finding or truth-seeking is likely to raise a quizzical eyebrow about the worthwhileness of studying the reliability of different kinds of evidence or ways and means of improving accuracy in judicial fact-finding; someone who doubts whether historical facts can ever be objective, may raise questions about the use of terms such as 'canons of evidence' or 'standards of proof' or 'criteria of relevance', in so far as they imply objective or, at least, trans-subjective criteria. If 'reality' is merely constructed by advocates and decision makers, rather than tested on the basis of evidence, why concern oneself with questions about evidence, proof and relevance? Someone who denies the possibility of rationality in decision making is likely to question the value of the study of logical aspects of probative processes. Not all of these doubts follow from sceptical premisses as a matter of logical necessity. For example, to suggest that rationality plays little or no part in practice in legal processes does not *ipso facto* invalidate all theories of legal reasoning; but it does put one on one's guard as to whether any particular theory contains dubious assumptions or gives a misleading impression about the part played by reason in such processes – and it raises questions about the worthwhileness of the enterprise. Someone who believes that the judgements of courts are mere rationalizations is not likely to be very interested in the logic of justification, not because he thinks that such an enterprise is invalid, but because he thinks that it is unimportant or trivial or irrelevant to his concerns. My primary concern in this paper is not to criticize the approaches under consideration. Rather this is a mapping exercise in which the main objective is to locate a variety of seemingly sceptical approaches in relation to each other and to orthodox theories of evidence and proof.

29   Twining (1978), esp. 189–92. The classic critique of polemical jurisprudence is by Karl Llewellyn:

Though

(a) jurisprudes are mostly lawyers, so trained in the rhetoric of controversy, with
   (i)   its selective, favorable posing of issues, and
   (ii) its selection, coloring, argumentative arrangement of facts, and
   (iii) its use of epithet and innuendo, and
   (iv) its typical complete distortion of the advocate's vision, once he has taken a case, so that he ceases to even take in any possibility which would work against him (as especially in the prevalent 'romantic' type of advocacy), that
(b) it has proved necessary to police their work as advocates by
   (i)   forcing them to define issues by a careful system of phrased pleading, served back and forth with opportunity for answer, under the supervision of a responsible and authoritative tribunal, and
   (ii) limiting their arguments to the issues so drawn, and
   (iii) confining the 'facts' to which they can resort to a record, and
   (iv) barring guilt by association, or by imputation, or without proof of particular offense, etc., yet
(c) in Jurisprudence every man
   (i)   states his own issue, misstates the other man's issue, beclouds the or–any issue, evades the or–any issue, etc., uncontrolled by procedure or by answer, or by authority (and cases where a jurisprude has stated an issue fairly are museum-pieces), and
   (ii) uses his rhetoric also without control, and
   (iii) is free to dream up 'facts' even by anonymous imputation, and
   (iv) consequently always rides his strawman down.
(d) Whereas in law one party always loses, or each must yield something, in Jurisprudence there is thus Triumphant Victory for All. This makes for comfort, if not for light. (*Law in Our Society*, 86–7, unpublished, 1950, quoted in Twining, 1973, 379–80)

30   Ibid.
31   Hart (1961), 135.
32   Twining (1973), 32, 255, 408. This was written before recent debates concerning critical legal studies.
33   Other examples of alleged myths as caricatures include 'the slot-machine theory of the judicial function', 'the myth of judicial neutrality' and 'the myth of logic'. A useful function may be served in showing *why* a particular belief is absurd, even if it is difficult to find evidence of widespread or even any adherence to the belief (e.g. Hart's treatment of rule-scepticism); but often this kind of approach leads to sterile polemics. A recent

example is J. A. G. Griffith's *The Politics of the Judiciary* (1977) which is marred by a tendency to interpret claims to 'neutrality' and 'impartiality' unduly strictly; by choosing an unnecessarily soft target, Griffith weakens the force of his argument and has made it easy for some of his critics to avoid its main thrust.

34 5.5.8. *'And–Not' is bad Jurisprudence.* In observation of any social scene, the complexity of material makes any *exclusively* single attribute or sequence highly improbable. 'And–not' is the traditional bane of sound Jurisprudence (and of lay thinking in general): 'Because it is A it is therefore *not* B' presupposes a thoroughly explored, exactly defined area of discussion, divided accurately and exhaustively into A and Not–A – which the current social scene almost never is. Examples: 'Good lawyers are born *and not* made.' (First half true sometimes; and *some* native capacity is indeed needed.) 'It is not law which shapes society, but society which shapes law.' (First half false; though much law has often failed to 'take'; but even then it may shape heavily in unforeseen directions: e.g. Volstead Act and gangsterism.) (Llewellyn 1950, reproduced in Twining, 1973, 516)

35 See *Law and the Modern Mind* (1930), *passim*, especially ch. 1. Frank contrasts 'the basic legal myth' with fields other than law where 'there is today a willingness to accept probabilities and to forego the hope of finding the absolutely certain' (p. 7). Frank attributed belief in this myth to most members of the Bar (and possibly of the general public) and acknowledged that many jurists before him had recognized that 'Law ... is at the best governed by "the logic of probabilities"' (ibid.). See further below, 109 ff.

36 A number of other important concessions and caveats are typically made by aspirational rationalists within the Rationalist Tradition.

1 The notion of 'rectitude of decision' involves no necessary commitment to the pursuit of truth as an over-riding value; it is standard to acknowledge that other values, such as the security of the state or preservation of the family or of confidential relationships, have to be 'balanced' against rectitude of decision as a social value. There is no consensus within the Rationalist Tradition about the relative priorities to be given to such competing values.

2 The notion of 'fact' is recognized as problematic: the distinction between questions of fact and questions of law is notoriously difficult; it is commonplace that triers of 'fact' are often called upon to decide whether conduct was reasonable or to make other judgements involving an element of evaluation, while the paradigm case of 'fact-finding' is concerned with allegations about *particular* past events, it is not assumed that all facts in issue are particular.

3 The claim that we have adopted 'the method of reason' in adjudication is a limited one. The 'method of reason' is contrasted with pure chance (Judge Bridlegoose) or brute force or appeals to the supernatural or 'the mechanical following of form' (Thayer's phrase). The claim relates to the aspiration and the design of the system; the standards of rationality are modest; it is generally accepted that closed system reasoning has limited applications and even enthusiastic Pascalians (see below) acknowledge that the conditions for pure mathematical calculation are rarely satisfied; few claims are made about the extent to which decision making in practice satisfies these standards of rationality; notions such as 'prejudicial effect' acknowledge the possible operation of irrational factors.

     The core of the Rationalist claim is that the maximization of 'soft' rationality in adjudication is a reasonable aspiration.

4 Emphasis on 'common-sense', 'knowledge about the common course of events', 'general experience', postulates both a general cognitive competence on the part of triers of fact and a widespread cognitive consensus within a given society – assumptions that are especially likely to attract criticism (see below, n. 136). This is an area particularly ripe for false polemics, if only because the assumptions and notions are vague and subject to exceptions. The assumption is that competence is general,

consensus is widespread, not that either is universal. Fuzzy targets invite scatter-shot attack. Suffice it to say here that showing that people from different backgrounds may draw quite different inferences from the fact of a youth running away from a policeman hardly goes further in undermining assumptions above cognitive consensus than showing that few people believe that buses have square wheels supports them. On cognitive competence see L.J. Cohen (1983), 1; on cognitive consensus see above, Table 2, and below, 114–5. See further Twining (1988), 1539–41. The notion of cognitive consensus has often been implicitly challenged in discussions of jury selection, where the values of potential jurors are also perceived to be important. The following represents a fairly typical statement:

> The theory underlying the core hypothesis, that the characteristics of jurors affect the decision they reach, can be stated fairly simply. A person's demographic background (socioeconomic class, race, religion, sex, age, education, and so forth) denotes a particular kind of socializing history for that person. If you are poor, young, black, and female, you will have been conditioned to view the world differently, to react to it differently, and to hold different attitudes compared with a person who is wealthy, old, white and male. These perceptions, attitudes, and values, in turn, help determine the decision you make as a juror. In addition to demographic characteristics, personality type (whether personality arises through genetics, psychodynamic development, or conditioning history) is thought to predispose a juror to a particular decision. If you are highly dependent on order, for example, you might be conviction-prone. It is unclear whether the theory holds that personality type determines the substantive preference one has (e.g. always wanting to be punitive) or whether it influences the way one processes the evidence (giving more weight to the government's evidence than to the defense's). Thus juror demographic characteristics, personality, and attitude are thought to have substantial impact on their decisions. (Saks and Hastie, 1978, 49.)

5   Acceptance of the postulates of the Rationalist model does not necessarily involve commitment to 'absolute' or unattainably high standards: just as probability is substituted for absolute certainty, so notions of objectivity, competence, impartiality and rationality can be treated as relative aspirations.

6   In so far as members of the dominant intellectual tradition of evidence theorizing have accepted the tenets of aspirational rationalism, this has not thereby necessarily committed them to *complacency* about the operation of their own system at a given time – Bentham, for example, developed his theory of adjudication as a basis for a radical critique of existing institutions and practices. This is crucial for the central argument of this paper for two reasons: first, it is part of my argument that a rationalist aspirational theory of EPF is not incompatible with scepticism concerning complacent claims about the actual operation of a particular system – indeed, it provides one set of standards for evaluation and criticism, and, secondly, that at least some alleged sceptics or relativists in pointing out gaps between aspiration and reality or in criticizing a particular system of adjudication or parts thereof are invoking something like the prescriptive model.

37   On the Hard-nosed Practitioner see further below, 206–7, 366 ff. Another example of hard-nosed pragmatism is the claim that the law systematically begs philosophical questions about truth and proof. For example, Doreen McBarnett (1981), 12–13, cites a fairly standard statement (by David Napley): 'While therefore the doctor and the scientist are engaged in an inquisitorial pursuit in which they are seeking the truth, the lawyer is engaged in an accusatorial pursuit to see whether a limited area of proof has been discharged.' She then comments: 'The justification lies not in any idealism that "the truth, the whole truth and nothing but the truth results", but in pragmatics. The courts are there not to indulge in the impossible absolutes of philosophy or science but to

reach decisions – quickly.' McBarnett's 'not ... but ... not ... but' involves the same kind of contrast as is made by the disappointed idealist. Statements like Napley's, thus interpreted, can easily be accommodated by the Rationalist Model, which explicitly sets standards falling short of certainty and 'impossible absolutes'. The dichotomies are false: because certainty ('absolute truth') is conceded to be unattainable, it does not follow that the enterprise is not concerned with the pursuit of the best attainable truth; because pragmatic concessions are made to the avoidance of vexation, expense and delay, it does not follow that the pursuit of truth is not a serious aspiration or that *for this reason* adversary enquiries are qualitatively different from medical, inquisitorial or scientific enquiries all of which, in different ways, also suffer from practical constraints. If 'fact-finding' in adversary proceedings is fundamentally different from such other factual enquiries it is not because practical constraints dictate acceptance of standards of proof below the ideal.

One example of a theory that suggests that the pursuit of truth is not the principal aim of legal process is the satisfaction theory of Charles P. Curtis (*It's Your Law*, 1954, 21): 'Justice is something larger and more intimate than truth. Truth is only one of the ingredients of justice. Its whole is the satisfaction of those concerned.' This view is criticized by Martin Golding and Robert Summers, in Bronaugh (ed.) (1978), chs. 9 and 10, both of whom accept the standard view that ascertainment of truth is a necessary ingredient of justice viewed as rectitude of decision, but that truth is sometimes subordinated to other values. This Golding calls the truth-finding theory. The disagreement, such as it is, relates to the primacy or priority of seeking 'truth' about the actual past rather than questioning whether truth is sought at all.

38   I have anecdotal evidence that this may be true of some individual evidence scholars. This separation of personal belief from professional convention may indeed be commonplace: it would be strange if all common law judges had identical philosophical views about matters directly relating to fact-finding. We are, however, only interested in such disparities in so far as they actually affect the discourse and actual behaviour of professional – and other – participants in legal processes. If a textbook writer, in following convention, does not believe what he writes, that it is merely of incidental interest to a study of the convention – in this case the Rationalist Tradition.

39   The main works on which this section is based are: Ayer (1956 and 1961); 'Statements about the Past' in Ayer (1963); Ayer (1980); Popkin, 'Skepticism' in *The Encyclopedia of Philosophy* (1967; ed. P. Edwards), vol. 7; Rescher (1980); Trigg (1973); Unger (1975).

40   Unger, op. cit., 1; cf. 242–3.

41   On the notion of 'legal truth', see below 249. On substituting 'Information in Litigation' (IL) for Evidence, Proof and Fact-Finding as an organizing concept see below, ch. 11.

42   Ayer (1961), 47.

43   Ayer (1956), 76. For a criticism of this argument see e.g. Trigg (1973), 145ff.

44   Cf. Ayer, id., 222.

45   Id., 76–8.

46   Id., 78–9.

47   Id., 81.

48   Id., 222.

49   Id., 78.

50   On the range of types of 'fact' that are the subject of dispute in adjudication, see below, ch. 8 and 11.

51   See above, 73.

52   On the relationship between Bentham's epistemological assumptions in writing about evidence and his theory of fictions, see Postema (1983) and *TEBW* 52–66. On whether Hume himself was necessarily an epistemological sceptic, see Ayer *Hume*, op. cit., *The Problem of Knowledge*, op. cit., ch. 3: 'Whatever scepticism Hume may have professed, there is no doubt that he believed in the existence of what may be called the physical objects of common sense', id., 35.

53 Michael and Adler may have been rather more eclectic than the others named in the text in their treatment of logic in their *The Nature of Judicial Proof* (1931).
54 Naess (1968); see also Unger (1973) and Lehrer (1973). On Nietzsche as sceptic, see Danto (1965), ch. 4. In Jurisprudence explicit epistemological scepticism is almost unknown, but some jurists – Hans Kelsen, for example – may be viewed as relativists or subjectivists in ethics, see Kelsen (1957); Raz 'The Purity of the Pure Theory' in Tur and Twining (1986). The main clientele of writers on judicial evidence would tend to be impatient of abstract doubts in so far as these inhibit practical action. In order to be able to get on with the job one has to proceed *as if* there is a real world, *as if* legal argument is really 'argument' and as if one is pursuing rationally defensible ends by rational means, whether or not one believes this to be the case, just as Bishop Berkeley sat down on chairs, Hans Kelsen no doubt 'reasoned' with his wife about their political views, and committed Pascalians regularly indulge in non-mathematical 'arguments'. A genuinely sceptical theory of evidence might be of great potential interest to theorists, but would have little appeal to practitioners. Most writers on evidence were, or wrote for, practitioners. Cf. Doreen McBarnett: 'Adversary advocacy helps solve the philosophical problem of reproducing reality quite simply by not even attempting it. Instead the search for truth is replaced by a contest between caricatures. Advocacy is not by definition about "truth" or "reality" or a quest for them, but about arguing a case' (1981, 16).
55 Rescher, op. cit., n. 39, at 249.
56 Id., 248–50.
57 Id., 249.
58 The main sources for the accounts of historiography in this section are: R. F. Atkinson (1978); Bloch (1954); Carr (1961); Danto (1968); Fischer (1970); Geyl (1955); Meyerhoff (ed.) (1959), a very useful anthology, and M. White (1964).
59 Cited Meyerhoff, op. cit., 13; discussed by Geyl, op. cit., ch. 1., Atkinson, op. cit., 13–17. Cf. Nevins's defence of objectivity against the 'crude policy of deforming history to suit an ideological purpose': 'The only history that can truly nourish, inspire and guide a people over a long period of time is written in a different spirit. It is produced with a high, not a low intention; in an earnest effort to ascertain the truth objectively' (1962, 28–9).
60 See generally M. White, op. cit.
61 See especially Cahn (1957), 3, 5–6; Frank (1945, 1953).
62 Becker (1955), 327–40; Beard (1934), 219–29. Both are reprinted in Meyherhoff, op. cit.
63 M. White in Meyerhoff, op. cit., 189.
64 Op. cit., n. 62.

65 What then is the historical fact? Far be it from me to define so illusive and intangible a thing! But provisionally I will say this: the historian may be interested in anything that has to do with the life of man in the past – any act or event, any emotion which men have expressed, any idea, true or false, which they have entertained. Very well, the historian is interested in some event of this sort. Yet he cannot deal directly with this event itself, since the event itself has disappeared. What he can deal with directly is a *statement about the event*. He deals in short not with the event but with a statement which affirms *the fact that the event occurred.* When we really get down to the hard facts, what the historian is always dealing with is an affirmation – an affirmation of the fact that something is true. There is thus a distinction of capital importance to be made: the distinction beween the ephemeral event which disappears, and the affirmation about the event which persists. For all practical purposes it is this affirmation about the event that constitutes for us the historical fact. If so the historical fact is not the past event, but a symbol which enables us to recreate it imaginatively. Of a symbol it is hardly worth while to say that it is cold or hard. It is dangerous to say even that it is true or false. The safest thing to say about a symbol is that it is more or less appropriate. (Meyerhoff, op. cit., 124–5ff.)

66 Id., 123.
67 Id., 122.
68 Ibid.
69 Ibid.
70 Id., 131.
71 Id., 125.
72 E.g., G.R. Elton on Carr (1969), 74ff.
73 Meyerhoff, op. cit., 143.
74 Danto (1968), ch. VI.
75 Id. After summing up Beard's argument, Dray comments: 'This would appear to be a very miscellaneous set of worries, to say the least, and it is far from evident that they are brought together with any one clear meaning of the term "objective" in mind' (Dray, 1964, 22).
76 Fischer, op. cit., 42–3n. Other leading critics of relativism are M. White and Danto, op. cit.
77 Cf. Geyl, op. cit., 28–9, on Leopold von Ranke:

> Historicism in the sense of an interpretation of history which acknowledges no standards outside the object, is abhorrent to me. I can see that Ranke, although not a historicist in that sense, has by his influence contributed to the development of that attitude of mind. Indeed, there is in his own presentation of the past enough of amoralism and passivism to give one frequent cause for impatience; and the illusionism, the spiritualizing of the brutish forces, leaves one with a feeling of dissatisfaction. Yet how admirable, nevertheless, is that serene matter-of-factness, that striving after comprehension, that openmindedness for historic phenomena other than those with which the writer himself felt in agreement – as a Protestant for the Papacy, as a German for the French absolute monarchy and for the English parliamentary monarchy, as a conservative sometimes for the French Revolution – qualities which have had a broadening effect on nineteenth century civilization and which (need I remind you?) are the complete opposite of the revolutionary fanaticism and doctrinairism of the men who half a century after his death threw Germany and the world into the catastrophe.

78 M. White, in Meyerhoff, op. cit., 197.
79 Nagel, id., 215.
80 Fischer, op. cit., 42–3.
81 The following is a good example:

> Essentially the law of evidence is concerned with the regulation of an investigation – that of fact-finding. This investigation is historical rather than scientific. The experimental methods of the natural sciences are not normally apt. When occasional resort is had to them, for example by the use of blood-tests or even of psychiatric evidence, this is strictly incidental to an enquiry as to past events. But to describe the fact-finding process simply as an historical investigation could be misleading: indeed, it has several characteristics which would be anathema to historians. There characteristics reflect, or should reflect, the context and purpose of the investigation. That purpose is not the mere acquisition of knowledge: it is the just settlement of a dispute. The results of the investigation have practical and often immediate consequences: they are likely to affect specifically the position of identifiable human beings. The context of the investigation is a trial, and, more particularly in common law jurisdictions, a trial conducted by adversary rather than inquisitorial methods. There are thus inherent constraints which the professional historian would find intolerable. These include the following: (1) Evidence is marshalled and presented very largely by interested persons. A party in civil proceedings and the accused in criminal proceedings is not impartial: he is concerned not so much with establishing the whole

truth as with winning his case. He can within fairly broad limits decide which evidence to offer and which to withhold. (2) A conclusion has to be reached one way or another even though the evidence may be inadequate. (3) It has to be reached quickly, and in a court of last resort it is final. (4) The tradition of trial by peers requires that the investigators be untrained. (5) The dogma that the trier of fact must judge according to the evidence seriously restricts the liberty of the investigators to inform themselves. (6) The evidence according to which they must judge is usually itself that of a non-expert and presented in the unfamiliar and somewhat forbidding atmosphere of a courtroom.

Adjudicative fact-finding smacks then of being an historical investigation carried out by untrained investigators required to act upon non-expert sources of information presented by biased protagonists, these untrained investigators being required to reach a decision which will be final and binding, to do so regardless of the adequacy of the evidence and to do so quickly. (Carter, 1981, 9–10; cf. Gulson, 1905, 214; Best, 1849 edn, Intro., s.2.)

82 Ch. Perelman (1963). It is sometimes said that 'judges decide, historians conclude'. While the central point about the differences in their roles is correct, the distinction can be drawn too sharply: historians have to make choices and judges are meant to justify their decisions on the basis of conclusions supported by reasons. Similarly, while it is no doubt the case that judicial decisions generally have potentially important practical consequences it is misleading to suggest that historians have no influence in the real world – in education and politics, for example.

83 Of course, the unique past event is the standard, rather than the universal, object of inquiry in judicial processes.

84 'From the epistemological point of view (also Engels wrote this) the fact that "Napoleon died on May 5 1821" is a trite truth (Plattheit), indeed, although it was a very sad or tragic fact for Napoleon and the Bonapartists. From the epistemological point of view also the truths of criminal judgment are "platitudinous truths" although they are significant, important or perhaps tragic from the social or individual point of view' (Kiraly, 1979).

85 See Bentham, *Rationale of Judicial Evidence* (J. S. Mill ed., 1827), Bk. I, ch. III.

86 E.g. J. Jackson (1983), 85; Zuckerman (1986) and Twining (1986b), 391–3.

87 Cf. the remarks of a legal historian:

> ... the isolation and selection of 'facts in issue' for trial is not of course the beginning stage of EPF, but an intermediate one quite far down the road, along which large numbers of people – legislators defining the liability, and establishing burdens of proof, the practices of bench and bar (or administrators and those dealing with them) in reducing elements of liability to certain stereotypes of proof-packages, witnesses in the particular case, their experts and their lawyers – have all been bringing to bear various interpretative theories and perspectives that have been sorting, packaging, interpreting, explaining, selecting, and, (unlike the historian, whose subjects are dead), actually impressing their own personalities on the 'facts'. I think the process is quite a lot like that of historical reconstruction, except much *more* complex and problematic, because the institutional setting, which is rather like that of a History Workshop, has to generate history under the maddest possible conditions – e.g. as a condition of the project, some outside bigwigs have initially excluded some kinds of work-product – such as explanations based on the characters of historical actors – as unacceptable; one has to rely as much as (or more than) most historians, on partisan witnesses; the project is interdisciplinary – i.e. it requires the services of lots of specialists in weird fields (experts) whose methodologies, interpretative schemes, and jargon are often quite alien and unintelligible to most people in the project and who keep trying to remake the rules to suit their own disciplines; the principal researchers are sworn adversaries, who *on principle* have to arrive at contrary versions of, or

interpretations of, the facts; but who paradoxically have to stipulate for budgetary reasons to some of the more controversial ones; and who keep trying to get the major sources of evidence to change their stories, etc. All this without even mentioning the complexities of fact-selection, interpretation, and explanation in the appellate opinion. The project therefore seems like a quite elaborate collective one in the construction of reality – the analogue to the historian is not just the decision-maker (judge or jury), but the whole crowd – lawyers, parties, witnesses, judge, jury – *not* excluding the lawmakers, who have set up the basic criteria of relevancy by defining the liability, setting up proof burdens, and establishing some basic canons of proof. (Robert Gordon, private communication to the author, 1983.)

88 The main sources for this section are: Frank (1930); (1933); (1938); (1942); (1945, revised 1953); (1947); (1953, in Ratner, ed.); (with Barbara Frank, 1957); Ackerman (1973); Cahn (1956) and (1967), 269ff.; Paul (1959); Schuett SJ (1957); Volkomer (1970). See further the entry on Frank (by the author) in Simpson (ed.) (1984).
89 Frank (1949), *Courts on Trial*, op. cit., *passim*.
90 For figures for England and Wales, see Zander (1980), chs. 1 and 2, updated in the 5th edn (1988).
91 See further, 'Taking Facts Seriously', above, ch. 2.
92 Frank (1949), 20; cf. id., 62.
93 Volkomer, op. cit., 18.
94 W. Seagle, cited by Volkomer, ibid.
95 In addition to his critics, this seems to be true of Cahn, Volkomer, Schuett, and, perhaps, Rumble. Exceptions include Bruce Ackerman, Robert Summers and Zenon Bankowski (1981).
96 Volkomer, op. cit., ch. 2.
97 Rescher, op. cit., 3.
98 Volkomer, ch. VI.
99 Op. cit., n. 88.
100 Schuett, op. cit., n. 88, at 29.
101 Frank (1943), chs. 12 and 13.
102 Id., v.
103 Frank (1949), ch. 3, at 29.
104 Frank (1930), xvi; cf. id., ch. XII; (1949), ch. III; (1945, revised 1953), *passim*.
105 Frank (1943), 175.
106 Id., ch. 2.
107 See especially Frank (1949).
108 Above, 148.
109 E.g., Frank (1949), 6.
110 Frank (1956), 921–4.
111 Frank (1930), xxviii.
112 Frank (1949), 6.
113 See especially id., ch. 12.
114 E.g., id., ch. 32.
115 Id., ch. 3.
116 Id., 23–4; on stories, see below ch. 7.
117 There is a useful list of Frank's principal targets in *Courts on Trial*, op. cit., ch. 31.
118 E.g. Frank (1949), ch. 1.
119 Frank (1930), 266.
120 Id., 268n.
121 Frank's prescriptions tended to be rather tame in comparison with his diagnoses; see, for example, *Courts on Trial*, op. cit., 422.
122 See Twining (1973a).
123 The main sources for this section are: Bennett and Feldman (1981); Berger and

Luckmann (1967); Binder and Bergman (1984); Cicourel (1973); Freeman (1978); Hollis and Lukes (eds) (1982); Luckmann (ed.) (1978); Mannheim (1936); McBarnett (1981); Turner (ed.) (1974).

124   Aristotle, *Nichomachean Ethics* v(vii), 2.
125   Marx's epistemology was never fully developed, but he was committed to the existence of a world independent of man's knowledge of it. See Plamenatz (1975), 78–9. Cf. V. I. Lenin:

> (1) Things exist independently of our consciousness, our perception, outside us ...
> (2) There is no difference whatsoever, and cannot be, between the phenomenon and the thing in itself we have not yet come to know.... (3) We must cogitate dialectically in epistemology just as in any other field of science, that is to say we must not assume that our cognition is complete and unchangeable; we must examine how knowledge arises from ignorance, how incomplete, inaccurate knowledge turns into more complete and more accurate knowledge. (*Materialism and Empiriocentrism*, cited by Kiraly, 1979, 67.)

Kiraly's work contains a useful survey of continental writings about 'the doctrine of truth in criminal procedure'.
126   Berger and Luckmann, 22.
127   Ibid.
128   Id., 13.
129   Id., 15.
130   Ibid.; cf. 26.
131   See esp. Introduction, *passim*.
132   Id., 26–7.
133   E.g. Cross (1979), 17.
134   This is the view taken by Michael and Adler and others. Some, like Cross, maintain that evidence has to be 'sufficiently relevant', thereby incorporating other tests. The difference is probably one of semantics, not substance.
135   Op. cit., 56. Bentham also uses the term 'stock of knowledge'.
136   Cohen (1977), 274–5; criticized in *TEBW*, ch. 3; cf. Binder and Bergman (1984), 82ff.
137   Berger and Luckmann, 16.
138   Id., 170; cf. Berger (1966), 55, 170.
139   Id., 41.
140   This theme is elaborated in Twining (1973), 275.
141   See, for example, the papers by Cicourel, Garfinkel, Zimmerman and Weider in Turner (ed.) (1974), Part III; cf. J. M. Atkinson (1978).
142   This is a theme of Trigg's *Reality at Risk* (1980) in which he argues the case for realism, and especially the notion of 'objectivity': 'There is a fundamental divergence between those who wish to "construct" reality out of man's experience, concepts, language or whatever, and those who start with the idea that what exists does so whether man conceives it or not' (vii). My own view is that at least some of those who apply 'constructionist' approaches to law do not need to commit themselves to the kind of position that Trigg criticizes but, as we shall see, they make statements that are vulnerable in this respect.
143   Op. cit., n. 123.
144   Id., 9.
145   Id., 13.
146   Garfinkel (1956), 420.
147   E.g. at 11.
148   Id., 13. See further on 'mistakes' and miscarriages of justice, below, 261 n. 148.
149   Id., 15.
150   For a more balanced treatment, see Binder and Bergman (1984). See below, ch. 6.
151   An example of a potentially illuminating study that is marred by grossly underestimating

the sophistication of orthodox views of legal process is Bennett and Feldman's *Reconstructing Reality in the Courtroom*, op. cit., n. 123. The authors claim that 'the use of stories to reconstruct the evidence in cases casts doubt on the common belief about justice as a mechanical and objective process' (Preface). This is to pick a rather soft target for attack and does not do justice to the sophistication of the legal literature on the subject. Bennett and Feldman are careful not to deny any place to empirical standards for evaluating evidence; rather they argue that stories serve as aids to *selecting* from a superfluity of information and to *filling in gaps* in that information; stories provide frames of reference for evaluating and interpreting evidence in terms of completeness and consistency. Unfortunately the authors did not direct their attention to the standard accounts by lawyers of how the problems of selection, incompleteness and inconsistency are supposed to be tackled. In particular, by ignoring almost entirely such lawyers' notions as facts in issue, materiality, relevance, burdens of proof, presumptions and, most surprising of all, the advocate's notion of 'the theory of the case', they fail to reach a point where issue is squarely joined with standard legal accounts. On stories, see further below, ch. 7.

152   That an empirically oriented 'constructionist' approach to legal process need not talk past traditional, unempirical writings by lawyers is illustrated by Doreen McBarnett's valuable study, *Conviction* (1981). McBarnett argues that there is not merely a gap between the law in action and the law in books, but an even more significant gap between the detailed rules of evidence and procedure and what she calls 'the rhetoric of justice'. I find her main argument quite persuasive, but the book is not entirely free from the kind of rhetorical exaggeration that she imputes to the official ideology. On the basis of a literalistic reading of selected passages in *Conviction* one might construct a set of propositions which provide what looks like a striking contrast with the core assumptions of the Rationalist Tradition: truth and reality are subjective and relative; conceptions of reality are multifaceted and unbounded; facts are constructs, as simple or as complex as lawyers make them; in the adversary system advocates are not concerned with 'truth', but with arguing a case – an edited version of reality, constructed from diverse sources, filtered through simplifying concepts such as relevance, standards of proof and facts in issue, and manipulated and organized into a persuasive argument and presented to the trier of fact in an acceptable form; the task of the latter is not to inquire into the truth, but to choose between two 'cases', caricatures of morality constructed and presented as competing versions of reality. 'Both in its concepts and its form the legal system copes with problems of proof and truth by redefining them.' The strength of a case is a function of the technical skills of lawyers, the resources available to each party, and 'the structural opportunities and limitations' offered by the legal system rather than of something inherent in the original situation that is purportedly being reconstructed. In this view, truth, justice and reason are part of the rhetoric of the system that is reflected neither in the detailed rules nor in the actual practices of the courts.

    This reconstruction of McBarnett's view, although it follows closely the language of the text, also smacks of caricature. Indeed, it would be difficult to make much sense of McBarnett's perceptive study if she were seriously committed to any strong version of any of the three kinds of philosophical scepticism discussed above: in her own descriptions she needs some notions of information, facts, accuracy, truth, proof, and science; as a sociologist her primary concern is more with understanding than with evaluation; but the very eloquence of her advocacy suggests a degree of commitment that sits uneasily with nihilism or an extreme form of ethical relativism; indeed, it is far from clear that she rejects the values embodied in the liberal democratic notions of justice which, in her view, the system fails to honour in its rules or practices.

153   Rabelais, *The Heroic Deeds of Gargantua and Pantagruel* (1542–52, Sir Thomas Urquhart's translation), Bk. 3, chs. 39–44.

154   Id., ch. 39.

155   Id., ch. 40.
156   Ibid. Sir Richard Eggleston, who may take credit for reminding us of Judge Bridlegoose, interprets Bridlegoose as 'putting himself under divine guidance which revealed itself in the fall of the dice' (1983), 1. It is true that Epistemon suggests, as a possible justification for the Bridlegoose Method, that the hand of Providence may reveal itself in the fall of the dice, but I favour a secular interpretation of the Judge's own view of the matter.
157   W. F. Smith (1918), 130–1; cf. Rabelais, op. cit., chs. 11–14.
158   Ibid.
159   In interpreting the Bridlegoose Challenge it is important to remember that it is not necessary that each side should have an even chance of winning; *semble* in civil cases this was the Judge's measure. Thus Bridlegoose can accommodate policies favouring one kind of error over another, e.g. preferring acquittal to conviction of the innocent.
160   E.g. Eggleston, op. cit., 1–2; Ellman and Kaye (1979).
161   On the conditions for the application of the calculus of probability generally, see Finkelstein (1978), ch. 1; Eggleston, op. cit., *passim*, esp. ch. 2.
162   It may be objected that it is a fallacy to assume that the prior probabilities in litigation are equal. Legal procedures are designed to filter out frivolous or groundless claims and charges, with the result that for any case that comes to trial the prior probabilities are not equal: few plaintiffs will ever get into court without any evidence to support their allegations; similarly most people who are prosecuted are in fact guilty. To which Bridlegoose might reply: 'First, what empirical evidence do you have to support such statements? Show me! Secondly, the rules of your system, as exemplified by burdens of proof, standards of proof and presumptions, frequently prescribe that the case should be decided *as if* the prior probabilities are even or, as in the case of the presumption of innocence, that the prior probabilities are to be treated either as equal or as favouring the defence, *despite* your claim that most people who are prosecuted are in fact guilty. Thirdly, if you wish to challenge the assumption that the prior probabilities should be treated as evenly balanced, please show me an agreed alternative basis for establishing the priors. Finally, it is not necessary for me to make such an assumption. In the circumstances of Mirelingues, it seemed to me to be a reasonable assumption to make. However, the rules for judging by the dice could be adjusted to fit different assumptions about prior probability, if only I knew what these assumptions were.' I am not concerned here to evaluate the validity of these arguments. It is sufficient for present purposes to show that there is scope for disagreement among reasonable men about what assumptions should be made about prior probabilities in evaluating evidence. Indeed one may ask whether doubts and difficulties surrounding the topic of prior probabilities do not reveal a chink in the armour of the Rationalist Tradition? On prior probabilities, see especially Kaye (1980); Tribe (1971) at 1368–70; Finkelstein, (1978) at 295–8.
163   See Kaye (1980), 601 for a critique of the notion that the 'more probable than not' standard equalizes errors between plaintiffs and defendants.
164   See above, n. 159. For the case against quantification of the standard of proof in criminal cases see Tribe (1971), 1329.
165   In the case of Toucheronde Bridlegoose conceded that one condition for the application of the doctrine of chances was not satisfied: he could not be relied on to read the dice correctly; but infirmity was a complete defence to such transgressions. W. F. Smith, op. cit., 130–2. Before examining this challenge in the light of recent debates about probabilities it may be useful to anticipate some obvious objections.

First, it may be asked, why should we take Bridlegoose seriously? Rabelais was a satirist who wrote with his tongue in his cheek; he is thought to have been arguing for appeals to broad principles rather than obscure and arbitrary technicalities. His own assumptions are quite compatible with aspirational rationalism. A simple answer is that there are some contemporary arguments that at least *prima facie* appear to lead to positions very close to Bridlegoose's brand of scepticism. Furthermore, Bridlegoose presents a direct challenge at a fundamental level to claims that we have a rational system of adjudication: 'Show me,' he says, 'that it is rational and that it is likely to produce better results in practice than throwing dice.'

Secondly, it may be objected, the doctrine of chances is not the correct aspect of the calculus of probability to apply to judgments of probability in forensic contexts; in most cases, it is Bayes's Theorem, or statistical calculations of frequency or some theory of subjective probabilities or wagering theory which is applicable. This objection is based on a confusion between using mathematics as the basis for reasoning towards (and justifying) probability judgments and throwing dice *instead* of 'reasoning'. The Bridlegoose challenge is that throwing dice ensures a higher probability of reaching correct *results* than do so-called 'rational' methods, irrespective of which theory of reasoning is espoused.

Finally, it may be objected, there are insuperable methodological and practical obstacles to testing the accuracy of the results of any system of adjudication. This objection may take several forms. One version is that a legal system sets its own standards and procedures for ascertaining 'legal truth'. There are no external methods for assessing the truth or accuracy or reliability of its findings. Truth is *determined* by adjudicative decisions; so long as the rules have been observed, what is determined to be true *is* true for this purpose.

A second version accepts that there are in theory external criteria for evaluating the accuracy or probability of adjudicative decisions – for example, by using the methods of historians to assess the probable historical truth of particular judicial determinations of fact. However, it is argued, no practicable method has yet been devised for making such assessments except in a few isolated cases. Thus we may come to the conclusion that as a matter of historical fact it was not James Hanratty who killed Michael Gregston, but no means has been or is likely to be devised for assessing the general reliability of adjudicative decisions by such criteria. I happen to think that such views are mistaken, but I shall not explore the reasons here. The relevant point in this context is that they constitute a refusal to meet Bridlegoose's challenge in its empirical aspect. The Judge says: 'Show me that your method produces better results than mine.' The objector says: 'That is not possible.' 'Exactly,' says the Judge, 'I have statistics on my side; you merely have faith in something you call Reason.'

166 Kaplan (1968); Finkelstein and Fairley (1970); see also Finkelstein (1978), op. cit.; Tribe, op. cit.; Eggleston, op. cit.; Cullison, op. cit. Earlier discussions include Ball (1961) and Ekelof (1964). For a bibliography see Twining (ed.) (1983), 156–7.
167 See generally Eggleston (1983), op. cit.
168 L.J. Cohen (1977); (1980), 91.
169 Williams (1979) (Parts I and II); Eggleston (1979), 678; L.J. Cohen (1980); Williams (1980).
170 See bibliography op. cit., n. 166 and 1 Wigmore *Treatise* (Tillers rev. 1983), s.37. See further Tillers and Green (1988).
171 R.F. Atkinson (1978), 67–8.
172 Finkelstein, op. cit., 63.
173 Wigmore (1937), 858ff.; *TEBW*, ch. 3.
174 Finkelstein, 63.
175 This is hinted at by Tillers, op. cit., n. 170. A different line of reply to Bridlegoose is suggested by Marcus Singer in discussing the censure of Judge William H. (Hawk) Daniels of Baton Rouge for flipping coins to determine verdicts, 'Judicial Decisions and Judicial Opinions' (1983, 22–3):

> Many judges have indicated that they would like on occasion to be able to decide cases in this way, and some have written learned articles extolling the advantages of the hunch or of guessing as a method of getting a just decision. Judges who write this

way about the practice of deciding cases and issuing opinions do not noticeably write fewer opinions than those who hold an opposite view, and that such a view has not had any appreciable effect on their actual practice is something to marvel at.

But let it be known – widely known – that judges decide cases regularly by flipping coins, and what will happen to the legal system? To answer this, we have to consider again the functions of courts of law, in the context of considering the aims of a legal system and why a legal system has courts of law. It is not enough for a legal system merely to decide cases. If it were, there would be nothing that could be said against deciding them by flipping coins. The second, third, and fourth functions I suggested – to interpret the law, to fill in the interstices in the law, and to determine legal validity – can be put aside in the present context as not essential to the functions of a court of law, though the second and third clearly are essential in a legal system considered as a whole. But it is not enough, as I have just said, simply to decide cases. It is also necessary, fifth, to decide cases *in accordance with justice*, and, sixth, in such a way as to *satisfy the public sense of justice* – that is, so that it will be generally believed, and for good reason, that cases are being decided in accordance with justice, or at least that an honest attempt is being made to settle cases in accordance with justice. But this means that it is being taken for granted, as an item of public faith in the society, that an honest attempt is being made to settle cases *on their merits*, and this presupposes, on the one hand, that there are merits, and, on the other, that these merits can be ascertained. A legal system in which cases are known to be decided by such methods as flipping coins could not long meet the condition of satisfying the public sense of justice, because it could not meet the condition of deciding cases in accordance with justice, and it would be known that it could not meet that condition. Knowledge of the practice would be a signal that either judges did not believe that cases had merits, or did not believe that they could ascertain them if they did, or did not believe that it was worth the trouble to ascertain them if they could. But people who want their day in court do believe, and very strongly, that their cases do have merits; the net result would be a crashing loss of confidence in the legal system.

176   'Standpoint' and related notions are considered in more detail in Twining (1973), 275 and Twining and Miers (1982), *passim*, esp. 64–71, 117–18, 172–83, 218–19.

177   Hart (1961), esp. 55–6, 86–8. The link between Hart's 'internal point of view' and the so-called hermeneutic approaches of social theorists such as Weber and Winch as well as philosophers (notably the later Wittgenstein and J. L. Austin) is admirably portrayed in D. N. MacCormick (1981), ch. 3.

178   Discussed in works cited above, n. 176.

179   Rawls (1955), esp. 6–7.

180   Twining and Miers, op. cit., n. 176, at 286–91.

181   Discussed in Twining (1973), 294–5.

182   There are some notable exceptions, e.g. for a discussion of relevance in sentencing, Streatfield (1961), paras. 267ff.; Shapland (1981). Once again, Bentham was ahead of his time. See his treatment of indicative evidence (evidence of evidence) in vi *Works* 214; vii *Works*, 164–5. The importance of standpoint in constructing arguments about questions of fact is developed in *Analysis*.

183   The distinction beween participants and observers is emphasized by Harold Lasswell, Myres McDougal and their associates in numerous writings. See, for example, McDougal and Reisman (1981), 43ff. See below, n. 188.

184   For examples of the breakdown of the distinction see, for example, Jacobs (ed.) (1970); Wilkins (1964).

185   However, expository works do not necessarily take much account of the needs of practitioners nor of desirable educational objectives for law students. See further Twining (1973), 293–9.

186 Within the category of participant-oriented theories a number of further rough differentiations can be made. First, a distinction may be drawn between 'design theories' and participant working theories (see further above, n. 36). The former deal with the design of the system as a whole or with particular aspects of it and are addressed to the legislator; the latter make recommendations to participants about ways of operating within a given system; such recommendations may relate to ways of furthering the objectives of the system, to what constitutes good practice (which typically contains a mixture of normative and prudential elements) or purely prudential advice on how to further one's own ends within the system, whether or not it furthers the ends or values of the system (e.g. tactical advice to advocates on how to use objections to break the flow of an opponent's examination or cross-examination). Much confusion arises in legal discourse because the theoretical objectives of the adversary system (on one view, to maximize rectitude of decision through disputation) are sometimes conflated with the objectives of partisan participants (to win). For example, the Hard-nosed Practitioner who claims that the trial is a game or his role is to win on behalf of his client may or may not be challenging 'truth theories' of the adversary process; if he is, it is not always clear whether the criticism is that the adversary system is a bad means of achieving rectitude of decision or that it is naïve or hopelessly optimistic or just plain wrong to postulate rectitude of decision as the primary objective of a system of adjudication (from the standpoint of the legislator). More commonly what is meant is that the practitioner's objectives are different from those of the system.
187 E.g. Campbell and Wiles (1976), 547–78.
188 Lasswell and MacDougal, op. cit., above, n. 183, claim to adopt the standpoint of 'the observer' and to be constructive, rather than critical. However, many – including the present writer – are sceptical of this claim. See further, Tipson (1974), 577–80.
189 Above, 92–3; cf. the difficulties for inter-disciplinary cooperation between members of a traditionally 'scientific' discipline like psychology and of a participant-oriented discipline like law.
190 That information is 'constructed' and 'processed' in litigation and other legal transactions is not quite such a new idea as sociological writers sometimes appear to suggest; witness, for example, the more sophisticated historical treatments of the use of the forms of action or Bentham's discussion of pre-appointed evidence. However, assertions of the kind that a witness's story or 'version of reality' has been 'transformed', 'translated' or 'distorted' in court proceedings need to be dissected carefully. A particular witness may have information (a) that is clearly irrelevant to the enterprise, judged by the criteria of relevance of each side and of the court; (b) that only deals with one small aspect of some broader picture, the prosecution's 'theory of the case', the jury's attempts to piece together the whole story or, more analytically, the evidence bearing on the facts in issue; (c) that is relevant to the facts in issue (or the prosecution's case or whatever), but is not so *perceived* by the professional participants; (d) that could be perceived as relevant by all concerned, but the witness is inhibited or prevented from providing it by some contingent feature of the proceedings, with the result that the witness is not given the opportunity to present the information or fails to produce it (because he or she is overawed or confused or inarticulate) or produces it, but what is said is misunderstood or distorted or its significance (in the system's own terms) is overlooked. It is also worth remembering that documentary evidence is less susceptible than oral evidence to such 'processing', and that provisions for pre-appointed evidence are intended specifically to minimize this kind of problem.
191 See further, Twining (1973).
192 See further, Twining and Miers (1982), 346–7.
193 On 'rectitude of decision' as an aspiration for all official decision making, see below, 201–2.
194 Mehan and Wood (1975), 68, cited in Trigg (1980), x.
195 Id., xvii.

196   I have argued elsewhere that where there is leeway for different interpretations of a case or a statute, the *appropriateness* of one of a number of possible interpretations is in large part a function of the role and objectives of the interpreter. In the same case a cautious solicitor and a bold barrister, both representing the same client at different stages, may each argue for wider or narrower interpretations of some rule; because the role of the solicitor is often to advise within a margin of error, while the role of the barrister in court is to argue in order to win. To suggest that different interpretations are *appropriate* for different participants, within the leeways of a range of possible interpretations, involves no necessary commitment to the view that there is never one *correct* interpretation for all participants. If the rule is clear the cautious solicitor, the bold barrister and even the tricky unhappy interpreter may all be stuck with the same interpretation. See Twining and Miers (1982), 171–81.

197   See below, 366 ff.

198   Hughes (1959), 430.

199   Berger and Luckmann, op. cit., 21–2.

200   See generally Hughes, op. cit., ch. 8.

201   Id., 431.

202   The distinction between 'concept' and 'conception' is usually attributed to Gallie (1956). It has been employed to good effect by jurists, e.g. Hart (1961), 155–9; Dworkin (1977), 134–7. See also Rawls (1972). In his very interesting critique of *TEBW*, Professor Dennis Galligan overlooks this crucial distinction when he states: 'Also, it is puzzling to see the Rationalist Tradition advanced as a product of a particular view of rationality which was established in the eighteenth century; it seems rather to be based on the view of rationality common to Western civilization' (Galligan, 1988, 264). He goes on to suggest that the only alternative is 'irrationality' or some version of scepticism. My argument was rather that the Rationalist Tradition adopted a particular *conception* of what constitute valid, cogent and appropriate arguments about questions of fact in legal contexts. That conception is broadly associated with Locke, Bentham, J. S. Mill and their successors. The main alternative considered in these essays relates to 'holistic' conceptions of fact-determination – which can be related historically to such varied thinkers as Hegel, the Scottish common sense school (see Glassford above, 77), Quine, Rorty and possibly Habermas. One does not need to trespass too far into a philosophical minefield to suggest that there is more than one conception of rationality abroad in our intellectual heritage. Far from being 'startling', this seems to me to be a modest claim. A bolder, less culture-bound approach, might take Clifford Geertz's *Local Knowledge* (1983), ch. 8 as its starting-point. E.g.

> And: other marketplaces, other *Anschaungen* ... such [legal] sensibilities differ not only in the degree to which they are indeterminate; in the power they exercise, vis-à-vis other modes of thought and feeling, over the processes of social life ... or in their particular style and content. They differ, and markedly, *in the means they use – the symbols they deploy, the stories they tell, the distinctions they draw, the visions they project – to represent events in judiciable form.* (id., 175, italics added)

Within our own legal culture, like Galligan, I am sceptical of most claims to philosophical scepticism that have been made by or about Anglo-American jurists; unlike him I am not convinced of the adequacy of the particular conception of rationality embodied in the Rationalist model.

203   *An Introductory View of the Rationale of Judicial Evidence*, VI *Works*, 5.

204   Many of these terms are recognized as problematic in more than one discipline; some may even rank as 'essentially contested concepts'. Within the discipline of law there is an extensive and, in some respects, rewarding literature on such difficult notions as 'fact', 'relevance' and 'probability'. Moreover, a highly sophisticated apparatus of concepts and distinctions has been developed, largely by judges and writers on evidence: standards of proof, presumptions, burdens of proof (and of persuasion),

materiality, admissibility, conditional relevance, legislative facts are leading examples. My impression is that only classical and modern rhetoric has so rich a heritage of carefully analysed terms. Yet we have a near-paradox. For this conceptual sophistication owes very little to orthodox jurisprudential analysis. By and large the attention of analytical jurists, as reflected in textbooks on Jurisprudence and the work of modern leaders of the field, such as H. L. A. Hart and Joseph Raz, has been directed elsewhere. The major exception, the notion of 'fact', is typically considered in the rather confined contexts of distinctions between fact and value, and fact and law. By and large, the theory of judicial evidence and its basic concepts have been neglected by mainstream legal theory. There is a simple explanation for this neglect. Orthodox analytical jurisprudence followed the Expository Orthodoxy in concentrating very largely on rules, on private law and on disputed questions of law. 'Legal reasoning' was concerned hardly, if at all, with disputed questions of fact or with the nature of argument and justification relating to other decisions in legal processes. Similarly, legal theory has had fruitful links with ethics and political theory, but has paid far less attention to the philosophy of mind and the philosophy of knowledge (including the philosophy of science and of history). It has been fashionable in recent years to dismiss analytical jurisprudence as old-fashioned, trivial and sterile. A broadened conception of law as a discipline cannot afford to dispense with conceptual analysis: rather it needs to insist that attention should be directed to elucidating and refining a much broader range of concepts. In developing its concepts evidence scholarship did rather well with at best spasmodic help from mainstream legal theory. Recent developments, as exemplified by the debate about probabilities, suggest that philosophers and legal theorists may be more willing in future to give sustained attention to the field of evidence.

205 Rescher (1980), discussed above, 102.
206 Fischer (1970), discussed above, 105.
207 Galligan (1988) is particularly good on the coherence of the tradition.
208 On distortions see Twining (1984), 281–2, and below, chs. 5 and 11. Silence has been the main strategy of defence by the Expository Orthodoxy against challenges by those who, in different ways, seek to broaden the study of law. It is an effective line of defence for a tough, coherent, well-established way of treating a subject. One response to silence is Ignoring. In polemical jurisprudence one debates with one's friends and talks past one's enemies. But there is far too much of potential value in the heritage of our literature on evidence for that to be a sensible option.
209 The two models can also be viewed, independently of any specific historical claim that is made about them, as a convenient heuristic device for mapping at a fairly general level a range of possible divergent views. The models were deliberately constructed in different ways. The statement of assumptions (Model II) was formulated in terms which kept as close as possible to recognizable positions of leading writers on evidence. The Rationalist model of adjudication (Model I), on the other hand, draws heavily on Bentham who in some respects took an extreme position. It is broken down into elements which consciously signal possible points of departure. It might be said to be deliberately provocative. One reason for this difference of treatment was that by and large the underlying assumptions of Model II are more clearly assignable to most writers on evidence and are subject to less controversy than those of Model I.
210 Dave Campbell has pointed out to me that the prevailing ideology and class-based pressures, in a society such as our own, can be interpreted as creating a situation in which there are competing versions of reality, but such an interpretation involves no commitment to philosophical scepticism.
211 John Jackson has suggested that it may be useful to isolate another kind of scepticism,

> perhaps a combination of 'nature-of-the-enterprise scepticism' and 'legal fact-scepticism', which claims that legal inquiries *are* qualitatively different from other fact-finding inquiries because there are so many goals and values apart from

truth-seeking in the legal inquiry. The claim is *not just* that pragmatic concessions are made to avoid vexation, expense and delay in the legal inquiry, since concessions like these and others are made in many inquiries, but that certain conflicting goals and values (for example demands for speedy *final* settlement, 'having one's day in court', 'winning', 'due process', lay participation in decision making, etc.) are such a part of the legal inquiry that the pursuit of truth is *necessarily* compromised. The view is one of a pessimistic rationalist who claims that these conflicts of value cannot be satisfactorily or rationally resolved until there is some *agreed* method of resolution which there is not at present because the participants within the system, taking different standpoints, and observers outside, cannot agree on priorities. (personal communication to the author, February 1984.)

If this essay had been written in 1988, I would have said more about 'nature-of-the-enterprise scepticism' and in particular the significance of institutional design, the manifest and latent functions of litigation and its uses by and consequences for different actors in different contexts.

212 *Acknowledgements*. In the long period of the gestation of this paper I have incurred more debts than can appropriately be acknowledged. Subject to the normal disclaimers about responsibility, I am particularly grateful to all those who contributed to discussions in seminars in Edinburgh, Kent, Miami, Warwick and Wolfson College, Oxford, and especially to Terry Anderson, Zenon Bankowski, Dave Campbell, Ken Casebeer, Richard DeFriend, Bob Gordon, John Jackson, Doreen McBarnett, Neil MacCormick, Christopher McCrudden, David Miers, Robert Stevens, Larry Taman, Peter Tillers and many other colleagues and friends for helpful criticisms and suggestions.

5

Identification and Misidentification in Legal Processes: Redefining the Problem

In recent years the problem of misidentification, especially in criminal cases, has attracted a good deal of attention from the media, lawyers, psychologists, and others. One influential, but by no means universally held, view of the problem might be stated in some such terms as these: From time to time an innocent man is convicted by a jury of a crime he did not – or probably did not – commit, on the basis, mainly or entirely of eyewitness testimony relating to identification. Typically this testimony is honest, but mistaken. It may be only half-a-dozen or so chaps a year, who suffer such miscarriages of justice and some of these are professional criminals who might well have been put inside for some other offence; no system of criminal justice can be expected to eliminate all mistakes, but our legal tradition and public opinion place a high value on safeguarding the innocent, even at the price of letting some, but not an unlimited number, of criminals go free. The problem peculiar to identification is that the value of the evidence is exceptionally difficult to assess. The task is to reduce the risk of error by taking measures to improve the law and procedure governing *evidence* of identification. In this view the main relevance of psychology to the problem of misidentification is thought to relate to the cognitive processes of individual witnesses (notably perception, attention, memory, bias, and suggestion) rather than to cognitive processes of other participants and interactive aspects of legal processes.

The purpose of this essay is to suggest that this orthodox view presents an artificially narrow definition of the problem and that future research and public debate about the problem of identification in legal processes would benefit from being set in the context of a comprehensive model of legal processes, and of a clearly articulated, integrated, theoretical framework; that information about the identity of a person or persons thought to be involved in some event or situation has a bearing not solely on adjudication of guilt or innocence, but on a wide variety of decisions each of which may have potentially harmful or unpleasant consequences for persons who are objects of identification; that such information needs to be regarded not only as evidence, but also as potential evidence and as information relevant to other decisions; and that the ways in which it is 'processed' and used and the operation of factors which affect its reliability or completeness (or other 'validity') need to be considered at every stage in the process. Finally, I shall argue that redefining the problem of misidentification in this way raises questions about the scale and distribution of the phenomena as they have been perceived in the Devlin Report on Evidence of Identification in Criminal Cases[1] and the debate surrounding that report.

The essay proceeds as follows: In the first section I shall consider the implications for perceptions of the problem of identification of adopting one of two different perspectives, which can crudely be designated as 'expository' and 'contextual' approaches to law. I shall argue that there are certain general tendencies and biases in the expository tradition that are reflected in part in the standard legal literature on the law of evidence, in contrast with most contemporary writing about legal processes which tends to be more in tune with a contextual approach; and I shall examine the extent to which these biases are found in the literature on identification. In the following section I shall sketch, in the form of an ideal type, a profile of a standard case of the problem of misidentification that reflects some of the biases both in the expository literature and in official or orthodox definitions of the problem – I shall argue that a broader 'information model' of misidentification may provide the basis for a more systematic and more realistic approach to the topic. In the final section the main elements of the problem of misidentification are re-examined in the light of the previous discussion and some implications of adopting a broader perspective in this context are suggested.

The analysis takes as its starting-point the Devlin Report and four very useful books on the psychological aspects of eyewitness testimony and identification by Clifford and Bull, Loftus, Yarmey and Lloyd-Bostock and Clifford.[2] Those four works, together with the chapters in the present volume, adequately survey the literature and provide a convenient basis for taking stock and considering future directions: for the purpose of this chapter these works will be taken as representative of the literature on identification. It is part of the thesis of this chapter that *some* discussions of identification have been influenced by some of the biases in the expository approach – notably a tendency to concentrate on adjudicative decisions in contested criminal cases and to view information about identity largely, if not solely, in terms of admissible evidence presented to a jury. However, it is important to emphasize at the outset that by no means all writers on the subject have taken so narrow a view of the subject. In particular this chapter should not be read as a critique of recent contributions by psychologists to the study of eyewitness identification and related problems. The psychological literature has not been entirely free of some of the narrow assumptions that are criticized here; but the main thrust of the chapter is to warn against some tendencies in legal literature and to sketch the basis for a broader perspective on the subject.

Two Perspectives on Law and Legal Processes

At some risk of over-simplification it is convenient to postulate two contrasting approaches to the study of law which are current in the United Kingdom and, with some more or less significant variations, in the United States and other parts of the English-speaking world. Each approach suggests a differing perspective on the problem of identification and hence on the potential contribution of psychologists and others. The first, which I shall refer to as the Expository Tradition, is sometimes known as 'legal formalism' or 'the black letter approach'. It has, at least until recently, dominated academic law in the United Kingdom during this century and it is exemplified by such standard works as *Cross on Evidence, Smith and Hogan on Criminal Law*, and *Salmond on Torts*.[3] In this view, the study of law consists predominantly of the exposition, analysis and, to a lesser extent, criticism of the rules of positive law in force in a given jurisdiction. Its protagonists would readily concede that history, the social sciences, and other disciplines are relevant to an understanding of law, but they tend to treat them as marginal and not really part of the specialized study of law. Thus the subject matter of evidence is the *rules* of evidence; *Cross on Evidence* for example, scarcely makes any reference to the logical, mathematical, epistemological, scientific, psychological or other 'non-legal' aspects of evidence and proof. Cross sharply differentiates the law of evidence from the law of procedure and from substantive law. Much legal writing about evidence proceeds on the assumption that if there were no rules of evidence there would be nothing for lawyers to study. Similarly, within the Expository Tradition, even the study of procedure has been largely confined to the rules of procedure. Few legal scholars have adhered rigidly and consistently to this view, but its influence has nevertheless been both pervasive and profound. It has not merely influenced legal education and legal scholarship, but has also provided the main underlying basis for the ways of thought and discourse about law of most practising lawyers and judges, even in the context of debates about reform.

An alternative approach (only one of several alternatives) I shall refer to here as the Contextual Approach.[4] The central unifying tenet of this approach is that rules are important – indeed a central feature of law – but for the purposes of understanding, criticizing or even expounding the law, the study of rules alone is not enough. Rather, legal rules, institutions, procedures, practices, and other legal phenomena need to be set in some broader context. What constitutes an appropriate context depends on the purposes of the study or other discourse in question. For example, if one is concerned to study the law of evidence in action, the rules of evidence need to be viewed in the context of the legal processes in which they in fact operate and those processes may need to be seen in the context of other social processes. In this view, the rules of evidence are only one small part of the subject of evidence and proof.[5] The rounded study of evidence, as part of the study of law, would include logical, philosophical, psychological, processual, and other dimensions. In order to make such a study coherent and manageable an overarching theory of evidence (or evidence and proof) is needed which provides a unifying conceptual framework, and, at the very least, maps the connections between these various aspects or dimensions.[6]

It is not necessary to canvass the much-discussed merits and limitations of these two different approaches;[7] but it is relevant to consider briefly certain tendencies or biases in the Expository Tradition that are to be found in some of the legal literature that has a bearing on the present subject. In its extreme form the Expository Tradition tends: (a) to be rule-centred; (b) to pay disproportion-ate attention to the decisions of appellate courts; (c) to treat jury trials as the paradigm of all trials; (d) to concentrate on events in the courtroom, to the exclusion of pre-trial and post-trial events; (e) to adopt a rationalistic and aspirational approach to problems of evidence rather than an empirical perspective; and (f) in discussing reform, to take existing rules and devices as the starting-point for response to problems, with a consequent tendency to be rather thin on diagnosis.

All of these tendencies are to be found to a greater or lesser extent in expository legal literature, as exemplified by orthodox treatments of the Law of Evidence; they are less marked in recent legal literature on judicial processes. I shall suggest that examples of some, but not all, of these tendencies have spilled over into recent discussions of identification.

Rule-centredness

We have seen that there is a tendency in the Anglo-American literature to treat the rules of evidence as constituting all, or nearly all, of the subject of evidence. It happens to be the case that the Anglo-American systems have by and large turned away from trying to regulate questions of *cogency* (or weight) and questions of *quantum* (amount) of evidence by means of rigid rules. (One of the few exceptions to this are the rules requiring corroboration in certain limited situations.) The great bulk of evidence doctrine is concerned with the rules of admissibility and exclusion – that is to say, rules governing what evidence may or may not be presented in what form and by whom to the decision maker.[8] This represents a partial victory for Jeremy Bentham, who argued that there should be *no* formal rules of evidence.[9] Since the middle of the nineteenth century there has been a general, if slow, trend in the direction of de-regulating evidence along the lines advocated by Bentham. However, as is well known, his victory has not been complete, especially in the United States. What is signific-ant in the present context is the fact that many aspects of presenting and weighing evidence are not governed by formal rules at all and that it is widely recognized that changes in the law of evidence represent only one of a number of possible strategies for tackling problems of misidentification. Thus, the Devlin Report conspicuously rejected the idea of a formal rule requiring corroboration of eyewitness identification testimony or of excluding such evidence; and it was generally sceptical as to whether much could be achieved by changing legal rules, except perhaps rules governing procedures of identi-fication parades.

The literature on identification is not strikingly rule-centred in the sense of focusing on formal rules: more attention has been paid to techniques for improving reliability of identification and to warnings about the pitfalls and dangers of eyewitness identification, independently of the formal rules of evidence. Nevertheless, some writers have from time to time talked as if this is part of the *law* of evidence. For example, Professor John Kaplan in his introduction to Elizabeth Loftus's *Eyewitness Testimony* treats the book as 'a contribution to the *law* of evidence' and implies it is strange that 'there are virtually *no* rules which govern what witnesses may say they saw with their own eyes'.[10] This is a harmless example of rule-centred talk. Ironically, Professor Kaplan himself has made a pioneering contribution to the discussion of probabilities and proof,[11] another topic concerned with evidence where significant steps have been taken away from the rule-dominated treatment of evidentiary issues in recent years. Elizabeth Loftus herself, in considering possible responses to the problem of unreliability of eyewitness testimony explicitly rejects formal rules of exclusion or of corroboration as remedies; she is dubious about the efficacy of cautionary instructions to the jury and she advocates, as the most important remedy, a more widespread use of psychologists as expert witnesses.[12] Suffice it to say here that problems of misidentification are only marginally concerned with the formal rules of evidence and that this has by and large been recognized in the literature.

'Appellate court-itis'

The American jurist Jerome Frank identified one of the major diseases of legal formalism as 'appellate court-itis' – that is, a tendency to concentrate far too much attention on the work of appellate courts and disputed questions of law (as exemplified by the commanding position in legal literature occupied by law reports), with a corresponding almost total neglect of the work of trial courts and of disputed questions of fact.[13] Not surprisingly, the literature on eyewitness identification is largely free of this bias; for example, the Devlin Committee cited barely a dozen appellate cases, while devoting nearly sixty pages to the detailed analysis of the total process involved in the cases of *Dougherty* and *Virag*, in striking contrast with most orthodox legal literature.[14] Elizabeth Loftus quite legitimately devotes a section to Supreme Court decisions on eyewitness testimony but fully recognizes that legal doctrine developed by the court is only a small part of the whole story.[15]

Jury-centredness

The first step away from 'appellate court-itis' is to shift attention from appellate to trial courts. There is a tendency in the orthodox literature on evidence to treat the contested jury trial as the paradigm case of all trials. This is understandable, though misleading, if only because the history and rationale of the rules of evidence are intimately bound up with the institution of the jury. Moreover rules of evidence tend to be applied more strictly in jury trials than in other proceedings. Nevertheless, this concentration on the jury has been strongly challenged by some writers. The American scholar, Kenneth Culp Davis has suggested that nearly all literature and discourse about evidence is dominated by 'jury thinking' and that this is inappropriate since only a tiny minority of all trials are jury trials.[16] The jury is less important in England than it is in the United States; an even smaller proportion of criminal cases, albeit many of the more serious ones, are tried by juries. The jury has almost completely atrophied in civil cases in this country and is on the decline in the United States.[17]

Apart from the obvious reason that juries tend to deal with more serious and more spectacular cases, another reason for the dominance of 'jury thinking' in much legal literature and public debate is that a high proportion of the contributors are judges and senior barristers, whose experience – at least their recent experience – has tended to be confined to jury trials. In the past academic lawyers have also tended to be prone to the biases of 'jury thinking', but recently increased academic attention has been paid to magistrates' courts and to tribunals.

Much of the literature on identification has been jury-centred. Psychologists writing on the subject such as Loftus, Yarmey, and Clifford and Bull, although they occasionally use examples from non-jury trials and other proceedings, sometimes seem to *assume* that eyewitness testimony of identification is presented to a jury. Even more striking is the fact that the Devlin Committee devoted only three pages out of nearly 200 to magistrates' courts and explicitly decided to limit their recommendations ('for the time being' [*sic*]) to trials on indictment. The main reason given for this was that disputes as to identity and disputes involving alibi evidence are rare in summary proceedings, but no evidence was advanced for these statements.[18] Thus it is fair to say that the bulk of literature about identification is strikingly jury-centred; whether this is justifiable will be considered below.

Court-centredness

The shifts from appellate courts to jury trials and from jury trials to all trials represent important steps in broadening the focus of attention of legal studies in the direction of a more balanced and realistic treatment of legal processes generally. An even more important advance has been to face the fact that what takes place in open court represents only one small part of legal processes and to follow through the implications of this perception. We all know that only a small minority of cases ever reach the stage of being contested in court and that the outcomes of contested cases are heavily influenced by events and decisions that have occurred before trial. Yet to an extraordinary extent orthodox legal literature and discourse have disguised these facts and their implications. This can be illustrated by contrasting standard works on evidence and on procedure. To put the matter in simplified form: the bulk of Anglo-American literature on *evidence* still tends to assume that the contested jury trial is the paradigm and to concentrate on events in the courtroom; on the other hand, nearly all modern Anglo-American literature on *procedure* considers total legal processes, starting with some initial situation or triggering event and following through a variety of stages of different kinds of process, often beyond formal adjudicative determinations of guilt or liability (or other determinations) to post-adjudicative decisions and events, such as sentencing, parole, and the enforcement of civil judgments.

During the past decade broader approaches have gained much wider acceptance in the United Kingdom, with the result that the dominance of the Expository Tradition has been quite successfully challenged, although first-class expository work is still, quite rightly, accepted as a respectable form of legal scholarship. This movement is quite neatly illustrated by the differences between three reports which have dealt, *inter alia*, with criminal evidence and procedure in recent years. The Eleventh Report of the Criminal Law Revision Committee (1972), which concentrated almost entirely on contested trials on indictment and on the operation of rules of evidence in court, is a fairly typical product of the Expository Tradition. In sharp contrast the later Report of the Royal Commission on Criminal Procedure (Philips Report, 1981) devoted more attention to police powers and pre-trial events and decisions than to proceedings at trial and was almost as much concerned with summary proceedings as with trials on indictment. The Philips Report in many respects is based on a contextual approach. Viewed thus, the Devlin Report can be treated as an example of a half-way house, combining features of both approaches; its analysis of the cases of *Dougherty* and *Virag* represents excellent case-studies based on a total process model and, in some respects, it took into account a variety of considerations; yet the Report is not entirely free of the biases and hidden assumptions of the Expository Tradition, as is illustrated by its concentration on contested jury trials and its failure to explore the scale and distribution of cases of misidentification.[19]

In so far as the debate on misidentification has concentrated on eyewitness *testimony*, and has treated identification parades solely as evidence-generating devices, it has tended to be court-centred. However, a shift towards a broader perspective is discernible in some recent writings.

Optimistic and complacent rationalism

Anglo-American evidence scholarship since the time of Jeremy Bentham has been remarkably homogeneous, not least in respect of its acceptance of the idea that modern methods of adjudication are 'rational'.[20] The dominant approach has been expository, as exemplified by the works of writers such as Starkie, Greenleaf, Taylor, Stephen, Phipson, McCormick and Cross. But Bentham's writings on evidence, Thayer's *A Preliminary Treatise on Evidence of Common Law* (1898), Michael and Adler's *The Nature of Judicial Proof* (1931), and Eggleston's *Evidence, Proof and Probability* (1978) are leading examples of an alternative tradition in which attempts have been made to go beyond exposition of the rules to deal with historical, logical, psychological, and other dimensions of evidence and proof. The greatest evidence scholar, the American, John Henry Wigmore, straddled both perspectives; his ten-volume *Treatise on Evidence* is generally regarded as one of the major achievements of expository scholarship; on the other hand, the historical aspects of the *Treatise* and his *Principles of Judicial Proof as Given by Logic, Psychology and General Experience* (later *The Science of Judicial Proof*) remain the single most important attempt since Bentham to establish a Science of Proof, based on a coherent general theory which covers both the rules of evidence and the non-legal aspects of probative processes.

Some of the best legal minds have contributed to this dual tradition of evidence scholarship. What is particularly striking about it is the remarkable homogeneity of the basic underlying assumptions of what may be termed the Rationalist Tradition of evidence scholarship. Almost without exception the leading Anglo-American scholars have, either explicitly or implicitly, adopted a view of adjudication which treats it as a rational process directed towards rectitude of decision, that is the correct application of valid substantive laws through accurate determination of the truth about past facts in issue (i.e. facts material to precisely specified allegations expressed in categories defined in advance by law).[21] This applies both to expository writers such as Phipson and Cross and those who were also interested in broader perspectives on evidence and proof, such as Wigmore.

The claim that the modern system of adjudication is 'rational' is best treated as a statement of what is considered to be an *aspiration* of the modern system; the aim is to maximize the rationality and accuracy of fact-finding in adjudication, so far as this is feasible and is compatible with other, overriding social values. Such aspirational rationalism does not necessarily involve a commitment to the view that the aspiration is always or even generally realized in practice. It is commonplace within the classical rationalist tradition to criticize the existing practices, procedures, rules, and institutions in terms of their failure to satisfy the standards of this aspirational model. Nor within this general framework of assumptions is there a general consensus on all particular issues; the intellectual history of Anglo-American scholarship and discourse has had its share of long-running debates,[22] but there has been an extraordinarily high degree of consensus within the tradition about the objective of maximizing rationality and accuracy in determination of questions of fact and about the underlying assumptions as to what this involves. To be an aspirational rationalist of this kind can reasonably be construed as involving a degree of optimism about the feasibility of the aspiration; in evaluating and considering possible improvements in existing legal rules, institutions, and practices it does not make sense to postulate completely unattainable goals. Optimism easily spills over into complacency and, with some notable exceptions (including Bentham himself), nearly all leading Anglo-American Evidence scholars have not only been optimistic about the feasibility of their ideals, they have also tended to be complacent about the basic design of the system and its actual workings and effects in practice. It is as if they had said: 'It is a poor show that a dozen or so chaps a year get gaoled or executed on the basis of unreliable identification evidence; we need to take steps to reduce the number of mistakes, but, after all, it is only a dozen or so ...'

It is important to notice that the Rationalist Tradition is not only rationalistic and optimistic, with a tendency to complacency. It is also aspirational and unempirical. The focus of attention in discussions of the logic of proof, and in debates about probabilities as part of those discussions, is on how people *ought* to reason in arguing, deciding, and justifying their decisions; it is not on how they in fact argue, decide, and justify. The study of logic is the study of what constitutes valid arguments; it is not the study of actual mental processes. One of the main reasons, I suspect, for the perennial uneasiness of relations between law and psychology is that, quite understandably, legal discourse is predominantly normative, while the dominant intellectual tradition of psychology is empirical. Lawyers, both academic and practising, are not primarily concerned with systematic description, explanation or understanding of events in the real world. Even in debates about the reform of particular rules a standard pattern is to move directly from the existing rule to a recommendation for 'improvement', with at best only highly impressionistic and superficial notions of its operation in practice. The dominant intellectual tradition in psychology being scientific – that is primarily concerned with systematic description, explanation and understanding and with the establishment and testing of empirical generalizations – it is conversely strong on the empirical and less concerned with the normative aspect.

The Rationalist Tradition of evidence scholarship is also unsceptical. Within legal discourse there is, however, a contrasting, but somewhat diverse strain of apparent scepticism. Rabelais's Bridlegoose threw dice to decide cases; Jerome Frank's 'fact-scepticism' emphasized some of the obstacles to predictability in judicial decision making; many lawyers view the adversary process more as a controlled form of battle in which the main objective of the contestants is to win rather than as a form of procedure designed to maximize the pursuit of truth through dialectical debate or disputation; contrasts between 'the law in books' and 'the law in action', between 'theory' and 'practice', and terms like 'the forensic lottery' are clichés in legal discourse. Before Karl Marx, Jeremy Bentham launched a full-scale attack on the mystifying devices of English law and procedure. Modern radical critics have carried on the tradition, arguing that many of the most cherished safeguards are merely a form of ideological façade and that 'adversary' proceedings are for a large part a myth. This alternative strand in legal thought is more in tune with the warnings by psychologists about the potential unreliability of various kinds of testimony than is optimistic rationalism. Yet, as I have argued in Chapter 4, many critical or seemingly sceptical writers tend to invoke the standards of prescriptive rationalism when criticizing existing practices or pointing to contrasts between aspiration and reality.

The way of the baffled medic: prescribe now, diagnose later – if at all[23]

In the Expository Tradition the existing rules of positive law are the natural starting-point for almost all legal discourse. There is a core of sense in the notion that one needs to know what the law is before starting to evaluate or to criticize it. But it is very easy to slide from this kind of attitude into a view of rules as things-in-themselves; once posited the law is the law independently of its origins or purposes. An alternative view of rules is to see tham as responses to problems, or as instruments designed to further certain purposes or policies. In this view it is almost always sensible to see particular rules or bodies of rules in the context of perceived problems to which they were a response or of the purposes which led to their creation. In evaluating or criticizing rules it is a good rule of thumb to identify and diagnose the problem before moving on to consider the adequacy or otherwise of the rule as a response to it. To study rules without reference to problems is like studying remedies without reference to diseases. Orthodox discussions of law reform follow the Way of the Baffled

Medic in so far as they substitute one prescription for another without any serious attempt to diagnose the problem.

The literature on reform of the law of evidence is replete with examples of this tendency. The standard weakness is to assume that the nature of the problem is self-evident and that the scale of its central factors is either well known or irrelevant. Thus the CLRC (Criminal Law Revision Committee) managed to treat professional criminals manipulating technical rules of evidence as typical of the behaviour of all persons accused of crimes. Nowhere in the literature on identification is there a full analysis of the nature, scale, and epidemiology of 'the problem of identification'. Typically the problem is *assumed* to be something to do with the unreliability of eyewitness testimony in jury trials; sometimes, as in the case of the Devlin Report, the nature of the problem is asserted with little by way of evidence or analysis. I shall endeavour to show below that the nature, scope, and scale of the problem of misidentification is by no means self-evident.

Many early discussions of identification parades provided, in a less obvious way, further examples of the operation of the fallacy of the Way of the Baffled Medic. So much attention has been focused, at least until recently, on this particular device that it has sometimes appeared as if the problem of identification is perceived as being co-extensive with some acknowledged defects and limitations of parade or line-up procedures and that the only, or at least the central, question is: How can the reliability of identification parades be improved? This is an interesting and legitimate question, but on its own it suffers from at least two limitations; it focuses on only one possible response to the problem of identification, assuming that one knows what the problem is; and it suggests that the only use of such procedures is to produce *evidence* of identification – whereas a study of decisions when and whether to hold parades might show that in some police areas there may be other objectives or uses; for example, the elimination of suspects or a decision to drop a case for want of evidence, or to persuade a suspect that the game is up. Where the identification parade is the starting-point of discussion there has perhaps been a tendency to take too much for granted both about the problem of identification and about the uses and latent functions of the device, to focus rather narrowly on a limited range of cases and to consider other possible devices, such as the use of photographs, too much in contrast with parades rather than to consider their potential in a variety of contexts. Starting from existing solutions, concentrating on only one of a possible range of devices, and not asking demographic questions about the phenomena under consideration are standard biases associated with the Expository Tradition.

Two Models of Misidentification

The contrast between the expository and contextual approaches to law may be reflected, at least in part, by contrasting views of what constitutes a standard case of misidentification. The analogy is not exact because, as we have seen, the orthodox definition of the problem does not simply reflect the tendencies and biases of an expository approach in its purest form. Nevertheless, it is possible to postulate a standard case, which is a fair reflection of the narrow view of the problem that was stated at the start of this paper. It may be helpful to depict this as an ideal type, consisting of a number of elements and to note some possible variants in respect of each element, as in table 3.

Three points about table 3 deserve comment. First, the standard case shares some, but not all, of the tendencies associated with the Expository Tradition (especially as illustrated by orthodox writings on evidence). In particular, it concerns an *incident* leading to a *contested case* tried before a *jury* in which the main role of the witness (W) is to provide *admissible evidence* of identification. The emphasis is on the objective reliability of evidence presented in *court*, and on *conviction* of innocent persons as the sole mischief of misidentification.

Second, in so far as psychologists and other writers on identification have tended to concentrate on examples which share all or most of the features of the standard case, they have also – perhaps unwittingly – shared some of the biases of the Expository Tradition. However, some researchers and commentators have pursued one or more variants of the standard case. For example, a good deal of attention has been paid to possible differentiating characteristics of witnesses, such as age, sex, and race: rather less attention has been paid to differentiating characteristics of subjects, except in regard to race.[24] Similarly as Baddeley and Woodhead have pointed out,[25] identification of persons may have special practical significance for certain occupations such as immigration officers, bank clerks, prostitutes, and the police. This raises questions both about the possibilities of improving the performance of such persons in providing reliable information and whether training or experience significantly improves capacity to identify. However, the crucial point here is that investigation of such variants has proceeded neither on a systematic basis nor in the context of some general theoretical framework. At best, it has tended to be *ad hoc* and uneven.

Third, the variants on the standard case point in a variety of possibly divergent directions. This raises the question whether what is needed is not a single polar ideal type, contrasting with the standard case, so much as a flexible model which can accommodate a variety of types of processes, of types of decisions within each process and of types of cases, including both the standard case and at least the more important variants of the kind indicated above. This involves a shift of perspective to a higher level of generality than is postulated by the standard case. What I wish to suggest is that the basis for such a perspective is to hand in a way that combines elements of contextual perspectives on legal process and some notions about information-processing borrowed from cognitive psychology and information theory: the result might be a composite 'information model', which is broader than, but incorporates, the traditional evidentiary model that is assumed in the standard case.

Let me revert briefly to the contrast between expository and contextual perspectives on law. Although the intellectual history of Anglo-American legal scholarship has not followed a single neat line of development, it is possible to pull out one thread which forms something of a pattern: this is a steady broadening of the focus of attention beyond disputed questions of law, represented by the standpoint of appellate court judges, through steadily wider

Table 3   Ideal type or standard case of misidentification and possible variants

Standard case	Some possible variants
A *witness* (W) of indeterminate age, sex, class, race, and occupation	W was middle-aged, male, myopic, middle-class, white, bank clerk or immigration officer;
sees	contact was by telephone or involved a combination of visual, aural, and other impressions;
an *incident*	W alleges that O was present in a particular vicinity, e.g. a theatre, a bar, a bed;
of *short duration*	over a period of hours or longer;
which becomes the subject of *criminal* proceedings	the issue of identification arose in a civil proceeding or a tribunal hearing or other proceeding, such as a university disciplinary hearing;
in a *contested* case	the case was not contested, for example O pleaded guilty or the case was settled out of court or proceedings were dropped;
tried before a *jury*	the (contested) hearing took place before a bench of magistrates or a professional judge or a court martial or other tribunal;
in which W *willingly*	W was coerced or bribed or compelled to testify;
gives *evidence*	the information given by W was used for purposes other than forensic evidence, e.g. as information leading to suspicion or investigation, or to neglect or elimination of a line of enquiry;
of the *identity*	it was sufficient for the purposes of the enquiry that O was placed within a certain class of people rather than was identified as a unique individual;
of the *accused* (O)	the object of identification was a *thing* (e.g. a car, a typewriter or a gun) or an *animal*;
a person of *indeterminate* age, sex, class, race, and occupation	O was a black, male youth or a one-legged elderly woman;
who was a *stranger* (i.e. previously unknown to W)	the subject was well known to W;
W's evidence is unsupported by other evidence of identification	W's evidence was corroborated or denied by other testimonial or circumstantial evidence;
and is *unreliable*	several factors in the particular situation enhanced the probability that the identification was reliable – e.g. W was an experienced or trained observer, the period of observation was substantial, O was already known to W, and so on;
but *results*	the information or evidence of W was not believed by the jury or other relevant participant(s);
in the *conviction* of O.	the *mischief* of the alleged misidentification was not that the subject was wrongly convicted or acquitted, but that he or she suffered *vexation* and/or *expense* and/or *delay* (with consequential injury) through being suspected or arrested or interrogated or charged or sued, or suffered some *other* serious damage, such as injury to reputation or loss of a job.

conceptions of different legal processes to a view of law in the context of society as a whole and, indeed, of humankind and of the universe. To put the matter simply: the focus shifted from disputed questions of law in appellate courts to disputed questions of fact tried before juries, to contested cases tried before courts without juries (and before other tribunals and arbitrators) to other methods of dispute-settlement. This broadening of the focus of attention to include other *arenas* was paralleled by a perception that even the most formal kind of legal process involved a sequence or *flow of decisions and events* involving a variety of *participants*. Such total processes, like stories, have no finite beginnings and endings other than those points selected, often arbitrarily, as suitable for the particular purpose at hand by the particular expositor, story-teller or whatever. In its most comprehensive and systematic version, as presented by Lasswell and McDougal,[26] the physical universe is the universe of discourse and any particular legally significant decision or event needs to be considered in the context of some larger legal process which in turn belongs to a broader totality of social processes.

Such contextual models of legal processes are, of course, quite commonplace today, even within legal scholarship. They are explicitly used, or assumed by implication, in most contemporary writing about identification. But the potential of such models has not been consistently and fully exploited in treatments of identification. A particularly revealing example is to be found in a recent book by a psychologist. In his chapter on 'Evidence and Truth in the Criminal Justice System', addressed to non-legal readers, Yarmey presents a model of 'Major Events and Proceedings Involved in a Criminal Prosecution' (figure 1).[27]

This flow-chart was designed to provide a general introduction to criminal process as one context in which eyewitness evidence is important. It is interesting in that some of the categories it uses – 'facts gathered', 'theories constructed', 'data analysed', 'evidence presented', 'facts', 'truths' – could equally well be fitted into an information-processing model of a kind that is to be found in books on cognitive psychology[28] or on information theory.[29] This suggests that it might be relatively easy to integrate a more sophisticated model of typical criminal processes (and models of other legal processes) with one or more standard models of information-processing, borrowed from other contexts.

For the purpose of a detailed analysis of problems of identification and misidentification, Yarmey's flow-chart would need to be expanded and refined in a number of ways. First, it is important to bring out the fact that by the time a witness comes to testify at the trial he or she has typically 'presented' at least some of his or her information on several previous occasions, for example in informal conversation, in interviews with the police and possibly with one or more lawyers, in depositions, perhaps at committal proceedings and so on. This is one reason why it is useful to think in terms not merely of witnesses testifying (*evidence*) but of the creating and processing of *information*. An adequate model for the purposes of the study of identification should indicate at least standard points in the process at which eyewitnesses report what they think they saw, what stimulated them to report, to whom, in what context and for what purposes.

It is also important to remember that information provided by eyewitnesses is relevant to a number of other decisions in criminal process – for example, the

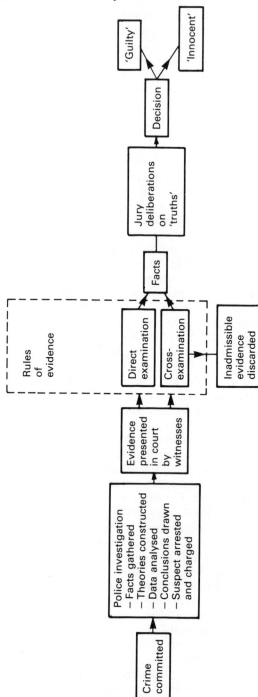

Figure 1   Major events and proceedings involved in a criminal prosecution (from Yarmey, *The Psychology of Eyewitness Testimony*, 1979; reproduced with permission)

decision to hold an identification parade, the decision to prosecute, the decision to charge, the decision to plead guilty or not guilty, the decision whether or not to call a particular witness and so on. Such decisions should not be seen merely as stages on the way to a jury verdict: they can have other direct consequences, some of which can surely be called 'consequences of identification'. Again an adequate model would include all the standard decisions and events which might have such consequences.

Yarmey's model follows convention in depicting standard processes as following a single linear pattern. A crime is committed – the police investigate – a suspect is identified, located, arrested, and charged – a case is prepared – and the evidence is presented in court. As readers of detective fiction will know, criminal processes do not follow a single pattern: in particular, the stages of an investigation follow in no set sequence and may overlap to a greater or lesser extent with preparation of the case against (or on behalf of) a particular suspect. Sometimes the story could be said to begin with a policeman seeing someone behaving suspiciously: if the starting-point is the finding of a dead body, it may or may not be clear at the outset that death was due to a criminal act and this can readily affect the sequence of investigation. Similarly police enquiries, formal 'interviews', identification parades and so on do not follow a single sequence – there are at least several different patterns. The immediate significance of this is that eyewitnesses play a variety of roles at different stages of pre-trial processes and this may have very significant impacts both on their own mental processes and on how information provided by them is treated or used.

The above analysis suggests that an 'information model' as a basis for a systematic approach to the subject of identification and misidentification in legal processes would need to satisfy the following conditions: it would need to accommodate all the main types of legal processes, rather than merely criminal processes; it would need to cover the main stages in each type of process, rather than concentrate on events in the courtroom; and it should be able to identify different points at which information relating to identification is provided, by whom and to whom, and how that information is processed and is used in a variety of types of decisions by different participants at different stages in the process. Furthermore it would need to point to the consequences of such decisions – especially the actual and potential mischiefs for the objects of identification. Finally, in deciding on the practical importance of particular research strategies, reforms, etc., some estimate would need to be made of the typicality and scale of the more important phenomena involved.

To produce such a comprehensive model would be an ambitious enterprise, which is beyond the scope of this chapter. However, it may help to concretize the discussion and suggest some possible ways forward by taking a fresh look at the problems of identification in the light of such considerations.

Redefining the Problem of (Mis)identification

It is a truism that the characterization, definition, and diagnosis of a practical problem depend on the standpoint, perceptions, concerns, and objectives of those doing the defining. 'The problem of identification' as it emerges from the literature has certain obvious characteristics. It is seen as a practical rather than a scientific or intellectual problem: the underlying concern is to improve legal processes rather than solely or even mainly to understand them better. It is seen mainly as a problem of design; and the standpoint is 'official' – not in any pejorative sense of that term – but, like Bentham's legislator, the standpoint is primarily of those responsible for the design and healthy operation of the system.

Eyewitness identification can, of course, be studied from a variety of other standpoints. It can, for example, be looked at from the point of view of the victim – as was done in part by Peter Hain.[30] It could be looked at from the point of view of police investigators or detectives or of prosecution or defence lawyers preparing cases, or of witnesses or of judges or jurors or of other participants in legal processes. It is also quite possible that the study of eyewitness testimony may produce insights, hypotheses, and findings which might be of theoretical significance in general psychology or in our understanding of legal processes.

To date, however, the primary focus has been on the practical problem of reducing the incidence of misidentification in the administration of justice; this is also the focus of this chapter. From that point of view, I wish to suggest that the problem has been defined in an artificially narrow way and that, while some of the limitations are justifiable on grounds of keeping the subject manageable, others are not. Accordingly let us look at some of the main ingredients of the 'problem' in turn.

The notion of identity

Wigmore, in what remains one of the best theoretical discussions of evidence of identity, stated:

Identity may be thought of as a quality of a person or thing – the quality of sameness with another person or thing. The essential idea is that two persons or things are for the moment conceived as existing, but that one is alleged, because of common features to be the same as the other; so that there is in fact only a single person or thing ... The process of constructing an inference of identification ... consists usually in *adding together a number of circumstances*, each of which by itself might be a feature of many objects, but *all of which together can most probably, in experience, co-exist in a single object only*. Each additional circumstance reduces the chances of there being more than one object so associated.[31]

In the present context it is not necessary to start, let alone to chase, any philosophical hares about the notion of 'sameness'. At least in respect of identification of persons such puzzlements rarely, if ever, raise any issues of practical consequence. However, it is worth noting that in some legal contexts the problem of what constitutes identity (of, for example, ideas, transactions, or things) is both familiar and important, as students of copyright, passing off, and Roman Law will know. So long as the problem of identification is confined to persons, the notion of identity may be taken for granted; if the subject is extended to things, then the matter may not always be so straightforward. Alger

Hiss's typewriter either was or was not the one on which the documents were typed; but that may not be true of a stolen car that has been dismantled or a metal object, such as a piece of silver plate, that has been melted down.

'Identifying'

If one looks at the 'problem of identification' in the context of legal process as a flow of decisions and events, it is obvious that a complex variety of mental processes and human actions are involved: seeing, hearing; acquiring, storing, interpreting, and retrieving information; recognizing; believing; asserting, communicating, describing, persuading; deciding; and so on. It is also obvious that the mental processes and actions of a variety of individual participants are involved and that they interact in complex ways. In the light of this it is worth noting two points about the concept of 'identification'. First, in the context of phrases like 'the problem of identification' it covers a complex range of mental processes and actions that need to be differentiated. Second, in some contexts statements of the kind 'X identified Y' may be ambiguous: such a statement could mean 'X *recognized* Y' or 'X formed the *belief* that Y was the same as Z' or 'X *decided* that Y was probably the same as Z' or 'X *asserted* that Y was the same as Z.'

It would not be appropriate here to attempt a systematic analysis of the main concepts and distinctions involved. But it is worth making the point that a systematic theory of identification in legal processes requires a quite elaborate conceptual framework which would need to draw on the language of both law and psychology. It would, for example, be necessary to integrate concepts and terminology from cognitive psychology (such as acquisition, retention, and retrieval of information) and from information theory (such as 'noise', 'signal', 'coding', and 'active'/'passive' information). Some standard concepts from decision theory and social psychology may also be useful, in addition to concepts and distinctions from legal discourse such as materiality, relevance, admissibility, and receivability; quantum, cogency, and corroboration of evidence; *factum probans* and *factum probandum*; and the whole panoply of standard procedural concepts. This is not intended as a plea for the jargonization of identification; rather it is to emphasize the truism that in this as in other spheres of inter-disciplinary work an important step towards an integrated approach is the harmonization of concepts from the relevant disciplines.

A further point about psychological aspects of the subject is suggested by the foregoing: several different branches of psychology are relevant to the study of identification. In recent years the psychology of eyewitness identification has spread beyond concentration on the cognitive processes of one actor, the witness, to include other established lines of psychological enquiry. Saks and Hastie (1978), for example, have been praised for directing attention to other actors, but have been criticized for concentrating too much on individual actors while neglecting 'the intricate web of relationships that bind and define different actors' (Loh, 1981). Clifford and Bull have pointed to several areas of social psychology that are directly relevant to the relatively narrow topic of person identification in contested jury trials. Broaden the perspective and other arenas may become relevant as well. This suggests that there is already in existence a substantial accumulation of concepts, theories, and findings in psychology, and elsewhere, some of which have not yet been perceived to be relevant to the subject of identification, at least in any sustained and systematic manner.

Identity of what?

The 'ideal' case and nearly all of the literature on eyewitness identification concentrates on what Clifford and Bull[32] referred to as 'person identification', and this is an advance upon the general assumption that all objects of identification are male. However, Loftus reports on some experiments in which identification and recognition of cars were involved and other examples are to be found in the literature.[33] Cases of eyewitness identification of objects or of animals can arise in practice and some of the psychological processes involved may be similar, if not identical. For many purposes it may be perfectly justifiable to focus primarily or exclusively on identification of persons – as I shall do from now on – but it is worth bearing in mind that many of the same considerations apply to identification of things; furthermore people are often identified or recognized through their close association with distinctive things, such as clothes.

Identification by what means?

Identity may be proved in court by circumstantial or testimonial evidence or by a combination of the two. As forensic science has developed, technological improvements such as fingerprinting, blood grouping, microanalysis of traces and the like have increased in practical importance; eyewitness identification may over time become correspondingly less important. Nevertheless it is likely to continue to have a role to play in investigation and in litigation, both civil and criminal, for the foreseeable future.

So far as analysing the problem is concerned only a few brief comments about means are needed. One point worth noting is that recognition is not solely visual; it is in theory possible to recognize another person by any one of the five senses; as a practical matter, as has often been acknowledged, identification may involve a *combination* of two or more senses, most commonly sight and hearing.[34] Accordingly, it may be artificially narrow or misleading to define the problem strictly in terms of *eye*witnesses.

Another form of combination needs also to be borne in mind. The paradigm case postulates that identification is based on the testimonial evidence of one or two eyewitnesses alone. However, the question of reliability of this kind of testimony remains in cases where there is a combination of testimonial and circumstantial evidence, especially where the circumstantial evidence alone is not sufficient to settle the issue. Thus even a rule requiring corroboration of eyewitness evidence of identity in certain kinds of case would not eliminate the need for guidance as to the likely reliability of a particular item of testimonial evidence in a given case. It is also worth noting that the problem of combining convergent evidence of different types has also puzzled logicians and other theorists of evidence.[35]

Finally it is worth remarking that much more attention has been given to date to evaluating the reliability of existing methods of eyewitness identification, such as confrontations, dock identifications, identification parades and the like than to inventing new devices or radically improving existing ones. In particular, discussions of the use of photographs seem on the whole to be rather unimaginative about the possibilities, perhaps because they dwell on the limitations of the photograph and the dangers of existing uses to which they are put rather than concentrating on how their advantages – especially cheapness, convenience, and flexibility – can be exploited and how procedures can be devised which offset or mitigate some of the acknowledged dangers and limitations.

The mischiefs of misidentification: who are the victims?

The paradigm case in nearly all of the literature on identification assumes that the only mischief arising from misidentification is the conviction of the innocent. Even if one extends this to other mistaken adjudicative decisions (such as the wrong person being held liable or even erroneous acquittals) this is an extraordinarily narrow conception of the mischiefs involved. Suppose, for the sake of argument, that Roger Orton was indeed the real Roger Tichborne, what were the consequences of the mistake? He was not only convicted of perjury and imprisoned: he lost his inheritance, his reputation and a good deal else besides; he was subjected to considerable expense and mental agony; and, in a sense, he even lost his identity. Peter Hain was acquitted of a charge of armed robbery, but can one seriously claim that he was not a victim of misidentification, given the anxiety, the expense, and the potential damage to his reputation that he suffered, in addition to what he refers to as 'the indignity and injustice of being hauled through the courts'?[36] Hain wrote a vivid account of his experience; he also described a number of cases in which misidentification led to evils short of conviction, thereby reminding us that even to be suspected, interrogated, arrested or threatened with prosecution can be an unpleasant, even traumatic, experience with a whole range of possible harmful consequences, financial, psychological, and otherwise. To treat mistaken adjudicative decisions as the only evils of misidentification is symptomatic of a narrow kind of formalism. Conviction and punishment of the innocent are among the great social evils; but they are not by any means the only ones. Add to Bentham's notions of the collateral pains of procedure – vexation, expense and delay – the notion of other harmful consequences, direct and indirect, of being involved as a party in legal processes and one has a more comprehensive conceptual basis for assessing the mischiefs of misidentification.

To broaden the enquiry in this way has important implications: it forces us to look at the consequences for the object of identification (and for others) at every step in legal process; it also transforms our estimates of the likely scale of the problem, for under 'victims' of misidentification are now included all those who have fallen under suspicion, who have been interrogated, harassed, arrested, charged, paraded, or have been involved in other unpleasant experiences in civil, criminal or other proceedings or in expense as a result of information derived from a witness. While the number of people wrongly convicted by a jury as a result of eyewitness identification may be as few as ten or a dozen over a year, the number who have suffered other evils of misidentification may number hundreds or even thousands. By broadening the notion of victims our perception of the nature and scale of the problem is transformed.

Two objections to this move need to be considered. The first is that it is reasonable to concentrate on mistaken *adjudicative* decisions, because these represent at once the most serious consequences of misidentification and the most easily remedied. No amount of improvement of the system can prevent innocent people falling under suspicion or being the subject of false allegations. A second possible objection is that to broaden the definition of the problem in this way renders it unmanageable.

To which one may reply: First, which is the greater social evil: an estimated ten or a dozen convictions of innocent persons each year or hundreds, perhaps thousands, mistakenly subjected to the vexations, expense, and other consequences of being involuntarily involved in legal processes? Even if one concedes that wrongful conviction of the innocent is necessarily always the worst evil – which is debatable – surely the potential scale of the wider problem is such as to demand at least as much attention.

Second, from several points of view it is artificial to isolate one harmful consequence of being involved unwillingly in legal processes from the other consequences. What the consequences that flow from a single, wrongful or mistaken identification are in a particular case is largely a matter of chance. For the individual victim the evil consequences tend to cumulate, whether or not the formal outcome is an unfavourable adjudicative decision. From the point of view of improving the system, almost any measure affecting the adjudicative stage will also affect other stages in the process: for example, there is a widely held view that one of the most important ways of avoiding wrongful convictions is to exercise more careful control over decisions whether or not to prosecute – but clearly measures affecting how such decisions are made have many potential ramifications in addition to the likely effect on wrongful convictions. The costs and benefits of almost any measure designed to deal with problems of identification cannot be rationally assessed by looking only at adjudicative outcomes.

Third, to broaden the definition of 'the problem of identification' may lead to a more realistic appraisal of the complexities of the situation, but this does not make it any less manageable than other important topics in legal process, such as confessions, plea-bargaining, and settlement out of court. Of course, there is need for specialized lines of research – for example into police identification of juveniles in some particular kinds of situation – but any particular research project and the evaluation of the significance of its findings need to be set in the context of some broader total picture.

Identification for what purposes?

In the orthodox view it is common to treat the information provided by eyewitnesses solely as *evidence* to be presented at trial. If, however, one looks at criminal process as a whole one is likely to find that such information is used in a variety of ways: eyewitness accounts and descriptions may provide the first leads for identifying a suspect or, anterior to that, for searching for potential suspects who correspond to a description; at a later stage information provided by the witness may lead to the elimination of particular suspects during the course of investigation and, as was dramatically illustrated by the Yorkshire Ripper investigation, false or misleading information may lead to the premature elimination of a suspect. As we have already seen, identification parades need not be solely evidence-generating devices; they may also be used to eliminate suspects or they may lead to the discontinuance of a case for lack of potential evidence. Even if evidence of positive identification at a parade were not generally admissible, or were inadmissible in a particular case because of some defect in the procedure, occasional parades might still be useful as part of the process of detection. Information provided by eyewitnesses also represents *potential evidence* which may have an important bearing on a number of pre-trial decisions, such as decisions to hold a parade, decisions to prosecute, decisions whether or not to plead guilty, and decisions whether to elect for summary trial or trial by jury. Thus in considering problems of identification in the context of criminal processes as a whole it is important to distinguish between the uses of information from eyewitnesses as *investigative information*, as *potential evidence*, and as *evidence actually presented* in court. There are no doubt other uses of such information in criminal processes and analogous distinctions also need to be drawn in the context of non-criminal processes. It is useful to see evidence and potential evidence as species of information provided by eyewitnesses, for that should serve as a reminder that the phenomenon under consideration is a particular form of human information-processing in a rather complex kind of social process.

Redefining the Problem

If one draws together the main strands in the foregoing analysis the following picture emerges: the starting-point of the process is a triggering event or situation in which one person, the witness, sees or hears another person, thing or animal, which on some subsequent occasion or occasions he or she is asked to describe or to state is the same as an object presented to his or her senses either directly, as in a parade, or through some representation such as a film, a photograph, a recording, a drawing or a description. It is generally recognized that a variety of factors tend to make such statements unreliable, even where the witness is disinterested. From this certain practical problems arise – for example, how to differentiate reliable from unreliable statements and how to improve the reliability of such statements.

Up to this point there is no difference of substance between the orthodox definition of the problem and the perspective advocated in this essay. It can readily be conceded that for certain purposes it is reasonable to confine the definition of the problem to *eye*witness identification of *persons* in *criminal* processes, so long as it is recognized that the processes of identifying other objects, by other means (such as voice or a combination of sense data) in other legal and similar processes are in many respects closely analogous. At the next stage, however, significant differences flow from the orthodox and broader perspectives. The former concentrates on identification statements as *evidence*, while the latter also includes the uses of such statements as *potential evidence* and as *information* relevant to a *variety of decisions* and other purposes. Similarly, if it is accepted that wrongful convictions are only one of the harmful consequences (*mischiefs*) that tend to flow from mistaken or dubious identification statements, then the population of *victims* is very substantially increased and attention is inevitably focused on *the whole process*, including events and decisions before and after trial. From this perspective it would be artificial to distinguish sharply between cases which are contested before a jury and other proceedings which take place before some other court or tribunal or which never reach the stage of a trial of the issue of identity. Even if a particular study concentrates on the trial stage in criminal proceedings, it will almost certainly be necessary to consider the trial in the context of the process as a whole.

The substitution of an explicit and broadly gauged 'information model' for the narrower, typically implicit, jury lawyer's 'evidentiary model' has a number of practical and theoretical implications for future research, for public debate and for practical action relating to the topic of identification in legal processes. First, at the level of theory, the information model may provide a better conceptual basis for an integrated multidisciplinary approach to the topic. Second, this kind of perspective fits rather more easily with much contemporary research and writing about legal processes than does the evidentiary model. This in turn may help cross-fertilization between several bodies of literature that have to some extent developed separately. For example, it may point to connections between psychological literature about eyewitness testimony and sociological, legal, and other literature about plea-bargaining and guilty pleas or about juvenile courts. It may also serve as a constant reminder of the enormous complexity of legal processes. Third, this broader perspective may indicate new lines of research for psychologists and others; it may also suggest that some existing bodies of research and literature have a more direct bearing on the study of identification, and vice versa, than has hitherto been generally perceived. Thus, on the one hand, relatively little is known about such specific matters as decisions to hold, or not to hold, identification parades and the consequences of such decisions or about the special features of juveniles as objects of identification. On the other hand, the potential broader implications of identification have yet to be systematically explored. Fourth, the 'information model' may provide the basis for a diagnosis and evaluation of the mischiefs of misidentification in legal processes that is at once more systematic and more realistic than that presented by the Devlin Report and similar policy documents. It may also open the way for a more free-ranging and imaginative approach to improving and inventing procedures, techniques, and rules for reducing the evils of misidentification in legal processes.

Since all this might seem rather ambitious, it is appropriate to end with some disclaimers. All I have tried to do in this chapter is to suggest that a fresh look needs to be taken at the problem of misidentification from a broader perspective than has generally been adopted in the past. A systematically constructed 'information model' (or series of models) has yet to be developed in this context, and this essay does no more than suggest some of the factors that might be taken into account in such an enterprise, for which, as a jurist, I have no special qualifications. Similarly a comprehensive, empirically based restatement of the problems of misidentification in England, or more generally, has not been attempted. Nor should anything that has been said here be taken as denigrating the very substantial advances in the study of the subject that have been made in recent years, especially by psychologists. All I have tried to suggest is that in so far as recent writings – as exemplified by the Devlin Report and the books by Yarmey, Loftus, and Clifford and Bull – have been influenced by 'the evidentiary model' of identification statements, some of the tendencies and biases of the expository tradition of academic law and jury-oriented practitioners have crept into the literature; in so far as they have broken away from the narrow focus of this model – as in many respects they have – the development of a broadly conceived 'information model' might provide a general perspective on the subject which is at once systematic and close to the empirical realities of the operation of legal processes.

NOTES

This chapter was published in 1983 in Lloyd-Bostock and Clifford (eds), *Evaluating Witness Evidence: Recent Psychological Research and New Perspectives* and is reprinted by kind permission of the publishers, John Wiley and Sons. The context was a stock-taking of research into witness psychology; the primary audience consisted of psychologists interested in the field. This provided both a stimulus and an opportunity to restate my general criticisms of traditional approaches in simple terms and to provide a concrete illustration of a general approach. Only minor changes have been made to the text and footnotes. Since 1983 the research and literature have continued to accumulate; for references see Wells (1988). There have been a few signs of a tendency to adopt broader perspectives: see, for example, Lloyd-Bostock (1988, 1988a) and the interesting article by Gross (1987). However, none of these go as far as is suggested in this paper. I am grateful to Peter Twining for assistance with this paper and to Michael King, Brian Clifford and Sally Lloyd-Bostock for helpful criticisms and suggestions.
1 Devlin (1976).
2 Clifford and Bull (eds) (1978), Loftus (1979), Yarmey (1979), Lloyd-Bostock and Clifford (eds) (1983). More recent works include Shepherd et al. (1981) and Wells (1988).
3 The editions discussed were Cross (1979); Salmond (1981); and Smith and Hogan (1978). The 6th edition of Cross (1985) contains a brief and somewhat dismissive discussion of probabilities at 149–51.
4 It might equally be referred to as Legal Realism, except that this term is often associated with a number of fallacies of which few, if any, leading Legal Realists were in fact guilty – such as the belief that talk of rules is a myth or that law can be defined in terms of prediction.
5 Broadening one's perspective typically requires redefining the scope of the subject and the choice of a new organizing category – in this context, the substitution of 'Evidence, Proof and Fact-Finding' (or something similar) for 'Evidence'. Wigmore divided the study of Evidence into two parts: The Science of Proof and the Trial Rules of Evidence; this, however, underemphasizes the procedural dimensions. See further, below, ch. 11.
6 Such theories have been attempted in the past, for example by Jeremy Bentham and John Henry Wigmore, but they have not caught on, partly because of the dominance of the Expository Tradition and partly because they are defective as theories in important

respects. Nevertheless there is sufficient in the heritage of the literature on evidence and on judicial processes to provide a starting-point for a broader approach to the study of identification.

7   See Twining (1974, and 1985a) for fuller discussions.

8   See further below, ch. 6.

9   Esp. Bentham *Rationale* and *TEBW*, ch. 2, 10; Loftus (1979), vii.

10   Loftus (1979), vii.

11   Kaplan (1968).

12   Loftus (1979).

13   Frank (1949).

14   The Devlin Report's analysis of the stories of Dougherty and Virag provides two case studies that deserve to become classics. Each follows the process from the initial crime through trial and appeal to the activities which eventually led to official acknowledgements that an error had been made and the payment of modest *ex gratia* compensation to the two men. The main focus in both accounts is on what went wrong and each reveals a catalogue of mistakes, accidents, and coincidences calculated to hearten inefficiency theorists, if no one else. In both cases misidentification played an important part, but they illustrate vividly how a series of mishaps and mistakes by different participants can combine to contribute not only to a wrongful conviction, but to failures to rectify errors on appeal and afterwards. The Report concludes that *R.* v. *Dougherty* was so badly bungled that it 'will never be a leading case on misidentification', whereas Virag's was nearly a 'copy book case' in which misidentification was not only the main factor, but 'was itself a case of some contributory errors'.

These two case-studies could be said to be based on an implied rather than an express, total process model. They clearly illustrate the complex interactions between events and decisions during different stages in the process, the contributions of different participants, and the importance of setting alleged examples of misidentification in the context of the story as a whole. However, it is debatable whether the rest of the Devlin Report gave adequate weight to all the implications of the lessons of these two case studies – especially in respect of some of the crucial decisions taken prior to trial in each case. Moreover, as had already been observed, by failing to make adequate demographic estimates of the main factors and actors in the situation, the Report provides no adequate basis for judging the typicality of the cases of Dougherty and Virag, except perhaps in respect of the importance of misidentification as a source of error as against other factors.

15   Loftus (1979), 180–7.

16   Davis (1964). Davis himself made numerous pioneering contributions to 'administrative evidence'.

17   In England and Wales the number of civil jury trials is rarely more than 15–25 a year. In 1973, 47 per cent of those sent to prison were sent by Crown Courts, 43 per cent were sent by magistrates, and 10 per cent were tried by magistrates and sentenced by Crown Courts. The great majority of these pleaded guilty. See generally Zander (1980), especially 1–5, 311–13. See now Zander (1988).

18   When a defendant can choose between summary trial or trial by jury, he is likely to be advised to opt for the latter in cases where there is a dispute about evidence of identity. Thus most contested cases of the kind in which a potential prison sentence is at stake are probably tried by Crown Courts. Against this must be set uncontested cases, cases tried before magistrates, in Juvenile Courts and in other tribunals, and cases which never reach trial, but in which a suspected or accused person has suffered substantial vexation and/or expense. No reliable statistics about the extent of such cases are at present available.

19   The reasons for these differences are complex and cannot be explored in detail here; they are in part due to the differences in composition of the two bodies; in part to the narrowness of the traditional definition of 'evidence' as a subject; and in part to a

generally heightened awareness that even questions about the admissibility of evidence at criminal trials can sensibly be discussed only when they are viewed in the broader context of some conception of criminal process as a whole. The differences in the definition of the problem in each report, including the way the terms of reference were drafted, reflected in large part a significant shift in perspectives.

20 Perhaps the *locus classicus* is Thayer's dictum: 'What was formerly "tried" by the method of force or the mechanical following of form is now tried by the method of reason' (Thayer, 1898, 198–9).

21 See above, ch. 2.

22 For example, debates about the privilege against self-incrimination, about illegally or improperly obtained evidence, about the nature of forensic 'probabilities', and about the rationales of the hearsay rule and its exceptions.

23 See below, ch. 10.

24 Lindsay and Wells (1983).

25 Baddeley and Woodhead (1983).

26 Lasswell and McDougal (1967), McDougal and Reisman (1981).

27 Yarmey (1979).

28 E.g. Lindsay and Norman (1977); Loftus and Loftus (1976).

29 E.g. Willmer (1970).

30 Hain (1976).

31 Wigmore *Science* (1937), 258–9.

32 Clifford and Bull (1978).

33 Loftus (1979, 1983). 'Radar Receivers' which warn motorists of speed traps are now widely advertised in the United States. One advertisement states: 'Although nine different errors have been documented for traffic radar, the most common source of traffic tickets is mistaken identity. It is hard to believe, but traffic radar does not identify *which* vehicle is responsible for the speed being displayed. It shows only a speed number and nothing else. The radar operator must decide who is to blame' (advertisement in airline magazine, 1989).

34 Clifford and Bull (1978); Clifford (1983).

35 E.g. L.J. Cohen (1977, 1980); Eggleston (1978, 1980); Tillers and Green (eds) (1988), *passim*; *TEBW*, Appendix.

36 Hain (1976), 29.

6

What is the Law of Evidence?

Introduction

Cross-cultural communication invites exchanges of stereotypes. A common kind of English joke involves trying to explain the mysteries of the game of cricket to foreigners. Conversely many foreign commentators treat cricket as a symbol of the English character. The English Law of Evidence is often presented as being even more bizarre and complex than the game of cricket. Anglo-American legal proceedings are often perceived as a kind of game, in which fair play and winning displace concern for truth and justice. The analogy has a core of truth in it; for English notions of fair play and American conceptions of due process have indeed played an important role in the development and survival of some of our technical rules of evidence. But like all analogies it can be pressed too far. Here, two important differences reflect central themes in this essay. On the one hand, I shall argue that our law of evidence is, in its fundamentals, much simpler than is commonly supposed. On the other hand, while I am prepared to give unqualified loyalty to the game of cricket, I share with most common lawyers a deep ambivalence about some important aspects of our law of evidence.

The purpose of this chapter is to try to demystify the modern English Law of Evidence by presenting a broad overview, shorn of the complexities and details that are the reason for its reputation. The standpoint is that of an expositor trying to give a clear and realistic introduction to this branch of English law to newcomers to the subject, whether they be law students or lawyers trained in a different system. I shall deal only incidentally with my views on the question: What should be our law of evidence? My central contention is that our rules of evidence consist of a series of disparate exceptions to a single principle of freedom of proof and that the exceptions are less important in theory and in practice than is sometimes suggested. The first part of this thesis follows James Bradley Thayer, the great American scholar, whose view is widely regarded as forming the basis of our modern law.[1] The second part – the argument of exaggerated importance – is largely attributable to historical trends in the organization of litigation since Thayer's time, in particular the decline of the jury; the increase of judicial discretion in fact-finding; and the growth in importance of tribunals and other arenas in contrast with the decline in importance of the contested trial.

The argument of exaggerated importance also reflects a difference in theoretical perspective on law. Thayer equated 'law' with binding rules created or authorized by state authority. Following Karl Llewellyn, I shall treat 'law' more broadly as a kind of *institution* which embodies not only rules, but also principles, procedures, practices, craft-traditions, devices, and ways of thought which are sufficiently established to be describable and which are specialized to performing a number of jobs or tasks in society.[2] The difference is mainly one of emphasis and perspective. Thayer treated questions of analysis of, argument about and presentation of evidence as falling outside the sphere of the Law of Evidence. This narrow view of the Law of Evidence may be correct in terms of his positivist conception of 'law'. The broader view of the subject of Evidence and Proof within the discipline of law includes all of these matters and much more besides.

What is conventionally conceived as the Law of Evidence is treated here as one part of a broader subject: Evidence and Proof in Litigation.[3] Each of these terms requires clarification.

Proof is the establishment of the existence or non-existence of some fact (a *factum probandum* or *fact in issue*) to the satisfaction of a legal tribunal charged with determining this fact in issue. The degree of satisfaction required is prescribed by the applicable *standard of proof*, for example, 'balance of probabilities' or 'beyond reasonable doubt'. Evidence is a means of proof. It has been defined as 'any matter of fact, the effect, tendency or design of which is to produce in the mind a persuasion, affirmative or disaffirmative, of the existence of some other matter of fact'.[4] The main examples of judicial evidence are statements by witnesses (testimony), things (real evidence), and documents presented to the tribunal as a basis for determining the issues of fact before it.

The Logic of Proof is concerned with the validity, cogency and appropriateness of arguments as the rational basis for persuasion towards making or justifying a decision or conclusion on a question of fact. From this perspective, both the facts in issue and evidence can be expressed in propositional form. An evidentiary proposition (*factum probans*) is *relevant* to a fact in issue (material fact or *factum probandum*) if it tends to support it or negate it, judged by the applicable principles of logic. The 'weight' or 'cogency' or 'probative force' of a single evidentiary proposition, or of a mass of evidence, refers to the strength or weakness of the support or negation. Questions of relevance (is there any connection?) and of weight (how strong is the connection?) are intimately related, but it is useful to keep them conceptually distinct.

'Litigation' in this context refers to formal proceedings to enforce the law or to pursue a claim in law through to a final determination by a court or other legally constituted tribunal. Litigation refers to the *total process* from the formal institution of legal proceedings (e.g. by the laying of a criminal charge or the issue of a writ) to a final order or act which makes the case *res judicata*. In practice, only a small minority of litigated cases involves a contested trial or a full hearing in court: a high proportion of civil claims is settled out of court or abandoned before trial; in the great majority of criminal cases the accused pleads guilty with the result that there is no trial of contested issues of law or fact, although the court will typically have to determine sentence.[5]

In modern times many legal proceedings fall under the jurisdiction of specialized adjudicative tribunals which perform the functions of courts, in important spheres such as employment, industrial injuries, immigration, welfare, land and tax. The important distinction, in this context, is between *adjudication* by a supposedly impartial third party and other methods of dispute settlement, such as negotiation, mediation and conciliation.[6] In so far as these tribunals are called to determine questions of fact, they are concerned with matters of evidence and proof. Accordingly, questions arise as to how such matters are and should be regulated and handled. A realistic picture of litigation in England needs to include all the main types of proceedings under the jurisdiction of adjudicative bodies and all stages in such proceedings.[7]

This chapter is primarily concerned with the situation in England and Wales (Scotland has a separate legal system with a different legal tradition); but much of it applies to jurisdictions that belong to the 'Common Law' family of legal systems. There are two particular reasons for referring specifically to the United States: first, modern thought about Evidence owes much to American scholars, especially James Bradley Thayer and John Henry Wigmore.[8] Secondly, some contrasts between the situations in England and the United States may help to illuminate the complex relationship between the law of evidence and the procedural and institutional contexts in which it operates.

The argument will proceed as follows: in the first part, Context, the subject of Evidence and Proof in Anglo-American litigation can best be understood in the context of (a) the diverse institutional and procedural contexts of litigation in the Anglo-American systems, including recent trends in respect of both; and (b) the underlying philosophical and ideological assumptions of Evidence discourse. In this essay these two contexts can only be sketched in very broad and simplified terms; paradoxically these sketches will underline a message of complexity: that litigation in England and the United States is complex, diverse and continuously changing. The task of this part will be to present a simple map of an exceedingly complicated terrain. In the second part Thayer's theory of the Law of Evidence will be considered critically in the light of developments since his day. In the third part a broader conception of Evidence and Proof in litigation will be sketched. It is claimed that this broader perspective can provide a deeper understanding and a more realistic picture of the actual operation of our institutions in respect of evidence and proof.

Context

The procedural context

An important recent book by a Yugoslav jurist, now resident in the United States, provides a useful theoretical framework for setting our subject in a broad context. Mirjan Damaska's *The Faces of Justice and State Authority* develops a way of describing and comparing systems of procedure in modern Western legal systems in terms of three theoretical models (or 'ideal types').[9] These relate to systems of government, structures of authority, and systems of legal procedure respectively. Damaska's three sets of distinctions can be briefly restated as follows.

Systems of Government can be characterized by the extent to which they approximate to or diverge from pure versions of 'the Managerial State', in which the role of government is to manage all important aspects of social life, and 'the Reactive State', in which the role of government is limited 'to provide a framework for social interaction'.[10] This corresponds with familiar distinctions between 'interventionist' and '*laissez-faire*' ideologies of government. Most modern Western societies have hybrid systems of government (and mixed economies) which lie somewhere between the two extremes. Even the United States departs in important respects from the 'ideal type' of the Reactive State; whereas the United Kingdom, despite recent incursions on the Welfare State, is in important respects somewhat closer to the Managerial model.

Systems of State Authority can similarly be characterized in terms of a distinction between hierarchical and coordinate authority. A reasonably clear example of the former is a bureaucratic state apparatus run by *professionals*, who are in a *hierarchical* relationship to each other, and who purportedly make most important decisions according to *precisely defined standards*. Coordinate authority is characterized by extensive *lay* (non-specialist) participation, *single levels* of 'horizontal' authority and resort to *undifferentiated community standards*, rather than formal rules. Again most actual systems of authority are hybrids. However, there are clear examples in particular spheres: for example, the English jury closely fits the coordinate model in that it is composed of ordinary citizens, its findings are only exceptionally subject to review or appeal ('the sovereignty of the jury') and its decisions, within its allotted sphere, are governed by 'common sense'. Significantly juries do not, indeed cannot, give reasons for their decisions. This contrasts significantly with the lower judiciary in countries like Italy and France, where the personnel are trained officials, whose decisions even on questions of fact have to be reasoned and are subject to regular review by and appeal to higher authority.

The third distinction, between 'inquisitorial' and 'adversarial' *systems of procedure*, is also commonplace. But Damaska departs from common usage, which tends to be both ambiguous and vague, by distinguishing these categories in terms of purposes rather than treating them as different means to shared ends.[11] The purpose of an 'inquest' is implementation of state policy in order to solve a problem; the purpose of a 'contest' is the legitimated resolution of a single dispute between identifiable parties. It is a truism of procedural scholarship that it is misleading to equate Anglo-American procedure with 'adversary' proceedings or systems influenced by Roman Law with 'inquisitorial' proceedings. English criminal procedure, for example, can be interpreted mainly in terms of the model of 'inquest' with a few 'adversarial' glosses, especially at the stage of a disputed trial – an event which occurs in only a small minority of cases. Damaska goes further than this: he argues that it would be surprising to find any modern state which had only one kind of procedural arrangement and, indeed, that examples of particular institutional arrangements which fit the 'ideal types' exactly are quite exceptional.[12] Most procedural arrangements, let alone most 'systems' of arrangements, are hybrids. Nevertheless these concepts, if used precisely, have considerable explanatory power.

These distinctions are, of course, potentially controversial; there is also scope for differences in interpreting and applying them to particular examples. That serves to underline the point that it is not possible to give an ideologically neutral account of a legal system. However, Damaska's central thesis may be less controversial and it is directly relevant to this essay. He argues that these different ideal types can combine in practice in a variety of ways: some combinations one would expect to be more 'comfortable', while others would almost inevitably give rise to serious tensions. For example, the Managerial State, hierarchical authority, and inquest fit together quite naturally; conversely there is likely to be regular tension between adversary proceedings and hierarchical authority. However, and this is the central point, there are many more workable combinations of relatively pure types than one might expect; many particular arrangements, as well as whole systems, represent mixes or compromises. For example, there is no necessary incompatibility between 'inquisitorial' procedure and a largely reactive state, on the one hand, or a largely coordinate system of authority on the other.[13] Many English tribunals are concerned with implementation of law relating to such matters as welfare, tax and immigration: cases typically come before them when a decision is challenged.[14] There is in a sense a 'dispute' and hearings have some 'adversarial' characteristics. We live in a world of hybrids. The English law of evidence and the ideological, institutional and procedural context in which it is situated, can be explicated in such terms.

It is often said that the peculiarities of the common law rules of evidence are attributable to two factors: the institution of the jury and the adversary system of procedure.[15] As a historical explanation of the origins and development of the law of evidence this is broadly true. However, as an explanation of its survival, and of its purported rationales, this can be misleading. In England, for example, such an account fails to explain the following features of the modern system:

1   The surviving traditional rules of evidence are mainly important today in respect of criminal proceedings. With a few exceptions, they apply to all criminal proceedings irrespective of whether these involve trial by jury, by lay magistrates or by professional judges.
2   Civil procedure in the court system is generally closer to the 'adversarial model' of procedure than is criminal procedure, but there are normally less than thirty contested civil jury trials per annum in England and Wales.[16] The decline in importance of the law of evidence in civil litigation is, in part, to be explained by the decline of the jury. But the question arises how far the surviving rules of evidence can be explicated in terms of 'adversarial' features of procedure.
3   A very large proportion of litigation, in the broad sense in which it is used in this essay, today takes place outside the formal court system, in tribunals, in

which many of the adjudicators are not qualified lawyers. There is a good deal of uncertainty in both theory and practice about the extent to which the technical rules of evidence apply to such proceedings.[17] However, it is generally true to say that tribunals operate in a context that is much closer to a system of 'free proof' than either criminal or civil courts. Accordingly the question arises: What is the relationship between the law of evidence and adjudication by lay persons (i.e. non-lawyers)?

We shall see later that there is some doubt whether there is any justification for continuing to talk of one 'Law of Evidence' instead of a series of laws of evidence, which are significantly different for the three main types of litigation, viz. criminal proceedings, curial civil proceedings and proceedings before adjudicative tribunals.[18] Without prejudging this important question, it is useful to underline the extent to which certain basic principles of procedure underlly all litigation. Adapting a recent formulation by Professor Sir Jack Jacob, the doyen of English proceduralists, one can summarize the most fundamental principles underlying English civil procedure as follows:[19]

1   *The principle of party autonomy*: subject to overall regulation by the Court, the parties and their lawyers retain the main initiative and control over the determination of the issues; the collection, selection and questioning of witnesses; and presentation of the suit (including negotiated settlement without approval or direction by the court). This principle is treated by most commentators as the main basis for distinguishing between 'adversarial' and 'inquisitorial' proceedings.

2   *The Court as umpire*: the role of the Court is 'inactive, passive, remote, neutral, independent'.[20] This is the converse aspect of the active role granted to parties and their lawyers by the first principle.

3   *The principle of specialization of functions*, with quite sharp divisions of functions between decisions on questions of law, questions of fact, and questions of disposition (e.g. sentencing); and between the role of different participants at pre-trial, trial and appeal; and, in England, between the role of solicitors and barristers. One important example of such distinctions is that, in jury trials, questions of law and procedure are for the judge, but the final determination of questions of fact is for the jury. Determinations of fact are only exceptionally subject to review or appeal.

4   *The principle of orality*, especially in respect of argument and of the cross-examination of witnesses in open court. It is sometimes claimed that the 'dialectical immediacy' of oral presentation and confrontation is the best means of arriving at rectitude of decision on questions of fact and law. It is important to keep the idea of *dialectical* exchange conceptually distinct from that of *adversarial* autonomy – although, in practice, the two are often combined.[21]

5   *The principle of publicity* at the stage of trial and appeal. Bentham wrote: 'Without publicity all other checks are insufficient: in comparison of publicity all other checks are of small account.'[22] Trials held '*in camera*' and restrictions on reporting of court proceedings are considered to be deviations from this principle and require justification. Sometimes such restrictions become a matter of political controversy. On the other hand, *pre-trial* proceedings, both in

184   *What is the Law of Evidence?*

civil and criminal litigation, generally fall outside this principle. For example, civil pre-trial applications are held in private ('in chambers') and the arcane nature of pre-trial proceedings is a major point of concern about the fairness of our system of criminal justice. One reason why many disputants prefer 'alternative' methods of dispute-resolution such as arbitration, mediation and settlement out of court is that these are less public than judicial trials.

6   *The principle that adjudicative decisions should be based on the issues, the evidence and the arguments presented 'in open court'*, rather than on a judgment of the whole person or on personal general knowledge or on knowledge of particular matters relating to this case obtained outside the courtroom.

7   *The principle of procedural fairness*: this elusive idea, embodied in such notions as 'due process of law', 'the rules of natural justice' and 'procedural rights', has been the subject of much theoretical concern and has been a source of recurrent controversy, especially where considerations of fairness have been thought to conflict with 'rectitude of decision' or with efficiency in implementation of the law.

These principles form the theoretical cornerstone of civil procedure in the English court system. None of the principles is absolute; much doubt and controversy have surrounded the weight and extent that should be given to each of them and how far they are in fact respected in practice in different kinds of proceeding. Similar principles, in simpler form, characterize proceedings before most adjudicative tribunals. The same basic principles govern criminal proceedings except that, as was noted above, such proceedings diverge in some important respects from the 'ideal type' of an adversarial contest. There are two particular concerns that underlie the design and operation of provisions for procedure and evidence in criminal proceedings. They reflect important differences between the purposes, values and contexts of criminal and civil litigation. It is worth articulating these as distinct principles:

8   *The principle of the protection of the accused against mistaken conviction*:[23] the presumption of innocence, the standard of proof beyond reasonable doubt, and many specific provisions of criminal procedure and criminal evidence are explained and justified in terms of this principle. Controversy is sharpest when the principle is thought to conflict with the public interest in convicting the guilty and in preventing crime. The concern is not, of course, peculiar to the common law. But many details of the common law of evidence need to be interpreted in relation to this principle and the tension between it and other concerns.

9   *The principle of the protection of suspects from illegal, unfair or improper treatment.* This principle relates especially to treatment of suspects by the police before trial and is a major point of intersection between the fields of evidence and procedure. Utilitarians may argue that this concern is susbsumed under the general objective of minimizing 'vexation' to *all* participants in legal proceedings, including witnesses, parties to civil litigation, victims, lawyers and officials as well as suspects. Similarly, some civil libertarians claim that this principle can be subsumed under a more general principle of procedural fairness or due process or a general theory of procedural rights. However, protection of suspects from mistreatment is such a pervasive concern of criminal evidence that it is worth articulating it in the form of a specific principle.

The theoretical context

As we saw in chapter 3, the common law of evidence, and the perception of Evidence as a distinct field of study, were relatively late developments. Many of the technical refinements, which led to the perception of the Anglo-American law of evidence as being peculiar, developed in the period 1770 to 1830. Nearly all specialized secondary writings about the common law of evidence since Gilbert have proceeded on very similar assumptions that belong to a remarkably homogeneous intellectual tradition that may be called 'The Rationalist Tradition of Evidence Scholarship'.[24] These assumptions relate, firstly, to the aims and nature of 'rational' adjudication and, secondly, to what is involved in 'proving' disputed matters of fact by 'rational' means.

The key ideas can be restated as follows: Firstly, the central *purpose* of adjudication is 'rectitude of decision', that is the correct application of substantive law to facts proved to be true on the basis of relevant evidence presented to the tribunal. However, the pursuit of truth in adjudication has to be constrained by other, 'extrinsic' values. These subordinate ends, or side-constraints, were summarized by the utilitarian jurist Jeremy Bentham (1748–1832) in the classic phrase 'vexation, expense and delay';[25] non-utilitarians have expressed some of the central values in terms of ideas of 'procedural fairness' or 'due process'.

Secondly, the pursuit of truth as a means to justice under the law is to be pursued by *rational* means. Evidence scholars have almost without exception adopted a conception of 'rational' fact-finding that comes from a single philosophical tradition, English empiricism, as exemplified by Locke, Bentham, John Stuart Mill and, in modern times, A. J. Ayer. Recently debates within philosophy, about epistemology, induction and rationality have once again spilled over into discussions of judicial evidence. For example, some sociologically oriented and critical theorists have questioned the conceptions of rationality underlying the Rationalist Tradition; some go so far as to question the possibility of 'rational fact-finding'. On the other hand, some students of statistics and decision theory have contended that arguments about evidence, since it is concerned with 'probabilities', should in principle fit mathematical models of reasoning and decision making. In order to keep presentation simple, this essay will by-pass these theoretical debates and proceed on the basis that the Anglo-American Law of Evidence broadly fits the ideal type of the Rationalist Tradition.

In so far as this is correct, certain features of that tradition deserve attention. Firstly, the idea that adjective law (evidence and procedure) is concerned with the correct implementation of substantive law (Truth and Justice under the Law) fits well with the ideology of Liberal Legalism, exemplified by the classic notion of the Rule of Law. But it fits equally well (if not better) with Damaska's ideal type of the managerial state in which adjudicators are bureaucratic officials charged with implementing state policy through the efficient application of precise rules. This need not surprise us; but it is significant in that it suggests that the idea that adjudication is concerned with the correct application of existing laws to true facts is shared by standard versions of liberal and socialist theories of law.[26]

Secondly, Civilian lawyers have pointed out that the set of assumptions embodied in the Rationalist Tradition fits civilian conceptions of procedure and evidence. Indeed, they ask, do they not fit the 'inquisitorial' systems of procedure better than 'adversarial'?[27] If so, how is it that the Rationalist Model is a rational reconstruction of the underlying assumptions of *common law* discourse about evidence? A short answer is first that common law procedural arrangements deviate in many important respects from the pure adversarial model, especially in Damaska's characterization; and secondly, a great deal of our law of evidence is concerned with side-constraints on the pursuit of truth (what Wigmore called 'rules of *extrinsic* policy') rather than with upholding rectitude of decision. Thirdly, the history of the Anglo-American law of evidence is marked by a series of long-running debates. At one extreme, Jeremy Bentham argued that all binding rules of evidence should be abolished. At the other extreme, it has been argued that the law of evidence embodies both the accumulated wisdom of centuries of practical experience and some fundamental notions of procedural fairness, especially in respect of safeguards of persons accused of crime. The latter include the presumption of innocence; the right to silence and the privilege against self-incrimination; exclusion of evidence of character (or disposition – including evidence of past convictions); the hearsay rule and, in the United States, the exclusion of evidence that has been obtained by illegal or unfair means. Such debates are often portrayed as differences between 'Right Wing' proponents of Law-and-Order and 'Left Wing' or Civil Libertarian defenders of the rights of persons suspected of crime. The issues are much more complex than that. However, the debates do fit a recognizable pattern: they are, by and large, debates *within* a single intellectual and ideological tradition; they are repeated across time and across geographical boundaries: for example, they have been repeated, with local variations, in England, Scotland, the United States, Australia, Canada, India – and, indeed, in nearly all common law jurisdictions; similarly recent arguments about criminal evidence in England in the period 1972–85 can be found in almost identical terms in debates in the first half of the nineteenth century. Not surprisingly, the outcome has almost invariably ended in compromise, a 'balancing' of the interests of the community in enforcing the criminal law and in avoiding the wrongful conviction of innocent persons. From time to time the balance shifts in one direction or another, with a general trend towards the reduction in scope and importance of the technical rules of evidence. However, no common law country has yet implemented Bentham's proposals for total abolition of the technical rules. One possibly surprising feature of those debates is that it is the proponents of 'Law-and-Order', generally regarded as conservatives or reactionaries, who claim to have reason on their side and who attribute the survival of the technical rules to the sinister economic interests of a privileged group, the legal profession.

Historical trends

The common law of evidence is a fairly clear example of Anglo-Saxon pragmatic evolution. Change has taken place more through case-by-case decision and piecemeal legislative intervention than through radical or principled reform. It is beyond the scope of this paper to attempt to catalogue, let alone to analyse, the many factors that have contributed to the developments that have taken place over the past fifty years. Some of the more immediate and obvious ones have already been alluded to: changes in patterns of litigation, the growth of tribunals, shifts in political opinion and some specific theoretical developments, for example. Others, perhaps less obvious, but also important, such as the computer revolution, membership of the European Community and changes in the legal profession cannot be dealt with here. However, four interrelated trends deserve specific mention in this context: the decline of the jury, the simplification and 'codification' of the law of evidence, the trend towards discretionary norms, and revival of academic interest in the subject.[28]

In nearly all common law jurisdictions except the United States, the jury has entirely or almost entirely disappeared from civil litigation. The general trend away from contested trials in criminal proceedings has led to a reappraisal of the rationale of the law of evidence, especially in respect of non-jury trials. However, it is important not to exaggerate the decline of the jury. First, the principle of the right to trial by jury in serious criminal cases is greatly valued in the Anglo-American system. For example, no major political party would advocate outright abolition of the jury in the United Kingdom and the *most important* contested criminal trials (though statistically quite small) are still tried by juries. The partial replacement of some jury trials by Diplock Courts in Northern Ireland is perceived as a symbol and a symptom of the continuing 'emergency'. Secondly, although the *origin* of much of our law of evidence is to be explained in terms of jury trial, the *continuance* of some important doctrines is usually justified on a variety of other grounds. Thirdly, because lawyers, police officers and other professional participants have been trained in the jury rules of evidence, they continue to treat the contested jury trial as the paradigm. Similarly, recent debates about the reform of the law of evidence have been dominated and distorted by 'jury thinking'.

Over the past century many common law jurisdictions have either codified the law of evidence or have put codification on the agenda. Among the most important examples is the Indian Evidence Act, 1872, which was adopted or imitated in the colonial period in a great many jurisdictions that were formerly under British rule. Most of these survive today. The Federal Rules of Evidence are now the foundation of the law of evidence in nearly all American jurisdictions. In England there is a traditional resistance to outright codification, but a number of important statutes – notably the Civil Evidence Act, 1968, and the Police and Criminal Evidence Act, 1984 – represent a similar trend. Law reform agencies in Australasia and Canada and some smaller states have also been considering major legislative reform falling short of codification.[29] All of these legislative reforms follow a general pattern: they purport to simplify, to narrow the scope of the rules of evidence and to move in the direction of substituting general principles and flexible standards for mandatory precepts. They differ in form and fall short of the extent of Bentham's anti-nomian thesis, but they have gone a long way in the direction that he advocated.

There has also been a distinct trend away from strict technical rules towards more flexible principles, standards, guidelines, balancing tests and 'rules of practice'. This is connected in part with the decline of the jury and the movement towards simplification and codification of the law of evidence. But it is also connected to broader trends. The reasons are complex and the process of change has been slow, but the trend can clearly be seen by comparing modern treatises on evidence with editions of the same work twenty or thirty years ago. This is made explicit by Colin Tapper, the editor of *Cross on Evidence*. Writing of the daunting task of taking over from Sir Rupert Cross he said:

[W]e both felt that the balance of importance of the law of evidence had shifted since the first edition was published in 1958. In civil proceedings the law of evidence had taken on a much less technical cast, and exclusionary rules have increasingly given way to the operation of discretion, guidelines and considerations of weight. The mainly matrimonial litigation which sustained most of the technicality is now a thing of the past ... Conversely more emphasis has been placed upon the different types of proceedings in which the law of evidence may be invoked and upon the nature and operation of the discretionary exclusion of evidence.[30]

This confirms that the general trend of change in the law of evidence has been consistently in the direction advocated by Bentham, but neither as systematically nor as rapidly as he would have wished. Later we shall have to consider how much of the surviving 'law' consists of mandatory precepts and whether these developments are compatible with the prevailing Thayerite view of the subject.

Finally, since about 1960 there has been a significant revival of academic interest in evidence after a long period in the doldrums. A new generation of evidence scholars has emerged from the shadow cast by the giants of the late nineteenth and early twentieth centuries. Debates about codification and reform stimulated both academic and political interest; adjacent fields such as forensic science, psychology and decision theory have developed rapidly; there have been important developments in respect of the 'new rhetoric' of Chaim Perelman and his associates, the theoretical and practical applications of statistics to problem of proof and, most recently, in connection with legal semiotics.[31]

The Thayerite View of 'The Law of Evidence'

In the Anglo-American tradition there have been four principal attempts to develop an explicit general theory of the 'Law of Evidence'.[32] Gilbert tried to subsume all the rules of evidence under a single principle, the 'best evidence rule'; Bentham saw the existing technical rules as an illogical and indefensible morass, and he argued that there should be no binding rules at all within the framework of the Natural System of Procedure; Stephen tried to find a coherent rationale for the whole of the Law of Evidence in the principle of relevancy. Thayer admired Stephen's enterprise, but agreed with Pollock's judgment that it represented 'a splendid mistake'.[33] Relevance was a matter of logic, not law and 'The law has no mandamus on the logical faculty.'[34] Thayer treated the rules of evidence as a mixed group of exceptions to a principle of freedom of proof. None of these four theories were purely expositions of existing law. Gilbert, Stephen and Thayer were rationalizers and systematizers who advanced creative interpretations of common law doctrine. Bentham considered that the technical rules defied rationalization as well as being indefensible. His theory was explicitly 'censorial' rather than 'expository'. Nearly all changes in the law of evidence since his day have been in the direction that Bentham recommended without going as far as he wished. However, nearly all modern writers on evidence in the common law would have accepted some version of Thayer's thesis and it has more or less explicitly provided the basis for most subsequent attempts to codify this branch of the law, including the Federal Rules of Evidence. Accordingly Thayer is the natural starting-point for interpreting the current position.

The Thayerite conception of the Law of Evidence has a strikingly narrow focus. It concerns processes *in court*; it is restricted to what facts may be presented to the court by whom and the manner of their presentation. It is not directly concerned with pre-trial and post-trial events. Many topics previously included in books on Evidence were exiled to procedure, pleading or substantive law, and in the United States to constitutional law. Underlying this conception are sharp distinctions between materiality, relevance, admissibility and cogency, each of which is governed by a different set of criteria. In constructing an argument on an issue of fact, a four-stage intellectual procedure has to be followed, with each stage belonging to a different sphere of discourse and allocated to a specific functionary. Thus in a contested jury trial the standard pattern is as follows:

Q1   What are the facts to be proved? (Facts in issue, ultimate *probanda*, material facts are all synonymous in this context.) This is the issue of *materiality*; it is governed by *substantive law* and is to be determined by the judge.

Q2   Of any fact offered as evidence or potential evidence: Does this fact tend to support or tend to negate one or more of the facts in issue? This is the question of relevance; it is governed by logic and general experience, and is a matter for the judge.

Q3   Of any fact offered as evidence or potential evidence: Is there a rule or principle that requires that this item of relevant evidence should be excluded because *either*
    (a)   it belongs to a *class* of inadmissible evidence; *or*
    (b)   it would be contrary to the policy of the law to admit this in the circumstances of the case?
This issue of *admissibility* is governed by the law of evidence, and is a question for the judge.

Q4   What *weight* should be given to this item of evidence (or the evidence as a whole) in the circumstances of the case? This is the issue of *evaluation of weight* (or cogency or probative force); it is governed by 'logic and general experience', and is a matter for the jury or other trier of fact. An alternative interpretation is that the criteria for weight of evidence are provided by probability theory, of which there are many versions.

Thayer's surgical narrowing down of the scope of the Law of Evidence was inspired ground-clearing. He then moulded what remained into a simple and coherent system, based on two principles:

(1) That nothing is to be received which is not logically probative of some matter requiring to be proved; and (2) that everything which is thus probative should come in, unless a clear ground of policy of law excludes it.[35]

The first principle (the test of relevance) is *exclusionary*, but is not strictly speaking part of the Law of Evidence: 'It is not so much a rule of evidence as a presupposition involved in the very conception of a rational system of evidence.'[36] The second principle is *inclusionary* and is the basic principle of the Law of Evidence. It mandates the reception of evidence supposed to be logically relevant to the facts in issue, subject to exceptions prescribed by law. The main role of technical rules of evidence is to prescribe the scope of the exceptions to the general inclusionary principle. Later we shall have to assess whether Thayer's formulation was too simple; but its great merit is that it is a magisterial simplification of what had traditionally been seen as a jungle of technicalities.

Thayer's explanation for the perceived complexity of the subject was essentially historical. While the exclusionary rules were logically exceptions to a general principle of inclusion, the historical process was different:

What has taken place, in fact, is the shutting out of the judges of one and another thing from time to time; and so, gradually, the recognition of this exclusion under a rule. These rules of exclusion have had their exceptions; and so the law has come into the shape of a set of primary rules of exclusion; and then a set of exceptions to these rules.[37]

These exceptions, and exceptions to exceptions, were justified on disparate grounds:

Some things are rejected as being of too slight a significance, or as having too conjectural and remote a connection; others, as being dangerous in their effect on the jury, and likely to be misused or overestimated by that body; others as being impolitic, or unsafe on public grounds; others on the bare ground of precedent. It is this sort of thing, as I said before – the rejection on one or other practical ground, of what is really probative – which is the characteristic thing in the law of evidence; stamping it as a child of the jury system.[38]

To these factors of *ad hoc* growth and diversity of reasons for exclusion was added the tendency for this branch of law:

to run over and mingle with other subjects, and to distress all attempts to clarify them . . . Rules, principles and methods of legal reasoning have taken on the color and used the phraseology of this subject, and thus disguised, have figured as rules of Evidence, to the perplexity and confusion of those who sought for a strong grasp of the subject. A bastard sort of technicality has thus sprung up, and a crop of fanciful reasons for anomalies destitute of reason, which baffle and disgust a healthy mind. To detail and scrutinize this topic of legal reasoning would tend to relieve our main subject of a great part of its difficulties and ambiguities.[39]

We need not be unduly concerned here with borderline problems of classification of legal doctrine. But three points about Thayer's conception of the scope of the Law of Evidence deserve emphasis. First, the core of Thayer's view of the Law of Evidence is concerned with the regulation of *reasoning* about disputed questions of fact at trial.[40] The Law of Evidence consists mainly of artificial limitations on free enquiry and ordinary reason in the process of arguing about and justifying decisions on such questions. Since the law, by and large, leaves judgements about relevancy and weight to logic and general experience, the 'excluding function' is the main role of the Law of Evidence.

Secondly, the converse of this last proposition is not the case. The law of evidence is only one of several grounds for excluding evidence. In litigation the issues are artificially and sharply defined in advance by substantive law and pleading; historians, physical scientists and others have no strong concept of materiality to limit their enquiries in such ways. More evidence is excluded on grounds of irrelevance than for any other reason; but relevance is a matter of logic, not law, even if lawyers tend to interpret relevance more strictly than most. It should also be remembered that Bentham, who wished to abolish all formal rules of evidence, was in favour of exclusion of evidence if it was irrelevant or superfluous or its adduction would have involved preponderant vexation, expense or delay judged by the standard of utility in the circumstances of the case.

Thirdly, Thayer indicates that questions of weight are not and should not be governed by rules of law, but are subject only to 'the ordinary rules of human thought and experience, to be sought in the ordinary sources, and not in the law books'.[41] In short, the law prescribes almost no rules for the evaluation of evidence.[42]

Thayer pruned the Law of Evidence in order to provide it with a coherent rationale. His successors built on his general theory, including the distinctions between materiality, relevance, admissibility and weight, but felt unable to sustain such a sharp distinction between evidence and procedure. Thus his pupil and disciple, Wigmore, presented his topical analysis of the system of evidence as follows:

The propositions of which evidence may be offered being thus given by the rules of substantive law and of pleading and procedure, and the law of evidence concerning itself solely with the relation between evidentiary facts and such propositions, the settlement of that relation obviously involves four distinct questions:

1 What facts may be presented as evidence? This is the question of admissibility.
2 By whom must evidence be presented? This is the question of burden of proof and, incidentally, of presumptions.
3 To whom must evidence be presented? This question involves the relation of function of judge and of jury, as respectively deciding upon law and fact.
4 Of what propositions in issue need no evidence be presented? This question includes the topics ordinarily termed 'judicial notice' and 'judicial admissions'.

The last three topics represent the borderline of what is in strictness the Law of Evidence. They involve and rest upon certain aspects of procedure that are independent of the evidential material. The question of who has the burden of proof, for example, is of a piece with the questions of who shall open and close the argument and of whether certain allegations require an affirmative or negative pleading. They form a part of a treatise on evidence merely because their material is chiefly evidential material and because their problems constantly have to be discriminated from the strictly evidential problems.[43]

By and large subsequent treatise writers and codifiers have followed Thayer in accepting a fairly restrictive view of the subject, but have followed Wigmore in including all or most of the 'borderline' topics.

A modern gloss on the Thayerite view: Philip McNamara

In a valuable article an Australian lawyer, Philip McNamara, has reformulated and glossed the Thayerite view.[44] His summary statement of his suggested 'Framework of the Rules of Evidence' mainly articulates current orthodoxy and is worth stating in full.

Framework of the Rules of Evidence

Since the beginning of the 20th Century, it has been true to say that, judged by their practical effect, the common law rules of evidence fall into the following framework:

1   There is one *principle of inclusion*: evidence is admissible and required to be admitted if sufficiently relevant to the facts in issue between the parties to be capable of assisting a rational tribunal of fact to determine the issues. This rule determines whether, as a matter of substance, information can lawfully be admitted by the tribunal of law and used by the tribunal of fact.

2   There is *one principle of exclusion*: information is not admissible in any form from any witness for any purpose if its reception is contrary to the public interest. This is the only principle which predicates that, as a matter of substance, information cannot be received by the tribunal of law or acted on by the tribunal of fact.

3   There are four principal rules which, to the extent to which they are independent of the inclusionary rule, restrict the use of *relevant evidence* once admitted:

    (a)   Evidence of an out-of-court assertion cannot in general be tendered to be used for the sole purpose of supporting the credibility of a witness;

    (b)   Evidence of an out-of-court statement cannot in general be tendered to be used for the sole purpose of proving the truth of matters asserted by the statement;

    (c)   Evidence that an actor or witness formed, expressed or holds a particular opinion cannot in general be tendered to be used for the sole purpose of proving the existence of the matter opined;

    (d)   In a criminal case evidence of the misdeeds of a defendant not connected with the events charged cannot in general be tendered to be used for the sole purpose of authorising the inference that the defendant has a bad character and is therefore guilty of the crime presently charged.

    It will be suggested that all but the second of these 'great canons of exclusion' are merely facets of the inclusionary rule.

4   There are rules as to the *competence and compellability of witnesses*: at common law, the parties and their spouses, children, lunatics, convicts and atheists were incompetent as witnesses. The competence and compellability of witnesses is now regulated by statute.

5   There are rules conferring *privileges* on competent and compellable witnesses to withhold relevant information: into this category falls the privilege against self-incrimination and the rules regulating legal professional privilege;

6   There are rules as to the *form* of evidence: for example, evidence of the contents of a document must, in general, be given in the form of the original document itself;

7   There are rules regulating *the manner of giving evidence*: for example, in general, a
    witness must give evidence on oath from memory and, in general, examination in
    chief cannot be conducted by the use of leading questions.

8   There are rules qualifying or restricting *the powers of the tribunal of fact*: into this
    category fall the rules as to presumptions, the rules as to burden and standard of
    proof, and rules of law requiring corroboration as a condition of conviction in certain
    criminal cases. In addition, there is the fundamental rule that the tribunal of fact
    must act on the evidence alone and not on its own knowledge.

9   There are rules of law and of practice conferring powers or imposing obligations on
    trial judges: for instance, the judge presiding over a criminal trial by jury has a duty to
    warn the jury as to its assessment of the credibility of the evidence of certain
    witnesses (complainants in sexual cases, children and accomplices) and as to the
    manner in which it uses evidence which lends itself to a proper use and to an
    improper use. In addition, the judge in a criminal trial has the power to reject
    relevant evidence pursuant to the judge's obligation to ensure that the trial is fair to
    the defendant.[45]

All but paragraph 3 of the first seven paragraphs can be interpreted as a
modern restatement of the Thayerite view of the Law of Evidence. Apart from
up-dating Thayer, McNamara glosses his theory in three main respects: First,
instead of treating the main exclusionary rules and discretions as a series of
disparate exceptions to the inclusionary rule, he suggests that '[r]elevant
evidence is required to be rejected as a matter of law if and only if it is contrary
to the public interest that it be received.'[46] While 'public interest' is an unruly
horse and there is no closed list of categories of evidence which must be
excluded on this ground, there are in fact only three established classes of
evidence which are generally rejected irrespective of the use for which they are
tendered, of the form of the evidence and the qualifications of the witness.
These are documents covered by 'public-interest immunity'; information
tending to disclose the identity of police informers; and 'information as to the
tenor of communications between estranged spouses aimed at achieving
reconciliation of their marital differences'.[47]

Secondly, McNamara introduces the notion of 'rules of use' and suggests
that most evidentiary rules that are treated as rules of admissibility are more
correctly interpreted as rules restricting the use of relevant evidence once it has
been admitted. For example, the hearsay rule prohibits the use of out-of-court
statements to prove the truth of such statements (subject to numerous
exceptions); but it does not prohibit the tendering of such statements for other
purposes, for example, to prove that the words were spoken. The connection
between admissibility and use is that certain categories of evidence will be
excluded if they are tendered solely for a prohibited purpose. Apart from being
a more accurate characterization of such rules, the concept of 'rules of use'
serves as a reminder that they are not a spent force once questions of
admissibility have been determined.[48] Rather they continue to restrict the
freedom of the parties and the tribunal of fact in important ways at all stages of
the trial.

Thirdly, McNamara differs from Thayer in treating presumptions, burdens
of proof and standards of proof as part of the Law of Evidence. In this respect
he is in accord with nearly all writers on evidence including Wigmore,

McCormick and Cross, in that they deal with these subjects in books (and codes) of Evidence. This is sometimes justified on grounds of practical convenience rather than of conceptual purity. I shall suggest later that Thayer's attempt to draw sharp distinctions between rules of evidence, procedure and substantive law was bound to fail and that for most practical purposes the classification of particular doctrines under one of those heads is of little or no importance.[49] However, there is one good conceptual reason for including at least most of these topics within this modified Thayerite view of the subject. From this perspective the Law of Evidence is that body of doctrine (rules plus) that regulates the reception and use of evidence in *argumentation and 'internal determination'* of disputed questions of fact. Presumptions, burdens and standards of proof, corroboration and, I would add, judicial notice all bear directly on these functions. Accordingly, they fit comfortably within a coherent view of the subject from this perspective.

The law of evidence is bedevilled by technical complexity and conceptual difficulties. Specialists may wish to take issue with some details of McNamara's re-interpretation of particular doctrines within his framework.[50] However, his restatement of the Thayerite perspective and his three main glosses all represent significant improvements on the original. The core of Thayer's insights is preserved, and some refinements are introduced that have considerable explanatory power. Accordingly, subject to one major caveat, this seems to me to be the clearest and most coherent modern formulation of the Thayerite thesis. Then I shall suggest an alternative perspective on the subject which suggests some important limitations to the Thayerite theory without necessarily invalidating it.

A further gloss on the Thayerite view: freedom of proof as the basic principle

The Thayerite theory can be interpreted as stating that the Law of Evidence consists of a series of disparate exceptions to a principle of free proof. McNamara's gloss suggests that those exceptions which deal with exclusion of evidence can themselves be subsumed under a single inclusionary principle, viz. that all relevant evidence may and must be admitted unless to do so would be contrary to the public interest. His other categories (3–9) can also be interpreted as setting artificial constraints on free proof.

If a body of law is conceived as constituting a series of exceptions to a single principle, it would seem natural to start by elucidating the nature and scope of that principle, before considering the exceptions. What, then, is 'free proof'? In a recent essay I have explored in detail some alternative conceptions of this relatively neglected concept.[51] In the present context, however, one can give a relatively straightforward answer that fits the Thayerite view of the Law of Evidence. 'Free proof' means an absence of formal rules that interfere with free enquiry and natural or commonsense reasoning. In the adversary system, where the parties have primary control over what evidence is presented in what form and what questions are or are not put to witnesses, the freedom of enquiry by judge, jury or other triers of fact is strictly limited. It is for the parties to determine whom and what they see or hear, but not how they evaluate and reason from evidence. This 'freedom' is largely the freedom of the parties and to a lesser extent that of the judge, jury or trier of fact. This is, of course, rather different from Bentham's model of the Natural System of Procedure, which was more inquisitorial in nature.[52] Nevertheless Bentham's attack on all binding rules of evidence, his 'anti-nomian thesis', provides the classic picture of a system of free proof in adjudication: no rules excluding classes of witnesses or of evidence; no rules of priority or weight or quantum; no binding rules as to form or manner of presentation; no artificial restriction on questioning or reasoning; no right of silence or testimonial privileges; no restrictions on reasoning other than the general principles of practical reason; no exclusion of evidence unless it is irrelevant or superfluous or its adduction would involve preponderant vexation, expense or delay in the circumstances of the particular case.[53]

This conception of 'free proof' is entirely compatible with the Thayerite picture of the Law of Evidence. In this context, there are two main differences between Thayer and Bentham: first, Thayer's main concern was expository: to explain and clarify the existing law. Bentham's project was censorial: to criticize and make the case for the abolition of the whole body of binding rules. Secondly, whereas Bentham could find no justification for any formal derogations from the principle of free proof, Thayer believed that a few limited exceptions were justified on grounds of policy.

That they shared the same basic picture of the nature of the common law of evidence, while disagreeing about how much was worth retaining, is reinforced by Thayer's most important disciple. John Henry Wigmore divided the subject of Judicial Evidence into two distinct parts: the Principles (or Science) of Proof, based on 'Logic, Psychology and General Experience' and the Trial Rules of Evidence.[54] The Principles of Proof, said Wigmore, were anterior to and more important than the Trial Rules. It is worth looking at both elements in this claim in detail.

Wigmore argued that it was better to study the Principles of Proof *before* studying the rules and, while he controlled the curriculum, his students at Northwestern had to take his course on Proof (Evidence I) before moving on to the Trial Rules (Evidence II).[55] This was not merely because it seems sensible to study a basic principle before considering exceptions to it. More important, the Science of Proof is logically anterior to the Trial Rules, as well as providing their underlying rationales (in so far as they had a rational basis). Thayer had made essentially the same point when he claimed that his two basic principles of evidence (the exclusionary and inclusionary principles) were not so much part of the Law of Evidence as necessary presuppositions of a rational system of evidence.[56] The exclusion of irrelevant evidence was a matter of logic not law; and there was a general presumption in favour of admitting all relevant evidence. In order to have a clear view of the Law of Evidence one needs first to understand these two basic principles of proof.

Wigmore also claimed that the Science of Proof was more important than the Law of Evidence.[57] I shall argue below that Wigmore understated this part of his case, even on his own terms, and that, if one adopts a broader perspective, 'the argument of exaggerated importance' becomes even more telling. At this stage it is sufficient to make the point that both Wigmore and, only to a slightly less extent, Thayer saw clearly that the Law of Evidence was truly a law of exceptions, not only in the sense that it consisted of a series of derogations from a basic principle of free proof, but also that these derogations were really quite limited in number, scope and practical importance.

Gruyère cheese and the Cheshire Cat: the argument of exaggerated importance

Thayer's picture of the Law of Evidence has dominated Anglo-American discussions of the subject during the twentieth century. In this view our Law of Evidence is a series of disparate exceptions to a single principle of free proof. 'Free proof', in this context, covers questions of admissibility and use as well as evaluation.[58] Normally the phrase refers to freedom from regulation by artificial, binding rules (mandatory precepts); but even on the broader conception of 'rules' of evidence adopted here, the extent of that freedom is quite remarkable. Even in Thayer's day the Law of Evidence was truly a law of exceptions; the silences were more extensive than the 'noise' that interfered with free consideration and evaluation of evidence and with principles of 'natural reason'. Consider, for example, the following points:

1   The first principle of the Law of Evidence is that only relevant evidence may be admitted or heard. But the test of relevance – what tends to support or negate the alleged facts that are in issue – is a matter of logic and not of law.

2   There are almost no rules of *evaluation* of evidence, that is rules that direct what 'weight' or 'cogency' or 'probative force' is to be attached to any type of evidence.[59] One reason why it has been felt that it is appropriate to leave determinations of questions of fact to the jury is that such determinations are best made on the basis of ordinary practical reasoning and commonsense knowledge.[60] Connected to this the old *rules of priority* – so far as they ever existed – have almost completely disappeared. There used to be a rule known as the 'Best Evidence Rule' which had the effect of creating a hierarchy of types of evidence: with official certified records at the top; then documents under seal; then written documents and so on.[61] Such distinctions can still be important in other parts of our law – as they are in most modern legal systems. But they do not now operate as rules of weight or evaluation.

Thus we have no principle that written evidence is to be given greater weight than testimonial evidence. We have no principle that testimonial evidence is to be given greater weight than circumstantial evidence. Nor is there any general principle of law that states that some kinds of witnesses are more credible than others. Generally speaking, the weighing of evidence is left to the logic and common sense of the trier of fact in the particular circumstances of the case. There are a few exceptions, but they are quite minor.

3   Next, there are almost no *quantitative* rules – that is rules prescribing the number of witnesses or the amount of evidence required to prove something. The main exception concerns what we call *corroboration* – that is a formal requirement that the testimony of a witness must be confirmed by at least one

other witness or by circumstantial evidence. What is very striking about our rules of mandatory corroboration is that they are very few in number and wholly exceptional. Examples include perjury; procuration of girls for prostitution; and, until 1988, facts testified by unsworn child witnesses (see the Criminal Justice Act, 1988). In a few cases, for example in respect of the evidence of accomplices, the judge must warn the jury of the dangers of reaching a conclusion without corroboration, but the trier of fact may nevertheless decide on the basis of the evidence of a single witness.[62] The point is illustrated by the example of eyewitness identification. Although evidence of eyewitness identification is almost universally recognized to be highly unreliable, I know of no jurisdiction in the common law world which has a formal rule requiring that this type of evidence *must* be corroborated. Warning as to the dangers is accepted as enough.[63]

Since Thayer's time the rules of exclusion have been increasingly curtailed. The great bulk of those that survive relate to criminal and not to civil proceedings. I do not wish to deny that some of these rules are important both in theory and practice. Some, such as the rules excluding coerced confessions and evidence of prior convictions, also have important symbolic and educative value in that they exemplify and reaffirm important procedural principles (due process; judge the act, not the actor; the presumption of innocence). Some significant categories of evidence are excluded some of the time, but it is only a tiny proportion of all evidence. However, I wish to suggest that even the limited Thayerite view encourages a tendency to exaggerate the importance of rules of evidence in litigation as a whole.[64]

On to this formalist account of our law, conceived in terms of rules, I wish to superimpose a realist gloss, which emphasizes the way important decisions are taken in practice in actual legal processes. Let us for a moment resort to metaphor. The Thayerite metaphor is of a great silence punctuated by spasmodic noises of varying duration and intensity or of a piece of Gruyère that consists of more holes than cheese. The realist metaphor is visual. In one of our classics of literature, *Alice in Wonderland*, one of the characters is the Cheshire Cat who keeps appearing and disappearing and fading away, so that sometimes one could see the whole body, sometimes only a head, sometimes only a vague outline and sometimes nothing at all, so that Alice was never sure whether or not he was there or, indeed, whether he existed at all.[65] In practice, our rules of evidence appear to be rather like that.

First, as you might expect, the rules are often ignored or broken or waived in practice. In civil proceedings some or most of the rules may be expressly or impliedly waived by the parties. In criminal cases it may be tactically dangerous to make technical objections; and in magistrates' courts, which try over 95 per cent of our minor criminal cases, it is a brave lawyer who raises technical points on the law of evidence.[66]

Next, there are other factors than non-observance in court. Much more important is the fact that only a tiny percentage of cases ever reach the point of being contested in proceedings in which the rules of evidence are meant to apply. In recent years there have been less than thirty contested civil jury trials per annum in England and Wales. And much less than 10 per cent of contested criminal trials are tried by juries – although these are the most serious and important ones. Just as significant is the fact that only a tiny percentage of cases ever reach the point of a contested trial: of civil cases, in which formal proceedings have been started, the vast majority are settled out of court. Similarly, and this is an important difference between the Anglo-Saxon and Continental traditions, where the accused pleads guilty, there is no trial. Between 60 and 80 per cent of criminal proceedings (the figures vary in different courts) culminate in guilty pleas.[67]

The law of evidence casts a shadow over pre-trial proceedings in ways which are imperfectly understood and hardly documented. Take, for example, a fairly ordinary case of someone suspected of shoplifting who had several previous convictions for this and other kinds of criminal offences. Generally speaking, those previous convictions may not be used at trial as evidence of his guilt on this occasion, if he pleads not guilty. But what effect does this rule have on other parts of the process? During the process of investigation his criminal record may be a key piece of information in making him a suspect and in guiding the police enquiries. At the moment when a decision has to be made whether or not to prosecute him, the information will probably be available to the prosecutor, who should discount it in assessing the likelihood of obtaining a conviction in a contested trial, but who may nonetheless treat it as relevant for other purposes.[68] The same bit of information will probably be relevant to a series of other pre-trial decisions, including the accused's decision whether or not to plead guilty, and the trial strategy of both prosecution and defence. If he pleads not guilty, but is convicted on the basis of admissible evidence presented to the court, the information about his prior record is produced (along with other general background information) as an important element in determination of sentence and it may be of practical importance in many other post-trial decisions, for example, whether and when he might be released on parole. Thus in a single, routine example of criminal process the same item of information may be inadmissible evidence for the purpose of determining guilt, may be discounted in some pre-trial decisions as potentially inadmissible evidence, but may play an important and legitimate role in a number of other important decisions in the total process. Often the exact nature of that role may be difficult to pinpoint.

Finally, a very great deal of our administration of justice does not take place in courts of law, but in administrative tribunals, before arbitrators, courts martial and the like. Here the Cheshire Cat image of the Law of Evidence really comes into its own. For in many such proceedings either the formal rules of evidence do not officially apply, but nevertheless exert an influence on the proceedings; or the tribunal is guided but not bound by the rules of evidence; or they exert a shadowy influence on the ways of thought and styles of argument. It is not uncommon for a barrister to arrive at a tribunal dealing with wrongful dismissal or welfare matters unsure whether all or any of the strict rules of evidence will be applied. In many of these arenas something close to a system of free proof operates a great deal of the time. The courts exercise a narrowly circumscribed supervisory jurisdiction over these tribunals, but generally speaking this does not extend to appeals against determinations of fact.

So far I have argued that our Law of Evidence consists of a rather limited and diverse mixture of exceptions to a principle of free proof, especially free evaluation of evidence; that the restricted group of surviving rules only apply in their full rigour in contested jury trials – which are a tiny part of all litigation; and even in such trials they are not always strictly observed. I have further suggested that a false impression of the nature and importance of the subject is given by the Evidence scholars. It is not only foreigners who are given a false impression; rather it is that we systematically mislead ourselves and our students.

Why should this be so? The key lies in changing conceptions of legal scholarship. We have seen that in criticizing the law of evidence in his day, Bentham was attacking mandatory precepts excluding *classes* of evidence and of witnesses. He was against formal regulation, but this did not preclude excluding evidence in particular cases on grounds of irrelevance, superfluity or preponderant vexation, expense or delay. Thayer's conception of the 'Law' of Evidence can reasonably be interpreted as extending beyond mandatory precepts to include general principles and flexible standards. What was striking about his perception was the narrowness of the scope of the Law of Evidence and the limited scope of this body of exceptions to the principle of freedom of proof. The general tendency of change since his time has been to erode this body of exceptions still further.

On this view Thayer was essentially correct, but he did not go far enough. From a broader perspective, the Thayerite Law of Evidence should be seen as only one small part of the subject of Evidence and Proof in litigation. From this point of view far too much attention has been paid to a limited number of 'paper rules' to the neglect of a number of topics of equal or greater theoretical and practical importance, such as what is involved in evaluating weight or the meaning and function of standards of proof and other standards for decision[69] or the nature of free proof.

The argument of exaggerated importance might be interpreted as leading to a version of 'rule scepticism' or 'radical indeterminacy'. This would be a mistake. The argument, as it applies in England, can be restated in four propositions:

1   The Law of Evidence is at least as remarkable for the extent of the matters which are *not* governed by formal rules or other legal norms (the silences) as for the matters which it does address.
2   The modern law of evidence contains few, if any, mandatory precepts; many of the most important surviving doctrines are more accurately described as flexible standards, guidelines or balancing tests.[70]
3   The law of evidence generally only applies in full force and directly to decisions by adjudicators (in their role as filters and ultimate triers of fact) in contested criminal jury trials and appeals therefrom. Such decisions represent a tiny and unrepresentative portion of important decisions in litigation.
4   Such norms as do survive are frequently waived or ignored or not treated as applying in full force (or at all) to many important decisions in litigation. Even where a rule of evidence has been found to have been breached, e.g.

evidence has been improperly admitted, this is only exceptionally treated as a sufficient ground for reversal on appeal.

Strong 'rule scepticism' – the belief that 'talk of rules is a myth'[71] – would involve a further proposition:

5   (a) Even those 'rules' of evidence which are claimed to survive do not in practice limit the freedom of adjudicators to decide as they please.

A modern variant of 'rule scepticism' is said to be 'the radical indeterminacy thesis'. This might be interpreted to apply in the present context as follows:

   (b) Every rule of evidence is open to a variety of interpretations from which any interpreter is free to choose at will.

Sometimes 'rule scepticism' is attributed to 'American realists', such as the young Karl Llewellyn, and 'radical indeterminacy' is attributed to leading members of the American Critical Legal Studies Movement. Such attributions are, in my view, generally unwarranted and misleading.[72] In order to avoid similar misinterpretations it is necessary to make it clear why the argument of exaggerated importance is different from and does not involve commitment to 5(a) or (b). In particular, it does not imply the proposition that all rules of evidence are 'radically indeterminate' nor the proposition that adjudicators are free to decide as they please. Nor does it follow from the argument that decisions taken in 'the shadow' of the 'trial rules of Evidence' are not and should not be influenced by these doctrines.

Firstly, the argument of exaggerated importance only claims that a misleading impression has been given about the *extent* of surviving mandatory precepts in the Law of Evidence. For example, the hearsay rule (even if interpreted as a rule of use) still serves to exclude a significant amount of potential evidence, especially in criminal cases (see now the Criminal Justice Act, 1988, ss. 23–6, and Keane (1989), ch. 12). Much of the surviving doctrine relating to competence and compellability of witnesses, privilege, prior convictions, and some of what remains of corroboration can similarly be interpreted as general mandatory precepts in this sense. It is reasonable to treat the duty of the judge to warn the jury about the dangers of identification evidence or the credibility of certain classes of witnesses (e.g. accomplices) as involving mandatory precepts even though they impose no duty on the ultimate triers of fact to ignore or disbelieve such evidence.[73] The crucial point is that, as a matter of doctrine as well as practice, the scope of such formal, technical mandatory rules is really quite limited.

Secondly, a very high proportion of surviving evidence doctrine consists of flexible standards, balancing tests and other norms that involve the exercise of judgment in the particular circumstances of the case. Thus, the Police and Criminal Evidence Act has substituted a flexible standard of reliability in the circumstances for a much more formal test of involuntariness[74] subject to a complete exclusion of confessions obtained by oppression. The similar fact rule has been interpreted in a way that involves balancing the likely prejudicial effect against the probative value of this evidence in the context of this case.[75]

Thirdly, some may challenge as over-inclusive McNamara's claim that there is only one principle of exclusion based on the public interest.[76] But, in so far as it is correct, 'public interest' is a notoriously vague term and the general tendency has been in the direction of balancing 'public interest' and other considerations in a specific context.[77] Again, English law has rejected a general rule excluding evidence obtained by illegal or improper means, but has left this to the residual discretion of the trial court to exclude evidence to ensure that the trial is fair.[78]

Fourthly, in addition to this general tendency to move towards more flexible norms, there is growing recognition that some 'rules' of evidence are either so vague or so unworkable as not to deserve to be called rules. The 'Best Evidence Rule' and the doctrine of 'Res Gestae' have been well described as 'evidentiary ghosts'.[79] Another example is the 'Opinion rule' which prescribes that non-expert witnesses must confine themselves to relating facts within their personal knowledge and their opinions or beliefs about the facts, based on experience are to be excluded. However, it is generally recognized that a sharp distinction between 'facts' and 'opinions' is conceptually dubious and impossible to maintain in practice. Accordingly, it cannot be treated as a rigid rule, and in practice a good deal of leeway is given to witnesses in this regard.[80]

The list could be extended. The central point is that the modern English Law of Evidence, in respect of both rules of auxiliary probative policy and of extrinsic policy, is much closer to what Bentham advocated than has been generally recognized. Galligan puts the matter well:

Bentham did not argue that rules be replaced simply by discretion, but rather by discretion structured through guidelines. Indeed, Bentham can be seen as a precursor of the lively debate of recent years as to the best mix of rules and discretion in any area of official decision-making, and his case for structured discretion has many supporters. It has come to be recognised, indeed, that guidelines can operate in different ways, ranging from factors to take into account as a matter of prudence, to factors that must be considered, through to instructions that have the force of rules except that the judge has the discretion to depart from them for good reasons. Considering the different forms and force of guidelines, it is a mistake to draw too sharp a distinction between rules on the one hand, and standards of lesser force and specificity on the other. Strict rules with an all-or-nothing quality are likely to have a minor role in any context of practical decision-making, and evidence is no exception. Decisions can normally be regulated without recourse to rules in a strict and narrow sense, and it is to be remembered that Bentham's strictures were against rules only in that sense.[81]

Galligan's statement provides a useful basis for the third reason for distinguishing the argument of exaggerated importance from rule-scepticism and radical indeterminacy. It does not follow from the proposition that the Law of Evidence is largely discretionary that in determining disputed issues of fact judges, other triers of fact and appellate courts are 'free to decide as they choose'. Discretion, as Galligan and others have argued, is not to be equated with arbitrariness:

On the assumption that one's choices must be reasoned, discretion consists not in the authority to choose among different actions, but to choose amongst different courses of action *for good reasons*. The course of action cannot be separated from the reasons, and therefore the standards on which it is based. If indeed the standards are settled in advance (and there are often good reasons why they should be) the decision must be made according to these terms and an appropriate course of action will follow.[82]

It is central to the ideas of the Rationalist Tradition that adjudicative decisions on questions of fact (and I would argue other important factual determinations in litigation) should, so far as is feasible, be the subject of argument, justification and evaluation according to rational standards. What is striking about such decisions is the extent to which they are structured in a standard way. More than in most forms of enquiry and decision making there are norms governing how the issues should be framed, what constitute valid and invalid reasons, how the weight or cogency of reasons is to be evaluated, and what are the standards for decision in a given context. Not only juries, and those who guide and address them, but all adjudicators are subject to essentially the same prescriptive model of reasoning. Moreover, aiming for rectitude of decision in respect of determinations of fact is not only an obligation of adjudicators but also of other officials charged with making important decisions in litigation – including, for example, prosecutors, administrators, sentencing authorities, appellate courts and so on.[83]

What is the source of these prescriptive standards of validity and cogency in reasoning? The answer given by the Thayerite view is as follows: the framing of factual issues for determination – the question of materiality – is governed by substantive law; the question of validity (what constitute admissible reasons) is determined primarily by ordinary canons of practical reasoning, subject to the exceptions prescribed by the Law of Evidence in the form of principles, standards, guidelines and a few mandatory precepts. In the case of adjudicative decisions, the standards for decision are incorporated in the standards of proof, which are also conventionally classified as forming part of the Law of Evidence. Various norms governing the manner, form and order of presentation and argumentation about evidence are allocated, somewhat randomly, to Procedure and Evidence.

The Thayerite view of the Law of Evidence, and its modern glosses, fall four-square within the Rationalist Tradition. His concept of the Law of Evidence as being concerned essentially with norms of reasoning provided the basis for rationalizing, systematizing and simplifying the subject. The argument of exaggerated importance does not fundamentally challenge this perspective nor is it seriously subversive of aspirational rationalism. However, it does suggest a number of ways in which the Thayerite view might be re-interpreted and modified.

First, if the primary focus of attention is to be reasoning about questions of fact, then it is surely unduly restrictive to concentrate solely or mainly on those norms which artificially derogate from general canons of reasoning appropriate to this context. That is to exaggerate the importance of the Law of Evidence relative to the other sources of norms which structure, guide and regulate argumentation about questions of fact. A simple way of doing this is to expand the conception of 'law' in this context to include all such norms – including the area designated by Wigmore as 'the logic of proof'. In this view, because the test of relevance is logic, it does not follow that it is not 'law'; because there are almost no positive rules governing weight or cogency, it does not follow that the applicable criteria do not deserve to be studied and debated as part of the subject of evidence within the discipline of law; because validity and cogency of reasoning in this context is based in large part on some very general principles of political morality, such principles deserve to be explicitly treated as forming part of this branch of 'the law'. In this view, Bentham's *Rationale of Judicial Evidence* is indeed a law book and the Law of Evidence is a sub-discipline of the general subject of 'legal reasoning' or 'lawyers' reasonings'.[84]

So much for the normative aspect of the Law of Evidence. The argument of exaggerated importance also has a 'realist' dimension. It reminds us that in order to understand this branch of the law in action one needs to consider all the important decisions that it affects, directly or indirectly, or fails to influence significantly when it is supposed to do so. Who in fact invokes, uses or ignores 'the law' of evidence in what context, for what purposes with what results? Such questions are an essential part of understanding and evaluating this branch of the law for the purposes of study, practice and reform. In so far as particular norms are ineffective, incomprehensible, offend the common sense of particular participants or have side-effects considered to be undesirable, such factors need to be taken into account in evaluating them as well as the aspirational values that they purport to serve. Conversely some doctrines may have direct or indirect, unperceived or unintended consequences that may be of positive value. Disappointingly little empirical research has been done in this area and some of the most important questions (e.g. about the actual operation of prejudicial effect)[85] are notoriously difficult to research. The 'realist' argument demands that these questions be addressed and some sort of assessments made, even if they fall short of scientific findings.

One law of evidence?

It is sometimes suggested that we have not one Law of Evidence, but a series of Laws of Evidence and that this needs to be recognized in legislation, in judicial development of the law, and in academic treatments.[86] Support for this view can be found in four rather different kinds of argument.

First, criminal, civil and other curial proceedings exist for different purposes and the values underlying the rules of evidence in each context should be fitted to these purposes.

Secondly, there are in fact many differences of detail between criminal and civil evidence, and between the Law of Evidence as it applies in courts and other tribunals. In particular non-criminal evidence doctrine is generally less extensive than criminal evidence.

Thirdly, the kind of 'total process' perspective that has been advocated in this essay leads to the conclusion that determination of the factual component of non-adjudicative decisions needs a greater differentiation between the contexts and roles of each kind of decision. For example, different standards for decision may be appropriate for decisions to prosecute, determinations of innocence or guilt, sentencing, appeal, parole and so on. Similarly the criteria of relevance and rules of admissibility may vary according to the kind of decision.

Fourthly, as we have seen, not only is it difficult to draw and maintain a sharp distinction between 'evidence' and 'procedure', but procedural and evidentiary issues are intimately related both in theory and practice. Accordingly, if evidence is to be reintegrated with procedure, then the Law of Evidence needs to be disaggregated and redistributed among the different sub-divisions of procedure. For the purposes of legislation, exposition and education, evidentiary issues and doctrines should be treated as sub-branches of the different branches of procedural law.

In England there has been a discernible tendency in this direction. We have, for example, the Civil Evidence Act, 1964 and the Police and Criminal Evidence Act, 1984; such practitioners' 'bibles' as *The White Book, Archbold,* and Stone's *Justices' Manual* incorporate the applicable rules of evidence; some, but too few, tribunals 'codify' the applicable provisions of evidence in their rule-books; not only police training but many academic courses concentrate almost exclusively on Criminal Evidence; and such tendencies are also observable in the academic literature.

There are clearly often good practical reasons for disaggregating criminal and civil and other aspects of the Law of Evidence for particular purposes. There are also reasons for regretting the artificial segregation of Anglo-American Evidence scholarship from adjacent fields of study. The question remains whether there is any justification for retaining 'Evidence' as a specialized field of study within the discipline of law.

It might be argued that we should defer to the contingent fact that there is a well-settled field with established specialists, entrenched courses and an extensive literature. Like it or not, it might be argued, Evidence as a subject is here to stay. Furthermore, tearing the seamless web is inevitably a somewhat arbitrary business and the distinction between Evidence and Procedure is no more artificial and uncomfortable than the separation of Tort and Contract, or Real and Personal Property. There are, however, some more positive reasons for continuing to treat Evidence and Proof in Litigation, and the Law of Evidence as part of that subject, as a worthwhile focus of attention.[87]

According to the modified Thayerite view explored in this essay the Law of Evidence is primarily concerned with reasoning about questions of fact. I have argued that we should treat the logic of proof and the notion of free proof as part of the 'law' of evidence – or at least as necessary preliminaries to its study. What is striking about adjudicative determinations of fact – by tribunals, criminal juries, magistrates and judges in civil cases – is that normative theory lays down almost uniform norms for structuring and evaluating the validity and cogency of arguments. The *concepts* of materiality, relevance, admissibility, cogency and standards for decision apply not only to adjudicative determinations of fact, but to all official decisions in which 'rectitude of decision' in respect of factual issues is an aspiration. There is thus a single paradigm for constructing, reconstructing, and evaluating arguments in respect of such determinations. Some elements of that paradigm are controversial – as is illustrated by the probability debates or the tensions between holism and atomism – but there is a consensus within aspirational rationalism that the general principles of commonsense reasoning apply, subject only to a relatively few technical limitations in different contexts.

The technical rules of evidence are not only exceptional, even in the unrepresentative context of the contested criminal jury trial, but these technical rules are also best understood as *exceptions* to a principle of free proof which itself can be explicated in terms of the basic concepts of the logic of proof. Similarly, while standards for decision, such as the criminal and civil standards of proof, may vary according to context, their function and logic remain fairly constant.

⎡It may be objected that different values apply to civil, criminal and non-curial proceedings and the suggested paradigm for rational fact-determination does not allow for this. This is not correct. The paradigm postulates the aim of rectitude of decision. In some contexts this purpose is overridden by other values – such as preservation of state security – and this is the rationale for 'rules of extrinsic policy'. In some contexts a high value is placed on avoiding misdecisions of one kind rather than another – for example, giving a higher priority to avoiding the risk of mistaken convictions rather than mistaken acquittals. Such purposes are furthered not only by standards for decision, such as the presumption of innocence and the criminal standard of proof, but also by 'rules of auxiliary probative policy', such as the exclusion of, or mandatory warnings about, classes of evidence considered to be prejudicial or unreliable. Nothing in the paradigm postulates that rectitude of decision is the only or a paramount value in all contexts. What it does is identify what is involved in making valid and cogent arguments when this is the objective.[88]⎤

Law for whom?

Whose behaviour and expectations are affected by those norms that form the Law of Evidence broadly conceived? Even on the narrow 'trial rules' view, several categories of participants are affected in quite complex ways. In the contested trial the focal point is the judge, in his multiple role of filter, umpire and guide, and the jury as ultimate trier of fact. Norms which are standards for decision, such as the standards and burdens of proof, directly concern the jury as ultimate triers of fact in the way that exclusionary rules do not. Bentham's 'admonitory instructions' are directed by the legislator to the trier of fact (via the judge in the case of the jury trials). Even with a single focal point there are many satellite standpoints: the criminal investigator's role is not merely to 'solve the problem' to his own satisfaction, but to collect sufficient potentially admissible evidence to secure a guilty plea or conviction in the event of a contested trial.[89] Barristers and other advocates need to have the 'trial rules' at their fingertips both in preparing for trial and in making instant tactical and other decisions, for example whether to put or object to a certain question. The actions of many other participants take place in the shadow of a potential trial, including 'the trial rules' – they have to *anticipate* decisions directly affected by evidentiary norms.

Thus the 'trial rules' affect behaviour and expectations before as well as at trial. One of the paradoxes of academic treatments of the Law of Evidence is that while the main *arena* for action is conceived to be the contested trial, one of the most important *sources* of authority and examples is appellate decisions. The main staple for classroom discussion, treatises, academic commentary and even debates on reform is the Law Reports rather than trial records. Ironically, a 'realist' justification is sometimes advanced for this. The Hard-nosed Practitioner, and his or her academic counterparts, suggest that the main practical significance of the law of evidence for the trial lawyer is to lay the basis for appeal by 'creating a record'. When an appellate court is inclined to reverse a decision on the facts at first instance it needs a good legal justification for so doing; the law of evidence is the main source of technical pegs on which to hang such appeals. One version of this view is elaborated in a leading American casebook on evidence as follows:

> Every experienced trial lawyer realizes as he or she goes into a litigation that his cause may not prevail at the trial level and that his client may wish to appeal to a higher court if, in counsel's opinion, errors occurring at trial contributed significantly to the unhappy outcome. An experienced trial lawyers knows, therefore, that he must be in a position to show a reviewing court precisely what happened during the trial (and perhaps also at any important pre-trial and out-of-court hearings or conferences). It follows that a lawyer must do two things at once – he must operate at two quite different levels – as he goes about the trial of his case. First, he must bend every proper effort to the winning of his client's case at the trial level, which means, essentially, that he must persuade the factfinder – judge or jury – of the rightness of his cause. Second, because counsel can never be absolutely certain of victory at the trial level, he must do everything he can to generate a record of the trial that will serve to convince a reviewing court that justice did not prevail in the court below.[90]

In a brilliant forty-page Appendix Professor (later Judge) Jon Waltz gives a lucid and revealing account of what is involved in 'making the record'.[91] No doubt, this is a valuable way of sensitizing potential trial lawyers to one of the main uses of the Law of Evidence at trial. It also serves as a reminder that both appellate and trial courts cast a shadow over earlier parts of the process *and* that the Law of Evidence has a potential role to play after trial or even final appeal – for instance, in decisions to re-open an alleged miscarriage of justice in the light of new evidence. However, this kind of 'realistic' treatment is not completely immunized from jury-thinking and appellate court-itis. It concentrates on appeals from contested jury trials and the potential use of the law of evidence to secure a reversal. In England the number of appeals against conviction by Crown Courts is just over 1 per cent and the success rate is very low. The percentage of civil appeals from the Queen's Bench Division and the success rate are both slightly higher.[92] The comparable American figures for jury trials, appeals and success rates are higher again, but are still strikingly small. By and large common law litigation approximates much more closely in practice to Damaska's ideal type of coordinate authority than hierarchical authority.

The general theoretical point is that in seeking to understand and evaluate evidentiary norms it is necessary to consider their role, use and impact, actual and potential, on all important decisions in litigation from normative, interpretative and empirical points of view.

We have already seen this illustrated with reference to identification,[93] confessions, and standards for decision other than standards of proof. One implication of the Cheshire Cat argument is worth spelling out in relation to adjudicative decisions by non-curial tribunals and *all* official decisions in respect of which rectitude of decision in fact-determination is a requirement or aspiration: to the extent that technical or artificial evidentiary norms, such as the hearsay rule, do not apply to them (or apply without full force), to that extent certain general principles, such as the norms of the logic of proof and the principle of humane and fair treatment of all citizens, become the main relevant norms. The intellectual procedures of modified Wigmorean analysis apply – with variations according to context – to an enormously wide range of official and other decisions in litigation and beyond. Both as aspirational norms and intellectual skills they are much more 'transferable' than the technical rules of evidence which gloss them in some contexts.

Thus the 'realism' of the Hard-nosed Practitioner, as illustrated by Waltz's analysis, needs to be balanced by the demographic 'realism' of a total process view of litigation.[94] The point of this example is not to 'trash' all orthodox treatments of the Law of Evidence, still less to suggest that jury trials and appeals are unimportant just because they are statistically atypical. There are some advantages in treating the jury trial as a paradigm for considering what is involved in argumentation and rectitude of decision in respect of questions of fact, just because the role of fact-determination is more clearly disaggregated from other roles in that context. The object is not so much to switch attention away from one focal point, but to draw attention to the potential for neglect and distortion if other important points in the process are ignored.

Let us consider a rather more controversial example – the meaning and significance of the presumption of innocence. Cross, in a typically robust fashion, deals with it as follows:

> When it is said that an accused person is presumed to be innocent, all that is meant is that the prosecution is obliged to prove the case to be beyond reasonable doubt. This is the fundamental rule of our criminal procedure, and it is expressed in terms of a presumption of innocence so frequently as to render criticism somewhat pointless; but this practice can lead to serious confusion of thought.[95]

If one is only concerned with evidence in disputed trials in relation to conviction and acquittal, this view may be correct, although it has not gone unchallenged. But is it the case that the principle that one is presumed innocent until proven guilty is only relevant to this one kind of decision? Does it not provide an actual or potential rationale for rules governing many other decisions – to arrest, to charge, to grant bail – and in other branches of law (e.g. defamation)? Should it not provide, more than it does in practice, one basis for decisions relating to bail and the way in which prisoners on remand are treated? While the more general principle of humane and fair treatment of all participants in legal processes including those who have pleaded guilty or have been convicted, is to some extent independent of and broader than the presumption of innocence – is not the principle one that should apply to the treatment of all suspects and accused persons at every stage in criminal process, not just in respect of arguments at trial? Of course, it has special importance at the point of determination of guilt or innocence; and it is probably not realistic to expect it to be applied without modification in some problematic contexts, such as the treatment of suspects on remand; but the value is an important one and its implications and applications need to be taken more seriously than they are in a wide range of contexts. The narrow interpretation given to it by Cross and some other writers on evidence does a disservice to an important general principle of our political morality.[96]

The future of the Law of Evidence

This essay is not primarily concerned with such questions as: Will the law of evidence survive? Should it? What should be its future? However, the foregoing analysis at least suggests some general indications.

The fact that there exists an established 'evidence industry' suggests that courses, treatises, codes and specialists on the Law of Evidence will survive in the common law world for many years to come. Nevertheless there are two general trends which suggest that in the long run its survival as a separate field of law is uncertain. First, as we have seen, the trend since Bentham's day has been steadily away from mandatory precepts and detailed technicalities in the direction of structured discretion and more flexible norms. Only in respect of Criminal Evidence is there considered to be sufficient technical detail to justify separate books and courses of a traditional kind. This trend in turn opens the way for the reintegration of the different bodies of evidentiary norms (Criminal Evidence, Civil Evidence, Evidence in Tribunals, Evidence in Arbitration, etc.) with procedure; in England this process is quite far advanced as illustrated by the separate treatment of criminal and civil evidence in important legislation and by the tendency of academic books and courses to concentrate on criminal evidence. On the whole the analysis presented here favours this development because of the difficulty of maintaining a clear and sensible distinction between 'evidence' and 'procedure' and, more important, because specifically evidentiary issues need to be considered in context – the multiple contexts of different types of proceedings and different stages in each proceeding.

However, some factors point in the opposite direction. While we clearly have a number of separate Laws of Evidence more or less suited to different kinds of proceedings, on the broad view of evidentiary norms suggested here they are linked together by a common framework of basic concepts and a single model, however theoretically problematic, of what constitute rational arguments about a disputed question of fact. The logic of proof remains relatively constant, as Thayer and Wigmore perceived in different ways, but it is subject to specifically legal intrusions, e.g. standards for decision, exclusionary norms, rules of competency, that vary according to context. For purposes of exposition and education it is clearly economical to consider these general aspects together, before considering the details of the operation of specific evidentiary norms in the enormous variety of contexts that comprise that complex set of social processes known as litigation. This strengthens the case for treating the principle of freedom of proof, the logic of proof and basic evidentiary concepts as an integral part, indeed the general part, of the law of evidence.

The Law of Evidence has been a battleground for many controversies. The most prominent and persistent debates, not surprisingly, largely concern Criminal Evidence. Some battles such as those over competency, the oath, civil hearsay, are largely over, at least in England. Some long-running controversies

– about presumptions, logical and legal relevancy, the meaning of 'real evidence' for example – in so far as they are still unsettled can be treated as primarily conceptual and classificatory puzzles that can be accommodated within the general or theoretical part of the Law of Evidence as it is presented here. The continuing 'probabilities debate' is more problematic. For, while it raises fundamental problems in probability theory and logic, it has important practical implications. The 'unreality' of some of these debates is in part attributable to over-concentration on naïve examples, such as the rodeo and blue and green bus problems, which do not take account of important procedural and other contextual factors.[97] But theories of probability are central to evaluation of evidence and to elucidating basic evidentiary concepts such as 'standards of proof', probative value and 'prejudicial effect'; and statistical evidence is of increasing practical importance in many different types of proceeding ranging far beyond the familiar examples of paternity, discrimination and fingerprinting.[98] The lawyer of today needs to be a master of elementary statistics. The general aspects of this can be accommodated within the logic of proof; particular applications need to be considered in their specific contexts.

Criminal Evidence remains the most important area of controversy. Here the disagreements are primarily political. The central issues relate to the relationship between and the priorities to be accorded to competing values. Utilitarians, following Bentham, tend to express this in terms of balancing the costs and benefits of rectitude of decision, on the one hand and vexation, expense and delay on the other. One weakness in Bentham's treatment was that he failed adequately to analyse and elaborate on what is encompassed by 'vexation'; another is that, even on his own terms, it can be argued that he miscalculated the extent and intensity of such 'vexations' as wrongful conviction, just as most modern treatments of litigation tend to underestimate the vexations or pains for most participants of being involved in litigation at all – the mischiefs of misidentification being merely one example. Modern economic analysis has produced much more sophisticated utilitarian assessments of both civil and criminal litigation. Many, myself included, do not think that even the most sophisticated versions of utilitarianism can adequately take account of some of the most important values that bear on the risks of wrongful conviction, fair procedures and acceptable treatment of suspects and of other participants in criminal process. One does not necessarily have to embrace a theory of procedural rights in order to maintain that a very high priority indeed should be given to the principles of non-conviction of the innocent and fair and humane treatment of all participants in litigation, including suspects. Rectitude of decision can, and in my view should, be an important value for non-utilitarians as well as utilitarians. Reconciling and balancing values and principles in criminal process is problematic for all of us.

It is not part of the present enterprise to suggest solutions to these problems. That, in my view, can best be done within the framework of a developed theory of criminal process or, more broadly of criminal justice. However, a broad perspective does have implications for the enterprise.

Firstly, while it makes sense to isolate evidentiary issues for some purposes, debating such topics as safeguards for the accused or the presumption of innocence or the right to silence or improperly obtained evidence is unsatisfactory within a narrow 'evidentiary' framework. Put simply, this is because the basic values involved transcend any distinction between evidence and procedure and, indeed, have more far-reaching implications. In designing a decent system of criminal justice it just does not make sense to consider 'disciplining' the police or the presumption of innocence or interrogation or even the right to silence from a purely evidentiary perspective. For this purpose, criminal evidence and criminal procedure need to be seen as interrelated parts of a single subject designated in some such terms as 'criminal justice'.[99]

In England in recent years two significant steps have been taken in this direction. First, consideration of 'reform' has moved towards a more integrated approach, exemplified by the differences in the frames of reference of the debates surrounding the Eleventh Report of the Criminal Revision Committee in 1972 and, its successor, the Royal Commission on Criminal Procedure and the resulting Police and Criminal Evidence Act, 1984. Whatever one's reservations about the outcome, the analysis and the public discussions were better grounded in the later debate by virtue of the broader frame of reference. Secondly, there are signs of a more principled approach to the study of Criminal Evidence, illustrated by the writings of scholars such as Ashworth, Dennis, Stein and Zuckerman. The search for principle to ground and to organize academic treatments represents a significant advance on the fragmented, incoherent and over-technical approach of an earlier generation. However, the field is still dominated by separate courses and books on 'Evidence' and 'Procedure', which concentrate on the formal rules and treat many of the broader aspects as falling outside their purview. We are some way yet from a coherent normative theory of criminal justice in which the basic values (in respect of detail and design) are carried through in a principled and realistic fashion. The general trend towards discretion needs to be balanced by a more robust affirmation of general principles.

In respect of civil and non-curial proceedings the historical trend has been steadily in the direction of a much simplified system, or set of sub-systems, in which derogations from the basic principles of rectitude of decision, free proof and minimization of vexation, expense and delay are officially derogated from only exceptionally and for good reason.[100] Some unnecessary complications and evidentiary ghosts still survive and there is a worrying vagueness about the status and applicability of the general law of civil evidence in many tribunals. Most of the pressing topics, such as discovery, are recognized as fitting most comfortably in Civil Procedure, a field which is belatedly becoming recognized in England as a fit subject for academic treatment. For most practical purposes the detail of civil evidence can be readily fitted under that rubric.

Earlier I reported Sir Rupert Cross as saying that he was working for the day when his subject was abolished.[101] The context was a debate on criminal evidence and I took issue with that admirable man partly for political reasons and partly because of his narrow conception of the subject. However, it is only fair to pay tribute to his massive contributions to the simplification and rationalization of the subject as he conceived it, especially in respect of civil litigation. A more generous interpretation might be as follows: for most purposes, it just does not make sense to treat the Law of Evidence as a subject apart from the different procedural contexts in which it operates; and the important values that should be the foundation of any healthy system of the administration of justice are likely to be better served by firm and explicit adherence to principle than by standing on technical doctrines which are largely fragmented, archaic and incoherent and which are often not observed in practice.[102]

Conclusion

1 Reasoning about disputed questions of fact in adjudication and in other important decisions in litigation is structured, regulated and guided by doctrines drawn from substantive law, procedure, logic, and the law of evidence. The latter is primarily concerned with four questions: What facts may be presented or considered as evidence? By whom must they be presented? To whom must they be presented? Of what propositions in issue need no evidence be presented? In respect of these questions no sharp distinctions can be drawn between the norms of procedure, evidence and practical reason.

2 The Law of Evidence consists of concepts, principles, standards, balancing tests, directory instructions, and rules and conventions of practice as well as mandatory precepts dealing with classes of evidence.

3 The Thayerite view of the Law of Evidence as a series of disparate exceptions to a principle of free proof is essentially correct if 'freedom of proof' is interpreted to refer to natural or commonsense modes of reasoning about questions of fact at trial and that the law constrains these only in a limited way. For example, the law limits the purposes for which certain kinds of evidence may be validly used (e.g. the hearsay rule) and by structuring, limiting and guiding the exercise of discretion in making decisions of fact.

4 The modified Thayerite view, advanced by McNamara, is also generally correct in suggesting that the great bulk of exclusionary rules can best be interpreted as rules which prescribe the exclusion, on grounds of public interest, of certain information from consideration as good reasons for decision. 'Public interest' covers either classes of evidence or types of situation or a balancing of interests in the circumstances of the case.

5 From this perspective Bentham's attack on all mandatory precepts was overstated, but is essentially correct in pointing to the importance of the particular circumstances of the case in respect of making correct decisions about weight, public interest and so on.

6 The Gruyère cheese view is essentially correct in emphasizing how little of the surviving Law of Evidence consists of mandatory precepts, especially in civil litigation. But this view underestimates the extent to which legal norms, broadly conceived, can structure and guide reasoning in legal processes.

7   The Cheshire Cat view emphasizes that a realistic view of the Law of Evidence needs to beware of over-formal or over-precise statements of the law because (a) of the flexibility of so much evidence doctrine and (b) the rules are often waived, breached or ignored and (c) many adjudicative tribunals are 'guided but not bound' by the rules of evidence. Most decision making by triers of fact is to a large extent discretionary; but the Cheshire Cat view may obscure the extent to which reasoning by and the discretion of all adjudicators is structured in a paradigmatic way.

8   Traditional treatises on Evidence treat the contested jury trial as the paradigm of all litigation. From the perspective of a total process model of litigation this is misleading in that jury trials are atypical of all trials, and contested trials are atypical of all litigation and adjudicative decisions are only one kind of important decision in the total process. However, there is an important sense in which adjudicative decisions are paradigmatic: not only do they 'cast a long shadow' over the prior proceedings, but they also serve as a general model for rectitude of decision.

9   Wigmore's claim that the logic of proof is anterior to the Law of Evidence also contains an important insight. The basic concepts of the Law of Evidence are also basic concepts of the logic of proof: in particular, materiality, relevance, admissibility, validity, cogency and standards for decision. Furthermore, if the Law of Evidence is a series of exceptions to general principles of practical reasoning, it makes sense to clarify and master these principles before considering the exceptions; and, in so far as the Law of Evidence is concerned with structuring, regulating and guiding *reasoning*, logic and epistemology are foundational to the subject. Accordingly, for most purposes, it is sensible to treat the logic of proof and the rules of evidence as two parts of a single subject.

NOTES

Parts of this chapter are derived from a paper entitled 'Evidence and Proof in Anglo-American Litigation'. Earlier versions were originally presented to legal audiences in Trento, Beijing and Warsaw during 1987–8. Attempting to explain the modern common law of evidence to lawyers trained in civilian and socialist legal systems was a great stimulus to developing a coherent overview of the field. In revising this paper for a more varied audience, I have retained the standpoint of a comparative lawyer introducing the subject to strangers, in the hope that this will illustrate the truism that foreign travel sharpens one's perceptions of one's own country. Among the many debts I have incurred, I am particularly grateful to Terry Anderson, Ian Dennis, Alex Stein and Adrian Zuckerman for comments on this version, and to Philip McNamara for permission to quote from his article.

1   J. B. Thayer (1898).
2   Llewellyn (1962); Twining (1973).
3   On the choice of an organizing category see below, ch. 11, where the case is made for treating evidence as a species of the broader category of 'information in litigation'.
4   Best (1849), s.11. For alternative definitions see 1 Wigmore, *Treatise* (Tillers rev. 1983), s.1.

5   For figures, see Zander (1988). On theories of litigation see below, ch. 11.
6   We need not concern ourselves here with the problem of borderline cases of adjudication, such as arbitration or quasi-judicial proceedings; the point is that a very great deal of the work of the application and enforcement of state law is today allocated to many kinds of tribunals that perform functions and have powers that have traditionally been associated with courts. See generally, Farmer (1974).
7   See above, ch. 5 and below, ch. 11.
8   Above, ch. 3.
9   Damaska (1986).
10 Id., 71.
11 Id., 3–6, 10–12; cf. 69.
12 Id., 224–5.
13 Id., 69.
14 Id., Introduction *et passim*.
15 E.g. *Cross on Evidence* (6th edn, ed., C. Tapper, 1985), ch. 1; Keane (1989), ch. 1.
16 Zander (1988), 403–9. The jury still plays an important role in American civil litigation. On the contrasts between England and the United States in this respect see Atiyah and Summers (1987), ch. 6.
17 For example, the Industrial Tribunals (Rules of Procedure) Regulations, 1985 (ss. 1985, no. 16) provide: 'Procedure at hearing: ... 8(1) the tribunal shall conduct the hearing in such manner as it considers most suitable to the clarification of the issues before it and generally to the just handling of the proceedings; it shall so far as appears to it appropriate seek to avoid formality in its proceedings and it shall not be bound by any enactment or rule of law relating to the admissibility of evidence in proceedings before the courts of law.' A useful discussion, referring specifically to Australia, but dealing with common law systems is by Enid Campbell, 'Principles of Evidence and Administrative Tribunals', in Campbell and Waller (eds) (1982), ch. 8. See also *Cross on Evidence* (6th edn 1985), 12–16, Logic and Watchman (1989).
18 The main differences between the civil and criminal rules of evidence are conveniently summarized in Phipson and Elliott (1986), ch. 2. There is a strong argument for treating the rules of evidence in criminal, civil and administrative proceedings independently in order to integrate them more closely with those different kinds of procedural context.
19 Jacob (1987).
20 Id., 156.
21 For example, a historian or scientist testing alternative hypotheses against available evidence may proceed dialectically, but not necessarily adversarially. 'Dialectics' refers to modes of reasoning; 'adversarial' characterizes the roles of different participants and, according to Damaska, the purposes of the enterprise.
22 Bentham (1827), vol. 1, 523–4.
23 I have borrowed the formulation from Zuckerman (1987), 68.
24 Ch. 4, above.
25 Esp. Bentham (1827).
26 For an interesting, but no doubt controversial, discussion see Damaska (1986), ch. VI.
27 See above, 81–2.
28 Some of these trends, for example the growth of discretion and the decline of the jury, already existed in Thayer's day and have gone further. Not all of these trends have represented linear developments: for example, academic interest in evidentiary theory has been spasmodic. See now Mengler (1989).
29 The piecemeal nature of the English colonial inheritance in respect of evidence in many small states is amusingly described by Professor Keith Patchett (1988). Patchett estimates that Tuvalu, with a population of 900 persons, three lawyers and no resident legally qualified judges, inherited twenty-seven English statutes dealing with evidence; to this have been added particular local provisions spread over more than fifty statutes (about a third of all local legislation). The Legal Division of the Commonwealth

214 What is the Law of Evidence?

Secretariat is currently preparing a simplified Evidence Code which may be adopted, with local variations, in many small states in the Commonwealth.

30 Cross (6th edn, 1985), Preface; cf. on USA Mengler (1989).
31 E.g. B. Jackson (1988) and symposium in the International Journal for the Semiotics of Law, vol. 2, no. 1 (1988–89).
32 See above, ch. 3.
33 Pollock (1899).
34 Thayer *Treatise*, 314.
35 Id., 530; cf. 266.
36 Id., 264–5.
37 Id., 265.
38 Id., 266.
39 Id., 273.
40 Id. Ch. VI is entitled 'The Law of Evidence, and Legal Reasoning as applied to the ascertainment of facts'.
41 Id., 275; cf. 272.
42 See above 67; see also *Treatise* 336, 558, 576.
43 1 Wigmore *Treatise* (Tillers rev., 1983), s.3.
44 McNamara (1986).
45 Id., 343–4 (quoted with permission of the author).
46 Id., 359. McNamara implicitly accepts Wigmore's useful distinction between 'Rules of Auxiliary Probative Policy' (concerned with rectitude of decision) and 'Rules of Extrinsic Policy' (concerned with giving priority to other values over rectitude of decision or at least balancing these competing values). McNamara argues (at 345) that most of the former rules fall under the inclusionary principle, 'subject to the qualification that, where in a criminal trial, the judge forms the view that there is a substantial danger that will put particular information to an irrational use (to the exclusion of its proper use) the judge should exclude'. In both categories, balancing tests predominate. Galligan (1988, 255–8), in arguing that the modern law of evidence is even closer to what Bentham advocated than I had suggested in *TEBW*, arrives at a similar conclusion by a different route.
47 Id., 360, citing *McTaggart* v. *McTaggart* [1949] P. 94. McNamara treats the rule governing 'without prejudice' communications as primarily a rule of use (ibid.) and makes a number of other caveats. *Semble* he treats the protection of public informers as independent of the doctrine of public interest immunity.
48 Id., 363.
49 Below, ch. 11.
50 McNamara's treatment of privilege and confessions may be considered controversial. His analysis may also need modification in respect of those areas of evidence doctrine that fall within the purview of American constitutional interpretation. However, it is suggested, his framework provides a valuable overview of the structure of the modern Anglo-Australian Law of Evidence. See now Ligertwood, *Australian Evidence* (1988) which seeks to show that by and large the Australian Law of Evidence is a principled, rational system which seeks to maximize rectitude of decision within the context of the adversary trial.
51 Twining (1988).
52 In a forthcoming work my friend Stefan Landsman proposes to argue that Bentham was a stronger supporter of the adversarial model than I suggest. I reserve my reply.
53 Bentham, however, recognized two privileges (public policy and confessions to priests). For a detailed discussion see *TEBW*, ch. 2 and note 71, below.
54 Wigmore *Science* (1937), 3; his first statement of this view was published as early as 1913 (Wigmore, 1913).
55 *TEBW*, 165.

56 Thayer *Treatise*, 264–5.
57 Wigmore *Science*, 4.
58 On 'freedom of proof' see Kunert (1966–7); L. J. Cohen in *FL* (1983), ch. 1; Twining, op. cit., n.51 (forthcoming). In contemporary usage at least four different usages of 'free proof' need to be distinguished:

1 free access to information. The obvious example is freedom of the trier of fact from rules excluding evidence or sources of evidence. The phrase is sometimes extended to include free access of parties to information, for example, through discovery procedures;
2 free evaluation of evidence: for example, freedom of triers of fact from formal rules of quantum or weight; or freedom of the jury to disregard the warnings or advice of the trial judge about the weight or credibility of particular items of evidence;
3 freedom to decide according to criteria of one's choice: for example, freedom from rules or standards governing burdens of proof and persuasion and formal standards for decision (such as standards of proof);
4 freedom from hierarchical controls: for example freedom of the triers of fact from appeal or review by a superior authority.

As we have seen, the English law prescribes some important exceptions to (1) and (3); only minimally seeks to regulate (2); and, compared to civilian systems, makes only limited provision for appeal and review in respect of findings of fact and treats such matters as belonging to procedure rather than evidence. Thayer was mainly concerned with (1) and (2).

59 On rules of weight, see Wigmore on Moore, above, 67.
60 Cohen (1983). However, determination of relevance which is governed by the same criteria, is left to the judge.
61 The classic discussion is Thayer *Treatise*, ch. XI. An important recent article by Dale Nance (1988) challenges this narrow interpretation of the 'Best Evidence Rule' and argues that reports of its demise are greatly exaggerated.
62 See the excellent discussions by Dennis (1984), Jackson (1988a) and Zuckerman (1989), ch. 10.
63 See above, ch. 5.
64 The modified Thayerite view of the Law of Evidence is that it consists of a series of disparate exceptions to a general principle of free proof. If this is correct, then it would seem sensible to start by elucidating the basic principle before considering the exceptions and exceptions to exceptions. Remarkably nearly all treatises and textbooks on evidence do not do this. They tend to take the principle for granted and proceed directly to considering the detailed rules. Wigmore got nearest to taking the idea of freedom of proof seriously when he argued that the Science of Proof is anterior to the Trial Rules of Evidence and in his teaching he practised what he preached. However, perhaps because of the influence of Thayer's artificially sharp distinction between 'logic' and 'law', Wigmore's most influential writings – the *Treatise*, the Code, and the textbook – did not treat freedom of proof as a legal principle and so did not elucidate its meaning nor use it as the explicit basis for organizing the subject. This affected the clarity of his exposition rather than its accuracy. The result was that 'freedom of proof' did not become a term of art and an opportunity was lost to present the subject as a coherent and essentially simple whole. Weinberg in Galligan (ed.) (1984) treats 'freedom of proof' as a category of meaningless reference (136–8). I disagree, but *semble* Weinberg would be satisfied by making Thayer's inclusionary rule the basic principle. Formally this might be correct, but it would obfuscate the point for which I am arguing.
65 Lewis Carroll, *Alice's Adventures in Wonderland* (1865). In ch. 8 of the story the Queen has ordered that the cat should be beheaded. At that point only the cat's head was visible. The executioner argued that you could only cut off a head if there was a body to cut it off from; the King argued that anything that had a head could be beheaded. Some

arguments about the abolition and reform of the common law of evidence are rather like that.

66   Carlen (1976).

67   Above, n.5.

68   Mansfield and Peay (1987); DPP *Code for Crown Prosecutors* (1986). Potentially inadmissible evidence of prior convictions is presumably discounted in coming to a judgement on whether there is a reasonable prospect of conviction; however, it is doubtful whether in practice such information is always discounted in deciding whether it is in the public interest to prosecute.

69   On standards for decision, see below 353 and *Analysis* ch. 6.

70   See above, n. 46 and Zuckerman (1989), *passim*; cf. Tapper in the Preface to the sixth edition of *Cross on Evidence* (1985), quoted above, 188.

71   Hart (1961), 133. Bentham was not a 'rule-sceptic' in this sense. The object of his attack was mandatory precepts (dealing with classes of evidence or of witnesses) addressed to the will of the trier of fact, but he strongly favoured cautionary 'instructions' addressed to the understanding. (See *TEBW*, 66–9.) At the start of *A Treatise on Judicial Evidence* he (or, more likely, his *rédacteur*, Dumont) stated explicitly:

> Let it not be inferred from these observations, that all forms should be abolished, and no rule admitted, except the discretion of judges. The forms and rules to be avoided are those, which lay a judge under the necessity of giving a judgment contrary to his conviction, and which render procedure the enemy of the law substantive. We shall afterwards see, what are the true safeguards, that should be raised round evidence and judgments. (3)

In the English translation of Dumont's *rédaction* the word 'rules' is used in a broad sense to encompass both mandatory precepts and 'directory' standards and other norms. In this context, 'discretion' is used in the strong sense of unregulated or unfettered choice; for Bentham favoured weak discretion in the sense of rational choices that are subject to guidance, justification and criticism according to general standards.

Bentham did not deny the 'reality' of the technical rules of evidence of his day. Indeed he claimed that they were pernicious as a patent source of misdecision. It is true that his famous account of the 'double-fountain principle' can be interpreted as a classic forerunner of modern arguments about indeterminacy (1827, bk. VIII, ch. XXII):

> Is interest objected as a ground of exclusion to a material witness? Here you are completely at your ease. There stand the cases, in two rows: on one hand, those in which the objection has been allowed – on the other, those in which it has been disallowed ... Exclude the witness, you bow to the name of Lord Kenyon, and with him pronounce the laws of evidence to be the perfection of wisdom: receive the witness, your bow points to Lord Hardwicke, and with him you confess your disposition to admit lights. (VII *Works*, 308)

However, the double-fountain principle was only one of eighteen devices of the technical system and Bentham explicitly stated: 'In practice, it has not yet stretched (it must be confessed) nor seems likely to stretch to so all-embracing an extent in the regions of Jurisprudence as to cover the whole field' (ibid.).

Bentham was highly sceptical of the *value* of binding rules, but he did not deny that some technical rules existed and influenced adjudication. Accordingly Bentham was not a 'rule-sceptic' in Hart's sense and it is misleading to claim, as I did in *TEBW*, that his anti-nomian thesis 'can be interpreted as a more radical form of rule-scepticism than is attributable to any American Realist' (66).

72   Twining (1973), *passim*, esp. 255, Appendix B; Kelman (1987), 214ff.

73 See *Cross on Evidence* (6th edn), 45–7, on the uncertainties about the scope and nature of the duty to warn.
74 Police and Criminal Evidence Act, 1984, s.74 (2).
75 Cross, op. cit., 338–9, discussing *DPP* v. *Boardman* [1975] AC 421; *R* v. *Sang* [1980] AC 402. The interpretation of these cases has been the subject of an extensive literature.
76 Op. cit., 363.
77 E.g. public interest immunity, see Cross, op. cit., 413ff.
78 Police and Criminal Evidence Act, 1984, 82(3), preserving the common law power. See further *Samuel* [1988] 2 ALLER 135; *Alladice* [1988] 87 *Cr. App. Rep.* 380.
79 Heydon (2nd edn, 1984), 8–9, 331ff. Zuckerman (1989) treats appeals to the 'Res Gestae' doctrine as a discretionary device for admitting evidence that would be inadmissible if the hearsay rule were strictly applied – i.e. a fictitious entity with practical effects. On the survival of a 'best evidence principle' see above, n. 61.
80 E.g. Keane (1989), ch. 15; cf. Thayer *Treatise*, 524.
81 Galligan (1988), 249, 256–7; cf. Mengler (1989).
82 Galligan (1986), 7.
83 Galligan (1988); see below, ch. 11, at 353.
84 This challenges positivists like Thayer, 279n. and J. Stone (1964) whose work on 'Lawyers' Reasonings' is confined to questions of law.
85 See, however, Teitelbaum et al. (1983).
86 E.g. Zuckerman (1989); see also ch. 4 above, 129.
87 See further below, ch. 11.
88 A great deal of what is most valued, or most controversial, in respect of the law of evidence centres round the importance and scope of the principle against mistaken conviction and the principle of protection of suspects and others against mistreatment (above, 184). A great deal of criminal evidence doctrine can be subsumed under these two principles; cf. Galligan, op. cit., n. 25, at 261:

> [T]he presumption of innocence, the burden of proof on the prosecution, the standard of proof beyond reasonable doubt – all reflect the special concern not to convict the innocent. That same concern has implications for other rules: those relating to similar facts, character, corroboration, restrictions of cross-examination of the accused, and confessions (to some extent), make more sense and are more justifiable than they otherwise would be, if they are viewed in the light of the principle against wrongful convictions. Each rule attempts to regulate the reception and use of evidence which, if freely admitted, would create a special risk of an unwarranted conviction. The principle against wrongful conviction explains why such types of evidence, which are normally of probative value and therefore admissible on the more general test of rectitude, are subject to restrictions. For that principle dictates that the aim of a trial be not simply a blanket notion of rectitude: it requires rectitude in the sense of ensuring, at least at a certain level, that convictions are rightly made even at the cost of acquittals wrongly made.

89 Above, n. 68.
90 Louisell, Kaplan and Waltz (1972), 1287.
91 Id., 1287–1328.
92 Op. cit., n. 5.
93 Above, ch. 5.
94 On the Hard-nosed Practitioner see above, ch. 4; on realism see below, ch. 11, 366–8.
95 Cross (1985), 6th edn, 114–15.
96 For further examples, see below, ch. 11.
97 Below ch. 11, at 362–3.
98 For example, Lempert (1988, 63) quotes the following extract from a 1986 LEXIS search on the use of statistical evidence in the United States: 'A search of published

opinions in federal courts with a computer-based legal information retrieval system reveals the dramatic growth since 1960 in cases involving some form of statistical evidence. Between January 1960 and September 1979 the terms 'statistic(s)' or 'statistical' appeared in about 3,000 or 4% of 83,769 reported District Court opinions. In the Courts of Appeals, the same terms appeared in 1,671 reported opinions.' See further, Barnes (1983).

99   See further below, ch. 11.
100   On different levels of 'official views' and their relationship to practice, see McBarnett (1981).
101   Above, 1.
102   Cross (1961), 33.

7

Lawyers' Stories

I understand that his strength as an advocate lay not in his powers of oratory, but in the reasoning and persuasiveness of the arguments by which he tried to bring the court round to his point of view. He continued to use his powers of persuasion when he was sitting as a Lord of Appeal and would come home and say that he thought that he had won his 'brothers' over to his side or 'so-and-so is still not convinced but I think he may be tomorrow.' He certainly persuaded his family that he was right. When he gave us the facts of a case and asked us what we thought about it, his way of presenting the problem was such that there was never any suggestion in our minds that the other side could have a leg to stand on.

E. Cockburn Millar on her father, Lord Atkin[1]

Might it be suggested that the central act of the legal mind, of judge and lawyer alike, is the conversion of the raw material of life ... into a story that will claim to tell the truth in legal terms?

James Boyd White[2]

Introduction

Once upon a time, Rhetoric was central to the humanities and forensic oratory was central to Rhetoric. In the long and complex story of rhetorical studies, the forum ceased over time to be the main arena and persuasive oratory was displaced as the main object of study. Conversely, the discipline of law lost touch with Rhetoric. Demosthenes, Cicero and Quintilian are almost entirely ignored in contemporary legal studies.[3] When jurists cite Aristotle, it tends to be the *Ethics* or *Politics* rather than the *Rhetoric*. Of course, practising lawyers still practise advocacy and they elicit, translate, construct, narrate, distort and attack stories as part of their art of persuasion. Legal theorists, on the other hand, have written a great deal about the reasoning of judges, especially appellate court judges, but have paid remarkably little attention to the argumentation of advocates, especially where it is the facts or the sentence rather than the law which is in dispute. 'Narrative' features hardly at all in discussions of legal reasoning; 'rhetoric' when applied to the discourse of a judge or even an advocate usually implies criticism.[4] One might infer from this that rhetoric and narrative have little or nothing to do with legal reasoning and so, by implication, are consigned to the dubious sphere of 'irrational means of persuasion'. On such a view, Lord Atkin's daughter's account of her father may be interpreted as an example of a skilful advocate, either through conscious trickery or unconscious bias, winning his family over by non-rational means. Is that the only or even the most plausible interpretation?

This essay is one of a series of exploratory studies of the role of narrative in general culture. It challenges any suggestion that narrative has a marginal role of dubious legitimacy in legal discourse; it also challenges the converse idea that constructing stories is 'the central act of the legal mind' as White and others have suggested.[5] The essay focuses mainly on one class of legal discourse, forensic advocacy in modern Anglo-American courts. In particular, it addresses the question: What, if any, are legitimate functions of narrative in *rational* argument by advocates on disputed questions of law and disputed questions of fact? In the course of what is a preliminary exploration, I shall suggest that narrative probably plays a variety of roles in advocacy: some of these roles are unavoidable and legitimate, but are more to do with communication than with rational argument and persuasion; that narrative can be used in ways that would be considered to be illegitimate or dubious, judged by conventional standards of ethical advocacy; but that narrative also has some important, legitimate contributions to make to rational argument by lawyers and that some of these roles fit uneasily with some standard accounts of lawyers' reasonings. The focus is normative rather than empirical; the examples used are illustrative rather than representative.

The discourse of advocates in court is only one kind of legal discourse. A wide variety of actors and commentators participate in law talk and talk about law in an even wider variety of contexts. Judges, law-makers, office lawyers, legal scholars, teachers of law, historians, journalists, novelists and all citizens regularly produce and consume legal discourse.[6] It is widely accepted by contemporary legal scholars that litigation is just one species of legal and law-related action and that what happens in open court is only one, often atypical, phase of the total process of litigation. There is debate among legal theorists as to how far the contested trial, the dialectics of adversary proceedings and the reasoned judicial decision are paradigmatic, or representative, or central forms of legal life and discourse. We need not enter these debates here, but it is relevant to state that I am personally sceptical of such claims.[7] For one message of this essay is a reminder of complexity. There are many kinds and contexts of legal discourse; there are many kinds and phases of litigation; any litigated case is likely to prove on examination to be an extremely complex kind of social process. It would be unwise to start on an exploration of the role of narrative in legal discourse by anticipating that there will be global or reductive answers.

My colleagues in law may think it surprising, even eccentric, to begin such an exploration by focusing on the discourse of advocates. For there are other types of legal discourse that are much better documented and more extensively studied and analysed. We have in reported judgments, in legislation, in legal textbooks and secondary writings about law, for example, a rich treasury of accessible and familiar texts. Compared to these, advocates' arguments are only spasmodically documented and, at least in modern times, they have been relatively under-theorized.[8] I accept that a systematic narratology of legal discourses, especially one that is to have a sound empirical base in concrete and representative examples of such discourses, has to engage with our general heritage of texts of different kinds and our stock of theorizing about them.[9] There are, however, two related reasons for using a different starting-point. Firstly, the situation, purposes, role and audience of the advocate in court are typically clearer or less problematic than those of the judge or the jury or the expositor.[10] *The primary task of the advocate is to persuade this tribunal to decide in favour of this client in respect of previously defined issues of law and/or fact and/or disposition.* By focusing on a relatively uncontroversial kind of actor one may be able to skirt, rather than plunge directly into, the morass of controversies surrounding theories of adjudication and other familiar areas of juristic debate. We shall not be able to avoid getting our feet wet, but we may be able to paddle before trying to swim.

A second reason is that a central concern of narratology is the role of stories in rational argument. While some aspects of the advocate's role are considered relatively unproblematic, questions about what constitute 'rational' and 'irrational', legitimate or illegitimate techniques or modes of persuasion are central, sharply posed questions in any theory of advocacy. In order to keep matters simple, I shall concentrate on three tasks of the advocate that are generally regarded as distinct: arguments about disputed questions of fact; arguments about disputed questions of law; and arguments about sanctions, such as arguments about the amount of damages to be awarded in a civil action or pleas in mitigation of sentence in criminal proceedings.

In legal theory the distinction between questions of fact and questions of law is recognized to be analytically problematic.[11] It is also recognized that determinations of fact and law in particular cases have an artificial all-or-nothing character (guilty/not guilty, liable/not liable). The winner takes all.[12] By contrast, the determination of sanction tends to be more open-ended, involving a choice between a range of possibilities within varying limits, such as maximum (and less frequently, minimum) penalties.

These distinctions have practical consequences for advocates. Whether a question is classified as one of fact, law or disposition may determine the arena, the audience, the timing and the style of presentation. In simplified form, questions of law are for judges; questions of fact are for the jury or other triers of fact; questions of sentence are usually for the judge. Elaborate rules govern which kinds of issue are subject to appeal or review in a higher court. There are reasons for adopting the working assumption that these three kinds of argument represent three different kinds of task, each with a distinct kind of discourse appropriate to it. Later we shall need to consider the relations between them.

A lexicon of advocacy

The discourse of advocacy, as found in manuals, trial records and informal conversation, contains relatively few terms of art. In so far as there is a distinctive vocabulary, much of it has recognizable roots in the formal rules of procedure and evidence, in classical and medieval rhetoric and in drama. Contemporary Anglo-American manuals of advocacy[13] contain a number of key terms that are useful for present purposes: theory, story, situation, scene, scenario, theme and thelema. Even the best English and American manuals tend to adopt an informal, often chatty, style in which precision is sometimes sacrificed to readability. A rather more exact vocabulary is needed for purposes of theoretical analysis. Accordingly, I propose to stipulate some definitions and make some distinctions that are more precise than ordinary usage.

Theory   An advocate's 'theory of the case' is his argument about the case as a whole.[14] It should be capable of being expressed in the form of a logical and coherent statement of the reasoning supporting the desired conclusion. A summary statement of such a theory should take the form of a précis of a complex argument. To take some simple examples:

1   Where the only issue is a question of fact:
    (a) 'The prosecution has failed to produce sufficient evidence that it was the accused who committed the alleged crime'; or
    (b) 'The evidence shows that my client was in another city at the time of the murder and therefore he could not be the murderer'; or
    (c) 'The evidence shows that the deceased was killed accidentally during the course of a struggle in which he was trying to stop the accused from committing suicide by shooting herself.'[15]
2   Where the only issue is a question of law:
    (a) 'Authority, principle and reason support the proposition that a professional person owes a duty of care to a non-professional in respect of advice given in circumstances X, Y and Z. The facts of this case are a clear example of this type of situation';[16] or
    (b) 'This case is new. It should be approached on principles applicable to modern conditions rather than on outmoded nineteenth-century precedents and values. Authority, principle and policy based on modern values support the proposition that the public interest should prevail over the private interest where there is a conflict between reasonable and long-established uses of land in the interest of the public at large (such as village cricket), and the private interest in enjoyment, without interference or risk of injury, or damage to adjacent property which has recently been developed.'[17]
3   In a plea in mitigation:
    'Notwithstanding the seriousness of the offence, the facts that my client has an unblemished record, has shown contrition, is unlikely to repeat the offence, has good prospects of employment and has a dependent family combine to support the conclusion that a custodial sentence would be inappropriate and could serve no useful purpose in this case.'

Manuals of advocacy, especially those concerned with trial techniques, stress the importance of developing and maintaining a clear and cohesive theory of the case as a whole: 'It is essential to develop a theory of the case before trial and act in accordance with it throughout the trial itself.'[18] The theory provides the basis for the advocate's strategy which will guide all his choices and actions throughout the proceedings.

This conception of 'theory' serves the function of isolating that aspect of advocacy which is concerned with rational arguments from other aspects, such as commanding attention, communication, questioning, persuasive presentation and various courtroom tactics. The conception is also analytically convenient in that it provides a convenient connection with theories of legal reasoning.

In standard, but not entirely uncontroversial, accounts of legal reasoning, the paradigm example of 'a case as a whole' takes the following form: 'If X then Y; if Y then Z.' Here X represents the *circumstances* governed by the rule; Y represents the *legal effect* (guilt or liability); and Z represents the *sanction* or consequence. For example, 'Whenever a person intentionally and with malice aforethought causes the death of another without lawful justification, that person is guilty of murder. Where a person is guilty of murder, that person shall be condemned to death (unless . . .).' On this view, the paradigm case of a disputed question of law is: 'What is the scope of X?' Or 'Do circumstances a, b, c, constitute a case of X?' The paradigm case of a disputed question of fact is: 'Does the evidence support the conclusion that X happened?' The paradigm case of an issue in sentencing is: 'Given X and Y, and in view of M_1, M_2, M_3 (mitigating factors) what is the appropriate punishment in this case?'[19]

Story   In the discourse of advocacy the word 'story' tends to be used rather loosely to encompass a party's or witness's version of what happened; or a chronological statement of a sequence of events; or a statement of 'the facts' of the case by a judge or advocate; or the formal allegations (the material facts) set out in the pleadings; or even the advocate's theory of the case.[20] In considering the role of narrative in forensic argument, it is important to give the term 'story' a more precise, restricted meaning. Adapting Ricoeur, I propose the following definition: 'A story is a narrative of particular events arranged in a time sequence and forming a meaningful totality.'[21] In this formulation particularity, time, change and connectedness are all necessary ingredients. But the connections between the events which make the story a totality need not be causal. In this usage, adapting E. M. Forster, 'The King died and then the Queen died' is not a story, but merely a chronological statement; 'the King died and then the Queen died of grief' has the necessary element of connectedness.[22] But so does the following: 'The King was reported to have died; the Queen died of grief; in fact the report was false, for the King had been feigning death in order to evade an assassination attempt.' Although this last narrative does not follow a strict chronological order and its connectedness does not depend on causation alone, it counts as a story. For the rest of this essay I shall equate narrative with story-telling: one narrates stories, but describes situations.[23]

There is an intimate relationship between 'theories' and 'stories', but it is important to keep them conceptually distinct. The distinction and the relationship can be illustrated by the closing speech for the Crown by Archibald Bodkin in the case of George Joseph Smith (the 'Brides in the Bath Case'). Smith was accused of murdering Bessie Mundy by deliberately drowning her in a bath in a rented house in Herne Bay. The crux of the case was whether her death was caused by accident or design. The defence theory was that she drowned during an epileptic fit. The evidence concerning the cause of death was circumstantial and inconclusive. In Bodkin's opening speech, and during the trial, the jury had been presented not only with the story of the course of the relationship between Smith and the deceased and of its aftermath, but with two other stories of deaths of Smith's 'brides' who had died in similar, unexplained circumstances. Bodkin's closing speech takes up only four paragraphs in the record. The last half reads as follows:

The prisoner and the woman being alone in the house, he had the opportunity of committing the crime. The motive of the prisoner has been demonstrated, the opportunity admitted, and the exclusion of accident proved. You are entitled to look at the evidence as to the two other deaths to see whether the death of Miss Mundy was accident or designed, and, if designed, for the benefit of whom? You can also look at that evidence to see whether the death was part of a system or course of conduct – horrible as it is to think so – of deliberately causing people's deaths in order that monetary benefit might ensue to him.

The three cases are of such a character that such a large aggregation of resemblances cannot have occurred without design. In each case the prisoner went through the form of marriage; in each case the ready money of the woman was either realized or drawn out of whatever deposit bank it might have been in; in each case there was a will drawn in favour of the prisoner absolutely; in each case the will was drawn by a stranger to the testatrix; in each case the victim insured her life or was possessed of property which did not make it necessary to insure her life; in each case there was a visit to a doctor shortly before the death, which, we contend, was unnecessary from the physical condition of the patient; in each case the women wrote letters to relatives the night before, or on the night on which they died; in each case there was an inquiry as to a bathroom drowning, and the prisoner was the first to discover it; in each case the bathroom doors were unfastened and the water was not drawn off until after the doctor had been; and in each case the prisoner was putting demonstrably forward the purchase of either fish, or eggs, or tomatoes to show that he was absent from the house in which his wife was lying dead; and in each case there was the prisoner's subsequent disappearance and the monetary advantage resulting or attempted to be made to result.[24]

This is generally regarded as a classic of advocacy. It is misleading to treat it as an example of narrative discourse. Rather it is more accurately described as an argument directed to a single issue (design). It proceeds by analysing and comparing three stories in order to fill a crucial gap in one of them, the story of the death of Bessie Mundy. Bodkin was *arguing* about one part of a story rather than narrating. The argument supports the prosecution 'theory' that Smith intentionally caused the death of Bessie Mundy. We could not give an account of the case without some notion of story – for it is a reasonably clear example of a jury having to choose between competing stories – but that is different from saying that Bodkin was here using story-telling as a technique of persuasion.

It may be objected that such notions as telling stories, stating the facts and narrating as they are ordinarily used in the discourse of advocacy do not correspond with the notion of 'story' as it was defined above.[25] For example, the predecessors of the serjeants-at-law were the *'narratores'* or 'counters' whose primary task was to present the plaintiff's *narratio* to the Court of Common Pleas. But the *'narratio'*, far from being a story, was a formal statement of claim that fitted a strictly limited set of categories. The primary skill of the *narratores* was 'in fitting the facts alleged by their clients into the appropriate mould'.[26] The art was not to tell stories, but to translate them. It was a sophisticated form of classification, more like form-filling than story-telling.

Similarly, in an argument on a question of law 'stating the facts' of the case before the court, or 'stating the facts' of some precedent used in argument does not necessarily involve telling a 'story' *stricto sensu*. For example, the material facts may concern a situation or state of affairs rather than a sequence of events; or the facts may be stated in a way which corresponds precisely with the elements of a crime or tort or other cause of action. Although typically presented less formally than the medieval *narratio*, a statement of the material facts of a case is only one step away from form-filling, especially in the case of written pleadings.

This line of argument raises two important issues. First, it can be readily conceded that there are many cases in which advocates are not involved in explicit story-telling at all. An argument about interpretation of a statute conducted at a general level; a defence based on a simple alibi; a plea in mitigation which emphasizes factors other than the accused's version of and attitude to the crime are all simple examples. Whether stories are necessary elements of an argument about 'a case as a whole' will be considered below.[27]

Secondly, can a sharp distinction be drawn between form-filling and story-telling? 'On 5 March X intentionally and with malice aforethought stabbed Y, who died from his wounds on 6 March' contains all the ingredients of the crime of murder and satisfies the formal definition of a story, viz. it is a sequential narrative of particular events that forms a whole. We normally expect stories to be more detailed, colourful and interesting, but analytically the bare-bones statement of alleged facts in a statement of claim or an indictment will often (but not always) satisfy the requirements of a 'story'.[28] Indeed the element of configuration or connectedness that make this account into a story is that the events narrated amount to a legally significant action, such as a murder.

Situation A situation is a state of affairs at a given moment of time. An account of a situation is like a snapshot or a picture. It is a configuration, but neither chronological sequence nor change are necessary ingredients. The distinction between 'situation' and 'story' is important in law, because the law is often concerned with momentary or static states of affairs. For example, someone may be responsible for a car with defective brakes or driving without a licence or owning a factory that violates Health and Safety Regulations irrespective of how the state of affairs came about.[29] Again, a plea in mitigation may focus wholly or in part on the situation of the defendant at the time of sentence and his or her likely future behaviour, without regard to his version of the story of the crime. Stories and descriptions of states of affairs have some shared features; but there are also important differences. However, most of what I have to say about stories in this context applies *pari passu* to descriptions of situations.

Scene, scenario, context   Advocates often talk in terms of 'setting the scene', 'developing a scenario', 'painting the canvas', and the like.[30] Sometimes what is meant is covered by or overlaps with the notions of 'story' and 'situation', as they were defined above. However, such talk typically suggests something additional in the way of 'background' or 'contextual' elements which are not essential parts of the story or situation, but which may nevertheless be helpful in understanding or grasping it. In fiction or drama or painting it is often difficult, if not impossible, to distinguish sharply between background and foreground, between scene and scenario, between context and substance. Legal argument on questions of law and of fact is supposedly characterized by strict and generally well-understood criteria of relevance which provide a basis for such distinctions.[31] One hypothesis, which we shall explore later, is that one function of narrative in advocacy is to allow in much more by way of context and background than is technically permitted in explicit argument.

Theme   'Theme' is another term that is used ambiguously in the literature on advocacy. Sometimes it is used to refer to the overall characterization of the situation or story or some element of it that appeals to a popular stereotype. For example: 'This is an example of a grasping landlord exploiting a helpless tenant'; or 'This is a case of property developers needlessly desecrating the countryside.' Another, more precise usage, which is useful in the present context, refers to any element that is sufficiently important to deserve emphasis by repetition. An English barrister gives a vivid account of what he calls 'the mantra', as follows:

In almost all cases there will be a key factor which has played a dominant role in the case from your point of view. It may be 'stupidity', 'fear', 'greed', 'jealousy', 'selfishness'. Pick your word, inject it into your opening. Put it on a separate piece of paper. Repetition will have a lasting effect. If you have hit the right note and have repeated it often enough, it will echo in the Jury's mind when they retire. It will be the voice of the 13th Juror. Try to hit the note as soon as possible in opening.[32]

Thelema   A constant refrain of manuals on advocacy is the importance of winning the trust and sympathy of the tribunal and of providing them with the means of reaching the result you want: '[A]im from the outset to capture and keep the sympathy of your audience.'[33] 'Aim to be the honest guide.'[34] 'You have got to be trusted.'[35] 'Maintain your status.'[36] 'Show them the way home.'[37] These are just some of such precepts set out in a recent introduction to *Advocacy at the Bar*. Such advice, typically presented in the form of discrete precepts, is usefully encapsulated by an American judge in a single concept:

Thelema is a generic term denoting the universe of things which can combine to create, in judge or jury, the desire to help. I pick an unknown word, which can precisely be defined without pruning away the semantic accumulations of similar words, such as; favor, appeal, sympathy, motive, beneficence, empathy and the like. The meaning of thelema, in Greek, is all of these things.[38]

Presentation and argument   I suggested earlier that the advocate's role in court is less problematic than that of other legal actors. It is to persuade this tribunal to decide in this case in favour of his or her client. It does not follow that the job is either simple or easy. In a contested trial it can be extremely complex, involving multiple tasks or sub-roles. In the popular metaphor of drama, the advocate may have to combine the roles of producer, stage-manager, actor, narrator and even, within limits, script-writer. In appellate cases and pleas in mitigation there are fewer participants, but the task is not necessarily easier. Indeed, Shapland reports that some barristers consider that 'doing a good mitigation is one of the higher tests of advocacy and is often very much harder to do than to do a successful contested fight.'[39] In so far as adjudicators are meant to decide on rational grounds, the task of the advocate is to persuade by rational means. On this view, the role of the advocate is to *present an argument* and that is implicitly recognized both in the notion of 'the theory of the case' and in the key role accorded to it in organizing and guiding the advocate's performance. However, especially in contested trials, the argument is not presented solely in terms of explicit argumentation. The story of a case is not merely told in the speeches of counsel: the evidence is typically presented by a succession of witnesses through direct examination, cross-examination and re-examination. Sometimes witnesses are allowed to 'narrate' their testimony, but often they are confined to answering questions. Some complain that they were prevented from telling their story.[40] In disputes on points of law the advocate has a much more straightforward role in presenting explicit argumentation, but even then part of the argument may proceed by question and answer. Similarly pleas in mitigation may involve not only a speech but also testimony and comments on written reports (such as social enquiry reports, medical reports, antecedent reports).[41]

In the present context this has a two-fold significance. First, an advocate's 'argument' may be more or less implicit and may have to be reconstructed from material that has been presented to the court. Secondly, the notion of argument needs to be distinguished from the manner and style of its presentation. Manuals of advocacy tend to devote far more attention to presentation than to construction of cogent arguments.[42] They emphasize the importance of attracting and retaining attention; of being clear, comprehensible and succinct; of body language and other non-verbal communication and of all that is encompassed by the notions of theme and thelema. There is, as we all know, much more to the art of persuasion than making logically cogent arguments. Clearly stories have a role to play in arousing interest, in maintaining attention, in winning thelema and in setting the context for argument. But, one may ask, what role, if any, do they play in *rational* persuasion? And, closely related to this, by what standards are we to determine the legitimacy or otherwise of the uses of narrative in advocacy?[43]

We have seen that not all arguments by advocates involve explicit story-telling. However, it is generally thought that story-telling is indeed a central skill of advocacy in respect of each of the three standard tasks with which we are concerned. Thus in a contested trial on disputed facts the prosecution is typically required, and the defence has the opportunity, to outline their respective 'cases' and very often this consists of presenting the facts in narrative form. At later stages in the trial counsel for each side may re-tell the story, or part of it, directly or have it told through witnesses. It is commonly said that in contested trials in the adversary system juries have either to choose between two competing stories or to construct a third from what has been presented to them.[44] In many criminal trials the defence takes the form of attacking or casting doubt on the prosecution 'story' without offering an alternative account.

Less obviously, narrative is recognized to be of critical importance in appellate advocacy (or other cases involving questions of law). 'The statement of facts is the heart' is a well-known dictum. Perhaps the classic statement is by John W. Davis, a highly respected leader of the Bar in the United States: '(I)n an appellate court, the statement of the facts is not merely a part of the argument, it is more often than not the argument itself.'[45] The precise meaning and significance of such precepts will have to be considered in some detail.

The role of stories in pleas in mitigation is recognized to be more problematic. Officially the prosecution's story has already been accepted and cannot openly be challenged. Where the accused has pleaded not guilty and has been convicted, he/she has already had an opportunity to tell his/her story and it has been rejected. The plea in mitigation has to be made in the context of an already defined version of what happened. Some mitigating factors may gloss or supplement the existing story, but others may relate to 'extraneous' matters such as the accused's past record, his present attitudes or situation and the likelihood of repetition of the offence. Where, however, the accused has pleaded guilty the situation is rather different. Although the truth of the prosecutor's allegations is acknowledged, it has only been in bare-bones form. The accused has not yet had a chance to present his/her version to the court and may wish to do so. While the truth of the charge(s) may not be directly challenged, there is generally some scope for putting the story in a different light by re-telling all or part of it in person or through the advocate.

Thus it is claimed that stories feature in all three kinds of advocacy, though with differing degrees of frequency and importance. However, it cannot be assumed that their role in each context is identical. Let us, then, look at some of these claims in more detail.

Arguments about Questions of Law: Stating the Facts

On the orthodox view a contested question of law involves a disagreement about the *general* scope of a rule or norm or principle (interpretation) or whether a *particular* set of facts fits within it (application). By convention, an argument about an issue of law is conducted on the basis that the facts are given – it proceeds *as if* the facts are true. Conversely, an argument about a disputed issue of fact proceeds *as if* the applicable law is settled. Both legal theory and legal practice recognize that these conventional distinctions are not unproblematic.

If in an argument about interpretation or application of law the facts are treated as given, what are we to make of the claim that the statement of the facts is 'not merely a part of the argument, it is more often than not the argument itself"?[46] The best-known, and probably the most theoretically sophisticated, explanation was advanced by Karl Llewellyn:

It is trite that it is in the statement of facts that the advocate has his first, best, and most precious access to the court's attention. The court does not know the facts, and it wants to. It is trite among good advocates, that the statement of the facts can, and should, in the very process of statement, frame the legal issue, and can, and should, simultaneously produce the conviction that there is only one sound result. It is as yet less generally perceived as a conscious matter that the *pattern* of the facts as stated must be a *simple* pattern, with its lines of simplicity never lost under detail: else attention wanders, or (which is as bad) the effect is submerged in the court's effort to follow the presentation or to organize the material for itself.[47]

This explanation contains at least three elements: securing the court's attention; framing the issue; and producing conviction. In the context of Llewellyn's wider theory of appellate judging and advocacy, there are two other points. First, he makes it clear that he considers that skilful statement of the facts is an element of *good* advocacy in the sense that it is legitimate and ethical and a hallmark of excellence. Llewellyn was much concerned with the ethics of advocacy and he was careful to distinguish those techniques which were, in his view, clearly legitimate from those which were illegitimate or of dubious legitimacy.[48] Secondly, Llewellyn maintained that what constituted a good argument by an advocate (on questions of law) and a good justification by a judge are to be evaluated by the same criteria. The role of an advocate is to advance the best justification for a decision. The statement of facts by the judge as much as by the advocate is (part of) the 'heart' of the argument.[49]

Let us, for the sake of simplicity, treat some elements of Llewellyn's theory as uncontentious. We can accept that it is both legitimate and important for an advocate to seek to secure the attention and interest of the court. We are not concerned here with examples of techniques of advocacy that Llewellyn would treat as clearly illegitimate, such as lying, deliberately misleading the court, inventing facts, or adopting diversionary or consciously obfuscatory tactics.[50] Our concern is with excellence, not just with effectiveness. Finally, let us proceed on the basis that there is at least a sufficient overlap between standards of excellence in argument, by judges and advocates, to justify looking at examples of statements of facts in reported judgments.[51] This is convenient, because texts of reported judgments are more accessible, extensive and familiar than verbatim reports of appellate arguments by advocates.[52]

If these points are accepted, at least two aspects of Llewellyn's explanation require clarification. What is the role of the statement of facts in framing the issues? And, why is the statement of facts considered so important in producing conviction about the answer to a question of law? The answers to both questions depend on one's view of the relationship between the general and the particular in legal argument in the common law tradition. Llewellyn's answer to the first question looks like a restatement of a familiar and orthodox position. His answer to the second has occasioned both puzzlement and controversy among jurists.

Llewellyn's position on the first question can be restated as follows:[53] it is a general principle of common law adjudication, subject only to a few exceptions, that courts will decide only questions arising out of actual disputes. Generally speaking, they will not give rulings on hypothetical facts or answer questions of law posed in general terms, divorced from some concrete fact-situation. The essence of case-by-case adjudication is to respond to problems that arise from some particular real life situation. Before legal argument begins the issues have been 'limited, sharpened and phrased in advance'.[54] But, as every common lawyer knows, there is considerable leeway as to the precise level of generality at which a question of law is posed and answered. In Llewellyn's terms the issues are *'reasonably but not rigidly clarified in advance'*.[55] The initial statement of facts, by advocate or judge, provides an opportunity for suggesting the categories to be used and the appropriate levels of generality for formulating with greater precision the problem or issue that arises from the facts. How one characterizes the problem depends upon how one characterizes the facts. To put the matter in formal terms: the statement of facts takes the form 'X happened'; the question of law is: If X happens, what is the legal effect? The answer to that question (one usage of the term *ratio decidendi*) takes the form: 'If X, then Y'. X is a common factor linking statement of facts, the question of law, and the applicable rule (the answer to the question of law). How X is characterized is crucial.

Up to this point this looks like a restatement of a familiar and orthodox view of common law reasoning.[56] But Llewellyn introduced a new concept, 'situation sense', which has occasioned a good deal of puzzlement and controversy. Some have adopted the term uncritically, but used it rather loosely; some have viewed it as impenetrably obscure or meaningless; some have rejected it as introducing an irrational or subjective or metaphysical element into theories of legal reasoning. I have explored some of the problems associated with Llewellyn's account of 'situation sense' elsewhere. Here I wish to concentrate on its function in respect of the claim that 'The Statement of Facts is the Heart'.[57]

What kind of statement of the facts of a case by a Grand Style judge or advocate satisfies the requirement of 'situation sense' and, because of this, 'can produce the conviction that there is only one sound outcome'?[58] The first requirement is that the facts of the particular case are stated in terms of categories that are directly translatable into a recognizable 'type-fact-pattern'.[59] The facts are categorized in such a way as to form a clear example of the situation seen as a *type*. Secondly, the type-fact- situation, so characterized, appeals to 'sense', 'reason' and 'justice' in such a way as to suggest a general solution to the problem raised by the particular case.[60] Factors in the unique story which are likely to arouse sympathy or antipathy – 'the fireside equities' – are filtered out or given a secondary role.[61] Thus X is a constituent in the process of translation from the statement 'X happened' to the statement 'This is a case of type X' and again to the statement 'Whenever X happens, Y ought to happen.'

But, it may be asked, what makes one particular characterization of X appeal to 'sense, reason and justice'? And, why should there be any difference in the persuasiveness or the cogency of an argument by presenting it in the form of a statement of the facts of the particular case rather than explicitly as a formulation of a general fact-pattern or as a rule?

Let us consider three possible ways of answering those questions that represent three different interpretations of the claim that 'the statement of the facts is the heart'.

The first, and weakest, answer acknowledges that there is no analytical difference in the characterization of X in statements of the kind 'X happened', 'This is a case of type X' and 'Whenever X happens, Y ought to happen.'[62] However, the advocate who takes care to formulate his statement of the facts in such a way achieves two things: First, a good foundation for the argument is laid at the very beginning. What is initially implicit can be made explicit by subsequent elaboration. Secondly, it ensures that there is complete harmony between the initial statement of the facts and the general proposition of law that is being argued for. The facts and the rule are not merely consistent; analytically they are the same. On this interpretation, the precepts we have been considering contain sound advice in exaggerated form. For the statement of facts is not 'the heart' of the argument, nor is it 'the argument itself'; rather it anticipates one crucial step in the argument, the formulation of the applicable rule.

A second interpretation is that the statement of facts allows implicit appeals to values or 'sense' (whatever that is) in a way which would be either less effective or perhaps even impermissible if it were done explicitly at a general level. Gerald Lopez puts the matter thus:

> While debate over what the facts mean (argument) is encouraged to be more explicitly persuasive than debate over what the facts are (story-telling), argument as an act of persuasion is constrained in most cultures in a way that story-telling is not ... stories by their very nature can appeal to what is, by convention, still taboo in a culture. Because facts themselves capture and reflect values, what cannot be argued explicitly can be sneaked into a story. Indeed the genius of story-telling as an act of persuasion is that it buries arguments in the facts. Stories can thereby circumvent the existing constraints on the meaning that can be given to the facts as found. Put differently, relevance is for a story a much looser standard than it is for argument.[63]

This is a perceptive account of some reasons why advocates consider the statement of facts to have an important role in the task of persuasion. But is this consistent with an ideal of argument that is legitimate, ethical, fair? Lopez acknowledges that 'this sounds very much like hypocrisy ... Yet in some ways hypocrisy is necessary to civilized life.'[64] On the other hand, jurists of an earlier generation have tended to emphasize articulation, explicitness and openness as important safeguards of honest and wise argument. 'Covert tools are never reliable tools', wrote Karl Llewellynn.[65] John Henry Wigmore, as we shall see, emphasized the utility of articulation of the implicit as a check on the validity and cogency of arguments about evidence.

A third interpretation makes a positive virtue of appeals to implicit, un-expressed or dimly perceived factors. In this view, far from being a matter of 'sneaking in' such factors or of licensed hypocrisy, narrative has a positive role to play in generating a pressure towards 'the inexpressible, the inexplicable'.[66] The most articulate proponent of the role of the inarticulate in legal argument is James Boyd White, a professor of both literature and law, who has developed a sophisticated, if somewhat idealized, view of the role of narrative in legal discourse.[67] Others talk in terms of appealing to intuition, emotion, or the imagination. Some rationalize this in terms of giving a legitimate place to appeals to 'irrational' considerations; others advance this in terms of differing conceptions of rationality.

Even Llewellyn's views fit this third interpretation. His glorification of the common law tradition and of the Grand Style of judging is based in part on the idea of courts being responsive to the nuances of complexity and change through a special sensitivity to facts that reaches beyond existing legal categories. I have argued elsewhere that one can only make sense of 'situation sense' by including in it some notion of 'judgment' that outruns our capacity to construct articulate and logical justifications for what is felt to be 'just' or 'wise' or 'to make sense'.[68] It is beyond the scope of this paper to explore whether Llewellyn can be rescued from charges of inconsistency in giving a place to such factors while emphasizing the value of articulation and explicit rationalization. Suffice it to say here that I believe that such a defence is possible because, in my view, there is no necessary incompatibility between rational reconstruction and giving play to the legal imagination in normative theories of advocacy and judging.

The judge as advocate: Lord Denning as hero and as deviant

A brief consideration of two of Lord Denning's most famous judgments may cast further light on the notion that 'the statement of facts is the heart'. No English judge in modern times has so regularly and so openly observed the precept that the manner of stating the facts of a particular case has a significant role to play in justifying decisions in disputed questions of law of general significance. His statements of fact have been highly praised, sharply criticized and treated with uneasy ambivalence by fellow judges and by academic commentators.[69]

In *Candler* v. *Crane Christmas* Denning MR (as he then was)[70] delivered a dissenting judgment which presented an interpretation of the duty of care that was, in due course, accepted by the House of Lords almost exactly in terms of his formulation.[71] It is widely regarded as a great dissent by a Grand Style judge that made legal history. The most famous passage in the judgment reads as follows:

... Did the defendants owe a duty of care to the plaintiff? If the matter were free from authority, I should have said that they clearly did owe a duty of care to him. *They were professional accountants who prepared and put before him these accounts, knowing that he was going to be guided by them in making an investment in the company. On the faith of those accounts he did make the investment, whereas, if the accounts had been carefully prepared, he would not have made the investment at all. The result is that he has lost his money.* In the circumstances, had he not every right to rely on the accounts being prepared with proper care, and is he not entitled to redress from the defendants on whom he relied? I say he is, and I would apply to the present case the words of Knight Bruce LJ in *Slim* v. *Croucher* (1860) 1 DeG. F. & J. 518, an analogous case ninety years ago, where he said: 'A country whose administration of justice did not afford redress in a case of the present description would not be in a state of civilisation' [italics supplied].[72]

This is widely regarded as an example of Lord Denning at his best. Before considering why this should be so, it is worth noting that this passage does not come at the start of the judgment. It contains Denning's third formulation of the facts of the case. The judgment begins with a statement of the facts in a single paragraph.[73] This is quite succinct, but more detailed than the version in the passage quoted above. It is a summary statement which through its language and emphasis seems calculated to win sympathy for the plaintiff. Someone reading it for the first time should have no difficulty in predicting the judge's decision; they may also find it quite persuasive. However, its ostensible function is to lay a foundation for a statement of the issue; for those facts 'raise a point of law of much importance'.[74] After framing the issue, Lord Denning proceeds to a much longer restatement of the facts in a narrative that takes up more than two full pages of the *All England Law Reports* (about 1,500 words). This very careful and detailed examination contains few 'rhetorical' flourishes; its main function is to make clear that in this case the accounts were intended to induce the plaintiff to invest in the company; and that the plaintiff's loss was 'caused' by this negligent advice. Few 'fireside equities' sneak into this detailed narrative. Its primary function is to establish that there is no doubt that this case does in fact constitute a clear example falling within the general rule for which Lord Denning is arguing.

Lord Denning next considers the decision in the court below, before restating the question of law ('of general importance')[75] to which this case gives rise. The passage quoted above comes at the start of his consideration of 'the law' on the matter and the authorities which, allegedly, support the defendant. His statement of the facts here is a third re-formulation. It is explicitly part of an argument, the gist of which might be rendered: 'Were it not for authority, I should have said that reason and justice and sense dictate that a duty of care exists in this kind of situation.'

He then turns to consider 'Authority'. Professor Patrick Atiyah has observed: 'When Lord Denning begins like this, one can be sure that he will then analyse the authorities in order to come out where he wants to, and this case was no exception. Skilful examination of the cases showed them to be either disting-uishable, or else inconsistent with the principles of *Donoghue* v. *Stevenson*.'[76] This, however, involved a bold reinterpretation of authority, rather than a 'timorous' analysis of the cases,[77] 'not designed to lead to a pre-determined conclusion, but to see what the cases had originally stood for'.[78] In this view, creative interpretation was required in order to ensure that reason and sense prevailed over a settled view of authority. Despite his hints at impropriety, Atiyah calls this 'one of the great dissenting judgments in the history of the common law'.[79]

What is the basis of this claim to greatness? The power of the argument lies not in any direct appeal to emotion through 'sneaking in fireside equities' or choosing emotionally laden terms. Rather it is persuasive because it suggests grounds both for extending and limiting liability in a type of situation which has the following elements: *reliance* by a *non-expert* on a *professional* in a relationship of *proximity* in which the professional gives *negligent* advice which he *expected* and *intended* would be followed by this plaintiff. The element of reliance links this to a general principle that is widely accepted as justifying liability; but, equally important, the other factors (professional, non-expert, negligence, proximity, expectation, loss) *limit* the scope of the situation and close the door on 'the floodgates argument' which had worried 'the timorous souls'. In short, Denning's formulation characterized and circumscribed the type of situation in which justice, reason and sense suggested that there should be liability. Most of the rest of the judgment is taken up with interpreting (or re-interpreting) earlier precedents and setting strict limits to the scope of the doctrine that he is advocating.

At first sight, Lord Denning's highly persuasive categorization of the facts in his third formulation neither violates any taboos nor expresses in particulars what is inexpressible at a general level. Rather it introduces and neatly encapsulates in simple and concrete terms the gist of an argument that is thereafter explicitly elaborated at a general level. On this reading, it seems to fit the first interpretation of 'the statement of facts is the heart', better than those of Lopez and White. This, I think, is too simple. For, I shall argue that, read as a whole, Denning's judgment gains some of its force from factors suggested by the other two interpretations.

In the first place, Denning saw this as a case of a conflict between justice and sense, on the one hand, and authority (as conventionally interpreted) on the other. 'The lawyer who argues from justice has a weak case'; but the lawyer who appeals to justice, sense and reason implicitly through the facts is often very persuasive. By judicious use of thelema and theme (*three* statements of the facts!) Denning's judgment appeals to 'reason, sense and justice' before he ever considers a single precedent. Anyone who doubts that his statements of the facts had a key role to play in his argument should try reading the judgment without these passages. 'Grand Style' or 'creative' or 'innovative' judges typically find themselves in situations in which all or most of the authorities seem to be ranged against them. It is a standard technique for them to use careful statements of the facts of the case at hand as part of their arguments for changing or re-interpreting the law. They tend to be at their most effective when, as in *Candler*, there is a high degree of consensus among 'laymen' as to what would be a just or sensible result in the particular case.

At first sight, *Candler* v. *Crane Christmas* looks unpromising as an example of a judge or advocate conveying more through a statement of the particular facts than can be captured by a purely abstract statement. For surely part of Denning's achievement was to identify and articulate the ingredients (professional and non-expert; proximity; reliance etc.) that constitute the new rule in an acceptable way. Undoubtedly that is part of the appeal of the famous passage. However, I wish to suggest that this is a good example of the appeal of the particular. For something *is* changed if we translate Denning's categorization of the facts into a statement of a general rule, as follows: 'A duty of care exists whenever a professional accountant prepares and puts before [a layman] accounts, knowing that he is going to be guided by them in making an investment and on the faith of these accounts he makes the investment and as a result he loses his money.' Analytically no change has been made in the course of translation. 'X happened and Y ought to happen' has become 'Whenever X happens, Y ought to happen.' But, whereas the particular statement seems unexceptionable, the general statement of the rule is likely to make lawyers uneasy. In this instance, the reason is clear. The formulation of the rule is too narrow: surely the rule, even in 1951, was not to be restricted to preparation of accounts for the purposes of investment by professional accountants. What of other professionals? Other forms of statement? Other purposes? Other kinds of loss? How far should the duty of care extend? In *Candler* Denning persuasively argued that there should be liability in this case, he suggested a general rationale for liability, and indicated some limits to the scope of the rule. But he left many details of the precise scope of the rule to be determined in future on a case-by-case basis. In an important sense, the general rule governing the situation was 'inexpressible' in 1951. For there is a difference between saying, 'This is a clear case of X', and providing a general definition of X.[80]

Miller v. *Jackson* Lord Denning's dissenting judgment in *Candler* v. *Crane Christmas* won almost universal acclaim and made legal history. A much later dissenting judgment, in *Miller* v. *Jackson*, is almost as well known, but represented a partial defeat.[81] The judgment is too long to reproduce here. Some of its flavour and the reasons for its notoriety can be gleaned from the opening paragraph:

In summer time village cricket is the delight of everyone. Nearly every village has its own cricket field where the young men play and the old men watch. In the village of Lintz in County Durham they have their own ground, where they have played for these last 70 years. They tend it well. The wicket area is well rolled and mown. The outfield is kept short. It has a good club-house for the players and seats for the onlookers. The village team play there on Saturdays and Sundays. They belong to a league, competing with the neighbouring villages. On other evenings after work they practise while the light lasts. Yet now after these 70 years a judge of the High Court has ordered that they must not play there any more. He has issued an injunction to stop them. He has done it at the instance of a newcomer who is no lover of cricket. This newcomer has built, or has had built for him, a house on the edge of the cricket ground which four years ago was a field where cattle grazed. The animals did not mind the cricket. But now this adjoining field has been turned into a housing estate. The newcomer has bought one of the houses on the edge of the cricket ground. No doubt the open space was a selling point. Now he complains that, when a batsman hits a six, the ball has been known to land in his garden or on or near his house. His wife has got so upset about it that they always go out at weekends. They do not go into the garden when cricket is being played. They say that this is intolerable. So they asked the judge to stop the cricket being played. And the judge, much against his will, has felt that he must order the cricket to be stopped; with the consequences, I suppose, that the Lintz Cricket Club will disappear. The cricket ground will be turned to some other use. I expect for more houses or a factory. The young men will turn to other things instead of cricket. The whole village will be much the poorer. And all this because of a newcomer who has just bought a house there next to the cricket ground.[82]

When I ask first-year students to read *Miller* v. *Jackson* as an example of Lord Denning's later writing, it stimulates a mixed reaction. Nearly everyone finds it enjoyable and interesting. Some find it persuasive, others think that it is 'over the top' or in some undefined way unjudge-like. Some see it as exhibiting prejudice or bias – in favour of cricket, against the Millers personally, or against property developers, or private property. When I point out that Lord Denning seems to have invented some facts (e.g. 'the animals did not mind the cricket'), omitted relevant facts (e.g. the Millers had a child,[83] they were not alone in complaining), and was guilty of exaggeration ('village cricket is the delight of everyone' – including the Millers?), most students agree that this is inappropriate behaviour for a judge. Would it be inappropriate for a barrister? Opinion tends to be divided. When I point out that in the course of the judgment he makes an elementary misuse of statistics,[84] they agree that invalid arguments are inappropriate for advocates as well as judges.

What of those who find it persuasive? The story as he tells it, does suggest that the Millers were being unreasonable, whereas the cricketers had in every respect behaved reasonably. Moreover, the Millers were newcomers who were trying to put a stop to a popular community activity that had been going on for seventy years ('newcomer' used five times; 'seventy years' six times – a clear example of 'theme');[85] 'thelema' is apparent too – is not the first paragraph alone calculated to win the sympathy of cricket-lovers, environmentalists, conservationists, ecologists, and lovers of tradition?[86]

There are some similarities between *Miller* v. *Jackson* and *Candler* v. *Crane Christmas*: in each Lord Denning perceived a conflict between what he calls 'the merits' and outmoded precedent;[87] in each he used his statement of facts as a foundation for framing the issue, for winning sympathy for one side and for weakening the force of prior adverse precedents before dealing with them explicitly. In each case he pinpointed the elements which provided a rationale for what he believed to be the right result. Reliance, proximity, negligence in *Candler*; long-established community activity; reasonable steps taken to minimize risk to neighbours; private individual purchasing adjoining property with notice of the activity and of the risk. However, whereas his performance in *Candler* is masterly, there are some weaknesses in *Miller*. It is not so much that in *Miller* he too overtly assumed the mantle of advocate, as that his argument is spoiled by poor advocacy. This is not merely because of the lapses which are even less acceptable from a judge than an advocate: inventing facts; not mentioning an awkward fact;[88] misusing statistics; and giving an impression of being unfair to the opposition. Nor is the essential weakness an unsuccessful striving after literary effect (law students, I find, are amused but not impressed). Rather he fails to make the strongest possible argument. There are two crucial weaknesses: first, he fails to meet head-on the main argument of substance (as opposed to authority) for the other side; is it reasonable for people living next to a sports field, whether newcomers or not, to bear the risk of injury to person or damage to property caused by cricket balls? Cumming-Bruce LJ found a *via media* by awarding damages, but refusing an injunction to prevent the playing of cricket.[89] Secondly, Lord Denning became so immersed in the particulars of the Millers' story, that he failed to step back sufficiently to satisfy Llewellyn's ideal of a Grand Style judge who categorizes the case in terms of the situation seen as a type in a way that suggests a solution. This could have been done along the following lines: 'This is a case of a long-established popular community activity which, despite all reasonable efforts to minimize risk of injury or damage to people and property on the adjoining land, cannot continue without an element of such risk.' One solution is to allow the activity to continue, but to make those involved bear the risk of damage.[90] This was in fact the final result.

Statement of facts

To conclude: the claim that 'the statement of facts is the heart' in arguments about questions of law is an example of an exaggerated statement that contains an important core of truth. It is exaggerated in two different ways: first, many statements of 'the facts' by advocates, as well as judges, are deliberately non-argumentative: that is to say that they set out to be 'impartial' or 'unbiased' or 'dispassionate'. Most judgments aspire to such relative neutrality; in proceedings by way of case stated a court will attempt a formulation which fairly raises the issue to be resolved by a superior court; in some jurisdictions both sides will agree on a statement of the facts; even some of Lord Denning's most colourful openings are designed to dramatize what he sees as a genuine dilemma rather than to lay the foundation for an argument justifying his decision one way or the other.[91] Of course, a skilful reader may be able to identify hidden clues or unconscious biases in the language of a purportedly fair statement of the facts. But that is very different from claiming that such a narrative is the heart of the argument.

The precept is exaggerated in another respect: even when narrative statements are clearly part of an advocate's argument or a judge's justification, it is wholly exceptional for this to be the main part of the argument, let alone 'the argument itself'. Legal argument typically consists of a mixture of authority reasons and substantive reasons.[92] Even those theories of legal reasoning which discount the importance of pure fiat – of authority unglossed by interpretation that spills over into 'substance' – would treat as wholly exceptional a case in which the gist of the argument is that the facts speak for themselves. At the very least, explicit argumentation will seize on one or two elements in the story for emphasis as key points in the argument – for instance, as a ground for distinguishing this case from others or for proceeding by analogy or for grounding a general reason of principle or policy. The facts at most are a component of the argument.

The analysis of *Candler* v. *Crane Christmas* and *Miller* v. *Jackson* suggests a further point. For these are examples of a judge using narrative to ground an argument appealing to 'substance' in a context where arguments based on authority appear to support an opposite conclusion. The judge who justifies his decision entirely or mainly on 'authority reasons' is likely to have less need to use his statement of the facts as an important part of his argument. In short, narrative is more likely to be important for advocates and judges who are concerned to attack, undermine or re-interpret authority (whether precedent or statute) than for those who can invoke it in a more straightforward fashion.

However, the precept contains an important core of truth. This goes much further than the mere claim that how the story of the particular case is told plays an important part in strengthening substantive reasons in some arguments on questions of law in path-breaking or historic or particularly hard cases. Rather my suggestion is that narrative can play many different kinds of roles in legal arguments.

The three different interpretations of the precept illustrate three such roles, without in any way claiming to be exhaustive. A statement of the facts of a case may do little more than anticipate in concrete terms what will later be explicitly formulated as a general rule: 'The facts are X' precedes 'wherever X, then Y.' Or, a formulation of the facts may appeal to 'reason, sense or justice' in a way that is rhetorically more persuasive than overt general argument.[93] The formulation in *Candler* appealed in a way that could be rationalized at a general level, but it was a statement of a clear example falling within a less clear general rule. The formulation in *Miller v. Jackson* involved some dubious appeals to 'fireside equities' – the particular plaintiffs were depicted as unattractive and unreasonable. In both of these cases narrative accounts of the facts of the particular case were being used, *inter alia*, as indirect means of weakening the force of adverse precedents. None of this is incompatible with the claim that focusing on the particular may also be a way of capturing 'the unexpressed' or 'the inexpressible'. *Candler* is an example of a common law judge in effect saying: 'This is clearly a case in which there should be a remedy. It is neither necessary nor desirable for me to delineate precisely the bounds of the general rule which should govern this and analogous kinds of situations.' The appeal of a case-by-case method of proceeding has appealed to most common lawyers and some philosophers over the centuries.[94] Narratology draws attention to the significance of the way in which we describe or characterize particular particulars.

Disputed Questions of Fact: Holism and Atomism in Arguments about Evidence

The distinction between questions of law and questions of fact is problematic at the level of analysis; it has important consequences in legal practice. Contests about facts are governed by different procedures, involve different actors and, in contested jury trials, multiple audiences – for the respective functions of judge and jury are governed by quite elaborate rules. In our legal culture decisions on questions of law are generally required to be supported by public justifications, whereas there is no such general requirement for determinations of fact. Thus, lawyers have good reason for treating argumentation about questions of law and questions of fact as quite different kinds of operation. Conventional legal discourse adds a further twist: when lawyers talk of 'appellate cases' this generally implies that the issues are related to questions of law; when they talk of 'trial practice', it is assumed that typically what is at stake is a dispute about the facts.[95] Such talk sometimes masks a much more complex reality.

This artificial separation of two intimately related spheres of legal discourse is reflected in secondary treatments. The massive theoretical literature on 'legal reasoning' deals almost exclusively with reasoning about disputed questions of law, sometimes without any acknowledgement that legal practice involves arguments about several other kinds of issues.[96] Discussions of reasoning about questions of fact – exemplified by recent debates about probabilities and proof – are largely dealt with in a separate body of literature, which belongs to a different intellectual tradition.[97] This artificial segregation has been maintained by a kind of fiction: just as arguments about questions of law proceed as if the facts are given, so arguments about questions of fact proceed as if the law is settled.

The complexities of the relations between narrative and argument are rather vividly exemplified in theorizing about judicial proof. Some of these can be illustrated by looking briefly at three apparently contrasting perspectives on the subject: Wigmore's account of the logic of proof;[98] a recent book entitled *Reconstructing Reality in the Courtroom*;[99] and the thesis, advanced by Abu Hareira and others, that many judgments about the evaluation of evidence are 'holistic' rather than 'atomistic' – and properly so.[100]

The great American Evidence scholar, John Henry Wigmore, developed a 'Science of Judicial Proof as given by Logic, Psychology and General Experience'. In his view there are two methods of organizing and analysing a mixed mass of evidence, 'such as is commonly presented in a judicial enquiry': the Narrative Method and the Chart Method:[101] 'The Narrative Method rearranges all the evidential data under some scheme of logical sequence, narrating at each point the related evidential facts, at each fact noting the subordinate evidence on which it depends; concluding with a narrative summary.'[102]

The Chart Method, which was Wigmore's own invention, involves restating the arguments about the evidence as a whole in the form of a list of propositions and depicting the relations between all the propositions in a single chart. The method is in essence an elaborate and rigorous form of rational reconstruction (or construction) of arguments in a manner which involves articulating every step of an argument and mapping the relations between all the parts.

Questions about the validity and the uses and limitations of Wigmore's Chart Method have been extensively canvassed elsewhere.[103] What is interesting in the present context is that Wigmore saw the Narrative and Chart Methods as alternatives, the former being in effect a more primitive and less rigorous version of the latter. 'The Narrative Method ... is the simpler method, more readily used by the beginner, and more akin to the usual way of describing an evidence problem.'[104] The Chart Method, by contrast, 'may not commend itself to some types of mind. It is the only true and scientific method.'[105] Wigmore made two main claims for the Chart Method: it enables one to see an argument as a whole and, through a process of disciplined articulation, it makes it easier to spot fallacies, unwarranted jumps and other weaknesses in a complex argument.

Wigmore saw narrative as no more than a rather casual form of analysis, organization and presentation of evidence. Story-construction and story-telling had no significant role to play in his 'Science of Proof'. In sharp contrast, the most extensive modern account of the role of narrative in contested trials maintains that 'The American criminal trial is organised around story-telling'.[106] Bennett and Feldman's *Reconstructing Reality in the Courtroom* explores in great detail and with some sophistication the theme of presenting and interpreting competing versions of reality in jury trials. The authors conducted a number of empirical studies about how cases are presented to and assessed by jurors in criminal trials in the United States. The underlying theory is based on the work of ethnomethodologists, such as Garfinkel, Cicourel and Saks, and on the ideas of Kenneth Burke.

Bennett and Feldman argue that the advocates and jurors typically use stories to organize the otherwise disjointed bits of evidence that are presented to them. This helps them to select, interpret and assess what would otherwise be a confusing and unmanageable mass of data. 'Stories organize information in ways that help the listener to perform three interpretive functions': to locate the central action of the story; to construct inferences about the relationships among the elements surrounding the central action; and to test the story as a whole for 'internal consistency and descriptive adequacy or completeness'.[107] The authors suggest that Kenneth Burke's 'pentad' of elements of social action – scene, act, agent, agency and purpose – provides an appropriate standard in this context: this general social frame of reference helps us to organize and evaluate the relations between the five elements in terms of their completeness and consistency.[108] Bennett and Feldman state their main conclusion as follows:

Judgments based on story construction are, in many important respects, unverifiable in terms of the reality of the situation that the story represents. Adjudicators judge the plausibility of a story according to certain structural relations among symbols in the story. Although documentary evidence may exist to support most symbolizations in a story, both the teller and the interpreter of a story *always* have some margin of control over the definition of certain key symbols. Therefore, stories are judged in terms of a combination of the documentary or 'empirical' warrants for symbols and the internal structural relations among the collection of symbols presented in the story. In other words, we judge stories according to a dual standard of 'did it happen that way?' and 'could it have happened that way?' In no case can 'empirical' standards alone produce a completely adequate judgment, and, there are cases in which the structural character-istics are far and away the critical elements in determining the truth of a story.[109]

In this account stories perform several functions: they serve as aids to *selecting* from a superfluity of information and to *filling in gaps* in that information; they are a vehicle for introducing judgments of value; and, above all, they provide essential *frames of reference* for organizing, evaluating and interpreting evidence. In this view, empirical evidence and logical analysis have a secondary role as checks on completeness and consistency. To put the matter simply in terms of our lexicon: Wigmore subordinates story to theory in his account of the logic of proof; Bennett and Feldman appear to subordinate theory (and even evidence) to story in their account of reconstruction of reality in the courtroom by advocates and triers of fact.[110]

A similar tension between narrative and argument, story and theory, underlies a new debate between 'holists' and 'atomists' in the theory of proof. In the Anglo-American tradition of discourse about evidence, by far the predomi-nant view of what is involved in organizing and evaluating judicial evidence has been 'atomistic'. That is to say, the construction and criticism of arguments about evidence, involves logical analysis of the relations between individuated items of evidence. In the extensive debate between Baconians led by Jonathan

Cohen, and Bayesians (and other 'Pascalians'),[111] both sides have assumed that it is (in principle) possible and meaningful to combine judgments of probability (conjunction, corroboration, convergence), to construct 'chains of inferences' and to evaluate evidentiary propositions. What has been at issue has been questions as to what are the applicable criteria for making and evaluating judgments about probabilities in the context of judicial proof.

Recently, however, M. A. Abu Hareira suggested that much evaluation of evidence is, and is rightly, configurative or holistic. For example, in evaluating the probative force of a 'mass of evidence' we do not and should not proceed by analysing the mass into separate 'items' and giving each item an independent probative value. Rather we consider the mass as a whole, as a gestalt or configuration, and assess its total probative force or plausibility in a manner which defies analysis.[112]

A rather different version of 'holism' is summarized by Peter Tillers as follows:

For our own part, we are inclined to believe that the effort to state systematically and comprehensively the premises on which our inferences rest may produce serious distortions in the factfinding process, in part (but only in part) because such systematic statement obscures the complex mental processes that we actually employ and should employ to evaluate evidence. It is not true that we can say all we know, and the effort to say more than we are able to say is likely to diminish our knowledge and our ability to use it. In our daily lives, we confidently rely on innumerable premises and beliefs that we often cannot articulate or explain, but our inability to express these premises and beliefs does not necessarily make them illegitimate or unreliable. The same may be true of many beliefs relied upon in the assessment of evidence by a trier of fact in the courtroom.[113]

These brief accounts of some very different perspectives on judicial evidence illustrate how questions about the role of narrative and stories are of considerable significance in this context. They should also serve as a warning against over-simplification. It is beyond the scope of this essay to explore these issues in detail. But it is relevant to the argument in the next section to outline a position that suggests, *inter alia*, that these apparently different perspectives have rather more in common than appears on the surface. Each contains elements lacking in the others. The 'holistic' approaches of Tillers and Abu Hareira have yet to be presented in the form of rounded theories. Each, in different ways, usefully directs attention to the relevance of fundamental philosophical issues about conceptions of 'rationality' and the place of notions such as configuration and coherence in rational argument. But we await a fully developed 'holistic' account of the role of analytical techniques in the evaluation of evidence.[114]

Wigmore's Chart Method is open to the criticism that, by failing to develop the notions of 'theory' and 'story', he gives the impression that his 'Chart Method' involves an almost mechanical application of ordinary principles of inductive logic. Anyone who tries to apply the method to a mass of evidence soon learns that Wigmore's theory provides almost no guidance in making *strategic* choices in constructing or criticizing a complex argument. He had a very crude view of narrative and he was surely mistaken in seeing 'the narrative method' as an alternative rather than as complementary to his method of analysis.

Bennett and Feldman's account has a converse weakness. They exaggerate the importance of stories in trials and underestimate the sophistication of good trial lawyers. Unfortunately they did not pay sufficient attention to the standard accounts by lawyers of how problems of selection, incompleteness and inconsistency are supposed to be tackled. In particular, by ignoring almost entirely such lawyers' notions as facts in issue, materiality, relevance, burdens of proof, presumptions and, most surprising of all, the advocate's notion of 'the theory of the case', they fail to reach a point where issue is squarely joined with standard legal accounts. Ignoring 'theory' leads them to exaggerate the role of stories in structuring understandings and decisions about disputed facts. Moreover, a Wigmorean can point out that general impressions are no substitute for meticulous detailed analysis in checking stories for consistency, coherence and completeness. Relying on stories to 'fill in gaps' could be interpreted as licensing just such unwarranted jumps and mere speculations that Wigmorean analysis can be used to expose. Finally, perhaps the best way of testing the plausibility of an argument or theory or story is to spell out in detail what precisely is being claimed. One of the best ways of exposing weaknesses in an argument is to articulate clearly what that argument is. This may be the main value of the Chart Method.[115]

All the theories mentioned here accept similar criteria of the credibility or plausibility of a theory or story: it must be compatible with uncontested or established particular facts; it must be internally consistent; it must be coherent; and it must be in conformity with what is variously referred to as 'general experience', 'the common course of events', 'common sense generalizations' or 'the stock of knowledge' in a given society. There may be scope for disagreement about the meaning and role of 'coherence' in such evaluations, and about the relative importance of these various criteria. But all of the views considered are open to interpretation as non-sceptical, cognitivist theories that treat the enterprise as one of enquiring about the correspondence of some version of events with a notionally external reality.[116] In this respect they may be out of tune with some of the more sceptical tendencies of post-modernist thought.[117]

In sketching a perspective that treats these seemingly different perspectives as to some extent convergent or complementary, I do not wish to give a false impression of consensus in this area. There are many unresolved questions and ample scope for genuine disagreements and differences at many levels in the theory of judicial proof. Rather I am suggesting that both narrative and explicit argument are almost bound to have a place in any prescriptive theory about arguing towards, arriving at, justifying and evaluating adjudicative decisions on disputed questions of fact. What precisely are the functions of narratives in this context and what are the proper relations between narrative and argument are open questions. My hunch is that the functions are diverse and the relations complex, but that they are closely analogous to those that we considered in connection with questions of law. My reasons for this are explored in the next section.

Making Sense of the Case-as-a-whole: Law, Fact, Value and Outcome

> [W]e can say that both the history and the tapestry are in this respect like a law case: the lawyer knows that to prove his (or her) case he must not only demonstrate the truth or probability of certain propositions of fact; he must present to the judge or juror a way of looking at the case as a whole that will make sense; and it must 'make sense' not merely as a matter of factual likelihood, but as a predicate to judgment, as a basis for action. While a case can in a technical sense be refuted by disproving one element or another, in practice the lawyer knows that he must do more than that: he must offer the judge or juror an alternative place to stand, another way of making sense of the case as a whole. To do his job, that is, the lawyer must both engage in an accurate retelling of the facts and make his own claim for what they mean.
>
> James Boyd White, *Heracles' Bow*[118]

So far I have followed legal convention by dealing separately with argumentation about questions of law, questions of fact and questions of disposition. The *basis* for the distinctions causes difficulty in legal practice as well as in legal theory, but the distinctions have important practical *consequences* in respect of allocation of functions between participants (e.g. judge and jury), rights of appeal, the doctrine of precedent and other matters.[119] The question arises whether such sharp distinctions make sense from the perspective of narratology or whether they break down within some such concept as the story of a case as a whole. I propose to argue that these differentiations are not merely artificial technicalities within legal discourse; they are relevant in the present context for identifying some differences both within and between stories of (or about) cases. But there is no escaping traditional juristic puzzlement about relations between law, fact and value.

One of the most powerful images in legal history is Holmes's Bad Man, an amoral citizen who is indifferent to the morality of his behaviour, the niceties of legal argument and procedure, or any questions about obligation to obey the law.[120] The Bad Man washes lawyers' discourse in cynical acid in order to arrive at a clear answer to a single selfish question: 'If I do this, what will happen to me?' The Bad Man is concerned only with what the organs of the State will do to him in fact, if he is caught. For him, 'the bottom line' is the outcome of the case. Imagine, for example, a petty criminal with a record of previous convictions, who has been arrested and charged with theft in circumstances in which the law is unclear, the evidence against him is problematic and sentencing practice for this kind of offence is indeterminate or variable. He meets his lawyer and tells her that his main concern is to keep out of jail. From his perspective, decisions whether to contest on the facts or on the law or both or to petition for leniency via a guilty plea are secondary considerations which he may leave to his lawyer.

From the lawyer's point of view there are some tactical choices to be made. The prosecution case is: 'If X, then Y, then Z. This is a case of X, therefore Y, therefore Z.' The defence can contest X and/or Y and/ or Z. What is involved in contesting on the facts, on the law or on sentence is very different in each instance, procedurally and in other ways. This is not just a matter of preparing and presenting three different kinds of argument, possibly to different audiences (judge, jury, magistrates, appellate court). One possibility might be a tacit or open plea-bargain: in exchange for not contesting X or Y, the prosecution (or the court) might agree to a non-custodial sentence, which is the lawyer's primary goal. In considering the case as a whole the lawyer might develop three very different kinds of theories: a theory of the law relating to the type of offence (Y); a theory about the evidence concerning the alleged incident (X); and a theory about mitigating circumstances (Z). While it would be unwise to have radical inconsistencies between these three possible lines of argument (for example to plead alibi in respect of X, and depression in connection with Z – 'my client was elsewhere at the time; he was depressed when he did it'),[121] the three theories could in principle have little or no overlap; in practice they are more likely to fit together as three fully integrated components of a single whole. The three lines of argument are all means to the same end (securing an acquittal or, at least, avoiding a jail sentence) in a single case and can be used to support each other. From the standpoint of the Bad Man's lawyer the distinctions between questions of fact, questions of law and questions of sentence are of practical importance. However, even from her standpoint, these distinctions and the decisions they entail operate within the context of some notion of the case as a whole. Conversely, the Bad Man may not be the only participant who is primarily concerned with the outcome; the prosecutor, in deciding to prosecute,[122] or the jury, in deciding whether to convict, may in practice base their decision on some global judgment about the Bad Man's deserts or the merits of the case rather than on a more differentiated approach that might restrict their role or the factors that they are meant to take into account. For example, the jury may return a 'perverse' or 'protest' verdict one way or the other because they think this law is an ass or that this prosecution should not have been brought or because they have taken against the accused.

How distinctions between law, fact, value and outcome break down in practice is vividly illustrated by Diana Trilling's account of the trial of Jean Harris, who was indicted for murdering her lover, Dr Herman Tarnower.[123] The case originally attracted attention because the accused was the head-mistress of a well-known school near Washington DC (Madeira) and the victim was even more famous as the author of a best-seller, *The Complete Scarsdale Medical Diet*. It is likely to continue to attract attention for many years to come, not least because many people believe that Mrs Harris was wrongly convicted. From the standpoint of the lawyer the case contained almost no questions of law. The crucial issue related to intention: did the evidence support beyond reasonable doubt the proposition that Jean Harris intentionally caused the death of Herman Tarnower? The prosecution argument was that Dr Tarnower's four wounds could only have resulted from deliberate shooting. Mrs Harris's story of the shooting was that she had come to Tarnower's house in order to have a last conversation with her lover before committing suicide in his garden; the conversation had gone badly wrong and Tarnower had been shot acciden-tally as he struggled to disarm her when she tried to shoot herself in his bedroom. There was no dispute that the pistol was Mrs Harris's. The issue of intent essentially turned on what happened in the space of less than five minutes in Tarnower's bedroom.

Diana Trilling suggests that Mrs Harris's lawyer, Joel Arnou, employed four different strategies in her defence: 'an old-fashioned compassionate defence; a defence based on social defence; what might by a stretch of definition be called an ideological defence (it dealt with Mrs Harris's dilemmas as a woman); and a defence based on physical evidence'.[124] Conspicuously absent was a psychiatric defence.[125]

The theory behind each of these strategies might be rendered by a Wigmorean analyst as follows:

1   Mrs Harris deserves your sympathy, therefore she should be acquitted;
2   Mrs Harris is a fine lady, therefore she did not commit murder;
3   Dr Tarnower deserved all he got. Mrs Harris acted rightly on behalf of all women. Therefore, the killing was justified;[126]
4   Dr Tarnower was accidentally shot in the course of a struggle in which he was trying to prevent Mrs Harris from committing suicide.

Diana Trilling claimed to be 'considerably estranged' by the first three strategies; 'I respected only the last of them.' Lawyers will recognize the first three as quite common courtroom tactics. They could point out that the second goes to Mrs Harris's credibility as a witness ('She is a good headmistress, renowned for her veracity; such people tell the truth; therefore you should believe her story').[127] However, they would agree that only (4) is legitimate and cogent as the main theory of the case. It is probably fair to say that this was the defence's theory and, in so far as the other strategies played a part they were ancillary. However, over a week of the trial was taken up with a parade of 'character' witnesses from Mrs Harris's school who, on Trilling's interpretation, were testifying on behalf of the school more than for the accused: 'They have no public choice except to treat the shooting of Dr Tarnower as "the tragic accident" that Arnou calls it, a temporary block in the otherwise unimpeded onward and upward march of education.'[128]

Perhaps even more significant is the lack of emphasis given in the closing speech for the defence to an account of the shooting itself: 'The story has taken no more than a minute or two, if that much, of Arnou's three-hour summation.'[129] On this interpretation the great bulk of the defence was taken up with attempts to secure thelema in terms which Wigmorean analysis quickly reveals to be based on defective logic. But it also suggests that the core defence theory relating to the fatal few minutes was wrapped up in the context of a story spread over several years and presented in a way which mixed fact, value and speculation within rather generous conceptions of relevance. It is reported that the jury focused almost entirely on the immediate circumstances of the shooting and decided that not all the shots could have been fired by accident.[130]

Some further complexities about the notions of 'case', 'case-as-a-whole', 'case-studies' and 'case-stories' can be illustrated by switching from the standpoint of the advocate to that of some outside observer, such as a student of law.[131] It is a common criticism of academic law in the Anglo-American tradition that it suffers from 'appellate court-itis';[132] law students and legal scholars pay too much attention to reports of appellate cases, whereas records and accounts of trials represent neglected materials of law study. In this context the distinction between 'leading cases' and *'causes célèbres'* is illuminating.[133] 'Leading cases' are precedents which have become landmarks in the development of legal doctrine either because they created or consolidated or gave authoritative approval to some resolution of a question of law of general significance. A few, for example, *Brown* v. *Board of Education*[134] or *R.* v. *Dudley and Stephens*,[135] are well known outside the legal profession; but these are exceptional. Most such cases are considered 'leading' only within the specialized culture of law. Most *causes célèbres*, on the other hand, whether famous or notorious or otherwise 'celebrated', are known to a much wider audience; for example *Dreyfus* or *Sacco and Vanzetti* or *Bywaters and Thompson* or *Alger Hiss* or *Jean Harris*. Almost all leading cases at common law were decided by appellate courts and feature in the law reports. Many *causes célèbres* have involved dramatic, much-publicized trials; most have little or no 'legal' significance; it is a matter of contingency whether they feature at all in the law reports. When they do, the report tends to give a rather thin account of the story of the case.[136]

Only a minority of cases featuring in the law reports count as leading cases. But, generally speaking in jurisdictions with selective law reporting, cases are selected for inclusion only if they have precedent value, that is they raised significant *questions of law*. The manner in which the reports are constructed, including the stories they tell, is determined in nearly every respect by this criterion of significance. *Candler* v. *Crane Christmas* and *Miller* v. *Jackson* are marginal examples of 'leading cases'. *Candler* paved the way for a later change in the law, but itself only reaffirmed the orthodox position that there was no duty of care for negligent misstatement. *Miller* v. *Jackson* is notorious because of Denning's performance, but its significance as a precedent is rather limited: it did little more than confirm the nineteenth-century doctrine. The law reports give us 'the facts' of *Candler* and *Miller*, but they do not tell us the complete stories of particular disputes. We do not know from that source what happened to Mr Candler or the Millers or the Lintz Cricket Club after their cases were decided. Nor, from the reports alone, can we tell what part these cases played in the story of the development of the law of negligence and nuisance.

Even on the most orthodox view of leading cases and other precedents, three different kinds of story are relevant to a reported case. The story of the original event or dispute which gave rise to the proceedings; the story of the litigation itself; and the story of the development of an area of law in which this precedent featured. We can rely on reports of cases *regularly* to tell only the first kind of story (the facts); even then the reported story may consist solely of allegations that have never been established by evidence – it is trite that the most famous of all English leading cases, *Donoghue* v. *Stevenson*, may be a monument to a mythical snail.[137] Yet, it is rather exceptional for a law report to be criticized for being incomplete. Judged by orthodox criteria of significance, law reports generally tell us all we need to know about a particular 'case'.[138]

This last point should prompt us to take a further look at the notion of 'a case as a whole'. An adequate report of a 'case' in the sense of a legally significant precedent does not need to give a full account of the proceedings nor of the dispute; it often does not even tell us the end of the story of the episode between the parties. Yet, from the point of view of legal significance, what is reported is the whole 'case'. What constitutes 'a case as a whole', even in a loose sense, depends on one's point of view and why the case is considered significant.

Some lawyers may think that this is belabouring the obvious. But a recent trend in legal scholarship suggests that the implications of this are not as obvious as they should be. The last decade has seen the publication of a number of notable contextual studies of leading cases. A conspicuous example is Brian Simpson's *Cannibalism and the Common Law*.[139] Such studies explore the historical context of the case in great detail and, in most instances, examine its aftermath and impact. Typically they cover all three kinds of story mentioned above: the story of the original facts; the story of the legal proceedings; and the story of the aftermath, including the legal aftermath.

They tend to make for good reading and they often change one's perception of the original case. Almost invariably they make the point that leading cases tend to become abstracted from their original historical context and take on a life of their own. Yet, as I have argued elsewhere, the significance of such studies is often unclear.[140] The reason is simple: leading cases are leading because they are legally significant. In-depth studies of the background of such cases, however scholarly, entertaining or illuminating they may be as slices of legal life, may add very little to our understanding of the general doctrine they produced. Their significance lies elsewhere and is sometimes obscure or unfocused. Law reports are centripetal; contextual studies are often centrifugal.

Contextual studies of leading cases are no different from other case-studies in lacking settled criteria of significance.[141] Indeed, it is leading cases and precedents which are exceptional in this respect. There are, of course, many different kinds of reasons why *causes célèbres* may be celebrated. They may have involved famous people or sensational events or dramatic trials or politically significant issues. Many retain their interest mainly as unsolved mystery stories. Some are significant as unequivocal or ambiguous symbolic events. America's leading *cause célèbre*, the *Sacco–Vanzetti* case provides a striking example.[142] It originally attracted attention as a potential miscarriage of justice.

Niccola Sacco and Bartolomeo Vanzetti, both Italian immigrant workers, were accused of murdering two men during a payroll robbery in South Braintree, Massachusetts, in August 1920. They were tried and convicted in April 1921. After a lengthy legal and political campaign to save them, they were eventually executed in August, 1927.

Few *causes célèbres* have generated such an extensive literature. The full transcript of the trial and subsequent proceedings has been published in several volumes. Lawyers involved in the case and prominent legal scholars, including Felix Frankfurter, John Henry Wigmore, Edmund Morgan and Karl Llewellyn published studies, including detailed analyses of the evidence. Many prominent figures were involved in the international protest. The case became the subject of so many novels, plays and poems that it prompted the comment that it was the only major literary event in the United States between two world wars.[143]

What is the legal, political and literary significance of the story of Sacco and Vanzetti? It has never been seriously doubted that a payroll robbery and murder took place in South Braintree on 15 August 1920. The central issue in the trial was a single question of fact concerning identity: were Sacco and Vanzetti (or one of them) involved in the crime? There were no substantial questions of law in the case, but many questions have been raised about the fairness of the proceedings, including some concerning admissibility of evidence. Legal opinion is split on these issues: 'The trial judge, the trial jury, the Supreme Judicial Court, and the Advisory Committee each and all decided every vital issue against [the accused].'[144] Most, but by no means all, legal commentators maintain that the trial involved serious violations of due process and that such evidence as there was linking the accused to the crime did not satisfy the standard of proof beyond reasonable doubt. There is still scope for disagreement about evaluation of the evidence relevant to the question whether as a matter of historical fact either or both were participants in the hold-up. From an orthodox legal point of view this does not differentiate the case from many other alleged miscarriages of justice. Karl Llewellyn, who campaigned actively on behalf of Sacco and Vanzetti, argued that the case was important not because it was unique, but because it was typical. It revealed serious institutional deficiencies in the administration of criminal justice in the United States.[145]

That is not why the story of Sacco and Vanzetti is 'celebrated'. Nor is it generally regarded as just another example of a mystery story. Rather it was treated (somewhat belatedly) and has continued to be perceived as a major political event. Sacco and Vanzetti became symbols of injustice. The significance of their story has, not surprisingly, been variously interpreted.[146] It has been taken to represent capitalist oppression of the working class; the non-acceptance of immigrants in American society; the persecution of political radicals; and conspiracy and corruption in 'the establishment', or just blind prejudice. In many commentaries, and in nearly all fictional accounts, it is assumed that this is a clear example of wrongful conviction of individuals who were innocent in fact as well as in law. Such interpretations often ignore distinctions between three kinds of miscarriage of justice in the courts: a person may be wrongly convicted because the court made a mistake of fact (in this case, that they got the wrong persons); or, whether or not as a matter of historical fact the accused did commit the crime, there was insufficient evidence to justify conviction according to the criminal standard of proof; or, whether or not the accused did commit the crime, the procedures followed were unfair. Many 'non-legal' interpretations of the *Sacco–Vanzetti* case tend to ignore these distinctions or treat them as trivial or irrelevant. On this view the important fact is that Sacco and Vanzetti were wrongly convicted and wrongly executed. The point of their story is the outcome: whether or not that outcome is attributable to factual error or insufficient evidence or procedural irregularity or other technical niceties or a combination of these is beside the point. They were victims of a great injustice.

This view needs to be taken seriously by lawyers as well as others. For the reasons for treating this case as important seem to be independent of such lawyers' distinctions. Surely, what matters is who they were (Italian, working-class, anarchists) and what happened to them (wrongful conviction and execution). Some of what is at stake here in this difference of views may be illuminated by considering Vanzetti's letters.

Bartolomeo Vanzetti's letters are among the classics of prison literature.[147] Written in touchingly fractured English, they have moved many readers with their combination of constant reiteration of his innocence with simplicity, concern for others, political awareness, and dignified acceptance of death. If one reads them on the assumption, or indeed as evidence, of Vanzetti's complete innocence, they constitute a powerful human document. If, however, one tries to read them on the contrary assumption that he was in fact one of the robbers, does this transform the collection into a work of monstrous hypocrisy? I do not think so. It could be that Vanzetti had come to believe in his own innocence and that this is a pathetic or tragic example of self-delusion. Or one can discount the protestations of innocence – perhaps as tactful, perhaps even necessary, white lies – and still respect his courage and dignity and concern for others. Or, is it perhaps the testament of a committed political activist who, well aware of his significance as a symbol of injustice, is consciously making his courageous last contribution to the cause? Opinions may differ on the plausibility of these different readings. But, I would suggest, the brute question of fact of his involvement in the hold-up is a central element in almost any interpretation of the story of Bartolomeo Vanzetti. Whether the 'point' of the story concerns the workings of American courts or political persecution of aliens and radicals or just an extraordinary person, it makes a qualitative difference whether the story proceeds on the basis that he was not in fact at South Braintree or that he was wrongly convicted because there was a reasonable doubt on the evidence or because unfair procedures were followed or because there were technical irregularities in the proceedings. Injustice established as a matter of historical fact is qualitatively different from miscarriages of justice that are solely deviations from the law's own standards.[148]

Jurisprudence and Narratology

Jurisprudence, viewed as the theoretical part of law as a discipline, is centrally concerned with the nature of legal discourses and their underlying assumptions. Legal discourses are of many kinds. This essay has principally been concerned with two specific kinds: 'arguments' by advocates and judges in court on questions of law and questions of fact. The conceptual difficulties associated with distinctions between 'law', 'fact' and 'value' are much debated in jurisprudence. On one view, with which I have some sympathy, arguments about questions of fact and questions of law are both species of practical reasoning with similar, but not identical, criteria of validity, cogency and appropriateness. However, the distinction between 'questions of fact' and 'questions of law' has very significant consequences for the discourse of advocates. How an issue is classified affects who addresses whom in what arena according to what procedural conventions and practices.

The modes of discourse in argumentation about questions of law and questions of fact in court are accordingly very different. Nevertheless there are some important structural and other similarities. In this essay I have tried to illustrate some of the variety of functions that narrative can play in both types of discourse and to a lesser extent in pleas in mitigation. It should not be a matter of surprise that in law, as in other parts of our culture, there are recurrent tensions between general and particular, fact and value, logic and rhetoric, and reason and intuition or imagination.[149] Nor should it come as a surprise that narrative plays a variety of roles in legal discourse or that in advocacy the relations between story-telling and rational argumentation are problematic. What may be more surprising to the outsider is to find that legal theory has almost entirely forgotten its roots in classical rhetoric; that theorizing about arguments on questions of law, questions of fact and sentencing occupy three largely disconnected bodies of literature; and that, in recent years, contacts between literary and legal theory have largely been confined to concern with the first kind of question. In considering what jurisprudence and narratology may currently have to offer each other in the Anglo-American context during the next few years, all of these factors are relevant.

The first message of the essay has been a warning of complexity. Not only are there many different contexts and kinds of legal discourses, but the specific context of advocacy – litigation – is itself extremely complex. Proceedings in court are of many different kinds and any particular example of courtroom discourse by lawyer, or judge or other participant, needs to be set in the context of the total process – the story of that particular piece of litigation. We have seen how even orthodox readings of the most familiar kind of legal text, 'cases' in the law reports, typically require differentiation of at least three kinds of stories: the story that gave rise to the proceedings ('the facts'); the story of the litigation (the proceedings); and the story of the development of the law which gives the case its significance (the case as precedent). Yet, as every lawyer knows, but we sometimes forget, law reports are highly selective, incomplete accounts of atypical cases, selected because they were 'hard', i.e. there was a doubt about the law. Quite often one does not learn of the final outcome of the proceedings, that is the resolution of the story of that particular litigation. The texts on which we draw for examples of arguments about disputed facts are more variable, less accessible, and even less likely to be typical of contested trials than the standard law report. Narratologists, beware!

The second lesson of this preliminary exploration is that it is easy to exaggerate the importance of narrative (*stricto sensu*) in legal argument. It plays important and multiple roles, sometimes in the foreground, sometimes as background. But some claims made for it are overstated: 'The statement of facts is the heart'; 'Juries choose between competing stories'; 'the central act of the legal mind . . . is the conversion of the material of life . . . into a story that will claim to tell the truth in legal terms' – these are all overstatements that exaggerate the roles of story-telling in legal argument, let alone other legal discourses. It is probably fair to say that 'story' and related notions have been neglected in legal theory. In so far as this is so, 'narratology' has something potentially significant to contribute – not least in stimulating lawyers to re-examine their conceptions of rationality. But it is unlikely that Law will become part of Narratology's Empire.

Thirdly, this essay has been almost entirely concerned with prescriptive theories of advocacy and argumentation. The focus has been on issues relating to what constitute legitimate, valid, cogent and persuasive modes of reasoning on disputed questions of law and fact. We have only touched incidentally on modes of persuasion in advocacy that may be perceived as clearly or arguably illegitimate or irrational. Narrative is no doubt sometimes used 'to sneak in' irrelevant or improper considerations, to conceal or divert attention from gaps or weaknesses in an argument, and in many other ways. Here, narratology may help to remind jurists of important issues about the ethics of argumentation. Such issues were central concerns of classical rhetoric, but have been relatively neglected in Anglo-American jurisprudence at least from this kind of perspective. These are just some possible lines of enquiry within normative jurisprudence.

Legal theorizing should not be and is not confined to normative questions. It is also concerned with understanding and interpreting law in the real world. In recent years actual examples of legal texts of different kinds have been subjected to scrutiny from a variety of perspectives. Ethnomethodologists, phenomenologists, semiologists, structuralists of many fashions, deconstructionists, literary theorists, hermeneuticists, and other inelegantly labelled academic entrepreneurs have exploited the rich heritage of legal texts with many fanfares and mixed success.

This essay is one of a series of explorations of the place of narrative in general culture. Can one expect to find something particularly illuminating or distinctive from the study of legal texts? Apart from the dual warnings about diversity and complexity, I have dropped a few hints about my own tastes. I happen to think that much of legal life and legal discourse is a part of general culture, far less distinctive, peculiar or unfamiliar to 'laymen' than is often suggested. So, for many purposes, legal texts can be treated as just one standard kind of cultural artefact which happens to be at hand. For example, just as social historians cull legal records as standard, relatively accessible sources of evidence about this or that aspect of social life, so one can find in the law reports an extraordinarily rich, well-documented anthology of 'real life' stories which can be analysed for all sorts of reasons unconnected with why they were originally preserved, constructed and published. However, if I had to settle for one reason why narrative in legal discourse has a special significance in culture, I would focus on the key factors of power, decision, publicity and argumentation. In no other sphere of social life are there to be found in such abundance practical decisions by powerful officials that have had to be argued for and justified in public and recorded in texts. Whether those texts are statutes, law reform documents, records and reports of trials, law reports or formal agreements, they share the elements of power, decision, recording and, to a lesser extent, public accountability and justification. Such legal texts are not unique in having these characteristics – witness for example election manifestos, (non-legislative) parliamentary debates, company reports – but as a body of literature they are unrivalled in their extent, detail and availability. Narratology seems to me to offer a fruitful lens for studying such texts; and, if legal narratology develops as a flourishing sub-discipline, it may even help to reunite legal theory with rhetoric. But that is another story.

NOTES

This essay was originally presented at the Seminar on Narrative in Culture organized by the Centre for Research in Philosophy and Literature, University of Warwick, in 1987. I am particularly grateful to Christopher Nash, Martin Warner and John McEldowney for stimulating my interest in the topic and for their guidance and comments on the original version. Later versions of the paper were presented, *inter alia*, at legal seminars at University College, London; the University of Miami; York University and the University of Windsor, Ontario. I am grateful to all those who participated in these seminars. The current version was largely completed in September 1987. I have profited enormously from discussions with or writings by, among others, Terry Anderson, Clarence Bennett and Martha Feldman, John Dewar, Reid Hastie, John Hoffman, Bernard Jackson, Gerald Lopez, Nancy Pennington, Stephen Penrod, Kim Lane Schepele, David Schum, Peter Tillers, James Boyd White and Steven Winter. Joanna Shapland's *Between Conviction and Sentence* was particularly valuable on pleas in mitigation. I have also made extensive use of manuals of advocacy; this revealing body of literature has been traditionally ignored by academics, perhaps because it tends to be 'anecdotal' and 'unscientific'. It has recently begun to be 'academicized' in the United States. However, Karl Llewellyn appears to be the only major theorist to have bridged the gulf between practitioners' cook-books and middlebrow legal theorizing. I have learned much from some writers on narrative, in particular Ricoeur, Danto and Rimmon-Kennan – but I have again been struck by a gap between this type of work and aspects of legal literature that deal with closely related, if not identical, questions.

So many issues and lines of thought have been suggested by these exchanges that it has been impossible to do justice to most of them in this essay, which is only my first venture into an enormous and seductive field. Some of the more significant writings are included in the bibliography. In the summer of 1987 Lord Denning very kindly agreed to be interviewed at his home by four of us on his conceptions of story-telling in advocacy and judging. The section on 'Lord Denning as hero and as deviant' was written before that interview and the text has not been altered, but a few points are mentioned in the notes. It is hoped that it will be possible in due course to report on that memorable occasion.

1   Millar (1957), 14–15.
2   J. B. White (1973), 859. Compare the claim of Fredric Jameson (1980): '[t]he all-informing process of narrative [is] the central function or instance of the human mind', cited by Nash (1987), 2.
3   The main exception is the 'New Rhetoric' of Chaim Perelman and his associates. See especially Perelman and Olbrechts-Tyteca (1971) and, more recently, Goodrich (1986, 1987), Bernard Jackson (1985, 1988) and others working in legal semiotics.
4   A notable example is Lord Diplock's rebuke, in criticizing Lord Denning's arguments in his dissenting judgment in *Gouriet* v. *Union of Post Office Workers*, as revealing 'some confusion and an unaccustomed degree of rhetoric', [1972] AC 1027, 1054.
5   White, op. cit., n.2; cf. Bennett and Feldman (1981).
6   Discussed, Twining (1984), 264–5.
7   Twining (1984), esp. 299.
8   In canvassing the literature of advocacy I have gained an impression of fragmentation rather than total neglect. The scene is the not unfamiliar one of bodies of literature talking past each other. In considering the role of narrative in arguments about disputed questions of law I have learned a great deal from the insights of Karl Llewellyn and James Boyd White. Despite a sense that White sometimes overstates his case (rhetorical exaggeration?), I am generally in sympathy with his impressive efforts to develop a humanistic rhetoric of law.
9   Non-lawyers should be warned that the great bulk of the jurisprudential literature on reasoning about questions of law (e.g. MacCormick, 1978) and on questions of facts (e.g.

Wigmore, 1937) is normative rather than empirical, and tends to be highly selective in its use of examples. See further, B. Jackson (1988), ch. 1.

10 I am here postulating that canons of ethics and the status of 'officer of the court' operate as side-constraints on this role of advocates in common law litigation to represent the interests of their clients. Although not unproblematic, the primary role is more easily grasped than the perennially controversial roles of the judge and jury. On the heuristic value of adopting the standpoint of advocate as a device for differentiating puzzlements about role from other concerns see Twining and Miers (1982), 286–91.

11 See generally Zuckerman (1986) and Jackson, Ockleton, White and Summers in Twining (ed.) (1983).

12 Ehrenzweig (1971).

13 This section draws on Du Cann (1964), Evans (1983), Jeans (1975), Mauet (1980), Rumsey (1986) and Stryker (1954). These are, of course, mainly examples of discourse *about* advocacy.

14 See *Analysis* ch. 3 and at 194–5, and below, 274 ff.

15 A reconstruction of the defence theory in the case of *Jean Harris*, below 245.

16 A reconstruction of a possible theory of the case for the plaintiff in *Candler* v. *Crane Christmas* [1951] 1 KB 164, discussed below, 232–5.

17 A reconstruction of a possible theory of the case for the defence in *Miller* v. *Jackson* [1977] QB 966, discussed below, 235–7.

18 Mauet (1980), 8. Recent research in Ontario suggests that manuals of advocacy and advocacy training have tended to underplay the importance of developing strategic plans as a basis for effective advocacy (N. Gold in Gold et al. 1989, 323).

19 Twining and Miers (1982), 136–40. Typically, determinations of X and Y take an all-or-nothing form, whereas (absent a fixed penalty or tariff) the appropriate sentence has to be selected from a range of possibilities. Orthodox theory recognizes deviations from the paradigm. For example, mixed questions of fact and law; judicial discretion in respect of application of a rule (e.g. discretion to exclude evidence) or of remedies (e.g. equitable remedies); interlocutory questions of procedure and so on.

20 These are different *usages* of 'story' commonly found in lawyers' talk. There are, of course, many *kinds* of stories, as the term is used in this essay. In the present context, it is especially important to distinguish between several types. First, stories about the events, or rather the alleged events, that gave rise to the proceedings ('the facts of the case'). Secondly, the story of the legal proceedings which may, of course, be one phase of some longer process, such as a long drawn-out dispute or feud. Thirdly, a party's or witness's version of events of which they have first-hand knowledge. There is an extensive literature about the ways in which our adversarial system of procedure can prevent or make it difficult for witnesses to tell 'their story' in their own way and in their own words (see below, n. 40). Fourthly, there are stories about the development of the legal doctrine applicable to the case. Such 'legal stories' sometimes form part of an argument by an advocate or judge *in* the case. (See e.g. Lord Denning in *Central London Property Trust Ltd* v. *High Trees House Ltd.* [1947] 1 KB 130.) Stories can also be told *about* the case, for example, explaining its significance as a precedent by setting it in the context of an account of the historical development of an area of law. Finally, the 'life-story' of a central participant, in more or less abbreviated form, may be treated as relevant in one phase of a legal proceeding (e.g. sentencing), but may be treated as irrelevant or inadmissible at a different stage (for example, there are complex rules governing the admissibility of evidence of character or disposition, including prior convictions, in relation to determination of guilt, but not of sentence). That this is not a comprehensive list of lawyers' stories can be easily seen by consulting the *Oxford Book of Legal Anecdotes* or *Great Legal Disasters* or any legal biography or collection of *causes célèbres*. In lawyers' clubland one can expect to hear a fairly predictable mix of war stories, anecdotes, jokes, gossip, legends, tales and myths. We are here mainly concerned with narrative accounts of the facts of a case and the use of narrative in legal argument ('legal stories', types 1–4).

21 Ricoeur (1981), 278–9.
22 Forster (1949), 82–3, discussed Rimmon-Kennan (1983), 16–19. Forster defines 'plot' explicitly in terms of causality; I have modified this in order to include narrations that are arguably totalities independently of notions of 'cause': in the third example, causation plays a part but is, arguably, not the 'point' of the story. Some writers, e.g. James Boyd White (1985), Kim Lane Schepele (1988) and Italo Calvino (1982), appear to maintain that all stories need a resolution or ending. While I am sympathetic to this view I have not included resolution as a necessary element in my conception of a story because in legal contexts there seem to be counter-examples: e.g. the facts of a case may raise an unresolved question, or an account of the development of a doctrine through a series of precedents may be presented as 'the story so far'. In both instances the telling of the story has a point, but not a resolution, as I understand that term.
23 'Narrative' is sometimes used more broadly to include accounts that are not stories. This paper is concerned with stories and story-telling in legal discourse; much of what is said here may also be true of other kinds of accounts.
24 *Trial of George Joseph Smith*, Watson (ed.) (1915), 261–2; cf. Bodkin's opening speech, 73–4.
25 See above 223.
26 Milsom (1967), 5–6. This probably over- simplifies the functions and discourses of *narratores*.
27 Below, 243 ff. Lawyers use the word 'case' in several different senses: one can bring a case (action), read a case (report), argue a case (argument), state a case (problem), win a case (action), or rely on a case (precedent). We have been considering reports of cases and case-studies. Let us call the genus 'case-accounts'. Such accounts share several features with stories: they have a unity; and they are supposed to have a point or meaning or significance. To say of a story or a case-account that it is pointless or meaningless or insignificant is generally to criticize it. Many case-accounts lack the time element of stories – they may concern situations or states of affairs; they may differ from stories in containing non-narrative materials – for example, arguments or diagnosis or solutions. But the elements of construction, configuration and of particularity linked to general significance make the analogy a close one. Stories and case-accounts *impose* beginnings and endings and resolutions and meanings on situations and events (but see above, n. 22). Within legal discourse, especially in the common law, different kinds of case-accounts play a prominent and varied role. For a different perspective on the concept of 'case' as a unit of discourse see below, ch. 11.
28 The use of stereotyped or mechanical or reconstructive stories, in e.g. traffic courts, may serve to simplify and speed up the process through 'typification'. See Brickley and Miller (1975), 693; Carlen (1976). I am grateful to an unidentified commentator at York University for this point.
29 Even in cases of strict liability, an account of how the situation came about may be relevant, for example, to ground a specific defence or as a mitigating or aggravating factor. It is, however, important to bear in mind that while attribution of legal responsibility normally relates to acts and omissions of identified legal persons, this is not always the case.
30 E.g. Patrick Bennett QC in Rumsey (1986); K. Evans (1983).
31 On whether lawyers have a peculiar notion of relevance, see Holdcroft and Zuckerman in Twining (ed.) (1983).
32 Bennett in Rumsey (1986), 3.
33 K. Evans (1983), 25.
34 Id., 36.
35 Id., 37.
36 Id., 43.
37 Id., 79.
38 The Hon. Charles L. Weltner in Rumsey (1986), 6. The primary meaning of θέλημα

(thelema) in classical Greek is 'will'; compare θέλγω (thelgo) 'to stroke with magic power, to charm, enchant, spell-bind, Lat. mulceo: to cheat, cozen', Liddell and Scott, Greek Lexicon (abridged).
39 Shapland (1981).
40 E.g. Danet (1980), 514–19; O'Barr (1982), 76–83, 137–48.
41 Shapland (1981).
42 E.g. K. Evans (1983), Du Cann (1984). American manuals tend to place more emphasis on preparation. The distinction between 'argument' and 'presentation' is related to, but does not quite correspond with, Aristotle's categories of logos, pathos and ethos. An 'argument' belongs to the sphere of logic in a broad sense; its validity and cogency are to be judged by whatever are achieved by the applicable principles of correct reasoning. Presentation refers to the method, style and techniques of communicating with an audience or audiences and, in relation to persuasion, is judged by its effectiveness in fact. Many of the precepts of advocacy relating to presentation, such as the importance of arousing and maintaining attention, of winning trust and of ensuring that one is understood are quite compatible with notions of 'rational persuasion'. To what extent such matters as thelema, themes, ethos and pathos belong to the sphere of persuasion by non-rational means is central to the theory of advocacy. See generally, J. B. White (1973), 810–21.
43 The concept of legitimacy is, of course problematic: see further below, 229–32.
44 E.g. Bennett and Feldman (1981), Preface and ch. 1.
45 J. W. Davis (1940, 1953), 181. Steven Winter has suggested to me the hypothesis that the 'best' advocates are more inclined to follow Davis's dictum in higher than lower courts. This corresponds with the notion of 'typification' as a means of speeding up the process in lower courts; see above, n. 28.
46 J. W. Davis, id.; cf. Paterson (1982), 52–65.
47 Llewellyn (1962), 341–2; cf. (1960), 238. The passage immediately preceding the quotations reads:

[The] real and vital central job is to satisfy the court that sense and decency and justice require (a) the rule which you contend for in this *type* of situation; and (b) the result that you contend for, as between these parties. Your whole case, on law and facts, must make *sense*, must appeal as being *obvious* sense, inescapable sense, sense in simple terms of life and justice. If that is done a technically sound case on the law then gets rid of all further difficulty: it shows the court that its duty to the Law not only does not conflict with its duty to Justice but urges along the exact same line.
   The great change during these last few years in the approach of the best advocates lies here. As little as twenty or even ten years ago [i.e. before 1945], leading appellate advocates were still apologizing in private for that necessity of their profession that they termed 'atmosphere' ... It is no longer a question of 'introducing atmosphere'. It is now a question of making the facts talk. For of course it is the facts, not the advocate's expressed opinions, which must do the talking. The court is interested not in listening to a lawyer rant, but in seeing or discovering, from and in the facts, where sense and justice lie. (Id., 341)

On sense, wisdom and justice see Llewellyn (1962), 59–61.
48 E.g. Llewellyn (1962), 85ff., 192, 256–60.
49 E.g. 126–8, 238.
50 Twining (1973), 261–3.
51 See below, n. 88.
52 One must, of course, beware of what Llewellyn called 'the threat of the available' (1962), 82–3. In this context, it is worth repeating that the examples used in this essay are not meant to be representative of day-to-day practice, in which, one suspects, explicit story-telling plays a more limited role than these illustrations suggest. Most lawyers and judges are more formalistic than Lord Denning and Karl Llewellyn.

53   See further, Twining (1973).
54   Llewellyn (1960), 29.
55   Ibid., note.
56   Twining and Miers (1982), ch. 7.
57   Llewellyn (1960), 238; Twining (1973), 216–27, 257–64.
58   Llewellyn (1960), 238.
59   Id., 59–61, 426–9.
60   Id., 60–1, 238, discussed Twining (1973), 216–27, 262–4.
61   Ibid.
62   Discussed Gottlieb (1968), chs. 3–4.
63   Lopez (1984), 32–3. This article illuminatingly explores stories and story-telling in order
     to illuminate 'the connections between how we perceive the world, how we persuade
     others, and how we make difficult choices ...' in problem-solving by lawyers seen as
     instances of human problem-solving (10, 2). The article centres on an example in which
     lawyers' sharp distinctions between questions of fact, law and disposition do not apply.
     The thrust of section IV of this paper is very much in sympathy with Lopez's analysis.
64   Id., 34.
65   Llewellyn (1960), 365, discussed Twining (1973), 227–9.
66   J. B. White (1973), 863–5; cf. J. B. White (1985), ch. 2 and 118–19. This idea may find
     some confirmation in psychological research on 'telling more than we can know', e.g.
     Nisbett and Wilson (1977).
67   J. B. White (1973), (1984), (1985). Some indication of White's perspective – he would
     not accept it as a definition – is expressed in this dictum: '[L]aw can be best understood
     as a set of literary practices that at once create new possibilities for meaning and action in
     life and constitute human communities in distinctive ways' ('The Judicial Opinion and
     the Poem: Ways of Reading, Ways of Life', 1985, 107). For an excellent critique of
     White's views see Sherwin (1988).
68   Twining (1973). There is now an extensive literature on Llewellyn's concept of 'situation
     sense'. One of the best discussions is Whitman (1987).
69   See especially, Jowell and McAuslan (1984), esp. 17–19, Robson and Watchman (1981),
     Harvey (1986). Lord Denning's own discussions of his style are also revealing, e.g.
     The Family Story (1981), 206–20. It is important to emphasize that the two cases
     discussed here are among the most striking of Lord Denning's judgments, and so cannot
     be taken as representative judgments of his output as a whole: still less can Lord
     Denning as story-teller be treated as typical of the style of English judges. See further
     note 52.
70   [1951] 2 KB 164, [1951] 1 All ER 426.
71   *Hedley Byrne and Co. Ltd* v. *Heller and Partners Ltd* [1964] AC 465. Lord Denning has
     denied that his judgment was written to persuade the House of Lords to overrule prior
     precedents on negligent misstatement (interview, July 1987). Nevertheless he is
     generally given credit for having persuaded them (e.g. Atiyah and Waddams, in Jowell
     and McAuslan, 1984, 57, 468).
72   [1951] 1 All ER at 428.
73   In the *Law Reports* the first paragraph is omitted. The paragraph reads:

In September 1946, the plaintiff invested £2,000 in a company called Trevanance
Hydraulic Tin Mines, Ltd. (which I will call 'the company'), and he has lost it all because
the company turned out to be a failure. He now brings this action against the defendants,
who are the company's accountants and auditors, claiming that he was induced to invest
the money because of erroneous accounts put before him by them and on the faith of
which he invested his money. The judge had found that the accounts were 'defective and
deficient' and presented a position of the company which was 'wholly contrary to the
actual position', that the accountants were 'in fact extremely careless in the preparation
of the accounts', and that the damage suffered by the plaintiff was 'plain', but,

nevertheless, the judge dismissed his claim because, in his opinion, there was no duty of care owed by the accountants to the plaintiff.

On the phenomenon of judges restating the facts (or doctrine), using different words see Llewellyn (1951), 47; Twining (1973), 235.

74   428.
75   Ibid.
76   Atiyah, op cit., 57.
77   The famous passage on 'timorous souls' and 'bold spirits' is at 432; Asquith LJ's riposte is at 442.
78   Atiyah, op cit.
79   Ibid.
80   cf. John Wisdom's account of 'case-by-case procedure' in his Virginia Lectures, discussed by D. C. Yaldon-Thomson in Bambrough (ed.) (1974), ch. 3.
81   *Miller* v. *Jackson* [1977] 3 All ER 340. This passage is discussed by Bernard Jackson (1988), 94–7, where he glosses but does not undermine my interpretation.
82   Id., 340–1.
83   [1977] 3 All ER at 346 (per Geoffrey Lane J), 350 (per Cumming-Bruce LJ).
84   'Despite these measures, a few balls did get over. The club made a tally of all the sixes hit during the seasons of 1975 and 1976. In 1975 there were 2,221 overs, that is, 13,326 balls bowled. Of them there were 120 sixes hit on all sides of the ground. Of these only six went over the high protective fence and into this housing estate. In 1976 there were 2,616 overs, that is 15,696 balls. Of them there were 160 six hits. Of these only nine went over the high protective fence and into this housing estate' (341). Later he states: 'He could not complain if a batsman hit a six out of the ground, and by a million to one chance, it struck a cow or even the farmer himself' (344). Innumerate lawyers and narratologists are invited to spot the fallacy.
85   At 340–5. In a recent interview (July 1987) Lord Denning indicated that at the time there was a lot of sympathy for the Millers and that he was concerned to right the balance. He graciously conceded that if his audience feels that he has overstated his case, then this is not good advocacy.
86   See B. Jackson (1988), 94–7 for a different interpretation.
87   In *Candler* the main, but not the only, adverse precedent was *Le Lievre* v. *Gould* [1893] 1 QB 491; in *Miller* v. *Jackson* it was *Sturges* v. *Bridgman* (1879) 11 Ch. D. 852.
88   J. B. White (1985), 116, says: 'An opinion that simply adopted one side's brief would not be worthy of the name.' This, however, underestimates the notion that the most persuasive advocate is the one who confronts the difficulties and surmounts them. Cf Llewellyn (1960), 241–5.
89   [1977] 3 All ER at 351.
90   Ibid.
91   E.g. *Lim Poh Choo* v. *Camden and Islington Area Health Authority* [1979] 1 All ER 332 (CA), 9.
92   Summers (1978), Fuller (1946).
93   Cf. Lord Atkin, op. cit., n. 1; B. Jackson (1988), 94–7.
94   See above, n. 80.
95   See e.g. Mauet (1980), Jeans (1975); cf. Weiner (1950).
96   A notable exception is MacCormick (1978, 1984).
97   See bibliographies in *TEBW* and Twining (1983) and Tillers and Green (1988).
98   Wigmore (1913, 1937).
99   Bennett and Feldman (1981).
100 Abu Hareira (1984, 1986); Schum and Martin (1982); cf. Tillers (1983), cited below, 241.
101 Wigmore (1937), 821.
102 Ibid.
103 *TEBW* (1985); Anderson and Twining (1987); Schum and Martin (1982).

104 Wigmore, op. cit., 821–2.
105 Ibid.
106 Bennett and Feldman (1981), dust jacket and preface. For a more moderate account see Hastie, Penrod and Pennington (1983), in which they develop a psycho-linguistic 'story model' of juror decision making.
107 Id., 41; cf. 67.
108 Id., 62–3.
109 Id., 33; cf. 65.
110 It could be argued that Wigmore and Bennett and Feldman are engaged in very different enterprises. Wigmore's Chart Method is a recommended intellectual pro-cedure for analysing, criticizing and constructing arguments based on evidence. It is part of a prescriptive 'logic of proof'. Bennett and Feldman purport to be presenting a sociological analysis of how lawyers, judges and jurors in fact 'reconstruct reality in the courtroom'. As such it is a contribution to an empirical, or interpretative, sociology of law. However, the connections are closer than appear on the surface. For Wigmore claims that what he is recommending is a usable, practical tool that reflects the practices of the best lawyers. His Chart Method is a systematization of good practice. Conversely, Bennett and Feldman, while primarily concerned with description and explanation, imply that the kinds of story-telling that they found in their data represent both inevitable and legitimate procedures for decision. They use their ideal types of 'case construction strategies' to explain (and by implication to criticize) deviant practices, such as disruptive and diversionary tactics (125–31) and the intrusion of bias into trial process (ch. 8). Accordingly, like Wigmore, they provide standards for criticizing the actual practices of advocates and triers of fact.
111 See n. 97 above.
112 Abu Hareira (1984, 1986).
113 Tillers (1983), 986n.
114 See works cited in n. 100 above and *TEBW* 183–5. Neither Abu Hareira nor Tillers denies a role to analysis and logical testing of the validity and cogency of arguments about disputed questions of fact. Like Bennett and Feldman, Abu Hareira appears to give such analysis a secondary place, as providing subordinate tests in a process in which attempts to individuate items of evidence in the process of evaluation involves an artificial, unwarranted and often dangerous attempt to dissolve the indissoluble. His theory echoes the traditional suspicion of practising lawyers of 'over-logical' approaches. Tillers, on the other hand, is self-consciously appealing to a different philosophical tradition in challenging the conceptions of rationality espoused by Wigmore and most participants in recent debates about probabilities. See now MacCormick (1980, 1984) and B. Jackson (1988).
115 See further Anderson and Twining (1987), *passim*.
116 There are two further points of agreement in all of the theories mentioned. All agree that one of the most important tests of the plausibility of a story or theory is its compatibility with uncontroversial or incontrovertible particular facts. It is a basic precept of advocacy (and detection) that one should confront uncomfortable facts (or evidence) both in constructing one's theory of the case and in presenting an argument. On the whole it does not pay to ignore or gloss over or try to divert attention from undisputed or credible facts. Rather one should explain them away or re-interpret them or acknowledge them, but seek to show that one's account is consistent with them. This is a different kind of 'consistency' from the internal consistency of the story considered apart from this evidence. Novels are generally supposed to be 'consistent', without having any direct connection with actual events in the real world. For a stronger version of a coherence theory see now B. Jackson (1988). Of course, many stories appeal to a community's stock of stories.
117 See generally, chapter 4 above and B. Jackson (1988).
118 J. B. White (1985), 160; cf. 174.

119 See generally, Summers and White in Twining (1983), Zuckerman (1986) and Guest (1987).
120 Holmes (1897), White (1985) warning against over-emphasizing the importance of outcome.
121 Cf. the morality tale of the lawyer's son who was charged with breaking the schoolroom window: 'In the first place, sir, the schoolroom has no window; in the second place, the schoolroom window is not broken; in the third place, if it is broken, I did not do it; in the fourth place, it was an accident' (*Punch*, cited Williams, 1973, 21).
122 On decisions to prosecute, see Mansfield and Peay (1987).
123 Trilling (1982). The following passage is an analysis of Diana Trilling's report of the Jean Harris trial as she observed it. The accuracy of the report is not in issue here. For a different view of the trial see Harris (1986). Diana Trilling's book about the case is a piece of impressionistic and imaginative reporting of the trial, presented as 'a work of social criticism'. 'My initial response was one of unqualified sympathy for the headmistress and I conceived the book in a spirit of partisanship' (9). As she sat through the trial and pondered what she had read and seen and heard, the work became transformed as she tried to make sense of the case. Her account needed a resolution, not just an outcome: 'Whatever one's judgment of Mrs Harris's guilt or innocence, or one's reaction to her as an individual, she was the person in this story who unmistakably had a fate, like a character in fiction. Dr Tarnower hadn't a fate; he had only an outcome, a conclusion to his life' (23). 'This story' is, of course, Mrs Trilling's story of Mrs Harris and her case. There have been, and no doubt will be, many others built on the same historical events. The point of the story in this particular interpretation is not the killing of Dr Tarnower nor the outcome of the trial nor the picture of American criminal process in action, but the character of Mrs Harris that was revealed by the courtroom drama and how it explained her behaviour before and during the trial. For Diana Trilling,

Mrs Harris has star quality ... without the armature of fiction, she can all too easily become a clinical study. She belongs to imaginative writing, where, as I say, Freud learned, as we learn, about character in conflict. Mrs Harris was unable to bring her inner contradictions into reliable working agreement, but our interest in her derives precisely from the unresolved opposition between her conscience and her impulses. She belongs to the novel in the way that Emma Bovary does, or Anna Karenina. They too were characters in contradiction. (435, 431)

What started 'as a story of sexual and social politics' (blurb) became transformed into 'faction', an imaginative and speculative interpretation of an interesting character. This, it seems, is the only way in which Mrs Trilling could make sense of her story-as-a-whole.
    Mrs Harris's recent book *Stranger in Two Worlds* (1986) is also an account of herself. It covers her early life, her career as headmistress and her experiences in prison. Only two chapters deal in any detail with the events immediately surrounding the death of Dr Tarnower and with her trial.
124 Trilling (1982), 422.
125 Id., 414–20.
126 The first three 'arguments' can be extrapolated from Trilling's account at 356, 233, 216–17; cf 420–38. Possible feminist interpretations of the case are only lightly touched by Trilling, e.g. 9–12.
127 Id., 422–3.
128 219–20, cf. 226.
129 Id., 357.
130 Newspaper reports.
131 On the different uses of 'case' in legal discourse see above n. 27 and below ch. 11.
132 The *locus classicus* is Frank (1949).

133   This theme is developed in Twining (1986).
134   *Brown* v. *Board of Education* 347 US 483 (1954), 349 US 294 (1955)
135   *R.* v. *Dudley and Stephens* 14 QBD 273 (1884), affirmed 14 QBD 560 (1885).
136   Compare the treatments of *Dudley and Stephens* in the law reports and by Simpson (1984).
137   The questions of law in *Donoghue* v. *Stevenson* [1932] AC 562 were decided by the House of Lords on the basis of the averments which were never put to the proof, i.e. the case was settled before 'the facts' were determined by a court.
138   Sykes and Heywood (1987) report that psychologists who have studied the phenomenon of story-understanding and recall, report that story grammar comprises four elements: setting, theme, plot and resolution. Reports of cases in the law reports can be readily analysed in these terms: the setting (S) represents the procedural context of the case; the theme (T) represents the issue of law which the court was called upon to determine and which is the basis for treating the case as a precedent (the point of the case); the plot (P) is the facts of the case; and the resolution (R) is how the court decided that issue of law for this and future cases. Thus a précis of *Candler* v. *Crane Christmas* could be rendered as follows:

S: In *Candler* v. *Crane Christmas* the plaintiff in an action for negligence appealed to the Court of Appeal against a decision of the Queen's Bench.
P: The defendants in the action were professional accountants who had negligently prepared a statement of accounts which gave a misleading picture of the financial position of the company. The accounts were prepared with the intention and expectation that the plaintiff would be guided by them in deciding whether to invest in the company. On the faith of the accounts he made the investment and as a result he lost his money.
T: The issue was whether a duty of care for negligent mis-statements is owed to the plaintiff in such circumstances.
R: The Court of Appeal decided that no such duty exists (Denning MR dissenting), but this decision was later overruled in *Hedley Byrne* v. *Heller* and the modern law of negligent mis-statement was born.

In this rendering, there are at least three stories. The story *in* the case (the facts); the story *of* the case as reported in [1952] All ER, and the story of the development of liability for negligent mis-statement, in which *Candler* v. *Crane Christmas* and Lord Denning's judgment in particular played an historic role. Each of these three stories can readily be made to fit the grammar (S), (T), (P), (R).

139   Simpson (1984).
140   Op. cit., n. 133.
141   Twining (1986c).
142   The literature on the *Sacco–Vanzetti* case is massive. The main sources of the discussion here are Joughin and Morgan (1948), Felix (1965) and Frankfurter (1927, 1961).
143   The remark has been attributed to H. L. Mencken, but I have been unable to trace the source.
144   Felix (1965).
145   Discussed Twining (1973), 341–9.
146   Felix states: 'The Sacco–Vanzetti case became a legend of innocence betrayed. It became more: a parable about betrayal in American society' (op. cit., 240). I would suggest that this is only one of many different, but overlapping, interpretations.
147   *The Letters of Sacco and Vanzetti* were published in 1924, edited by Marion Frankfurter and Gardner Jackson; the latter was in charge of the public relations of the Sacco–Vanzetti Defense Committee. Felix, whose interpretation of the case and of Vanzetti himself is less sympathetic than mine, commented: 'the published edition of the letters is a carefully edited fraction of the prisoner's epistolary production, which is crueler, rawer, less grammatical, more violent and more vital' (op. cit., 256).

148 Some writers argue that 'legal truth' is different from 'historical truth' and that trials are not concerned with historical truth. This is a mistake. One consequence of this view would be to deprive legal discourse of strong conceptions of 'mistake' or 'miscarriage of justice'. I may believe that Sacco and Vanzetti or Dreyfus or Luke Dougherty were victims of injustice on one or more different grounds:

1 There were technical irregularities in the proceedings which should, according to the rules, have been grounds for questioning the conviction. For example, an inadmissible confession or hearsay was admitted.

2 Unfair procedures were followed. For example, the trial was conducted in an atmosphere of prejudice against the accused.

3 The evidence adduced at trial did not satisfy the standard of proof beyond reasonable doubt.

4 As a matter of historical fact the accused was (were) innocent. For example, there was a mistake of identity; the crime was committed by someone else.

These are all four examples of miscarriages of justice. But accounts of great injustices would nearly always be qualitatively different, if claims of type (4) were ruled out. Legal discourse needs the categories of historical truth and historical error.

149 The suggestion that stories are one means of resolving such tensions fits in with the thesis of Clifford Geertz that the Western polarization of fact and law (and similar dichotomies) misleads us about the reality of our own processes. These may not be so very different from notions of judgment in other cultures that are expressed by such concepts as *dharma*, *haqq* and *adat* (Geertz, 1983, esp. chs. 4 and 8).

8

Anatomy of a *Cause Célèbre*: The Case of Edith Thompson

Strephon: And have you the heart to apply the prosaic rules of evidence to a case
    which bubbles over with poetic emotion?
Lord Chancellor: Distinctly. I have always kept my duty strictly before my eyes.
                                                                W. S. Gilbert, *Iolanthe*

Contrasts between the prosaic realities of the law and the worlds of poetry, romance, fantasy and imagination – worlds which are often depicted as representing quite distinct or separate realities – are commonplace in both legal and general literature. One rarely fails to raise a laugh if one tells students the story of the courtship of John Austin, the jurist, who wrote love letters to his wife in the style of a conveyancer.[1] Having attracted her attention in this improbable manner, he accompanied his proposal of marriage with a series of interrogatories which spelled out his manifold faults in dreary detail and asked if she accepted him as described, thereby at once winning her sympathy and estopping her in perpetuity from complaining about his defects. When Auden suggests in 'Law, say the gardeners, is the sun', that law is like love, it invites interpretation as a paradox.[2]

Such contrasts run through almost all of the extensive literature on *R* v. *Bywaters and Thompson*.[3] In that case Frederick Bywaters was hanged for murdering Edith Thompson's husband Percy, by stabbing him with his knife; Edith, his lover, was also hanged for either inciting or conspiring with him to do it, largely on the basis of the evidence of her love letters. A common view is stated by one writer:

The case of Edith Thompson caught the British legal system on its weakest side. That system is an admirable instrument for ascertaining facts, it is much less efficient in dealing with psychology ... Imagination is the lawyer's bugbear and literalism his occupational disease. For him life is governed not by passions but by statutes, and he likes to interpret individual actions as if they had their origins in icy reasons. [Great advocates are an exception] ... But in any generation great advocates are few, while stereotyped lawyers are two a penny. Rigid, narrow, formalistic and self-righteous they are particularly ill-suited to sit in judgment on a case which calls for sympathetic knowledge of the world.[4]

A similar contrapuntal tendency provides one of the main themes of an excellent novel based on the case, *A Pin to See the Peepshow*, by F. Tennyson Jesse. This has been re-issued as a feminist 'classic' by Virago Press.[5] It has also been the subject of a play which has been produced both on the stage and on television. Julia, the fictional counterpart of Edith, is presented as inhabiting two worlds: a world of prosaic realities represented by the dull domesticity of the respectable poor,[6] and a world of fantasy, both 'amazingly real and utterly unearthly',[7] symbolized by a child's peepshow, popular romantic novels and Julia's own letters in which fact, fantasy and passion were so inter-woven that her lover 'began to feel that something more definite and real was existing hundreds of miles away without him than the world he was actually in'.[8] The Law comes crashing into Julia's dreamworld to produce in turn an unreal nightmare so that lawyers' common sense makes out 'the parts about love to be nonsense and the parts that she knew were nonsense to be true? . . . and always with, apparently, that terrible fairness, but using words that to Julia seemed to make the thing appear quite different from what, in truth, it had been'.[9] The role of the impersonal forces of the law in the novel is summed up by an extract from a poem by Stephen Vincent Benét:

> No one can say
> That the trial was not fair. The trial was fair,
> Painfully fair by every rule of law,
> And that it was made not the slightest difference.
> The law's our yardstick, and it measures well
> Or well enough when there are yards to measure.
> Measure a wave with it, measure a fire,
> Cut sorrow up in inches, weigh content.
> You can weigh John Brown's body well enough,
> But how and in what balance can you weigh John Brown?[10]

In 'Lawyers' Stories' I argued that narrative plays an important and varied, but subordinate, role in arguments by advocates and judges in court in Anglo-American litigation. This essay explores a related theme: the uses and limitations of a particular kind of analysis in constructing and evaluating arguments about disputed questions of fact. Familiar tensions between reason and imagination, fact and value, narrative and argument, holism and atomism, and historical, legal and fictional truth will all resurface. But our main concern is to illustrate and evaluate a particular approach to evidence, which can be called modified Wigmorean analysis.[11]

The case of Bywaters and Thompson has generated a substantial literature. The reasons are obvious: it is interesting in itself – as a drama of love and murder and retribution; as a slice of social history; or as the story of a remarkable woman. It raises issues about the position of women, about capital punishment, about the significance of the orality of criminal proceedings in our adversary system, about the competence and impartiality of juries. It is also interesting as a puzzle: Was Edith Thompson rightly convicted of murder?

It is with this last question that we are here concerned. Such a focus may seem mundane and narrow. However, in the course of this apparently trivial pursuit I hope to show that the gaps between the prosaic world of law and the spheres of imagination and romantic love, and of those other familiar dichotomies, are not as sharp as they seem. In assessing the evidence against Edith Thompson, whether as lawyers or as historians, we need to interpret and make judgements about the personalities, the feelings of and the relations between the main protagonists. In order to arrive at any conclusions about the case we have to go beyond so-called 'hard' evidence and 'brute facts';[12] we have not only to weigh John Brown's body, but also to interpret the character, thoughts and intimate relations of John Brown.[13] It is, however, not part of my thesis that legal processes are particularly adept at handling intimate personal relationships nor that lawyers have some special insights into the world of imagination and emotion. *Bywaters and Thompson* provides ample evidence to the contrary: the story has plenty of examples of narrow-mindedness, insensitivity and lack of imagination; the impersonal machinery of law is vividly portrayed as crashing like a blind juggernaut into Julia's world in *A Pin to See the Peepshow*. In the actual case the trial was far from fair; it was conducted in an atmosphere of sexual prejudice and there is more than a little plausibility in the claim of Edith Thompson's counsel that his client was hanged, not for murder, but because of her immorality.[14]

Rather my thesis is that those who are concerned with the task of making judgments about the truth of allegations about particular past events, such as jurors, judges and historians, cannot avoid coming to grips with elusive matters which are sometimes felt to be beyond the reach of the law. In the case of Edith Thompson, in order to decide on her guilt or innocence as charged, we are inevitably drawn into weighing the characters of the main protagonists, into charting rather carefully and precisely the course of the relationship of Edith and her lover during their affair and into assessing the plausibility of a variety of generalizations, many of them highly speculative, about how lovers and seamen and married people behave.

The case of Edith Thompson is particularly suitable for present purposes. First, there is an historic doubt that is still unresolved. Secondly, we have direct access to the main evidence against Edith in the form of an extensive collection of letters to her lover. Thirdly, this evidence is extremely complex and extensive. As such it provides a fair test of the claim that Wigmorean analysis is a useful heuristic tool for organizing and analysing arguments about complex masses of evidence in a manageable way. Fourthly, some key passages – including several that were treated as particularly damning – require meticulous textual analysis. They provide a good test of the claim that the Wigmorean approach provides usable tools for rigorous microscopic analysis. Finally, both the evidence and the events we are concerned to reconstruct on the basis of that evidence appear to be particularly unpromising as objects for hard-nosed rational analysis. For these are not just the love letters of a simple lover or an articulate artist. Indeed, it has been doubted whether they are properly described as 'love letters' at all.[15] They are extraordinarily complex human documents, written at different times and suggesting a bewildering variety of moods and motives and manoeuvres. They include telegrams arranging meetings, newsy commentaries on her daily happenings, newspaper clippings and emotional outpourings, in various tones and voices. Moreover, Edith's style is strikingly uneven: sometimes it is jerky, allusive, extraordinarily vague or seems to be almost systematically ambiguous. Some of the letters, including some that are central to our enquiry, exhibit a stream of consciousness quality which adds to the difficulties of interpretation.[16] As one student put it: 'If one can analyse Edith's prose, one can analyse anything.'

The Facts[17]

About midnight of Tuesday/Wednesday, 3/4 October 1922, Percy Thompson, a London shipping clerk and his wife, Edith, were walking along Belgrave Road, Ilford, towards their home in Kensington Gardens. They had been to the theatre and had walked from Ilford Station.[18] The night was dark and the road was almost deserted. They were within 100 yards or so of their home when a man in a raincoat and hat came from behind them, pushed Mrs Thompson aside and approached Percy Thompson. What precisely happened between the two men is a matter of dispute. What is certain is that after some sort of struggle Percy Thompson collapsed on the pavement 50 feet further on and the man ran off. Edith's voice was heard by a neighbour crying, 'Oh, don't; oh, don't.'[19] Shortly afterwards she ran up to a group of people, also returning from Ilford Station, and cried out, 'Oh, my God! Will you help me; my husband is ill, he is bleeding.'[20] They woke up a Dr Maudsley in a nearby house and, on his arrival, some five to eight minutes later, Percy Thompson was found to be dead. He had been propped up against a wall by his wife. Mrs Thompson was in a confused and hysterical condition. When told that Percy was dead, she said: 'Why did you not come sooner and save him?'[21] Blood was gushing from the mouth of the deceased, but it was only after he had been taken to the mortuary that several knife wounds were found in his body. There were several slight cuts in the front of the body and two deep stab wounds in the back of the neck. One was 2½ inches deep and 1½ inches wide, passing upwards toward the right ear.[22]

The police called at the Thompsons' house at 3 a.m. She was in a very distressed state. She said that all she knew was that her husband dropped down and screamed out, 'Oh'. She said that she had thought that it was one of 'his attacks'. She denied that either she or her husband had a knife.[23] It was soon established that the assailant was Frederick Bywaters, a twenty-year-old clerk in the Merchant Navy. The following morning the deceased's brother had told the police of Edith's friendship with 'a young fellow named Bywaters' and, having found out that he had spent the evening with Edith's parents, the Graydons, some two miles from the scene of the crime, they detained him for questioning at 6 p.m. on 4 October. Detective Inspector Page searched Bywaters's room in his mother's house and found two notes (exhibits 9 and 10), five letters (exhibits 28, 47, 54, 58 and 60) and a telegram (exhibits 58 and 59).[24] Bywaters made his first statement, after caution, denying both knowledge of the crime and owning a knife. Mrs Thompson was arrested on the evening of the same day. On the following day she was shown some letters from her to Bywaters. She made a statement (exhibit 3). In this she denied seeing anyone at the time her husband fell; she gave an account of her relationship with Freddy Bywaters, admitting that they had corresponded on affectionate terms. Immediately after making a statement she was taken past a room in which she saw Bywaters. She said: 'Oh God, Oh God, what can I do? I did not want him to do it.'[25] After caution, she made another statement (exhibit 4) in which she said the man rushed out and pushed her away. She saw them scuffling. She recognized him as Bywaters by his coat and hat. Bywaters made a further statement (exhibit 6) on 5 October, after being told that he and Edith Thompson were to be charged with murder. He admitted to killing Percy after a struggle. 'Mrs Thompson must have been spellbound for I saw nothing of her during the fight.'[26]

The police found the knife on 9 October, as a result of statements made by Bywaters. On 12 October, they found a box on Bywaters's ship, the SS *Morea*, containing sixty-two letters and telegrams from Edith to Frederick, together with fifty cuttings from newspapers enclosed in the letters and a photograph of Edith. A number of the cuttings dealt with murder, mainly by poison. Three letters from Bywaters to Edith were found at her place of work. Rather over half of the letters and a selection of the cuttings were put in evidence by the prosecution. The defence decided not to put in the remaining 33 letters, but these are reprinted in Appendix 2 of *The Trial of Frederick Bywaters and Edith Thompson*, edited by Filson Young. Much of the interest of the case centres on these letters and cuttings, which constituted the main, but not the only, evidence against Edith.[27]

It is universally accepted that it was Bywaters who killed Percy Thompson. It is also not disputed that Edith and Freddy were lovers and that they both had a *prima facie* motive for killing Percy. Freddy pleaded not guilty on the ground that he had killed Percy in self-defence. Since Percy was unarmed at the time, it is hardly surprising that this defence failed. The interesting question was whether Edith was also guilty either on the ground that she incited Freddy to kill Percy or that they jointly planned to kill him.[28] It is clear from the letters that Edith and Freddy had been lovers for nearly two years; that Edith was very unhappy; that she wished to end her marriage and that she had expressed the view that she would not be sorry if Percy were dead.

The main facts about the three principal protagonists and of their relations with each other are not seriously disputed. But there is room for different interpretations of their characters, especially that of Edith, and of Bywaters's attitude to Edith at the time of the killing.

Percy Thompson was a shipping clerk, aged thirty-two at the time of his death. He had been employed by the same firm for twelve or thirteen years. He had married Edith Graydon, who was four years his junior, in January 1916. There were no children of the marriage. A tenant, Mrs Lester, reported that she had overheard several rows between Edith and Percy.[29] There were no servants, but a maid arrived for the first time on the day after Percy's death. Apart from the letters, there is not much evidence about Percy's character. He appears to have been a steady, respectable, dull, not particularly successful clerk who refused to give up his wife.[30] There is evidence that he was suspicious and jealous of Edith's relations with Freddy. She expressed fears that he would be violent and there is some evidence that he assaulted her on at least one occasion.[31] She speaks of 'submitting' to him sexually on a number of occasions, but also refusing him without repercussions.[32]

The evidence of those who knew her, of those who observed her in court and in prison, and of the letters themselves suggests that Edith Thompson had a striking personality. This, it seems, was also her image of herself. The undisputed facts about her include the following: She had worked as a book-keeper and manageress for a wholesale milliner's in Aldersgate for several years. She earned slightly more than her husband and was regarded by her employers as capable and industrious. There is evidence that she had several male admirers in addition to Freddy, but there is nothing to suggest that she had had extra-marital sexual relations with anyone but him. At the time of the murder Percy Thompson was thirty-two, Edith was twenty-eight and Freddy twenty. It is clear that Edith's marriage to Percy was not happy; it is less clear what price she was prepared to pay to escape from the security, comfort and respectability of her domestic situation. We have plenty of material on which to base judgements about Edith Thompson's character, but that material is open to a variety of interpretations.[33]

We have less information about her lover. Frederick Bywaters has been described as 'a clean-cut, self-possessed, attractive-looking youth of twenty with a good character and record.'[34] He had gone to sea before he was sixteen, and at the time of the murder was variously described as ship's writer, a clerk and a laundry steward.[35] During the period of his relationship with the Thompsons he was at sea for over half of the time and this was the occasion both for the protracted and intense correspondence between them and for possible fluctuations in their relationship. During the trial he instructed his counsel to conduct the case so as not to prejudice Edith's chances of acquittal.[36] This won him a lot of sympathy from public opinion, as reflected in the popular press, but it may possibly have damaged Edith's case, as he appeared as the dignified, loyal lover, whereas she was seen by some to be solely concerned with saving herself.

Edith Thompson and Frederick Bywaters were tried at the Central Criminal Court on 6–11 December 1922. They were both charged with the murder of Percy Thompson, Bywaters as principal, Edith as a principal in the second degree, because she was present at the killing.[37] A second indictment containing a number of counts, including charges against Edith of administering poison and broken glass with intent to murder were not proceeded with. The jury found both accused guilty, after barely two hours' deliberation. They were sentenced to death; ten days later the Court of Appeal rejected their appeals; and on 9 January – three months and six days after the death of Percy – Bywaters and Thompson were hanged.

The Sources

The bulk of the secondary literature on the case is by popular writers on crime – those who called themselves 'criminologists' until academics took over the term.[38] Several barristers, including Travers Humphreys, who was a junior counsel for the prosecution, wrote about it in their memoirs or in accounts of famous cases. It is discussed at some length in the biography of Curtis-Bennett, Edith's counsel. In addition to *A Pin to See the Peepshow*, F. Tennyson Jesse published an analysis of the case. So did Fenton Bresler, in his study of the exercise of the prerogative of mercy, *Reprieve*.[39]

A striking feature of this secondary literature is that the commentators are almost equally split on the question of Edith's guilt – a sharp contrast with many studies of *causes célèbres*, such as the Dreyfus case, Sacco and Vanzetti, and Adolph Beck, which are dominated by polemical writings claiming that a miscarriage of justice had occurred. Fenton Bresler, Montgomery Hyde and Travers Humphreys are among those who agreed with the Court of Criminal Appeal that Edith was guilty as charged.[40] J. P. Eddy suggests that she was probably not guilty of aiding and abetting this particular attack, but that she was responsible for continuous and protracted incitement. Filson Young, Marshall Hall, Tennyson Jesse, Ernest Dudley, Lewis Broad, Edgar Lustgarten and, most recently, René Weis, while differing on many points of detail, all argue that she was not guilty of murder and that she was the victim of moral prejudice. 'Mrs Thompson ... was hanged because of her immorality',[41] claimed her counsel – and most commentators have taken up the theme, typically suggesting that the prosecution lawyers, Mr Justice Shearman and members of the Court of Criminal Appeal were all blinded by their moralizing attitudes: 'It was as if they argued that here was a married woman who had gone to bed with someone other than her husband and gloried in it; obviously, therefore, she would want her husband out of the way and would conspire with her lover to murder him.'[42] The evidence, I shall suggest, was rather more damaging than that. Another feature of the commentaries, shared with most writing about *causes célèbres*, is that by and large they belong to the literature of popular entertainment rather than of serious scholarship. Some are very competent examples of this particular genre – carefully researched, often perceptive, usually readable. Since the main objective is to arouse interest or to make a case, detail tends to be sacrificed to readability and more emphasis is placed on amateurish psychological speculation than on the more mundane aspects of meticulous analysis of evidence, which can be tedious for readers of such works, for jurors and for those who attend public lectures.

Can a more scholarly or scientific approach add anything to our understanding of a case such as this? And can a close study of such material contribute anything to legal education or to a general understanding of law? I would answer 'yes' unequivocally to both questions.

The full transcript of the trial has been published in the *Notable British Trials* series; this includes all the evidence presented in court, together with a complete transcript of letters from Edith Thompson that were not put in evidence at the trial and the judgments of the Court of Criminal Appeal in the case (two appeals).[43] We thus have available to us what Wigmore called 'a mixed mass of evidence'.[44] This includes statements made by the two accused, the testimony of witnesses who were nearby at the time or immediately after the attack, a limited amount of circumstantial evidence, including the report of Sir

Bernard Spilsbury that there were no traces of either glass or poison discovered in the post-mortem examination.[45] The exhibits included the murder weapon, three letters from Freddy to Edith and Edith's letters to Freddy. There is also the evidence given by both accused at the trial. Some additional information, not given in evidence at the trial, will be ignored for present purposes.[46] Here I shall concentrate on those of Edith's letters that were put in evidence, but it is worth mentioning briefly that the other evidence establishes beyond reasonable doubt that it was Freddy who killed Percy,[47] that there is almost nothing to support, and a good deal to confute, Freddy's claim that he acted in self-defence,[48] that under cross-examination Edith admitted that she wished to give Freddy the impression that she had tried to make her husband ill[49] and that, while the testimony of both accused is an important aid to interpretation of some passages in the letters, there is little outside the letters to support the prosecution case and nothing that might be taken as determinative or dispositive in regard to the other main theories. Accordingly let us treat the letters as the main evidence against Edith and consider the other evidence presented at the trial as supplementary.[50]

The Letters

Sixty-two letters between Edith and Freddy, including the telegrams and short notes, were found by the police.[51] There were also fifty cuttings from newspapers on various subjects, ten of which dealt with cases of murder, mainly by poison. Only three of the letters were signed by Freddy. The remainder were communications from Edith to Freddy. Edith destroyed Freddy's letters; Freddy, for reasons which have been the subject of some speculation, did not destroy hers.[52]

The texts of these communications, including the newspaper cuttings, are reproduced in the record of the case. They occupy one hundred pages of small print – approximately 50,000–70,000 words – the bulk of them in Edith's deathly prose. Her communications start in August 1921 and finish with an undated letter that was written shortly before Percy's death (exhibit 60).[53] The bulk of the letters – especially the longer ones – occur when Freddy was on his ship; they span five different voyages over a period of thirteen months. One of the central problems of interpretation is whether one can infer important changes in the pattern of their relationship during the period. The bulk of the passages most damaging to Edith occurs in the earlier letters, including the extract from exhibit 17, written in early April – 6 months before the murder.[54] One line of defence for Edith was that the later letters suggest either that Freddy had cooled towards her or she was herself more resigned to a long-drawn out affair than in the early stages. I shall return to this later.

It is not disputed that certain facts are clearly established by the letters: that Edith and Freddy were lovers; that Edith was unhappy for much of the time; that she wished her marriage was at an end and that she had expressed the view that she would not be sorry if Percy were dead. The key issues in the case were whether the letters and other evidence proved beyond reasonable doubt that

Edith intentionally tried to incite her lover to kill Percy; whether the lovers conspired to murder him; and whether Edith herself had tried to poison her husband. Only a limited number of passages bear directly on these questions[55] – but they are open to a variety of interpretations and in interpreting them it is helpful to consider them in the context of the whole corpus of the surviving correspondence.

Partly because of their fragmentary nature, partly because of the elliptical and elusive content of some key statements ('Don't forget what we talked in the Tea Room. I'll still risk and try if you will'),[56] partly because of the jerky, inconsequential style of some of the most important letters, they are full of ambiguities: the main question in this context is whether it is possible by careful analysis to arrive at any firm conclusions about the central issues or at least to approach nearer to the truth or whether, as several commentators have suggested, they have no value at all as evidence, for they belong to a reality which is beyond the reach of prosaic lawyers and historians.[57]

Modified Wigmorean Analysis

In this case-study I shall apply a modified version of Wigmore's 'Chart Method' of analysing evidence. The original method has been extensively described and discussed elsewhere.[58] Here it is modified in three ways, the reasons for which will be explained as we proceed. First, no use will be made of symbols and charts. Second, clarification of standpoint will be treated as an essential ingredient in macroscopic analysis of the case as a whole. Third, there will be much more emphasis on the idea of 'theories' of the case. The proof of the pudding will be demonstrated in the cooking. This will involve the following steps: clarification of standpoint; definition of the ultimate *probanda*; outlining four main theories of the case, with some variant sub-theories, stories and themes; testing one of these theories, by way of illustration, through 'microscopic' analysis of three important items of evidence: the facts about the knife, one passage in Edith's last letter (exhibit 60) and the respective ages of the two accused; and finally suggesting some provisional conclusions on the basis of this partial analysis. This will not resolve the mystery; but I hope that it will show that even this incomplete and relatively straightforward exercise in analysis significantly narrows the possibilities and throws some light on the particular case and on some of the general themes that it illustrates.

Clarification of standpoint

The first step is to clarify the standpoint from which the analysis is to be undertaken.[59] For present purposes, I shall adopt the standpoint of a historian in 1988, confronted with a finite body of data – the record of the trial – and concerned to answer the narrow question: does the available evidence support beyond reasonable doubt the allegation that Edith Thompson was legally responsible for planning or inciting the murder of her husband?[60]

Adopting the standpoint of the historian has a number of advantages in this context: it precludes the necessity of the somewhat artificial role-playing that would be involved if we were to adopt the standpoint of counsel for one side or the other at the time of the trial. It enables us to consider points and theories not raised at the trial in a way that a rational reconstruction of the actual arguments of counsel and the trial and appellate judges would not. Further-more, the historian may define and pursue a single objective – the ascertain-ment of the truth on the basis of analysis of the available evidence (the data), without regard to the procedural complexities, multiple objectives and 'noise' factors that concern participants in actual trials. Adopting the standpoint of a historian can serve to isolate the task of analysis and evaluation of evidence from other tasks. However, in order to keep matters simple and to maintain a close connection with the context of the trial, I shall impose two artificial constraints on our enquiry. First, I shall confine my analysis to the evidence in the trial record. A 'real' historian would normally not accept any such limitation. Secondly, I shall concentrate on the single question whether Edith was guilty as charged. This question is, of course, by no means the only question about the case that might interest historians – but it is a central one which is very close to (though not identical with) the question posed to the jury in the case.

Framing the ultimate probanda

The next step is to identify the ultimate probanda – the material allegations on which our judgement of the case as a whole must rest. Historians have no concept of materiality.[61] They are free to frame their questions as they wish without formal constraints. In arguing in court about disputed questions of fact lawyers have no such freedom. The questions arising from the indictment (or other pleadings) are defined in advance by law.

Where the law is clear this can greatly simplify the tasks of analysis and argument, for it lays down clear and fixed touchstones of relevance. Where, however, the law is unclear, the task becomes much harder – indeed, a trial sometimes takes on the character of a game in which the rules are uncertain or constantly changing. In respect of Bywaters the law was clear enough. The prosecution had to prove beyond reasonable doubt that he had intentionally with malice aforethought and without lawful justification caused the death of Percy Thompson. The only points in dispute were whether Freddy acted in self-defence or under immediate provocation. The jury apparently had no doubts on this matter. Nor should they unduly trouble a historian. Percy was unarmed and there is no evidence to suggest that he had ever possessed a gun or that Freddy had any reason to think that he did. The evidence supporting provocation is almost as thin.

The case against Edith was less simple. She was charged as a principal in the second degree.[62] What this meant was that the prosecution had to prove (a) that Bywaters murdered Percy Thompson; and (b) that Edith was physically present at the murder; and (c) that she aided and abetted the murder. The first two requirements are relatively unproblematic, but the third contains the seeds of some genuine difficulties. Aiding and abetting, conspiracy and incitement are three areas of criminal law that involve notorious problems of interpretation and application.[63] In the trial and on appeal these difficulties barely surfaced, although a careful reading suggests that the trial judge took a much narrower view of the law than had been assumed by the prosecution or which the authorities at the time probably warranted. He directed the jury that they must be satisfied that Bywaters and Thompson had planned this attack, an interpretation which was surprisingly favourable to Edith.[64]

It would not be appropriate here to embark on a detailed historical and legal analysis of these difficulties. But it is important to touch on some specific points which illuminate the nature of our enterprise. The first precept of Wigmorean analysis is to formulate the ultimate *probandum* (or *probanda*) with the greatest possible care and precision. For these provide both one's touchstone of relevance and one's starting-point. Alter one's initial hypothesis and one may have to start all over again. Similarly, if there is some ambiguity or uncertainty at the start, this is likely to complicate the task significantly. One may, for example, have to construct separate arguments for a range of possible hypotheses.

Bywaters and Thompson provides a rather clear illustration. For, on most interpretations of the law, it was sufficient for the prosecution to establish any one of several different possibilities: for example, that Edith and Freddy planned this attack; or that Freddy acted in pursuit of a general plan to kill Percy when opportunity arose; or that Freddy murdered Percy as a result of Edith's incitement or 'within the scope of its authority'.[65] Our historian has to consider the evidence in respect of at least these three alternatives, as did the defence in the actual trial. That is one reason why this is a complex case.

The matter is even more difficult than that: whereas what constituted a conspiracy was reasonably clear in this case, the notion of incitement was and is notoriously difficult. The root of the difficulty is not just a matter of vagueness. It could be that the law provides a general, but vague, definition and leaves the application of the law to the jury as a question of 'fact'. However, research suggests that at the time there were several legal definitions, and that there was a conflict of authorities.[66] Even if one clears that hurdle, there are some further difficulties lurking behind the bland notion of 'a question of fact'. Is there not an inescapable evaluative element in an enquiry as to whether 'X *caused* Y to act in a particular way' or 'Y acted in *pursuance* of X's incitement'? One possible interpretation of the question of 'fact' can be stated in moral terms: 'Was Edith's conduct such that she was morally responsible for Freddy's act?'[67] In addition to uncertainty about the moral standards to be applied, there is a further layer of difficulty. For Edith's act in this case consisted of uttering words that are open to many interpretations. For example: 'I'll still risk and try, if you will.'[68] Risk what? Try what? By what criteria are we to determine the meaning of such opaque statements?

Thus the simple-seeming proposition 'Edith incited Freddy to murder Percy' reveals at least four different levels of difficulty. There is a different kind of difficulty in interpreting the meaning of Edith's alleged acts of incitement contained in her letters; and there is a further problem of interpreting Freddy's behaviour: Whatever Edith's intent, did Freddy act because of what she had written?[69]

What is our notional historian to make of all this? One potentially attractive solution is robustly to ignore these fine distinctions and to frame a single global question, such as; Is there any doubt that Edith was responsible for Freddy's action? In some cases such an approach might well be justified, for example, if it could be shown that, shortly before the murder, Edith had made one or more statements unequivocally urging Freddy to kill Percy or if there was an accumulation of evidence of persistent encouragement or pressure. However, such a robust approach will not do, if one is seriously concerned to enquire after the 'truth' about Edith Thompson. For, I shall argue later, perhaps the strongest evidence against her relates to incitement, but all the difficulties outlined above are relevant to interpreting and evaluating that evidence.

Perhaps the most sensible course, for present purposes, is to note the initial problem of framing one of the ultimate *probanda*, but to concentrate on outlining an overall strategy for analysing the evidence as a whole, leaving consideration of the detailed difficulties until later. One way of doing this is to consider how the arguments were in fact structured at the trial and to gloss these, through refinement and criticism, as we proceed.

In order to succeed on the charge of murder against both accused the prosecution had to satisfy the jury that the truth of the following propositions had been established beyond reasonable doubt:

1   that Frederick Bywaters deliberately and with malice aforethought killed Percy Thompson; and
2a   that Edith Thompson conspired with Frederick Bywaters to kill Percy Thompson either on this occasion or whenever opportunity arose; or
2b   that Edith Thompson intentionally incited Frederick Bywaters to kill Percy Thompson and the killing was within the scope of that incitement.

These three propositions were the facts in issue – that is the material allegations that the prosecution had to prove beyond reasonable doubt in order to succeed. The test of relevance of any item of evidence in this case is whether it tended to support or to negate one of these propositions.

In order to convict Freddy it was sufficient for the prosecution to prove the first proposition only. Although it was relevant to prove intent and motive to show that this attack had been planned or that there had been earlier attempts by either or both of them to kill Percy, these were not strictly necessary for the prosecution's case. At the trial there was no dispute about the cause of death or the identity of the killer; it was not even necessary for the prosecution to show that the attack was premeditated, as they claimed, so long as they established that it was intentional. Bywaters's defence was that he accosted Percy to ask him to agree to a separation or divorce, the argument developed spontaneously into a fight and he stabbed him in self-defence, as he thought Percy was about to draw a gun.[70] Since two of the stab wounds were in the back and there was no evidence to suggest that Percy had a gun on this, or any other occasion, it is not surprising that Freddy's story was not believed.

The case against Edith was more complex. In order to succeed the prosecution had to show that Bywaters was guilty of murder (proposition 1) *and* that Edith had either planned Percy's death with Freddy *or* had been responsible for inciting Freddy to kill him. In argument the prosecution, while presenting a story of continuous incitement leading to an attack that had been planned in advance, rather blurred the distinction between incitement and conspiracy – not surprisingly, for either was sufficient.[71] But Mr Justice Shearman in his charge to the jury implied that they should convict Edith only if they were satisfied that this particular attack had been planned in advance.[72] There is an ironic contrast between the unequivocal sententiousness of tone of the judge's charge[73] and his insistence that Edith should be convicted only on the basis of what I hope to show is by far the weakest of the possible theories of the case that are consistent with her guilt.

The judge exuded generalized disapproval indicating guilt, but then analytically posed the issue in such a way as to make conviction of Edith much harder, at least in theory. If, as seems likely, both the jury and nearly all subsequent commentators reacted more to the general attitude of the judge than to his precise words, that is doubly ironic.

Theories of the case as a whole

The next step is to consider, from the point of view of an historian, the range of colourably plausible hypotheses about the case as a whole, and the general lines of argument for and against each hypothesis – what we may conveniently refer to as the main theories of the case. The aim here is to provide a broad framework of competing general hypotheses or theories within which all the relevant evidence can be organized and weighed.

In adversarial criminal proceedings typically the prosecution presents its 'case' against the accused in the form of a coherent theory of what happened. In order to succeed they have to prove each of the material allegations beyond reasonable doubt; typically, but not necessarily, this involves persuading the trier of fact to accept their account of story as a whole. The theory of a case is typically an internally consistent collection of hypotheses that form a coherent argument, which supports the story.[74]

In order to counter the prosecution's case three main options are available to the defence, either independently or in combination: to *deny* the prosecution's story, either *in toto* or in some material particular(s), without offering an alternative, for example by submitting that there is no case to answer; to *explain away* the prosecution's story, for example, by admitting most of the hypothetical facts, but interpreting them in a manner consistent with the innocence of the accused (Freddy admitted killing Percy, but claimed that it was in self-defence); or to present a *rival* account of what happened in respect of one or more material facts (e.g. by presenting an alibi).[75] In practice many defences involve a combination of all three strategies, but sometimes these are not compatible with each other.

A theory in this sense relates to the case as a whole. It can serve a number of functions: it helps to organize the material; it provides a basis for selecting some of a mass of potentially relevant evidence for inclusion or emphasis – a subsidiary test of relevance; it may serve to fill in gaps in the available information with more or less plausible hypotheses; and it provides a general basis for testing internal coherence and consistency.[76] From the point of view of counsel each side's theories provide a strategic framework which guides, and often determines, many specific tactical choices.

In trials, when there are disputed questions of fact, typically the trier of fact is being asked either to select between competing theories of the case or to assess whether, on the basis of the evidence presented, the proponent has proved his version to the applicable standard. Historians do not work with the law's elaborate body of devices for guiding decision in situations of uncertainty in adversary proceedings: they do not have concepts such as materiality, conclusive or rebuttable presumptions, standards of proof, or burdens of proof or of production. However, the notion of competing theories or accounts fits a dialectical view of historical enquiries into truth.[77] One way of proceeding is to test a series of competing hypotheses against the available evidence and to select the most plausible one. In the present context, a series of alternative theories of the events in *Bywaters and Thompson* serves much the same function as they would in a real trial. Part of the complexity and fascination of the present case is that even at this general or strategic level there is room for considerable doubt and disagreement.

Four theories of the case

In order to simplify matters, out of the many different theories about the case which can be advanced, each with possible variants, let us outline four main ones, two favouring the prosecution (or the thesis that Edith was guilty as charged), two favouring the defence.[78]

1   *The conspiracy theory*: that *this* attack was planned by Edith and Freddy on the day before. Freddy set out carrying a knife with the intention of killing Percy as the Thompsons returned home from the theatre. Edith expected this attack because she had planned it. In most versions of this theory Edith was the 'master-mind', Freddy the instrument. The actual attack was the culmination of a long series of attempts to kill Percy. This was one of the theories advanced by the prosecution and the one that was emphasized by the judge in his charge to the jury. An important variant of this theory is that Edith and Freddy had agreed to try to kill Percy whenever opportunity arose, but that Edith had not necessarily planned or expected this attack.

2   *The incitement theory*: Edith may not have known of or expected this attack. But she had over a long period deliberately tried to persuade Freddy to kill her husband – working on him by direct incitement, by innuendo, by suggesting different ways of getting rid of him and by claiming – whether truthfully or not – that she was prepared to risk trying to kill him herself and that she had indeed made several unsuccessful attempts to do so. There was, in short, a protracted and continuous incitement of Freddy by Edith to get rid of her husband.[79] The particular timing and method of the attack were immaterial; Edith deliberately influenced Freddy to kill Percy. One variant is that there was some specific act of incitement that influenced Freddy on this occasion.

3   *The fantasy theory*: The attack on Percy was probably unpremeditated and was certainly totally unexpected as far as Edith was concerned. At no stage had

Edith tried to kill her husband; nor had she deliberately, recklessly or even inadvertently incited Freddy to do so. In this view many of the key passages had an innocent explanation, and even the potentially most damaging statements merely represent the outpourings of a vivid imagination *and* were so interpreted by Freddy. When Edith wrote to Freddy she entered a world of daydreams and make-believe and nothing that she said constitutes evidence of intent to kill or to incite Freddy to kill in the 'real' world.[80] They were, as Freddy unromantically put it, mere 'melodrama'.[81] A variant of this is that some of the passages are to be interpreted as references to attempts to kill Percy, but they were merely part of a game, possibly a sexual game, designed to give spice and excitement to their relationship ... and again this is how they were interpreted by Freddy.

4   *The broken chain theory*: This theory denies any connection between Edith's behaviour and Freddy's act.[82] At one or more points the alleged chain of connection is broken. The theory takes two main forms. One version consists of a straight denial of one or more key points in the prosecution's theory or theories without advancing an alternative account of what happened. An obvious example is a denial that the attack was premeditated.[83] An alternative version is to present a rival account of the attack (and of preceding events) which serves the same function. For example, Edith lived in an imaginary world of passion, daring actions and desperate measures, a world in which fact and fiction and fantasy were inextricably mixed. She gave full rein to her imagination in her letters, pretending, perhaps even imagining, that she had tried to kill Percy. All the possibly damaging passages are in the earlier letters which represent a particular phase in her relationship with Freddy. In this view it is not necessary to reach any firm conclusion as to what these passages might mean, whether for example she was claiming, whether truthfully or not, to have put broken glass in Percy's food; even if the most damaging interpretation is put on the key passages relating to incitement, conspiracy and attempted murder there is no sufficient connection between the actual killing and the letters because: (a) Freddy did not take them seriously; and/or (b) the relationship had entered a quite different phase in the period before the killing; all the passages which might bear a damaging interpretation were written six months or more before Percy's death; and/or (c) the actual attack was spontaneous rather than premeditated. Any one of these is sufficient to break the connection between Edith's letters and Freddy's act.

One may note in passing that there is a possible counter-theory to the broken chain argument – what one might call the unexploded bomb theory. Briefly this is that, even if only the early letters are evidence against Edith of conspiracy or incitement or attempted murder, and that at the time Freddy did not consciously take them seriously, nevertheless they had the effect both of sowing the idea and working on his emotions at the level of his subconscious so that he was like an unexploded bomb which was detonated in a moment of stress some time later. This theory raises some interesting questions about Edith's legal responsibility, if it is correct, but since it was neither raised at the trial nor has it been seriously canvassed in the literature, I shall not pursue it further here.[84]

To recapitulate briefly: the conspiracy theory suggests that this attack was either planned shortly before by both accused or was the culmination of a more general plan; the incitement theory suggests that this attack, whether or not it was planned or premeditated, was the direct result of a continuous and protracted campaign of incitement by Edith; the fantasy theory suggests that all the potentially damaging passages in the letters are either open to alternative, innocent, interpretations or were merely figments of Edith's heated imagination and were interpreted by Freddy as 'melodrama'. The broken chain theory suggests that whatever interpretation is put on the letters there was no direct connection between the killing of Percy and the letters (or Edith's other actions).

It is worth making some points about these general theories about the case. First, they are not all of the same kind. The first three each involved advancing a coherent account of what happened – constructing an integrated story that hangs together as a whole. So does the second version of the broken chain theory. There is scope for a few loose ends or ambiguities or gaps, but the overall plausibility or credibility of each theory depends in part on its internal coherence. Does the story *as a whole* form a unity and fit the available evidence?

The first version of the broken chain theory lacks this positive quality. Essentially it consists of a series of negative assertions about key elements in the other theories. It does not necessarily involve constructing an internally consistent story about what happened. One of the notable features of the trial is that, contrary to the strong advice of her counsel, Edith Thompson insisted on going into the witness box.[85] This had several catastrophic results. It gave the prosecution the opportunity to extract some damaging admissions from her; and she had to advance a single coherent account of what happened and to give her interpretation of key passages in the letters and to have these positive assertions challenged by the prosecution. She thus gave the prosecution a specific target to attack and made it difficult for the defence to cumulate doubt upon doubt about different elements of the prosecution's case. For the broken chain theory allows what amounts to a series of arguments in the alternative along such lines as these:

1 None of the relevant passages in the letters supports the view that Edith either tried or pretended to try to kill her husband.
2 Even if she had tried, the chain is broken because Freddy did not believe her.
3 Even if Freddy believed her, the chain is broken because he did not act on that belief at the time and there is no evidence of a connection between the letters and his behaviour on the night.
4 The evidence does not support the proposition that the attack was premeditated – that Freddy set out with the intention of attacking Percy; but even if the attack was premeditated the evidence does not support the contention that Edith had inspired Freddy's plan.

By giving evidence, Edith Thompson gave the jury the chance to choose which between two competing stories they found to be plausible, rather than to judge whether each of the key elements in the prosecution's case was established beyond reasonable doubt on the basis of the evidence. Or again, instead of arguing that a particular passage might mean A or B or C or D rather than E, as the prosecution suggested, the defence was committed to giving a single interpretation to each key passage and to having that interpretation challenged.[86] Almost all commentators agree that it would have been difficult to convict her if she had not given evidence.[87]

Of course, historians do not have the option of deciding not to call a witness. That is a matter of legal procedure. However, the broken chain theory could well provide a sufficient answer to our historian's question. For if one or other version of that theory is accepted as correct, according to whatever standard is thought appropriate, then it establishes that Edith was not guilty as charged.

Each of these 'theories' is a sketch of a complex argument. I have only noted some of the more obvious variants of each of these four main lines of argument. The range of possibilities is immense. There is considerable potential overlap between several of them. Enough has been said to illustrate how, even at this stage of general strategy, in constructing and criticizing this kind of argument, judgment and choice are unavoidable. There is nothing 'mechanical' about the art of analysing evidence. This is one reason for doubting Wigmore's claim that his Chart Method 'is the only ... scientific method'.[88]

Experience suggests some useful working rules of thumb in exercising the art at this strategic stage:

1 *'Strategy first, tactics later.'* Despite the kinds of complexities that have been illustrated, strategic 'theories' are powerful simplifying devices: they are a means of structuring and managing and selecting material, however extensive and complex it seems.
2 *'Proceed dialectically.'* The historian and the lawyer need to recognize the weak as well as the strong points in their own and rival theories.
3 *'Construct the strongest version that you can of each theory and identify its weakest points.'* What constitutes strength may, of course, be rather different for a trial lawyer and a historian.
4 *'Go for the jugular .'* That is to say select one or two or a few key points in an argument and concentrate on those.

Such precepts are commonplaces of advocacy[89] and, perhaps less explicitly, of analysis of evidence by historians and others. They are essentially heuristic techniques for making complex problems more manageable. All presuppose a reflexive view of the process: one cannot construct theories, judge their strength and identify key points without regard to detail. On the face of it the advice may seem to suggest moving from the general to the particular; in fact familiarity with the particular is almost always a pre-condition for clarifying the general.

Sub-theories, sub-plots and characters Each theory is dependent to a significant degree on one or more sub-theories. First, an assessment of Edith's character, or at least some important aspects, is relevant to each of them. For example, the fantasy and incitement theories depend very largely on the view one takes of Edith and a view of her character is relevant, though less important, to the conspiracy theory. It is not so important to the first version of the broken chain theory, which depends much more on an interpretation of Freddy's likely reactions to the letters and whether the attack was spontaneous or premeditated. Here the focus is more on Freddy, but an assessment of Edith's character is important for all the theories both as an aid to interpreting the letters and as part of interpreting the nature and course of their relationship. For example, both Edith and Freddy claimed that the phrase 'only three and three quarter years left' in Edith's very last letter (exhibit 60) referred to a suicide pact.[90] That phrase is relevant to all four theories. Whether there was in fact such a pact, whether Edith had suggested it, but Freddy had not taken it seriously or whether this is an example of Edith's alleged fantasizing depends in part on one's views of Edith's and Freddy's characters, in part on one's view of their relationship and in part on other evidence (for example, other passages ostensibly referring to the same topic).

The variety of interpretations of Edith's character to be found in the literature is both fascinating and bewildering. The prosecution – backed by the judge, and seemingly by the Home Secretary and most public opinion – saw Edith as an immoral, scheming, manipulative older woman – a sorceress, who insidiously and persistently worked on an impressionable, inexperienced younger man to kill her husband or to help her to kill him.

Filson Young, the editor of the record of the trial, suggests that Edith had too much and Freddy too little imagination. He asserts that Bywaters was a strong-minded, unimaginative, virile man of the world who kept Edith's letters with a view to blackmailing her (a highly speculative allegation).[91] In this view Edith lived in a world of make-believe and wishful thinking, which had no connection with her actual behaviour or intentions. ('A Borgia does not write, she acts', says Young.)[92] Freddy joined in this game of make-believe as an erotic game which also flattered his ego – he did not take Edith's claims or innuendoes seriously, but at the crucial moment fantasy spilled over into action – for action was Freddy's only reality. Other writers have compared Edith to Madame Bovary, and even to Marilyn Monroe.[93] What these various interpretations have in common is that they are highly speculative, confidently asserted, impressionistic judgements by amateur psychologists. There are passages in the letters taken singly which can be used to support each of these and no doubt many other interpretations. Nowhere in the literature is there any attempt to build up a careful picture of Edith's personality and behaviour on the basis of considering the evidence as a whole using any method other than impression.[94] It may be possible for psychologists (or psycho-historians) to construct a less speculative profile of Edith on the basis of the available evidence.

Another sub-theory concerns Freddy's character. Apart from points already mentioned this is relevant to assessing his credibility as a witness[95] and to whether the attack was premeditated or spontaneous (crucial to all but the fantasy theory, important for the broken chain theory and relevant to the other two).

Some sort of picture of the nature and course of the relationships between the main actors is also relevant at least as background to all the theories of the case; it is crucial to parts of the broken chain theory, in that this is greatly strengthened if one can show a cooling off on the part of Freddy after the most damaging letters were written (there is quite cogent evidence in favour of this)[96] and a calmer, less frenetic reaction on the part of Edith. However, even if it were accepted that at one stage Freddy has tried either to break off or to cool down the relationship ('Can we be pals, only', he had suggested in September)[97] there is a counter-theory, to the effect that there was a revival of passion later, backed not least by the fact that Freddy killed Percy. Without going further into detail here I wish to suggest that in order to assess the credibility of the broken chain theory *in toto* and responses to it, it is important to consider in meticulous detail the precise nature of the relationship at a number of stages in the story and to test the hypothesis that the early letters belong to a distinct phase which was significantly different from the state of the relationship in the days immediately before Percy's death.[98]

Macroscopic analysis: a preliminary stock-taking[99]

One of the main claims made for Wigmore's method is that it provides a powerful tool for organizing and mapping complex arguments based on *masses* of evidence.[100] The guiding rule of thumb is to start with the conclusions (the ultimate *probanda*, facts-in-issue) and to work down or back to the evidence.[101] The ideal type of an argument of this kind is pyramid-shaped with the apex being simpler than the base; in adjudication, there is typically only one apex (guilty/not guilty; liable/not liable), but usually multiple facts in issue are involved and we talk of these as the 'ultimate *probanda*'. It is almost always essential to define each fact in issue *before* proceeding to analyse the evidence relevant to it. To mix metaphors: a clearly defined apex provides a firm hook from which to hang an argument. The structure of the argument is (typically) as follows:

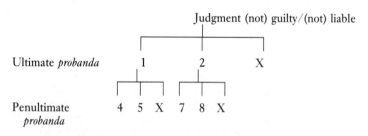

At first sight the preliminary stages of the analysis of the case of Edith Thompson may not seem to be a good advertisement for Wigmorean analysis as a simplifying device. The first stages have not been simple. But this is due to the nature of the case rather than the method. The case is usually considered to be complex because of the volume of the evidence and the difficulties involved in interpreting Edith's letters. The first stage in our analysis has revealed a number of further complications.

First, the ultimate *probanda* are more than usually complex. Many famous trials involve ultimate *probanda* in which the prosecution had to prove A+B+C+D, when only one element (e.g. identity or criminal intent) has been the subject of serious doubt or dispute.[102] In the case of Edith Thompson the facts in issue exhibit a more complex form: the prosecution case involved a mixture of necessary and sufficient conditions which can be represented as follows:

A (Freddy murdered P) + B [(i) *or* (ii) *or* ((i) or (ii) *or*, possibly, (iii))].

Secondly, some doubts surrounded the law governing the facts in issue: was it sufficient to prove a general conspiracy to murder Percy (B (i)) or did the prosecution have to prove that this attack was planned?[103] What precisely is the scope of the proposition 'E *incited* F'? Is the scope of 'incitement' a question of law, or fact, or mixed fact and law? And, although it was not raised at the trial, would Edith be responsible, if the prosecution established the 'exploding bomb' theory? This merely illustrates the general point that to the extent that the interpretation or application of the governing law is unclear, the task of constructing or evaluating arguments about disputed questions of fact becomes correspondingly more difficult.

Thirdly, the complexity of the ultimate *probanda* is reflected in the multiplicity of potential 'theories of the case', each of which has variants. What this means is that there are several potential possible lines of argument both for and against Edith. A 'comprehensive' analysis of the case would need to map and evaluate each of these arguments.

Fourthly, some of the lines of argument overlap: for example, as we shall see, the 'fantasy theory' may represent both a sufficient argument for exonerating Edith (in respect of both conspiracy and incitement), and a substantial prop for the broken chain theory. This is not uncommon in disputed cases involving multiple lines of argument.

Fifthly, in many *causes célèbres* the sole or main disputed issue relates to some relatively 'hard fact', such as identity or alibi or the death of the victim.[104] In this case we are dealing with the mental state of not one, but two people: did Edith intend ... etc? Was Freddy's act caused/inspired/done in furtherance of ... ? Proof of mental states is notoriously more elusive than proof of 'simple facts'.

Finally, as we have seen, some of the intermediate *probanda* that are potentially important in most of the theories involve interpreting the characters of and the relationship between the two main characters.

The case clearly illustrates how complications can arise at the top of the pyramid as well as at other points. Nevertheless the first steps in the analysis have imposed some order on to the material. Our standpoint has been clarified; the range of potential ultimate *probanda*, albeit unusually complex, has been laid out; four main theories of the case have been articulated, with scope left for dealing with variants of these where appropriate. We are now ready to proceed to the next stage.

Microscopic analysis: premeditation

All Wigmorean analysis involves selection; 'completeness' and 'comprehensiveness' are only relative matters in this context.[105] However, the purpose of this essay is to *illustrate* the application of this method to a particularly complex case. Accordingly, I propose to proceed highly selectively by concentrating on two small sectors of potential arguments about the case as a whole. Later I shall consider one simple fact, the difference in age between Edith and Freddy, to make some points about background generalizations and the relationship between analytical and holistic approaches.

First, let us look at just one element in the broken chain theory – the proposition (intermediate *probandum*) that 'Freddy's attack on Percy was spontaneous/unpremeditated' and the main evidence used by the prosecution to support premeditation. I shall use this to illustrate a number of points about Wigmorean analysis (e.g. generalizations, prejudice and the use of emotive language); but there is another reason for selecting this as a focal point. It is a maxim of advocacy that one should 'go for the jugular'.[106] If a reasonable doubt is established about the proposition that 'the attack was premeditated', then this breaks the connection between Edith's thoughts and actions and *all* the prosecution theories, except possibly the legally dubious and highly speculative 'exploding bomb' theory. This is one potential 'jugular' which could be sufficient to destroy all versions of the case against Edith. Whether or not the analysis achieves this result here – I leave that to the reader to judge – it may illustrate the potential value of careful microscopic analysis of one or more key points in a highly complex argument the main outlines of which have been firmly set by careful preliminary macroscopic structuring.

Let us start then by constructing the strongest argument that we can, based on the available materials, that Freddy's assault on Percy was unpremeditated. This sub-theory might be constructed in outline as follows:

1   When Freddy set out from the Graydons' he did not plan to meet Edith and Percy.
2   A planned murder would probably have: (a) been carried out in the absence of Edith; (b) been executed without a struggle; (c) been carried out in some other place.
3   Edith was genuinely surprised by the attack.
4   Freddy's purpose in meeting Percy was to ask him to grant Edith a divorce. The stabbing occurred during an unexpected struggle when the confrontation misfired.
5   Freddy's carrying of the knife was innocent.

All five props in this argument are consistent with Bywaters's conviction for murder and the rejection of his self-defence theory. These five theses are separable, but can be combined in various ways. I shall concentrate on (5), which was treated as crucial in the case. Suffice it to say, in my judgement, there is quite strong support for (3) and that there is little or nothing in the record to negate (1), (2) and (4), but there is little beyond Freddy's story to give them direct support, except some speculative generalizations which give weak support to (2) and (4).[107]

In order to convict Edith the prosecution had to establish not only that Freddy murdered Percy but also that the attack was premeditated. The two main props for the latter proposition are: (a) that the carrying of the knife was not innocent; (b) that there is clear evidence that this attack was planned. Establishing (a) or (b) or (a + b) beyond reasonable doubt would be sufficient for this purpose. Let us look at (a) and (b) in turn.

Table 4   Reconstruction of arguments about the knife

Prosecution	Defence
1 The attack was premeditated.	14 When B. arrived at Belgrave Road, he had no intention of killing P. T. (110, 142)
2 The murder weapon was a knife owned by B. (not disputed).	
3 B. put the knife in his pocket in order to kill P. T. (137).	15 B's carrying of the knife was innocent (142).
	16 *B. always carried the knife with him.*
17 a) B. contradicted himself (38–53). b) B's bias.	17 B.'s testimony (53).
4 *Possession of a knife of this kind is in itself suspicious (104).*	
5 The knife was a deadly weapon (35), a dagger (151), a stabbing instrument (151), a dreadful weapon (132).	18 The knife was an ordinary sheath knife used for many purposes (53).
6 a) The knife (exhibit 1.34).	6 b) The knife (exhibit 1.34).
7 The evidence of the wounds (22–3).	19 B.'s testimony (implicit, 53).
	20 Forster's (tool merchant's) testimony (32).
8 The knife was not a convenient thing to carry about (132, 137).	21 The knife fitted conveniently in the inside pocket of B.'s overcoat (137).
	22 B.'s testimony (implicit, 53).
23 [Nothing is known re size of coat pocket.]	23 The coat (exhibit 29).
9 B. purchased the knife in order to kill P. T.	24 B. purchased the knife for an innocent purpose.
	25 B. purchased the knife over a year before the attack.
	20 Consistent with Forster's testimony (above).
10 No evidence that B. showed it to anyone (132, 129).	10 a) No reason why B. should have shown it to anyone (137).
11 *If he had possessed it for long, there would have been evidence of jocular remarks (132).*	
26 a) B.'s bias. b) No corroborating evidence (132).	26 B.'s testimony (39, 53, 110).
12 B. was a ship's clerk, not a sailor [editorial intervention!] (110).	27 *It is not strange for a seafaring man, visiting foreign countries, to purchase a knife (110, 140).*
	28 B. took the knife abroad with him.
	29 B.'s testimony (53).
13 *No reasonable man living in London carries a knife like this in his pocket (140).*	30 *There are few sailors who do not possess a knife (110, 140).*

Notes: Explicit generalizations are in italics.
Figures in parentheses refer to page numbers of *Trial* (Young, 1923).

(a) The knife   Reconstruction of the actual arguments used at the trial in respect of the knife is particularly revealing. The prosecution argument was in effect: Bywaters had purchased the knife with the intention of killing Percy and he had put it in his overcoat pocket on the day of the murder for the same reason. The defence claimed that Freddy had bought the knife a long time previously, that he had taken it abroad with him on his last voyage, that he regularly carried it around with him and that it was natural that he should do so. The arguments actually used by counsel for each side and by the trial judge in his direction to the jury can be reconstructed as in table 4.[108] In the process of the arguments about premeditation, the weapon was variously described as an ordinary sheath knife, an English hunting knife, a deadly weapon, a dagger, a stabbing instrument, and a dreadful weapon. Interestingly, some of the more emotive terms were used by the judge.[109]

There were also some striking differences in the generalizations invoked in the context of considering this issue. Counsel for the prosecution suggested that possession of a knife of this kind is in itself suspicious;[110] in order to cast doubt on the suggestion that Bywaters had possessed the knife for some time, the prosecution suggested that if this were true it would have been a subject of jocular remarks;[111] the judge said: 'It is suggested that no reasonable man living in London carries a knife like that about in his pocket.'[112] Defence counsel, on the other hand, in the course of a single paragraph said: 'It is not strange for a sea-faring man, visiting foreign countries, to purchase a knife',[113] and, 'There are few sailors who do not possess a knife.'[114] The editor of the record in the *Notable British Trials* series commented on the last remark in a footnote: 'Bywaters was not a "sailor" in the technical sense. He was a clerk on board a ship, and had more use for a fountain pen than for a knife.'[115]

In the preceding examples not only is Bywaters variously categorized as a sailor, a sea-faring man visiting foreign ports, a clerk, and a man living in London, but quite different generalizations are invoked about the purchase, possession and carrying of knives. At the trial the jury had the opportunity to inspect the knife itself and thus could form their own judgement on its description and on the specific issue of whether it would fit conveniently in the pocket of Bywaters's coat. They could also check the accuracy of the various categorizations of Bywaters: for example, it is arguable that he was both someone living in London and a sea-faring man, who visited foreign countries, but the jurors were probably only slightly better placed than the modern reader for making confident judgments about the contemporary habits of merchant seamen or ship's clerks in respect of knives or of the likelihood that if someone possessed a knife of this kind for a considerable period it would be the subject of jocular remarks.

The example of the knife in *Bywaters and Thompson* is a simple example of the leeways for choice in selecting and in formulating generalizations as part of an argument about a particular issue of fact. It shows how there is room for the use of emotive terms, for distortion, and for selection by emphasizing different aspects of the same situation. Moreover, it is an example of invoking common-place generalizations, for example about the normality of carrying knives about London and of sailors possessing and carrying knives, about which the jury is expected to rely on its own version(s) of general experience in order to come to a conclusion. Clearly there is scope in this kind of context for the intrusion of bias, prejudice and sheer speculation.[116] Moreover, it is doubtful whether all the relevant background knowledge can ever be fully articulated. But, as Wigmore might have argued, what better basis is there for making such judgments?[117]

The date of purchase of the knife and the issue whether Freddy was carrying it with the purpose of attacking Percy was perceived by the main participants to be significant. Almost all the available information about it can be gleaned from the explicit arguments advanced in the case.[118] To this can be added a few further propositions: Mr H. W. Forster of Osborne and Co., tool merchants of Aldersgate, testified that his business sold identical knives for six shillings and had stocked them for about seventeen years.[119] Neither the defence nor the prosecution attempted to adduce evidence corroborating or negating Bywaters's statement that he had purchased the knife in November 1921, i.e. almost a year before the attack.[120]

A key-list of propositions relating to the propositions that (a) the purchase and (b) the carrying of the knife were both innocent, based on the available evidence, and constructed from the point of view of a relatively detached historian, might read as follows:

Purchase of the knife was innocent. The carrying of the knife was innocent.
1   The knife was bought in November 1921.
2   Freddy Bywaters (testimony, 53).
3   Freddy Bywaters carried the knife everywhere in England.
4   Freddy Bywaters (cross-examined, 71).
5   It was handy at sea and handy at home.
6   Bywaters (70).
7   Bywaters bought the knife from Osborne and Co.
8   Knives of this kind were sold by Osborne and Co.
9   Such knives had been stocked for about 17 years.
10 H. W. Forster (Director of Osborne's) testified to 8 and 9 (42).
11 Defence called no witness to corroborate Freddy's possession of knife since November 1921.
12 Shearman J (137).
13 'It was difficult to put the knife into any kind of pocket, except the side pocket.'
14 Shearman J (137).
15 Generalizations about the normality of carrying such a knife about – see page 283.

Prima facie this key-list adds little to the arguments presented in the case. However, it can be used as the basis for some other propositions which further weaken the premeditation thesis:

16 There is no evidence that Freddy Bywaters bought the knife on the day of the killing.
17 If Bywaters already owned the knife (1+16), he had it with him when he left home.

18   Bywaters carried the knife about with him from the time he left home until after the killing.
19   Bywaters had the knife on him during at least three social engagements (morning coffee and afternoon tea with Edith; visit to the Graydons).
20   The knife fitted easily in his coat.

All of this helps to bolster Freddy's claim that the purchase and carrying of the knife were both innocent. Furthermore, (17) suggests that the premeditation thesis requires that Freddy had formed the plan to attack Percy before he left home. Yet none of the several witnesses who saw him during the course of the day observed anything strange or unusual about his demeanour.[121] The net effect of all this, I would suggest, is to give some, albeit weak, support to this part of Freddy's story; it suggests that there is nothing in the evidence about the knife (other than the fact of its possession and use in the killing) which supports the premeditation thesis.

Against this background let us look more closely at Freddy's own account of the events leading up to the killing. At first he said that he had left the Graydons' at about 11 p.m. and had gone straight to East Ham station, catching a train to Victoria at 11.30 p.m. He had missed the last train to Gypsy Hill and had walked home arriving at about 3 a.m. (first statement, exhibit 5).[122] However, on the following day, after being told that he and Mrs Thompson were being charged with murder, he made the following statement after caution:

FREDERICK BYWATERS states: I wish to make a voluntary statement. Mrs Edith Thompson was not aware of my movements on Tuesday night, 3rd October. I left Manor Park at 11 p.m. and proceeded to Ilford. I waited for Mrs Thompson and her husband. When near Endsleigh Gardens I pushed her to one side, also pushing him further up the street. I said to him, 'You have got to separate from your wife.' He said 'No.' I said, 'You will have to.' We struggled. I took my knife from my pocket and we fought and he got the worst of it. Mrs Thompson must have been spellbound for I saw nothing of her during the fight. I ran away through Endsleigh Gardens, through Wanstead, Leytonstone, Stratford; got a taxi at Stratford to Aldgate, walked from there to Fenchurch Street, got another taxi to Thornton Heath. Then walked to Upper Norwood, arriving home about 3 a.m. The reason I fought with Thompson was because he never acted like a man to his wife. He always seemed several degrees lower than a snake. I loved her and I could not go on seeing her leading that life. I did not intend to kill him. I only meant to injure him. I gave him an opportunity of standing up to me as a man but he wouldn't. I have had the knife some time; it was a sheath knife. I threw it down a drain when I was running through Endsleigh Gardens.[123]

At the trial he gave a more detailed account of the struggle and the events leading up to it:

Until that moment had you had any intention of going to Ilford at all that night? – Oh, no. It kind of came across me all of a sudden. I arrived at Ilford station and crossed over the railway bridge, turning down York Road into Belgrave Road. When I got into Belgrave Road I walked for some time, and some distance ahead I saw Mr and Mrs Thompson, their backs turned to me. They were walking along Belgrave Road towards Kensington Gardens, and Mrs Thompson was on the inside of the pavement. I overtook them, and pushed Mrs Thompson with my right hand like that (describing). With my left had I held Thompson, and caught him by the back of his coat and pushed him along the street, swinging him round. After I swung him round I said to him, 'Why don't you get a divorce or separation, you cad?'

Where were your hands when you said that? – By my side; I had let go of him. He said, 'I know that is what you want, but I am not going to give it to you; it would make it too pleasant for both of you.' I said, 'You take a delight in making Edie's life a hell.' Then he said, 'I've got her, I'll keep her, and I'll shoot you.' As he said that he punched me in the chest with his left fist, and I said, 'Oh, will you?' and drew the knife and put it in his arm.

Did he do anything before you took the knife out? – Yes, he punched me with his left hand and said, 'I'll shoot you', going at the same time like that with his right hand (describing).

Why did you draw your knife? – Because I thought I was going to be killed. After I put my knife into his arm there was a struggle. All the time struggling, I thought he was going to kill me. I thought he was going to shoot me if he had an opportunity, and I tried to stop him.

We know of the wounds he received. Have you any recollection at all as to how the wounds at the back of the neck occurred? – I have not any exact recollection, but all I can say is I had the knife in my left hand, and they got there somehow.

During all this time after you had brushed Mrs Thompson away did you see her again? – I did not. She might have been 10 miles away for all I saw of her. After the struggle I suppose I ran away. I don't remember it definitely, but that is what happened.[124]

Bywaters's counsel, Mr Cecil Whiteley, did his best to argue on the basis of evidence that Bywaters used the knife in self-defence (justifiable homicide) or was provoked in the heat of passion after being assaulted by Percy (manslaughter).[125] The jury did not accept either of these versions. This is hardly surprising as they are not easy to reconcile with the nature and location of the wounds; there was no evidence that Percy ever had possessed a gun; and there is no hint of self-defence or provocation in Bywaters's original statements. Moreover, Bywaters's credibility was impaired by the evasiveness of some of his testimony, which may have been intended to protect Edith. Accordingly we can accept that he was rightly convicted of murder.

However, in respect of Edith, it was for the prosecution to prove that the attack was premeditated. Even if one totally discounts Freddy's evidence about the events of the evening (and his story of the period up to 11 p.m. was generally consistent and was largely corroborated by the Graydons), there is almost nothing to support the proposition that the atttack was premeditated. There was no evidence to support the proposition that the knife was purchased recently in order to attack Percy; there was no evidence in support of the proposition that Bywaters put the knife in his pocket that morning because he planned to attack Percy – the best that the prosecution could do was point out that there was no corroboration for his claim that he was in the habit of carrying it.[126] The alternative hypotheses about his state of mind (planned attack, loss of control in the heat of the moment) are essentially speculative. The evidence relating to the wounds may support an inference of intent, but it is about evenly balanced (and weak) in respect of the question of premeditation versus spontaneity. More information about the date of purchase of the knife, whether Bywaters did regularly carry it about, and its size in relation to the pockets of the overcoat might have helped one side or the other. However, on the basis of careful scrutiny of the available evidence, my conclusion is that it gives only weak support to either side and, on balance, it marginally favours Edith. Accordingly there is considerable doubt about this crucial aspect of both prosecution theories.

(b) Edith's last letter: the 'tea-room' passage (exhibit 60) The other specific prop of the premeditation thesis was the closing passage in Edith's last letter to Freddy (exhibit 60).[127] In presentation, the prosecution did not subject this to close scrutiny, preferring to concentrate on building up a general impression of a continuous process of encouragement and stimulation ('by precept and example, actual or simulated').[128] Edith incited Freddy and plotted Percy's death with him and this led directly to his death. In the case Edith's letters were admitted as evidence of motive and intent, but were used for other purposes, including as direct evidence of conspiracy.[129] Since the judge ruled that it was necessary to establish that Edith incited or planned *this* attack, the last letter in fact formed a crucial part of the prosecution case.[130]

I shall argue that the letter at the most gives only very weak support to the prosecution and that there is almost no other evidence to support the proposition that this attack was planned. It is worth subjecting one key passage to detailed scrutiny as an illustration of the potential methods and value of microscopic Wigmorean analysis.

There is some uncertainty about when this letter was written and when it was received; let us, for the sake of argument, take the timing most favourable to the prosecution: that it was written on the day before the killing (i.e. on 2 October) and received before Freddy left his mother's house on the 3rd.[131] It is reproduced in full at pages 297–99. The whole letter was the main evidence used by the prosecution in favour of the conspiracy theory. Let us focus on the following words which were relied on by *both* sides to support their case: 'Don't forget what we talked in the Tea Room, I'll still risk and try if you will – we only have 3¾ years left darlingest. Try and help.' The prosecution theory was that 'what' referred to killing Percy;[132] the defence claimed that 'what' referred to Freddy trying to find Edith a post abroad so that they could elope.[133]

If, from the standpoint of a historian, we take a fresh but careful look at this passage, it is clear that it is susceptible to quite elaborate textual analysis. Here I shall only sketch a possible approach. One might, for example, start by listing a series of propositions about possible referents of 'what' (also of 'risk and try', and 'try and help': risk what? try what? and so on) as follows:

1 'What' could refer to almost anything, i.e., there is no clear referent.
2 'What' could refer to killing Percy.
3 'What' could refer to getting a post abroad.
4 'What' could refer to eloping.
5 'What' could refer to a secret assignation.
6 'What' could refer to asking Percy for a divorce.
7 'What' could refer to a general conversation covering several or all of the above and possibly much else besides.
8 'What' could refer to whether to use poison or a dagger (Shearman, 151).

This probably covers the main possibilities, though the list is not exhaustive. There is a number of potential aids to interpretation which might give support to one or more of these hypotheses and eliminate others. Such aids include: the immediate context of these twenty-seven words; the context of the letter as a whole; the context of the whole corpus of letters and of particular passages in other letters (for example, Edith often uses the words 'risk and try'); one or other sub-theory about the state of the relationship between them; extraneous evidence might be sought from people who saw (or possibly overheard them) in the tea-room; the conduct of Edith and Freddy before and after the meeting; the occasion for writing the letter might also be investigated; and, of course, Edith and Freddy could be asked about the meaning of the passage.

Both the prosecution and the defence, in a very crude fashion, used something akin to textual analysis of the 'tea-room' passage in their arguments; but, in my view, they both cheated.

This passage is the main evidence in favour of the proposition that this particular attack was planned, i.e., the conspiracy theory. The prosecution emphasized the words 'risk', 'try', 'help' and 'only' in the passage itself to bolster the idea that this referred to a sinister conspiracy.[134] Then by taking a number of other words and phrases out of context ('great big things', 'he was suspicious', 'do something tomorrow night') and linking them to the fact of Percy's death and other letters, some of which were ambiguous and written over six months before, they suggested that the conversation in the tea-room was the culmination of a continuing conspiracy.[135]

The defence emphasized 'only 3¾ years' (strange if one was planning something immediate) and the fact that Edith and Freddy *both* testified that 'what' referred to eloping and risking her future with Bywaters,[136] but then counsel used the fact of the prosecution's misuse of this passage to cast doubt on their interpretation of all other passages, while carefully skipping over any explicit reference to any of the most damaging ones.[137]

Even more remarkable is Mr Justice Shearman's treatment of the passage; for he asserts, without any basis whatsoever and going well beyond what the prosecution had argued, that 'what' refers to whether it was better to kill Percy by means of poison or a dagger.[138]

A more careful analysis, using the aids mentioned above, can take us some way beyond this. First, we can quite confidently eliminate some of the possible hypotheses. For example, the judge's suggestion can be attacked on the following grounds:

1 it is sheer speculation, with no evidence to support it;
2 it involves a *petitio principii* in that it assumes what is seeks to prove;
3 it does not make sense of the passage: 'Don't forget what we talked in the Tea Room [about whether to use poison or a dagger], I'll still risk and try if you will – we have only 3¾ years left darlingest.'

Again, we can fairly confidently discard the first hypothesis that 'what' could refer to almost anything. The context of the letter as a whole, the context of the sentence, the general background of their relationship and the testimony of both Freddy and Edith all support the proposition that 'what' concerned some aspect of their relationship, rather than something else. It seems extremely unlikely that it referred to buying a motor car or that morning's world news, for example.

Of the remaining six hypotheses (2-7), only no. 2 favours the prosecution thesis that they were conspiring in the tea-room to kill Percy. No. 7 (general conversation about their situation) hardly constitutes evidence of conspiracy. The other four hypotheses all positively support the defence contention that the conversation had nothing to do with murder. Even if we totally discount the testimony of both accused that it referred to eloping (the 'risks' being financial and/or of social stigma), the context of the letter as a whole and the words 'only 3¾ years left' both tend to support the judgement that an innocent explanation is a good deal more likely than the prosecution's interpretation. At the very least, such factors seem to me to cast a reasonable doubt on that interpretation – yet this passage was the main item of evidence in support of the conspiracy theory. The passage supports the proposition that they met and talked seriously about their relationship, but it does not give any significant support to the proposition that they were conspiring to kill – it tends to negate it.[139]

Undertaking such analysis and reading about it can both appear wearisome to most people. It is much more entertaining to play with stories – and let Edith go hang. But this kind of approach can and does yield results. In this particular instance I do not think that it can do more than eliminate some of the possibilities and cast doubt on the wisdom of making any confident judgement about what was said in the tea-room; but in respect of other passages, including some that played a key role in the case, meticulous analysis can lead to the conclusion that one particular interpretation is very probably or almost certainly or even beyond peradventure, the correct one. However, in this particular case one's conclusions about different individual passages in Edith's letters tend to point in different directions. For example, the more carefully one studies the 'Marconigram' passage (Appendix B.1), the less easy is it to believe that Edith was *merely* fantasizing or playing games or that Freddy was not *actively* involved in whatever was being transacted between them at that time.[140] On the other hand, some of the other apparently damaging passages either become hopelessly ambiguous in the light of careful scrutiny or else seem to help Edith in one way or another. In short, it is unlikely that this kind of analysis will ever conclusively resolve all the doubts about Edith Thompson's guilt. In my view, it strongly substantiates the judgement that there is at least a reasonable doubt about it.

Generalizations: the example of age

For some readers the foregoing analysis may have been sufficient to persuade them that there is a reasonable doubt, or more, about the propositions that the attack was premeditated and was carried out in furtherance of a plan that was discussed in the tea-room. For some of them, breaking the chain in this way is sufficient to support the conclusion that Edith was wrongly convicted. Others may be less sure, perhaps because they are not persuaded by my analysis or because they do not feel that the proposition about premeditation is a (or the) 'jugular'. They may, for example, think that in some less determinate way Edith was legally and morally responsible for Freddy's act.[141]

This section explores some other features of 'microscopic' analysis and its relationship to macroscopic 'theories' and 'stories'. I suggested earlier that in order to test other parts of 'the broken chain' theory, as well as the other theories, it could be important to undertake a careful analysis of the relationship between the parties at different times. For example, the incitement theory is supported by a view of Edith being the dominant partner throughout the relationship. 'The 'fantasy theory' requires a very different picture of Edith as living in some kind of dreamworld, with Freddy either humouring her or not taking her seriously or perhaps joining in the make-believe as a sort of game. One way of 'breaking the chain' is to suggest that the earlier letters, including the potentially most damaging ones, belong to a quite different, perhaps more ardent, phase of the relationship.[142] A thorough analysis of the support for various interpretations of the course of the relationship could fill a book and will not be attempted here. Instead, a number of points are illustrated by looking in detail at the potential bearing of one simple fact on possible interpretations of the relationship.

At the time of the killing Edith was twenty-eight years old, Freddy was twenty. It was assumed on all sides at the trial that this information was relevant and admissible;[143] and, indeed, it would have been impracticable to exclude it even if its prejudicial effect outweighed its probative value. Not surprisingly, the 'older woman' theme played a key role in painting a picture of Edith as the dominant partner in the relationship. This was done both explicitly and implicitly, not only by the prosecution,[144] but also by the Lord Chief Justice on appeal. The following passage from the latter's judgment might be interpreted as implicitly relying on this fact:

With regard to the letters, in the opinion of this Court, there was more than one ground upon which the use of these letters could be justified. It is enough for the present purpose to say that it could be justified on this ground – that by means of them the prosecution were seeking to show that continuously over a long period, beginning before and culminating in the time immediately antecedent to the commission of the crime, Mrs Thompson was, *with every sort of ingenuity, by precept and example, actual or simulated, endeavouring to incite Bywaters to the commission of this crime*[145] [italics supplied].

'Common sense' suggests that the difference in the ages between the lovers was clearly relevant to this version of events. Many would consider it quite damning. But I shall argue, first, that the precise justification for treating this as relevant is far from clear and, second, that the same fact could also be used in support of the proposition that Freddy was the dominant partner.

Judged by the first reactions of several classes of law students, as well as nearly all commentators, it is quite natural to make the judgement that the fact that Edith was eight years older than Freddy tends to support the proposition that she was the dominant partner in the relationship (inference 1) and that this in turn supports the proposition that she incited him to murder Percy (inference 2).[146]

The issue is not the strength of these inferences, but whether the fact of age is relevant. What is the justification for the first inference? According to the standard view of inference assumed in the discourse of the Rationalist Tradition, an inference from one particular fact to another particular fact is normally justified by reference to a background generalization drawn from 'general experience'.[147] But what precisely might this generalization be? From the almost infinite number of possibilities, let us select just three candidates:

1   All older women dominate/manipulate younger men.
2   In love affairs involving a significant difference in ages, the older partner tends (nearly always/more often than not/sometimes?) to be the dominant partner (in almost all/most/some respects?).
3   Age is a significant variable in determining patterns of dominance and subservience in relationships between 28-year-old women and 20-year-old men.

In the absence of empirical research, one has to fall back on one's own stock of knowledge. My 'general experience' suggests that (1) gives strong support to the inference, but is almost certainly false. It is also expressed in the language of male prejudice; (2) is believable, but is speculative and vague and shows the inference to be, at best, very weak; (3) is *prima facie* plausible, but is also speculative and vague. Furthermore, it cuts both ways. Take, for instance, a fourth possibility:

4   Older women tend to be particularly vulnerable to manipulation by younger male lovers.

This last proposition is not a figment of my imagination. It is based on a confident assertion by F. Tennyson Jesse, as part of an argument that fifty-year-old Mrs Rattenbury was innocent of involvement in the murder of her husband by her much younger lover, Stoner. Jesse was a supporter of Edith Thompson, and a feminist, and in writing about the present case she made a similar assumption, but tended to leave it implicit.[148]

This example illustrates a number of points about this kind of analysis. First, 'relevance' (tends to support, tends to negate) denotes that there is some connection between propositions *in the context of an argument*. Secondly, one of the main functions of Wigmorean analysis is to clarify precisely what is being argued, by seeking to make explicit what is often left implicit. Thirdly, this process of articulation may lead one to revise one's evaluation of the strength of particular inferences or of some sector of an argument or of this argument as a whole. Fourthly, this process often reveals that in the course of an argument reliance is being placed on generalizations that on inspection turn out to be open to criticism as being, for example, highly speculative or prejudicial or vague or ambiguous or clearly false. Fifthly, it is difficult, if not impossible, both to *interpret* one specific phase of an argument (what is being argued?) and to *evaluate* the strength of a particular inference outside the context of the argument as a whole. This is one of the messages of 'holism'. Finally, this process of analysis and articulation has a subversive tendency in that it tends to reveal hidden weaknesses in what previously seemed plausible. But it is a tool which can be used in the process of constructing and refining arguments as well as of criticizing them. For example, the defence might have used the difference in age, coupled with other facts about Edith and Freddy, to build up an interpretation of the later letters as emanating from a vulnerable, anxious and unhappy woman trying to preserve a fading relationship – in my view, a quite plausible reading of the crucial last letter.

Ending

I have suggested that careful analysis of even such unpromising material as Edith Thompson's allusive, ambiguous and inconsequential love letters can at least reduce the range of plausible interpretations even if it cannot resolve all doubts. I would further suggest that such analysis is the best available way of getting as near as possible to the truth, but it was not the method used at the trial – nor is it a method which is well suited to our system of adversarial proceedings and oral presentation of evidence. In my view, the prosecution used selected passages unfairly by taking them out of context, by attributing particular meanings to them on the basis of innuendo, impression and bare assertion rather than analysis and argument. The reading aloud of the letters in court could create only a general impression, which is no substitute for careful study of the texts. Even if the defence had been handled more skilfully and if the emotional atmosphere and the pressure of time had been less, the basic flaw would have been the same: the *oral* presentation of such material, whether to twelve lay persons or to an experienced professional, cannot provide a satisfactory basis for the careful analysis and evaluation of the evidence.[149] Thus my conclusion is that dispassionate, logical analysis of even such unpromising material as Edith Thompson's letters is a possible, indeed even a necessary, method of trying to work towards the truth, but such a method is incompatible with oral presentation of the material – as much in a public lecture as in a courtroom.

This essay has not 'solved' the mystery of Edith Thompson. That was not its purpose. At most it can claim to show up some of the weaknesses of the arguments made at her trial and in much of the later literature. The case retains its interest partly because of its complexity and elusiveness. However, as a teacher and as a theorist, having exploited Edith over the years, I feel that I owe it to her to put on record some conclusions about her case. I believe that Edith Thompson was a victim of injustice in several ways. There is some evidence to support the view that there were occasions when she wished, intended and possibly even attempted the death of her husband. But this evidence is not cogent and most of it dates from a period remote in time from his actual death. The evidence against her at the trial was not cogent and clearly, in my view, fell below the criminal standard of proof; although the procedure was formally correct, the atmosphere before and during the proceedings was incompatible with my conception of a fair trial. Capital punishment is wrong; capital punishment for a *crime passionel* is particularly inapposite; execution for a *crime passionel* for which she was probably not responsible is a triple wrong. This may be contingent wisdom after the event, but at least it is based on disciplined reflection.

What other conclusions have I come to about the case after trying to analyse the available evidence, using the methods I have described? Without claiming to have completed an exhaustive analysis, I have done sufficient to arrive at some fairly confident judgements. In the circumstances I shall only report my conclusions rather than rehearse the arguments on which they are based.

First, all the theories of the case can be shown to rest on grounds that are at best highly speculative. In short, we are unlikely ever to be sure beyond peradventure of the truth about Edith Thompson.

However – and secondly – the evidentiary support for some theories is much weaker than for others. Of the theories that I have outlined it seems to me that the one with the least support is the one which provided the ostensible basis for Edith's conviction: that she and Freddy planned this attack. The main evidence for this relied on by the prosecution – the passage about the tea room – is at best ambiguous and of low probative value. There is strong negative evidence against it, not least other passages in the same letter, Edith's reactions at the time and the foolishness of choosing the particular place, time, weapon and general scenario for a carefully planned attack. The evidence relevant to the issue of premeditation – did Freddy set out with the intention of attacking Percy? – is inconclusive: it seems to me on the basis of available evidence more probable than not that he set out with no fixed intent; but we have seen how much speculation is involved in making such judgements.

To say that the evidence in favour of the conspiracy theory is weak is not the same as saying that the theory is untrue. It is merely to say that on the basis of the available evidence this is less probable than several other possible theories – some of which could also have justified holding Edith responsible. But there is one further consideration which might – paradoxically – give some tenuous support to the conspiracy theory. Let us call it the inefficiency theory.

One way of classifying mankind is into conspiracy theorists and inefficiency theorists. You may have guessed from the sceptical tenor of some of my remarks, that I have a bias towards inefficiency theory. Subjecting the record of Bywaters and Thompson to careful analysis does nothing to generate much optimism about the prospects for rationality in legal processes or in any other aspect of human affairs. From first to last the tale is one of foolishness, incompetence and irrationality – not merely the foolishness of the lovers, but the general human failings of nearly all the main actors, from Percy himself to the Home Secretary, Mr Bridgeman, who is reported to have refused a reprieve *because* he was a feminist and an opponent of capital punishment.[150] So it may be appropriate to end by presenting one further perspective on the story, in the form of a prose poem derived almost entirely from commentaries on the case:

If Only ... An Inefficiency Theorist's Lament on Bywaters and Thompson

... if only she had been upper class – or working class – or better educated – or even French, there would have been simpler solutions to her problems. If she had been male, of course, her particular problems would not have existed at all.

If only Edith had not married a man whom she did not love.
If only Freddy had not intervened in the quarrel between Edith and Percy;
If only Percy had thrown Freddy out immediately after the quarrel;
If only Edith had not written the letters;
If only Edith had not implied that she was keeping Freddy's letters or
had insisted that he destroy hers;
If only Edith had been more careful in what she wrote – 'A Borgia does
not write; she acts.'
If only either Edith or Freddy had been a competent poisoner;
If only Freddy, believing her talk of poison and glass to be 'vapourings'
and 'melodrama', had told her to stop it and shut up;
If only Edith could have made up her mind between comfort, respectability
and true love – and had decided to elope or to break off the relationship.
October 4th, 1922. If only Freddy, having decided to kill Percy, had:
Chosen a better venue
Used a more efficient weapon
Picked a time when Edith was not there
Arranged a plausible alibi
Used a weapon that could not be linked to him
Disposed of the weapon where it could not be found ...
If only Edith had maintained from the first her story about not seeing or
understanding or remembering any details of what happened ...
If only Freddy had destroyed the letters at his mother's house
And his blood-stained coat, which he continued to wear ...
If only Freddy had remained silent after being cautioned, instead of
making inconsistent statements.
If only Edith had stuck to her original story;
If only the trial had not been conducted in an atmosphere charged with
sexual prejudice;
If only the case for Edith had been prepared and presented more
carefully and cogently;
If only Edith had not insisted on giving evidence or had performed more
convincingly under cross-examination;
If only the jury had adopted the judge's test that Edith must have
planned *and* known of *this* attack on *this* occasion;
If only the Home Secretary had not been a logical man in favour of equal treatment for
women;
If only English law took a different view of *le crime passionel*;
If only the eternal human triangle had only three sides.

Appendix A

[~~Copy~~ *Indictment No.* 1.*]

𝕿𝖍𝖊 𝕶𝖎𝖓𝖌

AGAINST

FREDERICK EDWᴰ· FRANCIS BYWATERS

AND

EDITH JESSIE THOMPSON.

CENTRAL CRIMINAL COURT.

Presentment of the Grand Jury.

F. E. F. BYWATERS and E. J. THOMPSON are charged with the following offence:—

STATEMENT OF OFFENCE.

MURDER.

Particulars of Offence.

F. E. F. BYWATERS and E. J. THOMPSON on the 4th day of October, 1922, in the County of Essex, and within the jurisdiction of the Central Criminal Court murdered Percy Thompson.

[~~Copy~~ *Indictment No.* 2.†]

𝕿𝖍𝖊 𝕶𝖎𝖓𝖌

AGAINST

FREDERICK EDWᴰ· FRANCIS BYWATERS

AND

EDITH JESSIE THOMPSON.

CENTRAL CRIMINAL COURT.

Presentment of the Grand Jury.

F. E. F. BYWATERS and E. J. THOMPSON are charged with the following offences:—

FIRST COUNT:

STATEMENT OF OFFENCE.

Conspiracy to Murder contrary to sec. 4 of the Offences against the Person Act, 1861.

Particulars of Offence.

F. E. F. BYWATERS and E. J. THOMPSON on the 20th day of August, 1921, and on divers days between that date and the 2nd day of October, 1922, in the County of Essex, and within the jurisdiction of the Central Criminal Court, conspired together to murder Percy Thompson.

---

* This is the Indictment upon which there was Conviction.

† The accused were *not* tried on this.

SECOND COUNT:

STATEMENT OF OFFENCE.

Soliciting to Murder contrary to sec. 4 of the Offences against the Person Act, 1861.

Particulars of Offence.

E. J. THOMPSON on the 10th day of February, 1922, and on divers days between that day and the 1st day of October, 1922, in the County of Essex, and within the jurisdiction of the Central Criminal Court, did solicit and endeavour to persuade and did propose to F. E. F. Bywaters to murder Percy Thompson.

THIRD COUNT:

STATEMENT OF OFFENCE.

Inciting to commit a misdemeanour.

Particulars of Offence.

E. J. THOMPSON on the 10th day of February, 1922, and on divers days between that day and the 1st day of October, 1922, in the County of Essex, and within the jurisdiction of the Central Criminal Court, did unlawfully solicit and incite F. E. F. Bywaters unlawfully to conspire with her, the said E. J. Thompson, to murder Percy Thompson.

FOURTH COUNT:

STATEMENT OF OFFENCE.

Administering poison with intent to murder contrary to sec. 11 of the Offences against the Person Act, 1861.

Particulars of Offence.

E. J. THOMPSON on the 26th day of March, 1922, in the County of Essex, and within the jurisdiction of the Central Criminal Court, did administer to and cause to be taken by Percy Thompson certain poison or other destructive thing unknown with intent to murder the said Percy Thompson.

FIFTH COUNT:

STATEMENT OF OFFENCE.

Administering a destructive thing with intent to murder contrary to sec. 11 of the Offences against the Person Act, 1861.

Particulars of Offence.

E. J. THOMPSON on the 24th day of April, 1922, in the County of Essex, and within the jurisdiction of the Central Criminal Court, did administer to and cause to be taken by Percy Thompson a certain destructive thing, namely, broken glass, with intent to murder the said Percy Thompson.

Appendix B.1

Exhibit 17

Enclosure in letter dated 1/4/22

Dont keep this piece.

About the Marconigram – do you mean one saying Yes or No, because I shant send it darlint I'm not going to try any more until you come back.

I made up my mind about this last Thursday.

He was telling his Mother etc. the circumstances of my 'Sunday morning escapade' and he puts great stress on the fact of the tea tasting bitter 'as if something had been put in it' he says. Now I think whatever else I try it in again will still taste bitter – he will recognise it and be more suspicious still and if the quantity is still not successful – it will injure any chance I may have of trying when you come home.

Do you understand? I thought a lot about what you said of Dan.

Darlint, don't trust him – I don't mean don't tell him anything because I know you never would – What I mean is don't let him be suspicious of you regarding that – because if we were successful in the action – darlint circumstances may afterwards make us want many friends – or helpers and we must have no enemies – or even people that know a little too much. Remember the saying, 'A little knowledge is a dangerous thing.'

Darlint we'll have no one to help us in the world *now* and we mustnt make enemies unnecessarily.

He says – to his people – he fought and fought with himself to keep conscious – 'I'll never die, except naturally – I'm like a cat with nine lives' he said and detailed to them an occasion when he was young and nearly suffocated by gas fumes.

I wish we had not got electric light – it would be easy.

I'm going to try the glass again occasionally – when it is safe Ive got an electric light globe this time.

Appendix B.2

Exhibit 60*

Plain envelope

Darlingest lover of mine, thank you, thank you, oh thank you a thousand times for Friday – it was lovely – its always lovely to go out with you.

And then Saturday – yes I did feel happy – I didn't think a teeny bit about anything in this world, except being with you – and all Saturday evening I was thinking about you – I was just with you in a big arm chair in front of a great big

*The date of this letter is stated in *Trial* to be 3 October 1922, the day before the murder. The prosecution suggested that the meeting in the tea-room took place on Monday 2 October. Weis (171 – 2) argues convincingly that it was written before 5 p.m. on the Monday and that the meeting in the tea-room took place on Friday 29 September. See below 314.

fire feeling all the time how much I had won – cos I have darlint, won such a lot – it feels such a great big thing to me sometimes – that I can't breathe.

When you are away and I see girls with men walking along together – perhaps they are acknowledged sweethearts – they look so ordinary then I feel proud – so proud to think and feel that you are my lover and even tho' not acknowledged I can still hold you – just with a tiny 'hope'.

Darlint, we've said we'll always be Pals haven't we, shall we say we'll always be lovers – even tho' secret ones, or is it (this great big love) a thing we can't control – dare we say that – I think I will dare. Yes I will 'I'll always love you' – if you are dead – if you have left me even if you don't still love me, I always shall you.

Your love to me is new, it is something different, it is my life and if things should go badly with us, I shall always have this past year to look back upon and feel that 'Then I lived' I never did before and I never shall again.

Darlingest lover, what happened last night? I don't know myself I only know how I felt – no not really how I felt but how I could feel – if time and circumstances were different.

It seems like a great welling up of love – of feeling – of inertia, just as if I am wax in your hands – to do with as you will and I feel that if you do as you wish I shall be happy, its physical purely and I can't really describe it – but you will understand darlint wont you? You said you knew it would be like this one day – if it hadn't would you have been disappointed. Darlingest when you are rough, I go dead – try not to be please.

The book is lovely – it's going to be sad darlint tho', why can't life go on happy always?

I like Clarie – she is so natural so unworldly.

Why aren't you an artist and I as she is – I feel when I am reading frightfully jealous of her – its a picture darlint, just how I did once picture that little flat in Chelsea – why can't he go on loving her always – why are men different – I am right when I say that love to a man is a thing apart from his life – but to a woman it is her whole existence.

I tried so hard to find a way out of tonight darlingest but he was suspicious and still is – I suppose we must make a study of this deceit for some time longer. I hate it. I hate every lie I have to tell to see you – because lies seem such small mean things to attain such an object as ours. We ought to be able to use great big things for great big love like ours. I'd love to be able to say 'I'm going to see my lover tonight.' If I did he would prevent me – there would be scenes and he would come to 168 and interfere and I couldn't bear that – I could be beaten all over at home and still be defiant – but at 168 it's different. It's my living – you wouldn't let me live on him would you and I shouldn't want to – darlint its funds that are our stumbling block – until we have those we can do nothing. Darlingest find me a job abroad. I'll go tomorrow and not say I was going to a soul and not have one little regret. I said I wouldn't think – that I'd try to forget – circumstances – Pal, help me to forget again – I have succeeded up to now – but its thinking of tonight and tomorrow when I can't see you and feel you holding me.

Darlint – do something tomorrow night will you? something to make you forget. I'll be hurt I know, but I want you to hurt me – I do really – the bargain now, seems so one sided – so unfair – but how can I alter it?

About the watch – I didn't think you thought more of that – how can I explain what I did feel? I felt that we had parted – you weren't going to see me – I had given you something to remind you of me and I had purposely retained it. If I said 'come for it' you would – but only the once and it would be as a pal, because you would want me so badly at times – that the watch would help you not to feel so badly and if you hadn't got it – the feeling would be so great – it would conquer you against your will.

Darlint do I flatter myself when I think you think more of the watch than of anything else. That wasn't a present – that was something you asked me to give you – when we decided to be *pals* a sort of sealing of the compact. I couldn't afford it then, but immediately I could I did. Do you remember when and where we were when you asked me for it? If you do tell me, if you don't, forget I asked

How I thought you would feel about the watch, I would feel about something I have.

It isn't mine, but it belongs to us and unless we were differently situated than we are now, I would follow you everywhere – until you gave it to me back.

He's still well – he's going to gaze all day long at you in your temporary home – after Wednesday.

Don't forget what we talked in the Tea Room, I'll still risk and try if you will – we only have 3¾ years left darlingest.

Try & help
PEIDI.

NOTES

This chapter is a revised and expanded version of the Earl Grey Memorial Lecture, delivered at the University of Newcastle in January 1982, under the title 'Of Law and Love'. The change of title signals an increase in rigour at some cost in succinctness.

I am indebted to many people, too numerous to mention by name, for comments and suggestions made in informal discussions and in seminars and classes in several universities. Christopher Allen, Terence Anderson, Jill Cottrell, Ian Dennis and Alex Stein commented on the final drafts and made many useful suggestions. René Weis's *Criminal Justice: The True Story of Edith Thompson* (1988) (hereafter Weis) was published when the final draft was almost complete. This is by far the most substantial study of the case and it contains a great deal of new material. I have not altered the text of the essay in the light of the new evidence, except to correct some specific points of fact kindly pointed out to me by Dr Weis; a few references to his book are also included in the footnotes. Chapter 9 compares the approaches of Dr Weis and myself in order to make some points about the relationship between modified Wigmorean analysis and more orthodox narrative; it also considers a new interpretation of Wigmore's method that is being developed by Tillers and Schum.

1   Morison (1982), 8–9; Lotte and Joseph Hamburger (1985), 12–13; Waterfield (1937), 25–9.
2   Auden (1950), 91, 'Law Like Love'.

3 The most important source is Filson Young (ed.) *The Trial of Frederick Bywaters and Edith Thompson* in the *Notable British Trials* Series (1923) (hereafter *Trial*). This includes a transcript of the trial, a substantial introduction by the editor and the texts both of the letters put in evidence at the trial and of letters from Edith Thompson not put in evidence at the trial. It also contains the judgments of the Court of Criminal Appeal, dismissing both appeals. Other general works include:

Lewis Broad, *The Innocence of Edith Thompson: A Study in Old Bailey Justice* (1952), reprinted sub nom. *The Truth about Edith Thompson* (1957). The original edition includes an edited version of the letters put in evidence, while the paperback version (1957) contains only four letters.
Ernest Dudley, *Bywaters and Mrs Thompson* (1953).
Of the many contemporary newspaper accounts the reports of James Douglas, Editor of the *Sunday Express*, are particularly important.
Other, shorter, secondary discussions which I have consulted include: Earl of Birkenhead (F. E. Smith), *More Famous Trials* (1928), 65–78.
Fenton Bresler, *Reprieve* (1965).
Douglas G. Browne, *Sir Travers Humphreys: A Biography* (1960), esp. ch. 10.
J. P. Eddy, *Scarlet and Ermine* (1960).
Travers Humphreys, *A Book of Trials* (1953).
H. Montgomery Hyde, *United in Crime* (1955).
Stanley Jackson, *The Life and Cases of Mr Justice Humphreys* (1951), 148–56.
Edgar Lustgarten, *Verdict in Dispute* (1949).
Violet Van der Elst, *On The Gallows* (1937).
R. Wild and D. Curtis-Bennett, *Curtis: The Life of Sir Henry Curtis-Bennett QC* (1937).
For a discussion of other published and unpublished sources see Weis (1988), 313–16.

4 E. Lustgarten (1949), 127.
5 F. Tennyson Jesse, *A Pin to See the Peepshow* (1934, re-issued by Virago Press, 1979) (hereafter *Pin*; page references are to the Virago edition). *Pin* was also published as a play in 1948, but was banned by the Lord Chamberlain on first production, after a protest by Percy Thompson's brother. Ironically another play based on the case, *People Like Us* by Frank Vosper (1923) was running in London at the time, having had an earlier ban lifted. *Pin* was dramatized for television in 1973 by Elaine Morgan, who also wrote the introduction to the Virago edition. The story of *Pin* is told in Colenbrander (1984).
6 *Pin*, 82.
7 Id., 18–19.
8 Id., 364.
9 Ibid.
10 Stephen Vincent Benét, 'John Brown's Body', quoted in *Pin*, 313.
11 For general discussions of the nature, uses and limitations of this kind of analysis see *Analysis, passim: TEBW*, Appendix, and Schum and Tillers (1988) discussed below, ch. 9.
12 Such notions as 'brute facts' are, of course, problematic, Anscombe (1958). For present purposes it is sufficient to maintain that there is a useful working distinction to be drawn between two kinds of *probanda*: those which refer to 'simple' facts, such as identity (was it Sacco/Hanratty who ...?) and others which, even on their face, are more complex or elusive (e.g. motive, criminal intent or 'Did E *incite* F?'). On the conceptual difficulties associated with the notion of 'brute facts' see also above, 104–7.
13 Cf. Hilaire Belloc, foreword to Chassaigne, *The Calas Case* (1932), 13–14:

The interest of the Calas Case does not lie in the crude (and imaginary) elements of an obvious melodrama. No one worth listening to now believes that a man clearly innocent was put to death by wicked enemies. Nor does it lie in the violent emotions of the time, though the contemplation of these is a much more respectable subject than martyrdom. It lies rather in the example it gives of historical method and the opportunity for historical analysis. It is one of those questions which will presumably remain debated for a very long time without any fixed conclusion being arrived at. The continued discussion of the Calas Case is a model of that contrast in the use of evidence with which all those who engage in history are concerned.

Briefly, it is a model of the way in which historical evidence turns upon psychological judgment, of the way in which our acceptance of a witness's credibility, or of the greater value of one piece of his testimony over another, turns on our judgement of men.

The first rule to be put before anyone who has to read history, let alone to write it, is this: all historical evidence is a matter of psychology: all evidence whatsoever depends for its judgment upon the knowledge of the mind of man in general and of the mind of man in that particular society where the disputed event took place, and of the minds of individuals concerned.

14 'Mrs Thompson was hanged for immorality' is a remark attributed to Edith's counsel, Curtis-Bennett, by several writers (e.g. Broad, 219; Dudley, 123); cf. Wild and Curtis-Bennett, op cit., n. 3, who set this in the context of Edith's disastrous insistence on giving evidence (165).

15 Remark of the late Dean Soia Mentschikoff Llewellyn at a seminar on the case, University of Miami, 1981.

16 Exhibit 60 (Appendix B), part of which is analysed below, is a reasonably clear example of Edith shifting from topic to topic without always making clear transitions. Some other letters exhibit the same tendency even more clearly. However, the difficulties of interpretation can easily be exaggerated. It is part of my argument that careful textual analysis can provide the basis for reasonably confident interpretations of many, but not all, of the key passages.

17 This statement of 'the facts' attempts to present a relatively detached account in a way which leaves open the question of Edith's responsibility. It may not be completely impartial or neutral – for that is beyond my powers – but it is a long way from being the 'heart' of my argument (see above, ch. 7).

18 The Thompsons lived in 41 Kensington Gardens, Ilford. They were walking together along Belgrave Road at the time of the attack. There is nothing in the trial record to suggest that this was a surprising or unusual route to take from Ilford Station to their home; this is corroborated by maps and by a visit to the area and was emphasized by Edith's counsel (*Trial*, 123). The road was dark and deserted and, if there had been evidence that the route was unusual or strange, this could have been used to support the conspiracy theory. In the Court of Criminal Appeal the Lord Chief Justice stated: 'Now, the place where the body was found was about 50 yards from the Thompsons' house and 1250 yards from Ilford Station. *It was an indirect way from the station to the house* (*Trial*, 257, italics added). Other witnesses (at 18–19) were coming from Ilford Station along Belgrave Road shortly after the attack. There seems to be nothing in the evidence or on the map to support the Lord Chief Justice's statement. The route that they followed is still easily identified today.

19 *Trial*, 19–20 (testimony of Webber).

20 *Trial*, 18 (testimony of Pittard).

21 *Trial*, 20 (testimony of Dr Maudsley).

22 For details see Weis (1988), 181.

23 Edith's various accounts of the attack are to be found at *Trial*, 18–21, 35–7 (statements), 86–9, 103–4.

24 *Trial*, 33. Weis has unearthed some further letters.

25 *Trial*, 37.

26 *Trial*, 39.

27 Two of the most important exhibits are reproduced below, 297–9. See also above, n. 24.

28 The two indictments are reprinted below, 296. The Prosecution proceeded only with Indictment No. 1. The analysis presented here does not deal directly with the counts in Indictment No. 2.

302 Anatomy of a Cause Célèbre

29 *Trial*, 27–8.
30 *Trial, passim*. Douglas Browne, in his biography of Sir Travers Humphreys (1960) writes: 'From what is known of Percy Thompson it must be admitted that he seems to have been rather a bore – small-minded, a hypochondriac, fussy in the home, an unambitious shipping clerk who nevertheless was probably envious of his wife. Of his background and interests we hear nothing, and the impression that remains is a very dim one' (op. cit., n. 2 at 204–5). This expresses my own impressions almost exactly. See now Weis (1988), *passim* for a much richer account of the personalities and relations of the main actors.
31 *Trial*, 45–6 (Bywaters); 74 (Thompson).
32 E.g. *Trial*, 164, 167–9; cf. 199–200.
33 Apart from the material in the trial record and the letters, there is a great deal of contemporaneous journalistic writing about Edith based on other sources and several accounts of her last days (see Dudley, 125–7). Mary Size, the Deputy Governor of Holloway, discussed Edith with F. Tennyson Jesse during the writing of *Pin* (Colenbrander, op. cit., 189–90). There are also some photographs, the evidentiary significance of which is a matter of quite striking differences of opinion among my students. See now Weis (1988).
34 Filson Young, *Trial*, Introduction, xvii. See now Weis (1988), *passim*.
35 *Trial, passim*; cf. Weis (1988) for a more detailed account.
36 Broad, 109; Young, xxi; cf. Weis, 243.
37 See nn. 62, 66 below.
38 The impoverishment of Criminology because of disdain or neglect on the part of academic specialists of the contributions of journalists (such as Ludovic Kennedy) and humanistic interpreters (such as Tennyson Jesse) is a theme for another occasion.
39 See above, n. 3.
40 For references see n. 3. Lord Birkenhead's conclusion is revealing:

> Yet, admitting that she planned and plotted murder, recognising that if I had presided at the trial I should have directed the jury upon the same lines as Mr Justice Shearman, realising that, as a member of the Court of Criminal Appeal, I should, like the Court, have found no reason for quashing the conviction, I have still a small, lingering doubt whether Edith Thompson on that night was present at a crime which she had arranged or, indeed, whether she had any idea that any such crime would be attempted. But I was not present at the trial, and no amount of reading will be equivalent to seeing the witnesses and hearing them give evidence. And anyhow, she had the will to destroy her husband for the sake of her lover. (Birkenhead, op. cit., 75)

> This can be interpreted as representing the view, that whether or not Edith was technically legally guilty, she was morally responsible for her husband's death. This, in my view, provides ammunition for at least a residual form of positivism: this is not murder.

41 Above, n. 14.
42 Dudley, 87–8.
43 Op. cit., n. 3.
44 Wigmore *Science* (3rd edn, 1937), Part V, (cf. p.8).
45 *Trial*, 42–4. Bresler (1965), 177–81, reports that Sir Bernard Spilsbury recorded on his case-card for the post-mortem examination 'no disease found to account for fatty degeneration of organs'. He reports that Dr Donald Teare, a noted Home Office pathologist, surmised that 'it is highly probable that [Spilsbury] would interpret fatty changes as being due to poisoning rather than considering less sinister explanations' (cited, 178). Bresler suggests that this point did not come out in court because the Solicitor-General failed to put any questions about the degeneration in his examination of Spilsbury. He argues that the fact that the Crown had evidence that Edith had administered poison to her husband is supported by the inclusion of the fourth and fifth

counts in the second indictment (above, n. 28; these were probably drafted by Travers Humphreys, who would not have included them without evidence) and by the fact of the appearance of the Solicitor-General (who had little experience of criminal trials) – for it was traditional for either the Attorney-General or Solicitor-General to lead for the Crown in cases involving murder by poison. Bresler also suggests that Spilsbury probably communicated this information to the Home Secretary. He concludes: 'As the law then stood she was rightly hanged' (181).

There are two letters (exhibits 52, dated 14 July, and 55a, a cutting dated 20 September) which could be used as evidence of a continuing *interest* in poison, but these do not on the surface imply any attempt by Edith to administer poison. All the more damaging letters are earlier, and there is evidence to suggest that the course of the relationship had changed during the summer months. Even if we accept the proposition 'Edith had administered poison to her husband with intent to murder' as established beyond reasonable doubt, this provides only indirect support for the proposition that she incited or planned this attack and, most important, is quite consistent with the broken chain theory (below, 276).

There is, moreover, considerable doubt about the proposition. Bresler's account is highly speculative and is difficult to reconcile with Spilsbury's testimony which is quite emphatic on the points that he did not find 'any signs of poisoning' (43) and 'no trace whatsoever of any poison having been administered' (44). Even if not asked directly about fatty degeneration, he had the opportunity to advert to it and at the very least his testimony suggested an economy with the truth that is difficult to square with the speculation that he later communicated secretly with the Home Secretary. The above analysis is supported by Spilsbury's original report of 1 December 1922 (PRO Crim 1/ 206–58186) cited by Weis, 215. Browne and Tullett, in their biography of Spilsbury, op. cit., n. 3 suggest that Spilsbury believed that Edith had not attempted to poison Percy (267–8). A different view is advanced by H. Dearden (1934), 99–101, a grotesquely frivolous account of the case. Some commentators interpret Spilsbury's testimony as helping the defence, and the prosecution's handling of Spilsbury as an example of the Crown trying to minimize its impact (see e.g. Brandon and Davies (1973), 74–5).

46 See above, n. 33.
47 Admitted by Bywaters and corroborated by other testimonial and circumstantial evidence.
48 See text at 287.
49 *Trial*, 96 (probably the most damaging phase of Edith's cross-examination).
50 Other evidence adduced at the trial will be used as aids to interpretation of the letters.
51 *Trial*, 34.
52 E.g. Young, xxi *et seq.*; strongly doubted by Weis (personal communication).
53 Exhibit 60, reprinted in Appendix B.2. On the dating of this last letter see below, 314.
54 The letter contained an enclosure which is reproduced in Appendix B.1. In *Trial* it is stated to be postmarked 1 April, 1922. Weis dates this as 10 April; see below, 329 n. 50.
55 Arguably the most important are exhibits 15, 16, 17, 20, 22, 62 (including enclosures).
56 Exhibit 60, below, 299.
57 See below, n. 80.
58 Above, ch. 2.
59 On standpoint generally, see above, ch. 4.
60 On available evidence not tendered at the trial see notes 33 and 45.
61 Above, 106–8.
62 See Indictment No. 1, Appendix A. The fact that Edith was present and witnessed the killing made her a principal rather than an accessory, but the distinction was purely technical and did not affect the facts in issue in the case. *Trial*, 6.
63 See the brilliant analysis by Kadish (1985). For the position at common law, see generally, G. Williams, *Criminal Law: The General Part* (2nd edn, 1961), chs. 13–16.

64   *Trial* 133–55, esp. 155:

'You will not convict her unless you are satisfied that she and he agreed that this man should be murdered when he could be, and she knew he was going to do it, and directed him to do it, and by arrangement between them he was doing it. If you are not satisfied of that you will acquit her; if you are satisfied of that it will be your duty to convict her.

Cf. 127, where Shearman J interrupted the closing speech for the prosecution to say (in respect of incitement): 'It is necessary, of course, to be careful of words, and I do not feel inclined to take the matter at large.' In the context this was interpreted by the Solicitor-General to mean that the 'persuasion' lasted right up to the murder (128), but both gloss over the distinction between planning this attack and killing when an opportunity arose. See below, n. 72.

65   See now *R.* v. *Calhaem* [1985] QB 808; cf. *R.* v. *Clarkson* [1971] 1 All ER 1402.

66   My colleague Ian Dennis has usefully suggested the following analysis:

It appears that the prosecution case was that Edith was guilty of murder because she aided and abetted Freddy to kill Percy. The terms aiding and abetting embrace a number of methods of participating in an offence. Whatever the method of participation it is always necessary to prove criminal intent.

There is almost no evidence to support the proposition that Edith positively assisted Freddy at the time of the attack and substantial evidence to negate it. For practical purposes this theory can be eliminated. Alternative theories are based on conspiracy or incitement. One possible theory for the prosecution is that there was an agreement to murder Percy and that Edith was present at the attack in pursuance of that conspiracy. But even if there were evidence to suggest a prior agreement to murder it would be sufficient to exonerate Edith to cast doubt on either of the following propositions: (a) that the conspiracy continued to the time of the attack; (b) that Edith had the necessary criminal intent. As regards incitement it would be sufficient for the prosecution to prove that Edith had incited Freddy to kill Percy, and then to invite the jury to infer that she was continuing to do so up to the time of the attack.

Whichever theory is chosen it is necessary for the prosecution to establish *mens rea*. Thus, even if it were established that some passages meant that Edith was truthfully or falsely claiming to have tried to kill Percy, it is also necessary to establish that in making these claims she *intended* to incite or to agree with Freddy to kill Percy. The role of the 'fantasy' theory is to cast doubt both on the meaning of the damaging passages and on Edith's *mens rea*. The prosecution in fact seem to have treated the case as one involving a conspiracy to murder, using the letters to suggest incitement from which the conspiracy might be inferred.

See further, references in nn. 63 and 65 above.

67   For the distinction between complicity and causation see Kadish, op. cit., n. 63 at 404 ff.
68   *Trial*, 215, discussed below.
69   In case any reader should think this to be fanciful or unduly pedantic, consider the familiar historical puzzle about the death of Becket. Did Henry actually say: 'Who will free me from this turbulent priest?' (The source cited in the *Oxford Dictionary of Quotations* is 'History Books'). If so, what did he mean? If his words are evidence of a genuine desire for Becket's death, is that sufficient to hold him morally responsible for his murder? For a different and richer interpretation of the legend see Victor Turner (1974), ch. 2.
70   *Trial*, 54–5. Bywaters's Counsel, Cecil Whiteley, was probably trying, without much hope of success, to obtain a verdict of manslaughter.
71   At several points the Solicitor-General made it clear that either incitement or conspiracy was sufficient (e.g. *Trial*, 17 and 132–3).
72   In the passage cited above, n. 64, Shearman J's wording allows for a conspiracy to murder 'when he could be'. However, he places great emphasis on Edith's surprise and the talk in the tea-room (see especially 143–4, 146, 151–2, 155).

73   On the emotive use of language see below, 284.
74   See above, ch. 7.
75   Wigmore, op. cit., n. 44, at 31.
76   Above, ch. 7.
77   On the distinction between 'adversarial' and 'dialectical' see above, 213 n. 21.
78   The most important additional theory, not discussed here, is that the letters are of no evidentiary value or should not have been admitted in evidence.
79   E.g. *Trial*, 259 (Lord Chief Justice).
80   Most secondary writers who have argued that Edith was innocent have adopted some version of the fantasy theory, e.g. Broad, Dudley, Jesse, Young, and Weis.
81   *Trial*, cf. 49, 59, 64, 67–8, 117–18. Cf. Broad: 'He could recognise them for what they were – vapourings of her lively imagination' (65).
82   E.g. *Trial*, 123–4 (Curtis-Bennett).
83   'Pemeditation', in this context, is not a term of art; it was not a necessary element in proving that Bywaters's act involved 'malice aforethought'. However, if the act was spontaneous rather than planned that at least goes a long way, and is probably sufficient, to exonerate Edith. See below, 281 *et seq.*
84   See above, nn. 65 and 66. For a further example of an 'exploding bomb' theory, see Landsman (1986).
85   Young, xxiii; Wild and Curtis-Bennett, op. cit., n. 3, at 144–7.
86   See, for example, the analysis of exhibit 60 below, 288–90.
87   E.g. Young, xxiii–xxiv.
88   Wigmore, op. cit., 858.
89   E.g. the works cited above, 253 n. 13.
90   On suicide pact see *Trial*, 46–7, 59–70 (Bywaters); partly contradicted by Thompson (84). See now Weis (1988), 51, 229.
91   Young xv *et seq.*
92   Id., xix.
93   Elaine Morgan, *Pin*, 406.
94   This was written before Weis's excellent reconstruction.
95   Commentators differ on Bywaters's demeanour in the witness box and, in particular, how far what seem like rather unconvincing attempts to shield Edith in respect of the poisoning passages in the letters undermine the credibility of his account of the events of 4 October.
96   The evidence is too extensive to analyse here. I am inclined to agree with much of Lewis Broad's view of the course of the relationship (op. cit., chs. 1–4), but my argument is consistent with several other interpretations.
97   *Trial*, 210–11 (exhibit 28), commented on by Bywaters (68–9).
98   This has now been done admirably by Weis.
99   On macroscopic analysis see *Analysis*, Preface and ch. 5.
100 Wigmore *Science*, *passim*.
101 Wigmore, id., Part V.
102 A very high proportion of *causes célèbres* are much simpler than the present case in that the main historical doubt concerns identity.
103 Above, n. 64.
104 Above, nn. 12 and 102.
105 Cf. above, 104–9.
106 Cf. above, 278.
107 For example: 'premeditated murders are planned in such a way as to minimise the chances of detection' (2); 'the manner of Percy's death fits better the pattern of a spontaneous fight after a verbal exchange rather than the pattern of cold-blooded murders' (4).
108 See also below, 315, 330 n. 78.
109 'a knife with a leather sheath' (defendant at 53, cf. 140); 'hunting knife' (tool merchant

at 42); 'deadly weapon' (Shearman J, charge to the jury at 135); 'a dagger' (id., several times, at 151); 'a stabbing weapon' (ibid.); 'that dreadful weapon' (Solicitor-General for the prosecution at 132).
110 *Trial*, 140; cf. 132.
111 Id., 132.
112 Id., 140.
113 Id., 110.
114 Ibid.; cf. Shearman J at 140.
115 Ibid., note.
116 See *TEBW*, 213, n. 18, Bennett and Feldman (1981), ch. 8.
117 Tillers, op. cit., 988–91n.
118 The most significant gap is the size of the knife in relation to the pockets of Bywaters's coat. See now, Weis (1988), 179: 'The dagger [sic] consisted of a double-edged blade, which measured five and half inches and protruded from a four-inch long, chequered pattern handle.'
119 *Trial*, 42.
120 *Trial*, 53; cf. 132 (Solicitor-General, suggesting that this was not corroborated).
121 *Trial*, 24–5 (Mrs Lillian Bywaters); 25–7 (William Eustace Graydon).
122 *Trial*, 37–8 (first statement, exhibit 5).
123 *Trial*, 39 (second statement, exhibit 6).
124 *Trial* 54–5 (examined by Mr Cecil Whiteley QC).
125 *Trial*, 105–12.
126 *Trial*, 132.
127 Reproduced below, 297–9.
128 *Trial*, 127; cf. 259 (Lord Chief Justice).
129 *Trial*, 8.
130 Above, n. 72.
131 On Weis's analysis of the date of the letter and the meeting in the tea-room see below, 314.
132 *Trial*, 100, 132. However, the Solicitor-General was careful to say: 'Nothing I have said should give you reason to think that I wish to impress a single phrase, a single letter, beyond its proper importance' (132); contrast Shearman J (151).
133 *Trial*, 122 (Curtis-Bennett).
134 Especially *Trial*, 16, 100–1, 132.
135 *Trial*, 16.
136 Trial, 122–3. The letter contains other passages that are difficult to reconcile with a plan to kill Percy on 3 October ('its funds that are our stumbling block – until then we can do nothing'; 'Darlingest, find me a job abroad.' 'Do something tomorrow night, will you? Something to make you forget' (generally interpreted as taking another woman out). J. P. Eddy neatly used this passage together with the evidence that Edith was surprised by the attack to reject the conspiracy theory; however, he considered that her letters were 'evidence of a protracted and continuous incitement to Bywaters to commit the crime he did commit'. Accordingly he concluded that Edith should have been acquitted on the basis of the charge to the jury, but she was guilty of murder nonetheless (1960, ch. 15).
137 Above, n. 55.
138 *Trial*, 151.
139 This argument is put well by Eddy (1960), 130–2.
140 Below, 297.
141 See above, nn. 66 and 273.
142 See above, 276, and Weis (1988), *passim*, especially 75, 152ff.
143 E.g. *Trial*, 108–9 (Whiteley); 117 (Curtis-Bennett); and references in the next two notes.
144 Id., esp. 15; see also 9, 13, 14, 17. Age was a clear theme in the Crown's opening statement, but was given much less emphasis in the Solicitor-General's closing speech.

145 Id., 259.
146 Ch. 6.
147 See generally *TEBW*, 142–51.
148 F. Tennyson Jesse, 'Rattenbury and Stoner' in John Mortimer (ed.), *Famous Trials* (1984), 25: 'Nevertheless, the assumption of the Bywaters–Thompson case, that an elderly woman dominates her younger lover, still obtained at the Rattenbury trial. The truth is that there is no woman so under the dominion of her lover as the elderly mistress of a very much younger man.'
149 Typed transcripts of the letters were made available to the jury.
150 Bresler (1965), 176–7; Young, xxxix. The argument goes that, as a feminist, he felt that women should accept the consequences of their equality and, as Home Secretary, he was anxious not to jeopardize his position at a time when he was under attack for showing weakness in the case of Ronald True. Bresler argues that Bridgeman considered the case very carefully and may have been influenced by information not presented at the trial.

9

Thompson and Wigmore: Fresh Evidence and New Perspectives

This chapter develops themes from the preceding chapters through a commentary on two recent publications that raise important issues about narrative, holism and modified Wigmorean analysis. Section I interprets an important new study of Edith Thompson as a sophisticated application of the 'narrative method' and compares and contrasts this approach with my attempt to apply modified Wigmorean analysis to the case in chapter 8. In Section II I challenge the suggestion by Tillers and Schum (with whose ideas I am generally in sympathy) that Wigmorean analysis is essentially static and cannot adequately accommodate the complexities of legal analysis and the dynamic, temporal dimensions of legal process.

I   Edith Thompson: A Narrative Reconstruction

One hazard of academic life is to learn of an important work on one's subject shortly before or after completing a project. I was making final revisions to 'Anatomy of a *Cause Célèbre*' (hereafter *Anatomy*) in June 1988 when I learned of the publication of *Criminal Justice: The True Story of Edith Thompson* by René Weis.[1] This is by far the most substantial study of the life and death of Edith. Remarkably, Dr Weis and I are colleagues at University College, London, yet over a period of five years neither of us knew that the other was working on the case. Dr Weis is a lecturer in English literature. His interest was stimulated by the debate on hanging in 1983. His book is a scholarly contribution to the general literature on *causes célèbres* and is the first full-scale biography of Edith.[2] I had been using the case in teaching for rather longer; the first version of my paper was presented as a public lecture in 1982. Its main purpose was to illustrate a method of analysis; a subsidiary aim was to demonstrate the potential and the feasibility of using trial records as standard materials of study in legal education.

Criminal Justice contains much new information and many insights about

Edith Thompson. I share many of Dr Weis's values[3] and I agree with some, but not all, of his interpretations and judgements. We both conclude that Edith was probably wrongly convicted, but for somewhat different reasons. However, this essay deals only indirectly with the 'truth' about Edith Thompson. Rather its concern is methodological. It is a case study of the differences in approach of a jurist using modified Wigmorean analysis and a specialist in English literature using a sophisticated version of the 'narrative method' to reconstruct and present the 'True Story of Edith Thompson'. Others may make their own judgements about the value and interest of these two very different studies. My objective here is to explore quite briefly and report as honestly as I can what I think a first reading of Dr Weis's account has added to my understanding of the case in respect of the question: Was Edith guilty as charged? and, secondly, what modified Wigmorean analysis might have added to his account. This is a sort of 'thought experiment'. In order to reach for relative detachment I shall refer to both authors in the third person.

Criminal Justice is a substantial book of over 300 pages. It is published by a general commercial publisher, Hamish Hamilton, and is presented in a form designed to attract the general reader. It is based on extensive and meticulous original research and contains some conventional scholarly 'furniture': a table of contents, a Preface, two pages of acknowledgements, a list of illustrations, a 'Cast of Main Characters', an appendix on sources and an index based almost exclusively on proper names. Significantly it has virtually no footnotes. Even more significantly for present purposes it is presented as a story: the arrangement is chronological, starting with a description of Edith's parents and ending with a harrowing reconstruction of the execution of Edith and Freddy and a brief account of the subsequent lives of Edith's closest relatives. The whole forms a readable, coherent – and moving – narrative biography. Weis states: 'My readers will be the final arbiters of whether or not ... I have successfully allowed Edith Thompson to argue her innocence.'[4]

Criminal Justice differs from *Anatomy* in respect of, for example, purpose, length, style, source material, comprehensiveness, literary form and intended audiences. They are contrasting products of significantly different enterprises. There is, however, a solid basis for comparison, for both focus on the question of Edith's guilt, using her letters as the main, but not the only, evidence. One can thus compare and contrast two different ways of treating selected matters bearing on this question, with particular reference to the relationship between narrative, analysis and argument.

Standpoint

The first step in any such analysis is to clarify standpoint by asking: Who am I? At what stage in what process am I? What am I trying to do?[5] Partial answers to these questions in respect of *Criminal Justice* and *Anatomy* have already been indicated. However, posing the questions more sharply suggests some further affinities and contrasts. Both authors purport to adopt 'the standpoint of the historian' exploring the question of Edith's guilt from almost the same vantage-point: University College, London, in the 1980s.[6] Neither is a professional historian; both are liberal academics with a humanistic bent. They have produced works for publication at the end of rather different processes of research. Personal factors apart, some of their differences in perspective might be attributable to the kinds of differences one might expect between a legal and a literary mind: Twining more drily analytical; Weis more practised in the interpretation of literary texts and character. But, one may ask: Is it sensible to think in such terms or to draw sharp distinctions between legal and literary historical truth? Are not the similarities in standpoint much greater than the differences, given that they have both been addressing essentially the same central question?

Weis's story is based on extensive original research.[7] He has located an impressive range of materials in newspapers, official records (some made publicly available for the first time), 'evidence' to two Royal Commissions, Hansard, and, of course, the record of the trial (edited by Filson Young) and numerous secondary works, few of which, he says, add much to Young's volume. Weis can claim some notable *coups*: he has unearthed some new letters from Edith, Freddy, members of their families and others. Apart from their intrinsic interest some of these are directly relevant to the question of Edith's guilt. He has also interviewed a number of people who knew some of the actors or who were able to throw light on the environment of the main characters and the central action of the story. Almost as significantly, Weis reports that some potentially crucial documents are missing (including the originals of Edith's letters) and some official files are still closed.[8] Weis uses his material to give the fullest account to date of the background, biographies and personalities of the main actors, but both authors use the published version of Edith's letters as their primary source for the events leading to Percy's death.

The facts in issue: elucidating the question

Weis interprets the charge of murder against Edith almost exclusively in terms of conspiracy,[9] as did Mr Justice Shearman in his charge to the jury.[10] However, he interprets the relevance of conspiracy rather differently from both Shearman and Twining. The former directed that the jury should only convict if they were satisfied beyond reasonable doubt that the lovers had planned this attack. Twining suggests that it would have been sufficient to convict Edith if the jury was satisfied that Freddy acted in pursuance of a continuing conspiracy to kill Percy whenever opportunity arose. Weis tends to gloss over this distinction. He also treats the question whether Edith and Freddy had conspired to poison Percy in the period up to May as central to the question of Edith's guilt.[11] Twining on the other hand argues that under the broken chain theory, even if Edith were held to have attempted to poison Percy or to have conspired with Freddy to do so, these acts were too remote from the fatal attack to be sufficient to implicate her in the murder.[12] As the prosecution tried to argue, some of the early letters could be interpreted to support the theory of a protracted and continuing conspiracy, but the defence countered that the evidence failed to support the hypothesis that, if there ever was a conspiracy, it was continuing or that Freddy had acted in accordance with it. Twining differs from Weis in being much less confident that all the early letters are susceptible to an innocent interpretation, but believes that far less turns on them than Weis thinks.

Weis pays relatively little attention to the significance of incitement, both in respect of the murder and of interpreting some of the potentially most damning passages in the letters. Twining, on the other hand, argues that Edith was more vulnerable in respect of incitement than conspiracy, even without resort to the legally dubious, but psychologically plausible 'exploding bomb' theory.[13] However, on his analysis the chain was also broken in respect of incitement.

It might be argued that since the trier of fact was a jury of lay persons charged with rendering a general verdict, they would not in practice be concerned with such legal niceties. They made an undifferentiated (holistic?) judgment about Edith's legal (and moral) responsibility for Freddy's act and this is what society expects of juries. Accordingly this should also be adequate for an historian. On this view, Twining's differentiations are unduly legalistic and academic. Twining dissents. Such an argument is not qualitatively different from the judgment, which may well be historically correct, that Edith was 'hanged for adultery'.[14] In so far as our enterprise is rationally reconstructing the strongest possible arguments concerning Edith's legal responsibility for Percy's death, precision is very important indeed. The crucial point is that under Twining's interpretation of the law the prosecution had several alternative routes open to them and Edith's defenders need to deal with all the main alternatives. Wigmorean analysis requires as precise a clarification of the legal issues as legal interpretation will admit; and where, as in this case, there are multiple facts in issue, some of which are open to more than one interpretation, arguments have to be constructed about each of them.

Theories of the case

In *Anatomy* Twining outlines four main 'theories of the case', each with several possible variants and sub-variants: the conspiracy theory, the incitement theory, the fantasy theory and the broken chain theory.[15] A statement of a theory in this context means a summary statement of a general argument about the facts in issue. A theory in this sense is an analytic device of macroscopic analysis: for advocates, such theories typically form the basis of a strategy of argumentation; for historians and the like they are similarly a useful instrument for organizing complex material. In analysing the present case, outlining four main theories and their variants helps to clarify how each side had several different routes for reaching the conclusion for which it was arguing. Twining suggests that the broken chain theory is the most plausible of the four. It has the special advantage that it can be used to cumulate doubt about opposing theories without necessarily claiming to advance a fully coherent account of 'the truth' about Edith Thompson.[16] This theory was the main basis for the defence strategy at Edith's trial, but was undermined by her insistence on testifying and therefore being compelled to advance one account of key events and one interpretation of some passages in her letters. Most secondary writers who are sympathetic to Edith, including Weis, rely heavily on the fantasy theory. This has the most human interest and fits in with the function of general literature on *causes célèbres* which tends to be judged by its entertainment value as well as, or more than, its contribution to knowledge. Twining, however, believes that the fantasy theory is very difficult to sustain by evidence and argument.[17] It is both highly speculative and difficult to reconcile with some of the data. It is in his view the least cogent of the four main theories, although it is not as weak as the tea-room conspiracy theory.

Weis does not use the concept of 'theory' to differentiate between lines of argument. It is reasonable to interpret *Criminal Justice* as being based primarily on a version of fantasy theory with a few 'broken chain' points used to supplement his case.[18] As noted above, he does not differentiate very clearly between the various competing theories and their variants. This blunts the force of his negative attack on rival hypotheses and leads him to underestimate the importance of incitement in building up the case against Edith, especially in providing alternative interpretations of some of the letters.

On the positive side it is probably fair to say that Weis, by sustained and careful interpretation of Edith's letters, constructs the most plausible and best-supported version of the fantasy theory yet published. Most secondary writers assert rather than try to prove the fantasy theory and, in so doing, commit, or come close to committing, the fallacy of *petitio principii*. Weis, through skilful use of Edith's letters to document the theme of the constant intermingling of fact and fiction, at least provides an impressive number of texts to ground the thesis. His subtle reconstruction of Edith's character, not least through a perceptive use of her reactions and commentaries on the novels she has been reading,[19] lends support to the fantasy theory. At the very least he provides a coherent and plausible interpretation of the letters read as a whole that is consistent with this line of argument. However, it will be argued below, his interpretations too often involve assertion rather than argument. Moreover, the fantasy theory is by its nature heavily dependent on 'soft' psychological speculation which is in danger of foundering at crucial points when compared with rather 'harder' data.

A first reading of *Criminal Justice* suggests a further, ironic, twist. Weis's version of the fantasy theory, even if true, does not necessarily absolve Edith from legal responsibility. Even if those passages which suggest that Edith had tried to poison Percy or that she is 'dreaming' of Percy's death are accepted as mere fantasy, she is still responsible for communicating those thoughts in a form which might reasonably be interpreted as being factual reports on her acts or desires, for example, that she had tried to poison Percy or that she wished him dead.[20] Absent a positive defence of insanity such acts could legally ground a finding of incitement or conspiracy.[21] There are some hard facts that need to be explained away: Edith did make these statements; she admits to having tried to manipulate Freddy on a number of occasions, as lovers do; she did send at least nine cuttings about cases of murder by poison;[22] she did ask Freddy to send her 'things' which might be interpreted as poisons;[23] Freddy did supply her with some medicines;[24] Edith more than once expressed a wish that Percy was dead;[25] Freddy did kill Percy. The fantasy theory has a lot of explaining to do; it is inevitably speculative and fantasy can spill over into fact as easily as fact can spill over into fantasy – even if such a distinction can be maintained in legal or other discourse.[26] This is not to say that the fantasy theory is untrue nor to suggest that it has no explanatory power. But as an argument it is not very cogent.

Sub-theories, sub-plots and characters

In *Anatomy* Twining argues that an assessment of the characters of the main protagonists and of their relationships to each other is relevant to each of the main theories of the case. He reports a number of different interpretations of these matters that were implicit in the arguments at trial or have been advanced in the secondary literature, but he does not seek to develop them in detail.

Criminal Justice, on the other hand, adduces a wealth of new biographical and background facts, and builds up in fascinating detail a picture of Edith, Freddy and Percy, as well as many other members of the cast of characters. It contains a rich, perceptive and plausible account of all these matters which cannot but add to our understanding of the story, even if one does not accept all of the interpretations. At the 'macro' level, Weis's most striking achievement is to piece together a coherent and detailed chronological account of the course of a number of key relationships – not only between Edith and Freddy, but also between the lovers and members of their families and their circle of friends and contacts. Of particular interest is the detailed account of the course of the relationship between Edith and Freddy, including some significant new information about their attempts to communicate with each other after the trial.[27] Some of the detail may be irrelevant or tangential to the question of Edith's guilt, but the story is well worth telling at length for its own sake and Weis tells it very well. The final chapters have been justly praised as a devastating depiction of the horrors of capital punishment.

Not surprisingly, this meticulous reconstruction has implications for all of the main theories of the case. Although it is presented as an argument in favour of Edith's innocence, it also provides material that could be used for and against each of the main theories. To take but one example: Weis's account of the relationship between Freddy and Edith (which had even more ups and downs than had previously been noted)[28] supports the general thesis that the early letters are of very limited value in interpreting the events immediately preceding Percy's death.[29] It strongly negates any suggestion of either continuing conspiracy or protracted incitement. It gives some support to the contention that the prejudicial effect of the early letters outweighed their probative value and that they ought not to have been admitted at all.[30] On the other hand, given time one could argue that some parts of Weis's account could be used to argue that Edith was probably guilty of some of the lesser offences charged in the second indictment (which was not proceeded with) in the early phase of the relationship.[31] However, that is beyond the scope of this essay.

Weis's reconstruction of characters, relationships and sub-plots (including some new ones)[32] is very helpful in interpreting and making sense of many passages in Edith's letters. One does not need to accept all of his particular interpretations to recognize the value of these intermediate generalizations and of a coherent narrative as aids to developing well-grounded, mutually supportive interpretations of the meaning and significance of these elusive texts. The process is, of course, reflexive: one constructs a picture of a character or incident or sequence of events from the letters or other sources and uses these constructs to interpret the letters. This is quite compatible with a Wigmorean approach and Weis is arguably at his best at this level of analysis.

Microscopic analysis

Two main values are claimed for Wigmorean analysis: at the 'macro' level it helps to clarify the central issues and impose order on a mass of mixed evidence or data through the development of carefully formulated hypotheses, theories and sub-theories; at the 'micro' level it provides tools for sharply focused and detailed analysis of selected phases of an argument that have been identified as being potentially crucial or otherwise deserving special attention. At each level the main claim is that it helps to clarify what precisely is being argued as a preliminary to evaluating its cogency.[33] In *Anatomy* three particular examples were chosen to illustrate the application of microscopic analysis. Let us look at the treatment of just one of these in *Criminal Justice*, the last letter (exhibit 60) with particular reference to the 'tea-room' passage.[34]

Twining uses the last twenty-seven words of this letter as a vehicle for illustrating microscopic Wigmorean analysis. The passage was selected because at trial great emphasis was placed on it by the prosecution and the defence and Mr Justice Shearman, particularly in relation to the thesis that this attack was planned in the tea-room. Twining presents a fairly simple example of careful textual analysis, focusing particularly on the possible referents of 'what' in the phrase 'Don't forget what we talked in the Tea Room' and, in less detail, on the questions: 'Risk what?' 'Try what?' in the phrases 'I'll risk and try if you will' and 'Try and help'. He argues that by careful analysis of these twenty-seven words, backed by a range of contextual aids to interpretation (not least Edith's and Freddy's testimony at trial) the range of plausible interpretations can be narrowed and that, while the passage could refer to a plan to kill Percy, there are several more likely innocent interpretations. He concludes that the passage does not give any significant support to the conspiracy theory; if anything, it tends to negate it. Furthermore, the analysis suggests that the prosecution, the defence and the judge all used the passage in ways that do not stand up to close scrutiny.

Weis reaches a similar conclusion by a different route.[35] He reconstructs the context of the letter and the events to which the key passage refers. He argues plausibly, partly on the basis of new evidence, that the letter was written before 5 p.m. on Monday 3 October (ie. a few hours before the killing) and that the meeting in the tea-room took place on Friday 29 September and not on 3 October, as the prosecution had suggested.[36] He states, 'The Crown will mistakenly assume that the tea room conversation occurred on Monday afternoon, the day before the murder and that it ought to be *causally* linked to the tragedy.'[37] This is a partial *non-sequitur*. If it were accepted that Edith and Freddy had been conspiring to kill Percy a few days before his death, that would have been sufficient to implicate Edith. It is only marginally more damaging to claim that the meeting took place a few hours before the murder, rather than a few days. The dating of the letter and of the meeting involves only a minor and immaterial adjustment in the prosecution's version of the events. In this instance textual analysis is more helpful than contextual analysis, because the point at issue is what the passage means.[38]

The other specific points analysed by Twining can be dealt with briefly. Weis's account of Freddy's movements in the twelve hours before the murder is much more detailed but, like Twining's, casts doubt on the proposition that the attack was premeditated.[39] Weis produces some new information about the knife:

Getting a knife under the circumstances was hardly prima facie evidence to be used to convict, although his carrying it on this night was a different matter. The dagger itself consisted of a double-edged blade, which measured five and a half inches and protruded from a four-inch long, chequered pattern handle. The weapon caused a stir when it was produced in court, not least among the jury. The police might never have found it, had Bywaters not told them precisely where to look, unaware of the damage its visual impact would inflict on his case.[40]

Weis's account of Freddy's movements also supports the proposition that the knife fitted easily and inconspicuously in Freddy's coat pocket: Freddy left home about noon (a crucial moment in the premeditation thesis), met Edith twice, completed a few errands in the city,[41] dined with the Graydons, went out for a drink at a nearby hotel with Avis Graydon, Edith's sister, and made several journeys by public transport.[42] There is no evidence to suggest that anyone noticed that he was carrying a knife. All this in turn is at least consistent with Freddy's claim that he always carried it with him.[43] Weis invokes the defence's generalizations about merchant seamen carrying knives in foreign parts, but implicitly acknowledges that this does not in itself dispose of the proposition that possessing and carrying such a knife in London is in itself suspicious. It was a quite formidable instrument. Weis confirms that there is no evidence to support the suggestion that Freddy had purchased the knife recently for the specific purpose of threatening or attacking Percy.[44] All in all this corroborates Twining's contention that the evidence about the knife gives little support to the premeditation thesis; however, its nature and size (Weis follows Shearman in calling it a 'dagger') is damaging to Edith as well as to Freddy in the context of the premeditation argument as that bears on the conspiracy and broken chain theories.[45]

Weis places little emphasis on the difference in age between Edith and Freddy.[46] It is worth making two points about this: first, the availability of a great deal of specific information about the relationship reduces the significance of speculative generalizations about relationships between 28-year-old women and 20-year-old men (or however the matter is characterized). The fact of age is still relevant in interpreting the story as a whole and many events and letters. Factual detail downgrades but does not totally dispose of such 'common sense' background generalizations.

On the other hand, perhaps because he underestimates the significance of

316 Thompson and Wigmore

incitement, Weis never squarely addresses the crucial but complex question: Was Edith the dominant partner in respect of significant phases of the story? If she was, it is suggested, this could ground a different interpretation of some key passages in her letters from those advanced by Weis. To put the matter crudely: If one sees Edith as a manipulative, scheming or forceful woman who exerted or tried to exert influence over her younger, less experienced lover, this supports the thesis that several passages constitute incitement or solicitation to murder either by direct exhortation or by more or less subtle innuendo. This could significantly change the texture and emphasis of Weis's story, although she might still be rescued from responsibility for murder by the broken chain argument. Before applying this to a specific example, it is necessary to consider Weis's method of interpreting the letters.

Interpreting the letters

René Weis's enterprise is to reconstruct and present 'the true story of Edith Thompson'. He is openly sympathetic to Edith and explicitly claims to argue her case in her own terms.[47] *Criminal Justice* is in an important sense Edith's story and it is presented in a form which serves literary, humanistic and publishing values as well as the pursuit of a mundane kind of truth. It is a good read. In considering his 'method' it is accordingly important to distinguish between analysis and presentation and between narrative and argument. This is especially significant in the present context in that the main values claimed for the Wigmorean approach relate to analysis rather than presentation (for example it is more useful in pre-trial preparation than in presentation at trial);[48] furthermore, as was argued in 'Lawyers' Stories', while narrative may legiti-mately form part of a rational argument – stories may constitute arguments as well as be vehicles for presentation – narrative may also be used to 'sneak in' irrelevant or invalid factors or gloss over weaknesses in an argument or obscure what is being argued or serve other functions such as attracting attention, sustaining interest or winning sympathy.[49] It might be the case that while Weis's treatment of the case is more readable and eloquent, Twining's argument is more cogent.

In *Criminal Justice* Weis uses the letters as the main vehicle for presenting a coherent account of the story of Edith. Only exceptionally does he explicitly discuss alternative interpretations of these texts. If he had done so, it would have broken the flow in ways which would not only have reduced readability, but also impaired the coherence of his presentation. This is not to suggest that as a meticulous and fair-minded scholar he did not analyse and consider some competing interpretations and arguments for and against them. But it is fair to say that in dealing with the letters he generally reports his conclusions and only occasionally considers competing interpretations in detail. This opens up a whole range of issues that will not be pursued here. Let us rather illustrate some quite simple points with reference to a single passage.

Appended to a long letter, dated 1 April 1922,[50] but possibly written over several days, is a separate note which begins: 'Don't keep this piece.' The text of the note is reprinted in full in *Anatomy*.[51] It is worth reading carefully at this point. It has been widely regarded as the most damaging part of all Edith's correspondence ... by the lawyers in the case, by commentators and by several dozen intelligent law students, most of whom were sympathetic to Edith.

After summarizing the passage rather less scrupulously than usual, Weis comments as follows:

> That this piece of fantasy could ever be construed as part of a premeditated murder plot defies belief. Bywaters knew it was fiction and that she had herself tasted the quinine[52] in the tea to be able to give an accurate account of Percy's complaint. In the court the jury was told that 'the passage is full of crime'. Yes, as long as it is understood that 'crime' means 'imaginary crime'. It is never easy to separate fact from fiction in Edith Thompson's extensive and intense correspondence, and though outside evidence is available to help distinguish one from the other, the more intimately acquainted the reader becomes with the correspondence, the more complex its rash interweaving of fact and fiction is bound to appear. In most of our lives such a blurring is not uncommon. It is not always harmless. But it is seldom the matter of life and death into which it is developed here.[53]

This contrasts sharply with Twining's report of his reactions to the passage. He states: '[t]he more carefully one studies the 'Marconigram' passage, the less easy is it to believe that Edith was *merely* fantasizing or playing games or that Freddy was not actively involved in what was being transacted at the time.'[54] This merely reports a considered judgement reached after quite lengthy discussion in several classes. Rather than attempt an elaborate analysis of the whole passage, which *prima facie* contains several damaging statements, let us focus on one sentence and outline a strategy for construing it: 'I wish we had not got electric light ... it would be so easy.' To what might 'it' refer in this context? Nearly everyone who reads this for the first time concludes, in the context of the rest of the note, that 'it' means killing Percy (using gas) (interpretation 1). A strong case for this can be built up solely from the internal evidence of the passage. Other possibilities include making Percy ill (but not killing him) (interpretation 2),[55] but the talk of death in the previous sentence casts doubt on that. Some commentators have suggested that this – and some other passages – refer to Edith trying to abort herself (interpretation 3). Even if these other passages support the sub-theory that Edith was pregnant by Freddy (as Weis argues) or even that she experimented with unconventional methods of contraception, these interpretations do not make sense in this context. For example, how can one reconcile them with the *timing* of these actions ('I'm not going to try any more until you come back' ... 'I'm going to try the glass again occasionally')? And what of 'if we are successful in our action' (what action?) or the need to be careful in what Freddy says to Dan? And so on.

If 'it' does refer to killing Percy can this be explained away? One possibility is that Edith was *pretending* to try to kill Percy.[56] If so, why would she do this except to urge Freddy to try too? Or could this all be a joke ... a form of black humour or an April Fool? ... or a more elaborate game of make-believe? The last is the most common version of the fantasy theory; its application seems pretty dubious in this context. First, it seems likely from the context that Dan existed, that the 'Sunday morning escapade' actually did occur[57] and that Freddy did supply quinine and other drugs to Edith. It stretches one's credulity to suggest that the harmless elements are true but the damaging ones are fantasy. Secondly, whose fantasy? If only Edith's, how explain the passages that imply Freddy's participation ('About the Marconigram? – do you mean... ? ...What you said about Dan')? If this is a joint fantasy, how does this square with our general picture of Freddy, as the down-to-earth young fellow who dismisses Edith's 'vapourings' as 'melodrama'? The reader is invited to construct an argument that explains away this note as evidence which supports the proposition (a) that at that time Edith and Freddy were in fact conspiring to kill Percy; or (b) Edith was pretending that she has been trying to kill Percy in order to incite Freddy to risk and try too; or (c) that Edith on this, and other occasions, was telling Freddy that she wished Percy's death.[58]

To return to Weis's method. In this instance, he asserts rather than argues that the whole note is a 'piece of fantasy' and that Freddy knew that.[59] This is tantamount to a *petitio principii*. Furthermore, it is not clear what precisely he is arguing when he says that 'in our lives such a blurring of fact and fiction is not uncommon, but is seldom the matter of life and death that developed here'. Blurring of fact and fiction about the death of one's husband is not so very common and the coincidence of harmless fantasizing about such a death with his actual murder by the recipient of such fantasies is unique in my experience. On reconsideration, in my judgement the 'Marconigram' note does lend support to several elements in the incitement and conspiracy theories; it also raises some doubts about the fantasy theory itself, for the reasons stated. However, the timing of the note (six months before the attack) still leaves ample scope for the broken chain theory.

Many of Weis's interpretations of Edith's letters help to make sense of them and are much more convincing. However, he generally advances an interpretation on the basis of assertion or implicit argument without considering alternatives.[60] To have done otherwise with the great majority of letters would probably have been unrewarding as well as tedious. However, closer textual analysis of competing interpretations of selected key passages would almost certainly have refined his argument and might also have changed it.

Fresh evidence and new perspectives

Weis has collected a mass of new data and revealing insights and has skilfully woven them together into a coherent whole which for most readers is greater than its parts. Much of the new material fleshes out the background; some has a direct bearing on the central issue. Much of the new information helps to build a quite sympathetic picture of Edith; some of it could be used against her.[61] Some of the facts are 'hard' – such as the dimensions of the knife; other data are more difficult to evaluate. What, for example, is an historian to make of the following judgement of Margery Fry, who visited Edith in prison and afterwards became a committed abolitionist? According to Fry's biographer, Edith struck her 'as a rather foolish girl who had romanticised her sordid little love affair and genuinely thought herself innocent, discounting her own influence on her lover'.[62] For an historian, is this evidence that bears on the question of Edith's guilt?

The central themes of this book – the interplay of law, fact and value, of reason and imagination, of narrative coherence and atomistic analysis – have all resurfaced in this essay. What, if anything, does it suggest about the uses and limitations of Wigmorean analysis? My personal conclusion is as follows: *Criminal Justice* has added immeasurably to my knowledge and understanding of a case with which I already had an intimate acquaintance. It is an outstanding example of what Wigmore called the 'Narrative Method'. The argument of the book in respect of the issue of Edith Thompson's guilt would almost certainly have been sharpened and refined by the application of modified Wigmorean analysis in respect of clarification of the precise issues of law and fact, differentiating between several distinct theories of the case and the broad lines of argument that bear on them; and of selecting and subjecting to detailed microscopic analysis key phases of these arguments. Wigmorean analysis would have supplied a firmer foundation and clearer lines of argument around which to build Weis's detailed edifice. Finally, René Weis has reconstructed a version of events which contains the most careful, cogent and coherent case for Edith's complete innocence that has yet been made. His narrative also contains a good deal of material that could be used for several other lines of argument. For me, the effect of reading, reflecting on and reacting to Weis's account has been to strengthen my belief that some of Edith's letters could reasonably be construed as involving acts of incitement, but that Weis's account strengthens the case for the broken chain theory.

II   Analysis, Stories and Holism Revisited

'Next to the indeterminacy principle,' I told him, 'I have learned in recent years to loathe most the word "holistic", a meaningless signifier empowering the muddle of all the useful distinctions human thought has labored at for two thousand years.'

John Updike, *Roger's Version*

In 'Lawyers' Stories' I suggested that Wigmore underestimated the importance of narrative in legal argumentation while some other writers, such as Bennett and Feldman, have made exaggerated claims about the role of stories and narrative in this context. Rather, I argued, theories and stories, analysis and synthesis, atomism and holism are best regarded as complementary rather than as mutually antithetical. How far beyond this rather bland conclusion can the present case-study take us?

In a recent article, significantly subtitled 'Beyond Wigmore',[63] Tillers and Schum suggest that scientific analysis of complex proof processes, such as those involved in litigation, combines three distinct modes of analysis which they call legal structuring, temporal structuring and relational structuring. In their view, Wigmore made pioneering contributions both in respect of his systematic treatment of the Law of Evidence and the Chart Method. The latter represents a form of relational structuring, that is to say it provides a powerful tool for depicting the logical relationships involved in an argument about a mixed mass of evidence, but it has substantial limitations. They conclude that:

While Wigmore's chart method offers an illuminating account of relational analysis, it does not adequately portray the complexity of legal ordering of evidence and it also does not take into account the various temporal dimensions of the proof process. The result is that Wigmore's theory of proof only works in a relatively stationary world where facts-in-issue and evidence are held constant.[64]

Tillers and Schum also point to two further limitations of Wigmore's approach in respect to evaluation of the strength or cogency of arguments about evidence: he did not deal adequately with the criteria for evaluating the strength of particular inferences and of arguments about a case as a whole and he failed 'to provide us with some procedure for combining probative force assessments within and across chains of reasoning in an evidence chart'.[65] Accordingly, on its own, Wigmore's method is valid and important, but it needs to be supplemented by other tools of analysis, including methods that can be assisted by the use of computers. Tillers and Schum claim that they set out to praise Wigmore without burying him; their current research suggests that, with the aid of modern technology, they will in due course develop a much richer and more sophisticated method of analysing evidence that will indeed go far beyond Wigmore.[66]

I am generally in agreement with Tillers and Schum in their assessment of Wigmore's ideas and look forward with enthusiasm to their efforts to develop a more comprehensive approach to the analysis of evidence. The uses and limitations of Wigmore's method have been extensively canvassed elsewhere. The purpose of this section is to consider the present case-study in terms of Tillers's and Schum's three categories of analysis, with particular reference to the relationship between such analyses and stories and holism.

Chapter 8 was conceived and presented as a case-study of the application of 'modified Wigmorean analysis' to selected aspects of a case which was chosen for its complexity and for its potential 'to defy analysis'. Having set the scene by giving an account of the undisputed facts that led to the trial and execution of Bywaters and Thompson and of the sources that constitute the data to be analysed, I set out to illustrate the application of an intellectual procedure that involved (a) clarification of standpoint; (b) formulation of the ultimate probanda; (c) construction of alternative 'theories' about the case as a whole; (d) identification of selected 'sub-theories' and; (e) 'microscopic' analysis of three selected phases of arguments based mainly on evidence in the trial record. How does this relate to the three modes of analysis advanced by Tillers and Schum?

Temporal analysis

Tillers and Schum state:

Wigmore slighted one of the most central ingredients of inference: *time*. Time enters our picture in a number of important ways. First, the events underlying the matters at issue in a trial developed over time; beliefs about the temporal sequence in which these events are important inferential elements. Second, the advocate's analysis or structuring of arguments to be presented at trial is a *dynamic* process that also develops over time and in which many changes occur. Finally, the temporal order of evidence presentation to the fact-finding body is an important element, as every practising advocate recognizes ... The trouble is that Wigmore slighted the importance of narrative accounts and failed to recognize how such *temporal analyses* may be linked to the *relational analyses* his chart method allows.[67]

This raises a number of general issues that cannot be pursued here. For example, it is not entirely fair to Wigmore and one doubts whether all of these points can be properly designated as three modes of temporal *analysis*. Nevertheless, the central point is correct: relational analysis is essentially static – more like a snapshot than a moving picture. How was the time dimension dealt with in our case-study?

First, as every lawyer knows, in introducing the 'facts' that gave rise to a 'case' it is almost always necessary to present an account of the main events set in time, typically but not invariably in a chronological sequence. Thus in introducing the case of Bywaters and Thompson I tried to give a relatively detached account of 'the facts' *before* embarking on analysing the evidence relevant to the charge for which they were tried.[68] The account was legally incomplete in that it left out details that were crucial to determination of the contested issues in the case. I used this account to 'set the scene' – to provide a context in which arguments about guilt could be presented and analysed comprehensibly. I was unable to avoid presenting this in narrative form, but I tried to do so in a way that was as neutral as I could make it between the competing theories. No doubt some of my biases could be inferred from this account and the scene-setting was 'coloured' by the selection of facts and the language used to recount them. But I attempted not to use the story as a vehicle for presenting an argument. This statement of the facts was not 'the heart' of any of the main theories of the case. At other stages in the analysis other accounts of particular phases feature in a more or less articulated form (e.g. F's versions of the events of 3/4 October, the course of the relationship between E and F) or were left largely implicit (e.g. the history of the knife). The temporal relations of elements in such accounts are of a different kind from the logical relations between the evidence and the ultimate *probanda*.[69] In presenting accounts of cases Wigmore, not surprisingly, regularly used the 'narrative method'. His mistake was to treat it as an *alternative* to the Chart Method. What precisely is the relationship between the two methods will be considered further below.

Secondly, Tillers and Schum are quite correct in emphasizing the dynamic nature of legal processes and of the roles of advocates and judges. This is one reason for insisting on clarification of standpoint as a *preliminary* to analysis. One needs to ask: Who am I? At what stage in what process am I? What am I trying to do? The situation, tasks and needs of a trial lawyer change at every point in the overlapping processes of investigation, theory development, discovery, pre-trial preparation, and each stage of the trial and post-trial activities. As Terry Anderson has shown, and Tillers and Schum confirm, Wigmorean analysis can be useful at all stages of the process, but it tends to be more useful at the pre-trial preparation stages than for purposes of presentation during the trial.[70] The standpoint adopted in this case-study, an historian in 1988 considering the evidence in the trial record, side-stepped some of these complexities because it focused on a fixed body of data being considered in a *relatively* static process. This is not to deny that 'real' historians are also involved in complex and dynamic processes. Relational analysis requires temporary stasis.

Thirdly, time can and does feature in relational analysis. For example, the standard form of an alibi argument goes: 'X was in place Y at time Z; the crime was committed in place A at time Z; no person can be in two different places at the same moment of time; therefore it was not X who committed the crime.' In the present case, the date of the purchase of the knife, possible changes in the course of the relationship between Edith and Freddy, the timing of the meeting in the tea-room, the dates of the letters which suggested that Edith may have attempted to poison Percy are all examples of time featuring as a significant element in the various theories of the case. There is no reason why Wigmorean analysis cannot accommodate time as a factor in 'static' arguments.

Legal analysis

Tillers and Schum correctly point out that in the early stages of litigation there may be choices regarding charges, causes of action, defences and other aspects of determining the facts in issue. Furthermore, doubts or disagreements may arise about the implementation or application of legal doctrine in a given case. Until these matters are determined, there is likely to be a reflexive process between evaluation of the potential evidence and other information available to each side. In most litigation there comes a point when the pleadings or charges are settled and the factual issues are clarified. Where the substantive law is clear it defines the ultimate *probanda* and thus provides a relatively firm hook from which to hang arguments about the evidence.[71] However, where there are doubts about the law then the task of analysing and evaluating the evidence in the case is made much more complex, as is clearly illustrated by the uncertainties surrounding incitement and conspiracy in respect of Edith. Wigmore adopted the orthodox view that questions of materiality were a matter of substantive law and, quite reasonably, he presented his method of analysing evidence in respect of cases in which definition of the facts in issue was treated as unproblematic. Similarly, in order to simplify his presentation, he chose the point in the trial 'when the evidence is all in'[72] and all issues of admissibility had already been determined – a point at which there is a finite and relatively static body of data, at least in theory.

Relational analysis

I have suggested that locating the analysis at a relatively precise moment in time and identifying the ultimate *probanda* are *preliminaries* to analysis of evidence. The paradigmatic situation for using Wigmorean analysis postulates a specific point in the process and a given body of evidence (data) to analyse. As Wigmore recognized, it can be adapted for use in other contexts: for example, by detectives to formulate hypotheses and to identify information that they would like to have.[73] The present case-study satisfies the requirements of the paradigm case. What does it tell us about the uses and limitations of modified Wigmorean analysis?

In chapter 8 I tried to show with reference to Edith Thompson how Wigmorean analysis can help to sharpen the issues; structure the arguments; map their shape; articulate, and hence clarify and expose what precisely is being argued at every step and subject particular phases of an argument to meticulous scrutiny. Such uses of this kind of analysis are bounded by some fairly obvious limitations: analysis can generate fresh propositions, it can identify needed propositions, but it cannot create new data to fill in gaps in the evidence (e.g. information about the size of the pockets in Freddy's coat). At every stage of construction, reconstruction or articulation of an argument, selection and choice are inevitably involved and the criteria for such choices are largely external to the analysis. Not only is the method time-consuming and laborious (so that the technique itself has to be used selectively in practice), but many phases are susceptible to what looks like a potentially infinite regress. At several points of what may have seemed to some readers an excessively ponderous exercise, it has been necessary to renounce any claims to making a 'complete' analysis; even if this were theoretically possible, which I doubt, it would not be feasible even for the most leisurely scholar aided by the most sophisticated technology. Even scholars have to make choices and decisions.

Evaluation

My analysis of the case of Edith Thompson was 'informal' in the sense that I made no attempt to formalize the arguments in terms which might provide criteria for evaluation of the strength of particular inferences or arguments or theories. I reported my own considered judgements, appealed to 'common sense' or left it to readers to form their own judgements. My purpose was to illustrate a particular approach to structuring and analysing arguments based on evidence in complex cases; this approach claims to provide a preliminary basis for judgment rather than firm criteria for evaluating case-strength and inference-strength.

A 'theory of a case' is a general sketch or summary of an argument to support a given hypothesis or set of hypotheses (here the ultimate *probanda* concerning Edith's guilt). The criteria for evaluating an argument depend upon one's theory of logic and one's conceptions of validity, logical consistency, coherence and cogency. But before applying a particular set of logical criteria one needs to know what the argument is. The principal value of Wigmorean analysis is that it involves articulating *all* the components of an argument in the form of propositions and 'charting' (though not necessarily pictorially) all the relations between all the propositions thought to be potentially significant. Wigmore adhered to a particular tradition of inductive logic – that of Mill and Jevons – and he never seriously contemplated any alternatives. He has also been criticized for failing to give sufficient guidance about how one evaluates the strength of particular inferences, combinations of judgements of likelihood and the cogency of the argument as a whole.[74] It is beyond the scope of this essay to explore these philosophical issues about inference and probability – though a rigorous evaluation of any argument about Edith Thompson would ultimately be based on a particular theory of inferential logic. But I believe that Wigmorean analysis as a method of identifying what is being argued is sufficiently flexible to fit several different kinds of logical theory. Provided one accepts a view of inferential argument as being concerned with the relations between propositions, one can proceed by using one or other of several sets of criteria for making judgements about relevance, evaluating the strength of particular inferences and linking judgements of probability.

Support for this view can be found in the general literature on decision theory, which acknowledges that structuring a problem can for most practical purposes be separated from criteria for choosing between different 'solutions'. Similarly, while Wigmore looks like a rather simplistic Baconian, Tillers and Schum agree that this method is quite compatible with one or other versions of Bayes's Theorem and Lotfi Zadeh's notions of 'fuzzy logic'.[75] There is a further justification for using an 'informal' approach to evaluation. While formalization has a valuable role to play in respect of some kinds of microscopic analysis (for example revealing fallacies or misuses of statistics), I am personally sceptical of the idea that formal analysis is likely to be of much assistance in arriving at the best judgement one can about Edith Thompson's guilt or other complex cases. There are two reasons for this: first, on pragmatic grounds, one doubts whether formalized logical or mathematical analysis, even when valid and applicable, will add much of value in this kind of case. Secondly, *analysis* is not the only aid to 'good judgement' in such contexts.

There is, however, one challenge to the Wigmorean approach that needs to be confronted here. This is the assertion that the standard and correct way of evaluating the probative force of a mass of evidence is 'holistic' rather than 'atomistic'. One version of this view states that to individuate 'items' of evidence and express them in terms of propositions each of which can be given an independent value does not conform with ordinary practice and, as a matter of logic, involves one or more unwarranted steps. In this view, some masses of evidence are presented to and assessed by triers of fact as configurations or 'gestalts'.[76] Like stories, masses of evidence can be tested for their internal coherence and consistency and overall plausibility, but attempts to 'translate' masses of evidence and stories into atomistic arguments along Wigmorean lines are not only doomed to failure, but are also positively misleading. Some writers, for example Bennett and Feldman, assert that 'logic' and 'analysis' have a legitimate but subordinate role as tests of consistency and coherence.[77]

This kind of approach has a number of attractions, but I suggest that, in the form stated here, it greatly underestimates the reach and value of rigorous analysis. The case of Edith Thompson provides a particular vehicle for exploring what is at stake in this debate. On the one hand, the various theories about the case, the raw material on which they are based and some of the sub-theories and sub-plots referred to above seem to fit holism more comfortably than they do atomism. On the other hand, as we have seen, disciplined articulation and rigorous analysis can carry us quite far in organizing the materials, structuring arguments, eliminating possibilities and discounting certain theories of the case, even if they have not 'solved' the problem of Edith Thompson.

Here let us eliminate some possible grounds for unnecessary disagreement or misunderstanding. In actual trials and in most of the practical decisions of life few people, if any, have the time, stamina or ability to undertake rigorous analysis along Wigmorean lines. They proceed much more impressionistically and casually than that. At the trial of *Bywaters and Thompson* none of the letters were subjected to careful microscopic analysis. A few important passages were highlighted and different interpretations of their meaning and significance were advanced by counsel. But nothing approaching Wigmorean rigour was applied even to a single passage. Even the most enthusiastic Wigmoreans acknowledge that his method has only limited value in respect of *presentation* of arguments in court: its main uses, in the legal context, relate in legal practice to preparation, and in academic practice to rational reconstruction and *ex post facto* evaluation of arguments. It is not unreasonable to infer that in both preparation and presentation of their arguments the main professional participants were guided by models of advocacy that are rough and ready approximations of Wigmorean analysis. This claims to be an extension and refinement of good practice by advocates; none of the performances of counsel or members of the judiciary in the case can be held up as models of their kind, yet their arguments can be rationally reconstructed and criticized in Wigmorean terms without undue difficulty.[78]

Again, this method of analysis is consciously abstracted from the conditions and constraints of actual trials. The *mores* of the day, the particular atmosphere surrounding the case and the rapidity of the proceedings (less than 100 days separated Percy's killing and Edith's execution) hardly provided ideal conditions for painstaking, relatively dispassionate analysis. Perhaps, more significantly, few would expect a historian to undertake a complete analysis of all the evidence in *Bywaters and Thompson*. Some selection is necessary, even for leisured historians, and some place has to be given in such selection to such elusive matters as intuition and good judgement. But these, it may be suggested, are concessions to feasibility and the law of diminishing returns. What is at stake between atomists and holists is not how people in fact evaluate evidence, but what constitutes the best model for doing so. Wigmoreans do not challenge holism as a rough psychological description of how arguments are presented and decisions are often made. Its interest lies in its prescriptive claims.

A second possible source of misunderstanding lies in the use of the terms 'plausibility' and 'coherence'. Both holists and atomists generally seem to accept that one tests the credibility or plausibility of a theory or a story by reference to more general beliefs about the world, variously referred to as 'the common course of events', 'commonsense generalizations', 'the stock of knowledge' in a given society or 'our web of beliefs'. We have already seen some of the problems connected with these ideas. What seems to be at issue here is not the relevance or the reliability of such standards, but how far it is possible or desirable or dangerous to try to articulate them. Holism, at least in one version, emphasizes the difficulties and dangers of articulation and suggests that our capacity for making such judgments of fact outruns our capacity to describe the world in language.[79] Wigmorean analysis points to the value of articulation in clarifying what precisely is being argued and of bringing background general-izations into the foreground so that they can be subjected to careful critical examination. The example of the difference in age between Edith and Freddy provides a vivid illustration of this.

The broken chain theory also illustrates the relationship between theories and stories. Defence counsel or a historian relying on this theory does not need to construct a version of the events. The theory, in essence, states that whatever happened there was not sufficient connection between Edith's actions and Percy's death to hold her responsible. The 'chain' was broken at one or more points. Thus this theory can be used to cumulate doubts, some of which could be incompatible or uneasy bedfellows within a single story. Like the chestnut about the schoolboy and the broken window,[80] the argument runs: Edith's talk of poison and murder was mere fantasy; even if it were not, Freddy treated it as mere vapourings and did not take it seriously; even if he had taken some of her claims and urgings seriously, this was at an earlier phase of their relationship, which was now past; even if some recent letters supported the theory of continuing incitement or conspiracy, the killing was unconnected with them because it was spontaneous.

The prosecution also did not have to construct a single version of events. Their argument could have been essentially as follows: we do not claim to know exactly what happened, but there is no doubt that Edith was directly responsible for Percy's death whether by virtue of specific incitement or agreement or by a more complex cumulation of pressure in a relationship in which she was the dominant partner. This argument can fit several quite different stories, with varying sub-plots. There is an intimate relationship between theories and stories, as I have used them, but it pays to keep them conceptually distinct. It is not paradoxical to say: 'I have conclusive evidence that X killed Y, but I do not know the story of the killing nor of their relationship.'

One further point about the limits of Wigmorean analysis requires comment: the claim that some kinds of case 'defy analysis'.

For example, in what sense do any of the more plausible accounts of Edith Thompson's involvement in Percy's death 'defy analysis'? One interpretation might go as follows: in coming to a considered judgement about the particular conspiracy theory we need to develop a coherent picture of Edith Thompson's character that fits the suggestion that the 'tea-room' passage refers to killing Percy *and* that they were indeed conspiring to kill Percy in the tea-room *and* that Edith's behaviour at the time of the killing was quite consistent with her expecting this attack *and* all the other evidence that we have about Edith. We do not and cannot build up pictures of people's characters by listing discrete characteristics any more than we describe or evoke a person's face by analysing its elements. We have to use our imagination not merely to fill in missing ingredients but rather to create meaningful and recognizable totalities. Building up such pictures is an important element in making judgements about past events. The best judgements that we can make in this regard either outrun our powers of analysis or are different from them.

If Tillers and Schum can develop one or more computer programmes which can indeed link together static arguments in the dynamic process of litigation, as moving pictures link together stills, this will, indeed, be a significant achievement, which could be theoretically interesting and practically useful. However, to date their theoretical analysis does not take us very far beyond modified Wigmorean analysis.

NOTES

1 René Weis *Criminal Justice: The True Story of Edith Thompson*, London, 1988 (hereafter Weis).
2 On the literature on *causes célèbres* generally see above, 246–9.
3 The most relevant shared values are that we are both opposed to the death penalty (Weis emphasizes that his book is not primarily a polemic against capital punishment – at xii). We would firmly uphold the criminal standard of proof beyond reasonable doubt and have a general sympathy for Edith.
4 Weis, xi.
5 Twining and Miers (1982), 64–71, 116–18.
6 On the dangers of generalizing about 'the historian' see above, ch. 4. Twining's standpoint in *Anatomy* could be characterized as a student of Wigmorean analysis adopting the vantage point of an historian (i.e. operating in a context of free proof) considering the question: Was Edith guilty as charged? Weis adopts a similar vantage-point with regard to this question, but without the explicit methodological concern.
7 On sources, see Weis, x and 313–16.
8 By comparison Twining's efforts hardly count as historical research. He has read most of the secondary literature (but only a few newspaper reports), and he has focused almost exclusively on the published versions of the proceedings (trial and appeal) and of Edith's letters. He has had access to some additional primary and secondary legal sources, but with one possible exception (Fenton Bresler's *Reprieve*, 1965, discussed above, ch. 8, n. 45), agrees with Weis's judgment that most of the prior secondary literature adds little to Filson Young's volume. He also agrees that '(t)he most authentic tribute to Edith Thompson remains F. Tennyson Jesse's *A Pin To See The Peepshow*' (10), although he is more sceptical than Weis about its closeness to the likely historical truth. The potential significance of some of Weis's new evidence will be considered below. Weis relies heavily on Spilsbury's testimony (and notes) to support the thesis that if Edith had in fact tried to poison Percy this would have emerged in the post-mortem (215–16, 223, 226–7). He does not consider Bresler's argument that Spilsbury's case-card contains the statement 'no substance found to account for the fatty degeneration of organs' and that this implies that he suspected that this was attributable to poison. Twining is sceptical of Bresler's thesis and, on the basis of the 'broken chain theory', argues that even if Edith had really attempted to murder Percy this would not lend other than indirect and weak support to the prosecution case on the first indictment. It is not, however, entirely irrelevant, for it could be argued: she had attempted to murder Percy because: a) she wished Percy's death; b) she was capable of intent to murder; c) there was a continuing series of attempts to murder (see further ch. 8, n.45, above). Browne and Tullett (1951) suggest that Spilsbury believed Edith to be innocent (259 and 267).
9 Weis, 316.
10 *Trial*, 133ff., discussed above, 274.
11 E.O. Weis, ix–x, 215–16. Edith's supporters believed that Spilsbury's testimony would be sufficient to exonerate her (eg. 216, 226–7, 271). But, even if this testimony is given the most favourable interpretation, it does not on its own destroy either the conspiracy or incitement theories.
12 Above, ch. 8.

13   Above, 276. Some support for the exploding bomb hypothesis can be found in Weis's sources, e.g. 39–40 (impulsive action of FB in jumping ship); 177–87; 289 ('I lost my temper ... I just went blank and killed him', FB to his mother just before his execution).
14   Above, 264. Cf. Weis on Shearman (246), the Jury (247–8) and the Court of Criminal Appeal (260–1) *et passim*.
15   Above, 275 ff.
16   Above, 277.
17   Above, 279, 294.
18   See especially Weis, x, 58–9, 104–8, 112–13, 141, 148.
19   Especially on *The Fruitful Vine* (147–50) and *Bella Donna* (140–1).
20   It would still be necessary to show that these communications were made with criminal intent (see above, ch. 8, n. 66).
21   See above, ch. 8, nn. 63, 65, 66.
22   Exhibits 15a, 15b, 15c, 15d, 20a, 21a, 22a, 22b, 55a. Those relating to the death of the parson, Henry George Bolding (15a, 15b) had a local interest because suspicion fell on Dr Preston Wallis, a ship's surgeon, who had lived at Manor Park and treated Edith (Weis, 4, 83–4, 89). The others do not have such specific explanations, but need to be set in the context of a significantly greater number of cuttings dealing with other topics. The innocent explanation of the Wallis cuttings might be challenged by Edith's comment: 'It might prove interesting, darlint I want to have you only I love you so much try and help me Peidi:' (*Trial*, 171, exhibit 15); the same letter includes two cuttings about poisoned chocolates being sent to the Vice-Chancellor of Oxford (15c) – see also below, n. 56.
23   Exhibit 15. Weis acknowledges that in this letter Edith hints how easy it would be to murder her husband (84–5), but dismisses her remarks as 'silly'.
24   Weis's version of events includes the thesis that Edith twice became pregnant by Freddy, she suffered a miscarriage, and that some of the passages about poisons or medicines refer to abortifacients (68ff., 101–2, 124). If these interpretations are true this disposes of more sinister readings of some, but not all, of the early letters. The arguments for and against Weis's readings are too complex to deal with here.
25   See above, n. 20.
26   Cf. Weis's use of the fact/fantasy theme, discussed at 317.
27   Ch. 6.
28   E.g. Weis, 75–8, 110–11, 132, 136, 143, 161.
29   *Anatomy*, above, 279; Weis, *passim*.
30   The argument for excluding some of the early letters was put by Curtis-Bennett (*Trial*, 3–6). This was rejected by Shearman J and by the Court of Criminal Appeal. The Lord Chief Justice pointed out, rightly in my view, that there was 'more than one ground on which the use of these letters could be justified' (259). It is a matter for speculation whether a court today would be willing to exclude some of the early letters on the basis that their prejudicial effect outweighed their probative value (see Police and Criminal Evidence Act, 1984 s.78).
31   On the second indictment see above, 296. Edith seems most vulnerable on the second and third counts (Soliciting to Murder and Inciting to commit a misdemeanour), especially in respect of exhibit 15 (10 February 1922), and exhibit 17 (1 (?) April 1922), especially the 'marconigram' passage, discussed below, 317.
32   See especially n. 28, above.
33   See generally references above, ch. 8, n. 11.
34   Exhibit 60, quoted in full above, 297.
35   Weis 168–72, 241, 246–7.
36   Id., 171–2.
37   Id., 172.
38   Weis also makes some valid points about more serious misuses by the Crown of other passages in exhibit 60 and of other evidence, e.g. 171, 241, 245–6.
39   Id., 174–87.

40 Id., 179. The fact that the sheath was not recovered may have contributed to the impression that this was a 'dreadful weapon', Weis 207.
41 Id., 174.
42 Id., 177–8.
43 *Trial*, 70.
44 Weis 178–9, 206–7, 224.
45 Ibid.; see above, 284–6.
46 See, however, 223.
47 Weis, xi.
48 Id., 5.
49 Above, 227, 231.
50 Exhibit 17 was dated 1 April (*Trial*, 179). Weis convincingly argues that it is more likely to be 10 April (personal communication) as the earlier date does not fit in with his reconstruction of the events of this period. The letter is *prima facie* one of the most damaging to Edith, so incorrectly dating it is particularly significant.
51 Above, 297.
52 Weis points out that quinine was considered an abortifacient, but not a poison, although Edith may not have known this (86, 92). Another possibility is that 'quinine' was a code word for something more sinister, but this is conjectural. I find it difficult to make sense of the quinine passages.
53 Weis, 105.
54 Above, 290, cf. 312.
55 See *Trial* 95–6, where the most damaging passage in Edith's cross-examination occurs:

'It would be so easy darlint – if I had things – I do hope I shall.' What would be easy? – I was asking or saying it would be better if I had things as Mr Bywaters suggested I should have.
What would be easy? – To administer them as he suggested.
'I do hope I shall.' Was that acting or was that real? – That was acting for him.
You were acting to Bywaters that you wished to destroy your husband's life? – I was.
By Mr Justice Shearman – One moment, I do not want to be mistaken. Did I take you down rightly as saying, 'I wanted him to think I was willing to take my husband's life'? – I wanted him to think I was willing to do what he suggested.
That is to take your husband's life? – Not necessarily.
Cross-examination continued – To injure your husband at any rate? – To make him ill.
What was the object of making him ill? – I had not discussed the special object.
What was in your heart the object of making him ill? So that he should not recover from his heart attacks? – Yes, that was certainly the impression, yes.
The Court adjourned.

56 See Edith's admission above, n.55. Weis places great weight on Spilsbury's pathological evidence that there was no evidence of poison having been administered to Percy. Assuming that this is correct, this does not dispose of the hypothesis that Edith was claiming to have been trying to poison him in order to persuade Freddy to 'risk and try' too (60, 63, 79, 94). Weis does not deny this.
57 *Trial*, 183 and testimony of Edith and Freddy. *Semble*, Weis does not doubt that these incidents occurred, but gives them an innocent interpretation.
58 See above, 297.
59 Weis, 105.
60 E.g. 104–5.
61 E.g. 127, 158.
62 Weis, 293 (quotation from a biography of Fry). Weis agrees that the judgment seems rather harsh.
63 Peter Tillers and David Schum, 'Charting New Territory in Judicial Proof: Beyond Wigmore', 9 *Cardozo L. Rev.* 907 (1988) (hereafter TS).

64   TS, 907 (abstract).
65   TS, 939 (citing *TEBW* 180).
66   D. Schum and P. Tillers, 'Research on the Marshalling of Evidence and the Structuring of Argument' (unpublished paper, 1988, describing work in progress).
67   TS 942–3.
68   In the text I used the word 'account' rather than 'story' for a specific reason. In 'Lawyers' Stories', following Ricoeur, I confined the latter term to those accounts which contain three elements: temporality, particularity and configuration. A mere listing of events in chronological sequence is not a story; nor is a 'holistic' description or evocation of a scene or situation at a given moment of time. It is the configurative element in stories that links them to 'holism', rather than the temporal dimension. The holist's claim is that, if our objective is to come to the best judgement that we can about the truth of allegations about some particular past event, relational and temporal structuring of hypothetical accounts of the event (both of which can be analytical or 'atomistic') are typically not sufficient; a third element, 'configuration', is nearly always important and sometimes essential. In some sense, configuration defies analysis – see below.
69   Wigmore coined and used the terms 'prospectant', 'retrospectant' and 'concomitant' evidence to designate different temporal relations of evidence to particular facts in issue; see, e.g. *Science*, 52–4.
70   *Analysis*, ch. 5. Anderson suggests that the method of analysis currently being developed by Tillers and Schum may help to bridge the gap between Wigmore charts and conventional litigators' 'trial books'.
71   *Science*, 5, modified by Anderson and Twining, op. cit., to apply to all stages of legal process. Wigmore can hardly be accused of ignoring legal analysis in respect of materiality, but he may have underestimated the extent of reflexivity between 'legal' and 'logical' analysis.
72   E.g. *Science*, Appendices IV and V.
73   There have been extended debates within psychology about 'molar' and 'molecular' accounts of psychological phenomena, see Littman and Rosen (1950). How far these debates can illuminate the relations and differences between 'holistic' and 'atomistic' approaches to evidence is a question that must be reserved for some future occasion.
74   Discussed *TEBW* 180–3.
75   Tillers and Schum (1988), 921–2, 937ff., citing Zadeh (1965, 1983).
76   One version of this view is that, in some contexts thinking can get in the way of good judgement. This idea has been convincingly applied in respect of some sports (e.g. Galwey, 1975) and such matters as facial recognition. It is not implausible to suggest that similar considerations apply to making judgements about past events and that it sometimes pays to trust one's intuitions. This is a familiar issue in psychology, but I am not aware of any detailed research relating to specifically legal contexts. A suggestive analogy from ethics is John Rawls's notion of 'reflective equilibrium' (Rawls, 1977).
77   Bennett and Feldman (1981).
78   Terence Anderson suggests that this passage underrates the value of Wigmorean analysis for the practitioner:

The Wigmorean method is a practical tool, perhaps the only feasible tool, for testing a story for its weaknesses. The constraints of time and cost may ordinarily preclude a complete analysis of all the possibilities of the evidence in a case such as Bywaters and Thompson. Nonetheless, the discussion in chapter 8 suggests that the use of Wigmorean analysis to audit and test the key theories would have sharpened counsels' arguments and caused them to revise their stories.
For example, once counsel for Edith provisionally settled upon the fantasy and broken chain theories or some combination of the two as the most likely defence theories for Edith, microscopic analysis of the key points of the evidence that bears upon these theories becomes feasible and would probably have produced a more coherent theory

and story at trial. So too, once the 'tea-room conspiracy' is seen as a likely theory for the prosecution, 'atomistic' analysis of the 'don't forget what we talked in the tea-room' passage in relation to the other evidence becomes both feasible and practically called for.

Finally, the argument about the knife illustrates the point further. The legal structure of the case, under any view, made premeditation a crucial *probandum* for Bywaters and made the presence or absence of a planned attack critical for Edith. The potential significance of the fact that Freddy was carrying a knife at the time of the killing should have been apparent to counsel on both sides from the outset. The use of atomistic analysis early in the matter would have, to use Schum's term, abductively generated additional evidence that counsel for Bywaters (or the Crown) might have sought. For example, were any of Bywaters's shipmates aware that he carried a knife? The answer would presumably have been easily learned. Had it been learned, the necessary witnesses would have been called by one side or the other and the matter would not have been left to depend on speculative generalizations. (Personal communication to the author).

79 See *Analysis*, ch. 5 (especially the discussion of 'Trial Books').
80 Williams (1973) discussed above, 259 n. 121.

10

The Way of the Baffled Medic: Prescribe First; Diagnose Later – If At All

A Communication from Mr Bentham concerning Recent Proposals for Reform of the Law of Evidence

There are no reliable figures on the question whether 'Benthamite' is considered by the majority of readers of this essay to be a eulogistic or a dyslogistic term. It is accordingly hard to judge whether those who are currently applying this appellative to the recent Eleventh Report of the Criminal Law Revision Committee[1] are doing so in order to give it a spurious authority[2] or to undermine it through guilt by association.[3] The purpose of this note is to draw the attention of both factions to an account of a recent visit to Mr Bentham in his small hide-out somewhere in London. When communing with the distinguished jurist his visitor, whose integrity and perspicuity are unquestionable, noticed an expression of pain on Mr Bentham's visage when it was suggested that he was considered to be a progenitor of this document. Mr Bentham refused to give an explanation (which would in any case constitute inadmissible hearsay until he gets his way),[4] so we are left to speculate as to what the reasons for his distaste might have been.

Mr Bentham is explicitly cited only twice in the *Report*. First, a remark of his relating to the silence of the accused *coram judice* is quoted in favour of putting pressure on suspected persons to break their silence when being interrogated in police stations and like places – institutions which, it may be noted, are more sophisticated today than they were at the time the words in question were written.[5] Secondly, a passage from 'Swear Not at All' is misquoted,[6] but with apparent approval, in favour of the proposition that an oath should be replaced by an undertaking to tell the truth. However, the Committee decided to follow in the footsteps of the Law Reform Committee in making no recommendation for change on the ground that they regarded 'the question as a social rather than a legal one'.[7] One may confidently surmise that this distinction would be puzzling to Mr Bentham, for the question of abolishing the oath in civil or criminal proceedings would appear to fall no less within the province of the science of legislation than any other of the questions of reform considered by these august bodies of lawyers. There is no evidence to suggest that on this occasion the Criminal Law Revision Committee was indulging in false modesty in order to support a conservative position.[8] Better then to ask why, if the committee felt unqualified to deal with this issue of legislative policy, it did not question its own credentials in respect of the other issues of policy before it and decide to make no recommendations at all? By so doing it might have set a precedent calculated to increase the happiness not only of the newly discovered professional criminal class, but also of many others – not least those who for one reason or another have to plough through mystifying documents of this kind.

There is thus little direct evidence to support calling the *Report* 'Benthamite'. We must therefore dig deeper, but the time permitted for digging is short. The committee spent eight years over its work. At the end it was able to announce that 'criminals are far more sophisticated than they used to be'.[9] Progress, it seems has not affected our police in comparable fashion. It was rumoured[10] that our benevolent Government, anxious to protect us from this newly discovered threat (and solicitous for the interests of those who might waste their energies in opposing a *fait accompli*), had decided to enact the Committee's proposals with unusual despatch. More recently it has been rumoured that it is now proposed not to enact them at all, so that we can look forward to debate on the *Report* in perpetuity. Alas, our Editor is less flexible than our Government and his deadline has remained unchanged. Accordingly our search for 'Benthamite' characteristics in the *Report* has been rather hurried and there may be hidden affinities which have been overlooked.

A first reading of the *Report* suggests that, apart from the two explicit citations mentioned above, there are some further arguments which may have been borrowed directly from Mr Bentham, though without acknowledgement. The Committee's discussion of the sporting notion of fairness in criminal trials is strongly reminiscent of his account of 'the foxhunter's reason'.[11] Secondly, the Benthamite thesis that *Silence is tantamount to confession*, at least in the case of *non-responsion judicial*, is accepted with some modifications in the *Report*.[12] The Committee further invoke arguments in common currency, such as the advantages of the principle of orality in criminal trials[13] and the presumption of innocence,[14] which were also invoked by Mr Bentham, but he would no more lay exclusive claim to these than he would accept the whole *pot pourri* of arguments good, bad and indifferent, adduced in the *Report* in favour of its varied conclusions. In respect of *arguments* the crucial difference between Mr Bentham and the Committee is that the former's views are based on a relatively simple, coherent, articulated Theory of Evidence, whereas the latter's views are not.

This difference is illustrated by examination of the extent to which there is *coincidence of conclusions* between Mr Bentham's proposals made in the conditions of the early nineteenth century and those put forward by the Committee in the rather different circumstances of today. As is well known, some of his proposals have been incorporated into English Law over the years, without going as far as he would have wished, and at some considerable cost in complication. On the other hand in many important respects his advice has not

334 The Way of the Baffled Medic

yet been taken. The Committee's recommendations in some ways take the slow process of reform a step further in roughly the same direction as he indicated: the restriction of the right of silence *coram judice*, the extension of the competence and compellability of spouses, the extension of the admissibility of confessions, of certain types of hearsay statements, and of other relevant evidence previously excluded on grounds that it was unreliable or prejudicial are some of the specific proposals which move in the direction advocated by Mr. Bentham in his own day. For the most part on these matters he went further than the Committee, for his basic position was that there are only two grounds when exclusion of evidence is always proper: (1) when it is not pertinent; (2) when it is superfluous.[15] Otherwise all relevant evidence should be admitted *coram judice* unless this would be productive of preponderant vexation, expense or delay. His differences with the Committee would appear to be that their proposals, compared to his, in respect of the exclusionary rules are half-measures, which produce unnecessary complication, and which make too many concessions to the idea that unreliability should *per se* be a ground for exclusion. There are some specific differences between the Committee's and Mr Bentham's proposals: for instance, the Committee recommends the continued protection of communications between lawyer and client and no extension of the privilege to priests, journalists or psychiatrists.[16] Mr Bentham, on the other hand, favours extending the privilege to priests[17] and withdrawing it from the lawyer–client relationship.[18] His views on the position of journalists and psychiatrists are not known. Such differences are not fundamental and it can be safely concluded that there is a reasonably close affinity between Mr Bentham and the Committee on the situation *coram judice* – at least the similarities are more important than the differences.

It would thus be *quibbling* to deny that some of the Committee's main recommendations are Benthamite in tendency. But two important caveats must be entered in respect of the recommendations taken as a whole. The first relates to those parts of the *Report* which primarily concern extra-judicial matters.[19] Perhaps the most controversial of the Committee's proposals are those which would lead to the abandonment of the requirements for the two types of police caution and, related to this, to restrict greatly a suspect's 'right to silence' during interrogation.[20] The conditions under which interrogation is carried out today are not comparable with those in the early nineteenth century; Mr Bentham was more concerned with proceedings *coram judice*, than with pre-trial, but his discussion of extra-judicial examinations, confessions and silence suggest that it is far from clear that he would approve these recommendations of the Committee in the conditions of today. In particular the Committee's rejection of proposals that interrogation of suspects should be conducted before magistrates appears to be contrary to the general thrust of Mr Bentham's theory.[21] For to him the best security against abuse – the primary mischief feared by the opponents of these particular proposals – was publicity.[22] As he wrote in another context:

Without publicity, all other checks are fruitless: in comparison of publicity, all other checks are of small account. It is to publicity, more than to everything else put together, that the English system of procedure owes its being the least bad system as yet extant, instead of being the worst.[23]

It is the arcane and unchecked nature of the contemporary system of extra-judicial interrogation which is providing the single most important cause for concern about this part of the *Report*.

The second caveat is too complex to be pursued here. It is debatable to what extent Mr Bentham's Theory of Evidence is dependent on radical changes in the administration of justice, exemplified by the Natural System of Procedure and the doctrine of the single judge.[24] In other words, Mr Bentham's teachings on Evidence arguably postulate a system of judicature in which there would be few chances that the ignorant, slow-witted or feckless innocent would be in danger of being entrapped by a complex technical system. In so far as some of the safeguards which would be removed by the Committee were designed to protect such persons and in so far as there is a complex division of responsibility between police, judge, jury and others it is debatable whether the postulates of Mr Bentham's Theory of Evidence are satisfied. In short, a complex, technical system of judicature breeds technical safeguards. Change one, change both.[25]

Two strangely used citations, some scatter-shot arguments and a number of half-measures supply strong, but not conclusive, evidence that the *Report* as a whole deserves the appellative 'Benthamite'. The matter is not yet settled beyond reasonable doubt. What other factors might explain its confident use?[26] An admirer of Mr Bentham has suggested that it may be that *Love of Gadgetry* established the crucial link between the Committee and its imputed ancestor. For the *Report* recommends, subject to certain conditions, the admissibility of evidence of statements produced by computers and, on an experimental basis, the limited use of tape-recorders in interrogation of suspects.[27] The Committee was rather more cautious than Mr Bentham might have been expected to be in their attitude to these new-fangled gadgets, and their conceptions of an 'experiment' appear to be rather different from his; nonetheless it would indeed be quibbling to deny the label 'Benthamite' to these two important recommendations.

The link is established, the problem resolved. Why then the look of pain on Mr Bentham's face? Surely he of all people would accept that partial implementation of his proposals would be a lesser evil than their total rejection. One suggestion is that the *composition* of the Committee might have displeased him. While it is unlikely that he would have entrusted such a task to a body composed entirely of lawyers – indeed, it is doubtful whether, in his own day, he would have recommended the inclusion of any[28] – he is ever mindful of the influence of place and time in matters of legislation.[29] Today the *sinister interest* of lawyers in increasing their business is perhaps less of a threat than it was when he wrote. There are few signs of the direct influence of such sinister interest in the *Report*: indeed, it has been pointed out that the Committee missed a golden opportunity for increasing the work of the profession when they failed to recommend that a suspect should be entitled to insist on the presence of a solicitor of his choice during interrogation. Nor did they appear to think that there was occasion to recommend that the system of representation of accused in criminal proceedings was in need of extension.[30]

If any doubt should remain as to the Committee's disinterest, it can be set at rest by pointing out that in the process of simplifying the law for the sake of laymen, and especially jurors, it has drafted a Bill which few lawyers will find easy to understand. They have thus struck a double blow against the sinister interest of lawyers: whereas in the past this sinister interest has operated by maintaining a system of law so mysterious and complicated that *only lawyers could claim to understand it*, the Committee has reversed the process by inventing a device which, it seems, only laymen can understand. Thus they set out to demystify law through mystification of lawyers: 'It should be emphasized that provisions designed to simplify a complicated system of law cannot always themselves be expressed in simple terms.'[31] This important new doctrine of Simplification through Complexity must be welcomed by all who, like Mr Bentham, have the interest of undermining the legal profession at heart. Thus, while there might be grounds for asserting that the Committee was not well qualified to perceive the exact nature of the social mischiefs that reforms in the law of evidence might cause or cure (on which more later), there is little evidence to suggest that the sinister interests of *Judge and Co.* have substantially influenced this document.

Another possible reason for Mr Bentham's displeasure is that the *Report* exemplifies an approach to law reform which has seemingly become more common in recent times than it was in his heyday. For in his *Book of Fallacies* he did not consider worth mentioning what he might have termed The Way of the Baffled Medic: 'Prescribe First; Diagnose Later – If At All'. It is a fallacy much invoked by modern legislators for whom 'law reform' and the maximization of human happiness are quite unrelated activities. The *Report* itself gives hardly any indication of what precise social mischiefs the proposed reform of the Law of Criminal Evidence might help to resolve, what is the scale of these mischiefs, and the calculations on which it based its assumption, and it makes no *explicit* claim that the sum of human happiness would be increased rather than diminished – or indeed affected at all – by its proposals.

However, since publication of the *Report* much public debate has centred on which of a number of diagnoses best fits the announced prescriptions. Three runners lead the field at the time of writing: (1) The Police Morale Problem;[32] (2) The New Criminal Class Problem;[33] and (3) The Keeping the Right Wing Happy Problem.[34] The race is not yet over, for it will continue for many years even if the proposed legislation were to be enacted, but at the time of going to press the third of these runners had established a substantial lead.[35]

It is not only the *nature* of the problem, but its *scale* which is in question. For how without facts and figures can the Felicific Calculus operate? In a little known passage on the Poor Laws Mr Bentham compared our nation to that of a country whose inhabitants could not count beyond three. He continued:

Catch yahmee? – how many places of worship? is a question that, in a Turkish town upon the Danube (which being marked as a village in the map had surprised me by its magnitude) I took the liberty of addressing to the great man of the place – the Chief Officer of the Province. – *Chuck* – with a significant toss of the head – *Chuck* was the answer – *plenty*. This was all that the Chancellor of the Exchequer of Ruszug [?] knew, or seemed to think it worth any body's while to know, about the matter. The degree of information ... is unfortunately not peculiar to Turkish ground. Come back to England – address yourself to those who undertake to feed the hungry – feed them in a mass – feed them in a new style – and as it were with *manna* from the *clouds* – ask them how many mouths there are to feed – *Chuck* is still the answer: – *chuck* is the sum of knowledge.[36]

Come to our legislators in 1972 – ask them how many sophisticated criminals? – Chuck. How many cases contested by sophisticated criminals? – Chuck. How many ignorant, feckless, cowed or slow-witted accused are unrepresented? How many cases of improper methods of interrogation? How many cases of hardened criminals refusing to answer questions at all? What are the effects of the disciplinary principle?[37] On every factual assumption, on every item of information relevant to diagnosis of the problem, *Chuck, Chuck, Chuck* is still the answer.

Yet doubt lingers on. The diagnosis is defective, but the measures, though half, are Benthamite in substance. Why then the displeasure? One last possibility remains: that the object of our jurist's distaste was not the *Report* alone, but the whole debate of which the *Report* forms but a part. Permeating that debate is a view, which Mr Bentham would unhesitatingly reject, that the whole subject is not susceptible to rational discourse. The Committee attributed this view to all who submitted 'evidence' to it;[38] it dismissed these submissions as being based on faith and then in its own words 'we have ... necessarily gone our own way in deciding what to recommend',[39] which, as has been seen, is the Way of the Baffled Medic. Not to be outdone members of the Government first conveyed the impression that it had made up its mind *before* the public was given its brief chance to debate the *Report*, then reversed their position without giving reasons. Lemming-like 'liberals' leapt with alacrity into the trap which had been set for them, first by resorting to the Old Woman's Argument,[40] and secondly by espousing their own counterpart of the Way of the Baffled Medic – that is to say the Radical Chic Fallacy: Criticize First, Read Later – If at All. Sympathizers with the police invoked a novel version of the Foxhunter's Argument: Unfair to Hunters! On every side the forces of unreason marshalled for battle. Small wonder Mr Bentham frowned.

NOTES

This essay was written as a contribution to the debate on the eleventh report of the Criminal Law Revision Committee in 1972–3 (op. cit., n.1), and published by Butterworth in 12 *JSPTL* (NS) 348 (1973). The Committee's main recommendations were not adopted at the time and the debate has continued on and off since then. Although there have been some significant changes in both law and practice, the central issues are still almost permanent items on the political agenda in England and elsewhere; Bentham continues to be quoted out of context in discussions of 'the right of silence'; and positions which I support (on the basis of the twin principles of non-conviction of the innocent and protection of all participants in litigation against mistreatment) still tend to be backed by a mixture of good and bad arguments. On Bentham's views on these issues and my reactions, see *TEBW, passim* (especially index under silence and fallacies) and Twining (1988), 1536–9. See also Lewis (1988).

1   Cmnd. 4991 (1972), hereinafter referred to as (the) *Report*. During the debate on the *Report* in the House of Lords on 14 February 1973, the Lord Chancellor, the Lord Hailsham, spoke as follows: 'I was reading only the other day (thinking of this debate as I did so) an article in the current number of the *Modern Law Review* by Professor Hart on the relevance of Bentham to present day law. He represented Bentham as a prophet of rationalising law, or, as he put it, the demystification of law. I like to think of the Lord Chancellor's function like that – an enemy of jargon and jargonisation, a foe of imposter terms which cloud and fog the windscreen of clear thinking and prevent us from seeing the road ahead. I could not help noticing, incidentally, that at the end of his article Professor Hart came to the conclusion that the recommendations of the Criminal Law Revision Committee are indeed Benthamite, both in spirit and in substance, and that the recommendations which have caused so much controversy, and were recently condemned by the Bar Council, were largely recommended by him in 1828. In this connection he specifically mentioned some of the controversial recommendations in relation to hearsay, self-incrimination and the so-called right of silence that have been mentioned this afternoon', 338 HL Deb. (14 Feb.) 1584–5 (1973). The paper referred to was Professor Hart's Chorley Lecture on 'Bentham and the Demystification of the Law' (1973).
2   J. Bentham, *Book of Fallacies*, Part I, 'Fallacies of Authority', ch. I, 'Appeal to Authority, in what cases fallacious', II *Works*, 391. Unless otherwise stated all citations are to this edition.
3   Imputations of suspicious connections – (*noscitur ex sociis*), id., 416.
4   It must be conceded that there appears to be no decided case, not even from the United States, directly in point on the question whether evidence of a grimace respecting pedigree by a person already deceased is admissible under current doctrine respecting hearsay.
5   *Report*, para. 31.
6   Id., para. 280, cp. V *Works*, 192 (quotation attenuated).
7   *Report*, para. 279.
8   For arguments available to the Committee to sustain this position see *Book of Fallacies*, esp. Hobgoblin Argument (op. cit., 418), and Fallacies of Delay (id., 430ff.). It also appears from the *Report* that, in the view of our legislator, the Time is Not Yet Ripe for codification of Criminal Evidence (see paras. 12, 25), cf. Snail's Pace Argument, II *Works*, 433.
9   *Report*, para. 21.
10   E.g. *Sunday Times*, 6 August 1972.
11   *Report*, esp. para. 27, VII *Works*, 454. The Committee was less forthright on The Old Woman's Reason (hard on the guilty), id., 452.
12   *Report*, esp. para 31ff., 102ff. Bentham, VII *Works*, 25. Mr Bentham's arguments on this matter are complex. It is probably fair to say that he placed more emphasis than the Committee on the differences between the interpretation to be put on non-responsion judicial and non-responsion extra-judicial; in respect of the latter he entered some very important caveats on the doctrine 'silence is tantamount to confession', see esp. *A Treatise on Judicial Evidence*, 164–8 (English trans., 1825).
13   Para. 239.
14   E.g. para. 27.
15   *Treatise*, op. cit., bk. VII, esp. 230–1, *Rationale of Judicial Evidence*, bk. IX, esp. VII *Works*, 335ff. See above 214 n. 53.
16   Paras. 272–6.
17   VI *Works*, 98–9; VII id. 366–8.
18   VI id., 99–100; VII, 473–9.
19   See above, n. 12.
20   *Report*, paras. 28ff.
21   Id., para. 47. *Treatise*, op. cit., 161–4.

22 E.g. *Treatise*, op. cit., 163–5.
23 iv *Works*, 317, discussed by Halévy, (1955). M. Halévy's work contains the best secondary account of Mr Bentham's views on judicature, id., 376–403.
24 See Halévy, op. cit., n. 23.
25 Professor H. L. A. Hart challenges this suggestion (1982), 37n., on the ground that Bentham explicitly considers the right of silence in unreformed systems and concludes that its weakening effects on good laws is 'a greater evil than the conviction of greater numbers of offenders against bad laws or of innocent persons to which its abolition might lead' (citing vii *Works*, 454, 457, 522). I defer to his reading of Bentham in respect of silence *coram judice*, but would still maintain that an argument in favour of technical safeguards for suspects pre-trial, absent the safeguard of publicity, can be developed from Bentham's premises. Such safeguards, it is suggested, can be justified on both utilitarian and non-utilitarian grounds in some contexts.
26 No evidence has been forthcoming to suggest that *ignorance* of our jurist's views might have contributed to the association of his name with the *Report*. It is presumed that no modern lawyer would confidently use the term 'Benthamite' in relation to Evidence who has not at least read and carefully digested the 1,028 pages of *The Rationale of Judicial Evidence*, edited by Mr J. S. Mill and so compactly reproduced by John Bowring.
27 Paras. 48–51, 259.
28 vi and vii *Works, passim*.
29 Esp. i *Works*, 171ff.
30 E.g. para. 21.
31 Para. 25.
32 Diagnosis: there is a serious problem of police morale; the police think that easing the task of prosecution will boost morale. Prescription: keep the patient happy by giving him what he wants. Liberal Counter-Argument: The Police Image Problem. Diagnosis: public confidence in the police is seriously threatened at the present time. Prescription: retain the rules of evidence as they are. Committee: esp. para. 57 (cp. para. 52, minority arguments): There is no problem. See *Book of Fallacies*, op. cit., 431 (*ad quietem*).
33 Alias: The Mark Fallacy (as reported *Guardian*, 21 June 1972). Diagnosis: There is a new class (of unspecified size) of sophisticated criminals who abuse (with unspecified frequency) the safeguards designed to protect the (uncounted, countless?) weak, stupid, illiterate, spontaneous or slow-witted accused. Prescription: remove safeguards for all accused.
34 An ineffable problem, not openly discussed by the diagnosticians.
35 It has been plausibly argued that the *Way of the Baffled Medic*, as applied to the game of Law Reform, is in conformity with utility: the *intense* joys of prescription are outweighed by the almost infinite *duration* of speculative diagnosis. If diagnosis were to precede prescription the more *intense* pleasure would be reduced in respect of *propinquity* and *certainty*; with prescription first, utility is maximized. This argument is based on the as yet untested assumption that Law Reform affects the happiness only of the players and spectators of the game.
36 Bentham MSS, CXLIX (University College): 242–3. The passage continues:

So much for real conversation: – now for an imaginary dialogue. *John* – Come, Mary – the children be hungry – Come, bustle about, get 'em their dinner, Mary. *Mary* – Dinner? – Aye, that's what I wull – But, look ye d'ye see, how many be there of them, John – I say – how many children have us two got? – For my part, I don't know, not I – Dost thee know?
Were a dialogue of this stamp to be produced upon the theatre, and the scene laid in a Cottage, it would be spurned at as unnatural. In the humblest – in the worst-informed line of life – ignorance (it would be said) does not sink thus low. Among *individuals*, such language would be too silly for the merest simpleton. But *government* has never held – has never enabled itself to hold – any other.

37 *Report, passim.* The contrast between the way of the Baffled Medic and a more empirical
    approach is nicely illustrated by comparing and contrasting para. 68 of the *Report* with
    Dallin Oaks, 'Studying the Exclusionary Rule in Search and Seizure' (1970). Oaks and
    the Committee reach similar conclusions by different routes.
38 Para. 22
39 Para. 23.
40 Above, n. 11.

11

Rethinking Evidence

Introduction

When I took up Evidence, it was with the express intention of treating it as a case-study of the problems of 'contextualizing' any established field of law. The central question was: What might be involved in studying evidence within a broadened conception of law as a discipline? One of the lessons of the history of the American Realist Movement was that those who had tried to develop broad, inter-disciplinary approaches to the study of law, including 'the law-in-action', had failed to construct coherent alternatives to the law-as-rules orthodoxy that they sought to replace. The toughness of that orthodoxy was in part due to the fact that it was compact, coherent and manageable. At least, it seemed to be so. Realists, such as Holmes, Cook, Llewellyn and Frank, opened up a range of potentially fruitful lines of enquiry, but they failed to confront, let alone resolve, the Pandora's Box problem.[1] Accordingly a major aim of the project was to tackle the problem of coherence as part of a realist or contextual approach by developing a framework for an inter-disciplinary perspective on Evidence, Proof and Fact-finding in Law. A second concern was to clarify what it means to claim to be 'realistic' in this context, a question which seemed especially pertinent to an enquiry into the determination and construction of 'facts'.

I was fortunate both in my choice of subject and in my timing. For most of this century Evidence had the image among English lawyers of being a narrow, highly technical, often frustratingly unreal subject which was mainly the concern of judges and practising barristers. It was generally viewed as a clear example of 'lawyers' law'. I soon found that Bentham was much nearer the mark when he wrote: 'The field of evidence is no other than the field of knowledge.'[2] I hope that some of the fascination of its many ramifications has been communicated in these essays.

When in the early 1970s I first took up the subject, it seemed to be a rather neglected field.[3] There were few signs that we were on the verge of an explosion of interest in a variety of quarters. I knew little of rhetoric or epistemology or probability theory or witness psychology or forensic science and I had only a dim perception of their immediate relevance. There was almost no mention of them in the standard texts on the law of evidence. I had not even conceived of conversation analysis or semiotics or narratology or critical legal studies or fuzzy logic or expert systems. Mirjan Damaska's first path-breaking contribution was published in 1973; Jonathan Cohen's *The Probable and the Provable* appeared in 1977. David Schum started to contribute to legal periodicals only in 1979. The Wolfson Law-and-Psychology workshops organized by Sally Lloyd-Bostock also began in the late seventies. Peter Tillers's herculean revision of volume 1 of Wigmore's *Treatise* came out in 1983. I first encountered Sir Richard Eggleston in the late 1970s, Terry Anderson in 1981 and Philip Dawid in 1983/4. All of these individuals and many others started their work almost entirely independently of each other. But by the early 1970s we found ourselves to be part of an expanding international and inter-disciplinary network of scholars with converging interests in a field that had lain dormant for most of this century.

This explosion of new ideas and fresh lines of enquiry produced excitement, bewilderment and frequent temptations to dilettantism. It also sharpened the focus of my project. The claim that one was trying to develop a mapping theory naturally provoked the question: a map of what, for whom, to what ends? The advent of the 'New Evidence Scholarship'[4] provided a fairly obvious answer. For there was a clear need for a broad framework for charting the relationships between each of these new developments and longer-established lines of enquiry. A mapping theory could supply not only a framework, but might also provide some guidance to specialists from other disciplines about the nature, the extent and the pitfalls of the unfamiliar terrain on to which they had wandered. Furthermore it might shed fresh light on old questions and identify new or neglected questions worth exploring. Thus providing a general overview of a large and expanding area promised to be a modest contribution to the immodest enterprise of shifting the balance of attention in academic law.

The purpose of this essay is to make explicit the general perspective that has informed the earlier chapters and to examine its potential value and limitations as a contribution to understanding law. This will also serve to draw together the main themes of the book and indicate some possible directions for further exploration.

The basic elements of this perspective have already been introduced and some potential applications indicated. It has been suggested that it is illuminating to view questions about evidence and proof as questions about the processing and uses of information in important decisions in litigation. Information in litigation (hereafter IL) is substituted for 'judicial evidence' or 'evidence, proof and fact-finding' (EPF)[5] as the basic organizing concept for an area of study that deserves a more central place in the discipline of law than it has occupied until now. The following sections relate this perspective to a particular conception of legal theorizing, elaborate on the basic concepts of IL and consider some of its implications, applications and limitations.

Theorizing about IL

This book is intended as a contribution to Jurisprudence. What is meant by this claim? Jurisprudence can be usefully viewed as the theoretical part of law as a discipline.[6] In this sense it is synonymous with 'legal theory' but is broader than 'legal philosophy'. Theorizing and philosophizing can be seen as intellectual activities concerned with certain kinds of questions. A theoretical question can be defined as one posed at a relatively high level of generality. The most general and abstract kinds of questions are conveniently characterized as 'philosophical'. Somewhat less abstract questions belong to 'middle order theory'. Theoretical discussion also involves considering more or less particular illustrations, implications and applications of general ideas and, conversely, the general implications of particular examples.

Three points are worth stressing about this conception of theorizing as an activity concerned with relatively general questions. First, the main counter-point is between 'general' and 'particular', not between 'theoretical' (or 'academic') and 'practical'. There is no necessary connection or distinction between practical utility and levels of generality.[7] Secondly, particularity and generality are relative matters, as is illustrated by the metaphor of a ladder of abstraction. There are no sharp boundaries between 'philosophical', 'middle order', and 'applied' questions or theories. Such terms are merely broad indicators of positions on a continuum of generality; they are mainly useful because they are vague. As every lawyer should know, healthy discourse involves a constant interaction between relative generality and relative particularity.[8] Thirdly, if theorizing is viewed as an activity concerned with posing, re-posing, criticizing, reflecting on and answering general questions, 'theories' should not be assumed to be the only worthwhile outcomes of the enterprise. Of course, the development or construction of well-crafted theories of different kinds is one of the main functions of theorizing. In this context, 'a theory' refers to a relatively coherent, argued answer or set of answers to a general question or set of questions. But theorizing is concerned with questioning as well as answering; with digging out assumptions and presuppositions; with exploring logical implications, particular applications and other connections; with criticizing, as well as constructing, questions and answers and reasons; with charting relations between lines of enquiry; and with developing methods and tools for theorizing, such as techniques of conceptual clarification or the construction of models and ideal types.

Theorizing serves several different functions within the discipline of law.[9] These 'jobs of jurisprudence' include various kinds of intellectual history; 'high theory' or legal philosophy *stricto sensu*; middle order theorizing, including developing hypotheses for empirical research or working theories for legislators, judges and other participants in legal processes and activities. Other jobs include exploring relations and conducting conversations with neighbouring disciplines ('the lawyer's extraversion')[10] and constructing coherent frames of reference for law as a discipline, for legal discourse generally and for particular sectors, such as theories of contract or criminal law or evidence.

These categories may help to clarify the main purpose of these essays and of this essay in particular. *Theories of Evidence: Bentham and Wigmore* and the first four chapters of this book purport to describe, interpret and evaluate selected aspects of our intellectual heritage in respect of fact-determination in law. Because the primary concern is with contemporary issues, this is not strictly contextual history in the mode of scholars such as Quentin Skinner,[11] but one hopes that it may suggest some fruitful lines of enquiry for historians. In examining and interpreting one sector of our heritage of evidentiary texts I have tried to articulate their basic assumptions and presuppositions in a form that facilitates critical examination and indicates potential points of disagreement or difference from contemporary points of view.[12]

Some central themes of these historical forays and of the later essays bear directly on philosophical questions about reasoning, rationality and knowledge; about the nature of 'fact' (and fantasy) and how far some of our inherited concepts in this area stand up to critical scrutiny in the light of 'sceptical' challenges of various kinds. There has clearly been a philosophical dimension to these explorations, but they have never been only or even mainly philosophical, both because of the localization of these issues in specific legal contexts and because of the 'gravitational pull' of the concerns of different kinds of participants who want, even from theorists, at least general guidance on their activities in the form of strategies for action or working theories of legislation, adjudication, argumentation and so on. In practice the discipline of law tends to be participant-oriented because its primary clientele consists of actual or intending participants in the world of affairs.[13] Even those who call themselves 'legal philosophers' tend, quite understandably, to operate at a less abstract level than general philosophy. These essays are no exception. One result is that they draw on philosophy far more than they contribute to it.

The jurist John Austin made a useful distinction between 'particular' (or national) and 'general' (or comparative) jurisprudence: the former is confined to a single legal system, the latter is not.[14] The distinction is, of course, relative since general jurisprudence can be limited to two or more legal systems or to 'modern' or 'Western' legal systems; or it can make some claim to approximate to universality.[15]

In the picture of legal theorizing outlined here the great bulk of both general and particular jurisprudence falls within the sphere of 'middle order' theorizing because even quite general questions and concerns relate to specifically legal contexts and hence fall outside the sphere of philosophy *stricto sensu*.[16] One corollary of this is that 'middle order theory' covers a rather wide spectrum of levels of generality including, for example, a general theory of legislation such as that of Jeremy Bentham, a general theory of common law adjudication, such as that of Ronald Dworkin,[17] and a theory of American appellate court judging, such as that of Karl Llewellyn.[18] The breadth of the range of middle order theorizing is directly relevant here. The main questions and conclusions in the preceding essays can be interpreted as ranging over many levels of generality. For example, the historical thesis about the Rationalist Tradition is expressly confined to leading secondary Anglo-American writings on evidence over approximately two centuries (1754–1958), for that was the limit of the sample.

However, the claims for the 'ideal type' of Rationalist thought are more general, for it is suggested that it is a useful tool for analysing all common law discourse about 'judicial evidence' (including, for example, judicial decisions and reform debates) and, possibly, similar discourses in modern civilian and socialist legal systems.[19]

Again 'modified Wigmorean analysis' was presented as a useful intellectual tool for trial lawyers and triers of fact at various stages in litigation; with appropriate adjustments, it can also be used by detectives, historians and intelligence analysts, or indeed anyone concerned with drawing inferences from data.[20] It is a highly transferable tool of analysis.[21] Significantly its transferability is due to its being abstracted to some extent from the complex context of trial practice: it is easier to learn the technique if one postulates a world of free proof, a particular stage in litigation and a stable body of data. For just such reasons, however useful it may be, it can at best be only part of the armoury of a competent practitioner; on its own it does not provide the basis for a rounded working theory for trial lawyers or triers of fact.[22]

One further example, which will resurface in this essay, concerns the law of evidence. In chapter 6 Thayer's interpretation of the Anglo-American law of evidence was examined in the light of major developments since his death and the broadening of perspective involved in adopting a total process model of litigation. The thesis was explicitly restricted to modern English Law, though it seems likely that the main points would apply to most common law systems; ironically, the United States is the most likely deviant because of the survival of the civil jury trial and a rather pugnacious interpretation of adversary procedure.[23] My purpose was to present an overview and interpretation – a way of looking at this branch of law as it stands today – in order to help law students, foreign lawyers and others to make sense of it as a whole. That essay is not intended as a substitute for detailed exposition of what is, in parts, still a complex and technical subject. The main conclusion, that the logic of proof and the rules of evidence should be treated as a single subject, follows Thayer and Wigmore, but goes further in suggesting that these rules regularly bear on all decisions in litigation, not only or mainly in contested jury trials or even contested trials generally.[24]

Chapters 7–10 can be read as a series of forays which sought to explore some general themes in more specific or concrete ways. As such they are exercises in applied theorizing. Before considering the nature of an IL perspective and some of its potential implications and applications, it may be helpful to take stock by restating the main conclusions that have been suggested so far by these diverse explorations. This is done in the next section.

Taking stock

The main conclusions of the preceding essays may be restated as follows.

1   The study of fact-determination in legal processes is a large subject which deserves to be given a more central place in the discipline of law than it was accorded in the expository tradition.

2   The common law has been unusual in treating 'Evidence' as a distinct field of law, the subject of specialized codes, treatises, courses and experts. However, the subject has been narrowly conceived because (a) the Law of Evidence has often been treated as co-extensive with the subject of Evidence; and (b) the Law of Evidence has itself been narrowly conceived as consisting mainly of rules of positive law dealing primarily with questions of admissibility of evidence in contested trials.

3   Specialized Anglo-American scholarship and discourse about Evidence have tended to be based on a single, relatively coherent set of assumptions about adjudication and what is involved in rational fact-determination in this context:

(a)   These assumptions are largely rooted in post-Enlightenment thought, here characterized as optimistic rationalism.

(b)   Nearly all specialized Anglo-American writers on Evidence from Gilbert (1754) to Cross (1958) have conformed more or less exactly to the 'ideal type' of the Rationalist Tradition. Further research may be expected to reveal more deviants in respect of adjudication (Model I) than rational proof (Model II).

(c)   The central concepts and distinctions in the Rationalist Tradition – rectitude of decision, materiality, relevance, admissibility, weight/cogency, inference, probability, presumptions, and burdens and standards of proof – have been the subject of highly sophisticated analysis and development, which in many respects may not be matched in any other discipline.

(d)   The notion of rectitude of decision embodies values that can be expressed in terms of three *concepts* – truth, reason and expletive justice – that are almost universally held to represent the 'rational core' of adjudication. However, the particular *conceptions* of truth, justice and reason adopted or assumed by most writers in the tradition are regularly contested in philosophy.

(e)   Rectitude of decision and accuracy in fact-determination are central values not only of adjudication, but of nearly all official decisions. Adjudicative decisions and the logic of proof may provide a useful paradigm for considering questions about rationality in respect of structured decision making of all kinds.

(f)   By acknowledging that the law is concerned with probabilities not certainties, 'open system reasoning' (induction) rather than 'closed system reasoning' (deduction), and the balancing of rectitude of decision against competing social values the Rationalist Tradition created a tough and resilient conceptual framework that accommodated internal disagreements and has powerful defences against at least crude attack from the outside. However, questions arise as to how far the Rationalist model fits comfortably with:
(1)   adversarial as well as inquisitorial models of procedure;
(2)   non-utilitarian theories of process values or procedural rights;
(3)   holistic as opposed to atomistic conceptions of rationality;

(4) theories of litigation which depict it as an extremely complex form of social process which neither in respect of design or actual operation can be said to have a single direct end.

4 Specialized evidence writing has remained relatively isolated, despite the recognition of the problematic nature in many contexts of sharp distinctions between evidence and procedure, evidence and substantive law, fact and law, fact and value and fact and opinion. For certain purposes it is justifiable to abstract questions of fact and evidentiary issues for separate treatment, for example a code or statute on evidence, 'questions of fact' as a means of allocating roles (at first instance or on appeal) or for constructing or analysing arguments or research into the reliability of certain kinds of evidence or sources of evidence. However, sensitivity to the general context and the problematic nature of such distinctions is vital.

5 Specialized writing about the law of evidence became artificially segregated from adjacent fields by the end of the nineteenth century. This, combined with a rule-oriented, jury-trial conception of the subject, has certain benefits in respect of sophisticated and detailed treatment of particular topics. However, the costs have included:

(a) relative isolation from intellectual developments in adjacent fields;
(b) fragmentation of other lines of enquiry bearing on fact-determination, e.g. forensic science, the logic of proof, witness psychology, decision theory;
(c) neglect of important topics, for example, matters not covered by formal 'rules' (e.g. evaluation of evidence); the impact and shadow of the Law of Evidence on pre-trial and other decisions; fact-determination post-trial and in tribunals and non-jury trials; standards for non-adjudicative decisions involving fact-determination; and, until recently, neglect of fundamental theoretical questions;
(d) distorted perceptions of particular phenomena, e.g. confessions; standards for decision; the consequences of misidentification; the extra-judicial significance of the presumption of innocence; the latent functions of particular institutions, processes and norms (e.g. police interviewing as recruitment; the symbolic aspects of the right to silence).

6 The picture presented of our heritage of scholarship and learning about fact-determination, when viewed from a broader perspective, is of a series of related lines of enquiry that have lost touch with each other. In particular:

(a) Much of the more varied literature on legal processes neither regularly draws upon nor feeds into the specialized literature on Evidence. Sociologically oriented writings on legal processes and institutions tend to draw on different intellectual traditions and are generally more sceptical in tone. On close examination such scepticisms do not present sustained challenges at a fundamental level to the core concepts of the Rationalist Tradition (see above 3 (d)); they do, however, challenge both the optimism of aspirational rationalism and the particular conceptions that it has espoused.

(b)   Some researchers in other disciplines, e.g. witness psychology and to a lesser extent forensic science, have accepted simplistic and outdated models of litigation and fact-determination as the basis for their research.

7

(a)   The classical Thayerite view of the Law of Evidence is that it consists of a series of disparate exceptions to a general principle of free proof. Subject to a few exceptions and modifications this view still holds good provided that 'free proof' is interpreted to mean freedom from artificial constraints on free enquiry and natural reason, and that the 'law' of evidence includes not only mandatory precepts but also general principles, flexible standards, balancing tests and guidelines.

(b)   'Freedom of proof' implies neither arbitrariness nor strong discretion. Most important official decisions in litigation involving fact-determination are supposed to require at least structured discretion. Triers of fact and other official decision makers are subject to an overriding requirement of seeking rectitude of decision. 'Freedom of proof' does not imply freedom from the principles of logic, or principles of political morality or formal norms of substantive law or procedure.

(c)   If a branch of law consists of a series of exceptions to a single principle it makes sense to study the principle before considering the exceptions.

(d)   If Thayer was right in treating the Law of Evidence as being primarily concerned with reasoning and if Wigmore was right in treating the logic of proof as anterior to and more important than the 'Trial Rules' and if the logic of proof and the rules of evidence share the same basic concepts, it makes sense for most purposes of study, exposition and theoretical critique to treat the logic of proof and the rules of evidence as two intimately related parts of the same subject.

8   Modified Wigmorean analysis is a useful intellectual procedure for constructing, reconstructing, clarifying and criticizing arguments about relatively structured questions of fact. It is particularly useful as a device for organizing large 'mixed masses' of data and for subjecting selected phases of an argument to rigorous microscopic analysis. It is less useful in dealing with the evaluation of particular items of evidence or assessment of credibility of witnesses or in contexts where the benefits of meticulous analysis are outweighed by the costs.

9   'Stories' take many forms and play multiple roles in legal discourse. In the context of argumentation by advocates and judges stories are used for legitimate, dubious and clearly illegitimate purposes, judged by conventional criteria of the ethics of advocacy and of legal argumentation. Narrative and analysis are arguably complementary rather than alternative methods of reconstructing and arriving at judgements about past events on the basis of incomplete information.

10   One of the more encouraging developments in doctrinal Evidence scholarship is a renewal of interest in general principles. Some of the most important principles underlying a healthy law of evidence (such as the presumption of innocence, the protection of suspects and other participants in

criminal process from improper or unfair treatment and the non-conviction of
the innocent) should not be conceived solely or even mainly as evidentiary
principles, but as part of a more general framework of principles of political
morality.

'The New Evidence Scholarship' and the need for a mapping theory

In a preliminary stock-taking of our heritage of specialized evidence scholarship
in 1979, I suggested that, despite its many strengths, it was vulnerable to four
main lines of attack: it was too narrowly focused; it was atheoretical; it was
incoherent; and over-concentration on the rules of evidence has led to
'distortions and misperceptions of key evidentiary issues and phenomena'.[25]
Ten years on, I am inclined to modify this general statement in three main
respects.

First, while the charges of being atheoretical and incoherent can still be
levelled with some justification against a great deal of expository writing in the
first seventy-five years of the twentieth century, they do not apply to Bentham or
Thayer or Wigmore or to other less prominent figures, such as Jerome Michael,
or to quite a few nineteenth-century writers. The charge against most
twentieth-century Evidence scholars is more properly one of neglect of a rich
heritage, as is illustrated by the extraordinary disregard of Bentham's *Rationale*
and Wigmore's *Science*.[26]

Secondly, the charge of narrowness also needs qualification. Clearly neither
Bentham nor Wigmore could be accused of being narrowly concerned with
legal doctrine. And Thayer with his historical sensitivity and his concern for
practical reason hardly fits the prototype of the narrow expositor. However, all
three concentrated on *judicial* evidence, and in the case of Thayer, Wigmore
and their followers they treated the contested jury trial as the paradigm of the
arena in which the law of evidence operates and the law reports as the main
repository of their subject. It is symbolically apt that Wigmore should have
referred to the Law of Evidence as 'the Trial Rules'.

Thirdly, as was noted earlier, my criticisms of specialized Evidence scholarship were made at an early stage in the recent revival of interest in Evidence.
They have to large extent been overtaken by events. What, then, is this 'New
Evidence Scholarship'? To what extent is it vulnerable to charges of being
narrow, atheoretical, over-concerned with the rules of evidence, or incoherent?
The first three charges need not detain us: enough has been said to establish
that recent Evidence scholarship has been much concerned with theory, has
ranged far beyond legal doctrine and is informed by an extraordinary range of
disciplines. However, we need to look more closely at the nature and extent of
these new developments before considering whether they are, or can be made,
part of a coherent movement.

In 1986 Professor Richard Lempert, who has himself contributed much to
inter-disciplinary studies in law in general and Evidence in particular, wrote of
'The New Evidence Scholarship' in the following terms: 'Evidence is being
transformed from a field concerned with the articulation of rules to a field

concerned with the process of proof. Wigmore's other great work is being rediscovered, and disciplines outside the law, like mathematics, psychology and philosophy are being plumbed for the guidance they can give.'[27]

Lempert suggested that this new and exciting wave of Evidence scholarship was first stimulated by the advent of the Federal Rules and further developed by reactions to the notorious case of *People* v. *Collins*[28] which led directly to a series of lively, sometimes fierce, debates about the relationship of theories of proof to Bayesianism and other theories of probabilistic inference.

Lempert's statement appears to reflect a widely held American perception of recent developments. From the other side of the Atlantic 'The New Evidence Scholarship' seems to extend much more widely than that.

Undoubtedly, the literature on the Federal Rules and debates about probabilities are important examples of a widespread revival of academic interest in Evidence. But these represent only two strands in a much more varied picture. In recent years I have attended conferences or seminars exclusively devoted to Facts in Law (Durham, 1982), Probabilities and Inference (Boston, 1986), Semiotics and Legal Proof (Messina, 1987), Theoretical Aspects of Evidence and Proof (Oxford, 1988), and Freedom of Proof (Trento, 1988).[29] The excellent series of workshops on Law and Psychology sponsored by Wolfson College, Oxford, since 1979 has devoted a great deal of attention to evidentiary issues. I have been invited, but have not always been able to attend, academic events on Narrative in Culture, Legal Skills, Legal History, Criminal Process, Statistics, Forensic Science, and Expert Systems in Law in all of which issues of inference, proof and fact-determination have featured prominently. The topics covered in the first series of seminars on Evidence in Litigation at the Benjamin N. Cardozo School of Law in New York is similarly wide-ranging.[30] Further evidence of the extent and variety of inter-disciplinary interest in this general area can be found by looking at the publications since 1980 listed in the *select* bibliography at the end of this book. In order to interpret these developments, which seem to be related to each other in quite complex ways, it would be useful to have a map. But can all these different academic enterprises be fitted into a single coherent framework?

I would suggest that the main lines of enquiry that have excited interest in this general area can be subsumed under eight broad headings:

1 doctrinal analysis;
2 procedural scholarship, including Comparative Procedure;
3 sociological or socio-legal (including micro-economic) studies of legal institutions and processes;[31]
4 inference;
5 studies of discourse, including structuralist, deconstructionist, semiotic, rhetorical, narratological and phenomenological approaches;[32]
6 psychological research;
7 scientific and technological developments, including forensic science, computer applications and expert systems;
8 historical enquiries relating to all of the above.

Of course, this list is not comprehensive and it could be presented in different ways. For example, it does not make any specific mention of the philosophical or political dimensions of several of these groups. However, a framework which can accommodate all of these categories should be of some value if it can serve the following purposes: indicate points of connection between seemingly diverse lines of enquiry; subject such enquiries to critical scrutiny as to what questions are and are not being asked and how problems are defined; and provide a broad and realistic context for specialized lines of enquiry.

Before considering how far an IL perspective can serve these ends, it is worth taking a further look at the classics of evidence theory from this point of view. The three leading theorists of judicial evidence in the common law tradition all produced coherent frames of reference for their work. Bentham's theory of evidence was on the negative side an attack on all technicality; on the positive side it was part of a more general thesis about the natural system of procedure on the one hand and ordinary practical reasoning on the other. It is notable both for its internal consistency and for its clear integration with his grand design for all political and legal institutions and with his general philosophical position, of which the principle of utility and the theory of fictions were the main foundations. Internal coherence was and is one of its great strengths.[33] Nevertheless, Bentham's *Rationale* is insufficiently flexible and too rooted in its time to be suitable for present purposes.

Thayer's main concern was to construct a clear vision of the Law of Evidence on the basis of principle. In this he succeeded, at least in respect of admissibility.[34] While most subsequent treatise writers have accepted Thayer's basic ideas, their presentation of the law has tended to be confusing for two main reasons: first, they have generally not dealt explicitly with the principle of free proof, which provides the basis for a coherent view of the subject as a whole. Rather they have tended to focus on admittedly disparate exceptions without first studying the principle. Secondly, they have made some pragmatic concessions to a felt need to include some topics that Thayer had firmly expelled to 'procedure' or 'substantive law', such as the allocation of functions between judge and jury, cross-examination and some presumptions.[35] Such concessions were often quite sensible in the circumstances, but they have tended to be messy and to underline the artificiality of rigidly segregating evidence and procedure. Thayer's framework was also coherent, but it was confined to the Law of Evidence.

Wigmore took an important step in the direction of broadening the study of evidence by his division of the subject into two parts: the Science of Proof (consisting largely of the logical, psychological, scientific and commonsense dimensions of judicial proof) and what he called the Trial Rules. Like Thayer his underlying conception of the subject was to do with reasoning in adjudication: the 'science', and in particular the logic of proof, was anterior to the rules which could by and large be treated as being exceptional, artificial constraints on free enquiry and natural reason. Wigmore also made some pragmatic inclusions of borderline topics in his *Treatise*, but the underlying conception of the subject was a model attempt to construct a framework which was both coherent and inter-disciplinary.

To what extent could Wigmore's Science, suitably up-dated, provide a coherent framework for 'The New Evidence Scholarship'? The 'Science of Proof' was explicitly stated to be based on 'logic, psychology and general experience'.[36] This is broad enough to accommodate at least four of the eight heads of enquiry listed above. Thus Wigmore's conception of 'the logic of proof' as a subject can easily accommodate almost all of the recent literature on evidence and inference, even though he wrote before the development of modern interest in statistics, probabilities and inferential reasoning in the context of adjudication. Many new specific questions and answers have emerged from recent debates, but almost all of them relate directly to the central question of the logic of proof, viz.: What constitute valid, cogent and appropriate forms of reasoning about questions of fact in adjudication? Similarly Wigmore's conception of forensic psychology was confined to a narrow range of questions about the reliability of various kinds of testimonial evidence. However, his 'Science' could readily accommodate a broader view of forensic psychology that also gives attention to questions about decision making, communication and interaction in the court-room. Again, his notion of 'general experience' explicitly included forensic science, expert evidence, general knowledge and common sense generalizations; he also devoted considerable attention under this head to technological developments in such areas as fingerprinting, graphology and lie-detection.[37] There have, of course, been many specific developments in science and technology since his day, from genetic fingerprinting to computer data bases, but much of the literature is still informed by a perspective which is essentially the same as Wigmore's. The main arena is conceived to be the contested trial and the central concern is the reliability of such evidence presented in court. Wigmore clearly indicated the relationship between his Science and the Trial Rules (one does not need to agree with his analysis)[38] and he did not overlook the historical dimensions of the various components of his Science, although some of his history was somewhat sketchy. It is hardly surprising that he did not pay much attention to discourse analysis and related enquiries, but it would not be difficult to incorporate various kinds of courtroom discourse within an updated version of his Science. Thus a very high proportion of the main lines of enquiry in the New Evidence Scholarship could be fitted within Wigmore's conceptual framework without much difficulty and in a fashion which very clearly indicates their main points of interconnection. This is a classic example of what I mean by a mapping theory. Given that it was first outlined in 1911, it deserves to be recognized as a remarkable achievement.

The weakest point of Wigmore's Science is that it was based on simplistic assumptions about litigation and legal processes. Wigmore was learned in civil and criminal procedure, but his Science was in this respect narrowly focused and it was not informed by an adequate conception of the complexities of legal processes.[39] This was its Achilles' heel and is the point of departure for an IL perspective.

Constructing a mapping theory: choice of an organizing concept[40]

My project was originally entitled 'theoretical aspects of evidence and proof in adjudication'. Over time each element in the label has come under critical scrutiny. Opting for a total process model involved switching from one kind of decision to all important decisions in legal process and so substituting 'litigation' for 'adjudication'. This in turn meant finding alternative concepts to 'evidence and proof'. As we have seen, a single 'bit' of information that counts as admissible or inadmissible 'evidence' at the adjudicative stage may perform similar, but not identical, functions in respect of other decisions at other stages in the same process. Similarly a 'confession' may be the start of a process of cooperation with authority, the forerunner to a guilty plea (with or without bargaining) or, after retraction, may be admissible or inadmissible as evidence, or its reception may provide a ground for appeal. Again 'standards of proof' at the adjudicative stage are closely analogous to other 'standards for decision' at other stages; for example, the standards governing decisions to prosecute or rulings that there is no case to answer or an appellate decision that a verdict is 'unsafe and unsatisfactory' all serve similar functions to those served by the standards of proof, but both the standards and the contexts of their operation are different. They are, however, all linked by the notion of rectitude of decision.[41]

The substitution of 'information in litigation' (IL) for 'judicial evidence' or 'evidence and proof' meets these points. This is not merely a matter of labelling or taxonomy. Indeed, one does not expect that conventional labels will be dropped (I shall continue to refer to the 'law of evidence' for this reason) nor should one expect too much from a mere change of classification. What needs to be considered are the potential gains in illumination and coherence from adopting a perspective which takes a fresh look at a traditional field using three key concepts as the main lenses: litigation, decision and information.

Litigation: some warnings of complexity

The object of IL is the collection, construction, processing, uses of and argumentation about information in respect of important decisions in the context of litigation seen as a total process. It is sufficient for our purposes to paint the context in broad and flexible terms. For this purpose it is useful to draw on a theory of litigation which does just this. One example is that of John Griffiths, who has developed a total process model that takes account of modern developments in the sociology and anthropology of law. His concern was to construct a general sociological theory of litigation, external to any particular legal system, for the purpose of conducting 'scientific' empirical research, specifically into divorce proceedings and administrative appeals in Holland.[42] IL, while more narrowly focused in some respects, is concerned with normative and interpretative as well as empirical questions, in so far as these can be differentiated. But Griffiths's conceptual framework and his broad conception of litigation as a process provides a sophisticated and illuminating starting-point for mapping IL.

After considering some of the conceptual problems of developing such a theory, Griffiths suggests that 'normative claim' provides a more satisfactory baseline for analysis than 'dispute' or 'case':

A general theory of litigation, then, has as its object the social behavior entailed in the handling of normative claims. It will consist of a systematic set of propositions with respect to the quantity, variety and distribution of normative claims (input), the interactive processes which take place with respect to them, and the results of such processes (output).[43]

It is worth making some points about this theory without examining it in detail. First, it is very broad: the process starts at an early point, the making of a claim which may or may not lead to a dispute, and it is not confined to 'state law' or 'official' norms. Griffiths's conception of litigation includes claims made under social norms in, for example, traditional African societies or in 'non-state' arenas, such as schools or factories or family conclaves. The *focus* of these essays has been mainly on state law and institutions and on official decisions, but it has not been confined to them. There are significant advantages in setting IL in a broad context, but for my purposes it has been sufficient to adopt a somewhat more restricted concept of 'litigation', as a process which can for most purposes be said to start with a formal complaint and which, if pursued to a 'finish', culminates in the enforcement or non-enforcement of a final determination and order by an adjudicative tribunal.

Secondly, 'litigation' in Griffiths's usage cannot simply be contrasted with other modes of dispute-settlement, such as negotiation, mediation, conciliation, avoidance, elimination, exit, lumping it, diplomacy and war.[44] A single example of a litigious process may involve not only 'naming, blaming and claiming',[45] but also bipartisan negotiation and settlement, multi-party mediation and third-party arbitration or adjudication. This is as true in the most formal legal proceedings in modern societies as in other 'informal' or 'unofficial' processes. Once again a broader perspective helps to indicate similarities and connections.

'Process thinking' is a standard form of legal thought. It comes quite naturally to both practising and academic lawyers to think in terms of flows of decisions and events in time involving a variety of actors, institutions and arenas.[46] Even quite a simple linear process model of litigation is a potentially powerful tool of contextual thinking. For purposes of a mapping theory it has the following attractions:

1   It can accommodate the main typical standpoints of and decisions by participants in legal processes within a single framework.
2   It can provide a context in which particular decisions (such as adjudicative decisions) and phenomena (such as confessions) can be located in a broader picture.
3   It can be adapted quite easily to fit an information-processing model in which the progress of a 'bit' of information can be tracked along the process in which it may encounter noise, be filtered out, stored, coded, translated, modified or transformed in 'its' transition from an original perception or other triggering event to its reception by a relevant decision-maker. Thus the standard legal model can be harmonized with a standard way of organizing and presenting material from decision theory and information theory.[47]
4   The model can help to map points of connection and potential inputs from a variety of disciplines and specialized enclaves of knowledge.
5   It serves as a reminder that 'adjudicative decisions' are not co-extensive with 'legal processes', some of which may not involve adjudicative decisions.

For most purposes a simple linear model may be quite adequate. However, recent anthropological and sociological studies of litigation offer some salutary warnings of complexity. Griffiths illustrates some of the limitations of a single linear model of litigation. Concepts like 'case' and 'dispute' are not satisfactory as units of analysis just because they tend not to be neat units: like a story, a 'case' often does not have a clear beginning or ending; it is often part of a longer complex process like a feud or a political campaign; and it may have many ramifications.[48] Nor do the components of a 'case' remain static, for as the story develops the issues, the arenas, the participants, their roles and relationships and other elements may all change.[49]

Griffiths emphasizes another obvious point that is often overlooked:

The extended case method began by making the begin- and end-points of the conception of a 'case' problematic. '[T]he outcome of most conflicts and disputes' is, as Abel observed, not 'resolution' or 'settlement' but 'other conflicts and disputes, with at most a temporary respite between them' (Abel, 1973, 228) ... It would be wrong to suppose that the impossibility of understanding litigation processes in terms of isolated 'cases' is restricted to exotic circumstances of African tribes and so forth, where litigation takes place between entire lineages which have long-term relationships with each other encompassing repeated negotiation and litigation and requiring long-term strategies within which any individual case is a mere subsidiary incident ... As Galanter (1974) has emphasized the same is true in 'modern' settings for many institutional litigants such as insurance companies, legal services organizations, prosecutors and public defenders. But even where individuals are involved, as in the administrative appeals we are currently studying, we have every reason to suppose that litigation will often display the characteristics emphasized by the extended case method: a given 'case' will only be comprehensible as a phase in an extended relationship, comprehending among other things earlier conflicts and other interaction between an individual and a local government body, or between two individuals.[50]

Furthermore the process of litigation is not necessarily unilinear. Consider, for example, the aftermath of a quite commonplace 'messy divorce' in terms of the variety of actors, relationships, transactions and events involved and the complexity of the interactions between and the timing of all of these.[51]

The messages of complexity from anthropologists relate to allegedly routine disputes in 'simple' societies. Even the most formal accounts of modern legal systems remind us of the variety of types of claims, arenas, proceedings and procedures that fall within the ambit of litigation.

A further point, touched on in an earlier essay, is worth developing here.[52] Litigation, as we have seen, is sometimes contrasted with, but often includes, other modes of dispute-settlement. Setting litigation in the context of a total picture of dispute-settlement institutions and processes helps to maintain a balanced demographic picture (e.g. what percentage of civil claims reach the stage of the issue of a writ or other formal move?). It also serves as a reminder that the state does not have a monopoly on dispute-settlement.

There are further complicating factors. We have already seen that a single process may involve several modes of dispute settlement. This was not just a conceptual point. One reason for shifting the focus from adjudication to litigation was the familiar fact that a large majority of civil actions never reach trial and that in most criminal proceedings at common law, by reason of the guilty plea, the trial stage never happens, yet 'evidentiary' issues are involved. Similarly one need have only the most casual acquaintance with French or Italian courts to realize that what they mean by 'trial' is typically very different from English, let alone American, trials.[53] Furthermore such proceedings as inquests or public enquiries into disasters may or may not be usefully classified as involving 'litigation' or even 'disputes', but in all such proceedings questions of fact-determination arise and are often central. In order not to open Pandora's Box too wide, we may wish to make third-party decisions by officials a focus of specialized attention, but many of the concepts, insights and modes of thought central to IL so confined have direct implications for fact-handling or information-processing in analogous or related processes.

It is also worth asking whether litigation is only or primarily concerned with dispute-settlement. The boundaries of 'dispute' have to be stretched and stretched if the term is to include all criminal proceedings (especially where there is a guilty plea) or uncontested defamation actions to vindicate one's reputation, to mention but a few.[54]

A realistic picture of litigation recognizes its complexities in design as well as operation. What implications does this have for the prospects of IL as a coherent and manageable focus of attention? Has Pandora's Box been opened too wide? Even if one follows Griffiths in interpreting litigation very broadly – and it is not difficult to narrow the ambit for particular purposes – there is a single thread that constitutes the core of our concern: the factual element in decision making in this type of context.

Decision

> To a historian the most interesting thing about decisions is the fact that everyone is talking about them. No one interested in social ideas can fail to notice how large a part the word 'decision' has, of late, come to play in the vocabulary of moral and political discourse. It meets one on every page. Inevitably one asks, 'Why?'
>
> Judith Shklar[55]

It is hardly surprising that decisions and decision making have been a focal point of jurisprudence and the discipline of law. This is not solely because of the central, indeed exaggerated, place given to adjudicative decisions in Anglo-American legal thought. Legislative, administrative and many other kinds of public and private decisions and choices are also a focus of legal attention from many points of view; normative legal theory is centrally concerned with reasoning towards, justifying and criticizing adjudicative and other official decisions; official discretion in deciding has increasingly become a concern of public lawyers; rather more sporadically other decisions in legal process – such as decisions to prosecute, to plead guilty, sentencing and parole – have been the subject of specialized enquiry. It is difficult to conceive of law not giving a central place to decision making, but it is also worth noting that some American jurists in their 'revolt against formalism' tended to substitute 'decision' for 'rule' as the central concept of legal theory. This was most clearly exemplified in the

'Law, Science and Policy' approach of Lasswell and McDougal who advanced a view of 'law as a process of decision'. Historically this reflected similar trends in neighbouring disciplines.[56]

For the purpose of mapping connections between different lines of enquiry, 'decision' is particularly useful just because it is a focal point for so many disciplines: psychology, logic, political science, economic analysis, public choice theory, to say nothing of decision theory itself, have this shared point of contact. We have also seen that perhaps the main difference between judicial fact-finding and historical and scientific enquiries is that judges have a duty to decide in ways that have important practical consequences. For them decision is a form of action; scientists and historians mainly conclude.[57]

Decision making is also a focal point for actors in the real world. The actions of Holmes's Bad Man, notaries, tax advisers, policemen, advocates, witnesses, debt collectors and claims adjusters to a large degree centre on the decisions of judges and other officials. Their roles and their own choices are largely defined in anticipation of or in response to official decisions. To the extent that this is so, such participants and their choices can conveniently be treated as satellites of official decisions. In short, treating decisions and decision making as a focal point for study is an unremarkable, but extremely convenient, way of maintaining coherence and manageability.

Information

The original reason for substituting 'information' for 'evidence' was to emphasize the point that the same 'bit' of information could play multiple roles in the same process. At each stage it may be constructed, reconstructed, deconstructed, processed, filtered, presented, received and used in significantly different ways.

Information has some further advantages as an organizing concept. Firstly, as with 'decision', 'information' is a central concept of disciplines and sub-disciplines, such as cybernetics, information-processing, and various forms of intelligence gathering. This may suggest concepts, questions and hypotheses that have not yet been applied systematically to information in litigation.

Secondly, because it is somewhat broader than 'fact' and 'evidence', 'information' transcends sharp distinctions between 'fact' on the one hand and 'value', 'law' and 'opinion' on the other. The 'information' contained in Edith Thompson's letters or a social enquiry report is not confined to 'pure' or 'simple' facts, whatever those might be. Similarly in ordinary usage 'information' is neutral between atomism and holism. In some contexts it makes sense to talk of discrete 'items' or 'bits' of information, such as Edith's age or someone's address, but we also talk of 'flows' or 'streams' or 'banks' or 'pools' of information that have not been 'atomized' into 'bits'.[58] Questions about when and how one can sensibly isolate individuated 'facts' for a particular purpose cannot be avoided, especially where the primary focus is on factual information. But it helps to make the problems of making such differentiations fall within a field rather than define its boundaries.

Thirdly, substituting 'information' for 'evidence' indicates the need to broaden our focus beyond 'proof': standards of proof are only one species of the genus, standards for decision; 'the logic of proof' is a specialized sector of practical reasoning. IL is concerned with the factual element in all important decisions in litigation, but only exceptionally are questions of fact sharply distinguished from other questions for determination. When they are so distinguished, then the term 'fact' is often used in subtly different ways from ordinary usage. Thus lawyers use 'fact' differently in respect of defining the jurisdiction of a jury, indicating issues that are subject to appeal or review, and determining the status and value of a decision in the doctrine of precedent.[59]

Finally, the history of the study of the Law of Evidence shows how even expositors of legal doctrine had difficulty in delimiting their chosen field. Gilbert, Stephen, Thayer, Wigmore and many lesser figures struggled with the problem of segregating evidence doctrine from rules of procedure, pleading, substantive law and much else besides.[60] Bentham's sharp distinction between substantive and adjective law had a clear role in his general theory; but his manuscripts contain plenty of examples of indecision about where to draw the line between 'evidence' and 'procedure'.[61] Comparative lawyers sometimes treat the common law as unique in having developed the Law of Evidence as a distinct field of law, the subject of specialized codes, treatises, courses and even scholars.[62] As we have seen, it is not true that modern civilian systems 'have no rules of evidence'; for example, it is arguable that proof is in significant respects less 'free' in Italy than in England.[63] Rather, so far as legal doctrine is concerned, evidentiary issues are treated for most purposes as part of pro-cedure; and civilians as much as common lawyers have problems with the distinction between procedure and substantive law.

If the perennial problems of rending the seamless web of legal doctrine are especially difficult in respect of evidence, how much more difficult is it to make a neat surgical excision of 'Evidence' as a focus of inter-disciplinary study. Faced with this version of Pandora's Box it is not surprising that one reaction is to retreat back to a narrow formalism or to give up any attempt at coherence. An IL perspective may not solve all the problems of classification for purposes of specialized study, but it does provide a possible basis for a much closer integration of evidentiary, procedural and processual enquiries.

Some implications and applications

An IL perspective has implications and applications for other disciplines and for inter-disciplinary enquiries. I shall touch on these later. However, my immediate interest is with the internal concerns of the discipline of law. The case has already been made in general terms for recognizing the theoretical interest, the practical importance and the wider ramifications of IL in legal scholarship and legal education. This section develops this in relation to some specific topics.

Legal Philosophy[64]

Legal Philosophy *stricto sensu* is that part of Legal Theory that is concerned with the most general or abstract questions concerning law. The assumptions of the

Rationalist Tradition signal some clear points of contact with general issues of ontology, epistemology, logic, political morality, and social theory. In chapter 4 some potential connections with scepticism in philosophy were indicated, but it was suggested that few legal 'sceptics' are genuine philosophical sceptics in a strong sense. The recent debates on probabilities and proof and, in particular, Jonathan Cohen's writings on inductive logic in this connection are also contributions to the philosophy of science. At a slightly less abstract level, Mirjan Damaska's *The Faces of Justice and State Authority* explores the relationship between political ideology and systems of procedure at a relatively general level and in ways which have a direct bearing on general theories of litigation.

A central theme of the preceding essays relates to philosophical questions about reason, reasoning and rationality in legal processes: What constitute valid, cogent and appropriate reasonings about disputed questions of fact in adjudication and other legal contexts? What conceptions of reasoning and rationality have been adopted or assumed by writers in the Rationalist Tradition? How well do these conceptions stand up to critical scrutiny in the light of sceptical challenges or philosophical theories developed in a different intellectual tradition? To what extent is it possible and sensible to maintain at least working distinctions between questions of fact and questions of value or law or opinion in the context of adjudicative and other decisions in litigation? What is the relationship between reasoning about questions of fact, questions of law and other lawyers' reasonings in such contexts? For example, should reasoning about disputed questions of law and of fact in adjudication be viewed as closely analogous species of practical reasoning, governed by the same general principles subject to a few contextual variations? Or are the differences more fundamental? And so on.

These examples by no means exhaust the connections between philosophy and IL. It is noteworthy that the points of contact are in large part with areas of philosophy that have not traditionally been treated as central to Jurisprudence in the Anglo-American tradition.[65] At least until recently, the most sustained connections between Jurisprudence and philosophy have related to ethical, political and conceptual problems and to the nature of reasoning about disputed questions of law in hard cases.

IL is also concerned with practical reasoning, mainly about disputed questions of fact. Its links with probability theory, epistemology, historiography and the philosophy of science were for a long time relatively neglected by lawyers. Thus the resurgence of interest in this area involves extending the range of questions that may properly be regarded as central to the philosophical sector of Jurisprudence. At last there is growing recognition that it really does not make sense to confine the study of 'legal reasoning' to disputed questions of law – another example of the narrowing influence of the expository tradition. Out of this may develop a much broader and richer perspective on questions about the nature of practical reasoning in legal discourse. Justifying, arguing towards and appraising decisions on questions of fact, questions of sentencing, assessment of damages, parole, and many other important decisions in legal processes involve a complex mixture of philosophical issues about the nature of practical reasoning and of other kinds of questions about the nature of legal processes; these in

turn raise interesting and relatively neglected questions about the interrelation-
ship between forms and styles of reasoning and different kinds of practical
decisions. For example: To what extent do modes of reasoning accepted to be
appropriate to questions of law, questions of fact and questions of sentencing
exhibit the same logical structure? To what extent do contextual factors
generate different criteria of relevance and of appropriateness? Similarly the
questions raised about the relationship between the assumptions underlying the
Rationalist Tradition and other intellectual traditions could be broadened to
include more general questions about our conceptions of rationality in law.
How do these appear in the light of other intellectual traditions and of recent
developments in our own? Are they rooted in some particular historical conceptions or are they, as one commentator has boldly suggested, 'based on the
view of rationality common to western civilization'?[66]

Middle order theory

The difference between philosophical and middle order theory is a relative
matter of levels of generality. Middle order theorizing tends to be more
context-specific than philosophy, but can nevertheless encompass parts of
general as well as particular jurisprudence. Consider, for example, the continuum of questions about reasoning in general, about practical reasoning,
about practical reasoning about questions of fact in adjudication, and these last
questions in respect of adjudication by magistrates or industrial tribunals in
England and what constitutes the most cogent argument in a particular case. As
one moves down such a ladder of abstraction one moves further away from
'pure' philosophical issues and becomes involved with increasingly specific
institutional contexts.

Most of our heritage of 'general' and 'particular' jurisprudence falls within
this broad band of middle order theorizing in which concern with abstract
issues has to be combined with a grasp of contextual factors. Because the study
of law has tended to be oriented to the concerns of practice-minded participants, a great deal of our heritage of legal theorizing takes the form of
prescriptive working theories for different kinds of participants: witness
Bentham's theory of legislation (which included a design theory of adjective
law), the theories of (largely appellate) adjudication of Karl Llewellyn and
Ronald Dworkin, and Wigmore's Science of Proof (which was ostensibly
addressed to trial lawyers and, incidentally, to detectives). Interestingly our
main theories of litigation (Black, Abel, Galanter and Griffiths) and of
procedure (Damaska) have been empirical or interpretative rather than prescriptive, in so far as such distinctions can be maintained.[67]

IL as it has been outlined is a relatively clear example of middle order
theorizing, with prescriptive, interpretative and empirical aspects. Although it
has grown specifically out of the common law, especially Anglo-American,
tradition, many of its central questions and concepts could apply with more or
less adjustment to other Western legal systems and beyond. As such it has
potential implications for general and comparative as well as particular jurisprudence. However, in order to make the discussion more concrete and to

avoid some of the dangers of over-generalization, I shall restrict myself here mainly to English examples.

Broad perspectives and particular studies: the problem of the division of labour

It is beyond the scope of this essay to try to spell out the possible ramifications of an IL perspective for all the different lines of enquiry that have been identified as belonging to 'The New Evidence Scholarship'. I have already given numerous examples of particular applications; others are too obvious to need elaboration; yet others will be more readily apparent to, or remain to be worked out by, specialists in particular fields. However, something needs to be said about the relationship between IL and specialization.

In a penetrating critique of my *Theories of Evidence* Professor Dennis Galligan challenges the novelty, the utility and the manageability of a broad approach to evidence.[68] He claims that the idea that the study of evidence and proof should go beyond the legal rules to incorporate ideas from the social and forensic sciences is 'now orthodox' and he wonders 'whatever happened to the division of labour':[69]

If the attack is on narrowness in the sense of concentration on the rules of evidence, to the neglect of issues about their application in practice and the broader question of proof, then evidence scholarship, like all areas of legal scholarship, has come to realize the importance of these wider pursuits and the contribution of other disciplines. These changes are reflected in the literature which today is richer than ever before. This is all to the good, but it does not follow, as Twining seems to be suggesting, that one is precluded from entering the arena without first mastering – in addition to the law and practice of evidence – the philosophy of knowledge and logic, moral and political theory, probability theory, psychology, ethnomethodology, and statistics – to name but a few pertinent disciplines. All are of course relevant to evidence, just as they are relevant to any area of social or legal enquiry; but it does not mean that all have to be merged into one. There is still a place for the treatise as well as the study of probability, for the close analysis of exclusionary rules as well as their moral basis, for the psychology and dynamics of the courtroom as well as the organizational structure of the police-station. Each may advance and illuminate the other, but it is a mistake to think that broad generalization of an interdisciplinary kind is a substitute for close analysis of a selective kind.[70]

Galligan is perhaps more complacent than I am about the extent to which broad inter-disciplinary approaches have become orthodox in practice, but we both acknowledge the existence of the New Evidence Scholarship as a significant development. One hopes that enough has been said here to refute any suggestion that an IL perspective precludes rather than encourages 'close analysis of a selective kind' or that one has to be a polymath before one can embark on any specialized investigation. The claim that is being made here for IL is that it not only provides a basis for mapping – and possibly synthesising[71] – a rich assortment of seemingly diverse lines of enquiry, but also that it can provide a context for posing and re-posing questions and defining problems in illuminating and realistic ways. 'Narrowness' is harmful when it distorts perceptions or diverts energies away from significant issues into trivial pursuits or generates unnecessary puzzlements. An IL perspective claims to be an antidote to such ailments.

The imbalance and distortions that tend to result from viewing 'the problem of identification' from a narrow evidentiary perspective were indicated in chapter 5. Very similar considerations apply to almost all decisions and events pre-trial. An obvious example is the literature on confessions, the great bulk of which is written from an evidentiary perspective and is largely concerned with questions of admissibility.[72] Attention has regularly been diverted from what should be a central question for those concerned to understand the role of confessing in criminal process: Who 'confesses' what, to whom, in what form, in what circumstances and with what results?

Another example of the dangers of posing an issue too narrowly is the notorious 'problem of the gatecrasher' formulated by Jonathan Cohen in relation to the meaning of 'the preponderance of probabilities' in the civil standard of proof. This example has generated an extensive literature which is notable for an uneasy sense among commentators that there is something 'unreal' or 'artificial' about the problem.[73]

Cohen's example concerns a rodeo attended by 1000 spectators, 499 of whom have paid and 501 have not.[74] Cohen suggests that no legal system should, or is likely to, give a remedy to the rodeo operator against a randomly selected spectator in this situation, even though, on the basis of the 'naked statistical evidence' there is a 0·51 probability that the defendant did not pay. He appeals to lawyers' intuitions to support his argument that in this kind of situation it is inductive (Baconian) rather than mathematical (Pascalian) reasoning which is appropriate.[75] Cohen is probably right about lawyers' intuitions, both in respect to the rodeo problem and, more controversially, in respect of an aversion to relying on naked statistical evidence to determine individual cases. But these 'intuitions' are not necessarily to be explained solely, or even mainly, by reference to different modes of reasoning.

To the practising lawyer the rodeo example is unconvincing for several other reasons. It is unlikely that a rodeo operator would take legal proceedings over such a small sum. Since the allegation implies fraud, the standard of proof could well be higher than 'preponderance of the evidence'. It is unlikely that this would be the only evidence. If the defendant is available, why does he not testify? There should be other witnesses (the ticket attendants, other members of the crowd, etc.) who might well be sources of relevant evidence. There may, indeed, be a real problem about naked statistical evidence. At the very least, Cohen's example illustrates its vulnerability. For, if the defendant were to testify that he paid, even rather unconvincingly, the weight of the bare statistic would be significantly reduced.[76]

Furthermore, there are at least three kinds of background policy considerations that might help to explain our intuitive reactions to this case. There is a policy of the law that a plaintiff cannot recover more by way of compensation than the total loss suffered. If the rodeo operator were to sue all members of the crowd, using the same argument in each case, how could this policy be implemented fairly? Again, the law 'encourages' those who have relevant evidence to be forthcoming; some would argue that the rodeo operator should carry the risk of non-production of further evidence and be held not to have discharged his burden of proof. And might not the defendant have some procedural rights in respect of other potential co-defendants? In short, the rodeo example does not really support Cohen's thesis.

A Wigmorean lawyer would go one step further. In order to make sense of one sector of an argument, it needs to be set in the context of the argument about the case as a whole. In order to do this one needs more information than is provided by the rodeo chestnut which, like many academic examples, is artificially abstracted from the context of actual legal proceedings. Who is suing whom for what on what basis? One needs to know the answers to such questions before one can even decide whether the meaning of the civil standard of proof is in issue in this context.[77]

The rodeo problem (and to a lesser extent the similar green and blue bus problem)[78] does not make sense because it has been presented in a decontextualized way. Here 'lawyers' intuitions' may include a variety of considerations of procedure, policy and practicality that have little or nothing to do with the civil standard of proof. But what these intuitions might be cannot be confidently identified without more information about the context. Thus the example almost certainly does not illustrate the problem that it is meant to illuminate. This is not to say that the question of the meaning of the civil standard of proof at trial is either trivial or uninteresting.

A rather different example of an unsatisfactory body of literature is that dealing with the much-discussed problem of 'illegally or improperly obtained evidence'. The great bulk of it centres on the dilemmas of the judiciary in determining whether or not to use such evidence in given circumstances; the main source of the literature is the law reports and commentaries thereon. Nearly all modern writers explicitly or implicitly recognize that the Law of Evidence is likely to be largely ineffective in disciplining the police and other officials pre-trial and that the judiciary is likely to play only a marginal role in regulating the ways in which evidence is obtained in practice.[79] Undoubtedly, when such cases do reach the courts they pose difficult choices and raise important and interesting questions of principle. From an IL perspective 'the problem' is not only one of admissibility of evidence or of maintaining the integrity or perceived legitimacy of the judiciary. The central issue for those concerned to design a system for ensuring that official behaviour pre-trial conforms to a general principle of decent and fair treatment of all persons involved in criminal process is: What means of upholding this principle are likely to be effective without unduly hampering officials in carrying out the tasks that society has allocated to them? This involves detailed consideration of the situation in the round and of the kinds of factors that are likely to influence the relative effectiveness of many different means of control: procedural rules; criminal, civil and disciplinary remedies; training; resources; incentives and so on.[80] Similar considerations apply to attempts to understand how information relevant to decisions at each stage of a process is gathered, processed and used in practice. So viewed, the phenomena and problems are not primarily 'evidentiary'; it is odd to see the principle of decent and fair treatment of suspects and others being treated mainly as an evidentiary principle; it is even odder to see the main dilemmas in design and operation as centering on questions of admissibility.

One of the best recent discussions of illegally and improperly obtained evidence is by Adrian Zuckerman.[81] He gives an excellent account of the dilemmas facing judges in dealing with the admissibility and use of such evidence. He advances several cogent reasons why an exclusionary rule is unlikely to be effective in disciplining police and other official behaviour pre-trial. He makes a convincing case for the proposition that there is a value in subjecting police practices to public judicial scrutiny.[82] He even goes so far as to say that the reason why the courts find it difficult to confront the 'age-old question' is due to two principal factors: '[F]irst, a failure to come to terms with the nature of the problem, and, second, a reluctance on the part of the courts to look beyond the immediate confines of the law of evidence.'[83]

Zuckerman criticizes the courts for adopting a narrow evidentiary perspective, but he himself poses the issue from the same perspective – as a question of admissibility. His main concern is 'the legitimacy' of the administration of justice,[84] a much broader matter. The outcome is an uneasy tension between his 'broad' solution and his definition of the problem which follows tradition in adopting the kind of narrow evidentiary perspective that he criticizes. In short, I tend to agree with Zuckerman's answer, but not with his question.

It may be objected that the passage appears in a book on criminal evidence, which naturally concentrates on evidentiary issues, and that authors should not be criticized for their choice of subject. A brief answer to this is as follows: the vast bulk of the literature on 'illegally and improperly obtained evidence' adopts a similar perspective and, for this reason, exhibits all the symptoms of a topic that has been located in the wrong context. In this instance, there is a striking consensus in the literature that the judiciary, and the law of evidence in particular, can at best make a marginal contribution to the underlying problem. Yet there is very little systematic literature on that problem.[85]

Secondly, a broad IL perspective does not preclude highly specialized consideration of narrowly defined issues. In this instance, a chapter on this topic in an Evidence text might treat the following questions as central:

1 What, if anything, can an exclusionary rule or a discretion to exclude contribute, in the context of other (non-evidentiary) provisions, to the general objective of regulating official behaviour in obtaining information, potential evidence and evidence pre-trial?

2 In what circumstances and to what extent does the use of such evidence at trial run counter to principles or policies concerning the need to maintain the integrity or the perceived legitimacy of judges or other state officials? If there is a general principle of clean hands or non-contamination of the administration of justice, what is the scope, the weight and the rationale of that principle and how does it apply to the specific issue of admissibility?

3 How far are existing judicial doctrine and practice in regard to improperly obtained evidence consistent with a broader principle of integrity (or legitimacy or non-contamination) in analogous areas?[86] And so on.

The important point about this formulation is that none of these questions can be plausibly answered from a purely evidentiary perspective. IL is primarily concerned with question (1). The second and third sets of questions also raise issues of political morality that range far beyond the Law of Evidence, but in a different direction. Arguments about the specific issue of admissibility and use of such evidence cannot plausibly ignore these broader considerations. This does not mean that they cannot be dealt with in a sharply focused way within an orthodox textbook on judicial evidence. The adoption of a broader perspective does not preclude focusing on narrow questions. However, an IL perspective mandates concern with general questions about methods of obtaining and processing information in litigation.

Inter-disciplinary warnings

The main purpose of constructing a model of IL is to provide a framework for mapping a field within the discipline of law. The phenomena and questions within that field all pertain to litigation as one important form of legal process. The focus is legal but, of course, understanding the phenomena and posing, refining and suggesting answers to the questions is necessarily an inter-disciplinary activity. Specialists in other disciplines interested in, for example, inferential reasoning or information processing or discourse analysis or memory or story-telling will almost certainly choose to *organize* their enquiries within quite different frameworks. The IL perspective nevertheless has potential implications for anyone from another discipline who wishes to study phenomena or questions that fall within the scope of IL. Perhaps the most valuable service that a jurist can offer to extra-disciplinary visitors is to give some guidance about the nature and complexities of this particular context, i.e. litigation.

Inter-disciplinary warnings have been a recurrent theme of these essays: witness psychologists have been criticized for accepting too uncritically an unduly simple and unbalanced picture of litigation when addressing 'the problem of identification'.[87] Similar warnings might be offered to forensic scientists, although their close practical involvement with criminal investigation should generally have sensitized them to the varying uses of information at different stages of criminal process. Statisticians and lawyers have been warned of the peculiarity of lawyers' notions of 'fact' and how over-simple chestnuts, such as the rodeo and blue bus problems, generally take insufficient account of procedural complexities. Narratologists, semioticians and the like should be aware that there are many different contexts and modes of legal discourse (both law talk and talk about law) and that lawyers' stories perform many different functions and are told by a variety of functionaries.[88] Philosophers should take note that lawyers' reasonings are not confined to questions of law in hard cases. Historians and others may find that such notions as materiality and procedural norms are at least as important in explaining lawyers' handling of evidence as the rules of admissibility. There is already an extensive admonitory literature addressed to expert witnesses. One hopes, too, that these messages of complexity will curb over-enthusiasm on the part of Bayesians and decision theorists.[89]

These admonitions are certainly not intended to frighten off visitors from other disciplines who should be treated, like tourists in an underdeveloped country, as welcome guests rather than trespassers. Like any good nationalist, I am concerned to show off the splendours and subtleties of my home ground to visitors while trying to extract from them as much as possible that suits our local needs. Academic lawyers are, after all, in a relationship of dependency and interdependency with many other disciplines. Moreover, the peculiarities and uniqueness of fact-determination in legal contexts can easily be exaggerated. Just as nearly all of the conditions that give rise to doubts about interpretation of rules in legal contexts also arise in other contexts,[90] so the main problems, obstacles and puzzles surrounding fact-determination in legal processes are shared with other kinds of enquiry. Ironically, one of the reasons for the relative neglect of fact-determination in legal scholarship and legal education has been that there is relatively little about it that is unique or in special need of demystification: witness, for example, the explicit recognition in the Rationalist Tradition of the role of ordinary cognitive competence. The fallacy that underlies that neglect is the confusion between identifying what is characteristic or unique or peculiar about a phenomenon and trying to understand it.[91]

Realism revisited

This book is one emanation of a project that took the 'realism' of Karl Llewellyn and Jerome Frank as its starting-point. The aim has been to develop a 'contextual' perspective on an area of legal concern within a broadened conception of the discipline of law and to confront some factors – notably the problem of coherence – which, in my view, help to explain why the promise of American Legal Realism (one historical example of 'realism')[92] was not fulfilled. From time to time in the preceding pages terms like 'realistic', 'unrealistic', 'distortion', 'misperception', 'imbalance' have been used in evaluating general approaches and more specific treatments of particular topics. Without attempting a full-scale interpretation of what is involved in a realistic or anti-formalist approach to law in general, it is appropriate to try to clarify what is, and is not, being claimed about 'realism' and related terms here and to differentiate these from such standard targets as 'barefoot empiricism', 'naïve realism' and 'rule-scepticism'.[93]

One of the abiding concerns underlying 'realist' approaches is a sense of 'unrealism' about certain kinds of legal discourses. What is meant by the charge that a particular proposition or treatment is 'unrealistic'? There are plenty of examples of such charges in the preceding pages. For example, the Hard-nosed Practitioner and others regularly point to gaps between 'the law in books' and the 'law in action'; between what is said and what is done; between 'paper rules', interposed norms and actual practices; between 'aspiration' and 'reality'; and less discriminately, between 'theory' and 'practice'. Debates about the reform of the Law of Evidence have been said to be 'high among the unrealities', and I have suggested that orthodox treatments of such phenomena as confessions and identification parades have involved misperception or distortion or have overlooked important latent functions and so, by implication, have not reflected reality.

It is now widely recognized that such charges need to be differentiated: that we need, for example, to distinguish among complaints of triviality, irrelevance to particular concerns, narrowness of vision, over-optimistic idealism or utopianism, official mystification and concealment, and remoteness from actual events and consequences – to mention but a few. In short, charges of 'unrealism' are of different kinds and reflect a variety of standpoints and concerns.

There are, however, two common threads running through such complaints. First, they are all negative expressions of dissatisfaction; on their own they do not usually involve very clear positive claims. What for example is the referent of 'the law in action', or 'what is done' or that elusive term 'reality'? Do not these complaints too readily involve common sense assumptions that beg some of the central questions of interpretative sociology, such as: what is social reality? How is it constructed? By whom? What are the lessons of experience? What is involved in describing, interpreting and explaining them?

Sociologists of law, in discussing 'the gap problem', have elaborated this criticism in two ways.[94] First, such 'realist' talk assumes uncritically that a 'gap' between aspiration and reality or 'paper rules' and actual practice is necessarily to be deplored. Are not noble dreams or paper rules or ideal types or simple maps desirable or useful just because they do not perfectly mirror 'reality', whatever that is? Does 'realism' have as its ideal the same one-to-one relationship to the real world as the conception of the perfect map that was exactly the same shape and size as the territory it charted?

A second warning relates to the objects of realist attack. It is dangerous to take too much for granted about such targets as 'the law in books' or 'paper rules'. Doreen McBarnett has neatly shown that a careful reading of the relevant rule-books suggests that the detailed prescriptions of Scottish and English criminal procedure do not reflect the professed ideals of our criminal justice system – such as the Rule of Law and the presumption of innocence.[95] There is a gap between stated official aspiration and the detailed rules. Similarly, critical legal scholars have directed rather more attention to showing up the indeterminacy, contradictions or meaninglessness of the law in books without unduly concerning themselves with the law in action.[96]

Clearly a modern 'realist' who ignored such messages could justifiably be criticized as naïve. However, it does not follow that the sense of dissatisfaction underlying standard realist concerns is unfounded. When the Hard-nosed Practitioner claims that what is said in 'the books' or 'taught in school' just does not reflect her experience, such expressions of disbelief deserve to be taken seriously even if the complainant is silent or not very articulate about such experience or beliefs. There is no need for a sophisticated general theory or scientific research to sustain some basic complaints: for example, claims that 'jury-thinking' or 'appellate court-itis' or formalism can lead to distorted views of routine trials and confessing and identification parades can be sustained by quite simple facts and figures. This kind of 'demographic realism' falls far short of a sophisticated interpretative account of the phenomena in question. It may have served to strip away only one of 'reality's' many veils, but any account that fails to take account of the scale and distribution of the phenomenon under consideration or which treats the atypical as typical or the unrepresentative as representative is vulnerable to easily sustained charges of 'unrealism'. And any account of a body of legal doctrine that assumes that it affects the behaviour and expectations of only one or two kinds of participant, when that is just not the case, is similarly vulnerable.

In the course of my explorations I have made regular use of three standard devices of 'contextual' or 'realist' thinking: clarification of standpoint; thinking in terms of total pictures; and thinking in terms of total processes.[97] These devices, coupled with the assumption that for most academic and practical purposes in law the study of rules alone is not enough, justify labelling the approach in this book as 'realist' or 'contextual'. But 'realism' is not a distinctive form of legal theory nor, in my view, do these techniques amount to anything like a comprehensive methodology for the study of law.[98] They ought, however, to be part of the basic equipment of any student of law.

Once upon a time, lost in the labyrinth of a mid-western Law School, if my memory serves me right, at a return on one of the remoter staircases I came across an alcove with a sofa and chairs in it. It was called 'Reality Checkpoint'. One is free to interpret this as one will. I like to think of students coming there between classes to touch base with 'the real world'. It is as if on a summer's night a theatre-goer, in the interval of an absorbing drama, steps out into the street for a breath of fresh air. Each brings their own sense of reality to this point and, no doubt, different realities on different days. Maybe realism in law stands to Legal Theory as Reality Checkpoint stands to the classroom. It does not itself offer a rounded theory of or about law or life, but it furnishes a point of reference against which to check any theory for its plausibility or connection with what happens out there – if, of course, there is anything there. It is quite compatible with the idea that each of us sees the world around us with multiple lenses which construct, constitute or reveal many different realities. It helps to maintain connections in a down-to-earth way with actual events and practices and people in the world of fact, however varied, complex and elusive that world may be. So perhaps we should end with Calvino's beginning:

If on a winter's night a traveller, outside the town of Malbork, leaning from the steep slope without fear of wind or vertigo, looks down in the gathering shadow in a network of lines that intersect, on the carpet of leaves illuminated by the moon around an empty grave ... What story awaits there in the end? ... he asks, anxious to hear the story.[99]

NOTES

1   See above, ch. 1 at 5. One of the main thrusts of modern critical legal theory is to show up the incoherence (and alleged 'contradictions') of all legal discourse. Some critiques hit their target. I am quite prepared to accept the contingency of my own constructions, but I am less willing to surrender the search for coherent ways of looking at the world as a worthwhile aspiration.

2 Bentham, *Introductory View*, ch. 1.
3 Cf. Wright and Graham (1977), ch. 1; Lempert (1988), 61.
4 Lempert, id., discussed below.
5 See below, 352 ff.
6 The ideas in this section are developed in *LTCL*, chs. 4 and 11.
7 Of course, many ideas to be immediately usable have to be both concrete and precise. But general ideas and overviews can be of more practical utility than detailed ones when they serve economy or order or have a wide application; see further MacCormick and Twining (1986).
8 The *locus classicus* is J. Stone (1964), 267ff.
9 See further Twining (1974) and op. cit., n. 6.
10 J. Stone (1964), 16.
11 E.g. Skinner (1969, 1978).
12 Above, 73.
13 Op. cit., n. 9. See also chs. 4 and 5 (esp. 123–4), above.
14 Austin (1863).
15 One of the puzzles of contemporary legal theory is how far Ronald Dworkin's theory of adjudication can be plausibly interpreted as transcending particular (American or Anglo-American) Jurisprudence.
16 Op. cit., n. 6.
17 Dworkin (1977).
18 Llewellyn (1960). The theories of Dworkin and Llewellyn are mainly prescriptive. An example of empirical middle order theorizing is to be found in the ambitious project on the Comparative Sociology of the Legal Professions coordinated by Richard Abel and Philip Lewis. See Abel and Lewis (eds) (1988).
19 Above, 81.
20 *Analysis, passim*; Schum (1987).
21 On the theme of transferability of skills see N. Gold et al. (1989).
22 In *Analysis*, Wigmore's method is first presented in an abstract way and then in ch. 5 is 're-contextualised' into the specific context of an American attorney preparing for trial.
23 On the differences between litigation in England and the United States, see Atiyah and Summers (1987).
24 Above, ch. 6.
25 Above, ch. 1 at 3.
26 See generally *TEBW*.
27 Lempert (1988), 61. The context of this statement was the 1986 Boston symposium which was primarily concerned with 'The uses and limits of Bayesianism in the Law of Evidence' (see Tillers and Green, eds, 1988). Lempert was responding to a provocative paper by Professor Ronald Allen who had argued that the sense of malaise surrounding modern probability debates was due not so much to intractable disagreements about conceptualizing probability as to a need to re-conceptualize civil jury trials (Allen, 1988). In that debate Lempert argued that Allen's proposals might lead to some radical and undesirable changes in the rules governing civil trials (Lempert, 1988, 80ff.); while expressing some sympathy with Allen's approach, I argued that it was still too infused with jury-thinking, court-itis and atomistic models of reasoning to give an adequate account of the malaise. The 'unrealism' of some of the debates about rodeos, blue and green buses and other such chestnuts is largely due to their being divorced from a realistic sense of the context of actual litigation (see below). On this occasion Lempert argued that Allen had gone too far, while I argued that he had not gone far enough. Outside this very specific context I suspect that differences in our views of what constitutes a 'realistic' perspective on litigation are not very significant.
28 *People* v. *Collins*, 68 Cal. 2d 319, 438 P. 2d 33 (1968).
29 The first three of these conferences led to published symposia: Twining (ed.) (1983) (*FL*), Tillers and Green (eds) (1988) and B. Jackson (ed.) (1989).
30 The full title is the 'International Seminar on Evidence in Litigation' of the Jacob Burns

Institute of the Benjamin N. Cardozo School of Law, Yeshiva University, New York. The seminar is organized by Professor Peter Tillers. In its first two years the programme included contributions from academic lawyers, statisticians, information scientists, philosophers, practising attorneys and a Federal Judge.

31   The 'socio' in 'socio-legal' covers all the social sciences, including economics, anthropology, psychology and social history.

32   Studies of discourse include 'conversation analysis' of the kind developed by Atkinson and Pomerantz at Wolfson College, Oxford, in the early 1980s.

33   On the relationship of Bentham's *Rationale* to his general ideas see *TEBW*, ch. 2.

34   Above, ch. 6.

35   On the difficulties of separating 'evidence' and 'procedure' see above, ch. 6 and below, 358.

36   Wigmore *Science* (1913, 1937), subtitle.

37   Wigmore was influential in the development of what was then called 'police science' (Roalfe, 1977, 60ff., 85–7).

38   Wigmore *Science*, Appendix I, 923–46.

39   Wigmore's treatment of procedure in his *Treatise* and his other writings on the subject tends to be uninspired, if usually adequate in respect of the rules. He drew hardly at all on the literature on litigation and legal processes that was emerging towards the end of his career. His treatment of evidence in non-jury trials (vol. 1., s.4) sits uneasily within a framework that treats the contested jury trial as both the paradigm and the focal point of the subject.

40   One of the first steps in rethinking a field is to examine critically the traditional way in which it has been categorized; see, for example, Atiyah's substitution of 'compensation for accidents' for 'torts' or 'negligence' (Atiyah, 1970).

41   Galligan (1988), 252–4, 263–4.

42   Griffiths (1983), 146–7, 159–61.

43   Id., 169.

44   Cover and Fiss (1979).

45   Felstiner, Abel and Sarat (1980–1).

46   The view of processes as flows of decisions and events was developed by Harold Lasswell and Myres McDougal (e.g. 1967); McDougal and Reisman (1981). One hopes that the adoption of this conception of 'process' does not automatically condemn one to being labelled as an adherent of Law, Science and Policy or of the so-called 'Process School'.

47   E.g. Lindsay and Norman (1977), Loftus and Loftus (1976), Willmer (1970). The potential bearing of the information sciences on the processing and uses of information in decisions in litigation can be illustrated by three examples. First, the idea of a single 'bit' of information, such as a list of past convictions, which is used or not used at different points in a single process would be susceptible to analysis in terms of an 'influence diagram' which charts networks involving mixtures of inference and choice (see, for example, J. Q. Smith, 1988, ch. 5). Secondly, intelligence analysts, among others, have in recent years become sensitive to the idea of information feeding off itself to produce double or multiple counting of the same piece of evidence. For example, where weight is given to a cumulation of opinions from three seemingly independent sources which have in fact come to the same conclusion on the basis of information derived from the same single source. Such multiple counting of a single item of information is known colloquially as 'a self-licking ice cream cone' (see further Schum, 1987, ch. 8, 'Redundant Evidence'). Thirdly, Schum (*id.*, chs. 3, 5 and 11) explores in detail how the processing of information by different actors can affect its probative or inferential value – for example a policeman takes notes of what a suspect said in an interview and then writes them up later. I am indebted to David Schum for these points.

48   Griffiths (1983), 151–8.

49   A good example of a case-study in which the parties, the fields of law, the issues and the

arenas all change in the course of a single 'affair' is the film, *The Sunday Times Case* by Philip Britton and Ian Thompson (1984).

50 Griffiths (1983), 152–3.
51 Sampford (1989) in an important critique of the idea that law can ever be treated as systematic, takes me to task for presenting a unilinear model of decisions, tasks and roles (at 132–3). I agree that many legal processes are not so simple, but I still believe that flow-charts are useful devices for analysing and depicting legal processes.
52 Above, ch. 5.
53 Damaska (1986).
54 Abel (1973), Galanter (1983), Griffiths (1983).
55 Shklar (1964), 3.
56 Op. cit. n. 46.
57 Cf. above, ch. 4, n. 82.
58 See further Twining (1988), 1542–3.
59 J. Jackson (1983), Guest (1987), Zuckerman (1986).
60 Above, ch. 3.
61 E.g. MSS on 'forthcomingness' of witnesses and evidence (Twining, 1986a).
62 E.g. Duhamel and Smith (1959), ch. 5. Cf. Certoma (1986).
63 For example, in respect of rules of competency, Certoma (1986).
64 This passage is based on my 'Evidence and Legal Theory' (1984).
65 Kelsen's 'Pure theory' was for a long time debated in the United Kingdom with little or no reference to his epistemological concerns (see Tur and Twining, 1986). The intellectual climate of Anglo-American Jurisprudence has changed significantly in this regard in recent years.
66 Galligan (1988), 264. I disagree with this statement which fails to distinguish between concepts and conceptions of rationality, see above, ch. 4. The latter are 'essentially contested' in the Western intellectual tradition.
67 Conklin (1988), challenging sharp distinctions between empirical and normative approaches.
68 Galligan (1988).
69 Id., 250 and 264.
70 Id., 251.
71 Wigmore's *Science* provided a synthesis and a map; this essay purports only to sketch a map.
72 The most devastating critique that I have read of the literature on confessions was written by a student, Stephen Thomas, for my seminar at the University of Virginia in 1976. He concluded that very little of the legal literature had much to do with confessing and that hardly any of the psychological and theological literature moved beyond speculation. Perhaps the most instructive text is still Dostoyevsky's *Crime and Punishment*.
73 The example introduced in Cohen (1977) has been widely debated for over a decade. The discussions in Tillers and Green (1988) rather clearly illustrate the sense of unreality that characterizes such debates, see above, n. 27.
74 This passage is adapted from the Appendix of *Analysis*.
75 Cohen (1977), esp. chs. 7 and 11 and at 355–6.
76 Kaye (1980).
77 Some of these points have been made by different commentators; see the discussions in Tillers and Green (eds) (1988).
78 The blue and green bus problem is more easily translated into a realistic context, see *Analysis*, Appendix.
79 E.g. Cross (1985) (6th edn, ed. Tapper), 435; Zuckerman (1989). The best empirical study is still Oaks (1970). The problem has attracted much more attention in the United States because it raises important constitutional issues.
80 See, e.g. L. Lustgarten (1986).

81   Zuckerman (1989), ch. 16. Much of this chapter is based on lectures given in the 'Current Legal Problems' series, Zuckerman (1987), where it was not constrained by being in a text on Evidence.
82   Id..
83   Id., 342.
84   Id., 344–6, 350–2.
85   See, however, L. Lustgarten (1986) and literature cited there.
86   If a primary concern about the propriety of admitting and using tainted evidence is to do with the integrity of state officials or the state itself, interesting questions arise as to what constitute closely analogous situations that can be subsumed under a single principle. For example, which of the following are closely analogous: refusal to supply prisoners with syringes or condoms in order to check the spread of Aids; the licensing of prostitutes, gambling or abortion; taxation of illegal or immoral earnings or profits; charging VAT on pornography, hard drugs, alchohol or tobacco; granting immunities or privileges to members of the security forces or others in given circumstances? These examples were suggested by an interesting conversation with Andrew Choo.
87   Above, ch. 5.
88   Above, ch. 7.
89   Twining (1986b), dissenting from Ward Edwards (1986). Edwards's general approach is developed in Winterfeldt and Edwards (1986).
90   Twining and Miers (1982), *passim.*
91   *LTCL*, 63.
92   On the need to distinguish between 'legal realism' as a concept not limited to any specific time or legal system and American Legal Realism as an historical phenomenon see Twining (1985b). It is a common fallacy to treat 'realism' as an American exclusive.
93   Id.
94   Nelken (1981).
95   McBarnett (1981).
96   Peter Tillers has made the point (private communication) that in view of the fact that probability theorists, fact-sceptics and others concerned with fact-determination are interested in 'decisions in situations of uncertainty', it is surprising how little critical legal scholars, who claim to be interested in indeterminacy, have devoted attention to these issues. See also Tillers (1988).
97   See further Twining (1985).
98   Id.
99   Calvino (1981), 204.

Bibliography

Abel, Richard (1973) 'A Comparative Theory of Dispute Institutions in Society', 8 Law and Soc. Rev. 217.
Abel, Richard and Lewis, Philip (eds) (1988–9) *Lawyers in Society*: vol. 1, *The Common Law World*; vol. 2, *The Civil Law World*; vol. 3, *Comparative Theories* (forthcoming). Berkeley.
Abu Hareira, M. A. (1984) *A Holistic Approach to the Analysis and Examination of Evidence in Anglo-American Judicial Trials*, unpublished Ph.D. thesis. Warwick.
—— (1986) 'An Early Holistic Conception of Judicial Fact-finding', Juridical Rev. 79.
Ackerman, Bruce (1973) 'Law and the Modern Mind', 102 Daedalus 119.
Allen, Hilary (1987) 'The Logic of Gender in Psychiatric Reports in Courts' in Pennington and Lloyd-Bostock (eds), 104–16.
Allen, Ronald (1988) 'A Reconceptualization of Civil Trials' in Tillers and Green (eds).
American Bar Association (1979) *Lawyer Competency: The Role of the Law Schools*. Report of a Task Force of the ABA, Section of Legal Education and Admission to the Bar. Chicago.
American Law Institute (1939) 'American Law Institute Undertakes Code of Evidence', 25 ABAJ 380.
—— (1942) *Model Code of Evidence*. Philadelphia.
Anderson, Terence and Twining, William (1987) *Analysis of Evidence*, tentative edn. Miami.
Anscombe, Elizabeth (1958) 'On Brute Facts', 18 Analysis 69.
Appleton, John (1860) *The Rules of Evidence Stated and Discussed*. Philadelphia.
Archbold, J. F. (1822) *A Summary of the Law Relative to Pleading and Evidence in Criminal Cases*, 1st edn. London (40th edn. ed. S. Mitchell, 1979).
Aristotle (1926) *The 'Art' of Rhetoric* (trans. J. H. Freese). London.
—— (1967) *Nichomachean Ethics* (trans. J. A. K. Thompson). Harmondsworth.
Arnold, G. F. (1913) *Psychology Applied to Legal Evidence*, 2nd edn (1st edn, 1906). Calcutta.
Arnold, M. (ed.) (1981) *On the Laws and Customs of England*. Chapel Hill, NC.
Atiyah, P. S. (1980) *Accidents, Compensation and the Law*, 3rd edn (1st edn, 1970). London.
Atiyah, P. S. and Summers, R. S. (1987) *Form and Substance in Anglo-American Law*. Oxford.
Atkinson, J. Maxwell (1981) 'Ethnomethodological Approaches to Socio-legal Studies' in Podgorecki and Whelan (eds).
Atkinson, J. Maxwell and Drew, P. (1979) *Order in Court*. London.
Atkinson, R. F. (1978) *Knowledge and Explanation in History*. London.
Auden, W. H. (1950) *Collected Shorter Poems, 1930–44*. London.
Austin, John (1863) 'The Uses of the Study of Jurisprudence' in H. L. A. Hart (ed.), *The Province of Jurisprudence Determined* (1954). London.

Ayer, A. J. (1956) *The Problem of Knowledge*. London.
—— (1961) 'Philosophical Scepticism' in H. D. Lewis (ed.)
—— (1963) *Philosophical Essays*. London.
—— (1972) *Probability and Evidence*. London.
—— (1980) *Hume*. Oxford.
Baddeley, A. and Woodhead, M. (1983) 'Improving Face Recognition Ability' in Lloyd-Bostock and Clifford (eds).
Bain, Alexander (1882) *James Mill: A Biography*. London.
Baker, J. H. (1984) *The Order of Serjeants at Law*, Selden Soc., suppl. series, vol. 5. London.
Baldwin, J. and Bottomley, A. K. (eds) (1978) *Criminal Justice*. London.
Baldwin, J. and McConville, M. (1977) *Negotiated Justice*. London.
Ball, V. (1961) 'The Moment of Truth: Probability Theory and Standards of Proof', 14 Vand. L. Rev. 807.
Bambrough, Renford (ed.) (1974) *Wisdom: Twelve Essays*. Oxford.
Bankowski, Zenon (1981) 'The Value of Truth: Fact-scepticism Revisited', 3 Legal Studies 257.
Bankowski, Z., Hutton, N. and Mcmanus, J. (1987) *Lay Justice?* Edinburgh.
Barnes, David W. (1983) *Statistics as Proof*. Boston.
Bathurst, J. (1761) *The Theory of Evidence*. Dublin (later incorporated in Buller, 1772).
Beale, J. H. (1905) Review of Wigmore's *Treatise*, 1st edn, 18 Harv. L. Rev. 478.
Beard, Charles (1913) *An Economic Interpretation of the Constitution of the United States*. New York.
—— (1934) 'Written History as an Act of Faith', 39 Am. Hist. L. Rev. 219, reprinted in Meyerhoff (1959).
Beck, Anthony (1987) 'The Semiology of Law', 7 Oxf. Jo. Leg. Stud. 475.
Becker, Carl (1955) 'What are Historical Facts?' 8 The Western Political Qrtly. 327, reprinted in Meyerhoff (1959).
Belloc, Hilaire (1932) Foreword to Chassaigne.
Benenson, F. C. (1984) *Probability, Objectivity and Evidence*. London.
Benét, Stephen Vincent 'John Brown's Body', cited in Jesse (1979).
Benjamin, Walter (1970) *Illuminations* (ed. H. Arendt). London.
Bennett, Judge H. G. (1979) Report of the Committee of Inquiry into Police Interrogation Procedures in Northern Ireland. Cmnd. 7497. London.
Bennett, W. Lance and Feldman, Martha (1981) *Reconstructing Reality in the Courtroom*. London and New York.
Bentham, Jeremy (see also List of Abbreviations).
—— (1808) *Scotch reform*. London (2nd edn, 1811) v *Works* 1–53.
—— (1813) *Swear Not at All*. London (v *Works* 187–229).
—— (1824) *The Book of Fallacies* (ed. P. Bingham). London (II *Works*, 375–487).
—— (1825) *A Treatise on Judicial Evidence*, extracted from the MSS of Jeremy Bentham by Etienne Dumont and translated into English. London.
—— (1827) *Rationale of Judicial Evidence*, ed. J. S. Mill, 5 vols. London (VI and VII *Works*).
—— (1837) *Principles of Judicial Procedure*, ed. R. Doane. London (II *Works* 1–188).
—— (1838–43) *The Works of Jeremy Bentham*, ed. J. Bowring. Edinburgh.
—— (1838–53) *An Introductory View of the Rationale of Judicial Evidence* (VI *Works* 1–188).
—— (1968–) *The Collected Works of Jeremy Bentham*, prepared under the supervision of the Bentham Committee, University College, London. (London, 1968–82; Oxford, 1983–).
Berger, Peter (1966) *Invitation to Sociology*. New York.
Berger, Peter and Luckmann, Thomas (1967) *The Social Construction of Reality*. London.
Best, William M. (1844) *A Treatise on Presumptions of Law and Fact*. London.
—— (1849) *A Treatise on the Principles of the Law of Evidence*. London (8th English edn, ed. J. M. Lely, 1893).
—— (1856–8) 'Codification of the Laws of England', papers read before the Juridical Society, London.

Bienen, Leigh G. (1983) 'A Question of Credibility: John Henry Wigmore's Use of Scientific Authority in section 924a of the Treatise on Evidence', 19 Calif. Western L. Rev. 235.

Binder, David and Bergman, Paul (1984) *Fact Investigation*. St Paul.

Birkenhead, Earl of (F. E. Smith) (1928) *More Famous Trials*. London.

Black, Max (1952) *Critical Thinking*. Englewood Cliffs, NJ.

Blackstone, William (1765–9) *Commentaries on the Laws of England*, 1st edn, 4 vols. Oxford.

Bloch, M. (1954) *The Historian's Craft*. Manchester.

Blumberg, A. S. (1967) *Criminal Justice*. Chicago.

Bok, Sissela (1978) *Lying*. New York and London.

Bonnier, E. (1843) *Traité théorique et pratique des preuves*, 2 vols (2nd edn, 1852). Paris.

Borchard, E. M. (1932) *Convicting the Innocent*. New Haven.

Bradbury, Malcolm (1987) *Mensonge*. London.

Brandon, Ruth and Davies, Christie (1973) *Wrongful Imprisonment*. London.

Bresler, Fenton (1965) *Reprieve*. London.

Brickey, Stephen and Miller, Dan (1975) 'Bureaucratic Due Process: An Ethnography of a Traffic Court', 22 Social Problems 688.

Britton, Philip and Thompson, Ian (1984) *The Sunday Times Case* (film). London.

Broad, Lewis (1952) *The Innocence of Edith Thompson: A Study in Old Bailey Justice* (reprinted, 1957, sub nom. *The Truth about Edith Thompson*). London.

Bronaugh, R. (ed.) (1978) *Philosophical Law*. Westport, Conn., and London.

Browne, Douglas (1960) *Sir Travers Humphreys: A Biography*. London.

Browne, Douglas and Tullett, E. V. (1951) *Bernard Spilsbury: His Life and Cases*. London.

Buller, Sir Francis (1772) *An Introduction to the Law Relative to Trials at Nisi Prius*. London (see Bathurst).

Burke, Kenneth (1969) *A Grammar of Motives* (1st edn 1945). Berkeley.

—— (1972) *A Rhetoric of Motives* (1st edn, 1950). Berkeley.

Burns, Sandra S. (1986) 'The Expanding Domain of Negligent Misstatement', 8 U. Tasmania L. Rev. 127.

Burrill, Alexander M. (1856) *A Treatise on the Nature, Principles and Rules of Circumstantial Evidence, especially of the Presumptive Kind, in Criminal Cases*. New York.

Burton, F. and Carlen, P. (1979) *Official Discourse*. London.

Butler, William E. (ed.) (1987) *Justice and Comparative Law: Anglo-Soviet Perspectives on Criminal Law, Procedure, Evidence and Sentencing Policy*. Dordrecht.

Caenegem, R. C. van (1973) *The Birth of the English Common Law*. Cambridge.

Cahn, Edmond H. (1957) 'Jerome Frank's Fact-scepticism and our Future', 66 Yale L. Rev. 3.

—— (1967) *Confronting Injustice*. Boston.

Cairns, Huntington (1935) *Law and the Social Sciences*. London.

Calvino, Italo (1981) *If on a Winter's Night a Traveller* (trans. W. Weaver). London.

Campbell, Colin and Wiles, Paul (1976) 'The Study of Law in Society in Britain', 10 Law and Soc. Rev. 547.

Campbell, Enid and Waller, Louis (eds) (1982) *Well and Truly Tried*. Melbourne.

Carlen, Pat (1976) *Magistrates' Justice*. London.

Carr, E. H. (1961) *What is History?* London.

Carroll, Lewis (C. L. Dodgson) (1865) *Alice's Adventures in Wonderland*. London.

Carter, P. B. (1981) *Cases and Statutes on Evidence*. London.

Centennial History of the Harvard Law School, 1817–1917 (1918). Cambridge, Mass.

Certoma, G. L. (1986) *The Italian Legal System*. London.

Chadbourn, J. W. (1962) 'Bentham and the Hearsay Rule – A Benthamic View of Rule 63(4)c of the Uniform Rules of Evidence', 75 Harv. L. Rev. 932.

Chafee, Z. (1920–1) Book review, 34 Harv. L. Rev. 898.

—— (1922–3) Book review, 36 Harv. L. Rev. 1048.

—— (1931) Review of Wigmore's *Principles*, 80 U.Pa. L. Rev. 319.

Chamberlayne, Charles F. (1906) *Cyclopedia of Law and Procedure*. New York.
—— (1908) 'The Modern Law of Evidence and its Purpose', 42 American L. Rev. 757.
—— (1909) Book review, 20 Green Bag 627.
—— (1911–16) *A Treatise on the Modern Law of Evidence*, 5 vols. Albany, NY.
—— (1936) *Trial Evidence: The Chamberlayne Handbook*, 2nd edn. New York.
Chassaigne, Marc (1932) *The Calas Case*. London.
Cheshire, G. C. and Fifoot, C. H. S. (1969) *Contract*, 7th edn. London.
Christian, Edward (1819) *A Vindication of the Criminal Law and the Administration of Public Justice in England*. London.
Cicourel, Aaron (1973) *Cognitive Sociology*. Harmondsworth.
Clark, Charles (1940) 'Dissatisfaction with Piecemeal Reform', 24 Jo. Am. Judic. Soc. 121.
Clifford, Brian (1983) 'Memory for Voices' in Lloyd-Bostock and Clifford (eds).
Clifford, Brian R. and Bull, Ray (1978) *The Psychology of Person Identification*. London.
Cockburn, J. S. (ed.) (1977) *Crime in England, 1550–1800*. London.
Cocks, R. (1983) *Foundations of the Modern Bar*. London.
Cohen, L. Jonathan (1977) *The Probable and the Provable*. Oxford.
—— (1980) 'The Logic of Proof', Crim. L. Rev. 91.
—— (1980a) 'Bayesianism versus Baconianism in the Evaluation of Medical Diagnoses', 31 Brit. Jo. Phil. Sci. 81.
—— (1983) 'Freedom of Proof' in Twining (ed.) 1.
Cohen, Neil B. (1985) 'Confidence in Probability', 60 NYU L. Rev. 385.
Cole, P. and Pringle, P. (1974) *Can you Positively Identify This Man?* London.
Colenbrander, Joanna (1984) *A Portrait of Fryn: A Biography of F. Tennyson Jesse*. London.
Collingwood, R. G. (1939) *An Autobiography*. Oxford.
—— (1946) *The Idea of History*. Oxford.
Conklin, W. (1987) Book review. 7 Windsor Yearbook of Access to Justice 243.
Cook, Charles M. (1981) *The American Codification Movement: A Study in Antebellum Reform*. Westport, Conn.
Coons, Jack (1964) 'Approaches to Court-induced Compromise – The Uses of Doubt and Reason', 58 Northwestern L. Rev. 750.
Corbett, Edward P. (1965) *Classical Rhetoric for the Modern Student*. New York.
Corbin, A. L. (1914) 'The Law and the Judges', Yale Rev. 234.
Cover, R. and Fiss, O. (1979) *The Structure of Procedure*. Mineola, NY.
Cowen, Zelman and Carter, Peter (1956) *Essays in the Law of Evidence*. Oxford.
Criminal Law Revision Committee (1972) Eleventh Report: Evidence (General). Cmnd. 4991 (CLRC Report). London.
Cross, Sir Rupert (1961) 'Some Proposals for the Reform of the Law of Evidence', 24 MLR 32.
—— (1970) 'The Right to Silence and the Presumption of Innocence – Sacred Cows or Safeguards of Liberty?' 11 JSPTL (NS) 66.
—— (1973) 'The Evidence Report: Sense or Nonsense – A Very Wicked Animal Defends the 11th Report of the Criminal Law Revision Committee', Crim. L. Rev. 329.
—— (1985) *Evidence*, 6th edn, ed. C. Tapper. London (1st edn, 1958; 5th edn, 1979).
Cullison, Alan (1969) 'Identification by Probabilities and Trial by Arithmetic', 6 Houston L. Rev. 471.
Currie, Brainerd (1951–55) 'The Materials of Law Study', I and II, 3 Jo. Leg. Ed. 331; III, 8 id. 1.
Curtis, Charles P. (1954) *It's Your Law*. Cambridge, Mass.
Damaska, M. (1973) 'Evidentiary Barriers to Conviction and Two Models of Criminal Procedure', 121 U.Pa. L. Rev. 506.
—— (1975) 'Presentation of Evidence and Factfinding Precision', 123 U.Pa. L. Rev. 1083.
—— (1986) *The Faces of Justice and State Authority*. New Haven.
Danet, B. (1980) 'Language in the Legal Process', 14 Law and Soc. Rev. 445.

Danto, Arthur C. (1965) *Nietzsche as Philosopher*. New York and London.
____ (1985) *Narration and Knowledge* (incorporating *Analytical Philosophy of History*). New York.
Darrow, Clarence (1936) 'Selecting a Jury', reprinted in Jeans (1975) 167–72.
Davis, John W. (1940) 'The Argument of an Appeal', reprinted in *Jurisprudence in Action* (1953). New York.
Davis, K. C. (1964) 'An Approach to Rules of Evidence for Non-jury Cases', 50 ABAJ 723.
____ (1969) *Discretionary Justice*. Baton Rouge.
Dawid, Philip (1985) 'Probability, Symmetry and Frequency', 36 Brit. Jo. Phil. Sci. 107.
____ (1987) Appendix to Anderson and Twining.
Dearden, H. (1934) *Some Cases of Bernard Spilsbury and Others*. London.
Denning, Lord (1979) *The Discipline of Law*. London.
____ (1981) *The Family Story*. London.
Dennis, Ian (1984) 'Corroboration Requirements Reconsidered', Crim. L. Rev. 316.
____ (ed.) (1987) *Criminal Law and Justice*. London.
Devlin, Patrick (Lord Devlin) (1976) Report to the Secretary of State for the Home Department of The Departmental Committee on Evidence of Identification in Criminal Cases (the Devlin Report). HC 338. London.
____ (1985) *Easing the Passing: The Trial of Dr John Bodkin Adams*. London.
Diamond, A. S. (1971) *Primitive Law, Past and Present*. London.
Director of Public Prosecutions (1986) *Code for Crown Prosecutors*. London.
Dostoyevsky, Fyodor (1866) *Crime and Punishment* (trans. David Magarshak, 1951). London.
Dray, W. (1964) *Philosophy of History*. Englewood Cliffs, NJ.
Du Cann, Richard (1964) *The Art of Advocacy*. Harmondsworth.
Dudley, Ernest (1953) *Bywaters and Mrs Thompson*. London.
Duhamel, J. and Smith, J. Dill (1959) *Some Pillars of English Law*. London.
Dworkin, Ronald (1977) *Taking Rights Seriously*. London.
____ (1981) 'Principle, Policy, Procedure', in Tapper (ed.)
____ (1985) *A Matter of Principle*. Oxford.
____ (1986) *Law's Empire*. London.
Eddy, J. P. (1960) *Scarlet and Ermine*. London.
Edwards, P. (ed.) (1967) *Encyclopedia of Philosophy*, 4 vols. New York and London.
Edwards, Ward (1986) 'Summing Up: The Bayesian Society of Trial Lawyers', 66 Boston U. L. Rev. 937 (reprinted in Tillers and Green, eds, 1988).
Eekelaar, John (1984) *Family Law and Social Policy*, 2nd edn. London.
Eggleston, Sir Richard (1979) 'The Probability Debate', Crim. L. Rev. 678.
____ (1983) *Evidence, Proof and Probability*, 2nd edn. London (1st edn, 1978).
____ (1983a) 'Generalizations and Experts' in Twining (ed.) (1983) 22.
Ehrenzweig, Albert (1971) *Psychoanalytic Jurisprudence*. Leiden.
Eisenberg, M. (1976) 'Private Ordering Through Negotiation', 89 Harv. L. Rev. 637.
Ekelof, Per Olof (1964) 'Free Evaluation of Evidence', 8 Scand. Studies in Law 4.
Elias, T. O. (1962) *British Colonial Law*. London.
Ellman, Ira M. and Kaye, David (1979) 'Probabilities and Proof: Can HLA and Blood-group Testing Prove Paternity?' 54 NYUL. Rev. 1131.
Elton, G. R. (1969) *The Practice of History*. Sydney and London.
Empson, William (1828) Review of Bentham's *Rationale of Judicial Evidence*, 48 Edinburgh Rev. 457–520.
____ (1843) Review of Bowring's *Memoirs of Jeremy Bentham*, 78 Edinburgh Rev. 460–516.
Esmein, A. (1913) *History of Continental Criminal Procedure* (trans. Simpson). Boston.
Evans, Keith (1983) *Advocacy at the Bar: A Beginner's Guide*. London.
Evans, Sir W. D. (1803) *A General View of the Decisions of Lord Mansfield in Civil Cases*, 2 vols. London.
____ (1806) *Notes on Pothier on Obligations*. London (see Pothier).
Everett, Charles W. (1931) *The Education of Jeremy Bentham*. New York.

Farmer, J. (1974) *Tribunals and Government*. London.
Feeley, M. (1979) 'Pleading Guilty in Lower Courts', 13 Law and Soc. Rev. 461.
Felix, David (1965) *Protest*. Bloomington, Ind.
Felstiner, W., Abel, R. and Sarat, A. (1980–1) 'The Emergence and Transformation of Disputes: Naming, Blaming, Claiming...', 15 Law and Soc. Rev. 631.
Fenning, K. (1931–2) Review of Wigmore's *Principles* (2nd edn), 20 Georgetown Law Jo. 1092.
Field, R. H. (1970) 'The Right to Silence: A Reply to Professor Cross', 11 JSPTL (NS) 76.
Fifoot, C. H. S. (1959) *Judge and Jurist in the Reign of Queen Victoria*. London.
Finkelstein, M. O. (1978) *Quantitative Methods in Law*. New York and London.
Finkelstein, M. O. and Fairley, W. B. (1970) 'A Bayesian Approach to Identification Evidence', 83 Harv. L. Rev. 489.
Finkelstein, N. and Rogers, B. M. (1988) *Charter Issues in Civil Cases*. Toronto.
Fischer, D. H. (1970) *Historians' Fallacies*. New York.
Forster, E. M. (1949 edn) *Aspects of the Novel*. London.
Fortescue, Sir J. (1545–6) *De Laudibus Legum Angliae*. London (ed. S. B. Chrimes, 1942. Cambridge).
Frank, Jerome (1930) *Law and the Modern Mind*. New York.
—— (1933) 'Why not a Clinical Lawyer School?' 81 U.Pa. L. Rev. 907.
—— (1938) *Save America First*. New York.
—— (1942) *If Men Were Angels*. New York.
—— (1945) *Fate and Freedom* (revised edn, 1953). Boston.
—— (1947) 'A Plea for Lawyer-Schools', 56 Yale LJ. 1303.
—— (1949) *Courts on Trial*. Princeton (rev. edn, ed. E. Cahn, 1970. New York).
—— (1953) 'Some Tame Reflections on Some Wild Facts' in Ratner (ed.).
—— (1957) (with Barbara Frank) *Not Guilty*. Garden City.
Frankfurter, Felix (1927, 1961) *The Case of Sacco and Vanzetti*. Boston.
Freeman, M. D. A. (1978) 'The Social Construction of Truth: Some Thoughts on Jury Trials and Current Research into Juries', 1 Preston L. Rev. 3.
Fuller, Lon (1946) 'Reason and Fiat in Case Law', 59 Harv. L. Rev. 376.
—— (1978) 'The Forms and Limits of Adjudication', 92 Harv. L. Rev. 353.
Galanter, Marc (1974) 'Why the "Haves" come out Ahead', 9 Law and Soc. Rev. 95.
—— (1983) 'Reading the Landscape of Disputes', 31 UCLA L. Rev. 4.
—— (1986) 'Adjudication, Litigation and Related Phenomena' in Lipson and Wheeler (eds).
Gallie, W. B. (1956) 'Essentially Contested Concepts', 56 Proc. Aristotelian Soc. 167.
Galligan, Dennis (ed.) (1984) *Essays in Legal Theory*. Carlton, Victoria.
—— (1986) *Discretionary Powers*. Oxford.
—— (1988) 'More Scepticism about Scepticism', 8 Oxf. Jo. Leg. Stud. 249.
Gallwey, W. Timothy (1974) *The Inner Game of Tennis*. London.
Garde, Richard (1830) *A Practical Treatise on the General Principles and Elementary Rules of the Law of Evidence*. London.
Gardiner, Patrick (ed.) (1974) *The Philosophy of History*. Oxford.
Garfinkel, H. (1956) 'The Conditions for Successful Degradation Ceremonies', 61 Am. Jo. Sociology 42.
Geertz, Clifford (1983) *Local Knowledge*. New York.
Geyl, P. (1955) *Debates with Historians*. The Hague.
Gilbert, Sir Jeffrey (1754) *The Law of Evidence*. Dublin (3rd edn, 1769. London).
Glassford, James (1820) *An Essay on the Principles of Evidence and Their Application to Subjects of Judicial Inquiry*. Edinburgh and London.
Glazebrook, Peter (ed.) (1978) *Reshaping the Criminal Law: Essays in Honour of Glanville Williams*. London.
Gledhill, A. (1964) *The Republic of India: The Development of its Laws and Constitution*. London.
Gobbi, Claire and Twining, William (1981) *Adjective Law* (Report to Executive Committee of the Bentham Project), unpublished. London.

Goitein, H. (1923) *Primitive Ordeal and Modern Law*. London.
Gold, David M. (1979) 'Chief Justice Appleton', 18 Maine Hist. Soc. Qrtly. 193.
Gold, Neil (ed.) (1982) *Essays on Legal Education*. Toronto.
Gold, Neil, Mackie, Karl and Twining, William (eds) (1989) *Learning Lawyers' Skills*. London.
Golding, Martin (1978) 'On the Adversary System and Justice', in Bronaugh (ed.), ch. 9.
Good, I. J. (1950) *Probability and the Weighing of Evidence*. London.
Gooderson, Richard (1977) *Alibi*. London.
Goodrich, Peter (1986) *Legal Discourse*. Basingstoke.
—— (1987) *Reading the Law*. Oxford.
Gorphe, F. (1927) *La Critique du témoignage*. Paris.
Gottlieb, G. (1968) *The Logic of Choice*. Oxford.
Graham, Kenneth, Jr. (1983) 'The Persistence of Progressive Proceduralism', 61 Texas L. Rev. 929.
—— (1987) '"There'll Always be an England": The Instrumental Ideology of Evidence' (review of *TEBW*), 85 Mich. L. Rev. 1204.
Grasserie, R. de la (1912) *De la preuve au civil et au criminel en droit français et dans les législations étrangères*. Paris.
Greenleaf, Simon (1842) *A Treatise on the Law of Evidence*. Boston.
—— (1899) 16th edn, ed. J. H. Wigmore (vol. 1), J. Harriman (vols 2 and 3). Boston.
Greer, Desmond (1971) 'Anything but the Truth?' 11 Brit. Jo. Crim. 131.
Griffith, J. A. G. (1985) *The Politics of the Judiciary*, 3rd edn (1st edn, 1977). London.
Griffiths, John (1983) 'The General Theory of Litigation – A First Step', 5 Zeitschrift für Rechtssoziologie, Heft 2, 145.
Gross, Hans (1879, trans. Kallen, 1911) *Criminal Psychology*. London.
Gudjonnsen, G. and Drinkwater, J. (eds) (1987) *Psychological Evidence in Court*. Leicester.
Guest, Stephen (1987) 'Law, Fact and Lay Questions' in Dennis (ed.).
Gulson, J. R. (1905) *Philosophy of Proof*, 1st edn. London (2nd edn, 1923).
Hacking, Ian (1975) *The Emergence of Probability*. Cambridge.
Hain, Peter (1976) *Mistaken Identity*. London.
Hale, Sir M. (1682) *Pleas of the Crown*. London.
Halévy, Elie (1928) *The Growth of Philosophic Radicalism* (trans. Mary Morris). London (id, 1955, preface by A. D. Lindsay. Boston).
Hamburger, Lotte and Joseph (1985) *Troubled Lives: John and Sarah Austin*. Toronto.
Harris, Jean (1986) *Stranger in Two Worlds*. New York.
Harrison, Ross (1983) *Bentham*. London.
Harrison, S. B. (1825) *Evidence*. London.
Hart, H. L. A. (1953) *Definition and Theory in Jurisprudence*. Inaugural lecture, Oxford, reprinted 70 LQR 37 and Hart (1983).
—— (1960) *Bentham*. British Academy Lecture. London.
—— (1961) *The Concept of Law*. Oxford.
—— (1968) *Punishment and Responsibility*. Oxford.
—— (1973) 'Bentham and the Demystification of the Law', 36 MLR 2, reprinted in Hart (1982) ch. 1.
—— (1982) *Essays on Bentham*. Oxford.
—— (1983) *Essays in Jurisprudence and Philosophy*. Oxford.
—— (1984) 'Arthur Rupert Neale Cross, 1912–1980', LXX Procs. Brit. Academy 405.
Harvey, Cameron (1986) 'It all Started with Gunner James', Denning Law Jo. 67.
Hastie, Reid, Penrod, Stephen and Pennington, Nancy (1983) *Inside the Jury*. Cambridge, Mass.
Haward, L. *Forensic Psychology*. London.
Hawkins, W. (1716) *A Treatise of the Pleas of the Crown*. London.
Hay, Douglas (1975) 'Property, Authority and the Criminal Law' in Hay et al.
Hay, Douglas et al. (1975) *Albion's Fatal Tree*. London.

Hazard, G. (1965) 'Rationing Justice', 8 Jo. Law and Ecs. 1.

Hempel, Carl (1965) *Aspects of Scientific Explanation*. New York.

Heydon, J. D. (1984) *Cases and Materials on the Law of Evidence* (2nd edn). London.

Hoffman, John C. (1986) *Law, Freedom and Story*. Waterloo, Canada.

Holdcroft, David (1983) 'Relevance in Legal Proof', in Twining (ed.).

Holdsworth, Sir W. S. (1903–38) *A History of English Law*, 12 vols (misc. editions). London.

——— (1925) *Sources and Literature of English Law*. Oxford.

Hollis, M. and Lukes, S (eds) (1982) *Rationality and Relativism*. Oxford.

Holmes, O. W., Jr. (1897) 'The Path of the Law', 10 Harv. L. Rev. 457.

Honoré, A. M. (1981) 'The Primacy of Oral Evidence?' in Tapper (ed.).

Houts, M. (1955) 'A Course on Proof', 7 Jo. Leg. Ed. 418.

——— (1956) *From Evidence to Proof*. Springfield.

Hughes, Stuart (1959) *Consciousness and Society: The Reorientation of European Social Thought 1890–1930*. London.

Hume, David (1739–40) *A Treatise of Human Nature* (ed. A. Selby-Bigge, 1888). Oxford.

——— (1748) *Enquiry Concerning Human Understanding*. Edinburgh.

Hume, L. J. (1981) *Bentham and Bureaucracy*. Cambridge.

Humphreys, Travers (1953) *A Book of Trials*. London.

Hutchins, Robert M. (1933) 'Autobiography of an Ex-Law Student', AALS, reprinted in Hutchins (1936).

——— (1936) *No Friendly Voice*. Chicago.

Hutchins, Robert M. and Slesinger, Donald (1928) 'Some Observations on the Law of Evidence – Memory', 28 Col. L. Rev. 432.

——— (1928a) 'Some Observations on the Law of Evidence – The Competency of Witnesses', 37 Yale LJ 1017.

——— (1929) 'Some Observations on the Law of Evidence – Consciousness of Guilt', 77 U.Pa. L. Rev. 725.

——— (1929a) 'Some Observations on the Law of Evidence – State of Mind to Prove an Act', 38 Yale LJ 283.

——— (1929b) 'Some Observations on the Law of Evidence – Family Relations', 13 Minn. L. Rev. 675.

Hyams, P. (1981) 'Trial by Ordeal: the Key to Proof in the Early Common Law' in M. Arnold (ed.).

Hyde, H. Montgomery (1955) *United in Crime*. London.

Inbau, Fred E. (1981) 'John Henry Wigmore and Scientific Evidence', 75 Northwestern L. Rev. Supp. 8.

Ireland, R. (1980) 'First Catch Your Toad: Medieval Attitudes to Ordeal and Battle', 2 Cambrian L. Rev. 50.

Jackson, Bernard (1985) *Semiotics and Legal Theory*. London.

——— (1988) *Law, Fact and Narrative Coherence*. Merseyside.

——— (1988a) 'Narrative Models and Legal Proof', 2 Int. Jo. Semiotics of Law 225.

——— (ed.) (1988–9) Symposium: 'Approches du discours de la preuve en droit', 2 Int. Jo. Semiotics of Law, Nos., 3 and 4.

Jackson, John (1983) 'Questions of Fact and Questions of Law' in Twining (ed.).

——— (1988) 'Two Methods of Proof in Criminal Procedure', 51 MLR 549.

——— (1988a) 'Credibility, Morality and the Corroboration Warning' 47 Camb. LJ 428.

——— (1988b) 'Theories of Truth-Finding in Criminal Procedure: An Evolutionary Approach'. 10 Cardozo L. Rev. 475.

Jackson, Stanley (1951) *The Life and Cases of Mr Justice Humphreys*. London.

Jacob, Sir Jack (1987) 'Fundamental Features of English Civil Justice' in Butler (ed.).

——— (1987a) *The Fabric of English Civil Justice*. Hamlyn Lectures. London.

Jacobs, G. (ed.) (1970) *The Participant Observer*. New York.

James, George (1941) 'Relevance, Probability and Law', 29 Calif. L. Rev. 689.

James, M. H. (ed.) (1974) *Bentham and Legal Theory*, reprinted from the Northern Ireland Legal Quarterly, XXIV (1973). Belfast.

Jameson, Fredric (1980) *The Political Unconscious, Narrative as a Socially Symbolic Act*. London.
Jeans, James (1975) *Trial Advocacy*. St Paul.
Jesse, F. Tennyson (1934) *A Pin to See the Peepshow* (reissued, 1979). London.
―― (1984) 'Rattenbury and Stoner' in Mortimer (ed.).
Jevons, W. Stanley (1877) *The Principles of Science: A Treatise on Logic and Scientific Method* (2nd edn, 1907). London.
Jones, Burr W. (1896) *The Law of Evidence in Civil Cases*, 1st edn (5th edn, 1958; Supp., 1968). San Francisco.
Joughin, L. and Morgan, E. M. (1948) *The Legacy of Sacco and Vanzetti*. New York.
Jowell, J. and McAuslan, J. P. W. B. (1984) *Lord Denning: The Judge and the Law*. London.
Jurisprudence in Action: A Pleader's Anthology (1953). New York.
Kadish, Sanford (1985) 'Complicity, Cause and Blame: A Study in the Interpretation of Doctrine', 73 Calif. L. Rev. 324.
Kalven, H. (1958) 'Some Comments on the Law and Behavioral Science Program at the University of Pennsylvania', 11 Jo. Leg. Ed. 94.
Kamenka, E. et al. (eds) (1978) *Law and Society*. London.
Kaplan, J. (1968) 'Decision-theory and the Factfinding Process', 20 Stanford L. Rev. 1065.
Kaye, David (1979) 'The Laws of Probability and the Laws of the Land', 47 U. Chi. L. Rev. 40.
―― (1979a) 'The Paradox of the Gatecrasher and Other Stories', Ariz. St. U. LJ 101.
―― (1980) 'Naked Statistical Evidence', 89 Yale LJ 601.
―― (1988) 'What is Bayesianism?' in Tillers and Green (eds).
Keane, Adrian (1989) *The Modern Law of Evidence*, 2nd edn. London.
Keeton, George and Marshall, Roy (1948) 'Bentham's Influence on the Law of Evidence' in Keeton and Schwarzenberger (eds).
Keeton, George W. and Schwarzenberger, Georg (eds) (1948) *Jeremy Bentham and the Law*. London.
Kelman, Mark (1987) *A Guide to Critical Legal Studies*. Cambridge, Mass.
Kelsen, Hans (1957) *What is Justice?* Berkeley.
Kennedy, George (1963) *The Art of Persuasion in Greece*. Princeton.
―― (1972) *The Art of Rhetoric in the Roman World*. Princeton.
―― (1980) *Classical Rhetoric*. Chapel Hill and London.
Kenny, C. (1928) Book review, 3 Camb. LJ 318.
King, Michael (1981) *The Framework of Criminal Justice*. London.
Kiraly, J. (1979) *Criminal Procedure: Truth and Probability*. Budapest.
Krawietz, W., Scheskey, H., Winkler, G. and Schramm, A. (eds) (1984) *Theorie der Normen*. Berlin.
Kunert, K. (1966–7) 'Some Observations on the Origin and Structure of Evidence Rules under the Common Law System and the Civil Law System of "Free Proof" in the German Code of Criminal Procedure', 16 Buffalo L. Rev. 122.
Kurzon, Dennis (1986) 'How Lawyers Tell their Tales', 14 Poetics 465–81.
Kyburg, H. and Smokler, H. (eds) (1964) *Studies in Subjective Probability*. New York.
Lambourne, G. (1984) *The Fingerprint Story*. London.
Landsman, Stephan (1984) *The Adversary System: A Description and Defence*. Washington.
―― (1986) 'When Justice Fails' (The Haymarket Tragedy), 84 Mich. L. Rev. 824.
Langbein, John H. (1974) *Prosecuting Crime in the Renaissance: England, Germany, France*. Cambridge, Mass.
―― (1978) 'The Criminal Trial Before the Lawyers', 45 U. Chi L. Rev. 263.
―― (1983) 'Shaping the Eighteenth Century Trial: A View from the Ryder Sources', 50 U. Chi. L. Rev. 1.
Lasswell, Harold and McDougal, Myres (1967) 'Jurisprudence in Policy-oriented Perspective', 19 Florida L. Rev. 486.
Lea, H. C. (1878) *Superstition and Force*, 3rd edn. Philadelphia.
Lehrer, K. (1973) *Knowledge*. Oxford.
Lempert, Richard (1988) 'The New Evidence Scholarship' in Tillers and Green (eds).

Lempert, Richard and Saltzburg, Stephen (1977) *A Modern Approach to Evidence*, 2nd edn, 1982. St Paul.

Lenin, V. I. *Materialism and Empiriocentrism*, cited in Kiraly (1979).

Lerminier, E. (1830) *Introduction générale à l'histoire du droit*. Brussels.

Letwin, S. R. (1965) *The Pursuit of Certainty*. Cambridge.

Levin, A. Leo (1956) *Evidence and the Behavioral Sciences*, mimeo, U. of Pennsylvania Law School.

—— (1958) 'The Law and Behavioral Science Project at the University of Pennsylvania: Evidence', 11 Jo. Leg. Ed. 87.

Lewis, Andrew (1988) 'Bentham and The Right to Silence', 12 The Bentham Newsletter 37.

Lewis, H. D. (ed.) (1961) *Contemporary British Philosophy* (3rd series). London.

Ligertwood, Andrew (1988) *Australian Evidence*. Sydney.

Lindsay, P. and Norman, D. (1977) *Human Information Processing: An Introduction to Psychology*, 2nd edn. New York and London.

Lindsay, R. C. L. and Wells, G. (1983) 'What do we Really Know about Cross-race Identification?' in Lloyd-Bostock and Clifford (eds).

Lipson, L. and Wheeler, S. (eds) (1986) *Law and the Social Sciences*. New York.

Littman, Richard A. and Rosen, Ephraim (1950) 'The Molar–Molecular Distinction', 57 Psychol. Rev. 58.

Livingston, Edward (1833) *Introductory Report to the Code of Evidence*. New Orleans.

—— (1873) *Works* (ed. S. P. Chase), 2 vols. New York.

Llewellyn, Karl N. (1950) *Law in our Society*, unpublished course materials. Chicago (see Twining, 1973).

—— (1951) *The Bramble Bush*, 2nd edn. New York (1st edn, 1930).

—— (1960) *The Common Law Tradition: Deciding Appeals*. Boston.

—— (1962) *Jurisprudence: Realism in Theory and Practice*. Chicago.

Lloyd-Bostock, Sally M. (ed.) (1980) *Psychology in Legal Contexts: Applications and Limitations*. London.

—— (ed.) (1981) *Law and Psychology*. Oxford.

—— (1981a) 'Psychology and the Law', 8 Brit. Jo. Law and Soc. 1.

—— (1988) *Law in Practice* (*Psychology in Action* series). London.

—— (1988a) 'The Benefits of Legal Psychology: Possibilities, Practice and Dilemmas', 77 Brit. Jo. of Psychology 417.

Lloyd-Bostock, Sally M. and Clifford, Brian (eds) (1983) *Evaluating Witness Evidence*. Chichester.

Locke, J. (1975) *An Essay Concerning Human Understanding* (ed. P. H. Niddich). Oxford.

Loftus, Elizabeth (1979) *Eyewitness Testimony*. Cambridge, Mass.

Loftus, E. and Ketcham, K. (1983) 'The Malleability of Eyewitness Accounts' in Lloyd-Bostock and Clifford (eds).

Loftus, Geoffrey R. and Loftus, Elizabeth (1976) *Human Memory: The Processing of Information*. Hillsdale, NJ.

Logie, J. and Watchman, P. (1989) 'Social Security Appeal Tribunals: An Excursus on Evidential Issues', 8 Civil Justice Qrtly. 109.

Loh, W. D. (1981) 'Psycho-legal Research', 79 Mich. L. Rev. 659.

Lopez, Gerald P. (1984) 'Lay Lawyering', 32 UCLA Law Rev.1

Louisell, David W., Kaplan, John and Waltz, Jon R. (1972) *Cases and Materials on Evidence*, 2nd edn. Mineola, NY.

Low, Colin (1978) 'The Sociology of Criminal Justice: Progress and Prospects' in Baldwin and Bottomley (eds).

Lucas, J. R. (1958) 'On Not Worshipping Facts', 8 Philo. Qrtly. 144.

Luckmann, T. (ed.) (1978) *Phenomenology and Sociology*. Harmondsworth.

Lustgarten, E. (1949) *Verdict in Dispute*. London.

Lustgarten, Laurence E. (1986) *The Governance of the Police*. London.

Lyons, David (1973) *In the Interest of the Governed*. Oxford.

Macaulay, S. (1963) 'Non-contractual Relations in Business', 28 Am. Soc. Rev. 55.
McBarnett, Doreen (1981) *Conviction*. London.
McCloskey, Donald N. (1985) *The Rhetoric of Economics*. Madison.
MacCormick, D. N. (1978) *Legal Reasoning and Legal Theory*. Oxford.
——— (1980) 'The Coherence of a Case and the Reasonableness of Doubt', 2 Liverpool L. Rev. 45.
——— (1981) *H. L. A. Hart*. London.
——— (1984) 'Coherence in Legal Justification' in W. Krawietz et al. (eds).
MacCormick, Neil and Twining, William (1986) 'Theory in the Law Curriculum' in *LTCL*.
McCormick, Charles T. (1972) *Handbook of the Law of Evidence*, ed. Cleary et al. St. Paul (1st edn, 1954).
McDougal, M. and Reisman, W. M. (1981) *International Law Essays*. New York.
Mack, Mary P. (1962) *Jeremy Bentham: An Odyssey of Ideas 1748–1792*. London.
McKelvey, John J. (1897) *Handbook of the Law of Evidence*. St Paul (3rd edn, 1924; 5th edn, 1944).
MacNally, L. (1802) *Rules of Evidence on Pleas of the Crown*. Dublin.
McNamara, Philip (1986) 'The Canons of Evidence – Rules of Exclusion or Rules of Use?' 10 Adelaide L. Rev. 341.
MacNeil, Ian (1974) 'The Many Futures of Contract', 47 Calif. L. Rev. 691.
McRae, R. F. (1973) *Introduction to J. S. Mill's System of Logic*. Toronto.
Maguire, John M. (1947) *Evidence: Common Sense and Common Law*. Chicago.
——— (1963) 'Wigmore – Two Centuries', 58 Northwestern L. Rev. 456.
Maguire, John M. et al. (1973) *Cases and Materials on Evidence* (successor to Morgan and Maguire, 1934). Mineola, NY.
Maine, Sir H. (1892) *Life and Speeches of Sir Henry Maine* (ed. Whitley Stokes). London.
Mannheim, Karl (1936) *Ideology and Utopia*. London.
Mansfield, G. and Peay, J. (1987) *The Director of Public Prosecutions: Principles and Practices for the Crown Prosecutor*. London.
Marre, Lady Mary (1988) *A Time for Change*. Report of the Committee on the Future of the Legal Profession (The Marre Committee). London.
Marshall, J. (1980) *Law and Psychology in Conflict*, 2nd edn. Indianapolis.
Marx, Robert S. (1953) 'Shall Law Schools Establish a Course on "Facts"?' 5 Jo. Leg. Ed. 524.
Mauet, Thomas A. (1980) *Fundamentals of Trial Techniques*. Boston.
Mehan, H. and Wood, H. (1975) *The Reality of Ethnomethodology*.
Mengler, T. M. (1989) 'The Theory of Discretion in the Federal Rules of Evidence', 74 Iowa L. Rev. 413.
Merrills, John (1971) 'Fact and Fancy', 11 JSPTL (NS) 155.
Meyerhoff, H. (ed.) (1959) *The Philosophy of History in our Time*. New York.
Michael, Jerome (1948) *Elements of Legal Controversy*. Brooklyn.
Michael, Jerome and Adler, Mortimer (1931) *The Nature of Judicial Proof: an Inquiry into the Logical, Legal and Empirical Aspects of the Law of Evidence*, tentative edn, privately printed. New York.
——— (1934) 'The Trial of an Issue of Fact', 34 Col. L. Rev. 1224.
——— (1952) 'Real Proof', 5 Vand. L. Rev. 344.
Midgley, T. S. (1975) 'The Role of Legal History', 2 Brit. Jo. Law and Soc. 153.
Mill, John Stuart (1873) *Autobiography* (1924, ed. H. Laski). London.
——— (1973) *A System of Logic, Ratiocinative and Inductive* (*Collected Works*, ed. J. M. Robson et al.). Toronto (1st edn, 1843. London).
Millar, E. Cockburn (1957) 'Some Memoirs of Lord Atkin', 23 Glim 13.
Millar, Robert W. (1952) *Civil Procedure of the Trial Court in Historical Perspective*. New York.
Milsom, S. F. C. (1967) 'Law and Fact in Legal Development', 17 U. of Toronto Law Jo. 1.
——— (1969) *Historical Foundations of the Common Law*. London.
Mirfield, Peter (1985) *Confessions*. London.
Moenkmoeller, O. (1930) *Psychologie und Psychopathologie der Aussage*. Heidelberg.

Montesquieu, Charles Louis de Secondat, Baron de (1823) *De l'esprit des lois* (trans. Nugent), 2 vols. London (1st edn, 1748).

Montrose, James L. (1968) *Precedent in English Law and Other Essays*, ed. H. Hanbury. Shannon.

Moore, Albert J. (1987) 'Inferential Streams: The Articulation and Illustration of the Trial Advocate's Evidentiary Intuitions', 34 UCLA L. Rev. 611.

Moore, Charles C. (1907) 'Yellow Psychology', 11 Law Notes 125.

_____ (1908) *A Treatise on Facts: Or the Weight and Value of Evidence*. Long Island, NY.

Moore, W. Underhill (1923) 'Rational Basis of Legal Institutions', 23 Col. L. Rev. 609.

Morgan, Edmund M. (1924–5) Book review, 34 Yale LJ 223.

_____ (1939) (see American Law Institute) 25 ABAJ 380.

_____ (1940) Review of Wigmore's *Treatise*, 20 Boston U. L. Rev. 776–93.

_____ (1944) 'Judicial Notice', 57 Harv. L. Rev. 269.

_____ (1956) *Some Problems of Proof under the Anglo-American System of Litigation*. New York.

_____ (1961) 'Some Practical Difficulties Impeding Reform of the Law of Evidence', 14 Vand. L. Rev. 725.

Morgan, Edmund M. et al. (1927) *The Law of Evidence: Some Proposals for its Reform*. New Haven.

Morgan, Edmund and Maguire, John M. (1934) *Cases on Evidence* (later edns, 1942, 1951, 1957, 1965). Mineola, NY (see also Maguire et al., 1973).

Morison, W. (1982) *John Austin*. London.

Mortimer, John (ed.) (1984) *Famous Trials*. Harmondsworth.

Mueller, Gerhard O. (1969) *Crime, Law and the Scholars*. London.

Muensterberg, Hugo (1908) *On the Witness Stand. Essays on Psychology and Crime* (reprinted 1923). New York.

Muller, D.J., Blackman, D.E. and Chapman, A.J. (eds) (1984) Psychology and Law. Chichester.

Murphy, James J. (1974) *Rhetoric in the Middle Ages*. Berkeley.

Murphy, P. and Barnard, D. (1984) *Evidence and Advocacy*. London.

Naess, Arne (1968) *Scepticism*. London.

Nagel, E. (1959) 'The Logic of Historical Analysis' in Meyerhoff (ed.).

Nance, Dale A. (1988) 'The Best Evidence Rule', 73 Iowa L. Rev. 227.

Napley, Sir David (1983) *The Technique of Persuasion*, 3rd edn. London.

Nash, Christopher (1987) 'Slaughtering the Subject: Literature's Assault on Narrative', unpublished paper, Warwick Seminar on Narrative in Culture.

_____ (ed.) *Caught by the Tale*. London (forthcoming).

Nelken, David (1981) 'The Gap Problem in the Sociology of Law: A Theoretical Review', 1 Windsor Yearbook of Access to Justice 35.

Nelson, W. (1739) *The Law of Evidence*. London.

Nesbitt, George L. (1934) *Benthamite Reviewing*. New York.

Nesson, Charles (1985) 'The Evidence or the Event? On Judicial Proof and the Acceptability of Verdicts', 98 Harv. L. Rev. 1357.

Nevins, A. (1962) *The Gateway to History* (1st edn, 1938). New York.

Newell, Allen and Simon, Herbert (1972) *Human Problem Solving*. Englewood Cliffs, NJ.

Nielson, Kai (1973) *Scepticism*. London.

Nisbett, R.E. and Wilson, T. (1977) 'Telling More than We Can Know: Verbal Reports on Mental Process', 84 Psych. Rev. 231.

Nokes, G.D. (1967) *An Introduction to Evidence*, 4th edn. London.

Noonan, John T., Jr. (1976) *Persons and Masks of the Law*. New York.

Oaks, Dallin (1970) 'Studying the Exclusionary Rule in Search and Seizure', 37 U. Chi. L. Rev. 665.

O'Barr, William M. (1982) *Linguistic Evidence*. New York.

Ogden, C.K. (1932) *Bentham's Theory of Fictions*. London.

Ogden, C.K. and Richards, I.A. (1923) *The Meaning of Meaning*. London.

Ormrod, Sir Roger (1971) Report of the Committee on Legal Education (The Ormrod Committee). Cmnd. 4595. London.

Osborn, Albert S. (1922) *The Problem of Proof*. New York.

—— (1929) *Questioned Documents*. Albany, NY.

—— (1937) *The Mind of the Juror as Judge of the Facts*. Albany, NY.

Paley, Archdeacon W. (1809) *Principles of Moral and Political Philosophy*. London (1st edn, 1785).

Patchett, Keith (1988) 'Palm-tree Justice – A View from a Deck-chair in Law', 56 Commonwealth Leg. Ed. Assoc. Newsletter, App. I.

Paterson, Alan (1982) *The Law Lords*. London.

Pattenden, R. (1988) 'The Risk of Non-persuasion in Civil Trials: The Case for a Floating Standard of Proof', 7 Civil Justice Qrtly. 220.

Paul, J. (1959) *The Legal Realism of Jerome N. Frank*. The Hague.

Peake, Thomas (1801) *A Compendium of the Law of Evidence*, 1st edn. London (reprinted 1979).

Peczenik, A. (1979) 'Cumulation and Compromise of Reasons in the Law' in Pennock and Chapman (eds).

Pennock, J. Roland and Chapman, John W. (eds) (1979) *Compromise in Ethics, Law and Politics*, XXI Nomos. New York.

Perelman, Ch. (1963) *The Idea of Justice and the Problem of Argument* (trans. Petri). London.

Perelman, Ch. and Olbrechts-Tyteca, L. (1971) *The New Rhetoric*. Notre Dame.

Philips Commission (1981) Report of the Royal Commission on Criminal Procedure (Sir Cyril Philips, chairman). Cmnd. 8092. London.

Phillimore, John G. (1850) *The History and Principles of the Law of Evidence, as Illustrated by our Social Progress*. London.

Phillipps, Samuel M. (1814) *A Treatise on the Law of Evidence*, 1st edn. London (9th edn, 1843).

Phipson, S. L. (1892) *The Law of Evidence*, 1st edn (14th edn, ed. S. Phipson and W. Elliott, 1986). London.

Pitcher, George (ed.) (1964) *Truth*. Englewood Cliffs, NJ.

Plamenatz, John (1958) *The English Utilitarians*, 2nd edn. Oxford.

—— (1975) *Karl Marx's Philosophy of Man*. Oxford.

Plucknett, T. F. T. (1929) *A Concise History of the Common Law*. London (5th edn, 1956).

Podgorecki, A. and Whelan, C. (eds) (1981) *Sociological Approaches to Law*. London.

Pollock, Sir F. (1876) Review of Stephen's *Digest of the Law of Evidence*, 26 Fortnightly Rev. 383.

—— (1899) Review of Thayer (1898), 15 LQR 86.

Pomerantz, Anita and Atkinson, J. Maxwell (1984) 'Ethnomethodology, Conversation Analysis and the Study of Courtroom Interaction' in Muller, Blackman and Chapman (eds).

Popkin, R. (1967) 'Skepticism' in P. Edwards (ed.).

Posner, Richard (1977) *Economic Analysis of Law*, 2nd edn. Boston.

Postema, Gerald (1977) 'The Principle of Utility and the Theory of Procedure: Bentham's Theory of Adjudication', 11 Georgia L. Rev. 1393.

—— (1983) 'Facts, Fictions and Law: Bentham on the Foundations of Evidence' in Twining (ed.) 37.

—— (1986) *Bentham and the Common Law Tradition*. Oxford.

Pothier, R. J. (1761) *Traité des obligations*. Paris.

—— (1806) *A Treatise on the Law of Obligations, or Contracts* (trans. Evans). London (see also W. D. Evans, 1806).

Putnam, Hilary (1981) *Reason, Truth and History*. Cambridge.

Quine, W. V. and Ullian T. S. (1970) *The Web of Belief*. New York.

Quintilian (80–90 AD) *De Institutione Oratoria*.

Rabelais, F. (1542–52) *Gargantua and Pantagruel* (trans. T. Urquhart, 1913). London.

Radzinowicz, L. (1957) *Sir James Fitzjames Stephen* (Selden Society Lecture). London.

Rajchman, John and West, Cornel (eds) (1985) *Post-Analytic Philosophy*. New York.
Ram, James (1861) *A Treatise on Facts as Subjects of Enquiry by a Jury*, 1st edn. London.
Ranke, L. von (1824) *Geschichte der romanischen und germanischen Völker*. Leipzig.
Ratner, Sidney (ed.) (1953) *Vision and Action*. New Brunswick, NJ.
Rawls, John (1955) 'Two Concepts of Rules', 64 Philo. Rev. 3.
—— (1972) *A Theory of Justice*. Cambridge, Mass. and Oxford.
Raz, Joseph (1975) *Practical Reason and Norms*. London.
—— (ed.) (1978) *Practical Reasoning*. Oxford.
Reppy, A. (ed.) (1937) *Law: A Century of Progress*, 3 vols. New York.
Rescher, N. (1980) *Scepticism*. Oxford.
Ricoeur, Paul (1981) *Hermeneutics and the Human Sciences* (trans. John B. Thompson). Cambridge.
Rimmon-Kennan, S. (1983) *Narrative Fiction: Contemporary Poetics*. London.
Roalfe, William R. (1977) *John Henry Wigmore, Scholar and Reformer*. Evanston.
Roberts, Simon (1979) *Order and Dispute*. Harmondsworth.
Robinson, Daniel N. (1980) *Psychology and Law: Can Justice Survive the Social Sciences?* New York and Oxford.
Robson, P. and Watchman, P. (eds) (1981) *Justice, Lord Denning and the Constitution*. Farnborough.
Roebuck, J. A. (1828) 'Bentham's *Rationale of Judicial Evidence*', 9 Westminster Rev. 198–250.
Rolph, C. H. (1957) *Personal Identity*. London.
Romilly, Sir Samuel (1786) *Observations on a Late Publication, Entitled Thoughts on Executive Justice*. London.
—— (1810) *Observations on the Criminal Law of England*. London.
Rorty, Richard (1979) *Philosophy and the Mirror of Nature*. Princeton.
—— (1985) 'Solidarity or Objectivity?' in Rajchman and West (eds).
Roscoe, Henry (1827) *A Digest of the Law of Evidence on the Trial of Actions at Nisi Prius*. London.
—— (1835) *A Digest of the Law of Evidence in Criminal Cases*. London (16th edn, 1952).
Rosen, Fred (1983) *Jeremy Bentham and Representative Democracy*. Oxford.
Royal Commission on Criminal Procedure (Philips Commission) (1981). Cmnd. 8092. London.
Rumble, W. (1968) *American Legal Realism*. Ithaca, NY.
Rumsey, D. Lake (ed.) (1986) *Master Advocates' Handbook*. NITA, St Paul.
Rutter, Irvin (1961) 'A Jurisprudence of Lawyers' Operations', 13 Jo. Leg. Ed. 301.
Ryan, J. P. (1981) 'Adjudication and Sentencing in the Misdemeanour Court: The Outcome is the Punishment', 15 Law and Soc. Rev. 79.
Saks, M. J. and Hastie, R. (1978) *Social Psychology in Court*. New York.
Salmond, Sir John (1907) *Jurisprudence*, 2nd edn. London.
—— (1981) *Torts*, 18th edn, ed. R. F. V. Heuston and R. S. Chambers. London.
Saltzburg, Stephen A. and Redden, Kenneth (1982) *Federal Rules of Evidence Manual*, 3rd edn. Charlottesville.
Sampford, Charles (1988) *The Disorder of Law*. Oxford.
Sarkar, P. C. and S. (1971) *Law of Evidence*, 12th edn. Calcutta.
Saunders, D., Vidmar, N. and Hewitt, E. (1983) 'Eyewitness Testimony and the Discrediting Effect' in Lloyd-Bostock and Clifford (eds).
Saunders, J. S. (1828) Law of Pleading and Evidence in Civil Actions. London.
Schepele, Kim Lane (1988) *Legal Secrets: Equality and Efficiency in the Common Law*. Chicago.
Schiff, S. (1988) *Evidence in the Litigation Process*, 3rd edn. Toronto.
Schlegel, John H. (1979) 'American Legal Realism and Empirical Social Science: From the Yale Experience', 28 Buffalo L. Rev. 459.
—— (1980) 'American Legal Realism and Empirical Social Science: The Singular Case of Underhill Moore', 29 U. Buffalo L. Rev. 195.
Schuett, J. T. (1957) 'A Study of the Legal Philosophy of Jerome Frank', 35 U. Detroit L. Jo. 28.

Schum, David (1979) 'A Review of the Case against Blaise Pascal and his Heirs', 77 Michigan L. Rev. 446.
____ (1984) 'A Conversation with Wigmore about Psychology, Probability and the Law', Conference paper. Houston.
____ (1986) 'Probability and the Process of Discovery, Proof and Choice', 66 Boston U. L. Rev. 825.
____ (1987) *Evidence and Inference for the Intelligence Analyst*, 2 vols. New York and London.
Schum, David and Martin, Anne (1982) 'Formal and Empirical Research on Cascaded Inference in Jurisprudence: A Summary', 17 Law and Soc. Rev. 105.
Schum, David and Tillers, Peter (1988) 'Research on the Marshalling of Evidence and the Structuring of Argument' (unpublished).
Scott, Kenneth (1975) 'Two Models of Civil Process', 27 Stanford L. Rev. 937.
Shafer, Glen (1976) *A Mathematical Theory of Evidence*. Princeton.
____ (1988) 'The Construction of Probability Arguments' in Tillers and Green (eds).
Shakespeare, W. *Richard II*.
Shapiro, Barbara (1969) 'Law and Science in Seventeenth Century England', 21 Stanford L. Rev. 727.
____ (1983) *Probability and Certainty in Seventeenth Century England*. Princeton.
____ (1986) '"To a Moral Certainty": Theories of Knowledge and Anglo-American Juries 1600–1850', 38 Hastings LJ 153.
Shapland, Joanna (1981) *Between Conviction and Sentence: The Process of Mitigation*. London.
Shepherd, John W., Ellis, Haydn D. and Davies, Graham M. (1982) *Identification Evidence: A Psychological Evaluation*. Aberdeen.
Sherwin, Richard K. (1988) 'A Matter of Voice and Plot: Belief and Suspicion in Legal Story-telling', 87 Mich. L. Rev. 5.
Shklar, Judith (1964) 'Decisionism' in *Rational Decision*, VII Nomos 3 (ed. Friedrich).
Shulman, H. (1913–14) Book review, 23 Yale LJ 384.
Sidgwick, H. (1883) *Fallacies: A View of Logic from the Practical Side*. London.
Simpson, A. W. B. (ed.) (1984) *A Biographical Dictionary of the Common Law*. London.
____ (1984a) *Cannibalism and the Common Law*. Chicago and London.
____ (1986) 'The Common Law and Legal Theory' in Twining (ed.).
Singer, M. (1983) 'Judicial Decisions and Judicial Opinions', Crim. Justice Ethics 22.
Skinner, Quentin (1969) 'Meaning and Understanding in the History of Ideas', 8 History and Theory 3.
____ (1978) *The Foundations of Modern Political Thought*, 2 vols. Cambridge.
Smith, J. C. and Hogan, B. (1978) *Criminal Law*, 4th edn (6th edn, 1988). London.
Smith J. Q. (1988) *Decision Analysis*. London and New York.
Smith, K. J. M. (1988) *James Fitzjames Stephen: Portrait of a Victorian Rationalist*. Cambridge.
Smith, Sidney (1825) Review of Bentham's *Book of Fallacies*. 42 Edin. Rev. 367.
Smith, W. F. (1918) *Rabelais in his Writings*. Cambridge.
Smyth, Frank (1980) *Cause of Death: The Story of Forensic Science*. London.
Snyman, P. C. A. (1979) 'A Proposal for a National Link-up of the New Legal Services Corporation Law Offices and Law School Clinical Training' (with bibliography), 30 Jo. Leg. Ed. 56.
Stallybrass, W. T. S. (1933) Book review, 49 LQR 121.
Starkie, Thomas (1824) *Law of Evidence and Digest of Proofs in Civil and Criminal Proceedings*, 1st edn (4th edn, 1853). London.
Stein, Alex (1987) Book review, 22 Israel L. Rev. 245.
____ (1988) 'A Political Analysis of Procedural Law', 51 MLR 549.
Steintrager, James (1977) *Bentham*. London.
Stenning, Anders (1975) *Bevisvarde*. Uppsala.
Stephen, Sir James Fitzjames (1863) *A General View of the Criminal Law of England*. London. (2nd edn. 1890).
____ (1872) *The Indian Evidence Act, with an Introduction on the Principles of Judicial Evidence*. Calcutta.

—— (1876) *A Digest of the Law of Evidence*, 1st edn. London (12th edn, 1948).
Stephen, Sir Leslie (1895) *Life of Sir James Fitzjames Stephen*. London.
—— (1900) *The English Utilitarians*. 3 vols. London.
Stone, Julius (1964) *Legal System and Lawyers' Reasonings*. London.
Stone, Marcus (1984) *Proof of Facts in Criminal Trials*. Edinburgh.
Streatfield, Sir Geoffrey (1961) Report of the Interdepartmental Committee on the Business of the Criminal Courts. Cmnd. 1289. London.
Stryker, Lloyd P. (1954) *The Art of Advocacy*. Albany, NY.
Sully, James (1892) *The Human Mind*. London.
Summers, Robert S. (1974) 'Evaluating and Improving Legal Processes: A Plea for Process Values', 60 Cornell L. Rev. 1.
—— (1978) 'Two Types of Substantive Reasons: The Core of a Theory of Common Law Justification', 63 Cornell L. Rev. 707.
—— (1978a) 'Comment on "The Adversary System and Justice"' in Bronaugh (ed.), ch. 10.
—— (1984) *Lon Fuller*. London and Stanford.
Sutherland, A. (1967) *The Law at Harvard: A History of Ideas and Men 1817–1967*. Cambridge, Mass.
Swift, Chief Justice Zephaniah (1810) *A Digest of the Law of Evidence in Civil and Criminal Cases and a Treatise on Bills of Exchange*. Conn. (reprinted 1972).
Tapp, June (1976) 'Psychology and Law: An Overture', 27 Annual Rev. Psych. 359.
—— (1980) 'Psychological and Policy Perspectives on the Law: Reflections on a Decade', 36 Jo. Social Issues 165.
Tapper, Colin (ed.) (1981) *Crime, Proof and Punishment: Essays in Honour of Sir Rupert Cross*. London.
—— (1982) 'Proof and Prejudice' in Campbell and Waller (eds).
—— (1985) (see Cross, 1985).
Taylor, J. Pitt (1848) *Treatise on the Law of Evidence*. 1st end. London (12th edn, 1931).
Teitelbaum, L. E. G., Sutton-Barbere, G. and Johnson, P. (1983) 'Evaluating the Prejudicial Effect of Evidence', Wisc. L. Rev. 1147.
Thayer, E. R. (1913–14) Book review, 27 Harv. L. Rev. 601.
Thayer, James B. (1892) *Select Cases on Evidence at the Common Law*, 1st edn. Cambridge, Mass. (3rd edn., 1925) (see also Morgan and Maguire, 1934).
—— (1895) *Cases on Constitutional Law*, 2 vols. Cambridge, Mass.
—— (1898) *A Preliminary Treatise on Evidence at Common Law*. Boston (reprinted 1969).
—— (1927) *Legal Essays*. Cambridge, Mass.
Thibaut, J. and Walker, L. (1975) *Procedural Justice: A Psychological Analysis*. Hillsdale, NJ.
Thomas, P. A. (ed.) (1982) *Law in the Balance*. Oxford.
Thompson, E. P. (1973) *Whigs and Hunters*. London (revised edn, 1977).
Tillers, Peter (1983) 'Modern Theories of Relevancy', reprinted from 1 A Wigmore *Treatise* (Tillers rev. 1983), s. 37.
—— (1986) 'Mapping Inferential Domains', 66 Boston U. L. Rev. 883, reprinted in Tillers and Green (eds) (1988).
—— (1988) 'The Value of Evidence in Law', 39 NILQ 167.
—— (1988a) 'Prejudice, Politics, and Proof', 86 Mich. L. Rev. 768.
Tillers, Peter and Green, Eric D. (eds) (1988) *Probability and Inference in the Law of Evidence: The Uses and Limits of Bayesianism*. Dordrecht.
Tillers, Peter and Schum, David (1988) 'Charting New Territory in Judicial Proof: Beyond Wigmore', 9 Cardozo L. Rev. 907. See also Schum, D. and Tillers, P.
Tipson, F. (1974) 'The Lasswell–McDougal Enterprise: Toward a World Public Order of Human Dignity', 14 Virginia Jo. of International Law 535.
Trankell, Arne (1972). *Reliability of Evidence*. Stockholm.
—— (ed.) (1982) *Reconstructing the Past*. Stockholm.
Trautman, H. (1952) 'Logical or Legal Relevancy – A Conflict in Theory', 5 Vand. L. Rev. 385.

Tribe, H. Laurence (1971) 'Trial by Mathematics: Precision and Ritual in Legal Process', 84 Harv. L. Rev. 1329.

Trigg, Roger (1973) *Reason and Commitment*. Cambridge.

____ (1980) *Reality at Risk*. Brighton.

Trilling, Diana (1982) *Mrs Harris*. Harmondsworth.

Trusov, A. (1963) *An Introduction to the Theory of Evidence*. Moscow.

Tulloch, G. Gordon (1980) *Trials on Trial*. New York.

Tur, Richard and Twining, William (eds) (1986) *Essays on Kelsen*. Oxford.

Turner, Roy (ed.) (1974) *Ethnomethodology*. Harmondsworth.

Turner, Victor (1974) *Dramas, Fields and Metaphors*. Ithaca, NY.

Twining, William L. (1967) 'Pericles and the Plumber', 83 LQR 396.

____ (1973) *Karl Llewellyn and the Realist Movement*. London (re-issued London and Norman, Okla., 1985).

____ (1973a) 'The Bad Man Revisited', 58 Cornell L. Rev. 275.

____ (1974) 'Some Jobs for Jurisprudence', 1 Brit. Jo. Law and Soc. 149.

____ (1976) *Academic Law and Legal Development*. Lagos.

____ (1978) 'The Great Juristic Bazaar', 14 JSPTL (NS) 185.

____ (1980) 'Goodbye to Lewis Eliot: The Academic Lawyer as Scholar', 15 JSPTL (NS) 2.

____ (1980a) 'Debating Probabilities', 2 Liverpool Law Rev. 51.

____ (1982) 'The Rationalist Tradition of Evidence Scholarship' in Campbell and Waller (eds) 211.

____ (ed.) (1983) *Facts in Law*. Wiesbaden (FL).

____ (1984) 'Evidence and Legal Theory', Inaugural Lecture, University College, London, 47 MLR 261 (reprinted in Twining, ed., 1986).

____ (1984a) 'Why Bentham?' 8 The Bentham Newsletter 34.

____ (1984b) 'John Henry Wigmore' in Simpson (ed.).

____ (1984c) 'Jerome Frank' in Simpson (ed.).

____ (1985) *Theories of Evidence: Bentham and Wigmore*. London and Stanford (*TEBW*).

____ (1985a) 'Talk About Realism', 60 NYUL. Rev. 329.

____ (1985b) 'Taking Skills Seriously', 44 C'Wealth Legal Education Assoc. Newsletter, Appendix.

____ (ed.) (1986) *Legal Theory and Common Law*. Oxford (*LTCL*).

____ (1986a) 'Bentham's Writings on Evidence', 10 The Bentham Newsletter 34.

____ (1986b) 'The Boston Symposium: A Comment', 66 Boston U. L. Rev. 391.

____ (1986c) 'Cannibalism and Legal Literature', 6 Oxf. Jo. Leg. Stud. 423.

____ (1988) 'Hot Air in the Redwoods', 86 Mich. L. Rev. 1523.

____ (1988a) 'Legal Skills and Legal Education', 22 The Law Teacher 4.

____ (1988b) 'Adjudication between Freedom and Rules: Freedom of Proof at Common Law', Conference paper, University of Trento.

____ (1989) 'Rationality and Scepticism in Judicial Proof: Some Signposts', 2 Int. Jo. Semiotics of Law 69.

Twining, William and Miers, David (1982) *How To Do Things With Rules*, 2nd edn. London.

Twining, W. L. and Twining P. E. (1974) 'Bentham on Torture' (including 2 Bentham mss.) in M. H. James (ed.), reprinted from 24 NILQ 305 (1973).

Unger, P. (1975) *Ignorance: A Case for Scepticism*. Oxford.

Updike, John (1986) *Roger's Version*. London.

Van der Elst, Violet (1937) *On the Gallows*. London.

Volkomer, W. E. (1970) *Passionate Liberal: The Political and Legal Ideas of Jerome N. Frank*. The Hague.

Voltaire (1772) 'Essai sur les probabilités en fait de justice', Oeuvres complètes XXVIII (1879). Paris.

Vosper, Frank (1923) *People Like Us*. London.

Walker, M. and Brittain, B. (1978) *Identification Evidence: Practices and Malpractices*. London.

Walls, H. J. (1974) *Forensic Science*. London.

Waterfield, Gordon (1937) *Lucy Duff-Gordon*. New York.
Watson, Eric R. (ed.) (1915) *The Trial of George Joseph Smith*. London and Edinburgh.
Watt, J. (ed.) (1989) *The Legal Skills Sourcebook: A Bibliography*. Sydney and Windsor, Ont.
Weinberg, M. (1984) 'Evidence Scholarship and Theories of Adjudication – Towards an Integrative Jurisprudence', in Galligan (ed.).
Weinstein, Jack B. (1955) 'The Teaching of Fact Skills in Courses Presently in the Curriculum', 7 Jo. Leg. Ed. 463.
—— (1966) 'Some Difficulties in Devising Rules for Determining Truth in Judicial Trials', 66 Col. L. Rev. 223.
Weinstein, Jack B. and Berger, Margaret A. (1975–   ) *Weinstein's Evidence, Commentary on Rules of Evidence for the United States Courts and for State Courts*, 7 vols. New York.
Weis, René (1988) *Criminal Justice: The True Story of Edith Thompson*. London.
Wellman, Francis L. (1903) *The Art of Cross-examination*, 1st edn. New York (4th edn, 1936).
Wells, Gary L. (1988) *Identification Evidence: A System Handbook*. Toronto.
Whipple, Guy M. (ed.) (1910) *Manual of Mental and Physical Tests*. Baltimore.
White, Hayden (1987) *The Content of the Form: Narrative Discourse and Historical Representation*. Baltimore.
White, James Boyd (1973) *The Legal Imagination*. Boston.
—— (1984) *When Words Lose Their Meaning*. Chicago.
—— (1985) *Heracles' Bow: Essays on the Rhetoric and Poetics of the Law*. Madison.
White, Morton (1964) *Social Thought in America: The Revolt Against Formalism*, rev. edn. Boston (1st edn, 1959).
Whitman, James (1987) 'Commercial Law and the American Volk: A Note on Llewellyn's German Sources for the Uniform Commercial Code', 97 Yale LJ 156.
Wigmore, J. H. (see also List of Abbreviations).
—— (1899) S. Greenleaf, *A Treatise on the Law of Evidence*, vol. 1 (16th edn, ed. J. Wigmore).
—— (1904–5) *A Treatise on the System of Evidence in Trials at Common Law* (3rd edn, 1940). Boston.
—— (1908) 'A General Survey of the History of the Rules of Evidence' in II *Select Essays in Anglo-American Legal History*. Cambridge, Mass.
—— (1909) 'Professor Muensterberg and the Psychology of Testimony', 3 Ill. L. Rev. 399.
—— (1913) 'The Problem of Proof', 8 Ill. L. Rev. 77.
—— (1913a) *The Principles of Judicial Proof, as given by Logic, Psychology and General Experience* (2nd edn, 1931; 3rd edn, 1937, sub nom. *The Science of Judicial Proof*). Boston.
—— (1935) *A Students' Textbook of the Law of Evidence*. Brooklyn.
—— (1942) 'The American Law Institute Code of Evidence: A Dissent', 28 ABAJ 23.
—— (1983) (see Tillers, 1983).
Wild, R. and Curtis-Bennett, D. (1937) *Curtis: The Life of Sir Henry Curtis-Bennett QC*. London.
Wilkins, L. (1964) *Social Deviance*. London.
Williams, Glanville (1961) *Criminal Law: The General Part*, 2nd edn. London.
—— (1963) *The Proof of Guilt*, 3rd edn. London.
—— (1973) *Learning the Law*, 9th edn (11th edn, 1982). London.
—— (1979a, 1979b), 'The Mathematics of Proof', Crim. L. Rev. 297 and 320.
—— (1980) 'A Short Rejoinder', Crim. L. Rev. 103.
Willmer, M. A. P. (1970) *Crime and Information Theory*. Edinburgh.
Wills, W. (1838) *An Essay on the Rationale of Circumstantial Evidence*. London (later edns *An Essay on the Principles of Circumstantial Evidence*).
Wilson, W. A. (1963) 'A Note on Fact and Law', 26 MLR 609.
Winks, R. (ed.) (1968) *The Historian as Detective*. New York.
Winter, Steven (1988) 'The Metaphor of Standing and the Problem of Self-governance', 40 Stanford L. Rev. 1371.
Winterfeldt, Detlof von and Edwards, Ward (1986) *Decision Analysis and Behavioral Research*. Cambridge.

Wisdom, John (1956) *Other Minds*. Oxford.

Wittman, D. (1974) 'Two Views of Procedure', 3 Jo. Leg. Stud. 249.

Wright, Charles A. and Graham, K. (1977) *Federal Practice and Procedure*, vols 21–24 (1988 Supp.) St Paul.

Wright, Lord (1938) Review of *Wigmore's Science of Judicial Proof*, 24 ABAJ 478.

Wyckoff, D. B. (1915–16) Book review, 1 Cornell LQ 14.

Yarmey, A. D. (1979) *The Psychology of Eyewitness Testimony*. New York and London.

Young, Filson (ed.) (1923) *The Trial of Frederick Bywaters and Edith Thompson*. London.

Zadeh, L. (1965) 'Fuzzy Sets', 8 Info. and Control 338.

_____ (1983) *A Theory of Commonsense Knowledge*. Berkeley.

_____ (1983a) 'Fuzzy Logic as a Basis for Uncertainty in Expert Systems', 11 Fuzzy Sets and Systems 197.

Zadeh, L. et al. (eds) (1974) *Fuzzy Sets and their Applications to Cognitive and Decision Processes*. Berkeley.

Zander, Michael (1980) *Cases and Materials on the English Legal System*. London (5th edn, 1988).

Zeisel, Hans (1971) 'And then there were None: The Diminution of the Federal Jury', 38 U. Chi. L. Rev. 710.

Zemans, Frances K. (1980) 'Preparation for the Practice of Law in the United States: The Views Of Practitioners', Conference paper, Cardiff.

Zemans, Frances K. and Rosenblum, Victor (1981) *The Making of a Public Profession*. Chicago.

Zuckerman, Adrian (1981) 'Privilege and Public Interest' in Tapper (ed.).

_____ (1983) 'Relevance in Legal Proceedings' in Twining (ed.) 145.

_____ (1986) 'Law, Fact or Justice?', 66 Boston U. L. Rev. 487.

_____ (1986a) 'The Right Against Self-incrimination: An Obstacle to Interrogation', 102 LQR 43.

_____ (1987) 'The Transformation of the English Law of Evidence' in Butler (ed.).

_____ (1987a) 'Similar Fact Evidence: The Unobservable Rule', 103 LQR 187.

_____ (1987b) 'Illegally Obtained Evidence: Discretion as a Guardian of Legitimacy', 40 Current Legal Problems 55.

_____ (1989) *The Principles of Criminal Evidence*. Oxford.

Index

Index compiled by Jackie McDermott.